Gods in America

Gods in America

Religious Pluralism in the United States

EDITED BY CHARLES L. COHEN AND
RONALD L. NUMBERS

OXFORD
UNIVERSITY PRESS

OXFORD
UNIVERSITY PRESS

Oxford University Press is a department of the University of Oxford.
It furthers the University's objective of excellence in research, scholarship,
and education by publishing worldwide.

Oxford   New York

Auckland   Cape Town   Dar es Salaam   Hong Kong   Karachi
Kuala Lumpur   Madrid   Melbourne   Mexico City   Nairobi
New Delhi   Shanghai   Taipei   Toronto

With offices in

Argentina   Austria   Brazil   Chile   Czech Republic   France   Greece
Guatemala   Hungary   Italy   Japan   Poland   Portugal   Singapore
South Korea   Switzerland   Thailand   Turkey   Ukraine   Vietnam

Oxford is a registered trademark of Oxford University Press in the UK and certain other
countries.

Published in the United States of America by
Oxford University Press
198 Madison Avenue, New York, NY 10016

Library of Congress Cataloging-in-Publication Data
Gods in America : religious pluralism in the United States / edited by Charles L. Cohen and
Ronald L. Numbers.
pages cm
Includes bibliographical references and index.
ISBN 978-0-19-993192-7 – ISBN 978-0-19-993190-3
1. United States–Religion.   2. Religious pluralism–United States.   I. Cohen, Charles Lloyd,
editor of compilation.
BL2525.G627 2013
200.973–dc23
2013012875

1 3 5 7 9 8 6 4 2
Printed in the United States of America
on acid-free paper

This book was published with the support of the Lubar Institute for the Study of the
Abrahamic Religions at the University of Wisconsin–Madison.

Lubar Institute

for the Study of the Abrahamic Religions
University of Wisconsin–Madison

To the Memory of Paul Samuel Boyer:
Scholar, Colleague, Friend

CONTENTS

"Pluralism."

That was my one-word answer to the questions an editor had posed to me. "What is American religion about? What is the central focus of its story?"

He and I were pushing against a snowstorm in Manhattan on a day when cabs were unavailable but, against deadline, we were planning a book concerning five hundred years of religion in America. We decided that a huff-and-puff conversation could be a creative use of our breath and time.

So it was "pluralism," the topic to which essays in this book are addressed.

The editor turned his face and did me a favor by correcting me.

"'Pluralism?' You couldn't be more wrong. Pluralism is what sociologists and historians may think is what it's about." Later, over coffee, he elaborated, roughly as I recall it: "'Religion' is about praying when your spouse is dying, or leaping when a baby has been born. It is about the meaning of existence and celebrating Yom Kippur and calling on a chaplain and training the kids and.... 'Pluralism,' however, is a name for dealing with the groups that 'do' religion. It is very important, but Americans went through three or four centuries of life without even using the term in this sense. 'Pluralism' helps skein together the stories of the groups and the individuals within them; it is useful and important when a scholar or strategist needs and finds perspective on the human scene."

"Pluralism," as we just noticed, is what this book is about, as its authors serve to coordinate stories, and, yes, provide perspective. Properly understood, its use can help citizens better discern and interpret voting power, or motivate and sustain and sometimes end arguments. So long as people kill in the names of peoplehood and religion, inspire hatred or work toward peace in the domestic order, try to figure out where they belong in relation to "the others" in times of conflict or when they are bewildered about their identity, we need to learn more about pluralism. Anything that helps citizens reckon with the situation that is code-named "pluralist" deserves ponderings of the sort found so generously advanced by the authors in this book.

Rather than discuss American (and global) religious pluralism in sweeping and general terms, these writers bring us closer to the people in the stories that my editor on that stormy day had wanted me to notice. There are many ways to contribute to the understanding. Thus even one well-reasoned abstract essay on the subject can be of one kind of help to students of religious phenomena and affairs. What is especially valuable in the pages which follow is the comparative model; can we call it the pluralist approach to pluralism? So what does the story of "religion in popular culture" (Peter Williams's chapter) tell us to help us, when it is juxtaposed with the account of the Muslims in Yvonne Haddad's chapter, or with that of the Jews in Deborah Dash Moore's essay? The quick and succinct answer is: "Very much," but things get more interesting as these scholars detail movements and accents which differ so vastly from those of each other's groups—or, just as revealingly, when they overlap, parallel each other, or coincide.

Throw in the particular experiences of "women" in religion, as R. Marie Griffith finds them, whether as Protestants or in their location among women in politics, as assessed by Charles Lippy or, by now not much more of a stretch, among Catholics when viewed and written about by R. Scott Appleby.

Merely registering the presence of and telling some stories about these human clusterings in all their variety is only half the task. We could extend the list of groupings into the hundreds, as we find them in real life in America, and still not have located the main gift that most of these chapters provide. I have so far only pointed to diversity, and diversity is not the same as what these authors mean when they discuss pluralism. Diversity is an act of pointing and describing, as if to say, "There surely are a lot of religious groups out there!" or "look at how many identities are identified in America!" as if the authors here were only pointers and describers. "Pluralism," however, signals ways of doing things about the diversities of constituencies pointed to in these pages, or ways of thinking about and conceiving them.

Here is where the problems about pluralism become visible and the promise gets pondered. These problems and promises differ, depending upon the size of the religious groups, the length of time they have been in America, what they think of their neighbors as strangers, or of strangers as compatriots, colleagues, or agents of conflict. We learn right off from Amanda Porterfield that the diversity of approaches to the subjects in "Religious Studies" programs and departments forces some self-criticism and encourages some relishing of the scholars' own situations and histories.

One cannot avoid "pluralism" in religious studies, but one can turn study of it to good effect, as contributors to this volume have done individually and now do together. The concepts of pluralism which they address are constantly changing, so updates like the present work can be a reference for today. But I also like to picture what the scene will be in a few years, recalling as I do the historical events and proposals from recent decades. Reference to concepts like "pluralism" in indexes 50 years ago, when my generation started its work, dealt with an inherited category called "pluralism," but it then referred to philosophical and usually metaphysical usages as commented on by pioneers like William James. Then in the middle of the last century a number of philosophers and social scientists—Horace Kallen and Will Herberg being pathfinders in this case—developed the term "pluralism" as United States citizens were beginning to recognize that American religion could not be properly conceived as being contained only in the "Protestant" and then "Christian" and next the "Judeo-Christian" categories.

It is almost humorous and at the same time encouraging to see how terminologies shifted in organized discussions of religious pluralism and ways of dealing with it. It is as if they tried to contain the elements of pluralism by adding named groups to the smaller mix. In the 1960s the triad "Protestant-Catholic-Jew" had to be broken into until we read of improvisations such as "Protestant-Catholic-Jew-Muslim" or, on the other hand, of attempts at minimizing the diversity with coinages such as "Abrahamic faiths." That kind of concept does not begin to do justice to the realities of American pluralism that are now extant and expanding. Many of us entertain each other with geographical references of the sort that Bret Carroll calls to our attention. Example: when one spring I spoke of "pluralism" at Coe College in Cedar Rapids, Iowa, an audience member said she thought of the subject as being remote and only remotely of interest. Following up, the crowd was bidden to think of mid-Iowa representations of religious groups. So we heard volunteers remind us that a Hasidic community—later to be noticed nationally—resided not many miles north; that the Hindu-related University of Transcendental Meditation prospered a few miles south of where we were. And, startling to many only three decades ago, right in the city where we were was the oldest in-continuous-use mosque. My turn: I told of familiarity with the ethnic diversity which changed the context in once Catholic-Protestant "Western Christian" Fort Wayne, Indiana, where a Lutheran congregation was served by a pastor who was of gypsy provenance while the members were Burmese. Traveling on: to find one of the best-known and largest Somali Muslim populations in America, one goes not to the coasts but to the Twin Cities in Minnesota.

All these presences provoked mental adjustments among citizens in surrounding communities who had to learn how to live with these "strangers," or sometimes face up to new legal cases occasioned by religious complexities. Some of the pluralist situations could be exploited by those who sulked or raged with their "-phobias," as in "Islamophobia." Educators had to cope with linguistic problems in communities whose later-immigrant populations complicated life in their public schools but also with their place in the debates within their communities and nationally over "multiculturalism." Parents, educators, attorneys, politicians, and religious leaders had to learn how to ascertain the religious implications, mixed as they were with linguistic, cultural, and simply "ethnic" factors which helped characterize the various peoples. Several chapters here, for example those dealing with "law" and "diversity," make their contributions to this learning.

Of special interest to students and other observers of religion is the fact, demonstrated in and deducible from the accounts in this book, that while religion is supposedly diminishing as a useful category, "secularization" is having, if not the last word, then at least a late word about American society. This was to leave the phenomena noticed and dealt with in the scope of religious pluralism more visible, vivid, problematic, and more promising. As non- or anti-religion has also received much notice in the last two decades, publicity given to it has only enriched the discussions of religious pluralism. There is no place to hide from the controversies and advertisements relating to the pluralism. Since there is no place to hide, alert citizens welcome interpretations and guides to the life we now live among the groups that make up a civil (one hopes!) society. I commend this collection of essays to those who want to be increasingly equipped to deal with and (again, one hopes!) enjoy the nation and globe we are coming to know and to see changed constantly in the context of religious pluralism.

Martin E. Marty
The University of Chicago

CONTRIBUTORS

R. Scott Appleby is Professor of History and the John M. Regan, Jr., Director of the Joan B. Kroc Institute for International Peace Studies at the University of Notre Dame. A historian of religion who earned the Ph.D. from the University of Chicago in 1985, he is the author of *Church and Age, Unite! The Modernist Impulse in American Catholicism* (1992), *The Ambivalence of the Sacred: Religion, Violence and Reconciliation* (2000), and coauthor of *Strong Religion: The Rise of Fundamentalisms Around the World* (2003). He is coeditor of many volumes, including *The Fundamentalism Project* (1991–1995), and, most recently, *Catholics in the American Century: Recasting Narratives of U.S. History* (2012). He has been awarded honorary doctorates from the University of Scranton, Fordham University, and St. John's University, Collegeville, Minnesota. In 2010 he was elected to the American Academy of Arts and Sciences.

Paul Boyer was the late Merle Curti Professor of History, Emeritus, at the University of Wisconsin–Madison. He is the author of *Purity in Print: Book Censorship in America from the Gilded Age to the Computer Age* (1968, 2002); *Salem Possessed: The Social Origins of Witchcraft*, with Stephen Nissenbaum (1974), which won the John H. Dunning Prize of the American Historical Association; *Urban Masses and Moral Order in America, 1820–1920* (1978); *By the Bomb's Early Light: American Thought and Culture at the Dawn of the Atomic Age* (1985); *When Time Shall Be No More: Prophecy Belief in Modern American Culture* (1992), and many other works. He was associate editor of *Notable American Women, 1607–1950* (3 vols., 1971) and editor-in-chief of *The Oxford Companion to United States History* (2001). The author or coauthor of college and high school American history textbooks, he was series editor of the forthcoming *Oxford Encyclopedia of American History*. His last book, *American History: A Very Short Introduction* (New York: Oxford University Press, 2012), appeared posthumously.

Bret E. Carroll is Professor of History at California State University, Stanislaus, where he teaches American intellectual and religious history, as well as the history of gender and masculinity. He is the author of *Spiritualism in Antebellum America* (1997) and *The Routledge Historical Atlas of Religion in America* (2000), and editor of *American Masculinities: A Historical Encyclopedia* (2003).

Charles L. Cohen is Professor of History and Religious Studies at the University of Wisconsin–Madison and Founding Director of the Lubar Institute for the Study of the Abrahamic Religions. He has served on the Council of the American Society of Church History and of the Omohundro Institute of Early American History and Culture. He is the author of *God's Caress: The Psychology of Puritan Religious Experience* (1986), which won the Allan Nevins Prize awarded by the Society of American Historians, and coeditor of *Religion and the Culture of Print in Modern America* (2008, with Paul S. Boyer) and *Theology and the Soul of the Liberal State* (2010, with Leonard V. Kaplan). He is a Distinguished Lecturer for the Organization of American Historians.

John H. Evans is Professor of Sociology and chair of the Department of Sociology at the University of California, San Diego. He has been a visiting member of the School of Social Sciences at the Institute for Advanced Study in Princeton, N.J., and a post-doctoral fellow at the Robert Wood Johnson Scholars in Health Policy Research Program at Yale University. He is the author of the prize-winning *Playing God? Human Genetic Engineering and the Rationalization of Public Bioethical Debate* (2002) and *Contested Reproduction: Genetic Technologies, Religion, and Public Debate* (2010), and coeditor (with Robert Wuthnow) of *The Quiet Hand of God: Faith-Based Activism and the Public Role of Mainline Protestantism* (2002). He has also published a number of articles on opinion polarization in the United States over abortion, homosexuality, and related issues.

R. Marie Griffith, is director of the John C. Danforth Center on Religion & Politics at Washington University in St. Louis, where she serves as the John C. Danforth Distinguished Professor in the Humanities. She is the author of *God's Daughters: Evangelical Women and the Power of Submission* (1997) and *Born Again Bodies: Flesh and Spirit in American Christianity* (2004), editor of *American Religions: A Documentary History* (2007), and coeditor of both *Women and Religion in the African Diaspora: Knowledge, Power, and Performance* (2006) and *Religion and Politics in the Contemporary United States* (2008). Her next book is *Christians, Sex, and Politics: An American History*, expected in 2013.

Yvonne Yazbeck Haddad is Professor of the History of Islam and Christian–Muslim Relations in the Edmund A. Walsh School of Foreign Service at Georgetown University. She is the past president of the Middle East Studies Association and the American Academy of Religion, New England Region. She is a member of the Council on Foreign Relations. She is a recipient of the Distinguished Alumnus Award for Outstanding Achievement and Distinction in Service to the Profession, Boston University, School of Theology (2007) and Scholar of the Year: Canadian Corporation for Studies in Religion (2002). Her more than one dozen books include monographs such as (with Jane Smith) *Mission to America: Five Islamic Sectarian Communities in North America* (1993), and *Becoming American? The Forging of Arab and Muslim Identity in Pluralist America* (2011). She has also edited and coedited collections such as *The Muslims of America* (1993), *Islamic Law and the Challenges of Modernity* (1994), *Daughters of Abraham: Feminist Thought in Judaism, Christianity, and Islam* (2001), *Muslims in the West: From Sojourners to Citizens* (2002), *Religion and Immigration: Christian, Jewish and Muslim Experiences in the United States* (2003), *Muslim Women in America: The Challenge of Islamic Identity Today* (2006), and *Educating the Muslims of America* (2009).

Charles H. Lippy is the LeRoy A. Martin Distinguished Professor of Religious Studies, Emeritus, at the University of Tennessee at Chattanooga. He is the author or editor of more than two dozen books, including *Being Religious, American Style: A History of Popular Religiosity in the United States* (1994), *Pluralism Comes of Age: American Religious Culture in the Twentieth Century* (2000), and *Do Real Men Pray? Images of the Christian Man and Male Spirituality in White Protestant America* (2005). He is the coeditor, with Samuel S. Hill and Charles Reagan Wilson, of *Encyclopedia of Religion in the South* (2005), and a past president of the American Society of Church History.

Martin E. Marty is Fairfax M. Cone Distinguished Service Professor, Emeritus, at the University of Chicago, where he taught chiefly in the Divinity School for 35 years and where the Martin Marty Center has since been founded to promote "public religion" endeavors. He is a columnist for the *Christian Century*, on whose staff he has served since 1956 and in which his "M.E.M.O" column appears; editor of the semimonthly *Context*, a newsletter on religion and culture, since 1969; weekly contributor to *Sightings*, a biweekly, electronic editorial published by the Marty Center at the University of Chicago Divinity School; and a Lutheran pastor, ordained in 1952. He is the author of more than 50 books, including *Modern American Religion* (3 vols., 1986–1996), and *The One and the Many: America's Struggle for the Common Good*, as well as some five thousand essays, articles, papers, chapters, and forewords.

Stephanie Y. Mitchem is Chair of the Department of Religious Studies and Director of the African American Studies Program at the University of South Carolina. She is author of *Introducing Womanist Theology* (2002), *African American Women Tapping Power and Spiritual Wellness* (2004), *African American Folk Healing* (2007), and *Name It and Claim It? Prosperity Preaching and the Black Church* (2007). Her most recent publications include *Faith, Health, and Healing Among African Americans*, coedited with Emilie M. Townes (2008). She is a contributing editor of *Crosscurrents* and coeditor of the *Journal of Feminist Studies in Religion*.

Deborah Dash Moore is Frederick G. L. Huetwell Professor of History at the University of Michigan and Director of the Jean and Samuel Frankel Center for Judaic Studies. A scholar of twentieth-century American Jewish history, she is the author of *At Home in America: Second Generation New York Jews* (1981), *To the Golden Cities: Pursuing the American Jewish Dream in Miami and L.A.* (1994), and *GI Jews: How World War II Changed a Generation* (2004), a *Washington Post* Best Book of the Year. She has also edited several award-winning books, including *Jewish Women in America: An Historical Encyclopedia* (1997) with Paula Hyman, *Gender and Jewish History* (2010) with Marion Kaplan, and *City of Promises: A History of the Jews of New York* (2012).

Ronald L. Numbers is Hilldale Professor of the History of Science and Medicine, Emeritus, at UW–Madison. He is a past president of the American Society of Church History, the History of Science Society, and the International Union for the History and Philosophy of Science. He has authored and edited more than two dozen books, including, most recently, *Galileo Goes to Jail and Other Myths about Science and Religion* (2009), *Biology and Ideology from Descartes to Dawkins* (2010, with Denis Alexander), *Science and Religion around the World* (2011, with John Hedley Brooke), and *Wrestling with Nature: From Omens to Science* (2011, with Peter Harrison and Michael H. Shank). He is general editor, with David C. Lindberg, of *The Cambridge History of Science* (2003–).

Shawn Francis Peters earned a doctorate in history from the University of Wisconsin–Madison in 2007 and currently teaches in the School of Education at the University of Wisconsin. He is the author of four books: *Judging Jehovah's Witnesses: Religious Persecution and the Dawn of the Rights Revolution* (2000), winner of the Scribes Book Award and chosen as a "Notable Book of the Year" by the *Washington Post*; *The Yoder Case: Religious Liberty, Education, and Parental Rights* (2003); *When Prayer Fails: Faith Healing, Children, and the Law* (2007); and *The Catonsville Nine: A Story of Faith and Resistance in the Vietnam Era* (2012).

Amanda Porterfield is the Robert A. Spivey Professor of Religion and Professor of History at Florida State University. She has authored books in American religious history, the history of Christianity, and comparative religions, including *Conceived in Doubt: Religion and Politics in the Early American Nation* (2012), *Protestant Experience in America* (2006), *Healing in the History of Christianity* (2005), *The Transformation of American Religion* (2001), *The Power of Religion* (1998), *Mary Lyon and the Mount Holyoke Missionaries* (1997), and *Female Piety in Puritan New England* (1992). She is a Delegate of Oxford University Press, a past president of the American Society of Church History, and currently serves as coeditor, with John Corrigan, of the quarterly journal, *Church History: Studies in Christianity and Culture.*

William Vance Trollinger, Jr., is Professor of History and Religious Studies and Director of the Core Integrated Studies Program at the University of Dayton, where he also served as director of the Ph.D. Program in Theology. His work on American Protestantism includes *God's Empire: William Bell Riley and Midwestern Fundamentalism (1990)*, *Re-Forming the Center: American Protestantism, 1900 to the Present* (coedited, 1998), and "An Outpouring of 'Faithful' Words: Protestant Publishing in the United States" (in *Print in Motion: The Expansion of Publishing and Reading in the United States, 1880–1940*, eds. Carl Kaestle and Jan Radway, 2009). Forthcoming from Johns Hopkins is a book he is coauthoring with Susan Trollinger: *Righting America at the Creation Museum: Young Earth Creationism and the Culture Wars*.

Thomas A. Tweed holds the Harold and Martha Welch Endowed Chair in American Studies, with a concurrent appointment in History, at the University of Notre Dame, where he also is a Fellow in the Institute of Latino Studies and the Kroc Institute for International Peace Studies. He previously taught at the University of Miami, the University of North Carolina at Chapel Hill, and the University of Texas at Austin. He is the author of *The American Encounter with Buddhism, 1844–1912: Victorian Culture and the Limits of Dissent* (1992), *Our Lady of the Exile: Diasporic Religion at a Cuban Catholic Shrine in Miami* (Oxford, 1997), which won the American Academy of Religion's Award for Excellence, and *Crossing and Dwelling: A Theory of Religion* (2006). He edited *Retelling U.S. Religious History* (1997) and coedited *Asian Religions in America: A Documentary History* (Oxford, 1999), which *Choice* named an "outstanding academic book." Tweed's latest book, *America's Church: The National Shrine and Catholic Presence in the Nation's Capitol* (Oxford, 2011), also won the AAR's Award for Excellence. In 2012, he was elected vice president—and future president—of the American Academy of Religion.

Joanne Punzo Waghorne is Professor of Religion at Syracuse University, where she has taught since 2002. Her work on Hindu temples in the United States includes "The Hindu Gods in a Split-level World: The Sri Siva-Vishnu Temple in Suburban Washington, DC" (in *Gods of the City*, edited by Robert Orsi, 1999); "Spaces for a New Public Presence: The Sri Siva-Vishnu and Murugan Temples in Metropolitan Washington, DC" (in *American Sanctuary: Understanding Sacred Spaces*, edited by Louis P. Nelson, 2006); and *The Diaspora of the Gods: Modern Hindu Temples in an Urban Middle-Class World* (2004), which was awarded "Excellence in the Study of Religion, Analytical-Descriptive Category" by the American Academy of Religion in 2005. Her most recent work centers on Hindu gurus in the cosmopolitan city-state of Singapore. In 2007–2008, she was Visiting Senior Research Fellow (supported by a Fulbright-Hays Faculty Research Abroad Fellowship) at the Asian Research Institute, National University of Singapore.

Peter W. Williams is Distinguished Professor of Comparative Religion and American Studies and Faculty Affiliate in History, Emeritus, at Miami University, Oxford, Ohio. He is the author of *Popular Religion in America* (1980), *America's Religions: Traditions and Cultures* (1989, 2001, 2008), and *Houses of God: Region, Religion and Architecture in the United States* (1997), and coeditor of the *Encyclopedia of the American Religious Experience* (1988), the *Encyclopedia of American Social History* (1993), and the *Encyclopedia of American Cultural and Intellectual History* (2002). He is also editor of the series *Studies in Anglican History*, sponsored by the Historical Society of the Episcopal Church, and *Perspectives on American Religion and Culture* (1999). He has served as President of the American Society of Church History and as cochair of the North American Religions section of the American Academy of Religion.

Introduction

CHARLES L. COHEN AND RONALD L. NUMBERS

THE UNITED STATES IS generally recognized as the most religiously diverse nation on earth. *Religious Pluralism in Modern America* examines that phenomenon from a variety of perspectives as its dynamics have played out over the recent past. In this introduction, we set out a fuller historical context. To rephrase Carl Degler's long-ago assertion about capitalism, religious diversity came to the territory that became the United States in the first ships, but the nature and scope of that variety have changed markedly since Christians first met practitioners of native religions on the American strand. The "first diversity" consisted primarily of various Protestants gathered in regional denominational configurations, with a few localities essaying radical experiments that allowed different degrees of religious freedom. The American Revolutionary Settlement of Religion set up a constitutional framework that affirmed the value of religious liberty, facilitating the multiplication of different churches, but this development coincided with the flourishing of a Protestant nationalism, inherited from the British empire, that cast the United States as a "Christian" state whose liberties depended on minimizing the presence of non-Protestant faiths. The twentieth century's dramatic rise in the proportion of Americans adhering to non-Christian faiths (or none at all) played out amid this ongoing tension between the value placed on freedom of worship, which encouraged religious diversity, and ideologically driven concerns about maintaining the nation's historic Protestant identity.

A Protestant Baseline

European imperial competition laid the parameters for America's subsequent religious trajectory. In the beginning, Anglo-America comprised a "Protestant littoral" wedged between French Roman Catholics to the north, Spanish Catholics to the south, and Amerindians everywhere.[1] As the United States filled out its territory in the nineteenth century, residual religious communities left by the French and Spanish empires' ebb—métis in the Upper Midwest, Hispanics and missionized Pueblos in the Southwest—augmented the presence of Catholics, but the nation took its primary religious identity from British America's Protestant mélange. Conventional European thinking had, since late antiquity, held that political and social stability depended on religious uniformity—one church, one state—which by rights should have resulted in the Church of England exercising unchallenged dominion in the royal domains overseas. It did not. England's laxity in forming a coherent colonial bureaucracy for much of the seventeenth century included paying little heed to ecclesiastical administration, and by the time the Church came to dedicate itself to the task, religious diversity was already a fact on the ground, generated by England's own religious conflicts—which pushed Puritans, Quakers, Baptists, and Catholics as well as Anglicans into the migrant stream—and the incorporation of Dutch and Swedish Protestants following the capture of New Netherland.[2] Moreover, colonies like South Carolina advertised their willingness to tolerate non-Anglican Protestants as a means of attracting population and spurring economic growth. Anglo-America was thus a Protestant hodgepodge from the outset, and, since Protestants arrived first, they—and the circumstances of religious diversity—shaped the religious culture's ground rules: the centrality of the Bible as the supreme source of religious authority and, more expansively, a guide to personal life and national identity; the importance of the Reformed theological tradition; the prominence of religious experience and piety fashioned by being "born again"; the possibility (albeit often limited at first) of joining a church voluntarily; a willingness to tolerate different denominational perspectives on Christian truth; and the relative importance of lay governance vis-à-vis the power of ecclesiastical hierarchies.[3]

Regional differentiations appeared within the Protestant mass, somewhat linked to the strength of established churches (that is, those receiving privileges from the state).[4] By 1750 Anglicans could be found everywhere in Anglo-America, but they were politically and culturally most prominent in the South, where the Church had been established as early as 1619 in Virginia and elsewhere beginning with Maryland in 1692. The largest number of churches, however, belonged to the Congregationalists, concentrated almost exclusively in New England, where they formed the largest denomination in colonial times and constructed the most powerful establishment. In the eighteenth century, Anglicans, Baptists, and Quakers would win a grudging toleration, if not political and cultural equality. Rhode Island, on the contrary, from the outset eschewed establishment and welcomed "sectaries" of all stripes. The greatest diversity appeared in the Delaware Valley and its environs, a region not coincidentally the site of two major experiments in undoing the one church/ one state equation. Seventeenth-century Maryland allowed any professing Trinitarian Christians to settle, thus permitting Protestant settlers to lie down with Catholic rulers. In the eighteenth century Protestants took over the government, established the Church of England, and relegated the "papists" to second-class status, but the Catholics remained. Committed by its founder to a policy of toleration, Pennsylvania (and, less famously, New Jersey, as well as parts of New York) had no establishment; Presbyterians, Lutherans, German

Reformed, Mennonites and other German sects, and Dutch Reformed all clustered in the area along with the ubiquitous Quakers.[5] Philadelphia, not Boston, was, in Jon Butler's apt characterization, the "capital" of colonial Protestantism.[6]

Non-Christians were always present, but their numbers remained small and their cultural impact slight. Native peoples practiced a variety of faiths that defy easy generalization, but, in the Eastern Woodlands, at least, belief centered on enhancing one's own spiritual power by maintaining good relations with the spirits inhabiting the entire natural world. The perceived loss of this power by communities as well as individuals occasioned various revitalization movements in which charismatic "prophets" urged tribespeople to reject all aspects of Euro-American civilization, including Christianity. Beginning in the 1730s–40s, such movements continued over the next century as the line of American settlement moved inexorably west.[7] Christian beliefs did begin to infiltrate into some native practices, but Anglo-American missionaries converted a paltry number of Amerindians compared to what French Jesuits and Spanish Franciscans achieved.[8] Meanwhile, although hundreds of captives were adopted by Amerindian tribes and took on indigenous ways, virtually all colonists outside "Indian Country" regarded native religions as at best "heathenism," and at worst "devil worship." The arrival in New Amsterdam of Sephardic refugees fleeing the destruction of the Dutch colony of Recife in 1654 heralded the start of small Jewish communities, mostly in commercial centers such as Newport, Philadelphia, and Savannah. Britain permitted Jews to naturalize in the colonies in 1740, but their numbers remained tiny, at most reaching only 2500, 0.1% of the population, in 1776.[9] Michael Gomez has irrefutably established an Islamic presence in colonial America carried by enslaved Africans; what remains controversial, and perhaps unknowable, are their numbers, practices, and legacy.[10] Colonial Anglo-America established religious diversity as a norm for American life, but, as of the Revolution, that diversity remained hugely Protestant.[11]

The American Revolutionary Settlement of Religion

The American Revolutionary Settlement of Religion devised an unprecedented constitutional, legal, and political framework for organizing religious life, personal and institutional. Taking the religious diversity on the ground as a given and wishing to reduce the potential for sectarian conflicts that had riven European states, the Constitution and Bill of Rights permanently rejected the theory of one church/one state at the national level. The Constitution prohibited imposing religious tests as a qualification for office and, in a nod to Quakers, allowed officeholders to substitute an "affirmation" to uphold it instead of an oath. The First Amendment forbade Congress from creating an "establishment of religion, or prohibiting the free exercise thereof." These provisions did not originally obligate state governments, which, under the

Constitution's principles of dual sovereignty, enjoyed authority over their own internal arrangements. The states echoed the Federal Constitution in protecting the right to religious freedom, but, at the outset, most imposed a religious test, generally aimed at suppressing Catholics' holding office, and three New England states kept versions of their old church establishments. Within a generation, however, most of the test acts vanished, and the last establishment collapsed in 1833. In both the short and long runs, the Religious Settlement tilted toward increasing religious diversity by instantiating religious freedom as both a core value and a constitutionally protected right, and by removing official religious impediments to political participation. The Settlement did not, of course, give equal political credence to every religious body—candidates had constantly to win favor in the court of public opinion—but the state itself did not restrict political access to a favored religious caste.[12]

Nor did the Settlement eradicate a widespread sense that the United States was a Protestant Christian nation uniquely favored by God, and that reception of His continued blessings depended on maintaining that Protestant identity. One source of this belief issued from the idea that ancient Israel's national covenant had been transferred to America and that God would either reward or punish His people for their collective behavior. First theologized by the New England Puritans and restricted to regenerate church members, the idea gradually expanded to encompass the nation itself. A second source came from the British imperial ideology that regarded Britain as the freest society on earth and associated Protestantism with liberty, Catholicism with tyranny.[13] If the values Americans placed on religious liberty facilitated religious diversity, identifying the United States as a Christian country whose moral and civil institutions depended on maintaining perceived Protestant norms could act as something of a counterweight, underwriting anti-Catholicism, anti-Mormonism, anti-Semitism, Islamophobia, and hatred of atheists.[14]

Nineteenth-Century Developments

As Americans embraced the right of religious freedom and governments removed restrictions on belonging to certain faiths, what some scholars have called a "free market" for choosing one's religious identity took hold.[15] Its dynamics transformed the ecclesiastical landscape. Powered by theologies that emphasized humans' capacity to obtain grace, conceptions of the ministry that favored rough-hewn preachers who could turn sinners' hearts over university-trained didacts who could not, and a systematic deployment of the revival—a mechanism of mass evangelization and recruitment discovered in the eighteenth century and perfected in the nineteenth—the so-called "upstart sects," most notably the Methodists and the Baptists, grew dramatically. Comprising approximately 6.0% of the churches in 1770, Baptists by 1860 had grown to 23.4%, while Methodist numbers exploded from 0.8% to 37.9%. Meanwhile, the leading churches of the colonial period lost their numerical superiority; the Anglicans/Episcopalians declined from 14.3% to 4.1% over the same period, the Congregationalists from 25.2% to 4.3%. Evangelicalism— which may be loosely defined as a trans-denominational Protestant position deeply committed to the authority of the Bible, the urgency of proselytizing, and the necessity for sinners to undergo the experience of being born again— submerged more liberal Protestant movements; by one estimate, at least 85% of American churches in 1860 identified themselves as evangelical (though such a figure disguises major disagreements among them). Churches competed robustly with each other for "market share," but they also formed increasingly interconnected networks of voluntary associations, in so doing creating a trans-denominational front to spread the Word and effect moral reform. At the same time, the "evangelical surge," as Mark Noll has called it, reinforced the Protestant identity of the United States, cementing the Bible as a national icon and equating its texts with the founding documents of American republican institutions.[16]

Yet throughout the century, diversity among Christians inexorably increased. Protestantism's fissiparous tendencies coupled with religious innovation uncorked by the Revolutionary Religious Settlement account for much of the change. For instance, splits among Presbyterians about revivalism's validity helped spawn the Disciples of Christ, an entirely new denomination that embraced revivalism while moving in a rationalist direction theologically. African-Americans, relatively ignored by eighteenth-century proselytizers, became targets of the "Plantation Mission," engineered particularly by Methodists and Baptists, and entered those churches in droves. Discrimination by their co-religionists in the North led some African-Americans to form their own organizations, such as the African Methodist and African Methodist Episcopal Churches.[17] What Catherine Albanese has deemed "metaphysical religion" and argued for as a "third strain" alongside the mainstream churches and evangelicalism drew small groups of adepts and followers toward esotericism, the occult, and the heterodox. Swedenborgians and Transcendentalists combined numbered in the low thousands but gained intellectual prominence; Spiritualism appealed to a greater mass audience and may have counted some 50,000 loosely associated members as late as 1893.[18] Finally, Mormons, Christian Scientists, Seventh-day Adventists, and Jehovah's Witnesses pushed up to and beyond Christianity's conventional tripartite typology. These "American Originals," as Paul Conkin has called them, have increased religious diversity in the United States and across the globe.[19]

Immigration brought fewer new churches, but it added ethnic (and thus sometimes liturgical) diversity to existing bodies, like the Lutherans, and shifted balances within the pecking order of Christian churches. For the Catholics, it did both. The wave of Irish migrants in the 1830s–40s swamped the number of native-born Catholics and repopulated the ecclesiastical hierarchy; the "New Immigrants" arriving from Southern and Eastern Europe beginning in the 1880s broadened the Church's ethnic composition once again. Sometime between roughly 1850 and 1880, the Catholic Church became the largest single ecclesiastical institution in the United States, although the collected Protestant churches boasted more members (and still do).[20] The importance of immigration to building American Catholicism heralded the arc of Eastern Orthodoxy in the twentieth century.

Yet even as the types of Christians in America increased and the percentage of Protestants in the population began to drop, most late nineteenth-century Americans maintained their identification of the United States as a Protestant nation and had little ken of non-Christian religions beyond having a parochial awareness that somewhere existed Jews, "Turks" (or perhaps "Mahometans," not "Muslims"), "heathens" (which category capaciously included Buddhists, Hindus, and American Indians), and a handful of freethinkers who embraced no religion.[21] Those perceptions, and the demography that supported them, would change in the twentieth century.

From "Christian" to "Judeo-Christian"

Excepting the traditions of the American Indians, the first non-Christian religion to make a mark was Judaism. Augmented by migrations from Germany in the mid-nineteenth century and, more massively, from Eastern Europe a few decades later, their numbers reached nearly four million by the mid-1920s. Not surprisingly, it was Jews, in the first decade of the twentieth century, who first introduced the "melting pot" metaphor to describe American culture.[22]

As early as 1915 an immigrant Jewish sociologist, Horace Kallen, challenged the appropriateness of the metaphor because he regarded it as antidemocratic. In its place he recommended "pluralism," a term that increasingly came not only to imply religious and cultural diversity but also to indicate a positive attitude toward it.[23] During the years following World War II religious experts, especially academics, debated the question of "religious pluralism" in America, which some regarded as a "terrible evil" that divided the nation into competing denominations.[24] In 1951 an editorial in the mainstream *Christian Century* denounced pluralism as a "National Menace," while noting that "The idea of a plural society is so new to Americans that many will not even understand the term."[25] Marty E. Marty, always in the vanguard of American religious historians, described pluralism as follows:

> Americans like to speak of their religious settlement as one of pluralism, marked by tolerance. *Pluralism* is a rather recently applied term, necessitated by the presence of hundreds of competing religious groups and the freedom of citizens to have no religion at all. As long as Protestantism dominated the religious landscape, the choice of a term like pluralism could be postponed. Citizens spoke of *religious freedom* and *the separation of church and state*....Pluralism in colloquial language, means "any number can play." They can play on equal terms.[26]

Other observers saw pluralism as essential for winning the international war against communism. In the 1950s Columbia University's Arthur Hertzberg emphasized the need for the United States to adopt "a true religious pluralism in which men's beliefs and values can be subject only to the minimum restraint of public order."[27]

By this time some Americans were also beginning to refer to the "Judeo-Christian tradition." The first use of this expression in the *New York Times* appeared just a few months before the United States entered World War II, in comments attributed to Harold C. Urey, a Nobel Prize–winning chemist at Columbia University and the son of a lay minister in the Church of the Brethren.[28] As Deborah Dash Moore has explained, wartime experiences promoted the use of the phrase "Judeo-Christian tradition" as a way of identifying the three "fighting faiths of democracy." Symbolic of the newly invented tradition was an event association with the tragic sinking of the U.S. Army Transport ship *Dorchester*, torpedoed by a German U-boat in February 1942. "As the ship went down," writes Moore, "four chaplains—two Protestants, one Catholic, and one Jew—assisted the soldiers and sailors into the lifeboats, until they themselves went down with the ship...the four chaplains of three faiths worshipping together exemplified the creation of a 'Judeo-Christian tradition' that would come to express American ideals guiding the country's wartime mission." At funerals for unknown soldiers in the 1950s, three chaplains typically participated: a Protestant in English, a Catholic in Latin, and a Jew in Hebrew. Late in 1952 President-elect Dwight D. Eisenhower quipped to a Soviet colleague: "our Government has no sense unless it is founded in a deeply felt religious faith, and I don't care what it is. With us of course it is the Judeo-Christian concept but it must be a religion that all men are created equal."[29]

This newly invented tradition became enshrined in American culture with the publication in 1955 of the Jewish author Will Herberg's best-selling *Protestant-Catholic-Jew: An Essay in American Religious Sociology*, which described religious pluralism in America as "not merely a historical and political fact...[but] the primordial condition of things, an essential aspect of the American Way of Life, and therefore in itself an aspect of religious belief."[30] Not all Jews appreciated being yoked together with Christians, and some leading figures dismissed the notion of a common tradition as a "myth."[31]

The Turning Point: 1965

The religious demography of the United States changed dramatically in the wake of federal legislation during the Lyndon B. Johnson administration that opened the doors to millions of new immigrants. It all started naively in 1965, when the U.S. Congress passed a new Immigration and Nationality Act, which abolished the restrictive Immigration Act of 1924. The earlier law had established quotas limiting immigration largely to persons of German, British, and Irish nationality and created high barriers for those from Asia and Southern and Eastern Europe. The old law had the effect of separating families and restricting the entrance of skilled workers from outside of Western Europe. The new law, inspired by the growing civil-rights movement, abandoned the old quotas and allowed for the reuniting of families: husbands and wives, parents and children, brothers and sisters. Assured by Senator Edward M. Kennedy, the floor manager for the bill in the Senate, that levels of immigration would remain unchanged and that "our cities will not be flooded with a million immigrants annually," his colleagues overwhelmingly approved the bill by a vote of 76 to 18.[32] The new law capped the number of immigrants at 170,000 annually from the Eastern Hemisphere and 120,000 from the Western, with no more than 20,000 being allowed from any single nation. At the signing of the bill in the shadow of Ellis Island, President Johnson praised the measure for admitting immigrants "on the basis of their skills and their close relationship to those already here" rather than on their country of origin.[33]

Senator Kennedy turned out to be a false prophet. Under the new law millions of immigrants from all regions of the world, not just Europe, began flooding the country. Between 1966 and 2000, 22.8 million legal immigrants arrived. In the single decade of the 1970s Asian immigration, formerly a trickle, swelled to nearly 40% of the total, with the Korean population in the United States growing by 412.8%, the Filipino by 125.8%, the Chinese by 85.3%, and the Japanese by 18.5%. The bulk of the immigrants who entered between 1966 and 2000 were family members of recent immigrants, with 85% of them coming from the so-called Third World.[34]

Naturally, these new immigrants brought their religions—Islam, Buddhism, Hinduism, and many, many more—with them. "The United States has become the most religiously diverse nation on earth," announced the Harvard scholar Diana L. Eck in 2001.[35] As other experts quickly pointed out, this generalization was misleading. Indeed, according to Philip Jenkins, it was "flat wrong." While admitting that the massive post-1965 immigration had had "an enormous religious impact," Jenkins, a professor of history and religious studies, argued that its greatest effect was to swell the ranks of Christians:

> Far more than most secular observers yet appreciate, the vast majority of new immigrants are Christian or become so after their arrival on these shores. More catastrophic still, from the point of view of our secular elites, the Christianity that these newcomers espouse is commonly fideistic, charismatic, otherworldly, and (nightmare of nightmares) fundamentalist. In a wonderful illustration of the phenomenon of unintended consequences, the radical social policy of color-blind open immigration is producing rich benefits for religion of a powerfully traditional bent.

In other words, to adopt R. Stephen Warner's memorable phrase, the post-1965 world had witnessed "the de-Europeanization of American Christianity," not the swamping of the dominant religion.[36]

But non-Christian religions surged as well. Estimates vary wildly and controversially, but the usually reliable Pew Forum on Religion and Public Life in 2008 gave the following percentages for the most numerous non-Christians in America: Jewish 1.7%, Buddhist 0.7%, Muslim 0.6%, Hindu 0.4%.[37] Not all of these were new Americans. Many Buddhists, for example, came from non-immigrant families; and since 1930 tens of thousands of African-Americans have joined the Nation of Islam, which in the 1980s moved to the Muslim mainstream.[38]

The attacks of September 11, 2001, by Muslim extremists on the World Trade Center and the Pentagon prompted some skittish Americans to question the wisdom of embracing religious pluralism. The Right Wing's favorite historian, the evangelical preacher David Barton, drew the following "Lessons from the September Terrorist Attacks":

> In recent decades schools and public arenas have moved toward a completely inclusive pluralism, teaching that all of the 1700 different religions are equal and therefore deserve equal acceptance and respect. This tragedy shows the fallacy of that teaching. Not all religions are the same; not all have the same value systems; in fact, many directly oppose the value systems of others.[39]

Subsequent efforts to build an Islamic cultural center near the site of the destroyed World Trade Center, as well as concerns about the imposition of Sharia law in the United States, continued to fan the flames of distrust.[40]

Nevertheless, Muslims achieved widespread recognition. By the time of the attacks they had been serving since the early 1990s as chaplains in the U.S. armed services, and in 1997 President Bill Clinton had displayed the Islamic crescent on the White House grounds for the first time, along with a Christmas tree and a Hanukkah menorah. Airports began allocating space for mosques, and hospitals began catering to Muslim patients.[41] In 2006 the first Muslim, Keith Ellison (D-Minnesota), was elected to Congress—and was later sworn in while placing his hand on Thomas Jefferson's copy of the Koran.[42] That same year Mazie K. Horono (D-Hawaii) and Hank Johnson (D-Georgia) became the first Buddhists elected to the House of Representatives. In 2013 Horono moved on to the Senate, and Tulsi Gabbard (D-Hawaii) broke the congressional barrier for Hindus.[43]

By the new millennium scholars were suggesting that the phrase "Judeo-Christian" be discarded in favor of the "Judeo-Christian-Muslim tradition" or, more simply, the "Abrahamic faiths." Richard John Neuhaus, the influential Lutheran-turned-Catholic who edited *First Things*, mocked this move by predicting that Americans seeking religious inclusivity would soon be referring to the "Judeo-Christian-Buddhist-Hindu-Islamic-Agnostic-Atheist society." Neuhaus may not have been far off the mark. In 2010 the *New York Times* reported that at hearings of the Texas State Board of Education one woman argued that "Sikhism is the fifth-largest religion in the world and should be included in the curriculum."[44]

As more and more mosques sprouted up around the country, they were joined by an increasing number of Buddhist and Hindu temples.[45] Occasionally, these visible symbols of non-Christian faiths provoked protests and vandalism, but Americans generally tolerated them. In *American Grace: How Religion*

Divides and Unites Us (2010) the social scientists Robert D. Putnam and David E. Campbell report that "three quarters of Americans (76%) say they have no problem with the construction of a large Buddhist temple in their neighborhood"—but then note "that only a small number (15%) would explicitly welcome it in their midst."[46]

The "Nones"

With the possible exception of Wicca and other neo-pagan religions, no "religious" community has suffered more marginalization than those who do not believe in God: atheists and agnostics. (Alert readers may notice that even this book largely ignores them.) Today these religious skeptics make up roughly 6% of Americans, with another 14% reporting no particular religious affiliation. The roots of unbelief go back to the eighteenth century, when deists first appeared in the colonies. Then they constituted a tiny minority, but their ranks included such high-profile residents as Thomas Paine, Benjamin Franklin, and Thomas Jefferson. Although all of them professed belief in a creator god, they typically rejected any continuing involvement of the deity. Their contemporaries denounced them as "infidels." Organized deism declined in the early nineteenth century, only to be replaced in the second half of the century by "freethought" societies. The leading freethinker was Colonel Robert "Bob" Ingersoll, son of a Calvinist preacher and one of the most popular orators in America.[47]

Despite the growth of "secular humanism" and atheism in the late twentieth and early twenty-first centuries—symbolized by the celebrity of "new atheists" such as the American philosopher Daniel C. Dennett, the California-based neuroscientist Sam Harris, the British-American journalist Christopher Hitchens, and the British zoologist Richard Dawkins—unbelievers rarely received public recognition and were sometimes the objects of overt discrimination. The Boy Scouts of America denied them uniforms, and the U.S. military denied them a chaplain, despite their having a larger number in the armed services than Jews, Muslims, and Buddhists, each of which had at least one chaplain.[48] In 2007 California Representative Pete Stark became the first member of Congress to admit to being an atheist, declaring that he was "a Unitarian who does not believe in a Supreme Being." (In 2012 Krysten Sinema, a Democrat from Arizona who said she adhered to no religion, won election to the House of Representatives, becoming the first in Congress to identify publicly with the "nones.") In Barack Obama's inaugural address in 2009, the incoming president described the United States as "a nation of Christians and Muslims, Jews and Hindus, and nonbelievers," the first such recognition ever for nonreligious Americans.[49]

Although the reasons for rejecting religion are complex, unbelief seems especially popular among scientists. A recent survey by the sociologist Elaine Howard Ecklund of nearly 1700 elite American scientists found that 34% did not believe in God and that an additional 30% did not believe that there was any way to determine if there is a God—figures far higher than those for the U.S. population as a whole, which were 2% and 4%, respectively. In a new twist for such surveys, 22% of the atheists and 27% of the agnostics described themselves as "spiritual."[50]

Historians

Despite the growing evidence of religious diversity all around them, historians of religion in America only slowly awakened to what was transpiring. Winthrop S. Hudson's classic survey, *Religion in America*, nicely illustrates the gradual recognition. In the first edition, released in 1965, the very year Congress passed the Immigration and Nationality Act, Hudson mentioned in passing that by the end of the nineteenth century "even Buddhism had made its appearance on the Pacific coast"; he also devoted two paragraphs to "Esoteric Wisdom from the East," in which he noted the Buddhist-tinged Theosophical Movement, the Bahá'í faith, and the Vedanta Society, identified as "a Hindu cult." In the second edition, published eight years later, he concluded his book with a brief section on "Adjustment to a Pluralistic Society." Here he described how—largely as a result of the increasing presence of Jews—the United States had moved from "a Christian and even a Protestant nation" to a pluralistic one. "Perhaps one of the greatest contributions of Judaism to the United States," he opined, "will be to help other Americans understand how the United States can be a truly pluralistic society in which the pluralism is maintained in a way that is enriching rather than impoverishing." By the seventh edition, coauthored with John Corrigan in 2003, Hudson was devoting a lengthy section to "World Religions in America," describing twenty-first-century pluralism as "an exclamation point to the story" of religion in America.[51]

The same trend can be seen in Edwin Scott Gaustad's *Historical Atlas of Religion in America*. In the 1976 edition Gaustad included Jews in a section titled "Special Aspects of Religion in America" and briefly mentioned Buddhism in a discussion of Hawaii. However, a quarter-century later, a new edition coauthored with Philip L. Barlow included an entire section titled "Toward Pluralism":

> During the first decade of the 20th century more than 90 percent of immigrants continued to be Europeans, and the figure was still 80 percent at mid-century. A single generation later, however, a profound change had been wrought. One-third of Americans in 1990 were not of European heritage, and demographic projections indicated that non-whites would achieve an actual majority in the country by the middle of the 21st century.... In the 1980s, almost 40 percent of immigrants arrived from the Near East and Far East. In 1990 Asians constituted 22 percent of all persons born outside but residing in the United States. (Africans constituted 2.3 percent, Europeans fewer than 8 percent.)....Who can doubt that all this is profoundly influencing religion and the future of religion in America?[52]

Reflecting these changes, the new atlas added sections on Buddhism, Hinduism, and Islam—and lightly touched on Jainism, Sikhism, and Bahá'í.

The genie is out of the bottle; the pluralistic nature of American religion is too apparent for scholars, not to mention members of the general populace, to ignore any longer.[53] The United States may never give up its identity as a Christian nation, but Protestants are likely soon to drop below 50% of the population, at which point they will become a plurality. Yet the heritage of the past—the value placed on religious freedom versus a residual sense that Christianity (and, for some, Protestant Christianity) is prerequisite for ensuring American freedom and "greatness"—endures. Now is a good time to take stock of what the diversity of gods hath wrought—which is what the essays in this volume attempt to do.

This book grew out of a conference on "Religious Pluralism in Modern America" sponsored by the Lubar Institute for the Study of the Abrahamic Religions at the University of Wisconsin–Madison in April 2007. Besides the persons whose essays appear within, we would like to thank Diana Eck and Martin Marty, the two plenary speakers, and participants James Hitchcock, Jennifer Ratner-Rosenhagen, Katherine Carté Engel, Abbas Hamdani, and J. Rixey Ruffin, along with Sheldon and Marianne Lubar, founders of the Lubar Institute.

Notes

1 Much of what follows in this and subsequent paragraphs can be traced in Carla Gardina Pestana, *Protestant Empire: Religion and the Making of the British Atlantic World* (Philadelphia: University of Pennsylvania Press, 2009). See also Jon Butler, *Becoming America: The Revolution Before 1776* (Cambridge, MA: Harvard University Press, 2000), 185–224.

2 On the Church of England's struggles (and sometime successes), see John Frederick Woolverton, *Colonial Anglicanism in North America* (Detroit: Wayne State University Press, 1984).

3 On the Reformed tradition, see Paul Conkin, *The Uneasy Center: Reformed Christianity in Antebellum America* (Chapel Hill: University of North Carolina Press, 1995), though he defines "Reformed" too capaciously. For a classic study of denominationalism, see Sidney E. Mead, *The Lively Experiment: The Shape of Christianity in America* (Eugene, OR: Wipf and Stock, 2007 [orig. New York: Harper & Row, 1963]). For lay government, see James F. Cooper, Jr., *Tenacious of Their Liberties: The Congregationalists in Colonial Massachusetts* (New York: Oxford University Press, 1999), and Patricia Bonomi, *Under the Cope of Heaven: Religion, Society, and Politics in Colonial America*, updated edition (New York: Oxford University Press, 2003), 77–78.

4 These patterns can be followed in the maps placed throughout Edwin Scott Gaustad and Philip L. Barlow, *New Historical Atlas of Religion in America* (New York: Oxford University Press, 2001), Part I.

5 Thomas Curry, *The First Freedoms: Church and State in America to the Passage of the First Amendment* (New York: Oxford University Press, 1986), 38–53; Sally Schwartz, *"A Mixed Multitude": The Struggle for Toleration in Colonial Pennsylvania* (New York: New York University Press, 1987).

6 Jon Butler, "Protestant Pluralism," in *Encyclopedia of the North American Colonies*, 3 vols., Jacob Ernest Cooke, ed. (New York: Charles Scribner's Sons, 1993), vol. 3, 617.

7 Gregory Evans Dowd, *A Spirited Resistance: The North American Indian Struggle for Unity, 1745–1815* (Baltimore, MD: Johns Hopkins University Press, 1991).

8 James Axtell, *The Invasion Within: The Contest of Cultures in Colonial North America* (New York: Oxford University Press, 1985); Allan Greer, *Mohawk Saint: Catherine Tekakwitha and the Jesuits* (New York: Oxford University Press, 2005); Steven W. Hackel, *Children of Coyote, Missionaries of Saint Francis: Indian-Spanish Relations in Colonial California, 1769–1850* (Chapel Hill: University of North Carolina Press, 2005); Ramón A. Gutiérrez, *When Jesus Came, the Corn Mothers Went Away: Marriage, Sexuality, and Power in New Mexico, 1500–1846* (Stanford, CA: Stanford University Press, 1991).

9 Eli Faber, *A Time for Planting: The First Migration 1654–1820* (Baltimore, MD: Johns Hopkins University Press, 1992); for the population estimate, Jonathan D. Sarna, *American Judaism: A History* (New Haven, CT: Yale University Press, 2004), 375.

10 Michael A. Gomez, *Black Crescent: The Experience and Legacy of African Muslims in the Americas* (New York: Cambridge University Press, 2005), 3–200.

11 Chris Beneke, *Beyond Toleration: The Religious Origins of American Pluralism* (New York: Oxford University Press, 2008). See also Thomas S. Kidd, *God of Liberty: A Religious History of the American Revolution* (New York: Basic Books, 2010).

12 Frank Lambert, *The Founding Fathers and the Place of Religion in America* (Princeton, NJ: Princeton University Press, 2003); Edwin S. Gaustad, *Neither King nor Prelate: Religion and the New Nation 1776–1826* (Grand Rapids, MI: Eerdmans, 1993) [originally published as *Faith of Our Fathers: Religion and the New Nation* (San Francisco: Harper & Row, 1987)].

13 Pestana, *Protestant Empire*; Thomas S. Kidd, *The Protestant Interest: New England after Puritanism* (New Haven, CT: Yale University Press, 2004); Conrad Cherry, ed., *God's New Israel: Religious Interpretations of American Destiny* (Englewood Cliffs, NJ: Prentice-Hall, 1971).

14 On anti-Catholic sentiment, see Ray Allen Billington, *The Protestant Crusade, 1800–1860: A Study of the Origins of American Nativism* (New York: Macmillan, 1938); John Higham, *Strangers in the Land, Patterns of American Nativism, 1860–1925* (New Brunswick, NJ: Rutgers University Press, 1955); John T. McGreevy, *Catholicism and American Freedom: A History* (New York: W. W. Norton, 2003); and Philip Jenkins, *The New Anti-Catholicism: The Last Acceptable Prejudice* (New York: Oxford University Press, 2003). On anti-Mormonism, see Sarah Barringer Gordon, *The Mormon Question: Polygamy and Constitutional Conflict in Nineteenth-Century America* (Chapel Hill: University of North Carolina Press, 2002), and Spencer Fluhman, *"A Peculiar People": Anti-Mormonism and the Making of Religion in Nineteenth-Century America* (Chapel Hill, NC: University of North Carolina Press, 2012). On anti-Semitism, see Frederic Cople Jaher, *A Scapegoat in the New Wilderness: The Origins and Rise of Anti-Semitism in America* (Cambridge, MA: Harvard

University Press, 1994), and Hasia R. Diner, *The Jews of the United States* (Berkeley and Los Angeles: University of California Press, 2004), *passim*. On Islamophobia, see Peter Gottshalk and Gabriel Greenberg, *Islamophobia: Making Muslims the Enemy* (Lanham, MD: Rowman & Littlefield, 2008). The study of anti-atheism is less well-developed, but see Penny Edgell, Joseph Gerteis, and Douglas Hartmann, "Atheists As 'Other': Moral Boundaries and Cultural Membership in American Society," *American Sociological Review*, 71 (April 2006), 211–234, and Bryan F. LeBeau, "Becoming the Most Hated Woman in America: Madalyn Murray O'Hair," *Journal of American Culture*, 26 (June 2003), 153–170. See also Chris Beneke and Chrisopher S. Grenda, eds., *The First Prejudice: Religious Tolerance and Intolerance in Early America* (Philadelphia: University of Pennsylvania Press, 2011).

15 Roger Finke and Rodney Stark, *The Churching of America 1776–2005: Winners and Losers in Our Religious Economy* (New Brunswick, NJ: Rutgers University Press, 2007).

16 Mark A. Noll, *America's God: From Jonathan Edwards to Abraham Lincoln* (New York: Oxford University Press, 2002). The percentage figures have been calculated from Table 9.3, 166; the 85% estimate is on 170.

17 Sylvia R. Frey and Betty Wood, *Come Shouting to Zion: African American Protestantism in the American South and British Caribbean to 1830* (Chapel Hill: University of North Carolina Press, 1998).

18 Catherine L. Albanese, *A Republic of Mind & Spirit: A Cultural History of American Metaphysical Religion* (New Haven, CT: Yale University Press, 2007). For the number of Spiritualists, see Sidney E. Ahlstrom, *A Religious History of the American People* (New Haven, CT: Yale University Press, 1972), 490.

19 Paul K. Conkin, *American Originals: Homemade Varieties of Christianity* (Chapel Hill: University of North Carolina Press, 1997).

20 For a brief introduction to ethnicity within Catholic churches, see Finke and Stark, *Churching of America*, 134–139, and for the estimate of when the Catholic Church became the largest single church, ibid., 120.

21 Thomas A. Tweed, *The American Encounter with Buddhism, 1844–1912: Victorian Culture and the Limits of Dissent* (Bloomington: Indiana University Press, 1992), xvii–xviii.

22 Philip Gleason, "The Melting Pot: Symbol of Fusion or Confusion?" *American Quarterly* 16 (1964): 20–46, reprinted in Gleason, *Speaking of Diversity: Language and Ethnicity in Twentieth-Century America* (Baltimore, MD: Johns Hopkins University Press, 1992), 3–31; Edna Nahshon, ed., *From the Ghetto to the Melting Pot: Israel Zangwill's Jewish Plays* (Detroit, MI: Wayne State University Press, 2006), 215.

23 Diana L. Eck, *A New Religious America: How a "Christian Country" Has Now Become the World's Most Religiously Diverse Nation* (San Francisco: HarperSanFrancisco, 2001), 57, 70–73; William R. Hutchison, *Religious Pluralism in America: The Contentious History of a Founding Ideal* (New Haven, CT: Yale University Press, 2003), 1–4.

24 Willard L. Sperry, ed., *Religion and Our Divided Denominations*, vol. 1 of *Religion in the Post-War World* (Cambridge, MA: Harvard University Press, 1945), 28 (evil). The first appearance of the phrase "religious pluralism" in the *New York Times* is in a review of Sperry's book by Reinhold Niebuhr, "Practical Values in Religion," *New York Times*, September 2, 1945, p. 99.

25 Martin E. Marty, "Peace and Pluralism: The *Century* 1946–1952," *Christian Century*, 101 (October 24, 1984): 979–983, on 979.

26 Jackson W. Carroll, Douglas W. Johnson, and Martin E. Marty, *Religion in America: 1950 to the Present* (San Francisco: Harper & Row, 1979), 78, in a section written by Marty. For his more recent views on pluralism, see Martin E. Marty, *When Faiths Collide* (Malden, MA: Blackwell, 2005); and Marty E. Marty, *The Protestant Voice in American Pluralism* (Athens: University of Georgia Press, 2006).

27 Quoted in Irving Spiegel, "A.J.C. Leader Sees New U.S. Tensions," *New York Times*, April 18, 1959, p. 23.

28 "Berle Sees Nazis Losing Strength," *New York Times*, September 9, 1941, p. 26. The second mention came in 1945; the third in 1951.

29 Deborah Dash Moore, *GI Jews: How World War II Changed a Generation* (Cambridge, MA: Harvard University Press, 2004), 10, 118–121, 257–258 (quoting Eisenhower); Sarna, *American Judaism*, 266–267; Jack Raymond, "Unknowns of World War II and Korea Are Enshrined," *New York Times*, May 31, 1958, p. 1; Kevin M. Schultz, *Tri-Faith America: How Catholics and Jews Held Postwar America to Its Protestant Promise* (New York: Oxford University Press, 2011).

30 Will Herberg, *Protestant-Catholic-Jew: An Essay in American Religious Sociology* (Garden City, NY: Doubleday, 1955), 98–99. Two decades before the appearance of Herberg's book, the Protestant Everett Ross Clinchy published *All in the Name of God* (New York: John Day, 1934), which called for the recognition of Catholics and Jews but made no mention of Muslims, Hindus, or Buddhists. On the significance of Herberg's book, see Martin E. Marty, *Protestant Voice in American Pluralism*, 5. On the diversity of Jewish attitudes toward pluralism, see Joseph L. Blau, *Judaism in America: From Curiosity to Third Faith* (Chicago: University of Chicago Press, 1976), 8; Naomi W. Cohen, *Jews in Christian America: The Pursuit of Religious Equality* (New York: Oxford University Press, 1992), 240–244; Egal Feldman, *Catholics and Jews in Twentieth-Century America* (Urbana: University of Illinois Press, 2001), 136–144; and Yaakov Ariel, *Evangelizing the Chosen People: Missions to the Jews in America, 1880–2000* (Chapel Hill: University of North Carolina Press, 2000), 196. See also Mark Silk, "Notes on the Judeo-Christian Tradition in America," *American Quarterly*, 36 (Spring 1984), 65–85.

31 See, e.g., Arthur A. Cohen, *The Myth of the Judeo-Christian Tradition and Other Dissenting Essays* (New York: Harper & Row, 1970); and Jacob Neusner, *Jews and Christians: The Myth of a Common Tradition* (Philadelphia: Trinity Press International, 1991).

32 Quoted in Otis L. Graham, Jr., "A Vast Social Experiment: The Immigration Act of 1965," *NPG Forum*, October, 2005, p. 5, at www.npg.org/forum_series/vast_socialexp_immgact1965.pdf.

33 "Text of President's Speech on Immigration," *New York Times*, October 4, 1965, p. SU1; Roger Daniels, "The Immigration Act of 1965: Intended and Unintended Consequences," in *Historians on America: Decisions that Made a Difference*, ed. George Clack (Washington, DC: U.S. Department of State, 2007), 76–83, available at www.america.gov/publications/books/historiansonamerica.html. See also Roger Daniels, *Guarding the Golden Door: American Immigration Policy and Immigrants Since 1882* (New York: Hill and Wang, 2004).

34 Daniels, "The Immigration Act of 1965"; David M. Reimers, *Still the Golden Door: The Third World Comes to America* (New York: Columbia University Press, 1985), 116. See also Bill Ong Hing, *Defining America through Immigration Policy* (Philadelphia: Temple University Press, 2004), 93–111; and Aristide R. Zolberg, *A Nation by Design: Immigration Policy in the Fashioning of America* (Cambridge, MA: Harvard University Press, 2006), 337–381.

35 Eck, *New Religious America*, 4.

36 Philip Jenkins, "A New Religious America," *First Things*, No. 125 (August/ September 2002): 25–28; R. Stephen Warner, "The De-Europeanization of American Christianity," in Warner, *A Church of Our Own: Disestablishment and Diversity in American Religion* (New Brunswick, NJ: Rutgers University Press, 2005), 257–262; first published in *Christian Century*, February 10, 2004, under the title "Coming to America: Immigrants and the Faith They Bring." On Indian Christians in America since 1965, see Raymond Brady Willians, *Christian Pluralism in the United States: The Indian Immigrant Experience* (Cambridge, UK: Cambridge University Press, 1996). On the increasing ethnic diversity among Catholics, see Jay P. Dolan, *In Search of an American Catholicism: A History of Religion and Culture in Tension* (New York: Oxford University Press, 2002), 215–221.

37 *U.S Religious Landscape Survey*, 5, Pew Forum on Religion & Public Life, February 2008, at http://religions.pewforum.org/reports.

38 Ibid., p. 9 (Buddhists); Gutbi Mahdi Ahmed, "Muslim Organization in the United States," in *The Muslims of America*, ed. Yvonne Yazbeck Haddad (New York: Oxford University Press, 1991), 11–24; Mohamed Nimer, "Muslims in American Public Life," in *Muslims in the West: From Sojourners to Citizens*, ed. Yvonne Yazbeck Haddad (New York: Oxford University Press, 2002), 169–186; Gomez, *Black Crescent*. See also Edward E. Curtis IV, *Black Muslim Religion in the Nation of Islam, 1960–1975* (Chapel Hill: University of North Carolina Press, 2006).

39 David Barton, "Lessons from the September Terrorist Attacks," WallBuilders Newsletter, Special Edition, September 11, 2001, at www.wallbuilders.com/libissuesarticles.asp?id=144.

40 "Public Remains Conflicted over Islam," Pew Forum on Religion & Public Life, August 24, 2010, at www.pewforum.org; Carla Hinton, "Federal Judge Bars Oklahoma's Certification of Sharia Law Amendment," November 9, 2010, at http://NewsOK.com; Bob Smietana, "Near Tennessee Capitol, Faith Leaders Call for Stop to Anti-Shariah Bill," March 2, 2011, at www.tennessean.com.

41 Mohamed Nimer, "Muslims in American Public Life," in Haddad, ed., *Muslims in the West*, 169–186; Jane I. Smith, *Islam in America* (New York: Columbia University Press, 1999), 139, 158, 163, 175. See also "The Sheikh Maktoum Prayer Room," at http://my.clevelandclinic.org/pastoral_care/about/worship.aspx.

42 Neil MacFarquhar, "Muslim's Election Is Celebrated Here and in Mideast," *New York Times*, November 10, 2006, p. A28.

43 "Faith on the Hill: The Religious Composition of the 113th Congress," Pew Forum on Religion & Public Life, November 16, 2012, at www.pewforum.org, accessed March 4, 2013.

44 Eck, *New Religious America*, p. 65; Richard John Neuhaus, "In Lieu of Memoirs," *First Things*, No. 135 (August–September 2003), at www.firstthings.

com/issue/2003/08/augustseptember; Russell Shorto, "How Christian Were the Founders?" *New York Times*, February 14, 2010, at www.nytimes.com/2010/02/14/ magazine/14texbooks-t.html?em. Stephen Prothero, ed., *A Nation of Religions: The Politics of Pluralism in Multireligious America* (Chapel Hill: University of North Carolina Press, 2006), 9, dates the earliest such calls to 1988. The first reference to "Abrahamic faiths" in the *New York Times* appeared in Peter Steinfels, "Beliefs: Does a Plea for an Alliance of Science and Religion on Ecology Presage a New Kind of Coexistence?" *New York Times*, January 20, 1990, p. A12.

45 On the post-1965 growth of Asian religions in America, see Carl T. Jackson, *Vedanta for the West: The Ramakrishna Movement in the United States* (Bloomington: Indiana University Press, 1994); and Thomas A. Tweed and Stephen Prothero, eds., *Asian Religions in America: A Documentary History* (New York: Oxford University Press, 1999). On the early history of Buddhism in America, see Thomas A. Tweed, *The American Encounter with Buddhism, 1844–1912: Victorian Culture and the Limits of Dissent* (Bloomington: Indiana University Press, 1992).

46 Robert D. Putnam and David E. Campbell, *American Grace: How Religion Divides and Unites Us* (New York: Simon & Schuster, 2010), 513. See also Prothero, ed., *Nation of Religions*, 8. For instances of hostility, see Gurinder Singh Mann, Paul Numrich, and Raymond Williams, *Buddhists, Hindus, and Sikhs in America* (New York: Oxford University Press, 2001), 38.

47 "'Nones' on the Rise: One-in-Five Adults Have No Relgious Affiliation," Pew Forum on Religion & Public Life, October 9, 2012, at www.pewforum.org. On the history of deism and freethought, see Kerry S. Walters, *The American Deists: Voices of Reason and Dissent in the Early Republic* (Lawrence: University Press of Kansas, 1992); Susan Jacoby, *Freethinkers: A History of American Secularism* (New York: Metropolitan Books, 2004); and Susan Jacoby, *The Great Agnostic: Robert Ingersoll and American Freethought* (New Haven, CT: Yale University Press, 2013).

48 Margaret Downey, "Discrimination against Atheists: The Facts," *Free Inquiry* 24 (June–July, 2004): 41–43; James Dao, "Atheists Seek Chaplain Role in the Military," *New York Times*, April 27, 2011, pp. A1, A3. See also Tom Breen, "Army Group Says There ARE Atheists in Foxholes," Associated Press, April 1, 2011, at http://cnsnews.com/news/article/army-group-says-there-are-atheists-foxholes

49 Carla Marinucci, "Stark's Atheist Views Break Political Taboo," *San Francisco Chronicle*, March 14, 2007, at www.sfgate.com; "Faith on the Hill"; "Barack Obama's Inaugural Address," *New York Times*, January 20, 2009.

50 Elaine Howard Ecklund, *Science vs. Religion: What Scientists Really Think* (New York: Oxford University Press, 2010), 16, 58. On the history of science and unbelief, see Bernard Lightman, "Unbelief," in *Science and Religion around the World*, eds. John Hedley Brooke and Ronald L. Numbers (New York: Oxford University Press, 2011), 252–277. See also Ronald L. Numbers, "Science, Secularization, and Privatization," in Numbers, *Science and Christianity in Pulpit and Pew* (New York: Oxford University Press, 2007), 129–136.

51 Winthrop S. Hudson, *Religion in America* (New York: Charles Scribner's Sons, 1965), 226, 286–287; Winthrop S. Hudson, *Religion in America*, 2nd ed. (New York: Charles Scribner's Sons, 1973), 426–427, 440; John Corrigan and Winthrop S. Hudson, *Religion in America: An Historical Account of the Development of American Religious Life*, 7th ed. (Upper Saddle River, NJ: Pearson Prentice Hall, 2003), xiii

(exclamation point), 434–450. Corrigan and Hudson's inclusiveness did not extend to agnostics and atheists.

52 Edwin Scott Gaustad, *Historical Atlas of Religion in America*, rev. ed. (New York: Harper & Row, 1976); Gaustad and Barlow, *New Historical Atlas*, 258.

53 For a sample, see Eck, *New Religious America*; Robert Wuthnow, *America and the Challenges of Religious Diversity* (Princeton, NJ: Princeton University Press, 2005); Amanda Porterfield, *Transformation of American Religion: The Story of a Late Twentieth-Century Awakening* (New York: Oxford University Press, 2001); and Wade Clark Roof, ed., "Religious Pluralism and Civil Society," a whole edition of *The Annals of the American Academy of Political and Social Science*, 612 (July, 2007).

PART I | Overviews

CHAPTER 1

Religious Pluralism
in Religious Studies

Amanda Porterfield

AS I UNDERSTAND IT, religious pluralism is a term for religious diversity that imputes positive meaning to religion and encourages appreciative understanding of its many forms. Used to describe religious diversity in the United States, the term conveys respect for the contributions that religious traditions have made and continue to make to American society. Implying that religion is common ground in a shared democratic culture, people who use the term often convey idealism about democracy, and about religion's role in upholding it. This idealism presumes that different traditions are linked in a way that is hidden from clear view—as in, for example, "we all worship the same God." It also presumes that different traditions are intrinsically compatible; indeed, they are resources to be drawn upon for national unity and strength.

Religious pluralism thrives in academic settings where instructors lead students to slip imaginatively into different religious worlds and belief systems. Because students are expected to be open-minded learners respectful of others, the classroom is well-suited for the willing suspension of belief that enables people to explore other religions and their claims to meaning and truth. The academic practices of the classroom encourage students from different religious backgrounds to detach themselves, at least partially and temporarily, from their own beliefs in order to investigate the religious beliefs and practices of others. Removed from the communities, practices, and authority structures of lived religions, students in an academic class are more or less exempt from pressures to conform to and support the system of religious beliefs they are studying. Students can examine the structures, dynamics, contradictions, and effects of various belief systems, including their own, with an investigative spirit and sense of freedom that can be distinguished from the religious practices and confession of belief that characterize adherence to a particular religious tradition, group, or movement.

Classroom presentations of religious pluralism tend to highlight the esthetic dimensions of religion—the colors, sounds, sights, and poetry of religious expression, and the role that religion has played throughout human history in bringing human thought and feeling to expression. Such presentations accentuate the positive social aspects of religion and draw attention to the ways that religion draws people together in community, facilitating networks of support and cooperative activity. Commitment to religious pluralism as an interpretive framework encourages idealized representations of religion that deflect skepticism and social criticism of religion.

The repressive, violent, and antisocial aspects of religion are hard to ignore, but the significance of these aspects declines insofar as the purpose of interpretation is to appreciate religion's most enriching and beneficial aspects. As a model for thinking about religion and religious diversity, pluralism tends to lift up most inspiring and socially constructive aspects of religion, and downplay those aspects that fall short or fail to harmonize. Thus from a pluralist approach, Islamist fundamentalism is more of a distortion than an authentic expression of Islamic faith. The Ku Klux Klan is not a true Christian movement, despite what its members say, but a misrepresentation of Christian truths.

I would not want to deny the role that religious pluralism has played in expanding the horizons of many students, encouraging intellectual curiosity and open-mindedness, and genuine interest in understanding human beings and human cultures. In these important respects, religious pluralism fosters the liberal education, scholarly inquiry, and open exchange valued in academic life. Compared to exclusionary approaches to religion that hold up one faith tradition as true or superior and consider others false or inferior, religious pluralism marks an important advance in endeavors to understand peoples and cultures on their own terms. At the same time, though, religious pluralism operates to some extent like a religion itself, a conceptual framework of interpretation that rests in a universal and finally mystical understanding of religion and its essential importance for human existence.

In the United States, the institutional and emotional forces maintaining religion are considerable and, to some extent at least, the concept of religious pluralism supports these forces. Yet religion, especially in its form as religious pluralism, is also deeply allied with the work of critical inquiry. If enthusiasm for religious pluralism deflects skepticism about religion, it is also yoked to academic endeavors that have led to investigation of religious pluralism itself. With respect to the study of American religion, the more scholars have honed the concept of religious pluralism as a framework interpreting American religious history, the clearer its meaning as an influential form of religious idealism has become. Thanks to the work of many historians of American religion, we are now able to see how the idealism of religious pluralism developed over time as an important trend within American religious history.

In this chapter, I look at the historical antecedents of religious pluralism in Protestant idealism and show how the concept of religious pluralism emerged from Protestant institutions to operate as a dynamic factor in the growth of religious studies. I also show how historians of American religion came to define religious pluralism with increasing clarity in the process of grappling with the problem of comprehending growing religious diversity in the United

States. Their effort to study American religious pluralism historically not only contributes to better understanding of American religious history but also enables scholars of religion to critique the idealism that shaped the early growth of their field.

The Coinciding Histories of Religious Pluralism and Religious Studies

The emerging concept of religious pluralism played a dynamic role in the expansion or establishment of religious studies in many American colleges and universities after World War II. Growing enthusiasm for religious pluralism contributed to development of the study of religion as an important component of American academic life, and helped to shape the agendas and direction of that field. Conversely, the growth of religious studies after World War II contributed to enthusiasm for religious pluralism as a conceptual framework for interpreting the growth of religious diversity in the United States, and for advancing scholarly understanding of religious diversity around the world.

Before 1975, many of the faculty teaching religious studies in colleges and universities received their advanced degrees from mainline Protestant divinity schools, and the curricula developed in those schools provided models for curricular programs in religious studies. In preceding decades, in response to liberal Protestant concerns for ecumenism and universal religious understanding, mainline Protestant divinity schools had already transformed their courses on foreign missions into courses on world religions. Transplanted to colleges and universities, those courses on world religions grew after World War II in response to the booming interest in mysticism and Asian religions among college students, and as a result of widespread cultural approval of religion as an essential component of American democracy. Increasing enrollments in these courses fed the growth of religious studies programs, which increased by 90% between 1940 and 1970. Undergraduate enrollments in religion courses tripled in private nondenominational schools between 1954 and 1969 and at the same rate in public institutions beginning in 1964.[1]

Schools affiliated with mainline Protestant denominations played an important role in the early stages of this boom; denominations made grants to their affiliated colleges that required the development of new academic instruction in religion. Advocates of church support for the study of religion stressed the linkage between the academic study of religion and Christian education, arguing that studying different forms of religion would make church members better informed. "Churches often have a particular interest in the religion department," Randolph-Macon's Methodist president William F. Quillian acknowledged in 1953. "This is due to the perfectly understandable feeling that the religion department is a direct ally of the church in its program of Christian education." Quillian wanted the church to know, however, that religion faculty required intellectual freedom in order to fulfill their mission as teachers.

Rejecting the "authoritarian" strategies of teaching characteristic of "Roman Catholic institutions" and "more conservative Protestant institutions," Quillian believed that religion instructors ought "to present major alternative positions as honestly and clearly as possible." The instructor's job was to lead each student "to the realization that the final decision or choice is one which he must make." Quillian argued "that no limits be placed upon the range of heterodoxy permissible for individual instructors," with the sole proviso that the teacher be confident "in the validity of the Christian faith and of its power to win the day in free competition with alternative views."[2] Confident that liberal Protestant thought would "win the day," Quillian saw the academic study of "alternative" religions as a means of strengthening liberal Protestants in their faith.

Floyd H. Ross, professor of World Religions at the University of Southern California, pushed this line of thought further. Writing in 1953, the same year as Quillian, Ross thought that Christians had a lot to learn from other religions, and that instead of focusing on the inadequacies of other religions, Christians ought to look at other religions in a positive light and be prepared to take some lessons. "Few Christians have sought to understand the non-Christian religions *at their best*," Ross criticized. The task for students of religion was to take up that effort and advance their own faith in the process. In an interesting phrase, Ross linked appreciative study of other religions to the redemptive value of sacrifice: "We need to learn how to die to our concepts and our creedal conceits as new experiences make new concepts necessary."

Ross was confident that a new "synthesis" of religion would emerge once people let go of sectarian divisions and learned to hold on to those aspects of their faith traditions that truly contributed to civilization. He linked this self-critical and pragmatic approach to religion with Protestantism in its broadest, most universal sense. He praised medieval Jews for holding onto the civilizing aspects of their tradition and for being exemplars of the Protestant spirit. Lifting pluralistic wheat from sectarian chaff was "the true protestant function" of religion, Ross believed, quoting David Daiches. In the modern era, no group was better trained to exercise that function than scholars of religion.[3]

Scholars who advocated for religious pluralism through religious studies defined their work over against sectarianism. Rather than perceiving different religions as mutually exclusive roads to truth, proponents of pluralism in religious studies discerned an underlying compatibility, and argued for the importance of academic study as a means of drawing out that compatibility and thereby advancing interfaith cooperation. To some extent at least, this universalist approach to religion reflected Protestant understanding of the church as an invisible alliance of communities scattered throughout the world, working more or less independent of one another but also gathering cooperative momentum as time progressed.

In public universities, advocates of religious studies faced concerns from colleagues in other departments about how religion could be studied without inviting conflict between representatives of different religious groups. They responded to these concerns with an appeal to interfaith cooperation that would eventually develop into the fuller idealism of religious pluralism. Robert S. Eccles, assistant professor at the Indiana School of Religion in the early 1950s, explained how religion programs would build on the practice of interdenominational cooperation that mainline Protestants had developed over centuries. Those who feared bringing religion into public universities should know that "Exchanges of pulpits among ministers of different denominations is a familiar enough event." Such exchanges diminished rather than exacerbated sectarianism and were already providing the base of religious studies at some schools. Reporting on meetings held in 1950 to explore the issue of teaching religion as part of the academic curricula in public institutions, Eccles pointed to the University of Iowa as a model: "At this university credit courses are offered by a faculty of three instructors, one Protestant, one Roman Catholic, and one Jewish, all clergymen of their respective faiths."

As far as Eccles was concerned, the real sectarians in academic life were skeptics who refused to take a pluralistic view of their own subject matter and insisted instead on skeptical viewpoints not shared by everyone in their field. Psychologists who organized their departments for the sole purpose of advancing behaviorism came in for special chastisement. Partial himself to Jungian psychology as a helpful tool for the study of religion (as many other religionists of the time were), Eccles found behaviorists much more troublesome than fundamentalists. He assumed that fundamentalism had no place in a modern university, dismissing it as "a minority reaction within Protestantism" opposed to "interdenominational accord."[4]

Pluralism in Religious Studies as an Outgrowth of Protestant Idealism

As an emerging concept within religious studies, religious pluralism grew out of liberal Protestantism in two different senses. In one sense, it outgrew liberal Protestantism to become a form of idealism about religion and democracy that people of different religious traditions, including many non-Protestants, came to share. In this sense, religious pluralism emerged as a post-Protestant construct that avoided Protestant triumphalism and supersessionary rhetoric and promoted egalitarian respect for many different religions.

In another sense, religious pluralism retained important aspects of the Protestant idealism it grew out of; religious pluralism carried traces of Protestant idealism about denominations and millennialist expectations of a universal church, more or less hidden, scattered, and unfinished until the Second Coming of Christ. In North America, denominationalism flourished as an alternative to a national church, stimulating the growth of Protestant institutions and later serving as the institutional base out of which religious studies and the idealism of religious pluralism would develop.

The historian Winthrop Hudson traced the origin of denominationalism to seventeenth-century English separatists who held up the ideal of self-governing independent churches coexisting on more or less equal footing. When the Westminster Assembly convened in London to reform the Church of England in 1643, Hudson explained in 1961, proponents of self-governing churches spoke out against the idea of a national church. These spokesmen for independency argued that different opinions about church government were inevitable given the diversity and fallibility of human nature, and that Christians should not be required to deny their honest convictions and submit to doctrines or practices they believed to be erroneous. Open discussion of such differences might be God's way of producing light, they argued, just as "sparks are beaten out by the flints striking together."[5]

In eighteenth-century England and America, evangelicals popularized the term "denomination" to make the point that minor differences in Protestant doctrine and worship paled in comparison to the universal need for new birth. The Presbyterian evangelist Gilbert Tennent employed the term during the revivals he led in New Jersey during the 1740s. There was "one Church of Christ," Tennent declared, "but several branches (more or less pure in minuter points) of one visible kingdom of the Messiah." These branches or "societies," he explained, "who profess Christianity and retain the foundational principle thereof, notwithstanding their different denominations and diversity of sentiments in smaller things, are in reality but one." Making a similar point, the Anglican evangelist George Whitefield argued that the imperative of new birth in Christ overshadowed doctrinal differences and that differences between denominations would disappear in heaven. Preaching in Philadelphia in the 1740s, he demanded, "Father Abraham, whom have you in heaven? Any Episcopalians? No! Any Presbyterians? No! Any Independents or Methodists? No, no, no! All who are here are Christians."[6]

In America, enthusiasm for denominationalism as a form of religious organization coincided with growing acceptance of religious freedom and voluntarism. In the seventeenth and eighteenth centuries, many religious minorities welcomed religious freedom because of the opportunities for religious expression and church growth it offered. By 1830, most evangelicals had come to be persuaded that voluntary participation in religious life was more heartfelt than involuntary participation, and to embrace denominationalism as an evangelical strategy for church growth even in locales where the influence of their churches was already strong. Through benevolent organizations of various sorts, evangelicals worked to reform America and spread their faith throughout the world, often equating the voluntarism of evangelical social activism with democracy.[7]

Interdenominational cooperation grew along with the growing size and number of denominations. The heavenly ideal of a universal church existing with multiple branches encouraged cooperation among members of many of these different groups. United by a shared concern for personal conversion and active engagement in social reform, evangelical Methodists, Baptists, Presbyterians, and Congregationalists cooperated in numerous ventures and established interdenominational networks for the promotion of Sunday

Schools, foreign missions, temperance, abolition, and for the publication and distribution of religious tracts. In their idealism about people from different denominations working together to build God's kingdom, interdenominational organizations anticipated later forms of religious pluralism. In their many investments in education, and in their expansive interest in people around the world, interdenominational organizations also contributed to an intellectual commitment to knowledge about religion that would yield later fruit within religious studies.

Nineteenth-century efforts to promote interdenominational cooperation were not always successful, of course, and the more closely those efforts became associated with modern liberalism, the more resistance and disaffection they met. Conflict over how to interpret the Bible with respect to American problems of slavery and race, and with respect to "higher criticism" of the text emanating from Germany, drove liberals and conservatives apart. Liberal Protestants in the late nineteenth and early twentieth centuries moved forward in their plans for interdenominational organization to construct large bureaucracies and extensive systems of cooperative outreach that incorporated the social sciences and modern principles of social reform. By the end of the nineteenth century, their commitment to social activism had resulted in an Evangelical Alliance of unprecedented scope despite lack of participation by many conservative groups. As one of its chief promoters, Josiah Strong, described it in 1893, the Evangelical Alliance functioned as "a committee of churches" that included laypeople and ministers dedicated to the social teachings of Jesus and to "new and more scientific ways of thinking about humanity that would enable the people of the church to take up their full responsibility as Christians and finally realize their social mission."[8]

While expanding their own institutional outreach, these evangelical proponents of a modern, social gospel looked at other religions with increasing tolerance and intellectual interest. In organizations devoted to foreign missions, liberal-spirited evangelicals downplayed efforts to convert people from heathen darkness in order to focus on cooperative efforts to promote education and health care in many parts of the world. Outside the missionary context, more than a few liberal Protestants became enchanted with Vivekananda and other mystics from the East, and incorporated the study of other religions into their expanded understanding of the true meaning of Christianity. Such enthusiasm for spiritual growth, social progress, and world enlightenment was an important ingredient in American evangelical culture in the late nineteenth and early twentieth centuries.

In recent decades, it has become customary to equate evangelicals with intellectual and social conservatism. In January 2007, for example, an article in the *New York Times* defined evangelicals as "Protestants who believe that the Bible is literally true."[9] Before the First World War, however, evangelicals were some of the most modern and progressive religious thinkers in America and, in many cases, not biblical literalists at all. The liberal theology, social activism, and spirit of interdenominational cooperation characteristic of many evangelical Protestants in the late nineteenth and early twentieth centuries led to the founding of the Federal Council of Churches in 1908 and its successor, the National Council of Churches. Liberal evangelicals and the divinity schools they supported also paved the way for the extraordinary growth of religious studies after World War II and eventual establishment of academic programs in religion in most American colleges and universities.

The term "religious pluralism" took hold in the 1970s as multiculturalism and identity politics came to the fore on many college campuses. Affirmations of religious pluralism enabled faculty and students to endorse multiculturalism while minimizing some of the conflicts associated with identity politics. In their underlying respect for cultural difference and commitment to cooperativeness in response to that difference, proponents of religious pluralism carried forward a denominational approach to religion that had developed out of liberal evangelicalism, and, before that, seventeenth-century Protestant arguments that differences among churches might in fact amount to God's method for bringing greater insight to them all.

Religious studies is not the Evangelical Alliance. But in its development after World War II it carried some of that organization's legacy. Through the emerging interpretive framework of religious pluralism, instructors in religious studies broadened the Alliance's commitment to "new and more scientific ways of thinking about humanity that would enable the people of the church to take up their full responsibility as Christians and finally realize their social mission." With a similar hope in mind, proponents of religious pluralism assumed that all religions held essential elements in common, and that universal human religiosity was a good basis for social progress and peace. Such an idealistic approach to religion and religious difference was not something people could imbibe from news reports of religious activity in the world. But they could learn it in religious studies courses. The American college classroom was an ideal space for learning and practicing religious pluralism.

Philosophical theology from Europe contributed to this learning and practice. In the postwar period, the European-born scholars Mircea Eliade and Paul Tillich promoted variants of a romantic approach to religion that appealed to universal structures of human consciousness, and to a universal human quest for meaning at work in all the different cultures and religious traditions of the world. Their influence as writers and teachers in the United States carried considerable sway in academic studies of religion during its era of great expansion from the 1940s through the 1970s.

The Romanian-born philosopher Eliade was a student of Indian yoga and Siberian shamanism. Celebrating primitives and mystics as fully religious people, Eliade argued that critical, historical thinking made it difficult for modern Western people to fully experience "the sacred." In the hope that modern man could recapture more of the natural religiosity that primitives and mystics enjoyed, he advanced a systematic view of all religions as manifestations of "the sacred," which he defined in terms of epiphanies of spiritual insight.

The German-born Paul Tillich, who taught with Eliade for a short time at the University of Chicago in the 1960s after years as a celebrity teacher at Union Theological Seminary and Harvard Divinity School, defined religion as the "ultimate concern" at the root of every human life and manifest in every great work of human expression. Tillich linked awareness of this ultimate concern to the God underlying the gods of particular religious faiths, pointing to the depth of human consciousness as the realm out of which particular forms of human religious, cultural, and artistic expression emerged. Along with Eliade, Tillich affirmed the existence of a universal, ultimately mystical, realm of consciousness as the background against which particular religions, and all forms of human art and expression, ought to be revered. The teachings of these men influenced the academic study of religion at a critical juncture in its development, providing an idealist philosophical basis for conceptualizing religious pluralism and affirming its importance as a subject of study in American higher education.[10]

Along with these expansive philosophical affirmations, religious pluralism also derived support from the popular notion that religion was essential to American democracy. In this respect, religious pluralism developed as part of a larger cultural willingness to have "faith in faith" that was linked to postwar efforts to get along in a diverse society and uphold confidence in American freedom. In addition to encouraging democratic civility with respect to religion in the classroom, faith in faith served as an important element of national identity after World War II; beginning in the 1940s and 1950s, Harry Emerson Fosdick, Joshua Liebman, and other religious writers popular in the United States promoted faith as essential to confidence, success, and democratic cooperation.[11]

Religious pluralism crystallized as a concept in the context of this commitment to religion as a bulwark of democracy. While often critical of "Judeo-Christian" misunderstanding and disdain for other religions, proponents of religion in higher education often presumed that democratic civilization and religious faith went hand in hand, and that the study of religion would advance civilization through appreciation of the spiritual insights contained within the world's many faith traditions. As the United States exercised its military and economic influence around the world after World War II, religion programs increased in number and size and instructors in religious studies brought idealism about religious pluralism to the study of Hinduism, Buddhism, and other religions beyond the orbit of "Judeo-Christianity."

Eagerness to extract spiritual insight from its locales within different religious traditions coincided with the enormous boom in consumer goods of all kinds in the United States after World War II, and also with the waging of a Cold War against godless communism. The concept of religious pluralism became popular in the United States at a time when atheism was unpatriotic, when the religious diversity of the American people was increasing as a result of increasing numbers of new immigrants from Asia and new forms of religious experimentation at home, and when religious faith as an essential component of American democracy was often touted. As participants in this enthusiasm for religious faith, scholars of religion mined religious traditions for insight, and often paid more attention to lofty principles and glowing depictions of spiritual life than to how religious beliefs, practices, and institutions constrained people's lives and decision-making. Thus in the 1970s, for example, radiant portraits of Sufism by Huston Smith and Annemarie Schimmel enjoyed great popularity, but few religionists in the United States paid attention to the rise of Islamic militancy.[12]

At the same time, other intellectual forces were at work that led to tough questions about religious idealism and religious pluralism. While scholars of comparative religion might proceed under the assumption that different religious traditions were different expressions of a universal ground of being, historians of religion faced the problem of showing how religious ideals played out in behavior and institutional organization. Historians of American religion faced the additional problem of understanding how an increasing number of different religious ideals, behaviors, and organizations coexisted within the same society. Appeal to religious pluralism, and to its growth over time, was one way to pull the diverse strands of American religious history together. The employment of religious pluralism as an interpretive framework for tracing the accommodation of diversity in American religious history brought the term down to earth, so to speak, making it not only an idealized way of conceptualizing religion, but a subject for historical investigation.

Histories of American Religious Pluralism

Sydney Ahlstrom's monumental work, A Religious History of the American People (1972), served as a major stimulant to this historiographical process, laying important groundwork for subsequent histories of American religious pluralism. Although the index entry for religious pluralism in the book references only 16 out of 1158 pages, Ahlstrom's interest in the trajectory of increasing pluralism drove his effort to comprehend the whole sweep of American religious history. In this respect, A Religious History of the American People set the stage for Catherine Albanese's reconstruction of American religion in terms of pluralism and anticipated the more sharply focused histories of American religious pluralism written by William Hutchison, Diana Eck, and Charles Lippy. At the same time, Ahlstrom raised concerns about the divisive effects of religious diversity and religious radicalism that these historians of American religious pluralism sought, more or less strenuously, to lay to rest. Concerns raised by Ahlstrom anticipated some of the criticism of religious studies and religious pluralism later voiced by Russell McCutcheon, Timothy Fitzgerald, and D. G. Hart.

Winner of the 1973 National Book Award and chosen as the Religious Book of the Decade by The Christian Century in 1979, Ahlstrom's Religious History appeared at a time when the concept of religious pluralism had jelled, and it was possible to construct a history of American religion with that concept in mind. Ahlstrom brought the histories of numerous traditions and movements together in ways that highlighted parallel developments and called attention to the increased prevalence of pluralistic thinking about religion that resulted from the social turbulence of the 1960s and the decline in moral authority of an elite "Protestant Establishment." For Ahlstrom, pluralism was the assertion of diversity against the overweening claims of the Establishment; it was a protest movement as well as an affirmation of religious diversity.

Ahlstrom sympathized with the reasons for protest but feared the outcome. Deeply interested in the relationship between religion and democracy, Ahlstrom was particularly concerned to highlight the role that idealism about religion played in a society where citizens exercised moral responsibility for public life. Rather than lifting up religious pluralism as the culminating stage in the evolution of such public spiritedness, as Hutchison and Eck later would, Ahlstrom worried that religious pluralism was not a sufficiently strong or coherent base for a culture of shared responsibility for common life. At the end of his monumental effort to describe American religious history in all its diversity, he wished that, in the future, more evidence of the compatibility between religious pluralism and shared commitment to the common good would emerge: "one may hope," he wrote in the last paragraph of the book, for "increasing evidence that the American people, in their moral and religious history, were drawing on the profounder elements of their traditions, finding new sources of strength and confidence, and thus vindicating the idealism which has been so fundamental an element in the country's past."[13]

Ahlstrom traced the sense of shared responsibility for the common good, which he perceived to be quickly evaporating, to Puritanism, and he was keen to show how the ethical spirit of Puritanism led to the social gospel movement of the late nineteenth and early twentieth centuries rather than to fundamentalism. Proponents of the social gospel reformulated the Puritan sense of social responsibility in modern, secular terms, eager for everyone to participate in a democratic social covenant they understood to be derived from reformed Protestant ideas and institutions. For Ahlstrom, "the Social Gospel was anything but new. The major element in America's moral and religious heritage was Puritanism," he explained, "with its powerfully rooted convictions that the shaping and, if need be, the remaking of society was the Church's concern."[14]

Ahlstrom interpreted social gospel efforts to secularize Christian ethics as an endeavor to expand idealism about democracy, and make democracy work. As he portrayed them, proponents of the social gospel envisioned a secular ethic derived from reformed Protestantism as a shared idealism that people from different traditions could join. In their endeavors, investment in the supernatural and theological aspects of religion declined. Weak on "biblical exegesis and theological elaboration," proponents of the social gospel were less concerned about the transcendence of God and the qualifications for personal salvation through Christ than they were about the need "to find out the truth about society, and on the basis of that knowledge to chart programs for ameliorating the country's social woes." To that end, the social gospel "drew political science, economics, and sociology to its service and, wherever possible, sought to provoke in all social scientists a regard for the ethical implications of their work."[15]

Ahlstrom attributed the emerging emphasis on religious pluralism in his own day to an erosion of a shared sense of obligation to the common good; people looked to their particular religious traditions to compensate for the depletion of idealism about a common ground. In their attempts to fill the vacuum, revivalists called for personal salvation, rejecting the effort to secularize Christianity. With "the eclipse of the Protestant Establishment," which had dominated American culture in "its early colonial life, its war for independence, and its nineteenth-century expansion," Ahlstrom believed that America's fiercely anti-intellectual "popular revivalistic tradition" exerted "a kind of illicit hold on the national life." The Protestant Establishment had lost its political clout because of its failure to follow through on the social gospel—because of its failure to formulate a scientifically informed vision of social justice and because of its inequitable "social structures, legal arrangements, patterns of prejudice, and power relationships." As Ahlstrom wrote, he perceived American intellectuals experiencing an "unprecedented loss of confidence in American institutions" in response to inadequate forms of leadership, continuing problems of racism and poverty, and the escalation of the Vietnam War.[16]

Catherine L. Albanese's popular textbook, *America: Religions and Religion*, first published in 1981 and now in its fifth edition, offered an alternative to Ahlstrom's concerns about religious pluralism. As the first book to elevate pluralism to the level of the defining theme of American religious history, Albanese's textbook marked an important turning point in the study of American religion. "Over and over again, we have grown familiar with clichés about the fact and experience of pluralism in the United States," Albanese wrote in the preface to the first edition. "Yet when we look at America's history books—and more to the point here, America's religious history books—we find that they generally tell one major story, incorporating the separate stories of many peoples into a single story line arranged chronologically." Albanese dislodged that "one story" focused on "the Anglo-Saxon and Protestant majority—and perhaps those most like them—who dominated the continent and its culture into the later twentieth century," in order to tell a pluralistic story "of many peoples and many religious faiths." She was especially interested in bumping the Puritans off their central pedestal as the first people of American religion, and made a point of not introducing them until readers were well into her narrative.[17]

While Ahlstrom had worried about pluralism's disunity, Albanese discerned a "larger cultural religion of the United States," a "oneness" that everyone knew was there but found hard to describe. "The manyness and the oneness are interconnected," Albanese claimed, "each affecting the other and both together writing American religious history." In this and in other writings, Albanese appealed to idealism about America and also to metaphysical currents available for spiritually minded people to tap into. These currents not only accommodated personal and cultural difference; they also facilitated harmonic coexistence.[18]

To explain how "manyness" and "oneness" could be connected, Albanese opened her history with the proverb of the elephant that blind men could feel and describe parts of but not comprehend in its entirety. Annemarie Schimmel appealed to the same proverb in the opening paragraph of her popular book first published in 1975, *The Mystical Dimensions of Islam,* tracing the proverb to the Sufi poet Rumi and his description of the relationship between the mystical reality of Islam (the elephant) and Islam's various schools and sects (blind men).[19] Albanese noted that Buddhists as well as Muslims claimed this proverb as part of their tradition; she borrowed it from them to offer a more mystical and more confident picture of religious pluralism in America than Ahlstrom had presented. As Diana Eck later would, Albanese drew parallels between American religious pluralism and non-Western forms of mysticism. In linking American religious pluralism to a vision of many different truths coexisting as part of a larger whole, both Albanese and Eck drew on Mircea Eliade's emphasis on "the sacred" as an essential component of human life and on Paul Tillich's mystical understanding of the depths of human consciousness.

Trained as a scholar of modern Hinduism, Eck joined her knowledge and profound empathy for that tradition with her commitment to ecumenical understanding and cooperation as a divinity school professor and Methodist lay leader. In her book on religious pluralism in America published in 2001, her earlier CD on religious pluralism for college classes, *On Common Ground,* and the large-scale "Pluralism Project" at Harvard that has employed dozens of graduate students to gather data on U.S. religious communities, Eck has done more than anyone to promote appreciation for religious pluralism as a hallmark of American democratic life. As an indicator of her prestige and influence, President Bill Clinton awarded her the National Humanities Medal in 1998 for her work on the Pluralism Project.

Eck's 2001 book, *A New Religious America: How a "Christian Country" Has Become the World's Most Religiously Diverse Nation,* offered an historical overview of religious pluralism in America that explained how America had been transformed from a nation dominated by Protestant Christians to a more democratic nation in which many religious groups coexist in friendly equality and neighborliness. Acknowledging that this transformation was far from complete and calling attention to pockets of religious hatred that undermined democracy, the book nevertheless presented America's progressive march toward religious pluralism as a principal source of social harmony and national strength.

Eck's narrative tracked both the increasing diversity of religion in America and the progress Protestants made in accepting that diversity, showing how American ideas evolved from religious tolerance to melting pot assimilation and eventually to an egalitarian pluralism in which each religious group retained its distinctiveness and took responsibility for the common good. She devoted considerable space to descriptions of Hindu, Buddhist, and Islamic centers in the United States, and to particular stories of how twentieth-century Hindus, Buddhists, and Muslims made America home. She presented the diversity within these religions as compatible with the ideal of religious pluralism developed in liberal Protestantism. Thus the claim which begins her chapter on Hinduism "*E Pluribus Unum*, 'From Many, One,'" could easily come from the ancient Rig Veda, with its affirmation, "Truth is One. People call it by many names."[20]

Eck did not discuss the relationship between a religious system with many names for truth and a social system based on caste hierarchies, but that oversight was understandable in light of her effort to present different religions in the most positive light. Such positive constructions of religion served the idea that many religions were variants of one mystical reality. They also served the underlying argument that religion was fundamental to democracy and social cooperation.

Eck's definition of religious pluralism built upon the term "cultural pluralism" coined by Horace Kallen in 1915. In his essay, "Democracy *vs.* the Melting Pot," published in *The Nation*, Kallen made "cultural pluralism" a condition of democracy, contrasting it with assimilation, which he thought was not democratic enough. He described the democracy of cultural pluralism as an "orchestra" of cultures in which "each ethnic group" was a "natural instrument" and "the harmony and dissonances and discords of them all may make the symphony of civilization."[21] Eliding "religious" and "cultural," Eck followed Kallen's argument while updating his image of democratic pluralism as a symphony to that of a jazz session. Like the pluralism of democracy, jazz "is not all written out" and "requires even more astute attention to the music of each instrument" than symphonic music. As Eck asserted, "Learning to hear the musical lines of our neighbors, their individual and magnificent interpretations of the themes of America's common covenants, is the test of cultural pluralism." Appreciation of pluralism is the test of American democracy as well. "Our challenge today," she wrote, "is whether it will be jazz or simply noise, whether it will be a symphony or a cacophony, whether we can continue to play together through dissonant moments."[22]

In her use of Kallen's argument, Eck presumed an understanding of religion as a universal phenomenon more or less synonymous with culture and, by implication, essential to human nature. For Eck, religion was the kernel of ethnicity and culture; ethnic and cultural traits coalesced in religious difference. At the same time, she also viewed religion as having a universal aspect, and thus presented religion as a vehicle of expression enabling people to communicate across ethnic difference, a mode of experience enabling people to travel from one culture to another, and a common ground that people shared. As an example of religion as communication across ethnic difference, she quoted a New York taxi driver from Bangladesh who reported, "At the Masjid, Third Avenue comes to its knees." As an example of religion enabling people to travel across cultures, she described the journey of a young woman named Karen from Catholicism to a Southern Baptist church. From fundamentalist

Christianity, Karen moved to Islam, where she became "a living witness to the importance of *da'wah*," the call of Islamic teaching. And as an example of religion as common ground for people of different religious traditions, Eck cited the cooperative efforts of Muslims and Methodists in building Peace Terrace in Fremont, California, a worship center for both groups.[23]

In his 2003 book, *Religious Pluralism in America: The Contentious History of a Founding Ideal*, Eck's colleague at Harvard Divinity School, William R. Hutchison, elaborated on several of the main points in Eck's argument and went beyond her in analyzing the history of religious pluralism in the United States. While Hutchison maintained liberal valuations of religion and religious pluralism, he also opened religious pluralism to critical inquiry more fully than ever before by identifying it as an idealism and by emphasizing the contentious aspects of its history.

Drawn from classroom lectures and discussions with graduate students and faculty colleagues, Hutchison's *Religious Pluralism in America* envisioned religious pluralism as both a fruition of liberal Protestant idealism and a flowering of egalitarian respect and activism among people of different traditions. A culmination of decades of work as a teacher and historian of liberal Protestant thought in America, *Religious Pluralism in America* drew from Hutchison's earlier books on the American Transcendentalists, the liberalizing influence of foreign missions on American Protestant missionaries, and the "modernist impulse" in American Protestant thought. The mysticism of transcendentalists who thought all forms of spirituality dissolved into one, the respect for other traditions that some missionaries discovered to be consonant with Christ's message, and the effort by Protestant intellectuals to reform Christianity in response to the challenges of modern life all played important roles in Hutchison's understanding of how American religious pluralism had developed.[24]

As did Eck, Hutchison built his definition of religious pluralism on Horace Kallen's understanding of cultural pluralism as an essential aspect of democracy, and, like Eck, he appealed to Kallen's image of different instruments playing music together. Hutchison charted stages of progress in the history of religious pluralism along the same lines as Eck, but in more detail than she, moving from analysis of religious tolerance in the early republic, through discussion of the ideal of melting pot assimilation as it developed in the nineteenth century, to description of the newly expanded conceptualization of pluralism after 1960 as "a right of participation" that "implied a mandate for individuals and groups...to share responsibility for the forming and implementing of the society's agenda."[25] Like Eck, he emphasized the role that immigration and increasing religious diversity played in the development of pluralism, arguing that religious pluralism only matured as an ideal because people from outside the Protestant mainstream ascribed to it, and became equal partners in its construction.

Unlike Eck, Hutchison insisted that religious pluralism was an ideal, not the same thing as historical reality. And, as the subtitle of the book promised, he showed how Americans disputed this ideal from the preliminary stages of its development in the early republic to its full articulation in the late twentieth century. In line with his emphasis on the contentiousness of the ideal, Hutchison cited numerous examples of religious intolerance, ridicule, and exclusion. For all his emphasis on progress made in conceptualizing the ideal, *Religious Pluralism in America* was not a triumphal book.

In presenting liberal Protestantism as the matrix out of which the ideal of religious pluralism developed, Hutchison addressed Ahlstrom's concern about the relationship between pluralism and the loss of idealism about America. Hutchison made the struggle to affirm religious diversity central to the development of American democracy and carefully laid out the stages through which this struggle progressed. As the proportion of citizens from Anglo-Protestant backgrounds declined over the decades from a high of around 90% at the republic's founding, Hutchison showed how the meaning of pluralism expanded and how people from other backgrounds participated in defining it. In the course of its expanding history, religious pluralism was an important vehicle through which democracy moved forward.[26]

In another important study published around the turn of the century, University of Tennessee Professor of Religion Charles H. Lippy looked at religious pluralism even more dispassionately and pointed to a turning point in American religious history that enabled religious pluralism to become a cultural norm. Acknowledging that religious pluralism was "a natural development emerging from forces that had long shaped American religious life," forces that included diversity among Protestant groups and the legal guarantee of religious freedom and prohibition against religious establishment in the First Amendment to the U.S. Constitution, he nevertheless discerned a "cultural metamorphosis" occurring in the last third of the nineteenth century that "paved the way for dimensions of the variegated pluralism coming to fruition in the twentieth century." This watershed in the cultural understanding of religion occurred across religious traditions as religious diversity increased more dramatically than ever before as a result of new waves of immigration, and as religious life in all its diverse forms became more personalized. For many Americans, Lippy explained, "Personal experience replaced biblical revelation as the starting point for theological discourse; personal experience likewise superseded the community of the faithful as the buttress for belief."[27]

Lippy suggested that an important relationship existed between religious pluralism coming of age and the unity of American culture. As he stated in the concluding paragraph of his book, "it may well be that the greatest contribution made by the United States to global religious life is its demonstrating that however vast the pluralism, a vital religious culture can flourish. Pluralism does not undermine common life, but seems to enrich it."[28] In describing the historical process through which a personalized understanding of religion had come to pervade American culture, he presented that personalized understanding as the prerequisite for pluralism. While Eck would see religion itself as common ground in American culture, Lippy defined the common ground more precisely, arguing that what Americans shared was not religion per se, but an agreement about how religion ought to operate. For Lippy, this agreement allowed religion, in all its personalized diversity, to enrich common life.

Critics of Religion

The effort to understand religious pluralism historically is abetted by scholars who do not regard religious pluralism as a sufficient basis of cultural unity. Some of these scholars have criticized the arrogant idealisms of religion in light of the higher (and humbling) transcendence of God. These scholars might agree that respect for religious difference is important to democracy and can lead to healthy religious debate, but their insistence on the transcendence of God works against the notion that religious pluralism is a solution to cultural problems or a culminating stage of religious evolution.

In *America's God: From Jonathan Edwards to Abraham Lincoln* (2002), Mark A. Noll traced the sorry history of religious difference that led to the Civil War. Although his book is not about religious pluralism (the term does not even appear in the index), his critical approach to religion counters the idealism about religion associated with religious pluralism, and leads to an assessment of religion in America markedly different from that of historians who present American religious history in terms of the growth of pluralism. Setting religious claims to know the will of God against faithful acknowledgement of human fallibility and divine transcendence, Noll argued that Americans on both sides of the War confused religion with God and led the country to disaster by claiming that the Bible supported their own understanding of nationhood.[29] Along with George Marsden and other scholars whose understanding of American religious history is informed by neoorthodox thought, Noll commended the theology of Jonathan Edwards to his readers as an antidote against such attempts to substitute the cultural phenomena of religion for God. To those interested in "understanding God, the self, and the word as they really are," Noll reiterated the cry of an earlier Calvinist, Israel Holly, in 1770: "I would say, *Read Edwards!* And if you wrote again, I would tell you to *Read Edwards!* And if you wrote again, I would still tell you to *Read Edwards!*"[30] For Noll, Marsden, and other neoorthodox historians, religion (however pluralistic) ought to be judged by a higher standard.[31]

These neoorthodox historians carried forward some of Ahlstrom's appreciation for Calvinism, and some of his concern about religion. Ahlstrom emphasized the importance of individual responsibility for common life in Calvinist thought and practice and did not see anything like it in religious pluralism. In his discussion of the neoorthodox (Calvinist) movement of the 1930s, Ahlstrom argued that it laid the intellectual groundwork for the criticism of American imperialism that took hold in the 1960s. He appreciated the efforts made by Reinhold Niebuhr, H. Richard Niebuhr, and other neoorthodox thinkers to infuse the social gospel with "a more realistic awareness of institutional power, social structures, and human depravity" in ways that made these thinkers "at once more biblical in their standpoint and more utopian." Ahlstrom might have appreciated the work of Noll and Marsden in much the same way. He might also have seen them as bridge builders between two warring religious cultures in American society, as he saw neoorthodox scholars of an earlier generation; Ahlstrom observed that neoorthodox thinkers "opened communications not only with modernists who had all but decided that Christianity was obsolete, but also with conservatives who had all decided that true Christians must repudiate modern modes of thought and action."[32]

Not all recent proponents of neoorthodox theology would fit Ahlstrom's template of bridge building. In an acrimonious but important book on the academic study of religion, D. G. Hart, a church historian at Westminster Theological Seminary, argued that attempts to build bridges between modernism and Christianity, and to infuse academic life with true Christian principles, as he might say Noll and Marsden attempt to do, is futile. In his 1999 book, *How the University Got Religion: Religious Studies in American Higher Education,* Hart chided the neoorthodox thinkers of the 1930s for their failure to uphold Christian revelation against liberalism, when they had more of a chance, and presented scholars who continue to uphold orthodox values in the context of academic studies of religion as engaged in a hopeless struggle.

In Hart's opinion, the academic study of religion is a shoddy enterprise based on vague ideas about religion and religious pluralism and their contributions to democratic civilization. Calling for a halt on "trying to secure a religion-friendly university," Hart pointed to the origin of religious studies in mainline Protestant efforts to salvage the connection between religion and American culture that earlier generations of Protestants had taken for granted, and he condemned mainline Protestants for trying to water down religion to make it relevant in a modern world. Denouncing tenure and promotion as "so much hay and stubble" and calling "faithful academics" to abandon universities and commit themselves instead to the "enduring rewards" of "new heavens and new earth," Hart held out the prospect that stronger institutions of religious learning would appear as the liberal university crumbled under the weight of its corrupt standards and intellectual confusion.[33]

However quixotic his crusade against "the modern university," Hart's discussion of the origins of religious studies in mainline Protestantism makes an important contribution to the historiography of religious pluralism. His alienation from liberal interpretations of religion, and from liberal efforts to make the study of religion a humanizing influence in higher education, enabled him to discern idealistic assumptions within conventional concepts of religion and religious pluralism. Even more important, his history of the development of religious studies in the 1940s and 1950s contributes to an understanding of the relationship between that history and the historiography of American religious pluralism. As Hart discovered, advocates for religious studies in the 1940s and 1950s argued that the study of diverse forms of religion would serve as a vehicle for inculcating modern liberal democratic values. Religious studies would embody the American Council of Learned Societies' vision for the humanities as a "platform upon which democratically and liberally minded citizens throughout the country may now unite and move in greater harmony and efficiency toward our common goal."[34]

Other critics perceive religion and religious pluralism as theologically loaded concepts and attempt to deconstruct them without reference to anything more transcendent than cultural analysis. It may be no coincidence that sharply critical secular analyses of the religion concept, such as Russell T. McCutcheon's *Manufacturing Religion: The Discourse on Sui Generis Religion and the Politics of Nostalgia* (1997) and Timothy Fitzgerald's *The Ideology of Religious Studies* (2000), emerged around the same time as the histories by Lippy, Hutchison, and Eck that opened religious pluralism to further historical scrutiny, or that these studies coincided with Hart's harsh indictment. Unlike Hart, McCutcheon and Fitzgerald had no investment in perpetuating the Church, Christianity, or belief in God. Like Hart, however, they criticized religion as a sentimental, romantic concept—a kind of wishful thought about the way human beings understood the meaning of life—and they criticized religious studies as an elaborate system of institutional operation geared to uphold that thought.

While Hart criticized religion, religious pluralism, and religious studies for being antithetical to biblical revelation, McCutcheon and Fitzgerald criticized them for perpetuating mysticism and obstructing critical inquiry. McCutcheon wrote, "because the goal appears to be a theology of religious pluralism, the task at hand is not to develop a testable theory capable of explaining."[35] Fitzgerald connected this theology of religious pluralism with "the wider historical process of western imperialism" and with "the industry known as religious studies" that portrays "an idealized world of so-called faith communities—of worship, customs, beliefs, doctrines, and rites entirely divorced form the realities of power in different societies."[36]

Ahlstrom never imagined that the academic study of religion would be perceived as an insidious industry, or that religious pluralism would be seen as a theology in the service of western imperialism. Nevertheless, he did anticipate some of the analysis put forward by McCutcheon and Fitzgerald in his criticism of popular forms of religion that offered idealized worlds divorced from the realities of power. Although he believed that idealism was essential for a democratic American society to work, he did not link that idealism to religion per se, but rather to an increasingly secularized tradition of social thought derived from Protestant thinkers and institutions.

In some respects, the critics of religion, religious studies, and religious pluralism (Hart, McCutcheon, and Fitzgerald) on the one hand, and the proponents of religious pluralism (Albanese, Eck, and Hutchison) on the other represent two trajectories of thought about religion and religious pluralism that Sydney Ahlstrom attempted to reconcile. While Ahlstrom moved more in the direction of the affirmation of religious pluralism that Eck and Hutchison would take, his deep engagement with the history of American Protestant thought left him uncertain about religious pluralism as a solution to the problems of American democracy. Ahlstrom did not explore the historical roots of the concept of religion in the Enlightenment as Peter Byrne would do in 1989,[37] or caution against over-reliance on the term, as Jonathan Z. Smith would do in his famous distinction between map and territory in the study of religion.[38] But his panoramic history of religion in America provided a map that others would emulate, work against, or follow parts of in developing later histories of American religious pluralism.

Notes

1 Claude Welch, *Graduate Education in Religion: A Critical Appraisal* (Missoula: University of Montana Press, 1971), 168–178; for a history of connections between Protestant divinity schools and religious studies, see Conrad Cherry, *Hurrying Toward Zion: Universities, Divinity Schools, and American Protestantism* (Bloomington: Indiana University Press, 1995). Thanks to Shaun Horton for assistance with this section of the chapter.

2 William F. Quillian, Jr., "The Religion Teacher and the Churches," *The Journal of Bible and Religion* 21:4 (October 1953), quotations from pp. 227, 229, 231.

3 Floyd H. Ross, "A Re-Examination of Christian Attitudes Toward Other Faiths," *The Journal of Bible and Religion* 21: 2 (April 1953), quotations from pp. 79, 82–83.

4 Robert S. Eccles, "What is Sectarian Teaching?" *The Journal of Bible and Religion* 19:3 (July 1951), quotations from pp. 134, 136–137.

5 For discussion of the origin of denominationalism in English Separatism, see Winthrop S. Hudson, *American Protestantism* (Chicago: University of Chicago Press, 1961), 33–46, quotation from p. 41.

6 Hudson, *American Protestantism*, quotation from p. 45.

7 Amanda Porterfield, *Mary Lyon and the Mount Holyoke Missionaries* (New York: Oxford University Press, 1997).

8 Josiah Strong, *The New Era, or the Coming Kingdom* (New York: Baker & Taylor, 1893), quotation from p. 319.

9 The full definition of Evangelicals given: "Protestants who believe that the Bible is literally true, that salvation requires a 'born again' conversion, and that one must share that faith with others." *New York Times*, Sunday, January 14, 2007, p. 21.

10 Amanda Porterfield, "The Pragmatic Role of Religious Studies," *The Transformation of American Religion: The Story of a Late Twentieth-Century Awakening* (New York: Oxford University Press, 2001), 202–226.

11 Erin A. Smith, "Liberal Religion, Therapeutic Culture, and the World: Reading 'America's Preacher' at Home and Abroad," and Matthew S. Hedstrom, "The Construction of 'Judeo-Christian' Spirituality in Postwar America," unpublished papers in my possession.

12 Huston Smith, *Religions of Man*, 2nd ed. (New York: Harper & Row, 1965; orig. 1958); Annemarie Schimmel, *Mystical Dimensions of Islam* (Chapel Hill: University of North Carolina Press, 1975).

13 Sydney E. Ahlstrom, *A Religious History of the American People* (New Haven, CT: Yale University Press, 1972), quotations from pp. 1091, 1096.

14 Ibid., quotation from p. 787.

15 Ibid., quotations from p. 796.

16 Ibid., quotations from pp. 1090 and 1093.

17 Catherine L. Albanese, *America: Religions and Religion*, 3rd ed. (Belmont, CA: Wadsworth Publishing Company, 1999; orig. 1981), quotations from p. xv.

18 Albanese, *America*, quotations from pp. xv, 17. Also see Catherine L. Albanese, *Corresponding Motion: Transcendental Religion and the New America* (Philadelphia: Temple University Press, 1977); Albanese, *Nature Religion in America: From the Algonkian Indians to the New Age* (Chicago: University of Chicago, 1990); Albanese, *A Republic of Mind and Spirit: A Cultural History of American Metaphysical Religion* (New Haven, CT: Yale University Press, 2007).

19 Schimmel, *Mystical Dimensions*, 3.

20 Diana L. Eck, *A New Religious America: How a "Christian Country" Has Become the World's Most Religiously Diverse Nation* (San Francisco: HarperSanFrancisco, 2001), quotation from p. 80.

21 Horace M. Kallen, "Democracy *vs.* the Melting Pot" [1915], rpt. in Horace M. Kallen, *Culture and Democracy in the United States* (New York: Boni and Liveright, 1924), quoted in William R. Hutchison, *Religious Pluralism in America: The Contentious History of a Founding Ideal* (New Haven, CT: Yale University Press, 2003), pp. 20 and 194.

22 Eck, *New Religious America*, quotations from pp. 58–59.

23 Ibid., quotations from pp. 275, 271–272, 348–351.

24 Hutchison, *Religious Pluralism in America*; Hutchison, *The Transcendentalist Ministers: Church Reform in the New England Renaissance* (New Haven, CT: Yale University Press, 1959); Hutchison, *Errand to the World: American Protestant Thought and Foreign Missions* (Chicago: University of Chicago Press, 1987); Hutchison, *The Modernist Impulse in American Protestantism* (Cambridge, MA: Harvard University Press, 1976).

25 Hutchison, *Religious Pluralism in America*, quotations from p. 7.

26 In *Beyond Toleration: The Religious Origins of American Pluralism* (New York: Oxford University Press, 2006), Chris Beneke developed this point further.

27 Charles H. Lippy, *Pluralism Comes of Age: American Religious Culture in the Twentieth Century* (Armonk, NY: M.E. Sharpe, 2000), quotations from pp. 162, 14, 143. Catherine Albanese developed a parallel insight in the third edition of her text: "American cultural religion, as we know it today, roughly began to assume its shape in the late nineteenth century." By "American cultural religion," Albanese meant popular culture in its mythic dimensions and elements of sacred time and space. Albanese, *America*, quotation from p. 465.

28 Lippy, *Pluralism Comes of Age*, quotation from p. 162.

29 Mark A. Noll, *America's God: From Jonathan Edwards to Abraham Lincoln* (New York: Oxford University Press, 2002).

30 Ibid., quotation from p. 444.

31 George M. Marsden, *Jonathan Edwards: A Life* (New Haven, CT: Yale University Press, 2003).

32 Ahlstrom, *Religious History*, quotations from p. 948.

33 D. G. Hart, *How the University Got Religion: Religious Studies in American Higher Education* (Baltimore, MD: Johns Hopkins University Press, 1999), quotations from p. 251.

34 Hart, *How the University Got Religion*, quotation from p. 110.

35 Russell T. McCutcheon, *Manufacturing Religion: The Discourse on Sui Generis Religion and the Politics of Nostalgia* (New York: Oxford University Press, 1997), quotation from p. 117.

36 Timothy Fitzgerald, *The Ideology of Religious Studies* (New York: Oxford University Press, 2000), quotations from pp. 8–9.

37 Peter Byrne, *Natural Religion and the Nature of Religion: The Legacy of Deism* (London: Routledge, 1989).

38 Jonathan Z. Smith, *Imagining Religion: From Babylon to Jonestown* (Chicago: University of Chicago Press, 1982).

CHAPTER 2 | # Religious Pluralism in Modern America: A Sociological Overview

JOHN H. EVANS

IT SHOULD BE OBVIOUS to any sentient American that the United States is becoming more ethnically diverse. Only a slightly higher degree of attention is required to also notice that America is becoming more religiously diverse as well. Before one begins any examination of religious diversity in the United States, one must ask what the purpose of the examination is. What is it that motivates one to write in the first place? In American academic contexts, largely populated by social liberals, we can presume that the reason we write is not to examine religious diversity because we are concerned with how the minority religious groups are contaminating the beliefs of the majority. Rather, the presumption, deeply embedded in much of academic life, is that if we as a society understood each other better we would have less conflict and a more harmonious existence.

A report of the Harvard Pluralism Project on religion in Boston is exemplary. It begins by saying that "how we encounter religious and cultural difference is certainly one of the most important questions our society faces in the late twentieth century." Starting with the encounter with Native Americans, the report notes that "by the 1670s, the wars that would lead to the decimation of the Native population began. The first chapter in the history of cultural encounter was not an exemplary one." It then discusses how in the 1600s the "occasional Quaker, Baptist or Jew was 'warned out' of Boston," and how "between 1659 and 1661, four Quakers were hung on Boston Common." Eventually, "gone were the days when people of different beliefs could be 'warned out' of town, but prejudice and nativism continued to operate in subtle and overt ways to perpetuate tribalization and division. After more than a century, Boston's Catholic and Jewish communities are now very much part of the Boston mainstream, but the challenges of living in a society of religious, racial, and ethnic diversity have multiplied and are still very much on the agenda of Boston and other major cities." The report then goes on to discuss the growth of non-Western religious traditions in Boston, and, implicitly, the challenge this will create. "This process of encounter, dialogue, and transformation is critically important today as American cities begin to appropriate a new multi-religious reality."[1] Violence caused by misunderstanding lurks not too far beneath the surface here.

Many "solutions" to religious diversity in a society have been tried over the centuries. One solution has been "perfectionism," which holds that it is good to live a coherent ethical life, religious people have a substantive vision of such a life, and they hold that both state and society should help people to achieve this.[2] One way this is done is by limiting the development of competing value spheres: not only other religions, but competing secular ideas. In the sixteenth century they killed people from other religious groups to create a unitary society. Currently in some Muslim countries, perfectionism is enforced by making the practice of competing religions illegal. The religiously based wars of the sixteenth and seventeenth centuries in Europe, according to British historian Paul Johnson, "were based on the assumption that only a unitary society was tolerable, and those who did not conform to the prevailing norms, and who could not be forced or terrified into doing so, should be treated as second-class citizens, expelled, or killed."[3]

Obviously, this is not what most contemporary academics have in mind; it is rather their proper nightmare. The solution to religious diversity most common to academics, as well as at least in word by our society's leaders, is "pluralism." "Pluralism," in the words of Diana Eck, "is not just another word for diversity. It goes beyond mere plurality or diversity to active engagement with that plurality...without any real engagement with one another, neighboring churches, temples, and mosques might prove to be just a striking example of diversity.... Pluralism requires participation, and attunement to the life and energies of one another."[4] It is not a vision that America should be a "melting pot" that distills some lowest common denominator of religion, or what Will Herberg originally called a "transmuting pot" where Hindus, Buddhists, and others would become Christians like the dominant majority. Scholars interested in religious pluralism are explicitly or implicitly advocating a "salad bowl" and not a "melting pot." Pluralism understands the diverse religious groups in society for what they are, appreciating them and respecting them.

Numeric Diversity in American History

Pluralism becomes relevant as a strategy only if there is diversity to be managed. Religious diversity has been on the increase in the United States since colonial times. While America was not founded as a Christian nation, many of the colonies were, and, after colonization from Europe, America primarily contained Christians. These were not only Christians, but particular types of Protestant Christians. Religious pluralism originally meant diversity within Protestantism. In the colonial era there were Anglicans in some colonies, Presbyterians in others, Puritans elsewhere. The despised religious minorities of the day were not Muslims, like today, but rather Quakers and

Baptists, both of whom fled the Massachusetts Bay Colony to Rhode Island as a place of relative religious freedom. The first Jews arrived in the colonies in the 1650s. By today's standards, religious diversity in the colonial era operated within a very narrow band. This diversity also occurred primarily due to immigration, which is not the only way diversity has increased in U.S. history.

While the colonies started as primarily Protestant, there were also Catholics in the colonies, and their number increased markedly in the nineteenth century with immigration from European Catholic countries such as Germany, Italy, and Ireland. Protestantism also became more diverse with Lutheran immigrants from Northern Europe. For example, each national/ethnic/linguistic group would start their own Lutheran Church when arriving in the new world, and it wouldn't be for many generations that their ancestors—now all speaking English and thinking of themselves more as Americans than as Norwegians, Swedes, or Germans—would merge into collective Lutheran bodies.

Catholics began as an extreme minority, comprising 5% of the population and 14% of the religious adherents in 1850, then growing to 16% of the population and 28% of adherents in 1926.[5] As of 2001, Catholics comprised 24.5% of the population.[6] The era of rapid growth was, of course, also the era of large immigration from Catholic parts of Europe. Catholic growth in America also resulted from a higher fertility rate in all but the most recent decades.[7]

Of course, in addition to the emigration of various religious groups, one of the primary engines of religious diversity in the United States has been American religious inventiveness, itself spurred on by the religious freedom of America, where any person with a vision and charisma could try to start their own religious group. Perhaps the most famous geographic area in terms of religious invention is the "burned-over district" of western New York State. The term "burned-over district" was conferred on the area because it had "wave after wave of diverse religious excitements."[8] In this area Joseph Smith discovered the golden plates following the direction of the angel Moroni in 1827, eventually starting the Church of Jesus Christ of Latter-day Saints.[9] William Miller had many followers in the same area, and Miller preached that the second coming would occur in 1844. When that did not occur, the Millerites eventually transformed themselves into what are now called the Seventh-day Adventists, a group with a number of religious practices distinct from other Protestant groups.[10] A religious innovation appealing more to liberals and anticlericals was spiritualism, also born in the same area in 1847 when two young girls learned they could communicate with the dead.[11] American history is replete with such new inventions, but the point has been made: in the United States, much religious pluralism is the result of religious entrepreneurs creating new offshoots of existing religions.

American religion has not only had innovations, such as those above, which offer a fairly clear break with existing traditions, but also been many internal schisms that have resulted in more subtle religious diversity. For example, one source reports that there are 20 Baptist and 14 Methodist denominations in the United States.[12]

While religious diversity in the United States has often been judged in terms of the numerous types of Protestants, after World War II the divisions between these groups began to blur. If at the turn of the twentieth century a Methodist marrying a Baptist was a "mixed marriage," by the latter half of the twentieth century such distinctions were not quite so critical.[13] Instead, a new divide emerged between liberals and conservatives *within* each specific tradition. There were liberal Methodists and conservative Methodists, liberal Baptists and conservative Baptists. Although there is dispute over the nomenclature, the current divide runs between mainline Protestants and evangelical Protestants. So, to take one example, Hillary Clinton is a mainline Protestant United Methodist, and President George W. Bush is an evangelical United Methodist. Sociologists who examine the effects of religious affiliation conclude that this is the divide that has the greatest consequence in American life, not the divide between the various sub-traditions within Protestantism (e.g., Methodism, Lutheranism, Presbyterianism).

As is well known, the immigration patterns to the United States shifted markedly after a change in the immigration laws in 1965, which resulted in "a wave of new immigration that rivaled the one at the start of the 20th century in scope and magnitude."[14] Whereas the earlier waves of immigrants had come from the Christian countries of Europe, the new immigrants also came from countries where Christianity was not the dominant religion. While there were always members of non-Western religions in the United States, the numbers were tiny. After 1965, there were for the first time noticeable numbers of Muslims, Hindus, Buddhists, and members of other non-Western religions.

There is clearly some sort of cognitive threshold for a minority group to enter the consciousness of the majority group. This limit probably varies by how "different" the minority appears to the majority in terms of appearance and behavior. In terms of social perception, before the mid-1960s the numbers of Muslims, Buddhists, Hindus in the United States—to say nothing of Zoroastrians and adherents of Shinto—was essentially zero. The actual numbers were also objectively near zero. Of course, measuring the numbers of adherents to non-Western religions in the United States is difficult,[15] primarily because on average a survey of a few thousand households would net only five to ten respondents of a religious minority. Moreover, religious minorities are highly geographically clustered and often non-English speaking. One estimate in the year 2000 had approximately 0.5% of Americans claiming to be Muslim, 0.5% Buddhist, and 0.4% Hindu.[16] Another study had 0.6% of Americans claiming to be Muslim, 0.8% Buddhist, and 0.4% Hindu. The numbers of adherents of Baha'i, Taoist, Rastafarian, Sikh, and other religions are much smaller. The long-standing American religious minority in the majority's mind—Jews—comprises 1.3% of the population in one of the more recent studies.[17] In sum, before 1965 these groups would have been numerically unmeasurable. Now they can be measured, although they remain tiny minorities.

There is one highly distinct group in the religious landscape that is growing rapidly but is rarely referred to in studies of pluralism. Persons with "no religious preference" are probably the fastest growing group in the "religious" map of the United States. While hovering around 7% for 20 or so years, in the early 1990s the rate of nonaffiliation began to grow, topping 14% in 2000.[18] This group is far larger than all of the non-Western religions combined, and, as we will see below, it has been the most difficult group for the majority religious groups to contend with.

To summarize recent trends in religious diversity in the United States, Protestants have been declining, from 62% of the population to 52% between 1972 and 2002, Catholics have held steady at approximately 25%, Jews have remained in the 1.5 to 2.5% range, "no religious preference" has grown from 7% to 14%, and "others" have grown from around 2% to 7%.[19] Within the shrinking Protestant group, the mainline denominations have been shrinking faster than the evangelicals, primarily because mainline women have lower fertility rates than do evangelical women.[20] While percentages will vary depending on how one defines the various groups, at present, according to one survey, the U.S. population is 76% Christian, 14.1% "no religion," 5.4% "refused to answer," and 3.7% all other religions.[21]

The Presence of Religious Pluralism

Pluralism does not exist if different groups never encounter one another. If fifty million Muslims immigrated to the United States but remained isolated in enclaves with little or no interaction with the dominant religious community, the effects of that new increase in numeric diversity would be quite minor. Rather, pluralism is a strategy for dealing with diversity—a strategy of communication and understanding. Are people in a position to even start that conversation, or are they socially isolated from each other?

Within the Christian groups, the story of the twentieth century has been the increasing integration of *all* Christians into public life, and thus increasing exposure to the diversity that already existed in the United States. It has been mainline Protestants who have historically been the dominant religious group in American society, dominating professional, political, economic, and social life. This dominance has declined, making for a more inclusive public sphere. One way of demonstrating this slip in dominance, and the parallel rise of Catholics, evangelicals, and Jews, is to examine the religion of elite professionals. (This method is premised on the assumption that elite professionals have greater social exposure and interaction than others.)

James Davidson and his colleagues found that, in 1930–31, there were 3.3 times as many (mainline Protestant) Presbyterians in the Who's Who than there should be if all religions were represented according to their actual numbers in the general population. There were 6.3 times as many (mainline) Episcopalians and 5.6 times as many (mainline) Congregationalists as there should have been. In 1992–93, the Episcopalians had held steady in their overrepresentation, but the Presbyterians had slipped to only 2.75 times their target representation, and the Congregationalists to 2.6 times. More important for our narrative here, Jews had gone from 0.73 times (underrepresented given the Jewish population in the United States) to 6 times overrepresented. Catholics had gone from 0.13 times (massively underrepresented) to 0.85 (almost at parity). Due to the methods employed in their paper, it is difficult for someone else using their data to separate out evangelicals.[22] In a similar study of "American elites" in the fields of business, politics, intellectual life, and agriculture, between 1930 and 1977, liberal Protestants went from holding 54% of these positions to 32%, Catholics went from 3.7% to 16.4%, and Jews from 1.1% to 5.2%.[23]

Catholics and evangelicals have also become more visible because they are heading toward parity in educational attainment. Robert Wuthnow reported that data from 1980 showed that conservative Protestants and Catholics were converging on the mainline Protestants who had traditionally dominated higher education.[24] An analysis of a survey conducted in the year 2000 found no difference in the odds of completing a four-year college degree between evangelicals and mainline Protestants.[25] While the differences have been narrowing, the traditional gaps likely remain.[26]

Probably the most obvious location for the increasing presence of evangelicals and Catholics is in political debates in the public sphere. After many decades of avoiding politics, evangelicals and fundamentalists reentered American politics in the late 1970s and early 1980s with the formation of what has come to be known as the "religious right." Traditionalist Catholics, while never avoiding the public sphere as conservative Protestants had done, found kindred spirits on many issues, such as making abortion illegal. The apotheosis of the emergence of traditionalist Catholics and conservative Protestants as a political factor was the election of the explicitly evangelical George W. Bush to the presidency in 2000, with extensive backing from many evangelical groups. Due to the existence of the religious right, more Americans are probably aware of the beliefs of evangelicals than at any time in American history.

In sum, while the numbers of Catholics and evangelicals have not changed markedly in recent decades, their social exposure has changed markedly. Pluralism, as a strategy for managing this religious difference, could more realistically begin to take hold given the likelihood that members of the dominant majority would actually encounter Catholics and Jews in their everyday lives and find that such people had a social status akin to their own.

Many of the chapters in this volume are dedicated to non-Western religions such as Islam, Buddhism, and Hinduism, which remain extreme minorities in American society. However, for various reasons, probably having to do with their relative exoticness compared to the beliefs, appearances, and practices of the Christian majority, these groups have entered the consciousness of the American majority. Will pluralism as a strategy of dealing with this diversity prevail? Sociological studies of these non-Western religions suggest that the precondition of social exposure exists.

This condition is evident from a study of the degree of societal integration of Muslims, Buddhists, and Hindus in the United States which found that members of these non-Western religions have higher degrees of education than the Christian majority has—presumably because the immigration authorities prefer migrants with more education. Social isolation is also not the norm. The authors find that "the likelihood of being isolated from immediate neighbors is not statistically different among Muslims, Buddhists, or Hindus than among Christians," and that "members of non-Western religions are engaged in social interaction with the Christian population."[27] However, the degree of integration in the political sphere is less, with, for example, Asian Buddhists and Asian Hindus being less likely to vote than Christians.

Similarly, other studies show that members of non-Western religions are interacting with the majority population. In one survey of the United States, 56% of respondents claim to have had a "fair amount of personal contact" with Jews, 24% with Muslims, 15% with Hindus, and 14% with Buddhists. Thirteen percent said that they had had "no contact" with Jews, 32% had had "no contact" with Muslims, 41% with Hindus, and 44% with Buddhists.[28] Given how few members of non-Western religions actually live in the United States, it is striking that so many people claim to have met one.

Acceptance/Tolerance of Religious Others

In Diana Eck's vision, "pluralism goes beyond mere tolerance to the active attempt to understand the other."[29] Tolerance is, like social exposure, a prerequisite to pluralism. Is the dominant group tolerant of members of minority religions?

Over the years, more groups have been added to the dominant group in the United States through tolerance and acceptance. First it was Protestants who were asked to be tolerant of Catholics and Jews, and, for quite some time they were not particularly tolerant of either group. Now, however, Catholics and Jews are part of the accepted/tolerated mainstream. Evidence for this assertion comes from changing answers to a question that has been asked by survey researchers for decades: "if your party nominated a generally well-qualified person for president who happened to be [fill in a religious group], would you vote for that person?" Acceptance of a Jewish or Catholic candidate increased from approximately 50% in 1937 to almost all Americans by 2000.[30] Further evidence of increased acceptance and tolerance is the fact that, during a similar period of time, the rate of intermarriage between Catholics, Protestants, and Jews has also increased markedly.[31]

We lack the data to make claims about the change in the tolerance of non-Western religious groups in the United States; however, we can assess the contemporary situation. When a 2003 survey asked, "suppose you had a child who wanted to marry a Muslim who had a good education and came from a good family. Would you: object strongly, object somewhat, object a little, not object at all," 44% claimed they would "not object at all." The same question about Hindus resulted in 48% claiming they would not object at all. When asked, "suppose some Muslims wanted to build a large Muslim mosque in your community," 56% claimed that either they would welcome the mosque or that its construction would not bother them.[32] A similar question about a Hindu temple had 71% claiming they would either welcome or not be bothered by it.[33] How one interprets these results depends on whether one is inclined to see the glass half empty or half full. We could say that nearly half of the American people are entirely supportive of pluralism, given their answer to the questions about one's child marrying a Muslim or Hindu. On the other hand, there is a long way to go before the non-Western religions complete the path toward tolerance that Catholics and Jews have made over the past few hundred years. This conclusion is evident from the same survey, which shows that 38% of Americans favor "making it harder for Muslims to settle in the United States" and 23% favor "making it illegal for Muslim groups to meet in the United States." (By comparison, 20% wanted to make it illegal for Hindus and Buddhists to meet.)[34] Outlawing a religious group's meetings could be thought of as the inverse of religious tolerance and more like the "perfectionist" solution to numeric diversity.

Another "glass is half empty" analysis would consider hate crimes against religious minorities. Jews and Muslims in particular are subject to hate crimes,[35] and there is no need for examples here. Interestingly, the group on the religious landscape of whom Americans are least tolerant is not Muslims, as one would expect, but atheists. Susan Jacoby begins her history of the secularist and free-thought traditions in the United States by stating that:

> during the past two decades, cultural and religious conservatives have worked ceaselessly to delegitimize American secularism and relegate its heroes to a kooks' corner of American history. In the eighteenth century, Enlightenment secularists of the revolutionary generation were stigmatized by the guardians of religious orthodoxy as infidels and atheists. Today, the new pejorative "elitist" has replaced the old "infidel" in the litany of slurs aimed at defenders of secularist values. Since the terrorist attacks of September 11, 2001, America's secularist tradition has been further denigrated by unremitting political propaganda equating patriotism with religious faith.[36]

In a survey conducted in 2003, Americans were asked if a particular "group does not at all agree with my vision of American society." That atheists "do not at all agree" was the response of 39.6%. The next highest group was Muslims at 26.3%, followed by homosexuals at 22.6%, conservative Christians at 13.5%, recent immigrants at 12.5%, Hispanics at 7.6%, Jews at 7.4%, Asian Americans at 7.0%, African-Americans at 4.6%, and white Americans at 2.2%.[37]

The percentage who say they "would disapprove if my child wanted to marry" an atheist was 47.6%; 33.5% would disapprove of a Muslim marrying their child; 27.2% would disapprove of an African-American; and 11.8% would disapprove of their child marrying a Jew. The authors conclude that "atheists

are at the top of the list of groups that Americans find problematic in both public and private life, and the gap between acceptance of atheists and acceptance
of other racial and religious minorities is large and persistent."[38] This group
seems to be the one with whom most Americans will have the most difficult
time having a pluralistic relationship.

The Ambiguity of Pluralism

The function of this chapter is to give an overview or portrait of American religious diversity and pluralism, but not to make deep sociological claims about
pluralism itself. I will, however, make one limited point. I will present data
that, on one hand, can be interpreted as evidence of the increasing triumph
of pluralism in the United States, and, on the other, as evidence of one of the
greatest challenges for Americans to which pluralism (not diversity) leads.

In a 2003 survey, 74% of respondents agreed that "all major religions, such
as Christianity, Hinduism, Buddhism and Islam, contain some truth about
God." 42% agreed that "all religions basically teach the same thing." 46%
thought that "God's word is revealed in other writings besides the Bible, such
as the sacred texts used by Muslims or Hindus." 44%, however, insisted that
"Christianity is the only way to have a true personal relationship with God."[39]
In an even more striking survey, "75 percent of American adults said 'yes' when
they were asked, 'Do you think there is any religion other than your own that
offers a true path to God?'" In the same survey, 80% said that "such paths
were just as good as their own."[40] These data suggest that a large portion of the
Christian majority appears to respect other religions so much that they consider them correct on their own terms—they "contain some truth about God."

Here we must ask—is accepting that other religions are true a desired
response to the numeric diversity of religion? Is this to be celebrated? Diana
Eck thinks it is not necessary for her vision of pluralism. She says that "pluralism is not simply relativism. It does not displace or eliminate deep religious
commitments or secular commitments for that matter. It is, rather, the encounter of commitments."[41] The problem is that if you think that all religions are
true, then there is no particular reason for focusing upon your own. Wuthnow
quotes a campus chaplain who says that, if all religions are true:

> then it is easy to assume that "on Sunday you can be a Christian, on Monday you
> can be a Hindu, and on Tuesday you can be a Muslim and it's all okay." ... "I think
> most religious leaders would say you're not going to plumb the depths of a way
> to God or receive the benefits of a community or a discipline unless you make a
> commitment to one."[42]

Of course, the question is whether it is the sheer diversity of religion—or a pluralist response to this diversity—that leads to this relativism. Peter Berger and
Thomas Luckmann's hugely influential theory about the sociology of religion
can be used to explain, among other things, why increasing religious diversity

would, counter-intuitively, reduce the need for religious pluralism.[43] Religions, they assert, concern ultimate truths, the most deeply assumed facts about existence. Encountering people who do not share those assumptions—people from other religions—they posit, should inevitably erode one's faith that one's own assumptions are absolutely correct. This doubt, in turn, should lead to a decline in faith, and, as contact across religions increased due to increasing global communication, secularization would ensue. In my interpretation of their theory, increasing religious diversity leads to lower levels of religious commitment, essentially "solving" the problem of diversity and eliminating the need for pluralism. (Berger later had second thoughts about the theory he made so popular.)[44]

Many have modified this theory in subsequent years. Christian Smith argues that, when people evaluate the truthfulness of their beliefs, they consider the views not of everyone in society but rather those of their own particularly constructed reference group. Therefore, a decline of faith has not occurred, at least for certain religions in the United States, because the religious diversity in the modern world is not a threat—those in other religions are not considered when evaluating the truth of one's own religion.[45]

However, even if Smith is right, and religious diversity does not lead to a decline in certitude of the truthfulness of one's faith, pluralism may lead to such a decline. A Christian may know that a Muslim family lives down the street, and know that they have fundamentally different beliefs, but in Smith's theory they might not be considered part of the Christian's reference group. However, pluralism encourages the sort of communicative encounter about each other's religion that may well lead to the Muslim being considered to be part of the reference group. Pluralism, not diversity, may lead to the loss of certitude indicated by surveys that show a majority of religious persons believe in the truth of all religions.

There is not enough evidence about the impact of diversity or pluralism on the certitude of faith to reach strong conclusions. However, if pluralism does create less certitude about the distinctiveness of one's religion—about its truth—then pluralism may paradoxically be reducing the diversity for which it purports to be the solution. If all religions are considered the same by their own members, then one may ask why pluralism is even needed.

The Future of Diversity and Pluralism

The European colonization of America started out with a fairly high degree of religious uniformity. The religious diversity that then emerged in the colonial era took place largely within the Christian tradition, and this diversity was not always managed in the most harmonious way. Over time, most Christians and Jews came to be categorized as part of the dominant group that would or would not engage in a strategy of pluralism toward the new members of non-Western traditions that came on the American scene in force as of the mid-1960s. If history repeats itself—which it does not always do—the new non-Western religions will become part of the American "in-group," and the "in-group" will have to decide its stance toward the next type of diversity that appears on the American scene. At present, there does seem to be one group that may be particularly difficult to include as part of the "in-group": atheists.

Many social theorists would say that a society needs to have an out-group against which to define itself. That is, one cannot think of one's own group in the abstract without a comparison. For example, the identity of "American" presumes and requires a category called "non-American." The category of "we moral people" presumes and relies upon a social construction of a group of people who are not "moral people."[46] "The creation of the other is always necessary for the creation of identity and solidarity," claim the authors of the tolerance of atheists study.[47]

In the 1950s we had the communist other to define who "real" Americans were. In American history certain religious groups have served as this "other," most notably Catholics and Jews, and both are now a part of the "real American" category. Given the findings that Muslims are more acceptable to Americans than atheists, it seems that atheists are poised to be the "other" that Americans need to define themselves. In fact, all of the public discourse about religious pluralism may be creating the atheist as the other. Penny Edgell and her colleagues put it well:

> It is possible that the increasing tolerance for religious diversity may have heightened awareness of religion itself as a basis for solidarity in American life and sharpened the boundary between believers and nonbelievers in our collective imagination. It is also possible that the prominence of Christian Right rhetoric in the public realm has played the same role.[48]

Notes

1 Diana L. Eck, Elinor J. Pierce, and Alan G. Wagner, *World Religions in Boston: A Guide to Communities and Resources* (Cambridge, MA: The Pluralism Project, Harvard University, 2000).

2 Richard Madsen and Tracy B. Strong, "Introduction: Three Forms of Ethical Pluralism," in *The Many and the One*, Richard Madsen and Tracy B. Strong, eds. (Princeton, NJ: Princeton University Press, 2003), 2.

3 Paul Johnson, *A History of Christianity* (New York: Atheneum, 1976), 306.

4 Diana Eck, *A New Religious America: How a "Christian" Country Has Now Become the Most Religiously Diverse Nation on Earth* (San Francisco: HarperSanFrancisco, 2001), 70.

5 Roger Finke and Rodney Stark, *The Churching of America, 1776–1990: Winners and Losers in Our Religious Economy* (New Brunswick, NJ: Rutgers University Press, 1992), 114.

6 Barry Kosmin, Egon Mayer, and Ariela Keysar, "American Religious Identification Survey" (New York: Graduate Center of the City University of New York, 2001).

7 Mark A. Noll, *A History of Christianity in the United States and Canada* (Grand Rapids, MI: Eerdmans, 1992), 206.

8 Sydney Ahlstrom, *A Religious History of the American People* (New Haven, CT: Yale University Press, 1972), 477.

9 Jon Butler, *Awash in a Sea of Faith: Christianizing the American People* (Cambridge, MA: Harvard University Press, 1990), 242.

10 Ahlstrom, *Religious History*, 478–481.

11 Ibid., 488.

12 Eileen W. Linder, *Yearbook of American and Canadian Churches* (Nashville, TN: Abingdon, 2000), 170–172.

13 Robert Wuthnow, *The Restructuring of American Religion* (Princeton, NJ: Princeton University Press, 1988).

14 Robert Wuthnow, "Presidential Address 2003: The Challenge of Diversity," *Journal for the Scientific Study of Religion* 43, no. 2 (2004): 159.

15 Tom W. Smith, "Religious Diversity in America: The Emergence of Muslims, Buddhists, Hindus, and Others," *Journal for the Scientific Study of Religion* 41, no. 3 (2002): 577–585.

16 Ibid.

17 Kosmin, Mayer, and Keysar, "American Religious Identification Survey."

18 Michael Hout and Claude S. Fischer, "Why More Americans Have No Religious Preference: Politics and Generations," *American Sociological Review* 67 (2002): 165–190. My own analysis of the General Social Survey data used by Hout and Fischer concludes that this level of no preference remained stable at approximately 14% from 2000 to 2004.

19 Tom W. Smith and Seokho Kim, "The Vanishing Protestant Majority," *Journal for the Scientific Study of Religion* 44, no. 2 (2005): 215.

20 Michael Hout, Andrew Greeley, and Melissa J. Wilde, "The Demographic Imperative in Religious Change in the United States," *American Journal of Sociology* 107, no. 2 (2001): 468–500.

21 Kosmin, Mayer, and Keysar, "American Religious Identification Survey."

22 James D. Davidson, Ralph E. Pyle, and David V. Reyes, "Persistence and Change in the Protestant Establishment," *Social Forces* 74, no. 1 (1995): 167.

23 James D. Davidson, "Religion Among America's Elite: Persistence and Change in the Protestant Establishment," *Sociology of Religion* 55, no. 4 (1994): 429.

24 Wuthnow, *Restructuring of American Religion*, 86.

25 Kraig Beyerlein, "Specifying the Impact of Conservative Protestantism on Educational Attainment," *Journal for the Scientific Study of Religion* 43, no. 4 (2004): 511.

26 Pyle concludes that "despite some narrowing of difference among the religious categories on socioeconomic indicators, religious groups continue to be distinguished on the basis of their socioeconomic positions, and the overall religious group status ranking remains largely unchanged from the rankings of fifty years ago. Jews are at the top, followed by liberal Protestants, Catholics, Moderate Protestants, and Black and conservative Protestants at the bottom. Ralph E. Pyle, "Trends in Religious Stratification: Have Religious Group Socioeconomic Distinctions Declined in Recent Decades?" *Sociology of Religion* 67, no. 1 (2006): 76.

27 Robert Wuthnow and Conrad Hackett, "The Social Integration of Practitioners of Non-Western Religions in the United States," *Journal for the Scientific Study of Religion* 42, no. 4 (2003): 661, 664.

28 Robert Wuthnow, *America and the Challenges of Religious Diversity* (Princeton, NJ: Princeton University Press, 2005), 213.

29 Eck, *New Religious America*, 70.

30 Claude S. Fischer and Michael Hout, *Century of Difference: How the Country Changed in the Last One Hundred Years* (New York: Russell Sage Foundation, 2006), 200, 222.

31 Fischer and Hout, *Century of Difference*, 202.

32 41% said it would bother them a lot or bother them a little.

33 35% said it would bother them a lot or bother them a little.

34 Wuthnow, *America and the Challenges of Religious Diversity*, 219.

35 Wuthnow, "Presidential Address 2003: The Challenge of Diversity," 163.

36 Susan Jacoby, *Freethinkers: A History of American Secularism* (New York: Metropolitan Books, 2004), 1–2.

37 Penny Edgell, Joseph Gerteis, and Douglas Hartmann, "Atheists as 'Other': Moral Boundaries and Cultural Membership in American Society," *American Sociological Review* 71 (2006): 218.

38 Edgell, Gerteis, and Hartmann, "Atheists as 'Other'," 230.

39 Wuthnow, *America and the Challenges of Religious Diversity*, 191, 197.

40 Fischer and Hout, *Century of Difference*, 192.

41 Eck, *New Religious America*, 71.

42 Wuthnow, *America and the Challenges of Religious Diversity*, 100.

43 Peter L. Berger and Thomas Luckmann, *The Social Construction of Reality* (New York: Anchor, 1966).

44 Peter L. Berger, "The Desecularization of the World: A Global Overview," in *The Desecularization of the World: Resurgent Religion and World Politics*, ed. Peter L. Berger (Grand Rapids, MI: Eerdmans, 1999), 1–18.

45 Christian Smith, *American Evangelicalism: Embattled and Thriving* (Chicago: University of Chicago Press, 1998), 104–106.

46 Michele Lamont, *Money, Morals and Manners: The Culture of the French and American Upper-Middle Class* (Chicago: University of Chicago Press, 1992).

47 Edgell, Gerteis, and Hartmann, "Atheists as 'Other'," 231.

48 Ibid.

| Worlds in Space: American
Religious Pluralism in
Geographic Perspective

BRET E. CARROLL

THE SUMMER OF 2010 witnessed one of the most powerful and dramatic fire-storms in the history of American religious life. At issue: ambitious plans, spear-headed in part by the American Society for Muslim Advancement, to construct a $100 million, 100,000-square foot Islamic Center in lower Manhattan, about two blocks north of the symbolically charged place that Americans now call Ground Zero. There were at least two small and often overcrowded mosques nearby—Masjid al-Farah, squeezed between two bars, and Masjid Manhattan, in a base-ment near City Hall—and the building currently on the site, an old Burlington Coat Factory, had been used as a spillover prayer site since late 2009. Project organizers believed that the growth of the neighborhood's Muslim population now necessitated the proposed center. Long involved in interfaith initiatives, they envisioned something substantially more than the one-room prayer spaces already in place. This would be a complete community center and a locus of interfaith cooperation and understanding. As can be seen in Figure 3.1, its archi-tecturally striking structure would feature not the domes and minarets of tradi-tional Islamic mosques but an eye-catching white frontage both evocative of the arabesque motifs of Islamic architecture and, as the Star of David woven into it suggests, embracing of other religions. They proposed to call the space Cordoba House, after the medieval Spanish city home to a culturally fertile community of peacefully coexisting Muslims, Jews, and Christians. Its location so close to Ground Zero, said Feisal Abdul al-Rauf, imam at al-Farah and the cleric lead-ing the project, would broadcast a message of moderate Islam "opposite...to what happened on 9/11." Proponents and defenders saw in it a monument to American pluralism and First Amendment religious freedom, "an emblem for the rest of the world." The project received early encouragement from city offi-cials and the surrounding neighborhood, a nod from the local zoning board, and approval from the Lower Manhattan community board.[1]

But the project that began in supportive local zoning and commu-nity boards became the focus of a heated national and even international

Figure 3.1 Proposed design of Park51
Islamic Center.
Image courtesy of SOMA Architects.

controversy, carried on in physical space and cyberspace, after hostile blog-
gers labeled Cordoba House a "mega-mosque" and "a symbol of Islamic
conquest"—a "Ground Zero mosque."[2] Medieval Cordoba, they said, had
been above all a site of Muslim conquest, and the mosque constructed there,
like the center being proposed near Ground Zero, was a "victory mosque."
One congressional candidate that year thought Cordoba House signified
"not...reconciliation or understanding" but a "religious, ideological, and
territorial" claim for radical Islam. Ground Zero was "a graveyard, as sacred
as any American battlefield," suggested the mother of one September 11 victim. The center's location so close to it would amount, one critic claimed,
to "sacrilege on sacred ground." Former New York mayor Rudolph Guliani
called it "a desecration." For other critics, the problem was less a matter of
sacrilege than of the project's powerful visibility. A Muslim critic considered
it an "ostentatious architectural statement," a "towering Islamic edifice that
casts a shadow over the memorials of Ground Zero." Abraham Foxman, head
of the Anti-Defamation League, was surprisingly blunt: "Two blocks away
is basically in your face." Emotions on both sides of the issue ran high, for
those involved had charged the area with sacred meaning. A tactical name

change of the proposed building from Cordoba House to the more prosaic Park51 proved an ineffective palliative.[3]

Park51, still in the old Burlington Coat Factory building, eventually opened to the public on September 21, 2011, shortly after the tenth anniversary of the September 11 terrorist attacks and at a date intended to coincide with International Peace Day observances. The day passed without incident, but the debate had been exhausting. One September 11 family member complained that the process of deciding what to build at Ground Zero and how to commemorate the dead had been marked by fighting, competing interests, and politics, and felt that she had "wasted the past nine years of my life in meetings."[4] Such was the sometimes knotty process of sacralizing space, the often messy business of American religious pluralism. Nor was it over: as Park51 opened, some of those uncomfortable about the new center were moving to plant at Ground Zero a cross-shaped steel beam that survived the World Trade Center's destruction—the "Ground Zero Cross." (See Figure 3.2.) That effort, in turn, was being challenged by New Jersey–based American Atheists, who resisted on First Amendment grounds what they perceived as an attempt to give a specifically Christian and thus exclusionary stamp to a nationally significant public space. Park51 planners, meanwhile, continued working toward the construction of their spectacular new building.

The Park51 episode suggests that American religious diversity and pluralism—its symbolic expressions, its characteristic tensions and contests—play out nowhere more noticeably than on the landscape. Since the passage of the 1965 Hart-Cellar Act, which stimulated unprecedented levels of immigration from Asia, Latin America, the Middle East, and Africa, the churches and synagogues of a once "Judeo-Christian" United States have been joined by growing numbers of mosques, Hindu and Buddhist temples, Sikh *gurdwaras*, and Hispanic, Caribbean, African, and Asian Christian churches. By October 2011, according to the Pluralism Project at Harvard University, there were 2178 Buddhist temples and centers in the United States, 1701 Muslim mosques and Islamic centers, 741 Hindu temples and centers, 261 Sikh *gurdwaras* and centers, 109 Baha'i centers, 72 Jain temples and centers, 43 Taoist centers, and 40 Zoroastrian temples and centers, the vast majority of which had been founded in the last three decades.[5] In many cases these markers of the new American religious pluralism have been barely visible; they have sometimes been storefronts, sometimes suburban homes, sometimes converted warehouses. But a "crescendo of construction" since the 1980s has made them increasingly, purposefully, and sometimes insistently, visible structures.[6]

Such construction has often provoked resistance, and sometimes even destruction. In the most recent example, a self-described "Christian warrior" carried out an arson attack on an Islamic center in Corvallis, Oregon, in November 2010, with its accused perpetrator, who lived a block from the center, arrested for a hate crime.[7] Yet such episodes occur with unfortunate frequency and long predate the Islamophobia characteristic of the post–September 11 era. The annual government publication *Hate Crimes Statistics* regularly suggests

Figure 3.2 The "Ground Zero Cross."
Photograph by Samuel Li, http://en.wikipedia.org/wiki/
World _Trade_Center_cross, under Creative Commons
license (http://creativecommons.org/licenses/by/2.0/
deed.en).

that most religiously motivated hate crimes are directed against property rather than people, and *Racial and Religious Violence in America: A Chronology* lists numerous acts of arson and vandalism in its 650-page list of acts of violence.[8] Public interactions characteristic of the growing scope and visibility of American religious pluralism—whether cooperative, contentious, or downright violent—seem often to involve "turf." Particularly since the 1970s, controversies over where people can locate the spaces, symbols, and practices of their faiths, over how and whether people expressing their religion can impact the landscape, have erupted nationwide. These contests illustrate the workings of religious pluralism—defined here as the ongoing dynamic of interaction and exchange among diverse religious individuals and groups in a civic context that provides rules of engagement.[9] The process is evidently, perhaps inherently, characterized by interreligious tension, sometimes violent—even in the United States.[10]

The expanding scope, growing visibility, and increasing vociferousness and contentiousness of the new American religious pluralism have prompted alarm in some, celebration in others, and puzzlement and incomprehension in many more. Pondering the scene thirty-five years ago, Martin Marty suggested the extent of the confusion in reassuring his readers that American religious pluralism was not "a blur" or "crazy quilt." In 2007, after the passage of three more decades during which that scene became only more crowded, its voices louder and seemingly more cacophonous, Marty continued to see American religious pluralism as something which Americans are "upset about, hopeful for, bewildered by, and committed to." How is one to make sense of it all? Because the exchanges among the nation's faiths are so often about turf, anyone seeking to comprehend American religious pluralism must turn for insight sooner or later—at the outset, I would argue—to geography. Only in this way can we begin, in Diana Eck's words, "mapping the fault lines of America's diversity."[11]

Worlds in Space: Religious Pluralism and Spatial Dynamics

American religious pluralism, as suggested above, means not simply diversity (by definition a static fact) but an ongoing and complex dynamic involving encounter, engagement, and exchange among religious individuals and groups. Any attempt to understand this dynamic—indeed, to understand religion—must begin by recognizing that it is fundamentally spatial.[12] That is, like all areas of human activity and experience it occurs in and in relation to the space that constitutes the habitable surface of the earth. Saying so may seem to be stating the obvious, and is certainly not original: the centrality of space to American religion was suggested over a half century ago by historian of religion Sidney Mead.[13] But in the last decade and a half or so, religious studies has taken a "spatial turn," looking increasingly to geography for theoretical insight. That discipline focuses on the interrelationships between human activities and the earth's surface and has examined concepts and experiences of space with growing sophistication. Religion scholars have given more and closer attention to religion as a form of spatial behavior.[14]

Evident across a wide range of social and cultural studies, this spatial turn considers space not simply as an objective container for human activity but rather, in Klaus Benesch's words, as "a fundamental category of human life." Mead, steeped in consensus scholarship and the frontier thesis of American history, viewed space as a given—an objective, boundless, uniform reality void of inherent meaning—that had a considerable, perhaps decisive, "formative significance" in the development of American religious freedom and tolerance. But scholars in religion and other fields now understand space as a subjective experience, a situationally located social and cultural construction. Far from existing independently, it is, according to Henri Lefebvre, "produced" through active efforts at definition, appropriation, and control by human beings laboring to organize societies and cultures. Far from being boundless, argues geographer John Urry, "space is necessarily limited and there has to be competition and conflict over its organization and control." Far from being neutral, space is the arena of human territoriality—"a primary geographical expression of social power"—and, observes Michel Foucault, is "fundamental in any exercise of power." And, far from being homogeneous, it is inherently plural, hetero-geneous, and discontinuous. Just as cosmic space consists of worlds continu-ally forming and re-forming amid complexly interacting gravitational forces, human space is now being understood and explored throughout the social sci-ences and humanities as a "changing field of tensions and contradictions."[15]

The spatial turn has greatly sharpened our appreciation of just how basic space is, and of precisely how it is basic, to religion. Religion theorists have long suggested that religious experience is conceptually spatial insofar as it functions to provide believers with a sense of social, geographic, and cosmic orientation.[16] But as geographically sensitive scholars in the field have made us aware, religion is also fundamentally spatial in practice. Attempting, according to one definition, "to order life in terms of culturally perceived ultimate priori-ties," religion generates geographic, physical manifestations as believers seek, according to geographer Roger Stump, "spatial realization of their beliefs." Using space as "the medium within which…meanings become specific and concrete," people practicing and living their religions make themselves homes on the earth's surface—"world[s] of ritual, relationships, and symbols," as one spatially sensitive religion scholar has put it—in what amounts to an act of reli-gious imagination.[17] In short, human beings reify their religious commitments by creating worlds in space.

In doing so, they invest certain locations on the earth's surface, whether nat-ural or built environments, with particular spiritual significance through such ritual acts as worship, prayer, meditation, and sacrifice.[18] Performing this "cul-tural labor…in specific historical situations" transforms abstract, undifferenti-ated "space" into human "place"—"a piece of the whole environment that has been claimed by feelings"—in which people enact "the aspirations, needs, and functional rhythms of personal and group life." Through symbolic religious acts, "a world comes into being" as people "transform the previously unordered space into cosmos, a place imbued with meaning." Living and grounding their identities in places they "constantly imagine, describe, and construct," human beings develop deep and meaningful—spiritual and religious—attachments to them. Because believers necessarily imagine and construct religiously signif-icant places and spaces, religious systems and practices have "inherent spatial-ity" and "everyday, lived religion…depends crucially on place to constitute what it is."[19] A place set apart or claimed for religious or spiritual purposes is what scholars widely call a "sacred space."[20] Following Mircea Eliade, religionists once typically originated sacred space in an "irruption" of an essential "sacred" into the "profane" or "secular" human world,[21] resulting in a sharp differen-tiation between the sacred site of irruption and the surrounding space. While this "substantial" approach persists, more recent studies, beginning in geogra-phy and spreading to neighboring disciplines, have blurred its central polarity and questioned its essentialist assumptions, adopting instead a "situational" approach that grounds the creation of sacred space—typically understood as an act of conquest or appropriation—in "secular" human social, political, and cultural endeavors.[22]

If religion generates claims on space and space is limited, religious pluralism necessarily involves multiple, overlapping, competing, and often conflicting claims—a politics or geopolitics of sacred space in which individual and group claimants are required to engage, or at least remain mindful of, other claimants in the society. In other words, considered from a geographic perspective, religion is fundamentally a system of spatial interaction. As one religion scholar puts it, people live in space like "a deer in a clearing, alert, totally aware of her surroundings, instinctually sensible of the critical distance she must maintain from possible predators."[23] They exhibit territoriality—"a form of cultural strategy through which individuals and groups seek to exert control over the meanings and uses of particular portions of geographical space."[24] Religious territoriality allows believers to "articulate and resolve in immediate and practical terms the meanings around which they organize their faith," but it has also "provoked or reinforced tensions between distinct religious communities" and "led to the contesting of social spaces and the meanings applied to them" as some groups try to shape spaces in accordance with their own beliefs while others seek to minimize unwanted influences. Those who have staked a claim, invested a space with particular meaning, and transformed it into their own place may experience the presence of others as a "territorial encroachment," which "usually prompts a territorial defense whereby defenders try to reassert symbolically original place meanings." The multivalence of place, geographer Lily Kong reminds us, "requires an acknowledgement of simultaneous, fluctuating and conflicting investments of sacred and secular meanings in any one site." Sacred space is, then, "inevitably contested space." A particularly perceptive commentator in the Park51 controversy suggested as much in remarking that "Ground Zero is not a static shrine." We would do well, then, to think of the United States not as a single coherent space but rather as "an arena of multiple centers, changing environments, shifting geographical relations, and ambivalent symbolic orientations, all contested and at stake." Its religious life is an ongoing and complex spatial dynamic.[25]

The precise content of this dynamic, of course, has been conditioned by American religious history. That history began with subjugation of indigenous peoples, followed by the consolidation of colonies in which European Christians—above all, English Protestants—established geographic control and numerical, political, economic, social, cultural, and religious dominance. Although English Protestants were joined at the outset by Catholics, Jews, non-English Protestants, and Africans, and later by practitioners of the world's non-Western religions, the pattern of Anglo-Protestant dominance and marginalization of others remained facts of American life well into the twentieth century and left a deep and lasting imprint on American life. Only in the 1950s did Americans begin in sizable numbers to think of the country as "Judeo-Christian" rather than simply "Protestant" or "Christian," and the new immigration of the last third of the twentieth century is only beginning to displace that more recent perception. What this means is that, despite the pluralist vision of parity and harmonious exchange among the nation's religious groups, the actual geopolitics of religious space in the United States is grounded in a long-standing pattern of interreligious hostility and the "historically persistent" reality in multicultural America of well-established, deeply rooted power differentials.[26]

On the other hand, the dynamic of American religious pluralism has been equally driven by the widespread acceptance—if not always an active or heartfelt embrace—of diversity. A national commitment to religious tolerance developed out of the practical social and political realities of diversity during the colonial period, finding its definitive expression in the First Amendment guarantee of religious freedom.[27] This guarantee defined the national space as officially neutral, one in which any group could with equal legitimacy stake a claim. It also amounted to a set of rules of spatial engagement that has profoundly shaped the geographic manifestations and results of the pluralist dynamic. As if to underscore the recently amplified centrality of geography and space in its functioning, this arrangement has been supplemented by the Religious Land Use Act of 2000, intended to reduce burdens on religious exercise resulting from zoning laws and other land-use regulations. The national ideology of pluralism has changed over the past two centuries, moving from toleration (within a Protestant framework) to Anglocentric assimilationism to approval of religious difference,[28] but the underlying ground rules have remained the same.

Among forms of pluralism, religious pluralism by its nature generates particularly powerful emotional interactions and puts especially potent strains on the ground rules. This is, of course, partly because people's identities are at stake—particularly in pluralistic settings—and also because, as Harold Isaacs has noted, religious identity usually "appears enmeshed with other factors of great weight—race, land, nationality, history, power." But most distinctive to religious pluralism is the enormous significance with which many people invest their religious commitments and the associated spatial expressions. Martin Marty recently observed that religious pluralism is "often the most evocative of issues and provocative of conflicts" of all kinds of pluralism because "when citizens act in the name of a transcendent force or person—usually their God—they change the rules of the pluralist game and rule out those who do not share witness or obedience to that God." Their territoriality takes on a "distinctly compelling character rooted in the certainties of the[ir] worldviews and ethos," and they are inclined to view the spaces they claim "not merely as pieces of territory but as repositories of truth, authority, and legitimacy." Perceiving the ideologies by which they orient their actions and claim and define their spaces as absolute truths, believers are more defensive and reluctant to pursue and accept the spatial compromises necessitated by the American rules of engagement. A conflict over space "in essence becomes a conflict over religious truth" itself, and the potential for conflict is therefore enhanced. Furthermore, a pluralistic setting, according to several scholars, enhances the perceived importance of one's religious identity and magnifies commitment, heightening the potential for strong expressions of territorial possessiveness still further.[29]

An important recent change in the dynamic of American religious pluralism, and of the spatial politics at its core, has made it still more dramatic, intense, and challenging in the past three or so decades. As Richard D. Hecht explains, the radically expanded diversity of the American religious scene since the 1960s, together with the intensifying identity politics that grew from the civil rights movement, prompted a shift to a more "active" pluralistic style.[30] Departing from the more "passive" pluralism that preceded it, the nation's religious groups, especially those that perceive themselves to be excluded from the putative "mainstream," have increasingly sought not merely toleration but meaningful participation in American life. In geographic terms, active pluralism has translated into increasingly assertive efforts by minority groups to impress their religious worlds and meanings on public space, to stake and, when necessary, defend as equally legitimate their claims to the landscape—in short, to move an increasingly diverse United States in the direction of what scholars call "spatial equity" and "spatial justice."[31] "Religious ecological spaces had to be carved out in new ways, to make one's presence as a Muslim, a Buddhist, a Hindu, a Sikh, a Native American, and an African American in the nation."[32] It is in this context that the Muslim Public Affairs Council interpreted the Park51 controversy as "the civil rights moment for Muslims in this country" and refused to be "'forced' to move the location of Park51 to a 'Muslims Allowed' section of Manhattan."[33]

Driven by an expanding multiplicity of emotionally charged and increasingly assertive claims on limited space against a historical backdrop of Anglo-Protestant and "Judeo-Christian" cultural dominance—an environment that one historian of American religion has likened to a pressure cooker[34]—the nation's pluralist dynamic perhaps inevitably generates social, political, and cultural tension. And of course, this tension manifests itself in certain characteristic spatial patterns and practices. Groups seeking to carve out worlds of meaning, or to protect their worlds from perceived transgression or defilement amid the multiplicity of others occupying American space, have exhibited many kinds of spatial behavior, for all of which the nation's newspapers present evidence aplenty on an almost daily basis.[35] They have drawn imagined and often physical boundaries around themselves, forming enclaves, and have excluded others, sometimes forcibly. They have appropriated space for themselves and excluded or dispossessed others, sometimes violently, as in cases of arson, vandalism, desecration, or protest-driven seizure.[36] More positively, they have sometimes worked out more or less cordial space-sharing arrangements, in some cases with and in some without the intent of engaging in social or cultural exchange but in all cases with a commitment to avoiding conflict and seeking cooperative coexistence. One historian has usefully given the name "geographies of encounter" to the spatial dimensions and consequences of such "complicated cross-cultural engagement" and "competing quests for social and moral order."[37]

Because American public space is not amenable to exclusive claims under the ground rules of American religious pluralism, groups seeking to reify their religious worlds and staking their claims have often turned with particular urgency, as suggested at the outset of this essay, to building construction. In a "culture of religious pluralism," religion scholar Richard E. Wentz has observed, religious groups must rely on sacred buildings to express and preserve their identities. An officially pluralistic state and neutral public square make this form of spatial claiming especially important by forcing believers to create privately owned markers of their presence—to engage in acts of religious territoriality. In the United States, therefore, buildings have become "the most visible symbol of a religious community," resulting in an American landscape that "reveals the monuments of its religious diversity." Indeed, the function of these monuments as symbols, proclaimers, and protectors of religious identity, and as claims to a place in American space, is a key reason why the groups who create them deem them sacred. But their attempts to project their religious worlds tangibly in American space often brings them into tense encounter and, often, conflict. As the frequency and intensity of such interreligious interactions have multiplied, the nation's courts, town and city councils, and zoning boards—"site[s] of encounter and disputation"—have become the official mediators of modern American religious pluralism and shapers of its geographic expressions.[38]

In the remainder of this essay we will examine pluralism at work in American spaces: religious worlds struggling to establish and maintain themselves, sometimes avoiding and sometimes encountering one another, sometimes colliding and sometimes settling into gravitationally stabilized mutual orbit. Seeking to actualize their worlds in space amid a plethora of competing worlds, groups have claimed space and seized it; built it and destroyed it; borrowed, lent, leased, and donated it; shared it and fought over it; bounded it and opened it to others. Following geographer Roger Stump's suggestion that religion operates at different geographic "scales" that are "varied but interconnected,"[39] we will consider the dynamic at three distinct but interrelated geographic levels. We will begin with American religious regions—broad portions of the United States defined by characteristic styles of pluralism. These regions provide context for the two levels that follow. The first is geographies of intimate urban and suburban encounter; the second is the national level, where the meaning of the American space writ large is at stake. The closing section will briefly identify newer avenues of exploration, other scales of territoriality that are being mapped but remain largely undeveloped.

American Pluralisms: Worlds in Regional Space

For nearly a half century, one of the most frequently invoked concepts in geographic considerations of American religious pluralism has been that of region.[40] *Region* refers to a geocultural reality "born of natural geography, of past and present human history, and of the interaction between the two," and existing as "a function of the spatial location of people and the history of that spatial location."[41] In 1961, geographer Wilbur Zelinsky proposed a model of American religious regions consisting of seven broad zones, each with its own defining religious demography and culture: a New England region, a Midland region (with a Pennsylvania German subregion), an Upper Middle Western region, a Southern region (with Carolina Piedmont, Peninsular Florida, French Louisiana, and Texas German subregions), a Spanish Catholic region, a Mormon region, and a Western region.[42] Although this schema has been challenged by geographers and religionists—some proposing alternative models and others questioning the persistence of regional distinctions in an increasingly homogenized national space[43]—it remains influential, and the notion of American religious regions remains widely accepted.

Until very recently, regional approaches merely scratched the surface of American religious pluralism. Most have in fact been geographies only of American religious *diversity*, examining the spatial distribution or regional characteristics of religious groups but falling short of exploring the geographic manifestations and dynamics of pluralistic interaction and exchange. But recent work suggests that the nation's religious regions are definable not only by their demographic profiles but also by distinct, geographically and culturally conditioned styles of pluralism—characteristic kinds of alliances and tensions among the worlds occupying the regional spaces.[44] These regions, observes Mark Silk, "have different religious ecologies, based both on the numerical strength of the religious groups on the ground and on how these groups have interacted with each other over time in places subject to different social, economic, and environmental circumstances."[45] Although Silk defines them as clusters of states, they in many cases extend beyond such strictly defined boundaries and overlap each other. With these established (see Figure 3.3), we can go on to consider pluralistic encounters at the local and national scales—both of which, as we shall see, are regionally grounded.[46]

Located on the Atlantic seaboard and punctuated by several ports of entry, the *Mid-Atlantic* region (New York, New Jersey, Pennsylvania, Delaware, Maryland, and Washington, D.C.) has been a magnet for European, and later global, migrations. It has since colonial times been distinguished by its concentration of urban areas and its religious diversity. Peopled early on by Scotch-Irish Presbyterians, German Lutherans and Mennonites, Swedish Lutherans, Dutch Reformed, Jews, and English Quakers, Anglicans, and Catholics, all of whom usually separated themselves spatially, the region became characterized by strong links between religious and ethnic identity. The region's diversity and tendency to foster strong ethnoreligious identity were reinforced in the late nineteenth and early twentieth centuries by the "new immigration" of large numbers of incoming, ethnically diverse European Catholics and Jews. It is little wonder that this region generated the notion of a "Judeo-Christian" America and sociologist Will Herberg's famed 1955 proclamation of pluralistic parity among Protestants, Catholics, and Jews. While

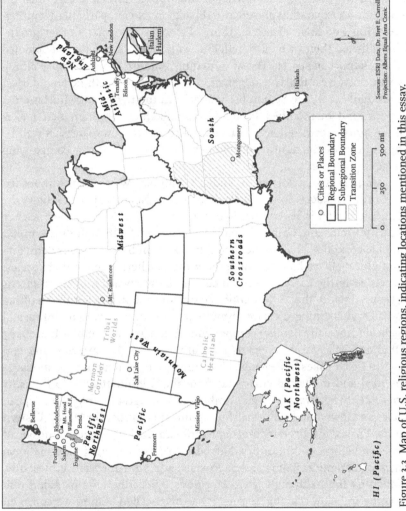

Figure 3.3 Map of U.S. religious regions, indicating locations mentioned in this essay. Based on *Religion by Region* series, edited by Mark Silk. Map produced by Alison McNally.

this formula became nationally accepted as normative, it was a particularly Mid-Atlantic product since its positing of the predominance of these three worlds was—and remains—more true of the Mid-Atlantic regional space than of the nation's other regional zones.[47] Since 1965, however, these three worlds have increasingly shared the region with newer arrivals. Catholics of various ethnicities remain heavily overrepresented, as do Jews, although strong infusions of orthodox and ultraorthodox sects in the New York metropolitan area since World War II have made the latter much more diverse there. Muslims have become an expanding presence in the region and are particularly numerous. Arriving Buddhists, Hindus, Latino Catholics, and many other groups have established their own ethnoreligious worlds in often densely populated urban and suburban spaces. The Mid-Atlantic remains a region whose pluralist dynamic involves "the daily negotiation of religious and ethnic boundaries" as its residents seek, the September 11 attacks in the region notwithstanding, to forge a kind of modified Protestant-Catholic-Jew paradigm that makes space for more recent religious arrivals.[48] The Park51 controversy, for all its rancor and extraregional impetus, typifies the growing pains accompanying this ongoing process.

The *Midwest* (Ohio, Michigan, Indiana, Illinois, Wisconsin, Minnesota, Iowa, North Dakota, South Dakota, Kansas, Nebraska) resembles the Mid-Atlantic region in its ethnoreligious diversity—particularly the presence of powerful Protestant, Catholic, and Jewish elements—though its dissimilar geographic conditions have generated differences of both religious demography and pluralistic style.[49] Adjoining both the northern and southern states, it was settled in the early nineteenth century by westward-moving migrants from New England, the Mid-Atlantic region, and the upper South, resulting in a broad and lasting Protestant diversity that included strong mainline and evangelical (especially Baptist) components. Extensive, flat, and fertile, cut by the Ohio and Mississippi rivers as natural transportation arteries, and bordering the Great Lakes, it developed both an agricultural landscape and large commercial and industrial cities that from the mid-nineteenth to the early twentieth century attracted large numbers of immigrants, mostly European Catholics and Jews along with small but significant numbers of Middle Eastern Muslims. Protestant diversity broadened into an intricate regional mosaic of religious and ethnic communities that today so closely approximates national averages in Catholics, Baptists, Pentecostals, African-American Protestants, and Muslims that, although Jews, Mormons, and adherents of Asian religions come in below national norms, it has been called "America's common denominator."[50] While Protestant and Catholic worlds remain the largest and continue to dominate the Midwestern public square, diversity has produced an equilibrium of forces among the worlds in this regional space that prevents any group from controlling the realm of public policy. Solidly pluralistic, this heartland region remains today the nation's "most balanced," the one "where the country comes together," America's religious as well as geographic center of gravity.[51]

At the other end of the continent, in the *Pacific* region (California, Nevada, and Hawai'i), a different combination of religious worlds and a different sort of pluralist dynamic developed.[52] Distance from the East and European influences, settlement by highly mobile easterners, proximity to Hispanic America and Asia, the conquest of Mexican and native territories and peoples (who remain significant demographic substrata), and Pacific ports of entry have combined to foster loosened religious commitments; institutional weakness; eclectic, innovative, and often individualized approaches to spirituality; pronounced cross-cultural borrowing; demographic levels of Mormonism, Buddhism, Hinduism, Sikhism, Islam, Hispanic Catholicism, and Hispanic and Asian Protestantisms far above national averages; relatively weak mainline Protestant groups; the absence of any form of Christian or "Judeo-Christian" dominance; and extreme diversity. California became particularly diverse: in 2000, over one quarter of its population was foreign born, and immigrants were arriving from 85% of the world's countries.[53] Depression-era and more recent "Sun Belt" migrations from other sections of the country, meanwhile, have given conservative and enthusiastic brands of Protestantism a solid presence in the region, especially in southern California, though these have sometimes dropped denominational labels or incorporated yoga and other Asian-derived elements to appeal to a culture of "seekers." The constant shifting and multidirectionality of forces in this regional space has made it a "crossroads of global religious and cultural encounters," "a borderland, a sociocultural place of complex and dynamic encounters and transformations" among worlds as protean as they are numerous.[54]

The vast, dramatic landscapes of the *Mountain West*, sparsely populated and punctuated by widely separated urban centers, spawned yet another arrangement of religious worlds and another kind of pluralism: a "libertarian" variety in which "each spiritual community stak[es] out its own turf."[55] The result is a regional space dotted by separate religious enclaves. United in regional religious consciousness only by a shared landscape that inspires veneration, holding "widely disparate values," and "co-existing more by necessity than commitment to a common cause,"[56] this region is best understood in terms of three distinct subregions: an "Old Catholic heartland" of New Mexico and Arizona, a "Mormon Corridor" comprising Utah and Idaho, and a "tribal world" of Colorado, Wyoming, and Montana. In Arizona and New Mexico, once part of New Spain and Mexico, the original Hispanic and indigenous worlds were joined during the 1930s by westward-moving southern evangelical Protestants seeking economic opportunity, expanding the Bible Belt toward southern California and prompting in New Mexico persistent Protestant-Catholic tension and, shortly after World War II, a legal battle over Catholic control of the public schools. Eventually, increased Latino immigration during and after the 1970s made New Mexico a world more uniformly Catholic while Sunbelt migrations made Arizona's religious space more like California's.[57]

Further north, Mormons, a minority religious group on the defensive against intense persecution in the nineteenth century, sought and then capitalized on geographic distance and insulation in the Great Basin. They staked out a vast space, tightly controlled that space by establishing a close relation between church and state—fully a theocracy until Utah's 1896 incorporation into the United States—and reified their religious world to a degree perhaps no longer possible for any group in pluralistic America.[58] Other religious groups, arriving later and in smaller numbers, proved unable to make strong spatial claims of their own. With a population two-thirds Mormon in its Utah portion, this regional space remains the least diverse and most nearly theocratic in the nation, with many small religious worlds more or less thoroughly locked like moons into the orbit of a single large one. Despite ecumenical outreach by the Church, other groups have been left feeling powerless in the face of the Church's use of its strength and resources to preserve what Mormons regard as their homeland and its sacred geography. Geography has fostered and reflected what one commentator considers "a quite un-American degree of religious tension and intolerance."[59]

While the Mormon space is dominated by a single massive world, the "tribal world," concentrated in Colorado, Wyoming, and Montana but stretching beyond their borders, consists of many small ones located at considerable distances from one another. This arrangement into separate religious enclaves is the combined result of the reservation system of the late nineteenth century, which organized Native Americans of the region into what were effectively ghettoes, and a revitalization of Native American spiritual life since the identity movements of the 1960s. Each reservation has become a unique religious space with its own particular geography, its own set of native practices, and its own cultural forms. Several cities built by whites have also evolved into enclaves: the powerful landscape of Boulder, Colorado, for instance, has become a mecca shared by Buddhists, Muslims, and a range of New Age and alternative spiritualities, while Colorado Springs developed in the opposite direction and is now headquarters to several evangelical advocacy groups. But it is the region's reenergized Native American religious worlds, typically defined with relation to specific sites on the natural landscape, that have driven a surge of "active" pluralist contests over space. Most concern access to and control of places claimed as sacred by Indians but owned—as is so much land in the Mountain West—by either the federal government or extractive business enterprises. Wyoming's Devil's Tower, northern Arizona's Big Mountain, and South Dakota's Black Hills, for example, have been the focus of repeated claims and counterclaims, both between different Indian groups and between Indians and non-Indians.[60]

The pluralism of the *Pacific Northwest*, consisting of Oregon, Washington, and Alaska, and projecting into northern California and the Sierra Nevada range, has developed from geographic conditions much like those of the Mountain West—a vast, imposing, awe-inspiring, and relatively unpopulated landscape—with the added feature of a particularly abundant biodiversity. A high proportion of religiously "unaffiliated" people has earned this region the nickname "the none zone" and left religious institutions there, as in other western regions, relatively weak in terms of public influence.[61] The result in the Northwest has been a pluralist dynamic distinguished by a high degree of interfaith collaboration born of practical necessity—an alliance of mainline Protestants, Catholics, and Reform and Conservative Jews that has been called an "interfaith religious establishment."[62] Committed to social justice issues during the 1960s, this establishment has more recently become absorbed into the region's emergent civil religion of spiritual environmentalism.[63] In this it works in alliance with the Northwest's large population of the unaffiliated, many of whom ground their commitment to wilderness protection in alternative New Age, Native American, survivalist, or secularist spiritualities.[64] This ecumenical cluster of worlds, cultivated in particular by the relatively recent arrivals of the region's cities and suburbs, meets with resistance from an evangelically inclined "counterculture" of rural, longtime residents whose livelihood is tied to the mining and logging industries and who seek to defend what they consider traditional Christian values. This tension between opposing worlds has been apparent in the region's characteristic spatial contests: controversies, often rancorous, over the definition and use of the landscape. These include disputes over the recently established Cascade-Siskiyou National Monument, the possibility of oil drilling in the Arctic National Wildlife Refuge, the impact of logging on spotted owl habitats, the Klamath Basin water crisis of 2001, and the fate of Yosemite's Hetch-Hetchy valley. To be sure, this bipolar contest over natural space is not all there is to the region's pluralist dynamic—Eastern religions, for example, are prominent here as in the Pacific region—but the debate between the two worlds so dominates public life that other communities feel compelled to enter the orbit of one or the other.

The geography of the *South* (Virginia, West Virginia, Kentucky, North Carolina, South Carolina, Georgia, Tennessee, Alabama, Mississippi, Florida) has fostered a different, though at times equally contentious, kind of pluralism.[65] The region's well-developed river system, mild climate, and interior Appalachian and Ozark mountains encouraged the development of rural and agricultural landscapes—featuring, outside the mountain areas, plantations and African-American slave labor—and a pattern of sparse settlement which proved congenial to the lay-led religious styles and congregational autonomy of the Baptist, Methodist, and, later, various Pentecostal denominations. All of these attracted whites and blacks alike, although racial tensions have in many cases produced separate congregations and even denominations characterized by distinct practices. Likewise, its relative lack of large urban areas and industries made most of it uncongenial to the "new immigration" of the late nineteenth and early twentieth centuries. Two key results were that southerners defined their region in opposition to the more modernist and urban North, and that, while Catholics and Jews streamed into the North, the pluralism of the South remained more narrowly Protestant and sharply biracial far into the twentieth century. It remains a region of low non-Christian diversity, a place "just about as evangelical as Utah is Mormon."[66] More to the point, however, southern pluralism has been powerfully defined by a joint evangelical religious world of Baptists and Pentecostals that has drawn even many in the nonevangelical denominations into its value system, and by a dichotomous and decidedly antimodernist division of American society into people of faith, who see themselves as defenders of "traditional religious values," and people deemed sympathetic to secularism. In the wake of the September 11 attacks, the region's conservative "culture warriors" added international Islam to their targets of mistrust.[67] Such perceived threats have put the evangelical world, for all its regional dominance, spatially on the defensive.[68]

Much the same can be said of that portion of the southern United States—Texas, Arkansas, Oklahoma, Missouri, and Louisiana—recently categorized as a discrete region called the *Southern Crossroads*,[69] although its proportion of Holiness and Pentecostal adherents is larger. The key distinction between the two regions is that between the "regional culture of confrontation"[70] and the readiness to lower church-state walls that characterize the latter, originally a frontier region settled by westward-moving southerners, and the more genteel, less confrontational style of the Old South. The two regions differ, too, in their patterns of diversity. In the South, African-American Protestant denominations figure more prominently, a legacy of the plantation landscape, and peninsular Florida, Virginia's D.C. suburbs, and other urbanized areas stand out as islands of diversity, the result of migration from other regions and recent immigration of Muslims, Hindus, Buddhists, and Latino Catholics. The Crossroads, more impacted by historic as well as recent immigration, has significant ethnically and spatially defined populations of Latino Catholics in south Texas, Latino and Vietnamese Catholics in northwest Arkansas, Cajun Catholics in Louisiana, and German and Irish Catholics in Missouri, all of which have increasingly responded to the powerful gravitational pull of the region's evangelical world of values.

The geography of *New England* (Massachusetts, Connecticut, Rhode Island, Vermont, New Hampshire, Maine), the smallest region, fostered a very different demographic and an opposite approach.[71] The water power available along its fall line, at the northern end of the Appalachian range and near already urbanized seaport areas, made it the first region to develop factories and industrial cities, especially in its southern half. This urban-industrial landscape in turn attracted large numbers of immigrants during the nineteenth century, especially Irish and, to a somewhat lesser degree, Italian Catholics. Tension between them and the dominant native-born Protestants led to the development of geographically parallel religious worlds; living in separate residential enclaves, Catholics built, in addition to their churches, their own schools, hospitals, and social service agencies. They also successfully worked their way into positions of political influence. Protestant-Catholic tensions subsided after World War II as the groups, having achieved a balance of power, settled into mutual orbit and agreed to remove religion from public life in the interest of maintaining civic stability. The two worlds retain decisive influence over this regional space and its pluralist dynamic: Catholics dominate numerically, making up over half of New England's religious adherents, while mainline Protestants, ecumenically organized since the nineteenth century in response to Catholic growth, with their churches still prominently located at town centers, remain the key participants in local affairs even though some congregations have struggled with declining membership in recent decades. Jews and African-American Protestants also figure prominently, especially in the region's more densely populated and urbanized southern portion, where they have since 1965 been joined by small but increasing, and increasingly visible, populations of Hindus, Buddhists, Muslims, and Sikhs. Conservative Protestantism, traditionally a weak presence in the Yankee heartland, is now making inroads among the whites of New England's rural north, appealing to southern New England's small but expanding population of urban and suburban Caribbean, Latin American, Asian, and Middle Eastern immigrants, and making common cause with Catholics on its moral agenda.

To understand these regional spaces—the relative sizes, positions, compositions, and gravitational relationships of the worlds within them—is to understand that, on one level, American religious pluralism can be understood as in fact consisting of an array of geographically defined pluralisms. This realization in turn prepares us to comprehend more fully the multiplicity of social and cultural contexts within which religious groups engage in "geographies of encounter" at the local and national levels. Indeed, region can be usefully understood as the crucial, pivotal geographic level in the nation's pluralist dynamic, reaching inward to shape local encounters and outward to shape spatial contests of national scope.

Close Encounters: Worlds in Local Space

Besides providing specific examples of regional pluralisms in practice, zooming in on localities—the cities, towns, and neighborhoods where interreligious encounters are most immediate—sharpens our appreciation of pluralism's geographic dimensions and spatial dynamics. At the local level, what is at stake in the pluralist dynamic is felt most directly. People may feel possessive of their national territory, geographer David Sibley has recently observed, but they are often (though not always) willing to share that space with those whom they perceive as different. At the local level, however, territorial possessiveness is more intense, and residents are more likely to allow "others" in only by invitation.[72] Sometimes invitations are extended, whether by choice or necessity; other times they are not. Even in an officially pluralistic national space, the encounter of religious worlds in local space is as apt to generate tension, even intolerance, as cooperation and dialogue.

The "active" pluralism of recent decades, in which religious groups seek public expression, visibility, and space more assertively, has made local encounters increasingly pointed. Because claiming space and making place typically require access to property—"that most important commodity of American life"—the dynamics of local pluralism have been perhaps most evident in zoning boards, town and city councils, and sometimes the courts. A new religious community in a locality, notes Diana Eck, "may first encounter its neighbors...in a city council or zoning board hearing." This arena of public interaction often provides a venue for "articulating, in concrete terms, some of the amorphous fears that residents may have about new neighbors."[73]

Among sites of local encounter, cities exhibit a particularly "intense religious pluralism." One reason is that a large population in a limited geographic area makes spatial claims highly competitive—a problematic situation since, as sociologist and pluralism theorist William M. Newman suggests, intergroup conflict "is directly proportional to the degree to which different social groups view each other as competitive threats to their social resources, to resources they wish to obtain, or to their basic social values."[74] Another reason for the pronounced dynamism of urban pluralism is the frequency of encounter with ethnic, racial, and religious difference. If, as some social geographers have suggested, the physical space neighbors occupy is inversely proportional to the likelihood of interaction among them, then densely populated but geographically limited urban spaces present a setting in which "one has no choice but to confront the religious 'other,'" resulting in an increased likelihood of perceived territorial encroachment.[75] Robert Wuthnow has, furthermore, recently pointed out that people's theological commitments may be challenged by living in close proximity to those of different faiths, thus magnifying the significance they attach to their religious allegiances.[76] Because the city compels encounters, residents feel not only crowded but often pressured to announce and express their cultural and religious identities, and to accentuate distinctions between their worlds and others'. This crucible-like effect makes cities "arenas of intense contestation," heightening the imperatives of active pluralism and the urgency of spatial claims.[77]

Further intensifying the geographic dynamics of urban pluralism is the high proportion of migrants and immigrants, for whom transforming the new space into place requires "strategies and tactics of cultural reterritorialization" in an environment of conflicting interests, aspirations, and claims.[78] Removal and distance from old surroundings, adjustment to new ones, and the density of the cityscape itself often magnify the cultural functions of religion and the need to create orienting worlds. An important result is the formation of compact, homogeneous ethnoreligious enclaves—for example, Miami's "Little Havana" or New York's "Little Odessa." As new arrivals in the nation's cities seek to establish or reestablish Muslim, Hindu, Jewish, Christian, Buddhist, or Afro-Caribbean worlds in new spaces amid many others doing the same, they appropriate space for purposes both negative and positive: on the one hand, they define and enforce "geographic and symbolic boundaries that distinguish the insider from the outsider, ethnically and racially as well as religiously";[79] on the other, they forge places for themselves as they develop, enact, and reify their religious orientations. The result is a complex patchwork of what Robert A. Orsi calls "urban religious cartographies"—overlapping arrangements of city space that sometimes coexist and sometimes conflict.[80]

A few examples of the urban pluralist dynamic at work will illuminate the broader regional contexts in which urban encounters occur, the defining features of pluralism in the city, and both the possibilities and limits of interreligious interchange. Consider first the place that came in the mid-twentieth century to be known as "Italian Harlem." Although dozens of ethnoreligious groups occupied this volatile area, Italian Catholics gave it their particular stamp through the annual midsummer *festa* of devotion to Our Lady of Mount Carmel.[81] Their own numbers declining and forced to confront growing numbers of Puerto Ricans during the 1940s and 1950s, they responded to the "logic of shared social, economic, and geographical circumstances" defensively, using an image of the Madonna paraded through the streets as an ethnic and territorial marker that would define their space and maintain borders they thought besieged.[82] The new arrivals, Italians feared, were using the rituals of Santería to steal power from the Madonna and the neighborhood from them. The Puerto Ricans, excluded from the parades, came to hate the *festa* and ignored the Madonna's passing. By contrast, neighborhood Italians of the 1980s, their grasp on the territory so decisively broken that they were no longer on the defensive, felt able to welcome to both the parade and the church itself Haitian Catholic immigrants who came from Brooklyn, bringing their Vodou idioms.

In Tenafly, New Jersey, meanwhile, Orthodox Jews faced resistance in 1999 when they sought to construct an *eruv*—to enclose a public space in wire strung on utility poles so as to allow them to carry personal items between their homes and synagogues on the Sabbath. Such appropriation had occurred before in the region without incident—by 1983, there were already about 400 *eruvim* in the United States—suggesting a pattern of nonconfrontational overlap of spatial claims. But in this case the Orthodox attempt to put their mark on the landscape sparked acrimonious public discussion in the borough council and produced an alliance of non-Orthodox Jews and non-Jews fearful that the *eruv* would attract more Orthodox, prompting a broader Orthodox claim to Tenafly. A frustrated Tenafly Eruv Association grew more aggressive, appealing over the borough to the county, which granted permission for the *eruv*. The incensed borough council responded by voting to dismantle the resulting *eruv*, and the case landed in court. Successive federal rulings concluded that the county had unlawfully allocated public space to religious uses and then that the borough council had acted with discriminatory intent. The Supreme Court's 2003 denial of the borough's request to hear the case secured the Orthodox a space that they had to stake out and defend through active pluralism and contentious, ultimately court-mediated, negotiation.[83] The mid-Atlantic emphasis on negotiating boundaries and the intensification of that process in specifically urban environments were painfully evident in both Harlem and Tenafly.

Salt Lake City, the hub of a vast desert subregion overwhelmingly dominated by a single religious world, is home to a different urban pluralist dynamic and has generated a different sort of geopluralist conflict. Here, minority groups must struggle particularly vigorously for public visibility against the Church of Jesus Christ of Latter-day Saints (LDS)—an entity that virtually monopolizes urban space. Their concern, therefore, is not only to draw protective boundaries around themselves, as in the case of Harlem's defensive Italians, but to pursue space aggressively. Although religious minorities' efforts to control public space tend to be "reflexive, and often defensive,"[84] the feeling of disempowerment resulting from their comparatively miniscule public presence led some of them to take the offensive in 1998. Their prompt was an attempt by the Mormon Church to purchase Main Street Plaza—the segment of Salt Lake City's Main Street between church headquarters and Temple Square and the "literal and symbolic intersection of church and state in Utah"[85]—and to ban non-Mormon proselytizing there. An easement still owned by the city within this stretch, they said, constituted a public forum where their free speech rights—their ability as small religious worlds to shine in a public space where their light would otherwise be washed out—were guaranteed. Attempting to assert the heterogeneity of the city which Mormons claim as a homeland, Salt Lake City's First Unitarian Church, Utahans for Fairness, and other groups won a 2002 federal court ruling that the area was public rather than sacred space.

Subsequent anti-Mormon activity there, however, led a sympathetic though non-Mormon mayor to allow Church regulation of the space, and in 2003 the city gave up the easement to the LDS Church, depriving non-Mormon religious groups of their limited public space. This development prompted the Unitarians, this time joined by the Utah Gospel Mission and the Shundahai Network, an environmentalist and healing group founded by a Western Shoshone spiritual leader, to sue again. They clearly felt their weakness. "There are barely enough Unitarians in the whole state to fill two Mormon wards," said the Unitarian Church's minister, who was anxious to clarify "how the Bill of Rights pertains to life in a city dominated by one religious culture."[86] The Unitarians eventually dropped the lawsuit in 2006, concerned that they would lose their case and that extending the controversy "would have underlined divisions in the city between the two religions."[87] Retreating to the defensive, they and other non-Mormons were left looking for other ways to make their point. These enhancements of the Church's already imposing public power and presence continue to resound in a region where religious minorities have long felt their spatial claims to be overlooked, defined themselves in opposition to the Mormon majority, and at times joined forces in anemic attempts to assert their combined power.[88] Mormon regional hegemony secure, meanwhile, Salt Lake City officials have moved to acknowledge on the public landscape the small worlds historically eclipsed in the LDS shadow. In This Is The Place Heritage Park, originally established to honor the area's Mormon past, representatives of Salt Lake City's Catholic diocese, Jewish synagogue, Greek Orthodox Church, and several Protestant denominations joined LDS leaders in June 2011 to dedicate a monument-studded Walk of Pioneer Faiths—a "landmark to ecumenism" recognizing nine Catholic, Jewish, and Protestant groups in Utah. The park's executive director said the Walk reflected the "inclusion that we see in our society." The Catholic representative understood well enough that the park is "especially sacred to members of The Church of Jesus Christ of Latter-day Saints," but an LDS elder emphasized that it also "belongs to all faiths."[89]

Perhaps the most assertive public attempt by a recently arrived urban religious group to stake a spatial claim was made in the southern region during the 1980s by Cuban-American practitioners of Santería. Established in Hialeah, Florida, in 1973, the Church of the Lukumí, Babalú Ayé, discovered the limits of contemporary American religious tolerance, and was forced to assume the offensive, when southern evangelicals resisted its attempt to place its Afro-Cuban world and its rituals of animal sacrifice. After the church opened its first public facility in 1987 in a conscious and active attempt to "bring the practice of the Santería faith...into the open," the city council, supported by fundamentalist Christians and animal rights activists, passed three ordinances banning ritual sacrifice. Evangelical critics hailed the move as evidence that "Jesus Christ Reigns Supreme in Hialeah." Effectively excluded from territory that conservative Christians claimed as theirs, the church withdrew to Miami in 1990. But after the Supreme Court overturned the ordinances in 1993, this "once-hidden faith leap[ed] out into the open" and became "very...public." In 1997 the church made a geographically striking declaration of victory by launching a new facility one block from the Hialeah city hall.[90]

Tension is not, of course, the only product of the urban spatial squeeze. In the small, often crowded cities of southern New England, where Jews are well established, mainline Protestant denominations are in decline, and newly arrived immigrant groups seek a toehold, living in close quarters is sometimes driving groups together. In New London, Connecticut, the full development of areas zoned to permit religious activity has left religious groups jostling for space and produced a complex spatial dynamic. Congregation Beth El, for instance, in a symbolic gesture of friendship, shares its space with the recently established Islamic Center of New London, which continues to seek space of its own. The United Methodist Church, meanwhile, struggling to maintain its building, has been driven by financial necessity to rent space to two new groups, which approach the situation with different attitudes. One, the Protestant Haitian Family Church of God, has little interaction with the Methodists and, indeed, seeks to maximize its autonomy by using the basement and its separate entrance; the other is the Hispanic Mission of Iglesia Bautista, whose pastor enjoys the resulting feeling of "unity in diversity." Located amid a dense urban geography, these two buildings proclaim both the limits and possibilities of American religious pluralism.[91]

If cities are arenas of pluralism amplified, suburbs constitute America's "interfaith frontier."[92] Consisting largely of Protestants, Catholics, and Jews when they began spreading across the landscape after World War II, they are now becoming multiethnic and multireligious neighborhoods as post-1965 immigrant groups migrate outward from their cities of initial residence or, in the case of highly skilled wealthy and middle-class groups, settle in them immediately upon arrival. Indeed, in what geographers recognize as "an important geographic reconfiguration," suburbs are now among the fastest-growing settlement areas for immigrant populations. These incoming ethnoreligious populations tend either to settle into concentrated "ethnoburbs"—ethnically distinct neighborhoods with ethnic institutions catering to group needs—or to scatter into geographically inchoate "invisiburbs."[93] In either case, their residents tend to be more open to the surrounding society, have greater contact with people of different backgrounds, and are more actively involved in community matters than are residents of the more self-contained enclaves. But at the same time their frequent concern to maintain cultural distinctiveness, their attempt to express ethnic identity by creating ethnic landmarks and signs on the landscape, and their willingness to join forces when they sense a threat to their rights, belie the classic "assimilation model" of immigrant socio-spatial behavior, according to which moving to the suburbs uniformly produces spatial integration and assimilation. Pluralism in suburbia is not so simple. Indeed, David Sibley argues in his recent analysis of "geographies of exclusion" that suburbanites' tendency to mind their own business may yield to episodes of "moral panic" in which they identify and target offending "liminal zones" and seek to eliminate or increase control of those they label as outsiders.[94]

Edison, New Jersey, offers a revealing Mid-Atlantic example of the religious tensions that may arise between long-time residents and newcomers. Here, some 11,000 South Asians arrived between 1990 and 2000, tripling the size of that group's presence in a town whose established populations of Irish, Italian, and Hungarian Catholics were comfortable with their time-honored position in the region's pluralist dynamic. Friction developed as the Indians claimed a place for themselves and their Hindu practices, created an ethnoburb, and transformed the local geography. Native residents dubbed a South Asian commercial district in nearby Iselin "Little Calcutta," South Asian businesses in the area were vandalized, and in the early 1990s the town council enacted ordinances to curb the annual Hindu festival of Navratri because it involved late-night celebrating. The local Indo-American Cultural Society fought back in court on First Amendment grounds and, in 1996 and 1997 rulings, had the ordinances overturned.[95] Other kinds of geographic tensions in suburbia have been more subdued, involving not so much interethnic hostility or religious practices as new and imposing buildings perceived as threats to established landscapes. In Norwalk, California, for instance, a Pacific region site where residents celebrated the West's Spanish heritage through their architecture, Hindus planning to build a temple with a lavishly decorated exterior were forced by the town to change the design for the sake of the surrounding style of the neighborhood. A similar concern for a geographic uniformity and regional feel led the San Diego zoning board initially to balk at the gold domes proposed for a new Sikh gurdwara.[96]

The Pacific landscape also reflects more positive facets of its regional pattern of multireligious encounter. A joint groundbreaking in Fremont, California, in April 1993 suggested cooperation and understanding between St. Paul's United Methodist Church and the Islamic Society of the East Bay as they prepared to build church and mosque side by side.[97] In Mission Viejo, meanwhile, the expansion of the religious demography beyond Protestants, Catholics, and Jews prompted the addition of an Islamic display to the city's annual Jewish and Christian holiday displays at the town gateway in 2000. At first, this development sparked a flurry of spatial claims by local Baha'is, atheists, and other groups, leaving the city council stymied in its attempts at mediation and unable to reach an equitable resolution. But in 2001, a week after the baffled council banned the displays, it found and enacted the space-sharing compromise it sought in a city park site that could accommodate ten to fifteen groups.[98]

These urban and suburban encounters, each prompting a process of negotiation over space and what activities would take place within it, suggest that the local geodynamics of American religious pluralism are part of the broader national conversation about religious freedom, social and cultural power, and the means of achieving spatial equity in an increasingly multicultural United States. Through their public religious displays and practices, Robert Orsi tells us, urban people—and, one might add, suburban people—announced the heterogeneity of their localities and staked a claim to living in a particular kind of nation.[99] Americans' attempts to create their own worlds at the local level coexist and interpenetrate with a shared commitment to a larger national space and community.

Contesting America: Worlds in National Space

Americans live their religious lives and engage in their pluralistic encounters not only in particular regional and local spaces, but also in a national space and on a national landscape that, as the lyrics of *America the Beautiful* suggest, they consider spiritually charged. The song suggests a geographic dimension to what religion scholars call America's "civil religion," defined by sociologist Robert Bellah as an institutionalized collection of sacred beliefs about the American nation that proposes a close relationship between God and the United States, seeks to confer cosmic legitimation on the nation, and finds expression in symbols and rituals.[100] But while it creates a religiously infused national orientation, it is at the same time regionally and locally embedded. Geographer Wilbur Zelinsky explains that, while America's religious-patriotic landscape is centered in the ritual core of Washington, D.C., American nationalism, particularly as it moved toward celebrating increasingly statist or centralist symbols of national identity and power, became rooted all over the country in a patriotic network of local sacred places.[101]

Zelinsky emphasizes this network's nationally unifying potential, but we must avoid *over*emphasizing it.[102] The realities of pluralistic competition for space and regional variation mean that definitions of the national space are perhaps inevitably contested.[103] However national in their significance, the local places that fascinate Zelinsky and other geographers remain fully immersed in their particular regional geographies and cultures and are therefore subject to the powerful regional and local cross-currents of the American pluralist dynamic. They reveal, in Rowland Sherrill's words, "a structural pattern of complex reciprocities between the stuff of univocal memory and the crucible of contemporary plural and competitive desires" in a "heterodox social world." Rather than carrying a single authoritative meaning, the sites are sacralized in a "democratic and pluralistic framework" in which "custodianship in the theological labors of 'patriotic orthodoxy'" contends with the "malleable memory" of a diverse society.[104] Because Americans seek to incorporate the national space into their particular religious worlds in the process of making places for those worlds in the national space, perception of the national space is a function of the world from which it is observed, and pluralistic contests over its meaning occur in specific regional and local settings. Indeed, different sorts of conflicts over the meaning of the national space are especially likely to erupt or to assume particular intensity in certain regions.

Some exchanges, for instance, pivot on the question of whether the United States is better defined as a specifically Christian (or "Judeo-Christian") space or a more spiritually multiform one. In the wake of the Hart-Cellar Act, there has been a growing call both in academe and in the wider culture to revise the "Judeo-Christian" model of the national religious scene in favor of a newer "multicultural" or "multireligious" model that sees the manyness of worlds in American space as the new reality.[105] Robert Orsi has suggested that this revisionist effort is most pronounced in the nation's cities, where public religious practices and displays are fundamentally attempts by immigrant and migrant groups to proclaim in urban geography the heterogeneity of American religious life and to join the national debate about pluralism and multiculturalism.[106] In response, conservative and fundamentalist groups, often drawing strong support from rural areas, have spoken with increasing insistence since the 1970s of a "Christian America," claiming the national space in the name of a single world. Religious fundamentalism in general tends to generate territorial claims or associations, geographer Roger Stump explained, because fundamentalists find them useful for giving their identity physical expression and for providing a focus for their struggle for influence. In the case of America's Protestant fundamentalists, the prospect of a multicultural society has heightened this territorial impulse and prompted them to integrate their territorial and religious identities on a national scale, making the kinds of public spatial claims typical of active pluralism.[107]

It is perhaps not surprising that the most dramatic spatial contests of this sort have occurred in the South and Southern Crossroads regions, where levels of diversity tend to be lower and Protestant evangelicalism constitutes the strongest force in the pluralist dynamic. The evangelical resistance to Hialeah's Church of the Lukumí, Babalú Ayé, mentioned earlier, is one example. A local columnist framed that issue nationally (and with clear exclusionist intent) in a pointed reminder to "satanic blood drinkers" that "We are One nation under God—not one nation under goats, chickens, pigs, ducks, or any other animal sacrifice," and that they "are welcome to leave THIS country."[108] Likewise, Alabama Chief Justice Roy Moore staked the fundamentalist claim when he installed an imposing monument of the Ten Commandments in the rotunda of the Alabama Supreme Court building. Moore's message was clear. The building, and thus Alabama itself, was a "Judeo-Christian" space; a similar Islamic monument, he said, would have no place there since "it wouldn't fit history."[109] Similar controversies erupted across the South and the Southern Crossroads, including in Georgia, Kentucky, Mississippi, Tennessee, and Texas, but Moore's actions suggest that his concerns were not so much merely regional as they were national with strong regional resonance. Expelled from office in 2003 for "willfully and publicly" resisting a First Amendment–based federal court order to remove it,[110] the pugnacious judge, aided by a Texas-based veteran's group, sent the monument on a national tour in 2004. As if to punctuate the route and its meaning with a symbolic exclamation point, he set the tour to end at the U.S. Capitol.[111]

The "tribal worlds" subregion of the Mountain West, meanwhile, has spawned tension-filled contests over whether American Indian spirituality or Euroamerican civil religion has stronger claim to the national space that both groups occupy. While the latter legitimates Euroamerican occupation of the territory that is now the United States, proponents of the former, in countercultural resistance, condemn Euroamerican mistreatment of Indians, see Euroamerican approaches to the land as exploitative and profane, and, in contrast to the dominant civil religion, regard precolonial rather than contemporary America as a utopian space.[112] The most pointed contest between the Euroamerican and Indian worlds in recent decades involves Mount Rushmore, technically located in the Midwest region as defined above but clearly participant in Mountain West–style pluralism and, indeed, located only about a dozen miles from South Dakota's border with Wyoming. Situated at the heart of the North American continent, the site, in which the Euroamerican claim to North America has literally been carved into the Black Hills, was intended by artist Gutzon Borglum and has been interpreted by many people in the United States as a "shrine of patriotism," a memorial to the "irresistible God-man movement" westward across the continent. The memorial's promoters, notably the Mount Rushmore National Monument Society (MRNMS), have sought to reinforce this reading of it by holding ceremonies about it in conjunction with such nationally significant dates as July fourth. Such "unadulterated" articulations of "patriotic faith" have made the "delicate effort to respect the pluralism of American life...particularly difficult" there.[113]

Since the 1970s, members of the American Indian Movement (AIM) have sought, in active pluralist fashion, to reorient public perceptions of the memorial and to challenge that form of American civil religion at one of its key symbolic centers. Using tactics of reoccupation, desecration, and purification, they have challenged what they consider whites' defilement of native space and attempted to restore the mountain's original sacred character. AIM activists occupied the memorial for several months in 1970, and again several other times in the 1970s (see Figure 3.4); in 1975, a bomb detonated at the visitor's

Figure 3.4 John Fire Lame Deer praying with peace pipe at Mount Rushmore, 1971. Photograph by Richard Erdoes, reproduced courtesy of University of Oklahoma Press.

center one day after a violent encounter at the nearby Pine Ridge reservation between Lakota Sioux and federal agents. Supporters of Mount Rushmore interpreted the actions of AIM as an invasion of public space, while AIM protesters claimed ownership and renamed the mountain Mount Crazy Horse. The AIM perspective has become more widely accepted among the Lakota than it was in the 1970s; many Lakota today speak of Borglum's desecration of the Sacred Paha Supa (Black Hills) of the Lakota Nation. On the other side of the contest, Roy Moore pointedly included Mount Rushmore among the stops on his national Ten Commandments tour (see Figure 3.5). Mount Rushmore scholar Matthew Glass concludes that "the sacred awareness which Rushmore's promoters hoped would advance national unity has been far from successful."[114] Rather, the sacralization process has been conflict-ridden, the only clear result being that pluralist spatial dynamics trumped the idea of a national symbolic geographic center.

A third type of contest over the national space involves the meaning of the land itself, pitting those who consider it inherently sacred—including "spiritual" environmentalists and Indian groups—against advocates of "dominion theology," usually conservative Christians, who believe that it was created for human use. As Bron Taylor explains, contemporary environmental conflicts entail "disputes about the nature of sacred space," "disagreements about the resulting human obligations," and diverging visions about whether the nation's sacrality can be located "in the landscape itself rather than in the U.S. nation-state."[115] This aspect of American religious pluralism, while nationwide

Figure 3.5 Judge Roy Moore's Ten Commandments at Mount Rushmore, 2004.
Photograph by David Ewing, reproduced courtesy of AVIDD.

in reach, has been particularly salient in regions where notions of sacred land-scape are most pronounced. In the Mountain West, for example, the prospect of Borglum's shrine of patriotism carved into the Black Hills prompted local residents to defend "God's statuary" over "any possible conception of mere man" and to plead that the Hills be left "as nature left them, deep, quiet, majes-tic, natural."[116]

Such contests have been even more frequent and intense in the Pacific Northwest because of the region's civil religion of spiritual environmental-ism, and because its high concentration of wilderness areas has generated a disproportionate number of public spatial contests. Movement and organiza-tion building have been especially vigorous there. Speaking for spiritual envi-ronmentalism, for instance, are Portland, Oregon's Earth and Spirit Council, whose "all-inclusive religious net" ranges "from Christianity to Judaism to Buddhism," and Interfaith Network for Earth Concerns, affiliated with the Ecumenical Ministries of Oregon.[117] The Interfaith Network has sponsored several conferences, such as the 1991 gathering held at Portland's First Presbyterian Church, First Unitarian Church, and St. Stephen's Episcopal Church, in which these denominations, joined by The Buddhist Peace Fellowship, the Oregon Environmental Council, and several Indian groups, declared that "the Earth is a sacred place."[118] A similar conference nine years later at Portland's Bethlehem Lutheran Church attracted ministers from across Oregon and Washington state and prompted Roman Catholic bish-ops from the region to draft a pastoral letter declaring the earth a "sacred shared space."[119] Even some evangelical Christians have embraced the cause, seeing in environmentalism a matter of "transcendent duty" and forming a "Northwest group" called Christians for Environmental Stewardship.[120] Other conservative Christians, in alliance with the timber and other extractive industries, have made opposing spatial claims through the Wise Use movement, which was born in the Northwest, and such Wise Use organizational arms as the Center for the Defense of Free Enterprise (based in Bellevue, Washington) and the Oregon Citizens Alliance (which has chapters in Washington state and Idaho).[121] In the courts and other public arenas, these two groups contest what constitutes American sacred space and who defines it—"who controls the land, and for what end."[122]

This regional spatial contest emerged into national prominence in the 1980s when the environmental group Earth First!, originally organized in Arizona in the late 1970s, became increasingly active in the Northwest. At the national level, it perceived a threat to its sacred space when Interior Secretary James Watt, founding president of the Wise Use–oriented Mountain States Legal Defense Fund, suggested that an imminent return of Christ rendered long-term environmental protection unnecessary. At the regional level, they launched a campaign in Oregon's Willamette National Forest in 1985 to oppose logging in old-growth forests and protect the habitat of the endangered spotted owl; joined members of the American Native People Organization and the Sacred Earth Coalition in 1989 to protest the expansion of a ski resort on Oregon's Mount Hood;[123] and, in 1992, joined by several Indian protesters in a prayer circle, blocked a logging company's access to a tract on Enola Hill, near Rhododendron, Oregon. But such activities met with opposition from those who, as one environmental activist recalled, argued in public hearings that "God had put trees in the forest for people to cut."[124] As spiritual environmentalists staked their spatial claims through symbolic tree sittings and roadblocks, caravans of logging trucks staked theirs by circling government buildings in Portland, Eugene, and Salem, Oregon, to protest a "radical environmental agenda."[125] The spatial contest even reached into the public schools when, for example, fundamentalist parents and the local timber industry in Bend, Oregon, resisted what they perceived as "Native American religion," "New Age religion," and a "mixture of Hinduism, eastern mysticism, and witchcraft" in "Earthkeepers," an environmental science curriculum whose name suggested the spatial claims informing it.[126]

These examples suggest that the religious meaning of the national space is as multiform and as much the stuff of public pluralistic wrangling as the religious culture within it, varying from individual to individual, group to group, locality to locality, and region to region. Further complicating the meaning of the national space and the geographic complexity of American religious pluralism are recent patterns of global migration and technological development, which have acted to blur the borders between the national space and the wider expanses beyond it.

America and Beyond: Worlds in Outer Spaces

Geographic perspectives on American religious pluralism are by no means confined to the local, regional, and national levels. We have become increasingly aware in recent years of several new approaches and developments that challenge us to stretch our thinking in new directions. We shall close with a brief survey of some of these emerging avenues for exploration.

One particularly important new approach, apparent throughout American studies, calls our attention to the nation's place in wider transnational and global communities and networks. American religious pluralism has always pointed beyond the nation, for its sources have been from the outset as much international as domestic. Such internal factors as the First Amendment and the identity movements of the 1960s have powerfully shaped its contours, of course, but religious life, Peggy Levitt has recently reminded us, regularly crosses borders and is not limited by geographic distances and boundaries.[127] Developments since 1965 have underscored her point, greatly amplifying the degree to which American religious space is part of, participant in, global space. Contemporary American immigrants integrate into the United States just as their forebears did, yet the dynamic of immigration has also changed dramatically. Transnationalism, increasingly convenient global travel, an emergent global media, and new telecommunications technologies have made possible to an unprecedented extent immigrants' continuing attachment to sacred places and religious communities outside the country; their ongoing interaction with fellow emigrants who settle in other parts of the United States; their maintenance of distinctive beliefs, practices, and values; and the solidification of global religious communities—Muslim, Hindu, Pentecostal and evangelical Christian, and others—in which they and other Americans can and do take part. It is with these developments in mind that scholars have increasingly spoken of "diasporic" religion, an increasingly common phenomenon in which the dispersal of peoples and their religions across the globe from a particular geographic point of origin transforms and generates new forms of religious community, ideology, and practice.[128] Transnationalism and diaspora have made "American religious pluralism and the globalization of religious life...part and parcel of the same dynamic."[129] National frameworks are becoming increasingly inadequate for fully understanding American religious lives. More than ever before, American religious worlds and American religious pluralism reach outside the nation's geographic boundaries and into transnational spaces.[130]

Nowhere is this reality more evident than in the nation's cities. Urban anthropologists speak of "world cities," places closely connected to other urban centers by the constant movement of people, ideas, and artifacts into and out of them made possible by rapid transportation, instantaneous communication, and global media. The result is what Ulf Hannerz has called an "intercontinental traffic in meaning," a system in which religious worlds, less bound than previously to geographically specific locales considered definitive "homes," can achieve transnational scope and interact at once in local, national, and global arenas.[131]

Further complicating spatial considerations of American religious pluralism is the advent of virtual space. We have barely begun to examine, let alone comprehend, the implications of cyberspace and the Internet for the formation and encounter of religious worlds, though it is already clear that those implications are profound. In religion as in other areas of human endeavor, interpersonal interactions become disembodied as they become electronic, raising the question not only of how to conceptualize this space in geographic terms but also of what electronic technology means for current notions of and actions in space.[132] Whatever the implications of this new spatial frontier for the way we think about conventional geographic space, recent events in Winter, Wisconsin, where the school board in 1998 blocked access to electronic information about Buddhism and Wicca, suggest that struggles over space—religious worlds making spaces, seeking legitimation of their presence, facing attempted exclusion—have carried over into it. American religious pluralism in all its complexity has entered cyberspace.[133]

Globalization, international travel, and electronic communications have all had the effect of erasing determinate, particular space and contributed to a new pattern of community formation recently identified by geographers: *heterolocalism*.[134] The term refers to the possibility that ethnic or religious communities can maintain close ties without spatial propinquity, scattered instead over large urban, national, or international domains. Surely this emerging sociospatial phenomenon, by changing the way that religious worlds locate themselves in and relate themselves to space, will affect the geographic dynamics of religious pluralism. Indeed, Barbara Metcalf, surveying changes in Islam as its adherents have become globally dispersed, has proposed the term "postmodern pluralism" to describe these developing heterolocal realities.[135] At least one study suggests that these new patterns have amplified the importance of buildings among groups seeking to establish religious communities in America.[136] But because they also challenge the notions of determinate and particular space on which our models of pluralistic engagement have so far been grounded, the precise contours of this new pluralism remain unclear.[137]

Two religious events of the early 1990s provide geographically striking examples of the new transnational, heterolocal realities of American religious pluralism. The first is the Muslim World Day Parade in New York City in 1991, which featured four floats. The first three were scale models of Islam's holiest mosques: Ka'ba in Mecca, al-Quds in Jerusalem, and Masjid Al-Haram in Medina. The fourth was of the anticipated new building for the Queens Muslim Center, which would soon relocate from a residential house in Flushing to a more expressively Muslim space featuring a dome, crescent moon, and minaret. The four floats together, three existing buildings and one being constructed in replacement of a far less visible structure, not only announced the spatial presence of Muslims in New York City and the nation but also identified them as a transnational community at once established in America and linked to the sacred places of Islamic tradition.[138] The 1990 consecration of the Sri Lakshmi Temple in Ashland, Massachusetts, described by Diana Eck, may be read similarly. The ritual featured a *kumbhabhishekha*—a sacred pouring of water over the temple towers and on the images of the gods within. What made the ritual striking was its use of the commingled waters of the Ganges, Mississippi, Missouri, and Colorado rivers. The simple ritual, attended by perhaps 3000 Hindus from across New England, created a new place at once transnational—Indian and American—and transregionally American.[139] The spatial orientation of this new religious world was at once inward, toward the heart of the North American continent, and outward, toward Hinduism's ancient homeland in South Asia's Indus valley. In New York and Ashland, American religion and world religion, American geography and world geography, were proclaimed one.

Of course, the September 11 terrorist attacks and subsequent backlash offer a harsh reminder that the experiences of American religious transnationalism and heterolocalism are not uniformly uplifting. The nation's pluralist dynamic received a powerful and violent jolt from a transnational and electronically savvy religious force that encompassed and connected people ranging geographically from the Middle East and South Asia to American cities and united in a belief that American cultural and political power were encroaching into distant places over which they had no legitimate claim. But however traumatic, September 11 has not necessarily "changed everything." Charles Cohen, director of the Lubar Institute for the Study of the Abrahamic Religions at the University of Wisconsin–Madison, commented that what September 11 did was to "put pressure on what is a very normal American dynamic in the way religious groups get integrated into American religious life."[140] The distinguishing characteristic of this newly pressurized environment has been largely a matter of—to quote one observer's description of the Park51 controversy's distinctive features—"the heat, the volume, the level of hostility."[141] Rather than proving utterly transformative, the post–September 11 strain has assumed the form of a national overlay that, the available evidence suggests, has left the fundamental regional and local patterns of American religious pluralism largely intact. A study of recent mosque controversies conducted by the Pew Forum on Religion and Public Life, for example, indicates that national anxieties about Islam have particular and predictably patterned regional resonance: resistance to mosque construction has been concentrated in the South, where the September 11 attacks only expanded the scope of the region's preexisting "culture wars" dynamic, and in urban areas of four other regions—the Mid-Atlantic, the Midwest, New England, and the Pacific—where larger Muslim populations have most impacted the landscape and heightened the likelihood of spatial tensions (see Figure 3.6).[142] The Park51 controversy, however intense and however transregional its reach, evidenced little that was incompatible with the established Mid-Atlantic religious dynamic—indeed, it was sparked online rather than by local resistance—and the well-publicized grand opening of the "victory mosque" may well be read

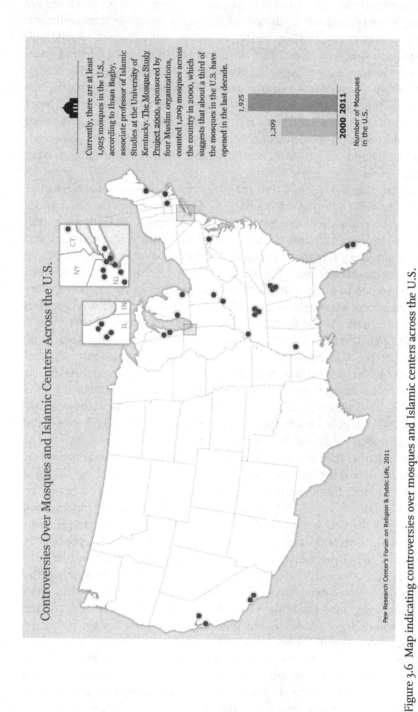

Controversies Over Mosques and Islamic Centers Across the U.S.

Currently, there are at least 1,925 mosques in the U.S., according to Ihsan Bagby, associate professor of Islamic Studies at the University of Kentucky. The Mosque Study Project 2000, sponsored by four Muslim organizations, counted 1,209 mosques across the country in 2000, which suggests that about a third of the mosques in the U.S. have opened in the last decade.

Number of Mosques in the U.S.

2000 1,209
2011 1,925

Pew Research Center's Forum on Religion & Public Life, 2011

Figure 3.6 Map indicating controversies over mosques and Islamic centers across the U.S.

Reprinted from: Controversies Over Mosques and Islamic Centers Across the U.S., Pew Research Center's Forum on Religion & Public Life, © 2011, Pew Research Center. http://pewforum.org/. Article available at http://features.pewforum.org/muslim/controversies-over-mosque-and-isl amic-centers-across-the-us.html.

as a triumph of the region's long-standing pattern of ever-widening multire-ligious coexistence.[143]

In other regions, meanwhile, characteristic regional spatial dynamics and signature contests of American pluralism that predate September 11 persisted a decade afterward. Near the Mountain West, United Native Americans hosted a forum to mark the fortieth anniversary of the 1970 occupation of Mount Rushmore, continuing their struggle to reclaim the Black Hills for their spiritual world. One forum participant found himself "fighting the same battles that my father and grandfather fought."[144] In the South, evangelical Protestants remain committed to their collision course with secularism as battles over court-house Ten Commandments displays continue to rage, most recently in rural Dixie County, Florida.[145] In Salt Lake City, Unitarians, their lawsuits against the LDS Church behind them, remain on the defensive, continuing their quest for space in the public square but keenly aware of the faintness of their religious world relative to Mormonism's sunlike regional dominance. Their omission from the group of religious denominations monumentalized on the landscape of This Is The Place Heritage Park's Walk of Pioneer Faiths left their offended minister asking "What About Unitarians?"[146] Ecumenism and environmen-talism continued their dynamic interplay in the Pacific Northwest in 2010 as Interfaith Network for Earth Concerns held its first Earth Care Summit in Portland, Oregon, while the Alaska branch of California-based environmental-ist group Interfaith Power and Light carried on its mission to defend polar bear habitats against the oil and gas industries.[147] At the local, regional, national, international, and cyberspace levels, the shock waves of September 11 jostled but did not rearrange the religious worlds of American space.

The decades since 1965 have clearly marked a watershed in American reli-gious history, and the perspectives of geography—an ongoing awareness of religion's inherent spatiality—will greatly enhance our efforts to grasp its full nature and import. The passage of the Hart-Cellar Act heralded both an expo-nential increase in the scope of American religious diversity and the onset of a new, "active" kind of pluralist interchange that together, mutually reinforcing, are revolutionizing the landscape. The precise dynamic appears to vary from region to region, from locality to locality. Diana Eck has suggested that our differences are not localized by geographical zones,[148] and insofar as pluralis-tic tension and exchange tap wellsprings of human behavior operative across regional or national lines, she is correct. But human behavior and the chal-lenges of American religious pluralism do indeed assume geographically con-ditioned, locationally specific forms, and our attempts to face these challenges must therefore be geographically sensitive. The spatial dynamics of American religious pluralism are more intense—religious claims on American space more numerous, more contentious, and yet more potentially productive of dialogue—than ever before. Seeing American religious pluralism through the lens of geography—understanding that it is fundamentally about groups seek-ing to turn spaces into places, about encounters of worlds in local, regional, national, and global space—therefore offers important insights as we continue pursuing the spatial equity that is the geographic promise of the First Amendment.

Notes

* An early draft of this essay was presented as a paper at "Religious Pluralism in Modern America," a conference sponsored by the Lubar Institute for the Study of the Abrahamic Religions, University of Wisconsin–Madison, in April 2007. Thanks to the Lubar Institute for providing crucial impetus and funding at the outset of this project, to Phil Barlow for initiating my invitation to that conference, and to Charles Cohen, Director of the Lubar Institute, for early encouragement and feedback. Thanks to Philip Barlow, Jon Butler, Philip Garone, Jennifer Helzer, Nicholas Howe, Amir Hussein, Patricia Killen, Ronald Numbers, Mark Silk, Bron Taylor, and the JAAR's two anonymous reviewers for their help in various stages of researching and writing this essay. Thanks also to Alison McNally for preparing the map used in Figure 3.3.

1 Ralph Blumenthal and Sharaf Mowjood, "Muslim Prayers and Renewal Near Ground Zero," *New York Times*, December 9, 2009, A1; Dan Margolis, "Islamic Center Has Broad Support in New York," *People's World*, August 17, 2010, http://peoplesworld. org/islamic-center-has-broad-support-in-new-york, accessed October 6, 2011.

2 Defenders of the proposed center point out that it is not so much a mosque as a community center that includes a prayer space, and that it is not located at Ground Zero. See "Is the 'Ground Zero Mosque' not even a mosque?" at PolitiFact.com, http://www.politifact.com/truth-o-meter/statements/2010/aug/23/ al-hunt/ground-zero-mosque-not-even-mosque/, accessed November 14, 2011.

3 Josh Nathan-Kazis, "Mosque's Plan to Expand Near Ground Zero Sparks Debate," *The Jewish Daily Forward*, June 4, 2010, http://forward.com/articles/128347/ mosque-s-plan-to-expand-near-ground-zero-sparks//, accessed February 22, 2013; Ilario Pantano, "A Mosque at Ground Zero?" *The Daily Caller*, June 18, 2010, http://dailycaller. com/2010/06/18/a-mosque-at-ground-zero/?utm_source=Online+Sign+Ups&utm_ campaign=17b5c66ae6-Ground_Zero_Mosque_Op_Ed6_17_2010&utm_ medium=email, accessed October 6, 2011; Lisa Miller, "War Over Ground Zero: A Proposed Mosque Tests the Limits of American Tolerance," *The Daily Beast*, August 8, 2010, http://www.thedailybeast.com/newsweek/2010/08/08/war-over-ground-zero. html, accessed October 3, 2011; Javier C. Hernandez, "Planned Sign of Tolerance Bringing Division Instead," *New York Times*, July 13, 2010, http://www.nytimes. com/2010/07/14/nyregion/14center.html, accessed October 3, 2011; Jonathan Mann, "Manhattan Mosque Plan Stokes Controversy," *CNN Politics*, August 6, 2010, http:// articles.cnn.com/2010–08–06/politics/mann.mosque.ground.zero_1_new-mosque -cordoba-house-state-religion?_s=PM:POLITICS, accessed October 7, 2011; Jeff Jacoby, "A Mosque at Ground Zero?" *Boston Globe*, June 6, 2010, http://www.boston.com/bos-tonglobe/editorial_opinion/oped/articles/2010/06/06/a_mosque_at_ground_zero/, accessed October 28, 2011; Jacob Gershman, "Sides Dig in Over Ground Zero Mosque," *The Wall Street Journal*, August 2, 2010, http://online.wsj.com/article/SB100014240527 48704702304575403853604214846.html, accessed October 2, 2011.

4 Miller, "War Over Ground Zero."

5 The Pluralism Project website is at http://www.pluralism.org.

6 Diana Eck, *A New Religious America: How a "Christian Country" Has Become the World's Most Religiously Diverse Nation* (San Francisco: HarperSanFrancisco, 2001), 21, 311.

7 Maxine Bernstein, "Man Accused in Hate Crime in Corvallis Mosque Arson," *The Oregonian*, August 25, 2011, http://www.oregonlive.com/pacific-northwest-news/index.ssf/2011/08/man_accused_of_hate_crime_in_corvallis_mosque_arson.html, accessed February 22, 2013.

8 Michael Newton and Judy Ann Newton, *Racial and Religious Violence in America: a Chronology* (New York: Garland Science, 1991). Editions *of Hate Crimes Statistics* dating back to 1995 can be found at the Federal Bureau of Investigation website: http://www.fbi.gov/about-us/cjis/ucr/ucr#hate. In 2002, Human Rights Watch published a study specifically of hate crimes against Muslims in the wake of the September 11 attacks (Singh 2002). The report concluded that "[m]osques and places of worship perceived to be mosques appeared to be among the most likely places of September 11-related backlash violence," and cited a survey that counted 104 such incidents—far more than the number of religiously motivated hate crimes against individuals—in the first week after September 11; Amardeep Singh, *"We Are Not the Enemy": Hate Crimes Against Arabs, Muslims, and Those Perceived to be Arab or Muslim after September 11* (Washington, DC: Human Rights Watch, 2002), 21.

9 Martin E. Marty, "Pluralisms," *The Annals of the American Academy of Political and Social Science* 612 (2007): 16; Robert Wuthnow, *America and the Challenges of Religious Diversity* (Princeton, NJ: Princeton University Press, 2005), 104.

10 Robert N. Bellah and Frederick E. Greenspahn, eds., *Uncivil Religion: Interreligious Hostility in America* (New York: Crossroad, 1987).

11 Jackson W. Carroll, Douglas W. Johnson, and Martin E. Marty, *Religion in America, 1950 to the Present* (San Francisco, CA: Harper and Row, 1979), 84; Marty, "Pluralisms," 16; Diana Eck, "The Multireligious Public Square," in *One Nation Under God? Religion and American Culture*, Marjorie Garber and Rebecca L. Walkowitz, eds. (New York: Routledge, 1999), 4.

12 The most recent and fully developed spatial analysis of religion is Roger W. Stump, *The Geography of Religion: Faith, Place, and Space* (Lanham, MD: Rowman & Littlefield, 2008).

13 Sidney E. Mead, "The American People: Their Space, Time, and Religion," *The Journal of Religion* 34, no. 4 (1954): 244–255.

14 Current scholarly approaches to space are grounded in the "humanistic" or "experiential" geography of Yi-Fu Tuan and others. Among the most important influential works in this area for religious studies are Yi-Fu Tuan, "Geopiety: A Theme in Man's Attachment to Nature and to Place," in *Geographies of the Mind*, David Lowenthal and Martyn J. Bowden, eds. (New York: Oxford University Press, 1976), 11–39; Yi-Fu Tuan, "Humanistic Geography," *Annals of the Association of American Geographers* 66, no. 2 (1976): 266–276; Yi-Fu Tuan, *Space and Place: The Perspectives of Experience* (Minneapolis: University of Minnesota Press, 1977); Jonathan Z. Smith, "The Wobbling Pivot," in *Map Is Not Territory: Studies in the History of Religions*, Jonathan Z. Smith, ed. (Leiden: E.J. Brill, 1978), 88–103; Jonathan Z. Smith, *To Take Place: Toward Theory in Ritual* (Chicago: University of Chicago Press, 1987). The "spatial turn" was heralded and guided in the late 1980s and early 1990s by Edward W. Soja,

Postmodern Geographies: The Reassertion of Space in Critical Social Theory (New York: Verso, 1989) and Henri Lefebvre, *The Production of Space* (Cambridge, MA: Blackwell, 1991), and expressed most decisively in the field of American religious studies in David Chidester and Edward T. Linenthal, eds., *American Sacred Space* (Bloomington: Indiana University Press, 1995).

15 Klaus Benesch, "Concepts of Space in American Culture: An Introduction," in *Space in America: Theory History Culture*, Klaus Benesch and Kerstin Schmidt, eds. (Amsterdam and New York: Rodopi, 2005), 12; Mead, "The American People," 244; Lefebvre, *The Production of Space*; John Urry, "Social Relations, Space, and Time," in *Social Relations and Spatial Structures*, Derek Gregory and John Urry, eds. (New York: St. Martin's Press, 1985), 30; Robert David Sack, *Human Territoriality: Its Theory and History* (Cambridge, UK: Cambridge University Press, 1986), 5; Michel Foucault, "Space, Knowledge, and Power," in *The Foucault Reader*, Paul Rabinow, ed. (New York: Pantheon, 1984), 252; David Sibley, *Geographies of Exclusion: Society and Difference in the West* (London and New York: Routledge, 1995), ix; Larry E. Shiner, "Sacred Space, Profane Space, Human Space," *Journal of the American Academy of Religion* 40, no. 4 (1972): 429.

16 Gerardus van der Leeuw, *Religion in Essence and Manifestation*, trans. J. E. Turner (Princeton, NJ: Princeton University Press, 1986); Mircea Eliade, *The Sacred and the Profane* (New York: Harcourt, Brace and World, 1957); Smith, *To Take Place*; Thomas A. Tweed, *Crossings and Dwellings: A Theory of Religion* (Cambridge, MA: Harvard University Press, 2006).

17 Robert H. Stoddard and Carolyn V. Prorok, "Geography of Religion and Belief Systems," in *Geography in America at the Dawn of the 21st Century*, Gary L. Gaile and Cort J. Willmott, eds. (Oxford, UK: Oxford University Press, 2003), 759–760; Roger W. Stump, *Boundaries of Faith: Geographical Perspectives on Religious Fundamentalism* (Lanham, MD: Rowman & Littlefield, 2000), 3, 207; Rowland A. Sherrill, "American Sacred Space and the Contest of History," in *American Sacred Space*, David Chidester and Edward T. Linenthal, eds. (Bloomington: Indiana University Press), 314; Barbara Daly Metcalf, ed., *Making Muslim Space in North America and Europe* (Berkeley: University of California Press, 1996), 3. The concept of "lived religion" has been the focus of increasing scholarly examination in recent years; two particularly relevant examples are David D. Hall, *Lived Religion in America: Toward a History of Practice* (Princeton, NJ: Princeton University Press, 1997) and Nancy T. Ammerman, *Everyday Religion: Observing Modern Religious Lives* (New York: Oxford University Press, 2006).

18 Eliade, *The Sacred and the Profane*; Tuan, *Space and Place*, 6; Yi-Fu Tuan, *Topophilia: A Study of Environmental Perception, Attitudes, and Values.* (Englewood Cliffs, NJ: Prentice Hall, 1974); Sherrill, "American Sacred Space and the Contest of History," 313–316.

19 Stump, *Geography of Religion*, 221; Rhys H. Williams, "Religion and Place in the Midwest: Urban, Rural, and Suburban Forms of Religious Expression," in *Religion and Public Life in the Midwest: America's Common Denominator?* Philip Barlow and Mark Silk, eds. (Lanham, MD: Rowman & Littlefield, 2004), 195.

20 Smith, "The Wobbling Pivot," 88; Alan Gussow, *A Sense of Place: The Artist and the American Land* (New York, NY: Seabury Press, 1971), 27; Tuan, *Space and Place*, 178; Carolyn V. Prorock, "The Hare Krishna's Transformation of Space in

West Virginia," *Journal of Cultural Geography* 7, no. 1 (1986): 129; Richard E. Wentz, *The Culture of Religious Pluralism* (Boulder, CO: Westview Press, 1998), 79; Louis P. Nelson, *American Sanctuary: Understanding Sacred Spaces* (Bloomington: Indiana University Press, 2006), 1–14; Stump, *Geography of Religion*, 26, 301–368. The concept of sacred space has been critiqued on the grounds that the inherent contextuality of lived religion renders such universal categories invalid. Geographer Roger Stump suggests that the term remains useful provided it be understood, as it is in this essay, "not as the expression of some sort of universal archetype, but rather as a religious component of the spatial imaginations of believers that takes different forms in different contexts" (Stump, *Geography of Religion*, 26). Peter Williams, meanwhile, has critiqued the term "sacred space" as having lost utility through overuse (Peter Williams, "Sacred Space in North America," *Journal of the American Academy of Religion* 70, no. 3 [2002]: 606–607).

21 Stump points out the advantages of using the neutral term "secular" to "profane," which carries sometimes pejorative connotations (Stump, *Geography of Religion*, 31 n.38).

22 Belden C. Lane, *Landscapes of the Sacred: Geography and Narrative in American Spirituality* (New York: Paulist Press, 1988); Chidester and Linenthal, *American Sacred Space*, 5.

23 Shiner, "Sacred Space, Profane Space, Human Space," 427.

24 Sack, *Human Territoriality*; Stump, *Geography of Religion*, 24–25, 221–300 (quotation on p. 222).

25 Stump, *Geography of Religion*, 27–28, 295, 349–362; John A. Jakle, Stanley Brunn, and Curtis C. Roseman, *Human Spatial Behavior: A Social Geography* (North Scituate, MA: Duxbury Press, 1976), 39; Chidester and Linenthal, *American Sacred Space*, 15; Javier C. Hernandez, "Planned Sign of Tolerance Bringing Division Instead," *New York Times*, July 13, 2010, http://www.nytimes.com/2010/07/14/nyregion/14center.html, accessed October 3, 2011; Lily Kong, "Mapping 'New' Geographies of Religion: Politics and Poetics in Modernity," *Progress in Human Geography* 25, no. 2 (2001), 212; Chidester and Linenthal, *American Sacred Space*, 31.

26 Wilbur Zelinsky, *The Enigma of Ethnicity: Another American Dilemma* (Iowa City: University of Iowa Press, 2001), 195.

27 Recent explorations of the relation between religious pluralism and the First Amendment include Ted G. Jelen, "The Constitutional Basis of Religious Pluralism in the United States: Causes and Consequences," *The Annals of the American Academy of Political and Social Science* 612 (2007): 26–41 and John C. Blakeman, "The Religious Geography of Religious Expression: Local Governments, Courts, and the First Amendment," *Journal of Church and State* 48, no. 2 (2006): 399–422.

28 William R. Hutchison, *Religious Pluralism in America: The Contentious History of a Founding Ideal* (New Haven, CT: Yale University Press, 2003).

29 Harold Isaacs, *Idols of the Tribe: Group Identity and Political Change* (New York: Harper and Row, 1975), 154; Marty, "Pluralisms," 17–18; Stump, *Geography of Religion*, 222, 363, 349; Steve Bruce, "The Poverty of Economism or the Social Limits of Maximizing," in *Sacred Markets, Sacred Canopies: Essays on Religious Markets and Religious Pluralism*, Ted G. Jelen, ed. (Lanham, MD: Rowman & Littlefield, 2002), 167–186; Jelen, "The Constitutional Basis of Religious Pluralism," 30–31; Rhys H. Williams, "The Languages of the Public Sphere: Religious Pluralism, Institutional

Logics, and Civil Society," *The Annals of the American Academy of Political and Social Science* 612 (2007): 44; Wuthnow, *America and the Challenges of Religious Diversity*, 2–3, 97.

30 Richard D. Hecht, "Active versus Passive Pluralism: A Changing Style of Civil Religion?" *Annals of the American Academy of Political and Social Science* 612 (2007): 133–151.

31 Myer Siemiatycki, "Contesting Sacred Urban Space: The Case of the Eruv," *Journal of International Migration and Integration* 6, no 2 (2005): 255–270; Edward W. Soja, *Seeking Spatial Justice* (Minneapolis: University of Minnesota Press, 2010).

32 Hecht, "Active versus Passive Pluralism," 143.

33 Common Cause of New York, "Press Statement on Behalf of New York Neighbors for American Values," August 25, 2010, http://readme.readmedia.com/Press-Statement-on-Behalf-of-New-York-Neighbors-for-American-Values/1702485, accessed October 3, 2011.

34 Patricia Bonomi, "Religious Pluralism in the Middle Colonies," Divining America, TeacherServe, National Humanities Center, http://nationalhumanities-center.org/tserve/eighteen/ekeyinfo/midcol.htm, accessed October 10, 2011.

35 The Pluralism Project maintains on its website an archive of "Religious Diversity News." Searches may be narrowed by theme; themes particularly relevant to pluralism's spatial dimensions include "Center Openings/Milestones," "First Amendment/Public Square," "Violence/Vandalism," and "Zoning." See http://www.pluralism.org/news/key_themes.php, accessed April 12, 2008.

36 Chidester and Linenthal, *American Sacred Space*, 14–18; Mary Douglas, *Purity and Danger: An Analysis of Concepts of Pollution and Taboo* (London: Routledge and Kegan Paul, 1966); Jakle, Brunn, and Roseman, *Human Spatial Behavior*, 39; Don Mitchell, *Cultural Geography: A Critical Introduction* (Malden, MA: Blackwell, 2000), 170; Sibley, *Geographies of Exclusion*; Zelinsky, *The Enigma of Ethnicity*, 195.

37 Tracy Neal Leavelle, "Geographies of Encounter: Religion and Contested Spaces in Colonial North America," *American Quarterly* 56, no. 4 (2004): 913–943.

38 Stump, *Geography of Religion*, 223; Eck, "The Multireligious Public Square," 9; Richard E. Wentz, *The Culture of Religious Pluralism* (Boulder, CO: Westview Press, 1998), 85; Barbara Daly Metcalf, ed., *Making Muslim Space in North America and Europe* (Berkeley: University of California Press, 1996), 17–18; Eck, *A New Religious America*, 326; Jay Johnson and Frank J. Costa, "Hindu Temple Development in the United States: Planning and Zoning Issues," *Journal of Cultural Geography* 17, no. 2 (1998): 115–123.

39 Stump, *Geography of Religion*, 223–224.

40 Wilbur Zelinsky, "An Approach to the Religious Geography of the United States: Patterns of Church Membership in 1952," *Annals of the Association of American Geographers* 51, no. 2 (1961): 139–193; Edwin Scott Gaustad, *Historical Atlas of Religion in America* (New York: Harper and Row, 1962); Wilbur Zelinsky, *The Cultural Geography of the United States* (Englewood Cliffs, NJ: Prentice-Hall, 1973); Raymond D. Gastil, *Cultural Regions of the United States* (Seattle: University of Washington Press, 1975); James R. Shortridge, "Patterns of Religion in the United States," *Geographical Review* 66, no. 4 (1976): 420–434; James R. Shortridge, "A New Regionalization of American Religion," *Journal for the Scientific Study of Religion*

16, no. 2 (1977): 143–153; Richard E. Wentz, "Region and Religion in America," *Foundations* 24, no. 2 (1981): 148–156; Roger W. Stump, "Regional Divergence in Religious Affiliation in the United States," *Sociological Analysis* 45, no. 4 (1984): 283–299; Roger W. Stump, "Regional Migration and Religious Commitment in the United States," *Journal for the Scientific Study of Religion* 23, no. 3 (1984): 292–303; Jerald C. Brauer, "Regionalism and Religion in America," *Church History* 54, no. 3 (1985): 366–378; Samuel S. Hill, "Religion and Region in America," *Annals of the American Academy of Political and Social Science* 480 (1985): 132–141; Roger W. Stump, "Regional Variations in Denominational Switching Among White Protestants," *The Professional Geographer* 39, no. 4 (1987): 438–449; Meredith B. McGuire, "Religion and Region: Sociological and Historical Perspectives," *Journal for the Scientific Study of Religion* 30, no. 4 (1991): 544–547; Philip E. Hammond, *Religion and Personal Autonomy: The Third Disestablishment in America* (Columbia: University of South Carolina Press, 1992); Catherine L. Albanese, *America: Religions and Religion*, 3rd ed. (Belmont, CA: Wadsworth, 1999), 325; Bret E. Carroll, "Reflections on Regionalism and U.S. Religious History," *Church History* 71, no. 1 (2002): 120–131; Mark Silk, "Religion and Region in American Public Life," *Journal for the Scientific Study of Religion* 44, no. 3 (2005): 265–270; Mark Silk, "Defining Religious Pluralism in America: A Regional Analysis," *Annals of the American Academy of Political and Social Science* 612 (2007): 64–81; Mark Silk and Andrew Walsh, *One Nation, Divisible: How Religious Regional Differences Shape American Politics* (Lanham, MD: Rowman & Littlefield, 2008).

41 Albanese, *America: Religions and Religion*, 325. I understand this definition of region to be free of the essentialism that for a time made many geographers highly critical of the concept. For the literature on the concept of region, see J. Nicholas Entrikin, ed., *Regions: Critical Essays in Human Geography* (Burlington, VT: Ashgate, 2008) and John A. Agnew and James S. Duncan, eds., *The Wiley-Blackwell Companion to Human Geography* (Oxford, UK: Blackwell, 2011), esp. chs. 7–10.

42 Zelinsky, "An Approach to the Religious Geography of the United States."

43 Sanford Labovitz and Ross Purdy, "Territorial Differentiation and Societal Change in the United States and Canada," *American Journal of Economics and Sociology* 29, no. 2 (1970): 127–147; William M. Newman and Peter L. Halvorson, *Patterns in Pluralism: A Portrait of American Religion* (Washington, DC: Glenmary Research Center, 1980); William M. Newman and Peter L. Halvorson, "Religion and Regional Culture: Patterns of Concentration and Change Among American Religious Denominations, 1952–1980," *Journal for the Scientific Study of Religion* 23, no. 3 (1984): 304–315; William M. Newman and Peter L. Halvorson, *Atlas of American Religion: The Denominational Era, 1776–1990* (Walnut Creek, CA: AltaMira Press, 2000), 30, 36.

44 Mark Silk, "Defining Religious Pluralism in America," 64–81; Silk and Walsh, *One Nation, Divisible*, passim.

45 Silk and Walsh, *One Nation, Divisible*, x.

46 The bleedover mentioned in the text underscores the coarseness and limits of a state-level approach to considering religion spatially, and to understanding cultural and religious regions, in the United States. Geographers Richard L. Nostrand and Lawrence E. Estaville have recently proposed "homelands"—like Silk's regions, defined culturally, but not tied to political boundaries—as "underlying today's pluralistic American society" (Nostrand and Estaville, *Homelands: A Geography of Culture*

and Place across America [Baltimore, MD: The Johns Hopkins University Press, 2001], quotation on p. xv). Some of Silk's regions bear strong resemblance to specific regional and subregional areas identified in their anthology.

47 Will Herberg, *Protestant, Catholic, Jew: An Essay in American Religious Sociology* (Garden City, NY: Doubleday, 1955); Mark Silk, "Religion and Region in American Public Life," 268.

48 Randall Balmer and Mark Silk, eds., *Religion and Public Life in the Middle Atlantic Region: Fount of Diversity* (Lanham, MD: Rowman & Littlefield, 2006), esp. 162, 163; Silk, "Defining Religious Pluralism in America," 66–68; Silk and Walsh, *One Nation, Divisible*, 2–3, 15–40 (quotation on p. 39).

49 Philip Barlow and Mark Silk, eds., *Religion and Public Life in the Midwest: America's Common Denominator?* (Lanham, MD: Rowman & Littlefield, 2004); Silk, "Defining Religious Pluralism in America," 78–79; Silk and Walsh, *One Nation, Divisible*, 11–12, 181–204.

50 Barlow and Silk, *Religion and Public Life in the Midwest*; Silk and Walsh, *One Nation, Divisible*, 181–204.

51 Silk and Walsh, *One Nation, Divisible*, 11; Silk, "Defining Religious Pluralism in America," 79.

52 Wade Clark Roof and Mark Silk, eds., *Religion and Public Life in the Pacific Region: Fluid Identities* (Lanham, MD: Rowman & Littlefield, 2005); Wade Clark Roof, "Pluralism as a Culture: Religion and Civility in Southern California," *The Annals of the American Academy of Political and Social Science* 612 (2007): 82–99; Silk, "Defining Religious Pluralism in America," 70–73; Silk and Walsh, *One Nation, Divisible*, 7–9, 109–134 (quotation on p. 11).

53 Silk and Walsh, *One Nation, Divisible*, 125.

54 Roof, "Pluralism as a Culture," 87; Silk and Walsh, *One Nation, Divisible*, 111.

55 Silk, "Defining Religious Pluralism in America," 78; Silk and Walsh, *One Nation, Divisible*, 10–11, 157–179.

56 Jan Shipps and Mark Silk, eds., *Religion and Public Life in the Mountain West: Sacred Landscapes in Transition* (Lanham, MD: Rowman & Littlefield, 2004), 139; Silk and Walsh, *One Nation, Divisible*, 226.

57 Richard L. Nostrand, "The Hispanic-American Borderland: Delimitation of an American Culture Region," *Annals of the Association of American Geographers* 60, no. 4 (1970): 638–661; Richard L. Nostrand, "The Highland-Hispano Homeland," in Nostrand and Estaville, *Homelands*, 155–167.

58 Donald W. Meinig, "The Mormon Culture Region: Strategies and Patterns in the Geography of the American West, 1847–1964," *Annals of the Association of American Geographers* 55, no. 2 (1965): 191–220; R. H. Jackson, "Religion and Landscape in the Mormon Cultural Region," *Dimensions of Human Geography: Essays on Some Familiar and Neglected Themes*, in Karl W. Butzer, ed. (Chicago: University of Chicago, Department of Geography, Research Paper 186, 1977), 100–127; Richard V. Francaviglia, *The Mormon Landscape* (New York: AMS Press, 1979); Lowell C. "Ben" Bennion, "Mormondom's Deseret Homeland," in Nostrand and Estaville, *Homelands*, 184–209; Richard V. Francaviglia, *Believing in Place: A Spiritual Geography of the Great Basin* (Reno: University of Nevada Press, 2003); Silk and Walsh, *One Nation, Divisible*, 162–169; see also Stump, *Geography of Religion*, 232–234, 262.

59 Silk and Walsh, *One Nation, Divisible*, 169.

60 Silk and Walsh, *One Nation, Divisible*, 11, 169–177; Stump, *Geography of Religion*, 359–360.

61 Patricia O'Connell Killen, "The Geography of a Minority Religion: Catholicism in the Pacific Northwest," *U.S. Catholic Historian* 18, no. 3 (2000): 51–71; Patricia O'Connell Killen and Mark Silk, eds., *Religion and Public Life in the Pacific Northwest: The None Zone* (Lanham, MD: Rowman & Littlefield, 2004); Silk, "Defining Religious Pluralism in America," 77–78; Silk and Walsh, *One Nation, Divisible*, 9–10, 135–155.

62 Silk and Walsh, *One Nation, Divisible*, 137.

63 Mark A. Shibley, "Secular but Spiritual in the Pacific Northwest," in Killen and Silk, eds., *Religion and Public Life in the Pacific Northwest*, 139–167.

64 Nicholas O'Connell, *On Sacred Ground: The Spirit of Place in the Pacific Northwest* (Seattle: University of Washington Press, 2003).

65 Charles Reagan Wilson and Mark Silk, eds., *Religion and Public Life in the South: In the Evangelical Mode* (Lanham, MD: Rowman & Littlefield, 2005); Silk, "Defining Religious Pluralism in America," 76–77; Silk and Walsh, *One Nation, Divisible*, 5–6, 63–84. The South has been considered a distinct religious region in Samuel S. Hill, *Religion and the Solid South* (Nashville, TN: Abingdon Press, 1972); John S. Reed, *The Enduring South* (Lexington, MA: Lexington Books, 1972), 57–81; Donald G. Mathews, *Religion in the Old South* (Chicago: University of Chicago Press, 1977); Ted Ownby, *Subduing Satan: Religion, Recreation, and Manhood in the Rural South, 1865–1920* (Chapel Hill: University of North Carolina Press, 1990); and Charles Reagan Wilson, *Baptized in Blood: The Religion of the Lost Cause, 1865–1920* (Athens: University of Georgia Press, 1980). See also Edward L. Ayers, Patricia Nelson Limerick, Stephen Nissenbaum, and Peter S. Onuf, *All Over the Map: Rethinking American Regions* (Baltimore, MD: The Johns Hopkins University Press, 1996), 62–82.

66 Silk and Walsh, *One Nation, Divisible*, 5.

67 Andrew Manis, "Southern Civil Religions," in Wilson and Silk, eds., *Religion and Public Life in the South*, 184–189.

68 Stump, *Geography of Religion*, 266.

69 William Lindsey and Mark Silk, eds., *Religion and Public Life in the Southern Crossroads: Showdown States* (Lanham, MD: Rowman & Littlefield, 2004); Silk, "Religion and Region in American Public Life," 268; Silk, "Defining Religious Pluralism in America," 73–76; Silk and Walsh, *One Nation, Divisible*, 6–7, 85–108.

70 Silk and Walsh, *One Nation, Divisible*, 94.

71 Silk, "Defining Religious Pluralism in America," 68–70; Silk and Walsh, *One Nation, Divisible*, 3–5, 41–62; Andrew Walsh and Mark Silk, eds., *Religion and Public Life in New England: Steady Habits Changing Slowly* (Lanham, MD: Rowman & Littlefield, 2004). See also Martyn J. Bowden, "The New England Yankee Homeland," in Nostrand and Estaville, *Homelands*, 1–23.

72 Sibley, *Geographies of Exclusion*, 90.

73 Eck, "The Multireligious Public Square," 9; Eck, *New Religious America*, 308; see also John C. Blakeman, "The Religious Geography of Religious Expression: Local Governments, Courts, and the First Amendment," *Journal of Church and State* 48, no. 2 (2006): 399–422.

74 William M. Newman, *American Pluralism: A Study of Minority Groups and Social Theory* (New York: Harper and Row, 1973), 112.

75 Rhys H. Williams, "Religion, Community, and Place: Locating the Transcendent," *Religion and American Culture: A Journal of Interpretation* 12, no. 2 (2002): 259; Jakle, Brunn, and Roseman, *Human Spatial Behavior*, 39.

76 Wuthnow, *America and the Challenges of Religious Diversity*, 2–3, 97; Williams, "The Languages of the Public Sphere," 44.

77 David H. Brown, "Altared Spaces: Afro-Cuban Religions in Cuba and the United States," in *Gods of the City: Religion and the American Urban Landscape*, Robert A. Orsi, ed. (Bloomington: Indiana University Press, 1999), 216.

78 Brown, "Altared Spaces," 157.

79 Lowell W. Livezey, "Communities and Enclaves: Where Jews, Christians, Hindus, and Muslims Share the Neighborhoods," in *Public Religion and Urban Transformation: Faith in the City*, Lowell W. Livezey, ed. (New York: New York University Press, 2000), 139. See also Emily Skop and Wei Li, "From the Ghetto to the Invisiburb: Shifting Patterns of Immigrant Settlement in Contemporary America," in *Multicultural Geographies: The Changing Racial/Ethnic Patterns of the United States*, John W. Frazier and Florence M. Margai, eds. (Binghamton, NY: Global Academic Publishing, 2003), 114, and Stump, *Geography of Religion*, 234–236.

80 Robert Orsi, "Introduction: Crossing the City Line," in Orsi, ed., *Gods of the City*, 47, 51.

81 Robert A. Orsi, "The Religious Boundaries of an In-Between People: Street *Feste* and the Problem of the Dark-Skinned Other in Italian Harlem, 1920–1990," in Orsi, ed., *Gods of the City*, 257–288; Joseph Sciorra, "'We Go Where the Italians Live': Religious Processions as Ethnic and Territorial Markers in a Multi-Ethnic Brooklyn Neighborhood," in Orsi, ed., *Gods of the City*, 310–340.

82 Orsi, "Religious Boundaries of an In-Between People," 263.

83 Myer Siemiatycki, "Contesting Sacred Urban Space," 255–270. See also Hecht, "Active versus Passive Pluralism," 144–148.

84 Stump, *Geography of Religion*, 268.

85 American Civil Liberties Union, "ACLU Returns to Court in Controversy Over Free Speech On Salt Lake City's 'Main Street Plaza,'" August 7, 2003, http://www.aclu.org/free-speech/aclu-returns-court-controversy-over-free-speech-salt-lake-citys-main-street-plaza, accessed October 10, 2011.

86 Donald E. Skinner, "UUs Fight for Free Speech in Salt Lake City," *UU World*, November/December 2003, http://www.uuworld.org/news/articles/2511.shtml, accessed October 10, 2011.

87 Donald E. Skinner, "Unitarian Church Drops Lawsuit over Mormon Plaza Deal," *UU World*, January 30, 2006, http://www.uuworld.org/news/articles/2573.shtml, accessed October 10, 2011.

88 Silk and Walsh, *One Nation, Divisible*, 168; see also Stump, *Geography of Religion*, 232.

89 Carole Mikita, "Walk of Pioneer Faiths Honors Heritage of 10 Religions in Utah," *KSL.com*, June 29, 2011, http://www.ksl.com/index.php?nid=148&sid=16178548, accessed October 14, 2011; Joseph Walker, "Utah Religious Leaders Celebrate Pioneers of Many Faiths," *Deseret News*, June 29, 2011, http://www.deseretnews.com/m/article/700148207, accessed October 14, 2011.

90 Brown, "Altared Spaces," 207–216, esp. 212, 213, 216.

91 Patrice C. Brodeur and Susan F. Morrison, "Shared Sacred Space: New Religious Communities versus the Planning and Zoning Commission of New London, CT," http://www.pluralism.org/research/articles/brodeur_article.php?from=articles_index, accessed April 12, 2008. R. Scott Hanson's study of Flushing, New York, has likewise called attention to the nature and limits of religious pluralism in densely populated and highly diverse urban settings; see "Public/Private Urban Space and the Social Limits of Religious Pluralism," http://www.ecologiesoflearning.org/images/aar/pdfs/RScottHanson.ReligiousPluralism.pdf, accessed July 25, 2008.

92 Eck, *New Religious America*, 374.

93 John R. Logan, *The New Ethnic Enclaves in America's Suburbs* (Albany, NY: Lewis Mumford Center for Comparative Urban and Regional Studies, 2001); Skop and Li, "From the Ghetto to the Invisiburb."

94 Sibley, *Geographies of Exclusion*, 39, 41.

95 S. Mitra Kalita, *Suburban Sahibs: Three Immigrant Families and Their Passage from India to America* (New Brunswick, NJ: Rutgers University Press, 2003), 10, 17–19, 28, 42.

96 Eck, "The Multireligious Public Square," 10; Eck, *A New Religious America*, 309, 310. See also Jay Johnson and Frank J. Costa, "Hindu Temple Development in the United States: Planning and Zoning Issues," *Journal of Cultural Geography* 17, no. 2 (1998): 115–123 and Joanne Punzo Waghorne, "Spaces for a New Public Presence: The Sri Siva Vishnu and Murugan Temples in Metropolitan Washington, DC," in *American Sanctuary: Understanding Sacred Spaces*, Louis P. Nelson, ed. (Bloomington: Indiana University Press, 2006), 103–127.

97 Eck, "The Multireligious Public Square," 11.

98 David W. Machacek, "Pacific Pluralism: Patterns of Change in American Culture and Social Institutions." Unpublished paper, annual meeting of the American Academy of Religion, 2002, 12; Roof, "Pluralism as a Culture," 82–83.

99 Orsi, "Crossing the City Line," 48.

100 Robert N. Bellah, "Civil Religion in America," *Daedalus* 96, no. 1 (1967): 1–21.

101 Wilbur Zelinsky, *Nation into State: The Shifting Symbolic Foundations of American Nationalism* (Chapel Hill: University of North Carolina Press, 1989). See also Edward T. Linenthal, *Sacred Ground: Americans and Their Battlefields* (Urbana: University of Illinois Press, 1991).

102 Don Mitchell, *Cultural Geography: A Critical Introduction* (Malden, MA: Blackwell, 2000), 30–31.

103 Stump, *Geography of Religion*, 284.

104 Sherrill, "American Sacred Space and the Contest of History," 322–323.

105 See, for example, Wentz, *Culture of Religious Pluralism*; Albanese, *America*, esp. 15–16, 21; Eck, *New Religious America*.

106 Orsi, "Crossing the City Line," 48.

107 Stump, *Boundaries of Faith*, 19, 194, 206; Stump, *Geography of Religion*, 266, 269–270, 285–286.

108 Quoted in Brown, "Altared Spaces," 212.

109 "Judge Suspended Over Ten Commandments," *CNN.com*, August 23, 2003, http://www.cnn.com/2003/LAW/08/22/ten.commandments, accessed February 11, 2008.

110 "Ten Commandments Judge Removed from Office," *CNN.com*, November 14, 2003, http://www.cnn.com/2003/LAW/11/13/moore.tencommandments, accessed February 11, 2008.

111 Wilson and Silk, *Religion and Public Life in the South*, 203–204. See also Derek H. Davis, "The Ten Commandments as Public Ritual," *Journal of Church and State* 44, no. 2 (2002): 221–228, and Stump, *Geography of Religion*, 269–270. The contests described in this paragraph illustrate well Catherine Albanese's suggestion that regional religious identities may emerge as a response to growing pluralism; see Albanese, *America*, 325.

112 Amanda Porterfield, "American Indian Spirituality as a Countercultural Movement," in *Religion in Native North America*, Christopher Vecsey, ed. (Moscow: University of Idaho Press, 1990), 152–164.

113 Matthew Glass, "'Alexanders All': Symbols of Conquest and Resistance at Mount Rushmore," in Chidester and Linenthal, eds., *American Sacred Space*, 161, 159, 165.

114 Glass, "'Alexanders All,'" 182.

115 Bron Taylor, "Resacralizing Earth: Pagan Environmentalism and the Restoration of Turtle Island," in Chidester and Linenthal, eds., *American Sacred Space*, 99.

116 Glass, "'Alexanders All,'" 158.

117 Mark O'Keefe, "Religious Groups Reach Out, Embrace the Environment," *The Oregonian*, February 3, 1996, A1.

118 Kristi Turnquist, "Conference Unites Environmental, Religious Groups," *The Oregonian*, November 12, 1991, D2; Kristi Turnquist, "Earth Is Called No. 1," *The Oregonian*, November 18, 1991, C1.

119 Michelle Cole, "Religious Leaders Seek Spiritual Link to the Earth," *The Oregonian*, February 5, 2000, C1.

120 O'Keefe, "Religious Groups Reach Out."

121 Ralph Maughan and Douglas Nilson, "What's Old and What's New About the Wise Use Movement," 2003, http://www.publicgood.org/reports/maughan.htm, accessed April 15, 2008; Dave Mazza, *God, Land, and Politics: The Wise Use and Christian Right Connection in 1992 Oregon Politics* (Portland, OR: Western States Center, 1993); Stephanie Hendricks, *Divine Destruction: Wise Use, Dominion Theology, and the Making of American Environmental Policy* (Brooklyn, NY: Melville House, 2005).

122 Taylor, "Resacralizing Earth," 98.

123 Jennifer Long, "American Indians Protest Expansion of Ski Resort," *The Oregonian*, August 28, 1989, D8.

124 Eric Gorski, "A Mission to Rescue Wilderness," *The Sunday Oregonian*, August 10, 1997, C4.

125 Eric Goranson, "Logging Protesters Arrested at Enola Hill," *The Oregonian*, November 28, 1992, D3; Mazza, *God, Land, and Politics*, 5.

126 Paul Rauber, "Friends of the Devil: Right-Wing Opposition to Environmental Education," *Sierra* 78, no. 2 (1993): 42. See also Stump, *The Geography of Religion*, 270.

127 Peggy Levitt, "Redefining the Boundaries of Belonging: The Transnationalization of Religious Life," in *Everyday Religion: Observing Modern Religious Lives*, Nancy Ammerman, ed. (New York: Oxford University Press, 2007), 103–120.

128 Thomas A. Tweed, *Our Lady of the Exile: Diasporic Religion at a Cuban Catholic Shrine in Miami* (New York: Oxford University Press, 1997); R. Stephen Warner and Judith G. Wittner, eds., *Gatherings in Diaspora: Religious Communities and the New Immigration* (Philadelphia: Temple University Press, 1998). See also Tweed, *Crossings and Dwellings.*

129 Peggy Levitt, "Redefining the Boundaries of Belonging," 107.

130 Roger W. Stump, "Spatial Implications of Religious Broadcasting: Stability and Change in Patterns of Belief," in *Collapsing Space and Time: Geographic Aspects of Communications and Information,* Stanley D. Brunn and Thomas R. Leinbach, eds. (London, UK: HarperCollins Academic, 2001), 354–375; Chidester and Linenthal, *American Sacred Space,* 29–30; Eck, *New Religious America,* 5; Machacek, "Pacific Pluralism," 8; Elizabeth McAlister, "Globalization and the Religious Production of Space," *Journal for the Scientific Study of Religion* 44, no. 3 (2005): 249–255; Peggy Levitt, *God Needs No Passport: Immigrants and the Changing American Religious Landscape* (New York: New Press, 2007); Stump, *The Geography of Religion,* 379–383.

131 Ulf Hannerz, "The Cultural Role of World Cities," in Anthony P. Cohen and Katsuyoshi Fukui, *Humanising the City? Social Contexts of Urban Life at the Turn of the Millennium* (Edinburgh: Edinburgh University Press, 1993), 68–69; Ulf Hannerz, "The World in Creolisation," *Africa* 57, no. 4 (1987): 546–559; Orsi, "Crossing the City Line," 36.

132 Lily Kong, "Mapping 'New' Geographies of Religion," 221–222.

133 Eck, *New Religious America,* 304; Williams, "Religion, Community, and Place," 250. See also Douglas E. Cowan, "Online U-Topia: Cyberspace and the Mythology of Placelessness," *Journal for the Scientific Study of Religion* 44, no. 3 (2005): 257–263.

134 Wilbur Zelinsky and Barrett A. Lee, "Heterolocalism: An Alternative Model of the Sociospatial Behaviour of Immigrant Ethnic Communities," *International Journal of Population Geography* 4, no. 4 (1998): 281–298.

135 Metcalf, *Making Muslim Space in North America and Europe,* 22.

136 Surinder M. Bhardwaj and Madhusudana N. Rao, "The Temple as a Symbol of Hindu Identity in America?" *Journal of Cultural Geography* 17, no. 2 (1998): 125–143.

137 Zelinsky and Lee, "Heterolocalism"; Zelinsky, *The Enigma of Ethnicity,* 132–151.

138 Susan Slyomovics, "New York City's Muslim World Day Parade," in *Nation and Migration: The Politics of Space in the South Asian Diaspora,* Peter van der Veer, ed. (Philadelphia: University of Pennsylvania Press, 1995), 157–176; Susan Slyomovics, "The Muslim World Day Parade and 'Storefront' Mosques of New York City," in *Making Muslim Space in North America and Europe,* Barbara Daly Metcalf, ed. (Berkeley: University of California Press, 1996), 205–209.

139 Eck, *New Religious America,* 87–94.

140 Annysa Johnson, "9–11 Alters Life for U.S. Muslims," *Milwaukee Journal Sentinel,* September 8, 2011, http://www.jsonline.com/features/religion/129504863.html, accessed April 9, 2012.

141 Laurie Goodstein, "Across Nation, Mosque Projects Meet Opposition," *New York Times,* August 7, 2010, http://www.nytimes.com/2010/08/08/us/08mosque.html, accessed April 9, 2012.

142 The study, which includes an interactive map, is at http://features.pewforum. org/muslim/controversies-over-mosque-and-islamic-centers-across-the-us.html, accessed October 6, 2011.

143 While every book in the recent *Religion by Region* series (2004–2008) alludes to the impact of September 11, none suggests that that impact fundamentally altered their respective regional religious cultures or pluralisms. Only the volume on the South identified a broad change after September 11, and it is an exception that proves the rule: the addition of an international anti-Islamic dimension to the region's long-standing "culture wars" pattern. See Manis, "Southern Civil Religions," 165–94.

144 Jason Tarr, "Native Americans Mark 40th Anniversary of Reclaiming Mount Rushmore," August 30, 2010, http://www.kotatv.com/Global/story.asp?S=13064126, accessed October 8, 2011.

145 Kimberly Moore Wilmoth, "Federal Judge Orders Ten Commandments Removed from Dixie Courthouse," *Gainesville Sun*, July 18, 2011.

146 Rev. Tom Goldsmith, "What about Unitarians?" *The Salt Lake Tribune*, July 29, 2011, http://www.sltrib.com/sltrib/opinion/52261737–82/unitarian-utah-church-lake. html.csp, accessed October 10, 2011.

147 Ecumenical Ministries of Oregon, "Summit Inspires Faith-Based Earth Care," 2010 http://www.emoregon.org/pdfs/INEC/2010_Earth_Care_Summit-Release.pdf, accessed October 8, 2011; Rev. Paul Klitze, "We Must Take Care of God's Creation," *Anchorage Daily News*, November 28, 2006, http://www.wolfsongnews.org/news/ Alaska_current_Events_1911.html, accessed October 11, 2011.

148 Eck, *New Religious America*, 336.

PART II | Protestantism, Catholicism, and Judaism

| Evangelicalism and Religious
Pluralism in Contemporary America:
Diversity Without, Diversity Within,
and Maintaining the Borders

WILLIAM VANCE TROLLINGER, JR.

NOT THAT MANY PEOPLE need convincing, but the 2008 American Religious
Identification Survey (ARIS) provides confirming evidence that evangelicalism in America is alive and well. In this survey, which involved 54,461 telephone interviews, the 76% of respondents who identified themselves as
Christians were asked a follow-up question: "Do you identify as a Born Again
or Evangelical Christian?" Forty-five percent answered yes. This number obviously includes a fair number of folks within "mainline" denominations and
within predominately African-American churches; more surprising, perhaps, 18.9% of American Catholics identified themselves as "born again" or
"evangelical." If one were to depend solely on the findings of the American
Religious Identification Survey, one could reasonably conclude that, when it
comes to religion, there are basically three types of folks in the United States:
Nonbelievers, Other Christians, and evangelical Christians (with only 3.9% of
Americans identifying themselves with non-Christian religious groups).[1]

It must be noted that, when it comes to evangelicals, the ARIS report is in
keeping with polling results over the past two decades, and in keeping with
what many scholars of and commentators on religion in the United States
have already noted, that is, since the mid-1970s evangelicals have been the
most dynamic, vibrant subgroup of American Protestants, with their influence
spreading far beyond the Protestant confines.[2] But this raises the question:
What do we mean by "evangelical"? Regarding the ARIS survey, the summary
report notes that—although interviewers did not supply respondents with definitions of "born again" and "evangelical" (just as they did not provide definitions of "religion," "Christian," and so on)—"born again" and "evangelical" are
"usually associated with a 'personal relationship' with Jesus Christ together
with a certain view of salvation, scripture, and missionary work." This serves
as a good working theological definition: evangelicals are Christians who

emphasize the necessity of having a particular and typically dramatic conversion experience, who hold a very high view of scripture and its authority (which often translates into language of understanding the Bible as being "literally" true), and who actively seek to share the Gospel with others.[3]

That 45% of all American Christians claim to be "evangelical" could suggest that this definition is too tidy, that some sizable minority of these Christians would not articulate their "evangelical-ness" in quite this way. That this would be the case is not surprising, particularly given that there is an inherent instability built into the term. Not only do the evangelical emphases on conversion (the "born again" experience) and the Bible as final authority (even literally true and inerrant) strongly encourage an emphasis on the individual and his/her understanding of the Christian faith, but such commitments have also militated against primary loyalty to an institution (e.g., denomination). Of course, these evangelicals have gathered together in faith communities, but these communities have always been contingent—open to being radically reshaped, abandoned, recreated by individuals or groups of individuals, with their own particular understanding of faith and the Bible. And as evangelicals move out into the world, spreading the Gospel, new ever-changing communities of various stripes of evangelicals are constantly being formed.

Given this definitional instability, given there is no "Evangelical" denomination, it is a challenge to ascertain how and where one should look to examine the impact of religious pluralism on evangelical Protestants. One approach is found in Christian Smith's 1998 sociological study, *American Evangelicalism: Embattled and Thriving*. In the best study of its kind, Smith and his collaborators used phone surveys and face-to-face interviews to conclude that self-identified evangelicals have higher levels of religious orthodoxy, confidence, and church participation than individuals in other religious traditions.[4] That is to say, evangelicals are thriving in this religiously pluralistic culture. But according to Smith, they are thriving not in spite of religious pluralism, not because they have sheltered themselves from religious pluralism. Instead, evangelicals—whose approach to the larger culture is one of "engaged orthodoxy"—are thriving *because* of religious pluralism. As Smith persuasively concludes, "it is precisely the tension-gathering confrontation between the activist, expansive, engaging evangelical subculture and the pluralistic, nonevangelical dominant culture that it inhabits—which to evangelicals seems increasingly hostile and in need of redemptive influence—that generates evangelicalism's vitality."[5]

American Evangelicalism: Embattled and Thriving provides a solid sociological foundation for understanding the impact of religious pluralism on American evangelicals. Building on Smith's work, taking as a given that evangelicalism thrives in a pluralistic environment, this essay seeks to look more closely at how evangelical opinion-shapers negotiate the issues raised by religious pluralism, how their discourse is affected by religious pluralism, and how they seek to make sense of the "increasingly hostile culture" to the broader evangelical public.[6] In this regard, and given evangelicalism's stake in maintaining an "orthodox" understanding of Christianity in its engagement with the wider culture, it makes sense to ask how evangelical theologians have responded to religious pluralism. As the Finnish theologian Veli-Matti Kärkkäinen has pointed out, "the relation of Christian faith to other living faiths" has been an "urgent issue" for evangelical theologians since the late 1980s. Kärkkäinen, a professor at Fuller Theological Seminary, asserts that some of this new-found interest grows out of the recent entrance of non-Christian faiths into the mainstream theological academy, which has resulted in evangelical scholars engaging in new and "fruitful dialogue" with scholars holding "views different from their own" on a variety of theological issues, including the theology of religions. But it is not simply an "academic" question for evangelical theologians. Because evangelicals, as Kärkkäinen puts it, "are the most mission-minded believers of all," and hence are frequently engaged in direct "encounter[s] with... followers of other religions," they are pushed to deal with the various theological questions attendant to the relationship of Christianity to other faiths.[7]

It is striking how often, especially since the early 1990s, evangelical theologians have proclaimed that the dramatic expansion of religious pluralism in the West makes these theological questions not only pressing but inescapable. "Religious pluralism feels like a new challenge for many of us because we have been culturally sheltered in the West," explained Clark H. Pinnock, a Canadian-American theologian, in *A Wideness in God's Mercy: The Finality of Jesus Christ in a World of Religions.* "It is a new experience for us to be meeting Sikhs, Muslims, and Buddhists in our streets and shops....[And it is this] religious pluralism [that] has gotten the theological pot boiling." Terry Muck, an evangelical expert on world religions, put it much more dramatically in *Those Other Religions in Your Neighborhood: Loving Your Neighbor When You Don't Know How* (a work designed for evangelical laypersons): "We Christians have been an uncontested majority in this country for so long that it is difficult to think of other religions challenging us here—in Chicago, Cedar Rapids, Lincoln, Austin, and Helena. This is, after all, America, founded on Christian principles by Northern European Protestants....The religious marketplace has [now] become very crowded....I do not think we are ready for the competition. It is time to get ready."[8]

William V. Crockett and James G. Sigountos sounded a similar alarm in *Through No Fault of Their Own: The Fate of Those Who Have Never Heard,* issued by the popular evangelical publisher Baker Book House. "Already pastors are facing many of the questions raised in this book," they wrote. "Large groups of people continually emigrate to the West, and increasingly we see them in our communities. These new immigrants have a religion, and it is not Christianity." However, they went on to note that because the "pluralistic nature of modern society decrees that their religion isn't so bad," and because of the American commitment to "freedom and self-determination," it "will not be easy to explain to the neighbors of these immigrants why we are trying to convert them to Christianity....It will be [very] difficult to explain why we are being 'intolerant.'"[9] Crockett and Sigountos summarize nicely an argument often made—explicitly or implicitly—by evangelical theologians and scholars grappling with the question of religious pluralism: not only are folks who hold to non-Christian faiths flooding America and the West, but governmental and legal structures that protect (even encourage) such religious pluralism combined with a "postmodern" culture that prizes pluralism for its own sake make it very difficult for Christians to make the case for the Truth of the Gospel, much less claim that other religions are wrong or that other religions will lead their adherents to hell.[10]

In *Four Views on Salvation in a Pluralistic World* Dennis Okholm (Azusa Pacific University) and Timothy Phillips (Wheaton College) declared: "Western societies demand that everyone assume [a] relativistic attitude so that each religion must treat the others as if they have salvific access to God. Popularly we call this political correctness."[11] This question of "salvific access to God" has preoccupied evangelical theologians at least since the early 1990s. As Kärkkäinen has observed, the "basic debate is about whether hope for eternal life can be extended beyond the borders of (confessing) Christians." Not only is there no traction among evangelical scholars for a pluralistic theology that "posits a 'rough parity' between religions," but all evangelical theologians agree on "the uniqueness of Christ" and "the biblical mandate of carrying on mission to all people." Despite (or perhaps because of) this consensus, Okholm and Phillips described "the debate within the evangelical academy regarding salvation and the unevangelized" as "fierce and intense."[12] On one side are theologians—Clark Pinnock and John Sanders are perhaps the best known—who have come to a position that can be identified (at least within the evangelical context) as "inclusivist," in which there is granted the "possibility of [individuals] attaining salvation" by "faithfully responding to God within the light given to them apart from hearing the Gospel." But such views have often produced a harsh response and remain very much in the minority. As Kärkkäinen persuasively asserts, a strong majority of evangelical "theologians and pastors still adhere to a more or less particularist paradigm," in which "not only is salvation found in Christ, but also a person has to make a personal response of faith [in Christ] in order to be saved."[13]

In short, the question of increased religious pluralism and the concomitant legal and cultural support for such pluralism have sparked a great deal of theological ferment among evangelical scholars, but the discussion has been carried on within fairly narrow bounds, and the commitment to a conservative theological understanding of Christianity vis-à-vis other religions remains quite strong. But what happens when we move a step or two away from the theologians? What happens when we move from an academic discourse to a more popular discourse aimed at a broad evangelical public?

One of the best places to look for such opinions is within the pages of *Christianity Today*. Founded in 1956 by Billy Graham and others as part of the neo-evangelical movement within American fundamentalism, by 2008 it had (according to its website) secured a circulation of 140,000, with a readership of 294,000. From its inception *Christianity Today* sought, quite self-consiously, to be **the** evangelical periodical. "My idea," wrote Graham, "was for a magazine, aimed primarily at ministers, that would restore intellectual respectability and spiritual impact to evangelical Christianity; it would reaffirm the power of the Word of God to redeem and transform men and women."[14] Over time the magazine expanded its focus beyond the ministers and other opinion-shapers to evangelicals in the pews, moving from questions of biblical interpretation and theology to issues pertaining to popular culture, the everyday life of middle-class believers, and—to use Mark A. Noll's memorable phrase—"celebrity-driven sanctity."[15] Although there is neither clarity about what it means to be evangelical nor an evangelical denomination, *Christianity Today* comes far closer than any other media source or institution to serving as the voice of American evangelicalism, reporting to insiders what is happening within the movement while also seeking (quite self-consciously) to determine the contours and boundaries of that movement.[16]

Using one decade of *Christianity Today* (1998–2008) as our guide, we find evangelicals growing more and more comfortable with the increased diversity within Christianity itself.[17] There is little evidence of distress over what the historian Philip Jenkins describes in *The Next Christendom* as Christianity's increasingly rapid shift to becoming a religion dominated by the "Global South."[18] This contrasts strikingly with the early years of the magazine, in which there was little recognition of Christianity outside the United States and Europe, except in the sense that the non-Western world provided venues for American missionaries to do their work. However, as Noll has observed, in 1975 "*Christianity Today* . . . ran five substantial articles on the Christian situation" in India, Latin America, Africa, and China. This trend toward worldwide coverage accelerated in the following years, with frequent references appearing to Christianity outside the West. On the occasion of the 25th anniversary of *Christianity Today*, a contributor drew attention to "the changing complexion of world missions," which reflected "the emerging leadership of the churches in the Third World and the end of colonialism."[19]

By the twenty-first century the growth of a global Christianity had become a regular theme in *Christianity Today*.[20] As Christopher Wright put it in a 2007 article tellingly entitled "An Upside-Down World," at "the start of the twenty-first century at least 70% of the world's Christians live in the non-Western world," the result being that, for example, "more Christians worship in Anglican churches in Nigeria each week than in all the Episcopal and Anglican churches" in the West, and that there are "ten times more Assemblies of God members in Latin America than in the U.S."[21] As Wright and other contributors pointed out, churches from "majority world" countries such as India, Nigeria, Brazil, and even Micronesia were now sending out Christian missionaries throughout the world, even into Europe and North America.[22] South Korea alone sent "more missionaries than any country except the United States" and served as a "potent vanguard for an emerging missionary movement that [was] about to eclipse centuries of Western-dominated Protestant missions."[23]

Perhaps there was so little angst about the demise of Eurocentric Christianity because *Christianity Today* contributors cheerfully understood that the emerging global church is, indeed, an evangelical church.[24] This sense of global evangelical triumph is reflected in the 2008 "Evangelical Manifesto: A Declaration of Evangelical Identity and Public Commitment," a document signed by a number of American evangelical luminaries, including David Neff, the editor-in-chief of *Christianity Today*: "We gratefully appreciate that...the great majority of our fellow-Evangelicals are in the Global South rather than the North, and that we have recently had a fresh infusion of Evangelicals from Latin America, Africa, and Asia."[25]

In places such as Latin America the growth of evangelical Christianity often came into conflict with (and at the expense of) the traditional enemy of conservative Protestants: the Roman Catholic Church. It is thus striking that there were virtually no attacks on and very few criticisms of Catholics. To the contrary, there was a very strong sense in the pages of the contemporary *Christianity Today* that evangelicals and Catholics—at least in the United States—were in the process of forming a happy rapprochement, a development in keeping with "Evangelicals and Catholics Together: The Christian Mission in the Third Millennium," a 1994 document signed by conservative Catholics and evangelical leaders.[26] Along with *First Things* editor Richard John Neuhaus, Charles Colson—a former Nixon Administration official and *Christianity Today* editor—played a prominent role in writing this statement. It delineated the ways in which evangelicals and Catholics agreed and disagreed theologically, mapped the road ahead for future conversations, and celebrated their "growing convergence," a convergence that owed much to their "common effort" to "protect human life" and oppose the "encroaching culture of death," including "abortion on demand" as well as "euthanasia, eugenics, and population control."[27]

One could conclude that this new-found cordiality was politically driven, meant to smooth the process of Catholics and evangelicals working together on behalf of the Religious Right and the Republican Party. Such an analysis has a great deal of merit, particularly when one considers the involvement of the likes of Colson and Neuhaus, and when one takes into account that "Evangelicals and Catholics Together" remained silent on issues such as capital punishment. But politics alone does not adequately account for the very clear sense in the pages of *Christianity Today* that the old Reformation conflicts were rapidly fading away. In the 1950s and early 1960s *Christianity Today*, like many other Protestant magazines, often displayed a strong anti-Catholicism, as seen in founding-editor Carl F. H. Henry's strident editorial in the wake of John F. Kennedy's election as president: "Rome never changes, [as] she is [always] determined to make the secular government her own agents of ecclesiastical gain...in accord with her ambitious concept of Church and State."[28] Two decades later these concerns remained, but the rhetoric had been tempered somewhat. In addressing the perennial question of whether the Pope was the Antichrist, a contributor wrote: "The modern papacy still presents at least some of the Reformers' problems [as] beneath the robes of the congenial churchman is a secular ruler."[29]

By the end of the century explicit anti-Catholicism had all but disappeared from the pages of the magazine. In this regard *Christianity Today* reflected what seems to have been a growing conviction among evangelicals that Catholics, while still theologically mistaken on such issues as justification by faith, shared with them a strong commitment to traditional Christian doctrine and practice.[30] More remarkably, some evangelicals thought that they had something to learn from Catholics. In the early twenty-first century the editors twice treated readers of *Christianity Today* to Christmas cover stories on the mother of Jesus: "The Blessed Evangelical Mary" and "The Mary We Never Knew." Executive editor Timothy George, author of the first piece, suggested that, "while we may not be able to recite the rosary or kneel down before statues of Mary," it is time for evangelicals to get beyond their fear of being "accused of leanings and sympathy with Catholics" and instead "recover a fully biblical appreciation of the Blessed Virgin Mary and her role in the history of salvation."[31]

It is also significant—and further belies the notion that all of this is simply a matter of politics—that reading these ten years of *Christianity Today* could easily give one the sense that American evangelicals now have little or no interest in seeking to convert Catholics. (Whether this is because evangelicals have recast Catholics in "their own image," or because of what William L. Portier and others have referred to as the growing phenomenon of "Evangelical Catholics," it is hard to say.)[32] Regardless, the traditional evangelical emphasis on soul-winning remains strong when one goes beyond the borders of Christianity. For example, *Christianity Today* published repeated calls for evangelicals to reject the notion, articulated in 2002 in a document produced by the National Council of Synagogues and the U.S. Catholic Bishops' Committee for Ecumenical and Interreligious Affairs, that Christians should cease efforts to "seek...the conversion of the Jewish people to Christianity," given that "Jews already dwell in a saving covenant with God."[33] Instead, and in keeping with the magazine's traditional stance on evangelizing the Jews, *Christianity Today* managing editor Stan Guthrie argued in 2008 that while there is "intense...pluralistic pressure to waffle" on the idea of "the necessity of faith in Christ for salvation," and while "we continue the good works of dialogue and practical ministries among our Jewish neighbors," let us also "renew our commitment to...sensitively but forthrightly persuade them to receive the Good News."[34] Guthrie also cosigned a document called "The Gospel and the Jewish People: An Evangelical Statement," sponsored by the World Evangelical Alliance and reprinted in an unusual full-page ad in the *New York Times*: "It is out of our profound respect for Jewish people that we seek to share the good news of Jesus Christ with them, and encourage others to do the same, for we believe that salvation is only found in Jesus, the Messiah of Israel and Savior of the World."[35] In all of this there were hints—as Fuller Theological Seminary president Richard Mouw acknowledged in an article entitled "The Chosen People Puzzle"—that within evangelicalism there was some tension, perhaps even ambivalence, regarding efforts to persuade God's "chosen people" to convert to Christianity.[36]

No such tension existed when it came to evangelizing religious groups further from Christianity. Although *Christianity Today* paid some attention to the matter of converting Hindus and other non-Christians, Muslims received by

far the most evangelistic attention, especially after the September 11, 2001, terrorist attacks.[37] In fact, 9/11 seemed to have opened a door for soul-winning, a
point reflected in a letter faxed by a Pakistani-American to *Christianity Today*
columnist Philip Yancey the day following the tragedy: "The most painful discovery for me about the Islamic faith has been its concept of militancy....As I
know now, violence does have a strong precedent in Islam....Do you think I
would find loving and open-minded friends in the church?"[38] According to the
magazine, this young Muslim's interest in Christianity was not anomalous.
A 2002 cover story, "Doors into Islam," announced that Christian missionaries were experiencing "fresh momentum in the spiritual battle of presenting
the gospel to the world's 1.2 billion followers of Islam."[39] Five years later the
momentum seemed to be continuing, thanks in good part—according to a survey of 750 Muslim converts to Christianity—to the love and kindness former
Muslims had received from Christians they had encountered, as opposed to
the repressive and even violent treatment they reported having received from
other Muslims.[40]

Most of the repression and violence described in *Christianity Today*, was
violence directed against Christians. The magazine's emphasis on persecution became much more pronounced over time. In the early years it devoted
much less space to anti-Christian repression and tended to focus on persecution of Christian missionaries in communist countries. But, as Noll has
noted, as the century progressed "the drama of persecution (first by communists, then by Muslims and Hindus) became a much more dominant
theme" in *Christianity Today* and other evangelical periodicals, with increasing
emphasis "on the persecution of national believers."[41] By 2000 *Christianity
Today* had become an extraordinarily thorough chronicler of the persecution
of Christians—primarily, but not exclusively, Protestant Christians—around
the globe, with virtually every issue containing one or more stories detailing
anti-Christian acts. For example, numerous stories appeared about Buddhists
attacking and oppressing Christians in such places as Laos, Myanmar, and
Sri Lanka, as did accounts of Hindu violence against Christians in India and
Trinidad.[42] Not surprisingly, Muslims came in for the most attention. Between
1998 and 2008 there were detailed references to Muslim persecution of
Christians throughout the world, including in Afghanistan, Algeria, Egypt,
Indonesia, Iran, Kenya, Lebanon, Malaysia, Nigeria, Pakistan, the Philippines,
Sudan, and Turkey. Some of these reports focused on legal repression, as in
a 2008 article on the Algerian government's decision to enforce a law bar-
ring "non-Muslims from worshiping," which resulted in the closure of "more
than half of the...country's 50 Protestant churches."[43] Others described acts
of horrific violence, as in a 2003 article about Muslim militiamen in Sudan
who routinely gang-raped and cut off the breasts of rural Christian women,
"as an example to others that this is what will happen to you unless you convert to Islam."[44]

The message was clear: although folks around the globe hungered for the
Gospel, life for Christians in the non-Christian world remained precarious

indeed. One could thus easily imagine *Christianity Today* holding up the United States as a shining example of religious freedom for all faiths, a country where pluralism flourished. But the magazine rarely celebrated America in this way. Instead, it commonly expressed a deep ambivalence about, even a palpable discomfort with, religious pluralism at home. The dominant message stressed that, in contrast to the freedom granted by the United States to Muslims or Hindus or Buddhists, the government often limited the free exercise of Christianity—and did so in the name of religious pluralism. The magazine found much of concern to report: courts (including, on occasion, the U.S. Supreme Court) prohibiting displays of the Ten Commandments on public grounds, banning prayers before city-council meetings and high-school football games, and eliminating references to God in high-school valedictory addresses, a practice that seemed to demonstrate that "Christian students" were not "fully members of the political community."[45] In addition, some colleges and universities refused to give credit for courses from Christian high schools, blocked Christians from distributing religious tracts, employed professors who refused to write graduate-school recommendations for biology majors who rejected evolution, and "derecognized" Christian organizations on campus in the name of a "pluralism that even the pluralists admit [is] not truly enforceable."[46] From time to time local communities sought to block the building of a church, state governments removed crosses from roadside memorials, and various government officials and business leaders—afraid of giving "offense" and being charged with creating a "theocracy"—made war on Christmas. As described by the magazine, government workers and store employees were "muzzled from wishing people 'Merry Christmas,' carols [were] squelched in city holiday parades, candy canes [were] confiscated from public school classrooms," all in an effort to erase any references to Christ from the public square.[47]

Editorial writers for *Christianity Today* sometimes offered more nuanced articulations of the argument that Christians in the United States were oppressed. For example, in the aforementioned piece on Christmas the editors went on to observe that what mattered most is "not the crèche on the lawn" but "whether we're encouraging people to make room for the Christ child in their hearts." Similarly, regarding the Ten Commandments, the editors reminded readers that "heeding the Commandments is far more important than displaying them."[48] More generally, in an editorial response to the "new atheism," they made the point that while liberalism—with its emphasis on tolerance—is "vapid," it does serve as "a safeguard" against militant antitheists. In a generally favorable assessment of David Limbaugh's book, *Persecution: How Liberals are Waging War against Christianity*—"Christians should be pleased with Limbaugh's high-profile recitation of a creeping anti-Christian bias in American society"—the editors noted that the author was "too gloomy" (neglecting positive signs, such as President George W. Bush's support for faith-based social service organizations), and they criticized the publishers for the "melodramatic" book title, writing that while what Christians are going through in the United States "can be called...injustice, liberalism run amok, or discrimination," in "no way" does it "rise to the level of persecution," especially when compared to what Christians elsewhere in the world were forced to endure.[49]

One person commended the editors for their "concern for persecuted brothers and sisters abroad," but went on to opine that the discrimination American Christians faced was simply the final stage before full-blown persecution; according to another reader, this day had already arrived: "Limbaugh's book is a realistic portrayal of what many U.S. Christians face on a daily basis. I'll call it what Jesus called it: persecution."[50] Notwithstanding editorial efforts to provide nuance, much material in the pages (including in the editorial pages) of Christianity Today reinforced such readers' understanding of what it meant to be Christian in America.

Especially egregious to some contributors to Christianity Today was the government's protection, indeed promotion, of homosexuality. How could it be, they reasoned, that a legal system that forbade high-school seniors from mentioning Jesus Christ in public addresses, insisted that physicians, when asked, provide lesbians with artificial insemination? Such rulings, they feared, foreshadowed the day when Christian doctors and nurses would be "pushed out of health care" entirely. It seemed incongruous that a corporate culture that prohibited employees from saying "Merry Christmas" could, in accordance with the "diversity and tolerance propaganda promoted by [their] human resource departments," command "millions of employees... not just to tolerate homosexual behavior but also to respect and even promote it."[51] A nation that tolerated "sodomy" could not be far from "legally sanctioned polygamy, incest, pedophilia, and bestiality." A country that repudiated "historic Christianity, the Bible, the Torah, and the principles of natural law that guided us so long" had, for all practical purposes, become "a pagan state."[52]

Christianity Today rarely mentioned that Christians remained the overwhelming majority in America and displayed no awareness of what it is like to be Muslim, Jewish, Hindu, or gay in America. Instead, the magazine frequently indulged in what Martin Marty aptly described in The Protestant Voice in Religious Pluralism as a "whining, griping, moaning, whimpering, and complaining" response to pluralism, which fueled "the 'politics of resentment' and the 'politics of nostalgia'" at the heart of the Religious Right.[53]

Anxiety about the loss of Protestant dominance and the rise of religious pluralism permeated the pages of evangelicalism's flagship journal. And it is striking the degree to which this anxiety reflected the same concerns troubling evangelical theologians: how to think about other religions in a time of rapidly increasing pluralism and of governmental and cultural support for such pluralism? But all of this had to do with pluralism outside the walls of Christianity. What about the pluralism that emerged from within evangelicalism itself? Even more than for Protestantism in general, pluralism has been part of the theological DNA of American evangelicalism; one might even say that evangelicalism is ontologically pluralistic.[54]

The great centrifugal impulse of evangelicalism, unrestrained or uninhibited by much in the way of institutional constraints, gave it much of its extraordinary energy. One result was the ever-increasing array of evangelical organizations that operated outside of denominational structures. We see this at the local church level, with the extraordinary multiplication of "non-denominational" or "independent" churches (a fact that has led many commentators to talk about contemporary Protestantism as having moved into a "post-denominational" phase). But beyond the local church, we see it in the stunning multiplicity of regional and national "parachurch" organizations and campaigns, most of which have as their primary purpose the bringing of individuals to a "saving knowledge" of Jesus Christ.

To read the flagship journal of evangelicalism is to become immersed in this "parachurch" world. And it is not just well-known and firmly established organizations—such as the Billy Graham Evangelistic Association, Campus Crusade for Christ, or Focus on the Family—that have received attention in *Christianity Today*. One gets a real feel for the entrepreneurial zeal within para-church evangelicalism when one reads about the Cowboy Church movement, which seeks to bring worship services to cowboys, ranchers, and "others who enjoy western culture," and which can include barn-style churches equipped with "old kerosene lanterns" and "antique saddles" on the walls. Another outreach program, *Festival con Dios*, featured a packaged Christian music road show that ran from 2001 to 2003 and that brought to cities throughout America a one-day festival of motorcycle stunt shows, bungee jumping, climbing walls, and "sloppily dressed rock bands."[55] Still another was the Lighthouse Movement, a collection of groups from more than 200,000 local churches that in 2000 sought to "reach every person in America with prayer, friendship, and a video depicting Jesus' life" (not to be confused with "Light the Highway," a 2007 prayer campaign involving hundreds of folks alongside Interstate 35, praying to make it the "holy highway" foretold in Isaiah 35:8).[56] In the wake of the 2001 terrorist attacks, evangelicals in Maryland established Nehemiah's Watchmen, a community emergency response team that sought to combine "search and rescue" work with sharing the Gospel. "In a situation like 9/11, that's when people are seeking God the most...and we can be there and share with them," explained the founder of the group. "You don't know if you'll be with someone when they take their last breath."[57]

Such organizations and campaigns reflected the evangelical willingness to use (almost) any means and any occasion to get the Good News out to the people. Perhaps inevitably, given the lack of ecclesiological constraints, some entrepreneurs pushed against or transgressed evangelicalism's (admittedly fuzzy) doctrinal and behavioral limits, a problem that the editors of *Christianity Today*, worried about pluralism inside the evangelical camp as well as outside it, explicitly addressed.

To take one example of how *Christianity Today* monitored evangelical pluralism, in 1979 Kip McKean in Boston founded the International Churches of Christ (ICOC), an offshoot of the "non-instrumental" (no musical instruments in worship) Churches of Christ. The ICOC (sometimes referred to as the Boston Movement) engaged in aggressive evangelistic practices, such as learning the schedules of college students deemed likely to convert and waiting for them outside their classrooms. In 1997 *Christianity Today* ran a lengthy piece on the ICOC, in which the author asserted that, despite the organization's claim to be evangelical, the ICOC may "be among the most dangerous" Christian movements in America. It not only practiced extreme evangelism but claimed "to be the only true Christian church," maintaining that salvation is dependent on baptism in an ICOC church. It also required that church members submit to an intrusive form of "discipling," during which members underwent "rigorous scrutiny by local church leaders who look for signs of godly living," thus giving church leaders the opportunity to intervene in all aspects of a member's personal life.[58] Nevertheless, by 2003 the movement had recruited 185,000 members. That year *Christianity Today* published a pair of articles detailing troubles within the ICOC, including "financial mismanagement, legalism, dishonest statistical reporting, and abusive teachings." The ICOC experience prompted the magazine to warn evangelicals that "it is extremely difficult for an aberrant Christian group [such as ICOC] with such an authoritarian structure to move into mainstream evangelicalism." In the end, membership began to decline, and McKean resigned as ICOC leader.[59]

Christianity Today also intervened directly in a controversy over whether or not the so-called Local Church Movement, a small Christian sect founded by Watchman Nee in China in the 1920s that grew to an estimated 250,000 members worldwide by the twenty-first century, was truly evangelical. Although leaders of the movement characterized themselves as evangelical, critics charged that they held to such un-Christian beliefs as claiming that true Christians become "part of God" and that the Local Church was "the only true church that God is satisfied with."[60] *Christianity Today* conducted its own investigation, reporting the results in 2006: "Just to be clear, the Local Church...is not even close to being a cult....CT editors have asked Local Church leaders doctrinal questions, and their answers were straightforward and satisfying. We agree with a Fuller Theological Seminary study that concluded the Local Group represents a 'genuine, historical, biblical Christian faith in every essential aspect.'"[61]

The nutritionist and religious leader Gwen Shamblin did not fare so well. In 1990 Shamblin, whose "luminous smile, big blonde hair, and petite figure" led one observer to describe her as a "Southern Barbie doll," turned her secular weight-loss workshop program into a Christian program designed for use in churches.[62] The program spread rapidly through evangelical churches in her native Tennessee and beyond, but the movement took off in 1997 with the publication of her first book, *The Weigh Down Diet*, in which she combined evangelical theology with a weight loss program. Her gospel was simple: it does not matter what type of food you eat; what matters is recognizing the spiritual void that prompts you to overeat (an act of rebellion against God); get right with God and the pounds will disappear. Her program exploded throughout evangelical America, with her book selling over a million copies, and with 30,000 churches organizing "Weigh Down" groups that sought to reach the overweight and the spiritually deficient.[63] By the end of the century the entrepreneurial Shamblin had become an evangelical superstar. Befitting her status, *Christianity Today* featured her in a 2000 cover story. In her nuanced article, "The Weigh and the Truth," Lauren Winner wondered about the lack of nutritional guidelines in the Weigh Down program, expressed concern with Shamblin's strong suggestion that God wants Christians to be thin, and observed that—for someone who had "become such an influential voice on spiritual matters"—she "has very little theological heft behind her teachings." At the same time Winner noted that "Christian dieting programs have helped many non-Christians come to faith." She also praised Shamblin for "doing the church a great service" by "teaching people to let God—not food—meet their deepest needs" and by helping "many Christians move into deeper relationships with God."[64]

Nuance notwithstanding, the cover story reinforced the notion that Gwen Shamblin was clearly within the evangelical fold. But even as "The Weigh and the Truth" was going to press, reports began circulating that the problems with Shamblin's theology were more serious than simply a lack of "heft." Questions intensified with the revelation that in an e-mail to her followers Shamblin rejected a traditional Trinitarian understanding of God, asserting instead a hierarchy within the Trinity. Although "we believe in God, Jesus, and the Holy Spirit," she wrote, "the Bible does not use the word 'trinity'...[and] the word 'trinity' [wrongly] implies equality in leadership, or shared Lordship....God is clearly the Head."[65] As the controversy escalated some evangelical pastors ordered Weigh Down workshops out of their churches, and the evangelical publisher of Shamblin's latest book, *Out of Egypt*, canceled publication.[66] In response *Christianity Today* intervened, contacting Shamblin in order to determine if she had indeed crossed the boundaries of Christian orthodoxy. A mere seven weeks after the initial cover story, and now with "Weigh Down Heresy?" on the cover, John Kennedy, who had served as news editor from 1992 to 1999, issued the verdict. Not only were the rumors of Shamblin's heterodoxy true, but, worse, she had made it clear that she was not going to back down. "People don't care about this," she was reported as saying. "They don't care about the Trinity. This is going to pass. What the women want is weight loss. They care about their bodies being a temple and their lives turned over to the Lord. That's what my ministry is about."[67]

As Kennedy later reported, "thousands of church leaders canceled Weigh Down classes after Shamblin publicly rejected the doctrine of the Trinity." However, as the historian R. Marie Griffith has observed, "the numbers of those choosing to retain Weigh Down or start it anew were high enough for her program to retain its title as the largest Christian diet plan on the market." Shamblin responded to the furor over her theology by creating her own quasi-denomination, the Remnant Fellowship, which by 2002 comprised ninety churches throughout the United States.[68]

The evangelical emphases on a "born again" experience and the Bible as final authority—along with a very weak ecclesiology—mean that evangelicals have a great deal of freedom to tailor their faith to their needs. As Baptist historian Winthrop S. Hudson has pithily observed, the great emphasis on "faith as a one-to-one relationship between God and the individual" has the "practical effect" of "mak[ing] every man's hat his own church."[69] Thus there is an instability at the heart of evangelicalism, an instability that gives evangelicalism much of its power and entrepreneurial energy. But when this instability interacts with the ever-increasing diversity both inside and outside the boundaries of Christianity, it produces anxiety about religious pluralism. One factor fueling the effort in *Christianity Today* and other evangelical publications to shore up the walls against enemies from within and without could be a sense that many younger evangelicals do not share their elders' anxieties about religious pluralism.[70] No one knows where the next generation will take evangelicalism, but we can be certain that a thriving evangelicalism does not mean an unchanging evangelicalism.

Notes

* The author wishes to thank the following individuals for their helpful comments and criticisms on earlier drafts: Ed Agran, Jake Dorn, James Heft, Brad Kallenberg, Bill Portier, Susan Trollinger, Sandra Yocum, various colleagues in the University of Dayton History Department, and the editors.

1 Barry A. Kosmin and Ariela Keysar, "American Religious Identification Survey 2008: Summary Report" (Hartford, CT: Trinity College Program of Public Values, 2009), 2–3, 9, accessible at www.americanreligionsurvey-aris.org. For a similar estimate, see the *U.S Religious Landscape Survey*, 5, Pew Forum on Religion & Public Life, February 2008, at http://religions.pewforum.org/reports.

2 See, for example, the 2005 Gallup Poll summary of polling results since the early 1990s, at www.gallup.com/poll/20242/Another-Look-Evangelicals-America-Today.aspx.

3 This definition draws on David Bebbington's oft-cited "quadrilateral," in which he defines "evangelical" as containing a commitment to conversionism, activism, biblicism, and crucicentrism (the latter referring to an emphasis on Christ's sacrifice on the cross). David Bebbington, *Evangelicalism in Modern Britain: A History from the 1730s to the 1980s* (London: Unwin, Hyman, 1989). The phrase "born again"—often understood as a synonym for "evangelical"—suggests that "conversionism" is the most significant side of Bebbington's quadrilateral.

4 Christian Smith et al., *American Evangelicalism: Embattled and Thriving* (Chicago: University of Chicago Press, 1998), 20–66. Looking beyond evangelicals per se, Robert Wuthnow's *America and the Challenges of Religious Diversity* (Princeton, NJ: Princeton University Press, 2005) is a wonderful study of how "we as individuals and as a nation are responding to the challenges of increasing religious and cultural diversity." Wuthnow divides Christians into "spiritual shoppers," "Christian

inclusivists," and "Christian exclusivists," with 50% of "exclusivists" claiming affiliation "with an evangelical denomination" (209).

5 Smith, *American Evangelicalism*, 151. Here Smith is directly challenging the "secularization paradigm," which asserts that as moderns come into contact with contrasting religious faiths the "truth" of their own faith becomes less convincing, thus reducing levels of religious commitment.

6 Thanks to Coleman Fannin for his assistance in examining the literature on the effects of religious pluralism.

7 Veli-Matti Kärkkäinen, "Evangelical Theology and the Religions," in *The Cambridge Companion to Evangelical Theology*, Timothy Larsen and Daniel J. Treier, eds. (Cambridge, UK: Cambridge University Press, 2007), 199.

8 Clark H. Pinnock, *A Wideness in God's Mercy: The Finality of Jesus Christ in a World of Religions* (Grand Rapids, MI: Zondervan, 1992): 9, 11; Terry C. Muck, *Those Other Religions in Your Neighborhood: Loving Your Neighbor When You Don't Know How* (Grand Rapids, MI: Zondervan, 1992): 9–10. See also Irving Hexham, "Evangelical Illusions: Postmodern Christianity and the Growth of Muslim Communities in Europe and North America," in *No Other Gods Before Me?: Evangelicals and the Challenge of World Religions*, John G. Stackhouse, Jr., ed. (Grand Rapids, MI: Baker, 2001): 138; Alister E. McGrath, "A Particularist View: A Post-Enlightenment Approach," in *Four Views on Salvation in a Pluralistic World*, Dennis L. Okholm and Timothy R. Phillips, eds. (Grand Rapids, MI: Zondervan, 1995): 153–154; Harold Netland, *Encountering Religious Pluralism: The Challenge to Christian Faith and Mission* (Downers Grove, IL: InterVarsity Press, 2001), 9–11; Dennis L. Okholm and Timothy R. Phillips, "Introduction," in Okholm and Phillips, eds., *Four Views on Salvation in a Pluralistic World*, 7; John G. Stackhouse, Jr., "Preface," in Stackhouse, ed., *No Other Gods Before Me?*, 11.

9 William Crockett and James Sigountos, "Are the Heathen Really Lost?," in *Through No Fault of Their Own?: The Fate of Those Who Have Never Heard*, Crockett and Sigountos, eds. (Grand Rapids, MI: Baker, 1991): 263–264.

10 See Elias Dantas, "The Incarnation of Christ and its Implications to the Ministry and Mission of the Church," in *Christ the One and Only: A Global Affirmation of the Uniqueness of Jesus Christ*, Sung Wook Chung, ed. (Grand Rapids, MI: Baker, 2005): 16–17; McGrath, "Post-Enlightenment Approach," 151; Muck, *Those Other Religions*, 154; Netland, *Encountering Religious Pluralism*, 12–14; Pinnock, *Wideness in God's Mercy*, 9; Anthony J. Steinbronn, *Worldviews: A Christian Response to Religious Pluralism* (St. Louis: Concordia, 2007): 156–157; and Mark D. Thompson, "The Uniqueness of Christ as the Revealer of God," in Chung, ed., *Christ the One and Only*, 90.

11 Okholm and Phillips, "Introduction," 9.

12 Kärkkäinen, "Evangelical Theology and the Religions," 205–207; Okholm and Phillips, "Introduction," 12.

13 Kärkkäinen, "Evangelical Theology and the Religions," 199–207. In this regard the theologians are in keeping with evangelicals in the pews, 94% of whom believe that "the only hope for salvation is through personal faith in Jesus Christ." Christian Smith, *Christian America?: What Evangelicals Really Want* (Berkeley: University of California Press, 2000), 202. See also Wuthnow, *Challenges of Religious Diversity*,

164–165; and James M. Penning and Corwin E. Smidt, *Evangelicalism: The Next Generation* (Grand Rapids, MI: Baker Academic, 2002), 49.

14 In Paul Robbins, "Welcome," at www.christianitytoday.com/anniversary/features/welcome.html.

15 Mark A. Noll, *The New Shape of World Christianity: How American Experience Reflects Global Faith* (Downers Grove, IL: InterVarsity Press, 2009), 147. In this quotation Noll is referring both to *Christianity Today* and to other evangelical magazines over the last few decades of the twentieth century.

16 William Martin, *A Prophet with Honor: The Billy Graham Story* (New York: Morrow, 1991), 211. For a summary of *Christianity Today's* origins and history, see Douglas A. Sweeney, "*Christianity Today,*" in *Popular Religious Magazines of the United States*, P. Mark Fackler and Charles H. Lippy, eds. (Westport, CT: Greenwood, 1995), 144–151 (where one will also find the Martin quotation).

17 As will be seen below, Noll's discussion in *World Christianity* of *Christianity Today's* treatment of global Christianity over the last quarter of the twentieth century is helpful in placing *Christianity Today*, 1998–2008, in its historical context. I have also examined the 1961 and 1981 issues of *Christianity Today* to identify ways in which the magazine has changed over time. Thanks to Justus Hunter for his assistance in this regard.

18 Philip Jenkins, *The Next Christendom: The Coming of Global Christianity* (New York: Oxford University Press, 2002).

19 Noll, *World Christianity*, 132–133; J. Herbert Kane, "'The White Man's Burden' is Changing Colors," *Christianity Today* 25 (July 17, 1981): 62. See also Samuel Moffett, "The Church in Asia: Getting on the Charts," *Christianity Today* 25 (October 2, 1981): 38.

20 Noll, *World Christianity*, 133–134, 143–144.

21 Christopher J. H. Wright, "An Upside-Down World," *Christianity Today* 51 (January 2007): 42.

22 One of the most interesting examples of this is the Redeemed Christian Church of God, a Pentecostal denomination founded and headquartered in Nigeria, which has sent missionaries and has established churches in more than 100 nations; as of 2008 it had 15,000 adherents in the United States, most of them Nigerian immigrants. Andrew Rice, "Mission from Africa," *New York Times Magazine*, April 12, 2009, 30–37, 54, 57–58.

23 Mark Hutchinson, "It's a Small Church After All," *Christianity Today* 42 (November 16, 1998): 46–49; Rob Moll, "Missions Incredible," *Christianity Today* 50 (March 2006): 28, 30.

24 In *World Christianity*, 13–14, 112–113, Noll argues that global Christianity "looks more and more like the [evangelical] Christianity in North America" less "because North Americans have pushed it in this direction," and more because "the newer regions of recent Christian growth" have followed "a historical path that Americans pioneered" in the nineteenth century, when "a conversionistic, voluntaristic form of Christian faith" came to dominate the American religious landscape.

25 "An Evangelical Manifesto: A Declaration of Evangelical Identity and Public Commitment," May 2008, at www.anevangelicalmanifesto.com/media/manifesto.htm. See also "Gospel Independence," *Christianity Today* 52 (July 2008): 20–21.

26 "Evangelicals and Catholics Together: The Christian Mission in the Third Millennium," *First Things* 43 (May 1994): 15–22. This document was followed by "Evangelicals and Catholics Together: The Gift of Salvation," *Christianity Today* 41 (December 8, 1997): 35–37.

27 "Evangelicals and Catholics Together," 19.

28 Carl F. H. Henry, "Editorials," *Christianity Today* 5 (March 27, 1961): 20–21. Henry's alarmist rhetoric was easily matched by the editors of *Christian Century*; see "Editorials," *Christian Century* 78 (October 11, 1961): 1196.

29 David P. Scaer, "The Pope as Antichrist: An Anachronism?" *Christianity Today* 25 (October 23, 1981): 66.

30 [Editors], "Honest Ecumenism," *Christianity Today* 44 (October 23, 2000): 28–29; Richard Mouw, "An Open-Handed Gospel," *Christianity Today* 52 (April 2008): 44–47.

31 Timothy George, "The Blessed Evangelical Mary," *Christianity Today* 47 (December 2003): 34–39, on 36; Scot McKnight, "The Mary We Never Knew," *Christianity Today* 50 (December 2006): 26–30. McKnight concludes his article with a list of recent books and articles by evangelicals regarding Mary, including Tim Perry's *Mary for Evangelicals: Toward an Understanding of the Mother of Our Lord* (Downers Grove, IL: InterVarsity Press, 2006).

32 William Portier, "Here Come the Evangelical Catholics," *Communio* 31 (Spring 2004): 35–66.

33 Consultation of the National Council of Synagogues and the Bishops Committee for Ecumenical and Interreligious Affairs, "Reflections on Covenant and Mission," *Origins* 32 (2002): 218–224. For a discussion of the controversy this statement generated within the Catholic Church, see John Pawlikowski, "Reflections on Covenant and Mission: Forty Years After Nostra Aetate," *Cross-Currents* 56 (Winter 2007): 70–94.

34 Stan Guthrie, "Why Evangelize the Jews?" *Christianity Today* 52 (March 2008): 76. See also David Brickner, "Elephant in the Room," *Christianity Today* 48 (May 2004): 67–68. On the magazine's earlier views toward the conversion of Jews, see, for example, Kenneth S. Kantzer, "Editorials," *Christianity Today* 25 (April 24, 1981): 12–15; and Vernon Grounds, "The Delicate Diplomacy of Jewish-Christian Dialogue," *Christianity Today* 25 (April 24, 1981): 26–29.

35 *New York Times*, March 28, 2008, A13. Thanks to Myrna Gabbe of the University of Dayton Philosophy Department for bringing my attention to this advertisement.

36 Richard J. Mouw, "The Chosen People Puzzle," *Christianity Today* 45 (March 5, 2001): 70–76.

37 Andy Crouch, "Christ, My Bodhisattva," *Christianity Today* 51 (May 2007): 34–37. It should be noted that, as with Jews, there was some discussion of efforts at Christian-Muslim dialogue, which typically emphasized the necessity of evangelicals' keeping in mind the theological gulf between the two faiths. See, e.g., Jocelyn Green, "Foreign Correspondence," *Christianity Today* 52 (March 2008): 21; and Stan Guthrie, "All Monotheisms are Not Alike," *Christianity Today* 52 (November 2008): 71.

38 Philip Yancey, "Letter from a Muslim Seeker," *Christianity Today* 45 (December 3, 2001): 80.

39 Stan Guthrie, "Doors Into Islam," *Christianity Today* 46 (September 9, 2002): 35.

40 J. Dudley Woodberry, Russell G. Shubin, and G. Marks, "Why Muslims Follow Jesus," *Christianity Today* 51 (October 2007): 80–85.

41 Noll, *World Christianity*, 133, 148.

42 "'Deceitful Propaganda,'" *Christianity Today* 45 (October 1, 2001): 68 (Laos); Manpreet Singh, "Anti-Conversion Conspiracy," *Christianity Today* 48 (May 2004): 20 (Sri Lanka); Sheryl Henderson Blunt, "'Destroy the Christian Religion,'" *Christianity Today* 51 (April 2007): 20–21 (Myanmar); Mary Cagney, "Hindu, Christian Tensions Rising," *Christianity Today* 43 (March 1, 1999): 21 (Trinidad and Tobago); Manpreet Singh, "Militant Hindus Assault Christians," *Christianity Today* 45 (February 5, 2001): 24 (India); Joshua Newton, "Hindu Leaders Crack Down on Conversions," *Christianity Today* 47 (November 2003): 34 (India); "Terror in Orissa," *Christianity Today* 52 (November 2008): 22–23 (India).

43 "Undue Attention," *Christianity Today* 52 (September 2008): 16.

44 "Submitting to Islam—or Dying," *Christianity Today* 47 (October 2003): 100. For other examples, see Alex Buchan, "Hostage Drama Exposes Christians' Vulnerability," *Christianity Today* 44 (December 4, 2000): 25 (Philippines); Stan Guthrie and Yunis Khushi, "Christians Massacred," *Christianity Today* 45 (December 3, 2001): 26 (Pakistan); "Out-of-Control Clerics," *Christianity Today* 48 (July 2004): 59 (Iran); Obed Minchakpu, "A Kinder, Gentler Shari'ah?" *Christianity Today* 52 (March 2008): 24–25 (Nigeria).

45 "Hang Ten?" *Christianity Today* 44 (March 6, 2000): 36–37; "Justices Turn Down Decalogue Appeal," *Christianity Today* 45 (July 9, 2001): 15; Marshall Allen, "Watch That Invocation," *Christianity Today* 47 (August 2003): 25; Deann Alford, "Pregame Prayer Barred," *Christianity Today* 44 (August 7, 2000): 19–20; "Invalidating Valedictorians," *Christianity Today* 45 (May 21, 2001): 35.

46 Dean Nelson, "Admissions Rejected," *Christianity Today* 49 (December 2005): 22–23; Sarah Pulliam, "Reading, Writing, and Rulings" *Christianity Today* 52 (October 2008): 17; Stan Guthrie, "University Forbids 'Offensive' Tracts," *Christianity Today* 47 (October 2003): 19; Ted Olsen, "Not Recommended," *Christianity Today* 47 (April 2003): 23; Randy Bishop, "Belief Police," *Christianity Today* 44 (June 12, 2000): 24; Andy Crouch, "Campus COLLISIONS," *Christianity Today* 47 (October 2003): 60–64, on 62.

47 Ted Olsen, "There Goes the Neighborhood," *Christianity Today* 46 (December 18, 2002): 21; Karen Schmidt, "Roadside Memorials Spark Religious Freedom Dispute," *Christianity Today* 44 (April 3, 2000): 20; "You'd Better Watch Out," *Christianity Today* 50 (January 2006): 29.

48 "God Reigns—Even in Alabama," *Christianity Today* 47 (October 2003): 35; "You'd Better Watch Out," 29.

49 "The New Intolerance," *Christianity Today* 51 (February 2007): 25; "Persecution Is a Holy Word," *Christianity Today* 47 (December 2003): 32–33. David Limbaugh is Rush Limbaugh's brother.

50 "Readers Write," *Christianity Today* 48 (February 2004): 10.

51 Sarah Pulliam, "Interview with David Stevens," *Christianity Today* 52 (October 2008): 19; John W. Kennedy, "Corporate Thought Police," *Christianity Today* 48 (January 2004): 26–27.

52 Charles Colson and Anne Morse, "Sowing Confusion," *Christianity Today* 47 (October 2003): 156; Harold O. J. Brown, "A Decisive Turn to Paganism," *Christianity Today* 48 (August 2004): 40–41.

53 Marty, *Protestant Voice in Religious Pluralism*, 71–72. William R. Hutchison makes a similar argument in *Religious Pluralism in America: The Contentious History of a Founding Ideal* (New Haven, CT: Yale University Press, 2003): 219–226.

54 I am indebted to my colleague Sandra Yocum for this pithy observation.

55 Linda Owen, "Worship at the O.K. Corral," *Christianity Today* 47 (September 2003): 63; Todd Hertz, "Evangelistic Circus in a Box," *Christianity Today* 46 (October 7, 2002): 18. *Festival con Dios* worked with the Luis Palau Evangelistic Association, which continues to organize evangelistic festivals that now include a service component designed to address needs in host cities; see Tim Stafford and Eric Pulliam, "Servant Evangelism," *Christianity Today* 52 (November 2008): 42–47.

56 "The Prayer Team Next Door," *Christianity Today* 43 (October 4, 1999): 17; Gary Tuchman, "Hitting the Road (Literally) With Some Faithful," at www.cnn.com/2007/US/12/19.

57 Sharon Mager, "Quenching Worst-Case Scenarios," *Christianity Today* 46 (November 18, 2002): 57.

58 Randy Frame, "The Cost of Discipleship?" *Christianity Today* 41 (September 1, 1997): 64–67. For a helpful summary of ICOC history and commitments, see Kevin S. Wells, "International Churches of Christ," in *The Encyclopedia of the Stone-Campbell Movement*, Douglas Allen Foster and Anthony L. Dunnavent, eds. (Grand Rapids, MI: Eerdmans, 2004), 418–419. On the ICOC's intervention in the family lives of members, see Kathleen E. Jenkins, *Awesome Families: The Promise of Healing Relationships in the International Church of Christ* (New Brunswick, NJ: Rutgers University Press, 2005).

59 John W. Kennedy, "'Boston Movement' Apologizes," *Christianity Today* 47 (June 2003): 23; Timothy R. Callahan, "'Boston Movement' Founder Quits," *Christianity Today* 47 (March 2003): 26–27. In monitoring such movements the editors and reporters of *Christianity Today* were, in a sense, functioning as evangelical bishops.

60 "The Local Church," in *The Encyclopedia of Cults and New Religions*, John Ankerberg and John Weldon, eds. (Eugene, OR: Harvest House Publishing, 1999): 211–212.

61 "Loose Cult Talk," *Christianity Today* 50 (March 2006): 27. See also Mark A. Kellner, "Local Church fights for Evangelical ID Card," *Christianity Today* 47 (February 2003): 24–25. As an indication of *Christianity Today*'s importance in the evangelical world, the publisher and the authors of the *Encyclopedia* responded immediately and forcefully to the magazine's verdict; see "Readers Write," *Christianity Today* 50 (May 2006): 12, 14.

62 Lauren F. Winner, "The Weigh and the Truth," *Christianity Today* 44 (September 4, 2000): 50–58, on 50.

63 R. Marie Griffith, *Born Again Bodies: Flesh and Spirit in American Christianity* (Berkeley: University of California Press, 2004), 176–177.

64 Winner, "The Weigh and the Truth," 50–58.

65 John W. Kennedy and Todd Starnes, "Gwen in the Balance," *Christianity Today* 44 (October 23, 2000): 15. The final five words of this quotation were found

only on the online version of this article: www.christianitytoday.com/ct/2000/october23/14.15.html.

66 Between *The Weigh Down Diet* and *Out of Egypt*, Shamblin wrote *Rise Again*, which, according to Marie Griffith, "vanished from bookshelves" in the midst of this controversy. *The Weigh Down Diet*, however, continued to sell. See Griffith, *Born Again Bodies*, 3.

67 Kennedy and Starnes, "Gwen in the Balance," 15.

68 John W. Kennedy, "Gwen Shamblin's New Jerusalem," *Christianity Today* 46 (December 9, 2002): 15; Griffith, *Born Again Bodies*, 182. On reports of child abuse in the fellowship, see Corrie Cutrer, "Faith-Based Child Abuse?" *Christianity Today* 48 (April 2004): 26. Although Shamblin herself was cleared of wrongdoing, in 2007 the accused Remnant couple were sentenced to life plus 30 years in prison for the death of their child; see www.religionnewsblog.com/17829/joseph-and-sonya-smith-sentenced.

69 Winthrop Hudson, *Baptists in Transition: Individualism and Christian Responsibility* (Valley Forge, PA: Judson Press, 1979): 142.

70 This certainly seems to be the case regarding homosexuality. The 2008 "Faith in American Politics Survey: The Young and the Faithful" reported that "among young evangelicals, a majority favor either same-sex marriage (24%) or civil union (28%), compared to a majority (61%) of older evangelicals who favor no legal recognition of gay couples' relationships" (Washington DC: Faith in Public Life/Public Religion Research, 2008), at www.faithinpubliclife.org/tools/polls/faps.

| Pluralism: Notes on the American
Catholic Experience

R. Scott Appleby

THE ONE TRUE CHURCH was not fully prepared for "the American experiment in ordered liberty." For at least 13 centuries prior to Columbus's historic voyage to the new world, popes and bishops had consistently held that the Catholic Church, founded by Jesus Christ and entrusted to Peter, the first pope (Matthew 16), was in full and authoritative possession of revealed truth. Saint Cyprian of Carthage, a bishop and martyr of the heresy-rich third century of the Christian era, pithily expressed the soteriological implications of this doctrine in the phrase *extra ecclesiam nulla salus*—there is no salvation outside the Church. The embellishment stuck.

Catholics living in the United States, like Catholics everywhere, therefore believed that because there was only one correct, or orthodox, Christian way of belief and practice, everyone else—especially Protestants, who should have known better than to follow the archetypal heretic, Martin Luther, and separate themselves from Holy Mother Church—was in serious theological error. "No salvation outside of the Church" meant, further, that the Protestants were in grave danger of losing their immortal souls.

Protestants at least had a chance, however.[1] Jews seldom rated a mention, with the notable exception of the Great Prayer of the Good Friday Liturgy, which read: "Let us pray for the Jews. May the Lord our God tear the veil from their hearts, so that they also may acknowledge our Lord Jesus Christ.... May they acknowledge the light of your truth... and be brought out of darkness."

In short, the *triumphalist* (we shall overcome our enemies) and *exclusivist* (for only our way is the correct way) orientation of Catholicism is a theological and social construct with deep historical roots.[2]

As mentioned, Catholics living in the United States fully shared in this orientation. But their sensibilities, from the very beginning, were shaped not only by the catechism, but also by contact and regular interaction with non-Catholics in the religiously plural colonies and in the new nation, which enshrined religious freedom in the First Amendment of the U.S. Constitution. "The abuses that have grown among Catholics," Father John Carroll, superior of the American Catholic missions reported to his Vatican superiors in 1785, "are chiefly those which result with unavoidable intercourse with non-Catholics and the examples thense [sic] derived: namely more free intercourse between young people of opposite sexes than is compatible with chastity in mind and body; too great fondness for dances and similar amusements; and, an incredible eagerness, especially in girls, for reading love stories brought over in great quantities from Europe."[3]

And yet certain aspects of the American character grew on Catholics. Daniel Carroll, John's brother, was a delegate to the Continental Congress and the Constitutional Convention, and urged ratification of the Constitution. After being named the first American bishop by Pope Pius VI in 1789, John Carroll pledged "to preserve in the hearts [of Catholics] a warm charity and forbearance toward every other denomination of Christians, and at the same time to preserve them from that fatal and prevailing indifference which views all religions as equally acceptable to God and salutary to men."[4]

The Catholic ambivalence toward American freedoms was reflected in competing strategies of adaptation. During the nineteenth and early twentieth centuries, notes the ecclesiologist Joseph Komonchak, the Catholic Church "constructed itself as a counter-society legitimated by the counter-culture of its basic faith."[5] Dogmas and religious practices were construed to emphasize their antimodernist, antiliberal—and anti-American?—meanings. Faced with a popular uprising in Rome and the Papal States, the newly elected Pope Gregory XVI (1831–1846 as pope) stood firmly against calls for elected assemblies and lay-dominated councils of state. *Mirari vos* (1832), Gregory's encyclical "On Liberalism and Religious Indifferentism," denounced the concepts of freedom of conscience, freedom of the press, separation of church and state, and other "liberal" ideas associated with the French priest Félicité de Lamennais and his newspaper *L'Avenir.*

Such ideas flew in the face of the basic assumption of the reigning neo-scholastic ecclesiology of Catholicism, namely that the clerical, hierarchical, and monarchical structure of the Church was divinely mandated. Pope Gregory was not alone in the conviction that this social structure was to be duplicated in the temporal order. Accordingly, Catholic bishops tended to support monarchical regimes against the new democratic movements sweeping across Europe, and they affirmed the official line that the divine origin of the papacy was the basis of the pope's temporal sovereignty over the Papal States.

Subsequent popes followed Gregory's lead. In *Quanta cura* (1864), also known as "the Syllabus of [Modern] Errors," Pope Pius IX repeated Gregory XVI's attack on "the madness that freedom of conscience and of worship is the proper right of every human being and ought to be proclaimed by law and maintained in every rightly-constituted society."[6] In 1885 Pope Leo XIII reaffirmed the rejection of religious liberty in *Immortale Dei*, an encyclical explicitly focused upon "the Christian Constitution of States."

This Catholic counter-ideology was embedded in the structures of an alternate society. Catholic organizations and movements multiplied, "to ensure that Catholics would primarily associate with one another and, thus immunized from the contagion of liberalism, be equipped to undertake the battle to restore Christ's rights."[7]

This construction of modern Roman Catholicism as a besieged fortress took distinctive form in the American context. Certain political and social questions arose and recurred throughout the nineteenth century. In settling and assimilating the waves of Irish, Italian, German, Polish, and other Catholic immigrants from Western and Eastern Europe, for example, would the Catholic Church rely on the local public schools, supported in part by taxpaying American Catholics? Or would Catholics shun that Protestant system in favor of their own parochial schools? Should Catholic nurses and doctors establish separate Catholic hospitals? What languages should be spoken in Catholic parishes, schools, orphanages? Running through these debates was the underlying question: How are immigrant Catholics to become more fully American without compromising or losing their faith, which seems so closely bound to ethnic and national origins?

These debates have been studied at length elsewhere.[8] For our purposes it is important to note that a minority of influential and well-placed bishops and priests (including the nation's most prominent Catholic prelate, Cardinal James Gibbons of Baltimore) adopted a positive, if not uncritical, attitude toward the freedoms of religion, speech, and assembly guaranteed in the U.S. Constitution. In the 1880s and 1890s they promoted the notion that church-state separation, religious voluntarism, and religious pluralism constituted near-ideal conditions for the flourishing of the Catholic religion in the United States. On several key issues concerning the assimilation of immigrant Catholics into the American mainstream these progressive Catholic leaders, who came to be known as "Americanists," opposed the bishops and priests who sought to preserve the European languages among the immigrant flock, rely on foreign-born priests and missionaries, and prohibit the participation of Catholic workers in mixed-religion labor unions.

While the Americanists won important battles—Gibbons, for example, stopped the Vatican from issuing a condemnation of the Knights of Labor, the largest union of the day—they did not succeed in changing the fundamental teaching of the Church on religious freedom and democracy. Nonetheless, these "Americanizers," by establishing a precedent for cooperation with Protestant civic and religious leaders, including the U.S. presidents from Grover Cleveland to Franklin D. Roosevelt, had an important influence on the sensibilities and lives of a rising professional class of Catholic educators, lobbyists, and bureaucrats. In turn, they laid the institutional foundations for Catholicism to emerge in the early twentieth century as a fully American and patriotic public presence in the social, cultural, and political life of the nation.

The Impact of American Pluralism on Twentieth-Century Catholics

In summarizing the concrete social experience of twentieth-century American Catholics as it relates to our topic, one might say that the experience of external pluralism triggered a recovery of the Church's long-forgotten internal pluralism. Religious diversity in the surrounding society prompted Catholics to justify, and even valorize, their place in that society by retrieving examples of tolerance and accommodation from a previously suppressed past.

As Catholics increasingly worked alongside Protestants in the factories, fought alongside them in the World Wars, studied in religiously plural land-grant colleges and state universities, and began to marry non-Catholics, the older logic of separatism and superiority began to lose its once-compelling force. The generation of American Catholics who came of age during and immediately following World War II was pivotal in this regard. This was the first generation that intermarried and attended public universities in significant numbers (thanks in part to the G.I. Bill) and moved from urban immigrant enclaves to suburbia in the 1940s and 1950s.[9]

Religious ideas and evolving social practice reinforced each other. On August 8, 1949, the Holy Office (the Vatican congregation charged with interpreting Catholic doctrine) condemned as erroneous the teaching of the American priest, Leonard Feeney, that Protestants were destined to eternal punishment. Had this been a U.S. Supreme Court decision, it would be described as a landmark ruling. According to the decree of the Holy Office, the Church continues to teach *extra ecclesiam nulla salus*. However, it hastened to add, *the interpretation of this dictum must be in accordance with the Church's mind.*[10] Protestants could be saved, as theologian Gregory Baum put it in interpreting the decree, "by their unconscious desire to be Catholic."[11]

The Holy Office was paying attention to "the signs of the times." That the attitudes and practices of ordinary postwar U.S. Catholics were changing rapidly, and rather dramatically, can be inferred by examining an inter-ecclesial debate that was raging at the time on the East Coast. While this debate was conducted at a high level of intellectual acuity, the contending priests were fighting about how ordinary Catholics should be educated and trained to interact with, and to think about, non-Catholic Americans. The exchange revealed what was at stake for Catholics in their mid-century confrontation with American pluralism.

On one side of the argument stood the American Jesuit, Rev. John Courtney Murray, S.J., who was considered something of a maverick. After all, the Church had long taught that "theological error has no rights" in a properly governed (i.e., Roman Catholic) state. The practical implication of this dictum was that non-Catholics who persisted in their heresy might be compelled to forfeit the full measure of their civil and political rights. And, indeed, the Church had shown little patience with the human rights reforms and democratic regimes of the later nineteenth and early twentieth centuries. It acquiesced in the authoritative regimes and policies that governed the European, Latin American, and African nations where Catholicism was strong. In liberal democracies, anti-Catholics had little trouble turning the church's own political philosophy against it. And in postwar America, Protestant and secular elites were joining forces to oppose "an organization that is not only a church but a state within a state, and a state above a state."[12]

In 1948 Murray, then a professor of theology at Woodstock seminary in Maryland, presented a paper at a gathering of Catholic theologians entitled "Governmental Repression of Heresy," in which he contended that it was *not* the duty of a good Catholic state to repress heresy even when it was practicable to do so. The majority of Catholic authorities, following the papal teachings, opposed Murray; his adversaries included French, German, Italian, and Spanish theologians of his own religious order. In the United States the leading expert on Catholic political philosophy prior to Murray had been Monsignor John A. Ryan, known as "the Right Reverend New Dealer" for his support of Franklin Delano Roosevelt's economic policies. Having studied *Mirari vos*, Ryan had concluded in 1941 that protection and promotion of Roman Catholicism is "one of the most obvious and fundamental duties of the State."[13]

Murray's opponents had a certain logic to their position, which David Hollenbach, S.J., one of Murray's intellectual heirs, summarizes as follows:

> The Roman Catholic faith is the true religion. It is good for people to believe what is true. The state is obliged to promote Catholic belief, and wherever possible to establish Catholicism as the religion of the state. Advocates of religious freedom are denying one of the cardinal premises of Roman Catholicism: they are rejecting the absolute truth of Catholic Christianity.[14]

Murray's most prominent (and fierce) opponents in America were Joseph Clifford Fenton (1906–1969) and Francis Jeremiah Connell (1888–1967). Fenton, ordained in 1930, began his teaching career in 1934, arrived at the Catholic University of America in 1938, and became editor of the *American Ecclesiastical Review* (*AER*) in 1944, serving in that capacity until he suffered a heart attack in 1963. He published 189 articles in the *AER* alone. Connell, a Redemptorist priest ordained in 1913, taught theology for 25 years before moving to Catholic University in 1940, where he authored an astounding 641 pieces, over 500 of which were answers to questions sent by the many priests who subscribed to the journal.

Products of a marginalized church that felt the sting of discrimination and still savored of its immigrant past, Fenton and Connell promoted a theology that enabled the Catholic community to make up in self-esteem what it lacked in economic and social status. Fidelity to the church and its teachings in a largely Protestant society necessitated the construction of a network of parochial institutions paralleling those of non-Catholic society. In this regard Fenton and Connell's relentlessly dualistic conception of the church's relation to the world served to explain and reinforce the segregation of Catholicism from the mainstream American society.

It is important to note that Fenton and Connell were not only theologians, but also pastors who influenced the pastoral practices of a generation of priests, which in turn affected the religious self-understanding of millions of U.S. Catholics. These two opinion-makers were dedicated to bolstering the social, cultic, and ideological barriers that, in their view, had protected the integrity of the Catholic Church within American society. The real threat to the Catholic subculture, they believed, lay in the undiscriminating religious environment created as a consequence of the nation's experience in the Second World War.

Coinciding with the coming of age of the first generation of American Catholics after immigration restriction, the war and its aftermath led to a new social mobility, economic prosperity, and a reinvigorated nationalist ideology—trends which Catholics experienced or embraced as readily as did other Americans. As a result, the Americanization of the Catholic community was accelerating just as Fenton and Connell were assuming their duties at the Catholic University of America and the *American Ecclesiastical Review.*

During the war Catholics and Protestants alike seized upon the rise of Nazism and the dramatic collapse of France before the German onslaught as illustrations of the moral and military decrepitude of an increasingly secular West. In a deft blending of traditional jeremiad and institutional special pleading, Protestants urged the citizenry to return to religion, and thereby strengthen the republic. The personal liberties and democratic polities of the West, it was argued, had been derived from a biblical anthropology that nurtured respect for the inalienable dignity of the human person. The fragility of the democratic experiments—amply illustrated in their ineffective response to totalitarian aggression—had to be countered with a strengthening of their spiritual and moral foundations. Catholic apologists, meanwhile, had been using socialism and communism as examples of human autonomy gone awry since the nineteenth century, and it was not difficult to incorporate Nazism into the litany of ills with which to flay liberalism. Fenton seized this opportunity, arguing that the perennial philosophy of Thomism is the "great weapon of civilization" for it provides "the fundamentals upon which an enduring civilization can be based."[15]

In wartime relief efforts and pastoral work no less than in sociocultural criticism, the menacing power of a revitalized paganism required a coordinated Christian response. Intercreedal collaboration during the war led to a makeshift ecumenism, the justifications for which were left to theologians of the several cooperating Christian denominations. The exigencies of this international crisis raised a "strictly theological issue" for Catholics, which John Courtney Murray posed as follows: "Can Catholics and non-Catholics form a unity by the fact of co-operation without thereby compromising the Catholic Unity of the Church?"[16]

What would count as compromise became the crux of the bitter debate between Fenton and Connell, and Murray. The former addressed what they saw as the intertwined problems of pluralism and indifferentism (i.e., the notion that no religion is necessarily better than another) by tempering postwar ecumenism and liberalism with a heavy dose of supernatural religion (with a corresponding emphasis on the exclusive and absolute truth-claims of Roman Catholicism). The priests also worried that the postwar economic prosperity enjoyed by lay Catholics, tied as it was to their social integration, required unacceptable compromises.

The outbreak of World War II had confirmed a generalized sense among Catholic intellectuals of crisis in the social order. Murray's call for interreligious cooperation was a carefully considered response to the needs of the moment. In 1941, however, Connell, lamenting the fact that "in present-day America the frequent intermingling of Catholics with non-Catholics is inevitable," wondered whether some Catholics, "in their laudable efforts to be broadminded and charitable toward the members of non-Catholic religious bodies, are not becoming unduly tolerant toward their doctrines. Is not the pendulum swinging from bigotry to indifferentism?" The wartime mobilization of millions of Americans hailing from diverse religious backgrounds had strengthened that troublesome spirit, he explained in a later article, and the principles of latitudinarianism were becoming powerful as a result of "above all, the governmental attitude so consistently practiced in all matters pertaining to religion, that all forms of religious belief are equally good."[7]

In response Murray argued that the received Catholic teaching on religious liberty, because it was not complete, was neither permanent nor irreformable. While consistent with the Catholic teaching since St. Augustine on the coercion of heretics, Murray noted, the official position ignored apostolic and sub-apostolic writings on the priority of conscience, as well as St. Thomas Aquinas's teachings on the duty to follow conscience. The American concept of church-state separation, he contended, was vastly more congenial to Catholic principles.[18]

In challenging Catholic theologians to reconsider the received doctrine in light of insights from the secular philosophy, Murray spoke of "the growing end" of authentic Catholic teaching, the place and moment where the internal pluralism of the great tradition crystallizes into a new and transformative insight into the tradition itself. "The theological task is to trace the stages of growth of the tradition as it makes its way through history...to discern the elements of the tradition that are embedded in some historically conditioned synthesis that, as a synthesis, has become archaistic," Murray wrote. "The further task is to discern the 'growing end' of the tradition; it is normally indicated by the new question that is taking shape under the impact of the historical moment."[19]

The "new question" that had confronted the Catholic Church for over a century was the relationship between "true religion" and the modern liberal state. Murray's argument against the received teaching drew a political distinction between society and the state, defining the former as made up of many diverse communities and forms of association (e.g., families, businesses, labor unions, and churches). State absolutism and totalitarianism occurred, he believed, when the state attempted to control society rather than serve it, as constitutional government requires.

In the fifties, even before these arguments were fully developed, Murray fell into disfavor with Cardinal Alfredo Ottaviani, prefect of the Holy Office. In 1954 Murray was effectively silenced when a Jesuit censor in Rome declared that his article, "Leo XIII and Pius XII: Government and the Order of Religion," could not be published. But other developments pointed to a change in the theological climate. The Feeney affair, for example, reflected a growing reluctance among Catholic officials to denounce non-Catholics, as well as a more inclusive attitude regarding membership in the Church. It also demonstrated, writes John T. Noonan, Jr., "that the literal reading of a hallowed formula could be mistaken, that theological terms are capable of expansion, that the development of Christian doctrine required spiritual discernment."[20]

While the debates between Murray and his opponents were unfolding in America, European Catholics, having suffered under fascism and communism, were also rethinking the relationship of Christian truth to human rights. Pope Pius XI, in the 1937 encyclical *Mit brennender Sorge*, addressed to the bishops of Germany, confirmed the "fundamental fact" that every person "possesses rights given by God, which must remain safe against every attempt by the community to deny them, to abolish them, or to prevent their exercise." During World War II, Pius XII invoked "the dignity with which God at the beginning endowed the human person." Totalitarianism had left Europeans suspicious of the state, the pope observed, and yearning for government that was "more compatible with the dignity and freedom of citizens." The United Nations' adoption of the Declaration of the Rights of Man reflected this attitude, as did the new postwar nations whose constitutions protected human rights, including the right of religious freedom.

In reading these signs of the times, the popes and bishops also drew upon a theory of Christian personalism, elements of which could be found in Christian tradition. In this they were guided by the French philosopher Jacques Maritain, whose writings on the state developed themes similar to Murray's (and who in fact cited the American Jesuit). In its care for the material welfare of the community the state is superior to any individual, Maritain wrote, but in its service to the spiritual welfare the state has limits set by the transcendence of the person. This ordination beyond any material need is the basis of human freedom. The state may not intervene to coerce a person in the person's search for the truth, he held, for it is the nature of a person to seek the truth freely. Maritain spoke to and for proponents of the idea of a Christian democracy in France, Italy, Germany, Belgium, and the Netherlands; his writings were also cited by Catholics in Latin America who sought to eliminate military dictatorships.

On January 25, 1959, Pope John XXIII announced plans for an ecumenical, or worldwide, council of the Roman Catholic bishops, and solicited suggestions as to what the council should consider. In light of the fact that "controversies have arisen about the relation of the Church to the modern State," as one bishop wrote to Rome, there was a need to "supply a new conception of this relation, as the old concepts in force are rooted in political matters no longer in force."[21] In 1960 a papal commission, led by bishops from Switzerland and Belgium, drafted a preliminary document on church-state relations that stressed tolerance as a virtue and discarded the ideal of a Catholic state as the enforcer of orthodoxy. "Perhaps the time has come," Murray wrote, "when we [Americans] should endeavor to dissolve the structure of war that underlines the pluralistic society, and erect the more civilized structure of the dialogue. It would be no less sharply pluralistic, but more so, since the real pluralisms would be clarified out of their present confusion. And amid the pluralism a unity would be discernible—the unity of an orderly conversation."[22] In crafting this invitation to dialogue, directed to U.S. Protestants and Jews—as well as to fellow Catholics—Murray understood himself to be extending but not over-turning traditional Catholic teaching. He was also identifying the theological and philosophical grounds upon which Catholics could finally and fully enter the American debate about freedom, truth, the common good—and the role of religion in shaping that debate.

Owing to the influence of his patron, Cardinal Francis Spellman of New York, Murray was allowed to join the deliberations of the Second Vatican Council at a crucial juncture; he was instrumental in convincing the assem-bled bishops that religious liberty, as proposed in the draft text under discus-sion, did not endorse "indifferentism." Nor would the bishops' endorsement of religious freedom exempt the individual from the obligation to seek the truth about God, which could be found in its fullness, Catholics continued to believe, only in the Roman Catholic Church. Rather, Murray insisted, the proposed text affirmed the right of the person to the free exercise of religion according to the dictates of the person's conscience, and guaranteed the person immunity from all external coercion in such matters.

Murray and his allies carried the day: *Dignitatis Humanae* (The Declaration on Religious Freedom), promulgated on December 7, 1965, ratified the postwar development of Roman Catholic doctrine on the inviolable rights of the human person, religious liberty, and the constitutional order of society. Endorsing the approach of Maritain as well as Murray, the bishops of Vatican II declared that human beings, directed as they are to God, "transcend by their nature the ter-restrial and temporal order of things." The civil power "exceeded its limits" when it presumed to direct or impede this relationship to God. Significantly, the council declared that the right to freedom belonged to groups as well as indi-viduals, because both human nature and religion have a social dimension.[23]

Pacem in Terris ["Peace on Earth"], Pope John XXIII's 1963 encyclical on "Establishing Universal Peace in Truth, Justice, Charity and Liberty," had rea-soned within a traditional "natural law" framework. By contrast, the architects of Vatican II's Declaration on Religious Liberty engaged the Enlightenment constitutional tradition of rights and liberties which affirmed the right of reli-gious freedom. By endorsing constitutional limits on the state and including religious freedom with other human rights, the Church embraced the full range of freedoms needed in the political order for the defense of human dignity. It did not forsake natural law, but situated it within an argument that embraced constitutional ideas previously tolerated but not accepted by the Church.

This development opened the way for subsequent transformations in Catholic political philosophy and social practice. By identifying innate human dignity, rather than theological orthodoxy and church membership, as the authentic source of civil rights and political self-determination, *Dignitatis*

Humanae made connivance with authoritarian (albeit pro-Catholic) regimes untenable. By proclaiming that the great tradition's understanding of the freedom of the church and the limits of the state was compatible with democratic political institutions, it aligned the modern church with democratic polities and against all forms of totalitarianism.[24]

Not least, the new doctrine of religious liberty opened the way for a genuine embrace of religious pluralism among American Catholics.

The Vatican II Generation and Beyond

This crowning achievement of Vatican II—providing the Catholic theological foundations for the practice of religious freedom and the endorsement of religious pluralism—could not have come at a more propitious moment in U.S. history. For waves of immigrants were about to intensify the diversity of the United States, and the U.S. Catholic Church, yet again.

By abolishing the National Origins Formula that had been passed by the U.S. Congress as part of its immigration restriction program in 1924, the Immigration and Nationality Act of 1965 opened the way for the new arrivals. A massive influx of "Hispanics" (Latinos hailing from Mexico, Central and South America, or the Caribbean), 70% of whom were Roman Catholic, led the way. By 2000 Hispanics in the United States numbered 35 million, making them the nation's largest minority; today, more than one in four U.S. Catholics are of Hispanic origin. Significant numbers of Catholic immigrants also arrived after 1968 from the Philippines, Vietnam, India, Haiti, and Lebanon. These groups changed the face of American Catholicism, especially in the western and southern regions of the country. The Vietnamese American Catholic community, for example, quickly organized tightly knit parishes in Orange County, California, New Orleans, and Houston to serve more than 250,000 Vietnamese immigrants.[25]

Meanwhile, the teachings of the Second Vatican Council were changing the way most American Catholics understood their faith, not least in relation to other religions. Vatican II's Dogmatic Constitution on the Church in the Modern World (*Lumen Gentium*) describes the Church as "the people of God," in such a way as to dissolve the direct correlation between sacramental baptism and official membership in the institutional Roman Catholic Church, on the one hand, and inclusion in "God's plan of salvation," on the other:

> The one people of God is accordingly present in all the nations of the earth, and takes its citizens from all nations, for a kingdom which is not earthly in character but heavenly. All the faithful scattered throughout the world are in communion with each other in the holy Spirit so that "he who dwells in Rome knows the Indians to be his members." Since the kingdom of Christ is not of this world (see John 18:36), in establishing this kingdom the church or people of God does not detract from anyone's temporal well-being. Rather it fosters and takes to itself, in so far as they are good, people's abilities, resources and customs. In so taking them to itself it purifies, strengthens and elevates them.

Lumen Gentium goes on to acknowledge that "the church has many reasons for knowing that it is joined to the baptized who are honored by the name of Christian but do not profess the faith in its entirety or have not preserved unity of communion under the successor of Peter." In addition, "those who have not yet accepted the Gospel are related to the people of God in various ways." Indeed, for example, "the plan of salvation also includes those who acknowledge the Creator, first among whom are the Moslems." Not least, "those who, through no fault of their own, do not know the Gospel of Christ or his church, but who nevertheless seek God with a sincere heart, and, moved by grace, try in their actions to do his will as they know it through the dictates of their conscience—these too may attain eternal salvation."[26]

The institutional impact of such declarations was wide-ranging and profound. On the level of official practice and rhetoric, the post-conciliar American Church adopted a wide range of internal reforms manifesting an ecumenical spirit, and established a series of unprecedented programs of collaboration with non-Catholics. Even before Vatican II had come to a close, Protestants and Catholics founded the *Journal of Ecumenical Studies* (whose first issue was winter 1964). New forums such as the "National Workshop on Christian Unity" were established for ecumenical dialogue and cooperation, and most if not all Catholic dioceses appointed an ecumenical officer to represent the diocese at these events and to coordinate ecumenical activities locally.

The changes flowed from the top down, and from the bottom up. "On the popular level, given the ecumenical spirit of the times," writes Michael J. Agliardo, S.J., "the rationale for maintaining a vast array of parallel Catholic institutional structures began to dissipate." He cites the case of the Catholic Sociological Association, founded in 1938, which rechristened itself in 1971 as the (more inclusive) Association for the Sociology of Religion. In general, former strictures against participation in non-Catholic religious ceremonies were dropped. "Baptism in non-Catholic Christian churches was recognized as valid," Agliardo notes. "And norms for marriage with non-Catholics were developed which emphasized a supportive pastoral tone rather than a punitive one." All this made a dramatic impression on the general Catholic population.[27]

Indeed, according to survey data, the so-called Boomer Catholics, or "Vatican II Catholics," those born between 1946 and 1964, as well as a larger share of their children (so-called "Generation X"), were (and remain) far more accepting of genuine religious pluralism—embraced as a good in itself—than the Church has actually given them permission to be. (Even *Lumen Gentium* insists that the fullness of Christ's Church "subsists in" the Roman Catholic Church, and warns Catholics that turning away from full communion with the Church jeopardizes their salvation.) The conviction that God has inspired other religions, including other branches of Christianity, became widespread among Boomer Catholics, whose religious identity was shaped in part by their understanding of the reforms.

As pluralism became a fact of life for most Catholics, indices of integration, and boundary-erosion, skyrocketed. In 1960, for example, the rate of intermarriage was 34%; by 1980 nearly 40% of all Catholic marriages were "mixed" and opinion polls showed that a majority of Catholics no longer felt that "as a general rule" it was better to marry someone of their own faith.[28]

Conservative Catholic polemicists accused these Catholic "pluralists"—those who do not believe that truth is fully or exclusively present in any one religious tradition—of the error of "indifferentism" feared by Fenton and Connell. These critics lament what they see as the "abuse" of Vatican II, one symptom of which, they claim, is the widespread practice of downplaying religious differences and minimizing the impact of the acceptance of heretical views on the body politic as well as the Church.

They may have a point. Prevalent among the mainstream Catholic laity, reinforced by sectors of the clergy and religious orders, is an attitude toward religious others that could be called an "inclusivist" orientation.[29] And that orientation has deepened over time. In a national survey of Catholic parishioners conducted in the mid-1990s, 58% of pre-Vatican II Catholics "strongly agreed" that "the Catholic Church is the one true church," while only 34% of Vatican II–era Catholics strongly agreed. Only 30% of Catholics born after the conciliar period strongly agreed with that statement.[30]

In several statements "the postconciliar pope" John Paul II (1978–2005 as pope) promoted the seminal texts of Vatican II, including the Decree on Ecumenism (*Unitatis redintegratio*) and the Declaration of the Church's Relationship to Non-Christian Religions (*Nostra aetate*); and he echoed the Decree on Ecumenism's endorsement of the ecumenical movement as "fostered by the grace of the Holy Spirit, for the restoration of unity among all Christians" (#1). According to the Decree, the Catholic Church recommends ecumenical dialogue "on an equal footing" (#9), not as the possessor of the truth wishing to convert other Christians. John Paul II was even stronger in support of *Nostra aetate*'s repudiation of historic discrimination against the Jewish people on the basis of assigning them blame for the persecution of Christ and in reaffirming the declaration that the Jews remain God's chosen people.

Yet John Paul II also warned against indifferentism and a "facile" ecumenism based on an incorrect understanding of pluralism:

> A legitimate plurality of positions has yielded to an undifferentiated pluralism, based upon the assumption that all positions are equally valid, which is one of today's most widespread symptoms of the lack of confidence in truth. Even certain conceptions of life coming from the East betray this lack of confidence, denying truth its exclusive character and assuming that truth reveals itself equally in different doctrines, even if they contradict one another. On this understanding, everything is reduced to opinion; and there is a sense of being adrift. While, on the one hand, philosophical thinking has succeeded in coming closer to the reality of human life and its forms of expression, it has also tended to pursue issues—existential, hermeneutical or linguistic—which ignore the radical question of truth about personal existence, about being and about God. Hence we see

among the men and women of our time, and not just in some philosophers, attitudes of widespread distrust of the human being's great capacity for knowledge. With a false modesty, people rest content with partial and provisional truths, no longer seeking to ask radical questions about the meaning and ultimate foundation of human, personal and social existence.[31]

The backlash against pluralism read as uncritical inclusivism deepened during the pontificate of Benedict XVI (2005–2013). Before his election as pope and while serving as the prefect of the Congregation for the Doctrine of the Faith (the former Holy Office), Cardinal Joseph Ratzinger issued the highly controversial *Dominus Jesus* (2000), which emphasizes the fullness of divine revelation in Jesus Christ mediated by the Catholic Church. According to the theologian Gregory Baum, the document insists that the Catholic Church "acknowledges religious pluralism only de facto (in fact), never de jure (by right). In the objective order, i) the Christian Churches are destined to the one true Church, which is the Roman Catholic Church, and ii) the world religions are destined to disappear through the conversion of their members to the Catholic faith." Nonetheless, in the present situation, Baum continues, "the Church is willing to engage in ecumenical and inter-religious dialogue because God's Spirit, acting outside the Church, is at work in these various communities. Yet Catholics engaged in such dialogue must tell their partners that if they wish to live in full communion with God, they will have to become Catholics."[32]

Ratzinger's view caused consternation in the Vatican and seemed to have little effect on the attitudes of mainstream American Catholics. Yet there has been a rearguard action, as it were, against certain aspects of the lived experience of pluralism in church and society. Conservative Catholics, for example, have been among the leaders of the political movement to enhance law enforcement against illegal immigrants living and working in the United States, to restrict legalization processes, and to strengthen security and interdiction on the border with Mexico.

The experience of internal pluralism—theological diversity within the American Catholic church—has also inspired conflict. Latino/a Catholics have complained of the continuing dominance of Irish-American Catholics in the American hierarchy and the slow growth of the number of Latino-American bishops. In Euro-American as well as Latino- and African-American parishes, the shortage of American-born priests has given rise to the importation of clergy from Nigeria, the Philippines, and elsewhere, to a decidedly mixed reception.[33]

The postconciliar practice of American Catholics affiliating only partially and occasionally with the parish and the diocese is not new, of course. U.S. Catholics have a long and often noble history of extra-parochial, extra-institutional presence and practice. But that kind of networking almost always occurred under Catholic auspices. It was rooted in, and expressive of, Church-sanctioned lay participation in labor unions, in schools, in business, in social justice witness and activism. Over the past 30 years, a pattern of alternative and sometimes expressly counter-ecclesial self-organization has become a viable option for Catholics from various cultural, class, and educational backgrounds.

No one ideology or theological perspective determines this pattern of affiliation. It can be seen in the women's movement and in Catholic feminism; in extra-ecclesial (not necessarily counter-ecclesial) Latino rituals, practices, and beliefs that exist in tension with official Church teaching; and in the willingness of young Catholics to participate in evangelical Protestant activities (e.g., retreats, Bible studies, fellowship) alongside, or in preference to, Catholic ministries.[34]

These liberalizing developments in turn have inspired "fundamentalist-like" reactions among certain sectors of the Catholic population. The selective retrieval of scriptures and traditions for ecclesial or political purposes, the hardening of religious boundaries, the energies devoted to naming and demonizing the impure or insufficiently orthodox, the facile reliance on "infallible" church authority to protect truth claims from rational scrutiny—all of these are familiar moves, designed to shore up religious authority and "truth." Scholars of religious fundamentalism have tracked these patterns in other traditions.[35]

The fundamentalist option, however, risks becoming yet another form of the ongoing individuation of religious identity—at base, it is a "make your own way" approach to spirituality and religion, dressed up in traditionalist garb. In popular culture, this form of radical individualism is now being "legitimated" by the expansion and celebration of pluralism. Ironies abound.

Notes

1 Gregory Baum, *Amazing Church: A Catholic Theologian Remembers a Half-Century of Change* (Maryknoll, NY: Orbis, 2005), 102–103.

2 The Council of Florence (1439–1445) taught that: "We firmly believe that no one existing outside the Catholic Church, neither pagans nor jews, heretics or schismatics, can participate in eternal life; instead they will go into the eternal fire 'prepared for the devil and his angels' (Matthew 25:41), unless they have become members of the Church before the end of their life." See Denzinger, *Enchiridion Symbolorum* (Rome: Herder, 1963), 1351.

3 John Carroll, "Report for the Eminent Cardinal Antonelli Concerning the State of Religion in the United States of America," in *Documents of American Catholic History*, John Tracy Ellis, ed. (Milwaukee, WI: Bruce Publishing Company, 1956), 153.

4 Quoted in Peter Guilday, *The Life and Times of John Carroll, Archbishop of Baltimore, 1735–1815* (New York: Encyclopedia Press, 1922), 384–385.

5 Joseph A. Komonchak, "Vatican II and the Encounter between Catholicism and Liberalism," in *Catholicism and Liberalism: Contributions to American Public Philosophy*, R. Bruce Douglass and David Hollenbach, eds. (New York: Cambridge University Press, 1994).

6 Pope Gregory XVI, quoted in John T. Noonan, Jr., *The Lustre of Our Country: The American Experience of Religious Freedom* (Berkeley: University of California Press, 1998), 27.

7 Komonchak, "Vatican II and the Encounter between Catholicism and Liberalism," 77.

8 See, *inter alia*, Jay P. Dolan, *The American Catholic Experience: A History from Colonial Times to the Present* (Notre Dame, IN: University of Notre Dame Press, 1992), 221–346.

9 For men born and raised Catholic the rate of marriage to non-Catholics increased from a low of about 22% for men born before 1930 to about 48% for men born during the 1950s. For women with a Catholic heritage, the rates of intermarriage range from about 31% for women born before 1930, to 46% for the 1950s cohort. William Sander, "Catholicism and Intermarriage in the United States," *Journal of Marriage and Family* 55 (1993): 1039.

10 Denzinger, *Enchiridion Symbolorum*, 3866–3873.

11 Baum, *Amazing Church*, 102–103.

12 Paul Blanshard, *American Freedom and Catholic Power* (Boston: Beacon Press, 1949), 4.

13 John A, Ryan and Francis J. Boland, *Catholic Principles of Politics* (New York: Macmillan, 1948), 319.

14 David Hollenbach, S.J. "The Growing End of an Argument," *America* 30 (1985): 364.

15 Quoted in R. Scott Appleby and John Haas, "The Last Supernaturalists: Fenton, Connell, and the Threat of Catholic Indifferentism," *U.S. Catholic Historian* 13 (Winter 1995): 23–48. This section of the present chapter is adapted from this article.

16 John Courtney Murray, S.J., "Intercreedal Co-Operation: Its Theory and Its Organization," *Theological Studies* 4 (1943): 257.

17 Francis J. Connell, C.Ss.R., "Catholics and 'Interfaith' Groups," *American Ecclesiastical Review* 105 (1941): 340–341; Francis J. Connell, "Pope Leo XIII's Message to America," *American Ecclesiastical Review* 109 (October 1943): 254.

18 Noonan, *The Lustre of Our Country*, 28; see also J. Leon Hooper, S.J., "The Theological Sources of John Courtney Murray's Ethics," in *John Courtney Murray and the Growth of Tradition*, J. Leon Hooper, S.J., and Todd David Whitmore, eds. (Kansas City, MO: Sheed and Ward, 1997), 106–125. This discussion of Murray and Vatican II is adapted from R. Scott Appleby, *The Ambivalence of the Sacred: Religion, Violence and Reconciliation* (Lanham, MD: Rowman & Littlefield, 2000), 42–47.

19 John Courtney Murray, S.J., "The Problem of Religious Freedom," *Theological Studies* 25 (1964): 569.

20 Noonan, *Lustre of Our Country*, 333.

21 Richard J. Cushing, Archbishop of Boston, quoted in Noonan, *Lustre of Our Country*, 335.

22 Murray, "The Problem of Religious Freedom," 570.

23 Appleby, *Ambivalence of the Sacred*, 47.

24 Ibid.

25 James T. Fisher, *Communion of Immigrants: A History of Catholics in America* (New York: Oxford University Press, 2007), 123.

26 "Dogmatic Constitution on the Church," in Austin Flannery, O.P., *Vatican Council II: The Basic Sixteen Documents* (Northport, NY: Costello Publishing Co., 1966), 18, 22.

27 Michael J. Agliardo, S.J., "Public Catholicism and Religious Pluralism in America: The Adaptation of a Religious Culture to the Circumstance of Diversity and Its Implications" (Ph.D dissertation, University of California, San Diego, 2008), 432.

28 James O'Toole, *The Faithful: A History of Catholics in America* (Cambridge, MA: Harvard University Press, 2008), 258.

29 The inclusivist and pluralist options are defined in Diana L. Eck, *Encountering God: A Spiritual Journey from Bozeman to Banares* (Boston: Beacon Press, 1993), 169.

30 James D. Davidson., Andrea S. Williams, Richard A. Lamanna, Jan Stenftenagel, Kathleen Maas Weigert, William J. Whalen, Patricia Wittberg, S.C., eds., *The Search for Common Ground: What Unites and Divides Catholic Americans* (Huntington, IN: Our Sunday Visitor Publishing Division, 1997), 126.

31 Pope John Paul II, *Fides et Ratio*, I:6.

32 Baum, *Amazing Church*, 119.

33 See Dean R. Hoge and Aniedi Okure, *International Priests in America: Challenges and Opportunities* (Collegeville, MN: Liturgical Press, 2006).

34 See, *inter alia,* Timothy Matovina and Gary Riebe-Estrella, eds., *Horizons of the Sacred: Mexican Traditions in U.S. Catholicism* (Ithaca, NY: Cornell University Press, 2002); Tom Beaudoin, *Virtual Faith: The Irreverent Spiritual Quest of Generation X* (San Francisco: Jossey-Bass, 1998); Robert A. Ludwig, *Reconstructing Catholicism: For A New Generation* (New York: Crossroad, 1995).

35 See, for example, "The Enclave Culture," chapter 1 in Gabriel Almond, R. Scott Appleby, and Emmanuel Sivan, *Strong Religion: The Rise of Fundamentalisms around the World* (Chicago: University of Chicago Press, 2003).

CHAPTER 6

Religious Pluralism
in American Judaism

DEBORAH DASH MOORE

THERE IS A STORY told about a wise rabbi who is approached by two Jews who have a dispute. The first Jew explains how he sees the matter. The rabbi listens patiently, nodding in agreement, and when the explanation is finished, he says, "you're right." Immediately the second Jew objects, "you didn't hear my side of the story" and launches into his account. The rabbi listens patiently, nodding in agreement, and when the explanation is finished, he says, "you're also right." Meanwhile, the rabbi's wife has overheard the dispute and she protests, "How can they both be right?" The rabbi turns to her and replies, "you know, you're right too." All three are right. Here is a form of pluralism that imagines not a binary system of truth and falsehood but one with multiple correct interpretations, or, as we might paraphrase, these and these and these are the words of the living God.

Well before Jews began arriving on the shores of North America, usually dated at 1654, Judaism was understood simultaneously as inherently plural and unitary. After all, according to tradition, Moses received two Torahs at Mt. Sinai, a written and an oral Torah. The latter was edited into two Talmuds, Palestinian and Babylonian. Yet the rabbis articulate a singular genealogy of transmission, from Moses through Joshua, and on to the prophets, the men of the Sanhedrin, and from them to the rabbis themselves.[1] Judaism's affirmation of faith, the Sh'ma, proclaims God's unity: Hear, O Israel, the Lord is our God, the Lord is One. And Jews have argued over many centuries with Christians about singular vs. plural understandings of God. In addition, many would contend that Jewish mystical tradition offers a pluralist understanding of God, Creation, and Redemption perhaps complementary to rabbinic interpretations.[2] Scholars of Judaism would multiply these examples of pluralism, pointing to important differences between Ashkenazi (or Northern and Eastern European) and Sephardi (or Spanish and Mediterranean) Jews, not to mention other less well-known groups such as Persian, Yemenite, and Iraqi Jews. With the rise of the Jewish pietist movement known as Hasidism in the late eighteenth century, Ashkenazi Jews split into two contending groups. On the one hand were the Hasidim who gathered around their charismatic leaders, and on the other hand were all those who opposed them, including many influential rabbis.[3] This division introduced additional forms of diversity within the group of Jews with the largest population at the end of the nineteenth century. These pluralistic tendencies found expression in the United States.

Types of Jewish Pluralism

In thinking, then, about Judaism and pluralism in the United States, several contexts overlap involving multiple understandings of pluralism. First there are Judaism's own diverse traditions that coexisted often uncomfortably, forced to accommodate each other in part because of external pressures on Jews as a minority group that made them assume collective responsibility vis-à-vis a non-Jewish state and society. Anti-Semitism held Jews together despite their differences. Second there are American traditions of pluralism grounded in the First Amendment to the Constitution, usually presented as freedom of religion and freedom from religion. Yet these exist within a spectrum of American civil religion that ranges from national unity to accommodation of diversity to promulgation of a Christian society.[4] Third there are efforts within twentieth-century American public culture to move from toleration to acceptance of the legitimacy of non-Christian religions as part of the distinctive fabric of American life.[5] Fourth there is most recently a willingness among some Americans to go further to speak of a positive good that comes from diverse religious traditions. We might liken this contemporary perspective on pluralism in the United States to the willingness of Jews to recognize that there are multiple, contradictory, truths within Judaism. Only in the case of contemporary American pluralism, its proponents seem ready to argue not only that there are multiple, contradictory, truths in all of the many religions that find expression in the United States, but also that this is a good thing.[6] By contrast, the rabbi in the story refrains from commenting on whether so much pluralism, so many truths, is a good to be valued rather than a fact to be accepted.

What makes the American experience particularly interesting for Jews involves the structure it provides for religious pluralism within Judaism together with a framework for situating Jews and their religious differences within the nation. Separation of church and state as well as religious tolerance and freedom influenced how Jews thought about themselves as Americans and Jews. The possibilities of national unity and religious diversity that developed largely among Protestants, even as practiced in the colonial era, gave Jews room to experiment with various types of pluralistic accommodation. "Already in the late colonial period," writes historian Jonathan Sarna, "American Judaism had begun to diverge from religious patterns that existed in Europe and the Caribbean. The American Revolution, the ratification of the Constitution, the passage of the Bill of Rights, and the nationwide democratization of religion that followed from these developments further transformed Jewish religious life." Sarna argues that the shift in the 1820s from a unified "synagogue community" to a pluralistic "community of synagogues" proved to be the "first dramatic turning point in the history of American Judaism."[7] Although he emphasizes the impact of political developments on religious trends, one could also point to the significance of Protestant religious disputes upon revolutionary politics and thus indirectly upon American Jews.

Yet even before this shift to congregationalism occurred, Jews were developing forms of pluralism responsive to their new situation in North America. For example, as Daniel Ackermann points out, in Charleston, South Carolina, the city with the largest Jewish population in the colonies at the end of the eighteenth century (roughly 500–600 Jews), members of the city's only congregation, Kahal Kadosh Beth Elohim (Holy Congregation House of God) expressed their understanding of pluralism in a new synagogue building they constructed in 1794. The synagogue's exterior, modeled upon that of one of the city's foremost churches, albeit without the steeple, proclaimed Charleston Jews' sense of place as well as their willingness to borrow styles of Christian architecture. KKBE's spire, visible on the skyline but not overreaching, symbolized the congregation's "aspirations for full integration into the city's civic and religious life." Charleston Jews identified through their architecture with the city and accepted a design demonstrating that Judaism participated in the town's public culture. The synagogue's interior, however, reflected resolution of a different pluralist dilemma. Many of KKBE's members came from Ashkenazi backgrounds, yet they wanted Jewish visitors, especially merchants of Sephardi backgrounds with whom they traded, to feel comfortable in their synagogue. Sephardi practice structured the internal space of a synagogue by placing the ark containing the Torah scrolls on the eastern wall and the *bimah*, the platform where the Torah scroll was read, close to the western wall. This placement invited a long walk from ark to bimah with the scrolls each Sabbath and holy day, allowing members of the congregation to feel the Torah's presence, God's presence, among them. Ashkenazi congregations, on the other hand, moved the bimah to the center of the synagogue, physically centering the reading of the Torah. So where should Charleston Jews locate their bimah? The answer—not quite in the middle but not at the end—split the difference between two Jewish practices. It represents an early effort at pluralist accommodation.[8]

When another generation proposed religious innovation, however, those in charge were less inclined to compromise. Thirty years after KKBE built its new synagogue, a group of young native-born men petitioned for changes in religious practices within the synagogue, changes somewhat more radical than adjusting the placement of the bimah. They requested "a more rational means of worshipping the true God" for themselves and their children. They wanted a religious service that included English as well as Hebrew, so that worshippers might understand the prayers, and a sermon on the weekly reading of the Torah, so that the American-born generation might comprehend Jewish teaching. They also desired more decorous behavior in synagogue, less talking and arguing, not to mention a shorter service. Having attended Lutheran and Catholic services in the city, they were impressed with what they had encountered and sought to emulate these Christian styles of worship. "We wish not to *overthrow*, but to *rebuild*;" they explained, "we wish not to *destroy*, but to *reform*...we wish not to *abandon* the institutions of Moses, but to *understand and observe them*." Then, in a concluding stab, the men wrote that they wished "to worship God, not as *slaves of bigotry and priestcraft*, but as the enlightened descendants of that chosen race."[9] The metaphor of slavery surely raised hackles among the congregation's leadership, which did not identify with their black slaves and would have resented a comparison of traditional Jewish religious worship with slavery. Not surprisingly then, although the petitioners included their sons, the congregational leaders turned them down. Failing to introduce religious change, the younger generation established the Reformed Society of Israelites.[10] Although it lasted less than a decade, its establishment points to another type of religious pluralism that would subsequently flourish among American Jews.

I begin with these two examples from Charleston to raise a comparative question. Why did accommodation and compromise triumph in one instance while in the other situation resistance sparked schism? Both, I would suggest, represent expressions of religious pluralism among American Jews, despite their different outcomes. In the first case, immigrant leaders seek unity through accommodation even as they incorporate Christian styles; in the second case, an American-born generation seeks change inspired in part by Christian practice and provokes opposition. Looking at Jewish religious pluralism in the United States, I think that we can identify several sources of diversity as well as multiple outcomes. Immigrant Jews brought religious traditions with them but often remained flexible in implementing Old World practices. This flexibility encouraged pluralistic practices, especially where there were not enough Jews to sustain uniformity. Of course, as the numbers of Jews multiplied, so did diversity. In the early years differences stemmed from the great traditions of Ashkenazi and Sephardi customs. By the middle of the nineteenth century, diverse practices reflected ethnic and regional traditions (for example, German Jewish and Polish Jewish and Hungarian Jewish). When mass immigration from Eastern Europe was in full swing at the end of the century, local religious traditions of towns and even occupational groups marked differences among Jews. Indeed, when Jews came from such a large city as Bialystok, time of arrival signifying how "green" and unacculturated one was mattered as well as age. Newcomers formed their own prayer groups of peers because they felt uncomfortable within more established ones. Religious practice and local identities merged.[11] Yet all of these customs remained sufficiently flexible for practitioners to make room for variations. The diversity that flourished reflected Jewish desires for inclusiveness as much as for familiarity.

When we look at generational conflicts, especially those that stem from American-born children opposing their immigrant parents, we see more sharply drawn lines. Here religious pluralism among American Jews often finds expression through alternative institutions. It is a form of structural pluralism that does not necessarily reflect ideological commitment to unity through diversity. Native-born generations of Jews with immigrant parents continually appear because mass immigration extends across most of a century, from the 1840s through 1924, when restrictive legislation radically reduced the numbers of immigrants. Responding to their situation as Americans and children of immigrants, Jews are ready to experiment with Judaism to make it more institutionally and experientially available to themselves and to their children. The Reformed Society of Israelites of Charleston may have been the first, but it is surely not the last group of Jews to seek to improve upon parental practice with idealistic innovation.

Another example of father-son conflict can be seen in the establishment of the Ethical Culture Society. In this case, its founder, Felix Adler, grew up in a Reform Jewish family. In the years after the Civil War, his father, Samuel Adler, served as rabbi of Temple Emanu-El, the leading Reform synagogue in New York City, now home to the largest Jewish population in the United States. Felix started out following in his father's footsteps, until he stumbled over the question of whether God exists. Yet rather than try to petition his father, or anyone else within Reform Judaism, for changes reflecting his doubts about God, Adler embarked on an alternative program, beginning with regular Sunday lectures in 1876. Excluding prayer and ritual, he proposed a "common ground" where all could meet. "Diversity in the creed, unanimity in the deed."[12] That was his slogan. It points to a division of belief and practice as a way of accommodating diversity. Irrespective of theology, ethical behavior was universal. "This is that practical religion from which none dissents." Supported primarily by young Jews, many of them members of Temple Emanu-El, Adler went on to build a new religious movement that initially rejected ritual and moved "beyond particularism," in historian Michael Meyer's words. When Adler constructed the hall and school to house his Ethical Culture Society, he chose a site on the west side of Central Park opposite the place where Temple Emanu-El stood on the east side of the park. Architecture metaphorically located father and son. Many argued that these forms of religious pluralism led Jews out of Judaism and into a Christian America.[13]

Adler's case raises the issue of when religious pluralism within Judaism spills over into religious pluralism without Judaism. When does schism produce not another variant of Jewish tradition but a form of practice or a set of beliefs that does not elicit consensual acceptance among Jews more widely? Are there moments when the American constitutional model of support for religious diversity fails to guide American Jews as they contemplate an increasingly pluralistic Judaism in the United States? Most Jews accepted American legal ideas about separating church from state and protecting religious freedom as descriptively and prescriptively normative. How did those norms constrain Jews? What, we might ask, are the limits of pluralism within American Judaism? An examination of indigenous American Jewish religious movements and contemporary responses to them may suggest some answers.

However, before exploring those trends, it would be helpful to review common understandings of the main forms of acceptable religious pluralism in Judaism in the United States after World War II.

The Impact of World War II

The war itself exerted a powerful impact on Jewish religious pluralism. The war structured Jewish religious pluralism and promoted a form of ecumenism among Jews of all religious backgrounds, including a sizable number of those of no religious background. Military service recruited all types of Jews from all over the United States. Integrated into the armed forces, Jews quickly learned that they were a small minority, something not necessarily part of the consciousness of Jews growing up in large cities like New York. Somewhat isolated and lonely, and eager for a taste of home, Jewish soldiers and sailors found ways to accommodate each other's religious preferences. Military standard operating procedures encouraged Jewish inclinations to compromise because its guidelines required Jews to respect each other's differences. Jewish diversity of necessity congregated under one roof since the American armed forces recognized only one category of Jew, a classification that it labeled "Hebrew." Recruits were free to have their dog tags stamped with an H or not. Those choosing to identify included secular Jews and radical Jews, Zionist Jews and Socialist Jews, as well as religious Jews of all stripes.[14]

When the United States mobilized after the bombing of Pearl Harbor, American Jews also organized to provide chaplaincy services. The reorganized Committee on Army and Navy Religious Activities (CANRA) of the Jewish Welfare Board (JWB) took responsibility for recruitment and supervision. CANRA encouraged each of the rabbinical associations to recruit chaplains. Thus rabbis trained in Reform and Conservative seminaries worked together with Orthodox rabbis. Many admitted that the armed forces introduced them to each other as well as to Christian clergy. Although there were notable tensions, serving as chaplains did stimulate a spirit of cooperation among Reform, Conservative, and Orthodox rabbis, a spirit that endured for decades after the war ended.[15]

At a time when boundaries between Orthodoxy and Conservatism were still fluid, CANRA institutionalized both Jewish denominationalism and cooperation among rabbis.[16] It established a special committee of three rabbis representing Reform, Orthodoxy, and Conservatism to answer religious questions posed by chaplains.[17] The tripartite division of Orthodox, Conservative, and Reform soon became standardized. It allowed the JWB to develop consensus on a wide range of religious matters. CANRA's director considered its abridged Jewish prayer book to be one of its most important accomplishments. "In its final war-time revision it represents a remarkable achievement," he wrote, "namely the agreement of the responsible Reform, Conservative and Orthodox rabbinate on a common prayerbook."[18] Such cooperation existed on the ground as well. "For a brief period at one time there were three Jewish Chaplains at this depot," Reform rabbi Chaplain Harold Saperstein observed in his Jewish New Year's letter to his congregants back home. "We joined in our services and though in civilian life one had served an orthodox congregation, the second a conservative, and the third a reform, we were aware not of differing interpretations but only of our common Jewishness."[19] Emanuel Rackman, an Orthodox rabbi who led a neighboring congregation in Lynbrook, agreed with Saperstein. "Jewish unity was an ideal that we not only espoused but lived," he recalled. Rackman credited his years in service for teaching him how to live in harmony with other Jews. "We learned this together in our military experience," he affirmed, "and never forgot it."[20]

Rabbi Rackman's affirmation should remind us that Jewish religious pluralism and unity remain related. Religious differences can flourish under a common identification as Jews, such as the one enforced by military service. But what Saperstein called "our common Jewishness"—a sense of membership in the Jewish people (klal yisrael), a shared history, and a commitment to ensuring a Jewish future, that is, a world with Jews—could also bind Jews together and allow for religious diversity. The salience of these values appears most vividly in the extensive array of Jewish organizations established by American Jews and usually classified by them as secular. These include not only philanthropic organizations but also social and political groups as well as economic and even neighborhood associations. Membership in these organizations depends less upon religion than upon ethnic, ideological, or social connections. Jews involved in what is often called the "organized Jewish community" need not practice Jewish religion. Indeed, the scholar and educational leader Jonathan Woocher argues that organizational life more often requires commitment to key "beliefs, myths, and rituals which legitimate" its work and mobilizes support "for its endeavors" than religious observance. Woocher claims that enough consistency can be found in these beliefs, myths, and rituals to constitute what he calls "civil Judaism." This form of Judaism flows from a recognition and acceptance of Jewish religious pluralism as well as experiences of participating in a common social order as American Jews. "Out of this sense of unity" emerges a spiritual quest: "an effort to endow the commonality which is felt and actions which are undertaken as a society with transcendent significance in their own right."[21]

Alongside Jewish organizational life which flourished after World War II, the tripartite structure of religious pluralism in Judaism crafted during the war also endured, perhaps most visibly in the Synagogue Council of America, an organization that sought to implement pluralism and unity on a national level. At its establishment in 1926, Reform, Orthodox, and Conservative Jews could identify many areas of common concern and agree upon initiatives. After World War II one of those initiatives involved promoting a day of mourning to memorialize the Holocaust. Although the Holocaust would acquire even greater public visibility and salience in the United States in the years after 1973, during the postwar decades all three religious movements sought to remember the genocide of European Jews. Poetry and prose were incorporated into memorial services for martyrs during the Day of Atonement as well as into the Passover Seder.[22] Similarly, the Council encouraged integration of the establishment of the State of Israel into the Jewish religious calendar through observing Independence Day in May. The common ground of the Synagogue Council reflected the experiences of a generation that had gone through the war and believed in Jewish religious pluralism as a positive good contributing to Jewish unity.

Yet new challenges to this considerable achievement were brewing. Some of these would come from the consolidation of the movements of Reform, Conservative, and Orthodox Jews. As these movements elaborated their institutional frameworks beyond that of a rabbinical seminary, congregational union, and rabbinical association, they simultaneously were articulating their self-conscious awareness as separate, competing movements with distinct aims.[23] Other challenges came from a generation of native-born American Jews impatient with all three major movements in Judaism, while additional challenges emerged from Jewish refugees from Nazism, recent arrivals in the United States. What had existed previously as variations on the practices of orthodoxy, conservatism, and reform gradually emerged as full-fledged alternatives to them.

Challenges to Pluralism

A group of *Haredi* Orthodox initiated these new trends with an important salvo attacking the pluralist achievements of the war years even before the fighting in the Pacific theater had ended. In June 1945 a religious court (*Bet Din*), composed of members of the Union of Orthodox Rabbis of the United States and Canada (*Agudat Harabbanim*), an organization of Yiddish-speaking rabbis, convened at the Hotel McAlpin in the heart of Manhattan's midtown. Its purpose was to pass judgment on Rabbi Mordecai M. Kaplan and the *Sabbath Prayer Book* that he had published in May. Distressed at Kaplan's radical changes in the traditional *siddur*, or prayer book, the rabbis issued a formal writ of excommunication (*herem*) against him. They accused the founder of Reconstructionism of "atheism, heresy, and disbelief in the basic tenets of Judaism."[24] Then, having declared Kaplan a heretic, they burned his prayer book, although it contained the holy name of God. Their actions, surprisingly, reverberated beyond the Jewish community due in part to a *New York Times* report.[25]

The *Agudat Harabbanim* intended the *herem* to affect only Jews who cared about such matters, Jews whom they wished to influence. It represented a political and religious act designed to strengthen their authority. These orthodox rabbis strenuously resisted Kaplan's efforts to create a pluralist, inclusive American Judaism. By condemning him, they affirmed a particularist form of Judaism that effectively emphasized the irrelevance of American values to Jewish canonical boundaries and their enforcement. They spoke only as Jews and thought they addressed only Jews within their religious orbit. Instead, their actions evoked chagrin among a much wider circle of American Jews. These Jews interpreted the ban, and particularly the burning of the prayer book, as an outrageous attack on cherished American values of freedom of speech, an attack that ironically echoed recent Nazi practices vividly etched in public consciousness. Burning the prayer book short-circuited discussions of its contents as many Jews rallied to support the American concept of freedom of religion, applying it across and within Judaism itself.[26]

Kaplan's *Sabbath Prayer Book* did radically challenge traditional orthodox understandings. Its editors, Rabbis Ira Eisenstein and Eugene Kohn, deliberately transformed a traditional *siddur* into a pedagogical vehicle. They recognized that their new prayer book disrupted Jewish uniformity but argued that other considerations took precedence. "We too are eager to preserve the Jewish worshiper's sense of oneness with Israel and the feeling of a common destiny, which the services of the traditional synagogue have always fostered," they wrote in their introduction. "But due regard must be paid to certain other considerations besides the unity of Israel and the continuity of its spiritual tradition." Indeed, they argued, unity should not depend on uniformity. "Many modern Jews have lost, or all but lost, their sense of need for worship and prayer," they observed. "They rarely attend religious services, and even when they do, their participation is perfunctory. The motions survive; the emotions have fled." Since worship sustained spiritual values among Jews, and the traditional prayer book had failed to hold Jews, "new forms of Jewish liturgical expression" were required. A prayer book had to inspire Jews to believe in God, which the editors understood meant "a Power both in and beyond nature which moves men to seek value and meaning in life." And a prayer book had to make Jews conscious of "being members of the Jewish people, that we sense our kinship with it, that we accept a personal share in its history and destiny."[27] For Kaplan, that meant Hebrew prayers, a commitment to Zionism, and a connection to Jewish culture. Thus the editors removed most of the additional Sabbath service to make room for supplementary readings. Of the 565 pages, 330 contained supplementary readings. Among these were entire services for such American holidays as Memorial Day, Independence Day, and Thanksgiving.

It was a deliberately pluralist prayer book and explicitly American, but close enough to the traditional one to be seen as a provocation by the Union of Orthodox Rabbis of the United States and Canada, who rejected pluralism as antithetical to Judaism and sought through the ban to assert their authority among observant American Jews, the ones who really mattered. In an attempt to rationalize their actions, the president of the Union indicated, "the *herem* was intended to prohibit" the prayer book's use "in synagogues where it might otherwise be confused with the traditional prayer book."[28] Unlike the Reform prayer book, which was sufficiently different from a traditional *siddur* in its format and extensive use of English, Kaplan's *Sabbath Prayer Book* possessed potential to entice believing Jews, or so they feared.

Here was an anti-pluralist posture that sought separation of practicing Jews from such religiously observant heretics as Kaplan. At the Jewish Theological Seminary, the Conservative movement's institution where Kaplan taught, the ban elicited support among several scholars. However, the Seminary's president refused to fire Kaplan. Not only did Louis Finkelstein fail to honor the ban by shunning Kaplan, he also subsequently turned to Kaplan and invited him to articulate a rationale for the Conservative movement. In the wake of the ban and book burning, Finkelstein explicitly championed pluralism among American Jews and an end to Jewish isolationism. Cooperation among Jews and between Jews and Christians in the United States would lead to the deepening of faith in Judaism and to "devotion to the true spirit of the Prophets among our neighbors."[29] The ban and book burning produced unanticipated results, stimulating the Conservative movement to reject the separation advocated by the *Aggudat Harabbanin* and to adopt Kaplan's ideas regarding religious pluralism. The Conservative movement in the postwar world embarked on extensive and diverse forms of outreach to American Jews: establishing a University of Judaism in Los Angeles, setting up a system of summer camps, creating a leadership training program, rallying the center of American Jewry under a pluralist banner. At the same time, Finkelstein encouraged the growth of a liberal Judeo-Christian tradition in the United States, one that treated Judaism as an equal to Protestantism and Catholicism.[30]

Despite the growing commitment of Conservative Jews to religious pluralism, in the 1950s Reconstructionists, followers of Rabbi Kaplan, began to organize into a loosely-knit federation of congregations and fellowships or *havurot*. Although affiliation with another (usually Conservative) congregational union was required for membership, the federation encouraged a consciousness among its members of their common goals and shared commitments. Within a decade many were ready to support a Reconstructionist Rabbinical Seminary, which opened in 1968 in Philadelphia, and to declare the independence of Reconstructionism as a religious movement rather than an intellectual tendency in American Judaism.[31] The historian Jack Wertheimer observes that becoming an independent movement propelled Reconstructionists to adopt far more radical positions than those espoused by Kaplan, in part because many of Kaplan's ideas found widespread acceptance among American Jews who remained connected to other Jewish denominations. Ironically, Wertheimer wrote, "a movement that began as the most sharply defined ideological group within American Judaism now serves as an umbrella for Jews of varying perspectives."[32]

A second visible alternative appeared in the postwar decades with the transplantation of several Hasidic sects to the United States as a result of World War II. Reluctant to leave Europe for an unkosher land, they fled Nazi persecution and murder, escaping with difficulty to foreign shores. They reconstituted themselves in the United States as best as possible, many of them settling in the borough of Brooklyn. One can look at the gradual transformation of such Brooklyn neighborhoods as Williamsburg, Crown Heights, and Borough Park as part of an increase in religious pluralism within Judaism. Single neighborhoods now hosted as many as a dozen different Hasidic sects, groups that previously had been scattered across a broad landscape and many European countries. This concentration produced both conflict and cooperation.[33]

Among the most prominent Hasidic groups are the Lubavitch Hasidim headquartered in Crown Heights, Brooklyn. The widespread success of its outreach program, Chabad, across the United States and the world gives Lubavitch Hasidim exceptional visibility. Chabad adapted new media to pursue its goals of reaching nonobservant Jews to convince them to adopt Lubavich orthodoxy. Their innovations included videotaping the talks of Rebbe Menachem M. Schneerson to extend the possibility of experiencing his presence to his devoted followers, mitzvah mobiles on city streets to invite Jews passing by to say prayers, and extensive Internet educational programs open to all. In addition, Chabad seeks to be the Jewish presence in the public square, usually through the erection of large Hanukkah menorahs as a counterpoint to Christmas trees. Schneerson's charisma stirred messianic hopes among his followers, and near the end of his life many were convinced that he was the long-awaited messiah.[34]

Both Reconstructionism and Hasidism contributed to a third form of Jewish religious pluralism that emerged in the 1960s and 1970s: Jewish Renewal. From Reconstructionism, Jewish Renewal accepted an insistence on egalitarianism between men and women along with the idea of small groups of like-minded Jews gathering not in congregations but in fellowships. From Hasidism, the renewal movement borrowed forms of worship, especially an emphasis on expressive spirituality, informality, mysticism, and wordless prayer. The combination stimulated members of the postwar generation to innovate and experiment. "Do-it-yourself Judaism" acquired many advocates (not to mention critics) in the 1970s. Eventually, feminist groups, *havurot*, neo-Hasidic groups, and new age spiritual practices would coalesce into a loosely connected but identifiable movement called Jewish Renewal. Based partially in the Conference for Alternatives in Jewish Education, partially in the national Havurah movement, and partially in a number of retreat centers with influential rabbis as leaders, Jewish Renewal introduced diverse practices into American Judaism. Its national organization, ALEPH: Alliance for Jewish Renewal, coordinates information for several dozen communities throughout the United States. Often lay-led, its peer-group structure speaks directly to an American-born and bred generation.[35]

A fourth form of Jewish religious pluralism also developed in these years, a product of suburbanization and of the writings and leadership of Rabbi Sherwin Wine. Like Felix Adler, Wine rejected belief in the God of Israel; unlike Adler, Wine created a religious movement within Judaism. Humanistic Judaism emphasizes ethics but does not avoid ritual; instead it adapts Jewish folkways, the name Mordecai Kaplan had given to *mitzvot* (commandments). Like Reconstructionism, Humanistic Judaism has separate religious structures, including a rabbinical seminary, a congregational union, and an organization of rabbis. In some ways Humanistic Judaism might be seen as building upon the practices of secular Jews who rejected Jewish theology but whose lives followed a Jewish rhythm in the years before World War II. Yet suburban living, especially its nuclear families, also contributes to Humanistic Judaism's approach.[36]

There are additional forms of Jewish religious pluralism beyond the seven mentioned here. Compared to the hundreds of thousands who identify with Reform, Orthodoxy, and Conservatism, the three indigenous American Jewish religious movements and transplanted Hasidic sects enroll very small numbers of American Jews. Rather they exert influence through their beliefs and practices.[37] Diversity flourishes among American Jews, a product of American attitudes toward religion, but the United States seems particularly hospitable to pluralist forms of Orthodox Judaism. For example, *Haredi* Jews who emphasize yeshiva study instead of secular education for men represent an influential stream. They help to create a spectrum of Orthodox behaviors, with modern Orthodoxy at the liberal end and extreme sectarianism and rejection of contemporary society at the conservative end. Although no single issue separates these different streams, the presence or absence of television might serve as a symbolic marker of attitudes toward American society that distinguishes modern orthodox from ultra-orthodox Jews. Alternatively, one could say that separatist Orthodox Jews live in American society and are apart from it, while the integrationist Orthodox live in American society and are a part of it.[38]

The rise of feminism in the 1960s and 1970s reconfigured Jewish pluralism, especially within the liberal movements. It also helped to distinguish liberal Judaisms from Orthodox Judaisms. As feminism won converts to its vision of equality and as egalitarianism in Jewish ritual and education spread, attitudes toward women increasingly sharpened boundaries between Jewish religious groups. Thus Reform, Reconstructionist, Conservative, and Humanistic Jews gradually came to recognize women as rabbis and cantors by the late 1980s.[39] At the same time, modern Orthodox Jews opened the study of sacred texts to women as equal, albeit usually separate, partners. By the beginning of the twenty-first century, a number of modern Orthodox congregations were experimenting with new forms of female religious leadership, including separate women's worship services. By contrast, those committed to stricter lines of gender separation have increased restrictions on women in the name of distinctiveness and modesty.[40] Not only women's equality but also the equality of gays and lesbians within Judaism has come to demarcate distinctions between liberal movements on the one hand and more traditional movements on the other. The 2008 decision of the Conservative movement to accept gays and lesbians for ordination aligned it with the liberal movements.

But attitudes toward pluralism itself are as important as specific denominational divisions among American Jews. Structural pluralism—the array of religious affiliation available to Jews in the United States—has not accompanied a broad ideological commitment to religious pluralism as either an inherent or instrumentalist good. The ideal of Jewish unity in diversity as embraced by rabbis who served as chaplains during World War II suffered in the past quarter century. Instead, structural pluralism exists alongside increasing stridency as spokesmen for different forms of Judaism have adopted exclusivist positions denying legitimacy to many Jews who don't share their beliefs and practices. In the name of the continuity of the Jewish people, these particularist Jews willingly write off groups of Jews with whom they disagree. For example, a full-page advertisement "Pluralism=Disunity" proclaimed loudly and clearly attitudes of an Orthodox coalition group, One People (*Am Echad*).[41] There are Orthodox rabbis, especially *Haredi* ones, who refuse to participate in local councils of rabbis because these boards include Reform and Reconstructionist rabbis. Nor do they merely boycott. They explicitly criticize more accommodating Orthodox rabbis for participating. Thus pressure is exerted to maintain a single standard for Jewish unity that does not recognize diverse practices. These attitudes accompany a rejection of the Judeo-Christian tradition, a concept that found expression during World War II. This ideal construct framed Jewish, Catholic, and Protestant cooperation in the spirit of American democratic aspirations.

Jews and the Judeo-Christian Tradition

Much as military service during World War II established a spirit of religious pluralism among American Jews as a positive good, the armed forces also invented what became known and accepted as the "Judeo-Christian tradition." It would come to express American ideals guiding the country's wartime mission. The four chaplains of three faiths—Protestant, Catholic, and Jewish—who went down to their deaths on the troop ship *Dorchester* in 1943 while worshipping together symbolized that tradition. In the face of death, religious differences no longer mattered. However one prayed, whether in English, Latin, or Hebrew, the same God heard the prayers. Similarities outweighed differences. All Americans, the "tradition" proclaimed, believed in the Fatherhood of God, the Brotherhood of Man, the individual dignity of each human being, and "positive ethical standards of right and wrong" existing apart from "the will of any man."[42] Throughout the war, chaplains would preach these values as emblematic of American democracy and of the "Judeo-Christian tradition." What had formerly been three distinct religious traditions would now become part of a collective, distinctively American "tradition." As an example, the lifeboats of the *Dorchester* carried a waterproof package of pocket-sized Protestant, Catholic, and Jewish Testaments.[43] Worshipping together in life, under stress of future and past combat, would require dedication to mutual understanding beyond sharing a lifeboat and different versions of scripture, of course. Both chaplains and enlisted men would have to work together to establish the "Judeo-Christian tradition" as standard operating procedure in the armed forces. Formidable religious differences had to be both respected and surmounted. Doctrinal disagreements had to be accommodated and subordinated to the demands of war and military requirements.[44] It would not be easy. Yet despite significant difficulties, the armed forces succeeded in creating a tripartite tradition of three fighting faiths of democracy so that by the end of the war, many Americans accepted the reality of the Judeo-Christian tradition.[45]

That framework sustained significant Jewish contributions to religious pluralism in the United States. Until the end of World War II, anti-Semitism possessed widespread respectability among Americans of varied backgrounds. Expressing dislike of Jews, excluding them from universities and suburban neighborhoods, restricting their employment opportunities and vacation choices, even vilifying them as traitors on the radio or attacking them in the streets rarely produced serious consequences. Given the small size of the Jewish population and its urban concentration in the United States, most Americans had never met a Jew, and few knew much about Judaism. The end of the war demonstrated vividly the horrors of racist anti-Semitism as reports of the murder of six million Jews reached the United States. At the same time, Jewish veterans returned home unwilling to put up with discrimination and prejudice. They were ready to join with African-Americans to fight for civil rights. Other American veterans agreed with them. It was time to improve American democracy, to stop persecuting its non-Christian minority. Each year after the war saw a decline in anti-Semitism.[46] Growing acceptance of the Judeo-Christian tradition facilitated this process because it provided a new position for Jews and Judaism within American society.

The concept of the Judeo-Christian tradition championed in the 1950s by President Dwight D. Eisenhower included Judaism as equal to Protestantism and Catholicism. Especially in the post–World War II years, Jews pressed hard for greater separation of church and state, bringing cases in the courts to take religious practices out of the public schools. Prayer, Bible reading, holiday observances, and religious invocations were successfully challenged as unconstitutional abridgements of Thomas Jefferson's famous "wall of separation."[47] Jews pushed for these changes based on their understanding of the Judeo-Christian tradition, seeking to separate what was explicitly and exclusively Christian from what was Judeo-Christian and shared equally by three faiths. As Sarna notes about American Jews' "Christmas problem" or "December dilemma," the struggles involved how to accommodate two equally compelling American demands: "the need for national unity" versus "the value of religious diversity."[48] Jews recognized that Christmas was the one American holiday with particularist roots, yet they did not just want to reject the spirit of the season. Their strategies for coping with the holiday reveal both the strengths and limitations of the Judeo-Christian tradition. Among those strategies was promotion of Hanukkah as a Jewish alternative to Christmas. But Jews were less successful in winning recognition for such important Jewish holidays as Rosh Hashanah, the Jewish New Year, except where they made up a substantial percentage of public school teachers, as in New York City.

However, the postwar Jewish consensus on the importance of separation of church and state frayed considerably in the latter decades of the twentieth century as outspoken Orthodox figures pressed for state and federal aid for parochial schools. Similarly, the Chabad practice of erecting large public expressions of Judaism, such as Hanukkah menorahs, also chipped away at long-standing Jewish preferences for a neutral public square devoid of religious symbols. Currently, American Jews argue as much with each other as with other Americans over how to maintain religious freedom for individuals and pluralism among and perhaps even within groups.[49]

The establishment of the State of Israel in 1948 and its decision to accept a chief rabbinate with two chief rabbis, one Ashkenazi and the other Sephardi, also influenced Jewish pluralism in the United States. The Israeli model does not separate religion and state, writes Jewish law into state law (especially in areas of personal status), allocates public monies to support several types of religious educational systems, and provides exemptions from military service for religious Jews. These practices limit religious pluralism in Israel and deny legitimacy to religious movements with which many American Jews affiliate.[50] In 1981, in response to efforts by Orthodox groups in Israel to extend their power to invalidate conversions to Judaism performed by non-Orthodox rabbis outside of Israel, American Jews mobilized to protest. Rabbi Gerson Cohen, Chancellor of the Jewish Theological Seminary, summed up the situation: "It is indeed ironic that the Jewish people who fled religious tyranny and persecution should have to encounter, in the Israeli government, the only democracy in the western world in which Jews are not free to practice their religion as they wish."[51]

Although American Jews were slow to export their understandings of Judaism, the 1981 controversy spurred efforts that have increased in the past 30 years to win recognition for American forms of Judaism. These struggles have included feminist challenges to male-dominated public prayer space in Jerusalem, opposition to Israeli rejection of conversions to Judaism performed by Reform, Conservative, and Modern Orthodox rabbis, and expressed resentment over Israeli unwillingness to bestow the title "rabbi" on non-Orthodox American rabbis. Ironically, "many nonreligious Jewish Israelis who identify and sympathize with the Reform movement," writes Ephraim Tabory, "do so primarily because of its fight against the religious establishment, and not necessarily because of their interest in a true religious alternative to Orthodox Judaism."[52] Even Reform leaders abet such attitudes. Rabbi Richard Hirsch argues that conversions to Judaism, one of the disputed areas, should be left to the Orthodox. His position "is that the Jewish state comes first, and Jewish rights come before human rights."[53] Thus pluralism among Jews is contested as an ideal and as a practice by treating pluralism as if it were an issue relevant only to common denominators among humans generally. But pluralism is about shared variability, not shared commonality.

The question of pluralism becomes even more complicated when one views Judaism within the framework of a religiously diverse American society. For years Jews have been the most visible and outspoken non-Christians in the United States. In the early decades of the twentieth century they contributed significantly to theoretical considerations of pluralism. The work of the philosopher Horace Kallen proposed a model of cultural pluralism emphasizing the viability of ethnic diversity in creating an American democracy. As a secular Jew, Kallen cared less about religious diversity, but he did argue persuasively that religious freedom required that groups be free to maintain their own culture. After the war, Jews used the Judeo-Christian tradition as a common context to articulate their values of religious pluralism.[54]

In the last third of the twentieth century Jewish views shifted toward Christians, both Protestants and Catholics. These changes reflected Jewish responses to increasing intermarriage with Christians, the growing political strength of evangelicals, and the Vatican's efforts to revise its teaching on Jews and Israel. Perhaps the most dramatic expression of this new viewpoint can be found in the statement "Dabru Emet" (Speak the Truth). Published in 2000 in a full-page newspaper advertisement, it appeared on the eve of the Jewish New Year of Rosh Hashanah endorsed by over 100 men and women, mostly rabbis from various backgrounds as well as some scholars. "It is time for Jews to reflect on what Judaism may now say about Christianity," they averred. After all, Jews and Christians worship the same God. Moreover, both Christians and Jews seek authority from a shared sacred scripture, accepting the moral principles of Torah. Working together for peace and justice also characterizes both religions. But "Dabru Emet" tackled more controversial issues as well. It affirmed that Nazism "was not a Christian phenomenon" and that reestablishment of a Jewish state was the most important event since the Holocaust. Finally, "Dabru Emet" admitted the impossibility of resolving the issue of the messiah. Here Jews and Christians parted company over what "Dabru Emet" called a "humanly irreconcilable difference." Both Christians and Jews will not be able to settle their disagreement until God redeems the entire world. In the meantime, the signers of the statement urged mutual respect for each other's traditions, affirming that a new relationship between Jews and Christians would neither weaken Jewish practice nor lead to syncretism.[55] The signers of "Dabru Emet" sparked controversy among both Jews and Christians in their forceful articulation of a pluralist position that proclaimed religious diversity as a positive good. "Dabru Emet" embraced an open American society and extended recognition to Christianity as a true faith. Yet it also affirmed the significance of Israel for American Jews as well as the importance of the impact of the Holocaust on Jewish religious perceptions of Christians.

In *Jew vs. Jew*, journalist Samuel Freedman takes a very different position from that taken by the signers of "Dabru Emet." He concludes, "in the struggle for the soul of American Jewry, the Orthodox model has triumphed." He means that those American Jews who will flourish in the future will be those who have accepted "the central premise of Orthodoxy that religion defines Jewish identity." Freedman cites a 1996 "Statement on the Jewish Future" that places Torah among the list of five "fundamental values" for Jewish continuity while "omitting the concept of *tikkun olam*, healing the world with social justice." Contrast this with Woocher's optimistic list of seven fundamental tenets of civil Judaism that emerged from his overview of American Jews in the 1980s: 1. Unity of the Jewish people; 2. Mutual responsibility; 3. Jewish survival in a threatening world; 4. Centrality of the State of Israel; 5. Enduring value of Jewish tradition; 6. Tzadaka (or *tikkun olam*); and 7. Americanness as a virtue.[36] The 1996 statement includes the unity of the Jewish people but ignores both Israel and America and limits its recognition of pluralism to Reform and Conservative Judaism.[37] American Studies scholar MacDonald Moore argues that this form of "nouvelle tribalism" based on the fear that "American Jews cannot cope, as Jews," with an open society, reflects a startling retreat from pluralist visions that Jews often championed as Americans.[38] It also prematurely allocates victory to a militant minority at a time when debate continues to characterize American Jews and new forms of diversity continue to emerge.

The Limits of Pluralism

Among the issues dividing American Jews regarding the limits of pluralism within Judaism probably none has generated as much conflict as intermarriage. Intermarriage has been seen as a catastrophe (Benjamin Netanyahu, in his first tenure as Israeli Prime Minister, even characterized it as "a silent Holocaust"), irreparably weakening American Jews and consigning them to future insignificance. It has served as the focal problem behind the communal rallying cry of "continuity." It has prompted Reform and Reconstructionist Jews to recognize patrilineal descent, departing from centuries-old Jewish practice that determined Jewish identity based on maternity. It has also caused some American Jews to reconsider a long-standing Jewish aversion to seeking converts. Increasingly, American Jews are ready to accept and even welcome "Jews by choice," a phrase that often refers to incoming converts. Intermarriage has provoked bitter battles over communal resources for "outreach" as well as sharp debates about how to count intermarried Jews. But rarely has intermarriage been discussed in the context of Jewish attitudes toward non-Jews, that is, in terms of American religious pluralism. The openness of American society, its lack of anti-Semitism, and the willingness of Americans to accept Jews, seldom elicit comments from Jews except in terms of posing challenges to Jewish survival as a distinct group.[39]

Since a 1990 population survey that revealed an intermarriage rate of 50%, American Jews have been in the throes of a "continuity crisis." The phrase expresses fears that the number of American Jews is declining as well as aging, leading to a future without Jews or with only a handful remaining in the United States. In its most compact form, the complexity of the current continuity crisis gets reduced to a single question of "Who Counts." That is to say: Who does the counting? Who is counted? Who matters? Where are the limits of pluralism and who remains within the Jewish circle? These questions often provoke bitter debate. In 2006, for example, the sociologist Steven M. Cohen published an article called "A Tale of Two Jewries: The 'Inconvenient Truth' for American Jews." Cohen argues not only that the division between intra-married and intermarried is significant but also that the latter have no future as Jews.[60] The article prompted responses questioning the wisdom of such a bifurcated view of American Jews. As the sociologist David Schoem notes, "Our analysis is deeply flawed if we can only see the Jewish people through the lens of in-married or interfaith married, or if we can only see the Jewish people as religiously observant or not." He goes on to decry the "unrelenting" division of Jews into "core" and "peripheral," categories adopted by demographers and often referenced in discussions of American Jews.

> Let's identify these so-called peripherals: they are Jewish single parents, Jewish couples and adults without children, non-wealthy Jews, including poor and middle class Jews, Sephardi Jews, gay and lesbian Jews, Jews who attend public schools and afternoon Hebrew school rather than Jewish day schools, less traditionally observant Jews, Jews from the midwest, west coast, and southern U.S., small-town and rural Jews, Jews in Europe, Russia, and South America, most Reform Jews, non-white Jews, secular Jews, most Jewish women, and the list goes on of categories of Jews identified as peripheral and made to feel marginal in and by the American Jewish community.

"Personally," he concludes, "I abhor these categories, but if I had to choose, I'd rather throw my hat in with these so-called peripheral Jews."[61] Schoem's list articulates a panoply of Jewish diversity ignored in binary divisions of in-married and out-married, core and peripheral. He challenges an approach that insists on dividing Jews into two groups, one acceptable and the other not.

Contending views toward belief in the messiah, specifically whether the messiah has come, have also challenged the limits of pluralism. American Jews have often defined themselves vis-à-vis Christians as not believing in Jesus as Christ. Even "Dabru Emet" draws that line. However, while many still think in such terms, the appearance of Jews for Jesus and similar groups that seek to participate in Jewish organizational life (including, for example, some local boards of rabbis) has sparked discussion among liberal Jews over where to draw boundaries. "In the final analysis," concludes religious studies scholar Yaakov Ariel, energetic Christian "missionary endeavor had exposed the vulnerability of Jewish continuity in a free, open culture in which religious affiliation had become increasingly a matter of choice and not inherited obligation and in which the social boundaries between Jews and Christians crumbled and no longer worked to reinforce religious identity."[62] The appeal of belief in a messiah who has come also confronts Hasidic Jews, especially Lubavitch Hasidim. The death of Menachem Mendel Schneerson, the Lubavitcher rebbe, in 1994, failed to quiet messianic speculations among many of his followers. David Berger, a modern Orthodox Jew, found ongoing belief in the rebbe's messiahship so fraught and dangerous that he wrote an entire book exposing this segment of Lubavitch Hasidim. Stopping short of recommending excommunication, Berger urged the orthodox Jewish world to shun them.[63] Berger's *cri d'coeur* has largely gone unheeded. Messianic anticipation flourishes, as a recent full-page advertisement in the *New York Times* suggests.[64] Few American Orthodox Jews have protested these expressions of belief in the rebbe as messiah. Furthermore, these controversies have diminished neither the power nor effectiveness of Chabad. Does Jewish pluralism include those who believe the messiah has come?

Other forms of eclecticism arouse fewer passions. The fusion of Judaism and Buddhism, nicknamed "Ju-Bu," gets a respectful hearing from diverse American Jews.[65] Jewish Renewal members lead the way in incorporating such Buddhist activities as meditation and controlled breathing into Jewish observances. Reform and Reconstructionist Jews also experiment with such embodied practices. Jews have also adapted such religious models as the twelve-step program of Alcoholics Anonymous, using it as a means of inviting Jews to adopt increasing levels of religious observance (such as keeping kosher).[66] Other therapeutic approaches to religion draw on Jewish and Christian sources, as historian Andrew Heinze has shown.[67] Feminist god-language as well as feminist midrash and theology find acceptance within liberal Jewish religious movements, and are included in their prayer books. By contrast, Wiccan practices have been deemed beyond the pale.

There is, finally, what one might call Hollywood Judaism, an eclectic blend that imagines Judaism as spiritual recreation, a leisure activity and form of conspicuous consumption. Although many of these practices began in postwar experimentation in Los Angeles, they have continued to flourish.[68] The spreading popularity of Kabbalah reflects some of this tradition as does the extraordinary appeal of bar and bat mitzvah ceremonies (including, of course, the lavish parties). Such celebrity Judaism influences public perceptions of Jews in the United States and tells us something about religious pluralism. It taps into inchoate desires of Jews and others for a different form of spirituality, one attuned to postmodern possibilities of identity and community.

Undoubtedly, structural pluralism is flourishing among American Jews even as an ideological commitment to unity in pluralism struggles for acceptance. Many American Jews still subscribe to an ideal of a Jewish community as a house for many types of religious Jews articulated by Mordecai M. Kaplan. The consensus of the postwar period that recognized three major denominations in American Judaism endures in many aspects of Jewish organizational life. Jews generally agree that Jewish organizations should provide kosher food for Jewish communal activities, honor the Sabbath on the seventh day, celebrate Jewish life-cycle events (although here eclecticism and egalitarianism have introduced changes), follow the Jewish calendar, support those in need, champion Israel, and pursue social justice. But beyond these areas, and even within them, debate and dissension flourish. The political power of an Orthodox religious establishment in Israel serves as a potent alternative exclusivist model to the pluralism of the United States. Although Jewish liturgy repeatedly reminds Jews to look to Zion for teachings of Torah, when many

American Jews contemplate the contemporary reality of Israeli religious life, they see a world lacking religious freedom, something they value highly as Americans. Such transnational pressures challenge American Jews. Is there a form of religious pluralism that might address Jewish religious conflict beyond the borders of the United States? Ongoing bitter arguments among Jews within and without the United States suggest that perhaps the rabbi of the story was right. These and these and these are true. Jews just need to figure out how to live with such knowledge.

Some scholars suggest that Jews are moving into a post-denominational world because Reform and Conservative Judaism are moving closer to each other in ways reminiscent of pre–World War II Conservative and Orthodox Judaism. Despite these trends toward convergence in religious behaviors and beliefs, the types of compromises and flexibility that characterized immigrant Jews toward religious practice and that might be considered pre-denominational do not really typify American Jews today. Jonathan Sarna argues that "Jewish unity is far from dead," despite contentious disputes. He highlights three historic strategies employed to preserve Judaism: tradition in an American idiom; reforming tradition and Americanizing it; and emphasizing bonds of peoplehood rather than religion. All three sought to accommodate diversity in unity.[69] These approaches to pluralism have not disappeared. Judaism in the United States is diverse and multiple, competitive and fractious. It is most definitely pluralist but more in an older sense of diversity and not due to an inherent value that accepts the legitimacy of multiple religious truths. Yet if Jews continue to work to build a religiously pluralist United States, they may succeed in providing models for American Judaism as well.

Notes

1 Pirke Avot, 1:1.

2 Gershom Scholem, *Major Trends in Jewish Mysticism* (New York: Schocken Books, 1946), pioneered modern scholarship on Jewish mysticism.

3 Glenn Dynner, *Men of Silk: Hasidic Conquest of Polish Jewish Society* (New York: Oxford University Press, 2006).

4 See Robert N. Bellah, "Civil Religion in America," reprinted from the Winter 1967 issue of *Daedalus* in *American Civil Religion*, Russell E. Richey and Donald G. Jones, eds. (New York: Harper & Row, 1974), as well as other essays in the volume.

5 William R. Hutchison, *Religious Pluralism in America: The Contentious History of a Founding Ideal* (New Haven, CT: Yale University Press, 2003).

6 This volume bears witness to such a viewpoint, as does the conference on pluralism out of which it emerges. See also Diana Eck, *A New Religious America: How a "Christian Country" Has Become the World's Most Religiously Diverse Nation* (1997; reprint San Francisco: HarperCollins, 2002).

7 Jonathan D. Sarna, *American Judaism: A History* (New Haven, CT: Yale University Press, 2004), xvii, xviii.

8 See Daniel Kurt Ackermann, "The 1794 Synagogue of Kahal Kadosh Beth Elohim, Charleston, SC: Reconstructed and Reconsidered," *American Jewish History* 93, no. 2 (June 2007): 159–176, quotation on p. 166.

9 Quoted in James W. Hagy, *This Happy Land* (Tuscaloosa: University of Alabama Press, 1992), 131. Emphasis in the original.

10 Deborah Dash Moore, "Freedom's Fruits: The Americanization of an Old-time Religion," in *A Portion of the People: Three Hundred Years of Southern Jewish Life*, Theodore Rosengarten and Dale Rosengarten, eds. (Columbia: University of South Carolina Press, 2002), 10–21.

11 Daniel Soyer, *Jewish Immigrant Associations and American Identity in New York 1880–1939* (Cambridge, MA: Harvard University Press, 1997), 49–80.

12 Quoted in Horace L. Friess, *Felix Adler and Ethical Culture: Memories and Studies*, Fannia Weingartner, ed. (New York: Columbia University Press, 1981), 49.

13 See Benny Kraut, *From Reform Judaism to Ethical Culture: The Religious Evolution of Felix Adler*, Monographs of the Hebrew Union College, 5 (Cincinnati, OH: Hebrew Union College Press, 1979). Quotation on p. 109.

14 Deborah Dash Moore, *GI Jews: How World War II Changed a Generation* (Cambridge, MA: Harvard University Press, 2004), 118–155.

15 Deborah Dash Moore, "Jewish GIs and the Creation of the Judeo-Christian Tradition," *Religion and American Culture* 8 (Winter 1998): 31–54.

16 On the fluidity between Conservative and Orthodox, see Jeffrey S. Gurock, "From Fluidity to Rigidity: The Religious Worlds of Conservative and Orthodox Jews in Twentieth-Century America," in *American Jewish Identity Politics*, Deborah Dash Moore, ed. (Ann Arbor: University of Michigan Press, 2008), 159–204.

17 These included what to do about Sabbath and holiday observance, marriage and divorce, conversion, and finally, death and burial. The three rabbis were Solomon B. Freehof, Leo Jung, and Milton Steinberg, representing Reform, Orthodox, and Conservative Jews respectively.

18 Phillip Bernstein, *Rabbis at War: The CANRA Story* (Waltham, MA: American Jewish Historical Society, 1971), 18.

19 Harold Saperstein to Friends of Temple Emanu-El, September 14, 1944, American Jewish Archives.

20 Emanuel Rackman, "Preface," *Witness from the Pulpit: Topical Sermons, 1933–1980*, Marc Saperstein, ed. (Lanham, MD: Lexington Books, 2000), xii.

21 Jonathan S. Woocher, *Sacred Survival: The Civil Religion of American Jews* (Bloomington: Indiana University Press, 1986), vii, 13.

22 Hasia R. Diner, "Before 'The Holocaust': American Jews Confront Catastrophe, 1945–62," in Moore, ed., *American Jewish Identity Politics*, 88–99.

23 Jack Wertheimer, *A People Divided: Judaism in Contemporary America* (New York: Basic Books, 1993).

24 Joshua Trachtenberg, "Review of the Year 5706, Part One: The United States, Religious Activities," *American Jewish Year Book* 47 (1945–46), 217.

25 *New York Times*, June 22, 1945, A15.

26 Zachary James Silver, "The Excommunication of Mordecai Kaplan: How an Act of Intolerance Paved the Way toward Cultural Pluralism in Post-war America" (Honors Thesis, Jewish Studies Program, University of Pennsylvania, May 3, 2005), 39–48, 78–81.

27 "Introduction," *The Sabbath Prayer Book*, Mordecai M. Kaplan and Eugene Kohn, eds. (New York: Jewish Reconstructionist Foundation, 1945), 1–5.

28 Quoted in Trachtenberg, "Review of the Year 5706," 217.

29 Quoted in Silver, "The Excommunication of Mordecai Kaplan," 117.

30 See the articles in *Tradition Renewed: A History of the Jewish Theological Seminary*, Jack Wertheimer, ed. (New York: Jewish Theological Seminary of America, 1997), especially "The Finkelstein Era," by Michael B. Greenbaum, 163–232, and "The Unfinished Symphony: The Gerson Cohen Years," by Paula E. Hyman, 235–268.

31 Charles Liebman, "Reconstructionism," *American Jewish Year Book* (1970), 35–45.

32 Wertheimer, *A People Divided*, 169.

33 Egon Mayer, *From Suburb to Shtetl: The Jews of Boro Park* (Philadelphia: Temple University Press, 1979).

34 Sue Fishkoff, *The Rebbe's Army: Inside the World of Chabad-Lubavitch* (New York: Schocken, 2003).

35 Sarna, *American Judaism*, 345–352.

36 Sylvia Barack Fishman, *The Way into the Varieties of Jewishness* (Woodstock, VT: Jewish Lights Publishing, 2007), 173–191.

37 For example, in 1954 Rabbi Aaron Kotler led 11 yeshiva heads in issuing a prohibition against Orthodox cooperation with non-Orthodox rabbis, especially in such interdenominational efforts as the Synagogue Council of America. Wolfe Kelman, "The Synagogue in America," in *The Future of the Jewish Community in America*, David Sidorsky, ed. (Philadelphia: Jewish Publication Society of America, 1973), 165–166.

38 Jeffrey S. Gurock, *Orthodox Jews in America* (Bloomington: Indiana University Press, 2009), 226–272; Fishman, *Varieties of Jewishness*, 127–152.

39 Sylvia Barack Fishman, *A Breath of Life: Feminism in the Jewish Community* (New York: Free Press, 1993), 121–180.

40 Gurock, *Orthodox Jews in America*, 273–311.

41 Cited in Samuel G. Freedman, *Jew vs. Jew: The Struggle for the Soul of American Jewry* (New York: Simon & Schuster, 2000), 289.

42 Frank L. Weil, "Greetings," *A Book of Jewish Thoughts* (New York: Jewish Welfare Board, 1943): vii–viii.

43 *The Chaplain Serves*, Office, Chief of Chaplains, Army Service Forces, War Department, March 1, 1944, 44; Bernstein, *Rabbis at War*, 136. The Catholic Douay translation included the sentence, "Jews are the Synagogue of Satan," which Jewish chaplains protested.

44 "Not only were differences taken for granted," reported one rabbi after naval training, "but with the proverbial 57 varieties of religious denominations represented, each group was *expected* to be different." This man discovered that the philosophy was "harmony, not uniformity." Quoted in Randall Jacobs, "Religion in the Navy— Differences are the Norm," *The Jewish Veteran* 13, no. 12 (August 1944): 17. Emphasis in the original.

45 Kevin M. Schultz, *Tri-Faith America: How Catholics and Jews Held Postwar America to its Protestant Promise* (New York: Oxford University Press, 2011).

46 Leonard Dinnerstein, *Antisemitism in America* (New York: Oxford University Press, 1994).

47 Naomi W. Cohen, *Jews in Christian America: The Pursuit of Religious Equality* (New York: Oxford Univesity Press, 1992).

48 Jonathan D. Sarna, "Is Judaism Compatible with American Civil Religion: The Problem of Christmas and the 'National Faith,'" in *Religion and the Life of the Nation: American Recoveries*, Rowland A. Sherrill, ed. (Urbana: University of Illinois Press, 1990), 157.

49 David G. Dalin, ed., *American Jews and the Separationist Faith* (Washington, DC: Ethics and Public Policy Center, 1993).

50 Charles S. Liebman and Steven M. Cohen, *Two Worlds of Judaism: The Israeli and American Experiences* (New Haven, CT: Yale University Press, 1990).

51 Quoted in Hyman, "The Unfinished Symphony", 254.

52 Ephraim Tabory, "The Legitimacy of Reform Judaism," in *Contemporary Debates in American Reform Judaism: Conflicting Visions*, Dana Evan Kaplan, ed. (New York and London: Routledge, 2001), 232.

53 Quoted in Tabory, "Legitimacy of Reform Judaism," 232.

54 The *Harvard Encyclopedia of American Ethnic Groups*, Stephan Thernstrom, ed. (Cambridge, MA: Harvard University Press, 1980) presents good evidence of these perspectives. See especially the entries on "Pluralism: A Humanistic Perspective," by Michael Novak; "Pluralism: A Political Perspective," by Michael Walzer; "Assimilation and Pluralism," by Harold Abramson; and "American Identity and Americanization," by Philip Gleason.

55 http://www.icjs.org/what/njsp/dabruemet.html, accessed August 15, 2007.

56 Woocher, *Sacred Survival*, 67–68.

57 "A Statement on the Jewish Future," was anchored in an article by Jack Wertheimer, Charles Liebman, and Steven M. Cohen, "What to Do About Jewish Continuity," in *Commentary* and a meeting at Jewish Theological Seminary of Jewish leaders and intellectuals to express a "countervoice" to prevailing opinion on what constitutes Jewish continuity. The Statement was formulated and released in August 1996. See *A Statement on the Jewish Future: Text and Responses* (New York: American Jewish Committee, 1997).

58 Quoted in Freedman, *Jew vs. Jew*, 338–339.

59 Deborah Dash Moore, "Intermarriage and the Politics of Identity," *The Reconstructionist* 60 (Fall 2001): 44–51.

60 Steven M. Cohen, "A Tale of Two Jewries: The 'Inconvenient Truth' for American Jews," Jewish Life Network/Steinhardt Foundation (November 2006/ Cheshvan 5767).

61 David Schoem, email communication, June 9, 2007.

62 Yaakov Ariel, *Evangelizing the Chosen People: Missions to the Jews in America, 1880–2000* (Chapel Hill: University of North Carolina Press, 2000), 252–269, quotation on p. 269.

63 David Berger, *The Rebbe, the Messiah, and the Scandal of Orthodox Indifference* (London: Littman Library of Jewish Civilization, 2001).

64 *The New York Times*, March 30, 2007, A17.

65 For example, Alan Lew's spiritual autobiography, *One God Clapping: The Spiritual Path of a Zen Rabbi*, with Sherril Jaffe (New York: Kodansha America, 1999) or Rodger Kamenetz's classic account of his 1990 visit to the Dalai Lama, *The Jew*

in the Lotus: A Poet's Rediscovery of Jewish Identity in Buddhist India (San Francisco: HarperCollins, 1995).

66 For example "Chew by Choice," in Riv-Ellen Prell, "Communities of Choice and Memory: Conservative Synagogues in the Late Twentieth Century," in *Jews in the Center: Conservative Synagogues and their Members*, Jack Wertheimer, ed. (New Brunswick, NJ: Rutgers University Press, 2002), 294–302.

67 Andrew Heinze, *Judaism and the American Soul: Human Nature in the Twentieth Century* (Princeton, NJ: Princeton University Press, 2004).

68 Deborah Dash Moore, *To the Golden Cities: Pursuing the American Jewish Dream in Miami and L.A.* (New York: Free Press, 1994), 123–152.

69 Jonathan D. Sarna, "American Judaism in Historical Perspective," in Moore, ed., *American Jewish Identity Politics*, 139–156, quotation on p. 152.

PART III | Islam, Buddhism, and Hinduism

CHAPTER 7

Muslims and American
Religious Pluralism

Yvonne Yazbeck Haddad

IT IS CLEAR BY now that the attacks of September 11, 2001, on the World Trade
Center and the Pentagon have fostered new reflections on Islamic theological discourse throughout the Muslim world on issues of violence, tolerance,
diversity, and pluralism. Some of the discourse was a response to the universal
condemnation of the ideology the terrorists claimed was inspired by the teachings of Islam. The new discourse engaged Muslim scholars both overseas and
in the diaspora who were disturbed with the yoking of Islam with militancy
and terror. While Muslims overseas have generally continued to contextualize the violence as a reaction to American neocolonial policies in the Muslim
world, diaspora Muslims, given the prevailing Islamophobia and the security
measures sanctioned by the PATRIOT Act, have downplayed the intricacies
of the "why" of the violence in an effort to dissociate and distance themselves
from the perpetrators. They have sought to repossess a role in defining their
own faith and take it back from the Muslim extremists as well as from those
who thrive on demonizing Islam.[1]

The urgent reexamination of the ideological constructs of diaspora Islam is
now in process, addressing similar charges against Islam and Muslims coming out of different contexts. Since Muslims first began to come to the United
States, they have had to respond to a variety of events overseas, such as the
Arab-Israeli conflict, the Salman Rushdie Affair, and the Iranian Revolution,
all of which tarred them by association. In the aftermath of 9/11, promoting
tolerance and pluralism became an imperative as Muslims were confronted by
rising xenophobia and Islamophobia, in part a consequence of the propaganda
for the Global War on Terrorism (GWoT). At the same time, such reflections
became a necessary shield as government security measures targeted Arabs
and Muslims through profiling, censoring Islamic texts, monitoring mosques,
freezing assets of Muslim NGOs, and instituting procedures for search and
seizure, arrest, deportation, and rendition of suspects. These government
security measures have isolated Muslims and placed them in what one Muslim
called a "virtual internment."[2]

Another impetus for such reflection is the demand of certain sectors of American society that the U.S. government get into religion-building, namely to help reformulate and promote an alternative "moderate Islam" that can fit the description of "a religion of peace."[3] Thus the goal of these reflections is not only to prove that Muslims living in the West are loyal citizens, but more importantly that they share American values and are not associated with the teachings of those targeted in America's declared Global War on Terrorism, who have been variously labeled as extremists, fundamentalists, jihadists, terrorists, and proponents of an Islamo-fascist Islam.

The new diaspora discourse on pluralism displays a strong awareness of the need for a pluralistic interpretation of Qur'anic verses that have been used by extremists to justify their terrorist actions. This is seen as crucial not only to assuage the doubts and apprehensions of the general public, but also in a more important way to address the reality of the diversity within the North American Muslim community itself and the challenge of forging a united constituency. Islam is projected as a way of life and a culture, which thus provides guidance on issues of "diversity, unity, harmony, tolerance and peace."[4]

Responses to accusations that Islam is a violent religion have been addressed since the nineteenth century in various venues and in different languages throughout the Muslim world as Muslims have attempted to respond to the challenges of Western encroachment on their lands as well as their civilization and culture. The presentation of Islam as moderate, tolerant, and pluralistic was not invented in the heat of the moment as an answer to the intense scrutiny Islam and Muslims undergo during periods of crisis. Rather, it has a venerable place in the heritage of Islam. It asserts unequivocally that if some Muslims promote ideas of vengeance and hate in the name of Islam, it is due to their misunderstanding and misinterpretation of the Islamic sources, the teaching of the Qur'an and the Prophet Muhammad, as well as the historical record of Islamic civilization.

This chapter will provide an overview of the wider context in which the discourse on pluralism in Islam became an important defensive measure in the modern world and of the crises that fostered reflections on the topic. It will provide a brief discussion of the Qur'anic verses used to buttress arguments and undergird the claims for Islamic pluralism. Contemporary Islamic interpretations that were incubated and nurtured overseas have been transplanted by Muslims living in the diaspora. These theological constructs of the meaning of certain Qur'anic verses and cultural norms were formulated in particular contexts and in response to direct and indirect challenges. Whether consciously or unconsciously, they are the intellectual sources and in some cases precedents of the discourse produced by writers in the diaspora, especially by bicultural Muslim intellectuals, both immigrants and émigrés. The last section of the chapter will focus on the material generated in the diaspora among immigrant and convert Muslims who are responding to the ways in which the Western public has impugned Islam and its teachings after 9/11.

Pluralism and the Muslim Encounter with Colonialism

The Muslim encounter with colonialism is part of the identity formation of most Muslims in today's world. It is an essential part of the modern efforts at nation-building in Muslim countries, having a prominent place in history and civics textbooks. The encounter is portrayed as violent in nature, with powerful Western armies encroaching on and subduing peaceful Muslims in an effort to monopolize their natural resources, restructure their economies, and gain strategic advantage over other competing European nations. The colonial venture and Muslim resistance to subjugation have given rise to a literature that sees European colonialism masked under the guise of a benevolent project to bring democracy to people living under autocratic rule, to liberate the women of Islam from bondage to men, to provide modern education, and to foster civic organizations in order to uplift Muslim societies. Whether operating under the banner of the French "civilizing mission" or the British "white man's burden," Western expansion into Muslim territories is at times depicted as having a religious agenda carried out by colonial bureaucrats and Christian missionaries, considered the two "archenemies of Islam,"[5] who sought to liberate Muslims from their religion.

Thus colonialism is held culpable for defaming Islam and projecting its own aggression on Muslims, promoting ethnic and sectarian divisions as part of the policy of divide and rule. The colonial venture is seen as anything but pluralistic. Rather it has promoted division and sectarianism, while insisting that Western worldviews are superior and must supersede all others. Colonial bureaucrats aimed at restructuring Islamic societies and casting them in their own image. Muslims believe that Western nations do not practice the pluralism that they now preach. The mistreatment of Muslims living in the West today, holding them responsible for the acts of extremists overseas, is seen as one more manifestation of that attitude. Just as nationalism was invented by the West to divide the Muslim world into discreet entities, some Muslims say, so pluralism is seen as a recasting of the perennial efforts by the West to undermine Islam.

To resist the West's project, a significant amount of Islamic literature was produced throughout the twentieth century. This literature tends to be defensive and polemical in tone. It addresses the issues raised in the West about the adequacy, efficacy, and validity of Islam as a religion for the modern world, defending it as capable of generating a renaissance to confront the new challenges facing Islamic societies and bring them to parity with the West. It responds to Western charges that Islam advocates holy war, jihad against non-Muslims, and has legislated the subjugation of women and minorities.

Writing in response to such charges at the turn of the twentieth century, the modernist reformer Muhammad 'Abduh (1849–1905) insisted that Islam favors forgiveness and that fighting is sanctioned only for putting an end to aggression against Islam and Muslims, as well as to maintain peace. Jihad, he argued, is not aimed at forcing people to convert to Islam, or punishing those who disagree with Muslims. Christian history, on the other hand, is replete with massacres and the killing of old men, women, and children. Muslims can boast that there has not been a single Islamic war that sought the annihilation of others.[6] 'Abduh argued that when Muslims conquered a territory, they practiced Islamic tolerance and allowed its people to worship and practice their faith and maintain their customs. While it is true that non-Muslims were required to pay the *jizya*, or poll tax, they were guaranteed security and protection in return.[7] Muslim rulers instructed Muslim armies to respect those who were in convents and monasteries, he wrote, and they proclaimed the sanctity of the blood of women, children, and noncombatants. The teaching of the Prophet forbids hurting covenanted non-Muslims, *dhimmis*; the Prophet Muhammad said that "He who harms a *dhimmi* is not one of us."[8] Unlike Christianity, Islam provides for freedom of religious thought. Even though a statement by a Muslim may appear in a hundred ways to make him a *kafir* or unbeliever, 'Abduh insisted that, if there is even one way that can be accepted as belief, then he cannot be called an unbeliever.

Pluralism and the Muslim Encounter with the Cold War

By the middle of the twentieth century, the colonial and the missionary presence in Muslim nations came to an end. Islamic literature increasingly referred to the colonial incursion as part of the "intellectual or cultural invasion," *al-ghazu al-thaqafi*.[9] It portrayed Western educational, cultural, and social institutions introduced in Muslim nations as part of a sustained campaign to root out religion. Western leaders were accused of not being satisfied with military and political domination, but of aiming at the eradication of Islam, its culture, civilization, and intellectual expression. As such, Westerners did not practice pluralism or promote equality between Western and Islamic cultures. Rather, they assumed the roles of teachers, reformers, and enforcers of their own ideas and beliefs. They also claimed that Western values are universal and that all alternate values must aspire to match their level.

By this time many Muslim intellectuals had adopted nationalism and Marxism as a buffer against colonialism. This move, however, created a backlash among Islamists, who saw these intellectuals as agents of European interests insofar as they divided Muslims into nationalities and set them against each other. Islamists accused the nationalists of advocating radical secularization and the eradication of any vestiges of religion. Buying into antireligious ideology, they were, in effect, duped by outside forces bent on destroying Islam.[10] Islamism became an important response to safeguard Islam against disintegration. Islamists, in turn, were supported by American policy, which viewed their efforts as a necessary impediment to the spread of socialism and Marxism.

One of those Islamists was the Egyptian intellectual Sayyid Qutb, whose works have been translated and disseminated throughout the world. Qutb originally advocated Islam as an alternative to capitalism and Marxism, but he later revised his ideology and decreed an Islamic imperative, a comprehensive, holistic vision that offered Islamic answers to social, economic, political, and cultural problems. The Islamic imperative, as Qutb saw it, supersedes materialistic systems, capitalism, and Marxism. It asserts a parallel promise of a better future, one guaranteed by God to the believers, a promise that has been vindicated in history as demonstrated by the greatness of the Islamic empires. Qutb attacked what he saw as the perversion of Christianity. In Fi Zilal al-Qur'an, a 30-volume commentary on the Qur'an, he depicted Christians as extremists because of their claim that God has a son.[11] He accused them of being duplicitous for their refusal to govern by the laws and dictates that God has revealed, preferring to follow their own whims. For Qutb, governing by any law other than the shari`ah amounts to disobedience and apostasy.[12] As the final revelation from God, the Qur'an abrogates and supersedes all other revelations.[13] Thus he viewed the world from a bipolar perspective: on the one side is the abode of Islam, dar al-Islam, where Islamic law is implemented regardless of the religious affiliation of the citizens, and on the other the abode of war, dar al-harb, where Islamic law is not implemented.[14] He thereby set up the justification of using violence against those who do not govern by what God has revealed.

Whereas 'Abduh had defended Islam against accusations of intolerance and aggression, and promoted the idea of Islam as a religion of peace, Qutb—writing in the context of torture in Nasser's prisons in the 1960s—justified jihad as armed resistance. By decreeing laws based on socialist ideology, said Qutb, Nasser was an apostate. He saw the struggle against Nasser's regime, which violated God's dictates, as a just cause. Qutb argued that the sword verses (S. 9:5, 29, 36) constituted the final revelation dealing with the relation of Muslims to non-Muslims. People of the Book (Jews and Christians), having sanctioned what has been forbidden by God, are unbelievers, kuffar. They have forfeited their right to protection; they must either convert to Islam or pay the jizya. Those who refuse can be killed, and Muslims who emulate the deviant ways of the People of the Book can expect the same fate.[15] Qutb wrote that the Qur'an warns Muslims about the reality of their enemies and of the war these enemies wage against Muslims because of their doctrine.[16] While Muslims are asked to be tolerant of the People of the Book, they are not to take them as friends.[17] He was dubious about efforts at dialogue and compromise. Those who seek to bring about good relations among religious people misunderstand the meaning of religion. Islam alone is acceptable, and no other religion can be recognized.[18] Therefore, no covenant with people of other faiths can be accepted unless it has this condition.[19] Furthermore, the Islamic imperative does not tolerate coexistence with falsehood. It must obliterate all impediments while providing freedom of choice. True liberation comes when people choose Islam out of conviction.[20]

This interpretation of Islam as articulated by Sayyid Qutb persists today in the ideology of Islamic revolutionary groups such as al-Takfir wa al-Hijra, al-Jihad Islami, al-Qaeda, and the Taliban. These groups continue to condemn those who do not subscribe to their interpretation of Islam as *kuffar*, persons who willfully and intentionally cover the truth of Islam. That ideology became justified in the eyes of revolutionary Muslims in the wake of the 1967 Arab-Israeli War. The militancy and violence of the continuing conflict has evoked a strong response within Islamist circles.[21]

The 1967 Arab defeat brought about a major reassessment and the rise of a body of self-critical literature in the Arab world. It blamed Arab failure on the premise that the nation states had put their faith in nationalism and socialism and abandoned Islam. Some authors wrote that the Israelis were victorious because of their devotion to their religion and their insistence on fashioning a Jewish state while Muslims had abandoned the idea of a Muslim state. This idea soon gave way to anticolonial, anti-imperialist, and anti-Zionist themes centered on mobilizing the masses who were disenchanted with the new international order, which allows the United Nations to be the arbiter of justice. The fact that Israel was allowed to hold on to lands conquered through a "pre-emptive strike" was perceived as a conspiracy against Muslim rights and a violation of universal proclamations of the United Nations. For an increasing number of Muslims, it became a time to reassess, to grieve over a loss of innocence, to mourn fresh victims, and to come to terms with the death of hope. The international order, they concluded, does not treat Muslims and non-Muslims equally.[22]

With the death of Nasser, Sadat became president of Egypt. He proceeded to remove the socialists from positions of power, bringing the Islamists out of prison and giving them a prominent role in society. For Sadat, Islamism was the firewall that would hold socialism at bay. Islamists demanded the establishment of an Islamic state in Egypt and the implementation of the *shari`ah* as the law of the land. It was thought that the only way to curb the excesses of authoritarian rulers was to place restrictions on their legislative authority. In Islamist literature, the Qur'anic verse: "This day, I have perfected your religion for you and completed my favor upon you and chosen Islam as your religion" (S. 5:3) was seen as sanctioning the canonization of the *shari`ah* and its implementation in society. Even the venerable al-Azhar, the intellectual center of Sunni Islam, generally accountable to the authorities in power, issued a statement on the subject: "Not to implement the revelation in God's Book and judge by His decrees is *kufr* (unbelief). If a person refuses to believe in it, doubts its divine origin, professes that it is not valid for judgment, ridicules it, says that it is inappropriate except for the society or the age in which it was revealed or other similar statements or actions he oversteps the boundaries of the ordinances of God."[23]

Pluralism Debates in the Aftermath of the Iranian Revolution

The 1979 Islamic Revolution in Iran jolted Western nations as they began to reassess the reality of Islamic militancy and the power of Islamic ideology to garner the devotion of the masses and undermine puppet regimes. The success of the revolution encouraged Islamist groups throughout the Muslim world who preached that God will give the victory to those who believe, if they but believe. The ability of the Iranian Revolution to get rid of the Shah, depicted as the mightiest of tyrants, protected by the United States, the most powerful nation in the world, could be replicated if Muslims focused on being better Muslims and resisted efforts to impose foreign values. Its success also provided a formula for victory, a prototype that could be replicated in other places under puppet regimes accountable to American interests. Islamic groups began to demand the institution of an Islamic state. This generated concomitant hostility toward Christians who were not happy with such developments. Books were published in critique of Christian doctrine, and Christian properties came under attack. It also nurtured hostility between Sunnis and Shi`a.

While traditionalists consulted and republished treatises in Islamic literature on conflict resolution, *adab al-ikhtilaf,* a new genre of literature was developed in the 1980s to deal with the crisis following the Iran Revolution and rise of jihadist Islamist groups.

The term *ta`addudiyya,* now translated as "pluralism," was first coined by secular Arab intellectuals to parallel the Western concept of pluralism. (Earlier usage of the term was mainly in reference to multiple wives, *ta`addud al-zawjat.*) Pluralism was cast into the Arab market of ideas as a challenge to the growing Islamization of society, the demand for establishing an Islamic state and the adoption of the *shari`ah* as the law of the state. It was first used as part of the title of a symposium convened by the Jordanian Center for Research and Information in 1986.[24] Several other symposia followed in Jordan and Egypt.[25] By the 1990s, discourse on pluralism had become indigenized. Islamists were using the term to explore issues of conflict and difference in Islamic society as well as the legitimacy of a multiparty system in an Islamic state.[26] In 1992 the Labor Party in Egypt held a symposium on Islam and Pluralism.[27]

By 1993, Dr. Muhyiddin Atiyyah, editor of *al-Muslim al-Mu`asir* magazine, had compiled a bibliography of 122 titles related to pluralism.[28] Several conferences were funded by European governments and civic organizations to consider the role of pluralism in Islamic thought. As a consequence, it became the buzzword of the 1990s.[29] It joined a venerable list of concepts conceived and popularized in the West, then idealized and exported for foreign consumption, such as modernity, democracy, nationalism, normalization, secularism, human rights, women's rights, minority rights, privatization, and globalization. These concepts are generally seen as challenges to developing countries, their adoption posited as a sign of having successfully joined the ranks of civilized nations.[30] Muslim intellectuals addressed these challenges as soon as they were posited. They are perceived as new hurdles to be cleared in an effort to prove that Islam not only measures up to Western norms, but that Islam is the pioneer in setting norms. The authors generally rummage through Islamic history and texts in search of parallels they can recommend or sanctions that can be invoked to support their arguments. Their own differing ideological perspectives determine whether they see Western values as antithetical to, compatible with, or in fact the very essence of Islam.

The Islamist debates on pluralism have addressed such matters as universal pluralism—whether the Islamic state can maintain normal relations with governments who promote non-Islamic or un-Islamic ideas and practices; political pluralism—whether the Islamic polity can tolerate political differences within its ranks without disobeying the commandments of God; sectarian pluralism—whether the Islamic majority, the Sunnis, can tolerate the differences in religious interpretation represented by Islamic sectarian groups; gender pluralism—whether women have a public role in an Islamic state and when they can be allocated equal rights to those of men; and religious pluralism—whether the Muslim nation can afford equal status and opportunities for religious minorities (namely Christian) in a reconstituted Islamic state, allowing them the role they acquired under nationalist governments.[31] The pluralism discourse also addresses such issues as the peaceful rotation of authority, public approval through elections and nominations, separation among the several branches of government, peaceful coexistence among various groups, and respect for human rights.[32] Islamists have also developed new and moderate positions, such as a pluralistic vision that allows for the rotation of leadership among different parties and a call for new jurisprudence that incorporates the People of the Book as full citizens in a Muslim state.

One of the most important of the contemporary Islamists who has written on tolerance in Islam is Muslim Brotherhood activist Yusuf al-Qaradawi. From his current position in Qatar, he has gained extensive influence over diaspora Muslims. His popular website, IslamOnline, provides a bank of fatwas, legal opinions, and cyber-counseling for Muslims in the diaspora.[33]

Al-Qaradawi has become controversial, since he provides different fatwas on Islamic behavior for Muslims who live in Islamic countries and those who live in the diaspora. His 1983 book *Ghayr al-Muslimin fi al-Mujtama'al-Islami* (Non-Muslims in an Islamic Society), for example, was published during a tense period in Egypt when Islamic groups were harassing the minority Coptic Christian community.[34] Al-Qaradawi based his analysis on historical precedent of the covenant, `ahd, through which People of the Book (Jews and Christians) are guaranteed security by the Muslim state even though they are not forced to convert. Thus, he argued, Copts have Islamic citizenship, enjoying the freedom to practice their own faith at the same time that they are subject to Islamic law. They are guaranteed personal and communal security and their property rights must be respected. Al-Qaradawi based this interpretation on S. 60:8–9, which affirms the essential Islamic principles of toleration, justice, and mercy.[35] Muslims, therefore, do not have the right to punish those who hold differing doctrines.[36] People of the Book, while enjoying these rights in an Islamic state, have specific duties under the *shari`ah*. Among them is the paying of the poll tax, *jizya*.

Some interpreters had argued that this tax was imposed by God because of the basic inferiority of the People of the Book since they refuse to accept the religion of Islam. Al-Qaradawi interprets it instead as a way in which Christians can contribute to the welfare of the state, since in an Islamic state they are not drafted into the army and are not subject to the obligations of *zakat*, tithing and jihad. Furthermore, non-Muslims must be subject to the regulations of the *shari`ah*. Specifically, they cannot collect interest on their investments, cannot be involved in any occupations that involve the selling or importing of forbidden substances such as alcohol or pork, and cannot hold official positions of a religious nature such as head of state or judge among Muslims. Also, Christians must not offend the religious sensibilities of Muslims by wearing or showing their religious symbols in obvious or inappropriate ways. This includes the proscription on displaying crosses or other Christian paraphernalia in public places, or demonstrating their religion too overtly. Christians must not consume wine or pork publicly or sell such commodities to Muslims, and they must not speak negatively about Islam.[37]

According to al-Qaradawi, however, this principle of not offending religious sensibilities is not reciprocal. Muslims do not have to be sensitive to Christians if it requires ignoring the commandments of God in the effort not to offend the People of the Book. Tolerance does not mean that the essential differences between religions should be ignored. The essential oneness of God must be affirmed at all times, the Christian notion of the trinity notwithstanding. Stressing commonalities, said al-Qaradawi, can lead to contradiction, separation, and even destruction.[38]

Other Islamists defined pluralism as the affirmation of difference, of freedom, and of peaceful coexistence. "Pluralism in its general philosophy is a natural truth, a universal law, a legal way of life and a divine mercy," wrote Zaki Ahmad.[39] It was promoted as a foundational principle of nature evident in the revelation of the Qur'an, which affirmed the equality of all humanity, regardless of color, language, rights, or lineage; all are equal before the law. Thus the essence of the divine plan for humanity as revealed in the Qur'an was interpreted to be pluralism. The Qur'an revealed that one of God's signs is his creation of the world composed of different nations, ethnicities, tribes, and languages (S. 30:22; 48:13). Difference in the divine plan is not for discord or war, but a sign of God's mercy that humans may have a better understanding of one another. Or as Fahmi Huwaydi puts it, Islam is pluralistic "because he [God] willed us to be different."[40]

Muslim Discourse on Pluralism in the United States

In the United States, advocacy for a pluralistic interpretation of Islam and engagement with non-Muslims, whether in interfaith dialogue, social welfare projects, or political activity on the local level in organized Islamic communities, had been eclipsed by a more conservative interpretation of Islam. This was the interpretation propagated by the Muslim Student Association (MSA) and its subsequent organization, the Islamic Society of North America (ISNA), as well as the Islamic Circle of North America (ICNA), the Tableeghi Jamaat (TJ), and Muslim American Society (MAS). These organizations were founded by immigrants who came after the 1965 revocation of the Asian Exclusion Act. Initially, they sought guidance from Muslim scholars overseas, committed to Islamist worldviews, lectured at Muslim conventions, and weighed in on living as a Muslim in a non-Muslim environment. The earliest to lecture against assimilation in the Untied States were two scholars from the subcontinent: Abu al-A`la al-Mawdudi and Hasan Nadvi. They believed that Muslims are at risk of losing their faith in the American secular environment. Another lecturer was Muhammad al-Ghazali of the Muslim Brotherhood of Egypt, who addressed one convention with, "I bring you greetings from the abode of peace to you who dwell in the abode of war." Subsequent dignitaries were more open and promoted tolerance. Rashid al-Ghannushi of Tunisia and Hasan Turabi of the Sudan, for example, urged immigrant Muslims to engage with American society since it provided a hospitable environment.

The majority of American Muslim authors who have addressed issues of pluralism in the United States have done so from the confines of academia. They include immigrants or émigrés from all over the Muslim world who have found a home in the United States and an environment conducive to research, reflection, and publishing without the constraints of government censorship. The earliest to address the issue of pluralism in Islam were Isma`il al-Faruqi and Fazlur Rahman, both émigrés who were unable to return to their home countries due to political exigencies. Rahman was deemed too liberal for the Pakistani government, which was engaged in cobbling together an Islamic state after the War of Independence, and al-Faruqi had been a mayor of a Palestinian town seized by the Israelis. Both gained an international reputation and became very influential as Muslim students from all over the Muslim world flocked to American campuses to study under their guidance. To varying degrees, they participated in interfaith dialogue and, at times, trialogue, where they became engaged in defending the faith against its American detractors and responding to queries and challenges from their colleagues.

Al-Faruqi was initially an advocate of Arab nationalism. After experiencing the American reaction to the 1967 Israeli preemptive attack on three Arab states, however, he became disappointed in America's response to what he saw as an invasion of the rights of the Palestinian people, and he lost hope for their redress through the United Nations and American mediation. He embraced the Islamic ideology in the early 1970s. Islamism universalized the Arab-Israeli conflict, changing it from a struggle in the Middle East to a cause that could be championed by the whole Muslim world.

For al-Faruqi, Islamic civilization is a witness to Muslim tolerance and provides an actual model of a culture where other religions have thrived. "The *modus vivendi* which Islam provided for the world religions in Madinah, Damascus, Cordoba, Cairo, Delhi and Istanbul is certainly worthy of emulation by the whole world," he wrote.[41] Unlike Western civilization, Islam tolerates difference. "Compared with the histories of other religions, the history of Islam is categorically white as far as toleration of other religions is concerned."[42] Islam respects Judaism and Christianity, their founders and scriptures, not out of courtesy but as a foundational acknowledgment of religious truth. They are not "other views" that need to be tolerated, but de jure, "truly revealed religions from God." This consideration is not out of the necessity of social, political, cultural, or civilizational concerns, but a religious acknowledgment. "In this Islam is unique. For no religion in the world has yet made belief in the truth of other religions a necessary condition of its own faith and witness."[43]

Al-Faruqi asserted that Islam's contribution to interreligious dialogue in the world is "very, very significant," since it has experience throughout history with the widest variety of religions and ethnicities. Starting with its relationship to Judaism and Christianity, as prescribed in the Qur'an, Islam extended its engagement and tolerance to other religions based on the shared beliefs in God and the Qur'anic affirmation that all human beings are religious by nature.[44] This al-Faruqi based on the Qur'anic reference to Islam as the natural religion, *din al-fitra*, innate to human nature. "For the first time it has become possible for the adherent of one religion to tell an adherent of another religion: 'We are both equal members of a universal religious brotherhood. Both of our traditional religions are *de jure*, for they are both issued from and are based upon a common source, the religion of God which He has implanted equally in both of us, upon *din al-fitrah*.'"[45] From this perspective, the Muslim looks at the non-Muslim not as "a fallen, hopeless creature, but as a perfect man capable by himself of achieving the highest righteousness."[46]

Al-Faruqi did not think that Christians reciprocated these sentiments. He was critical of Vatican II and dismissed it as "too modest a contribution," as it did not engage seriously in dialogue. The fact that it asked Catholics to stop calling non-Christians by bad names was not necessarily a great achievement, since politeness in modern society is a prerequisite, as are courtesy and mutual respect. The assertion of deference for Islam is not sufficient to produce an "admiring trance." Al-Faruqi found the statement referring to Muslims to be insufficient, as it was placed in the company of archaic religions.[47] After 14 centuries, he said, Vatican II has in a "condescending and paternalizing manner" decreed that "Islam is a tolerable approximation of Christianity," with salvation still only to be found within the church.[48] While al-Faruqi promoted ideas of tolerance and a pluralistic interpretation of the Qur'anic verses, he felt that it is the duty of Muslims in the United States to propagate their faith and share their beliefs with Americans because they had a message that can elevate American society. "For the Muslim, the relation of Islam to the other religions has been established by God in his revelation, the Qur'an. No Muslim therefore may deny it; since for him the Qur'an is the ultimate authority."[49]

Al-Faruqi affirmed that while God could have created one uniform universal system, he decreed a perpetual pluralism in civilizations, systems, and laws (S. 5:48, 69). It is his divine will that different cultures compete in striving to bring about a virtuous society. From this perspective, Islam does not seek the negation or the eradication of "the other," since God created difference as a means of fostering competition in virtue among the nations, a fact that guarantees progress (S. 2:251).[50] Furthermore, he said, God favors moderation, as is demonstrated by the fact that he made Islam a middle community (ummatan wasat), one that avoids extremes.

As Muslims were once again called upon to address issues of pluralism, diversity, and tolerance in the 1980s and explain the treatment of religious minorities by the Islamic Republic of Iran, the takeover of the Mosque in Mecca, and the attacks on French and American troops in Lebanon, al-Faruqi cautioned that religion and politics should be separate. "Do not mix up Islam and Iran. Do not say in one breath Islam and events in Saudi Arabia." He gave the example of the internment of the Japanese during World War II as a political expediency similar to the treatment of minorities in Iran and Saudi Arabia.[51]

Not all of al-Faruqi's contemporaries on the American scene agreed with him. Fazlur Rahman, who taught at the University of Chicago, for example, was not satisfied with the traditional exegesis of the Qur'anic verses, especially those that have been interpreted as advocating supersession. He noted that the Qur'an deplores the fact that religions are divided within themselves, as well as from each other. According to Rahman, humankind is one but became divided with the advent of prophets bringing their messages. His interpretation that God willed that messengers come with messages that divide people was truly innovative (S. 2:213). The Qur'an leaves no room for exclusivist claims by various faith communities, said Rahman (S. 2:211, 113, 120). "The Qur'an's reply to those exclusivist claims of proprietorship over God's guidance, then, is absolutely unequivocal: Guidance is not the function of communities but of God and good people, and no community may lay claim to be uniquely guided and elected" (S. 2:124).[52]

Pluralism Discourse in the 1990s

Several factors helped usher in a surge in writings on the Muslim concept of pluralism in the 1990s. These include the publication of the *Satanic Verses* by Salman Rushdie that generated Muslim rage in India and the United Kingdom. American Muslims became aware that they were not sheltered under the canopy of political correctness, since few people supported their condemnation of Rushdie's denigration of the Prophet. The American public perception, on the other hand, was that Muslims were intolerant and did not believe in freedom of speech.

Another impetus for producing discourse on pluralism in Islam was the disintegration of the Soviet Union. A new enemy was needed for the United States, now the sole power in the world, to vanquish. Bernard Lewis and Samuel Huntington, among others, identified Islam as a worthy enemy and a potential threat to American power. Fear of the presence of Muslims in the West brought together a confluence of two important political interest groups in the United States—Zionists and right-wing Republicans. The two ideologies coalesced into what later formed the policies implemented by the neoconservatives as a response to the attacks on 9/11.

Muslim ideological reconstruction in the 1990s was in part a response to the Gulf War. The American response to Saddam Hussein's invasion of Kuwait was supported by many Muslim nations who joined the American initiative to roll back the occupation. The war made evident major fissures in the ranks of Muslim nations and people. While most governments and their official muftis supported the American intervention, many independent religious leaders, along with the majority of the populations in Islamic nations as well as those living in the diaspora in the West, were against it. The war intensified the divisions between Gulf Arabs and those living in the Northern tier. It set up Sunnis against Shi'is. It split Muslims in the diaspora, many of whom were loath to see Saudi Arabia allow western forces to "re-occupy" Muslim territory.

As a consequence of the Gulf War, which was opposed by the leadership of the American Muslim communities, financial support from Saudi Arabia and the Gulf states was cut off. This had a transformative effect on the Muslims in the United States. They became independent and began to establish Islamic institutions in the United States, including political action committees, as they sought to participate in the public square.

The growth in the number of Muslim intellectuals in the United States was another factor that increased reflection on and production of material on pluralism. The public debates about Islam as the next threat, along with the propaganda for war, spiked the demand for courses on Islam on American campuses. And as religious studies departments began to expand their offerings, they hired Western-educated Muslim scholars to staff these teaching positions. Most of those hired were immigrants or émigrés. A substantial number belonged to Shi`i branches of Islam, some of whom were part of the emigration of South Asians expelled from Uganda by Idi Amin. Other important contributors to the discourse have been Sunni African Muslim immigrants such as Sulayman Nyang from Gambia, Abdullahi An-Naim from the Sudan, and Farid Esack from South Africa. Each has made a distinctive contribution to the debates that bear the imprint of their African experience. A few are from an Arab background, including Mahmoud Ayoub of Lebanon, Fathi Osman, and Khalid Abou al-Fadl, both of Egypt.

Fathi Osman advocates a pluralistic Islam grounded not in fear or isolation, but in engagement with American society and exploration of new ways of leadership and participation in it. For Osman, the theology of pluralism begins with the affirmation that all humans are descendants from the same pair. The Qur'an talks about the dignity of all humans as "children of Adam," even though they may not believe in God. He concedes that consensus on all matters is impossible and different views will continue to prevail because God willed it that way. Meanwhile, "God's grace lies not in the abolition of difference in beliefs and views, nor in changing human nature which He himself has created, but in showing human beings how to handle their differences intellectually and morally and behaviorally."[53] There is no reference in the Qur'an for meting out death for apostasy, says Osman; rather, a death sentence is valid only in case of a crime against the state. He affirms that "Freedom of belief cannot be genuinely secured unless abandoning the faith is unrestricted; the same as embracing it is not imposed."[54]

Mahmoud Ayoub acknowledges that the Qur'anic text includes verses that are both exclusive and inclusive, and ascribes the apparent contradictory interpretations to the context in which they were written.[55] He writes that the Qur'an is more accepting of Jews and Christians than adherents of other religions because they are monotheists. It guarantees their reward on the last day. He notes that other religions may be accepted if they call for worship of the one God, but this pluralistic openness does not extend to polytheists.[56]

Writing prior to 9/11, Abou El Fadl, in the *Authoritative and Authoritarian in Islamic Discourse: A Contemporary Case Study*, addresses the issue of tolerance within the Muslim community in the United States. He says that the Qur'an makes it quite clear that the truth is accessible to all people regardless of gender, class, or race. He has been criticized for objecting to certain exclusive interpretations of Islam, such as Wahhabism, particularly at a time when Muslims have been under pressure from Western writers such as Harvard historian Samuel Huntington and Islamophobe Daniel Pipes.[57]

Surveying the writings of public intellectuals of the last decade of the twentieth century, Sulayman S. Nyang of Howard University sees an accelerated interest in pluralism as a consequence of changes taking place in the world. He identifies several converging realities that push toward pluralism: globalization that has brought humanity closer together by tearing down the walls of separation, a phenomenon brought about by the communication revolution; the growing awareness of the poor of the world and of the material possibilities they began to seek; the dissatisfaction with secularism and the growing quest for spiritual meaning; and the increased awareness of other religions now gathered under the same roof as a consequence of international migration.

At the same time, Nyang identifies factors that have limited Muslims' response to pluralism and caused them to be less attracted to American values. Muslims share with American conservatives a revulsion at American popular culture—identified as a "libertinism" that encourages sexual promiscuity. They are also turned off by American materialism, which places a premium on "excessive acquisitiveness." Furthermore, they find American textbooks problematic; they "wish to keep their children from the triple problems of religious indoctrination, drugs, and sexual promiscuity" and seek to remove anti-Muslim materials from the textbooks. They also are reluctant to embrace "excessive individualism," which they perceive as undermining the importance of the family and the maintenance of a cohesive society. They seek to maintain dietary restrictions in part as a protection against gluttony. "In the special case of American Muslims, those who adhere faithfully to the halal diet see fewer opportunities in the eateries than their more voracious neighbors, who consume swine as easily as they imbibe alcohol."[58]

Despite such impediments to enthusiastic engagement in American plural-ism, Nyang enjoins Muslim leaders to participate in dialogue over issues of common concern with the larger population. He especially puts the onus on them to share their particular perspective on life and urges them to participate in forums on American campuses and to reach out to their neighbors and coworkers.[59] Nyang notes that "triumphant Islam" has tended to forget that Islam at its core, as it was in its Meccan formative period, is pluralistic. Return to the true teachings of the Qur'an and the practice of the prophet Muhammad does not mean that one can compel others to follow a doctrine, but rather pro-motes freedom of religion as the Qur'an proclaims when it says that "there is no compulsion in religion."[60]

Another African intellectual who found a home in the American academy is Farid Esack, who writes out of the context of the struggle for liberation in South Africa. Esack's pluralistic definition of Islam includes both race and econom-ics as he talks about the liberation of people "who eke out an existence on the margins of society" from economic exploitation.[61] He prescribes pluralism as not just "joyous intellectual neutrality," but as the endeavor to liberate people and to work toward healing societies that are racially divided, patriarchal, and economically exploitative. Esack faults traditional exegesis in promoting the doc-trine of supersession, which has circumvented the Qur'anic verses that promote the recognition of other religions. Pluralism for Esack does not mean the liberal embrace of all "others" as equal. The struggle in South Africa demonstrated that some interpretations must be opposed because they suppress people.[62] The barometer for exclusion, he says, is social justice, not religious commitment.

Also contributing to the conversation about pluralism is African Muslim Abdullahi An-Na`im, professor of Islamic Studies at Emory University. He is the disciple of Mahmoud Taha, founder of the Republican Brothers, who was executed by the Sudanese government because his liberal ideas were deemed heretical.[63] In the United States, An-Na`im's ideas are not shared by the gen-eral Muslim population, who question his criticism of Islamic doctrines and the *shari`ah*, holding that universal values should be the norm. He argues that Muslims need to generate new ideas in order to mainstream Islam and make it consistent with currently accepted universal norms. Rather than insisting that the world should adjust to their norms that were formulated in a different context centuries ago, or to reformulate them and enwrap them with mod-ern discourse that maintains their superiority, An-Na`im urges Muslims to align Islamic values with the universal norms. He insists that the status of non-Muslim religious minorities under *shari`ah* is not congruent with cur-rent universal standards of human rights, that what obtains cannot be justi-fied on claims of Islamic cultural relativism. Religious minorities should not be subject to Muslim cultural norms that are not consistent with the relevant universal standards. It is not only possible, but also imperative, that the sta-tus of non-Muslims under *shari`ah* be reformed from within the fundamental sources of Islam, namely the Qur'an and Sunnah, the teaching and example of the Prophet Muhammad.

At issue for An-Naim are several laws and practices that the *shari`ah* uses to restrict religious minorities. He notes that the religious minorities "are not allowed to participate in the public affairs of an Islamic state. They are not allowed to hold any position of authority over Muslims, although Muslims may, and do, hold such positions over *dhimmis* (non-Muslims). *Dhimmis* may practice their religion in private, but they are not allowed to proselytize or preach their faith in public. A *dhimmi* is allowed and even encouraged to embrace Islam, while a Muslim may never abandon Islam.[64] The modern world has necessitated a revision of the *shari`ah,* since the problems have changed; the traditional answers are no longer valid.[65] Unlike al-Qaradawi, who promotes a dual interpretation, An-Naim seeks a radical reinterpretation of Islamic law that can help Muslims in the diaspora adjust to the exigencies of their situation.

For An-Naim, such reform would at once be both Islamic and fully consistent with universal human rights standards.[66] He is therefore critical of Muslim insistence on implementing the *Shari`ah*, which he finds as discriminatory against non-Muslims, since it renders them inferior and teaches that their lesser status is divinely inspired. "It would be heretical for a Muslim who believes the *shari`ah* is the final and ultimate formulation of the law of God to maintain that any aspect of that law is open to revision and reformulation by mere mortal and fallible human beings. To do so is to allow human beings to correct what God has decreed."[67]

Abdulaziz Sachedina of the University of Virginia notes in his seminal work *The Islamic Roots of Democratic Pluralism,* published prior to the attacks of 9/11, that the Qur'an provides a basis for a democratic pluralistic global community. The universal Islamic model demands coexistence among people of different religions as part of the divine plan for humanity.[68] He argues that Islam has a unique characteristic that proceeds from the unity of God, a fact that unites the Muslim community with all humanity.[69] Pluralism is thus part of the divine mystery, and, as such, it is not merely a matter of tolerance of difference, but of accepting others "in fellowship towards the divine."[70] He, too, sees that this foundational principle of the Qur'an has been obscured by the doctrine of supersession devised by the traditional exegetes. He rejects their claim that the verses of the Qur'an that promote pluralism were abrogated by others revealed at a later date, saying that "of the 137 listed verses that are claimed to have been abrogated, in reality not even one of them has been abrogated."[71] Furthermore, he notes that the Qur'an assures Christians and Jews who believe in God and the Last Day that they will be saved (S. 2:62); there is nothing in the Qur'an that suggests that the Qur'an abrogated the previous scriptures of the Jews and the Christians.[72]

Building on the same Qur'anic reference used by al-Faruqi regarding the Islamic concept of *din al-fitra*, Sachedina argues that *fitra* affirms that each human being is endowed with a sense of knowledge and discernment of good and evil, as well as the relationship of humans to the divine. All humanity is therefore predisposed toward monotheism. He faults the two major branches of Islam, Sunnis and Shi`a, for impeding human progress, the Sunnis by affirming and practicing exclusivism and the Shi`a by insisting on certain prerequisites and qualifications for interpreting the Qur'an. Their exclusive claims to truth have impeded human recognition of the divine mandate for pluralism that can promote peace in a violent world.[73]

The Pluralism Discourse after 2001

For Muslims in the West, September 11 appears to have convinced onlookers that religious expression can be associated with religious fanaticism and that Muslim fanaticism is an anti-American and therefore a global threat.[74] This perception was aggravated by events in Afghanistan such as the wanton destruction of the Buddha statues in Bamyan by the Taliban and the public execution of a woman. The image of Muslims bent on holy war, intolerant of other faiths, and subjugators of women became seared into the American consciousness, exacerbated by the American government's propaganda for war. Questioning American policies in the Muslim world became tantamount to treason. President Bush announced on November 6, 2001, "You are either with us or against us,"[75] hardly a clarion call for pluralism. American values are governed by American interests. Muqtedar Khan of the University of Delaware believes that the United States uses pluralism as an ideology that it seeks to impose on less powerful nations as part of its global reach. In a sense, says Khan, pluralism is a tool of propaganda which supersedes truth and belies its power relationship with the Muslim world. The United States does not seek real international pluralism and does not tolerate other views.[76]

In his post 9/11 book, Abou El Fadl returns to the topic of pluralism, putting more emphasis on the relation of Muslims to non-Muslims. He tries to dissociate Islam from the Saudi, Wahhabi interpretation promoted by the perpetrators of 9/11. Wahhabi-inspired publications have been available for American Muslim consumption in books, pamphlets, and magazines as well as on the Internet. Admitting that there are verses in the Qur'an that are exclusionary, El Fadl tries to put them in context. As al-Faruqi and Rahman had done earlier, he reaffirms that diversity and difference are the essential teachings of the Qur'an. He notes that, while the Qur'an posits claims of the absolute truth of the revelation, it does not deny that there might be "other paths to salvation." And since the Qur'an states that there is no compulsion in religion, it is the duty of every Muslim to emphasize the tolerance of Islam, recognizing that nonbelievers should not be subjugated.[77]

Some Muslims have called for initiatives to forge common norms. Husain Kasim of the University of Central Florida calls for dialogue between Muslims and other Americans that can lead to the "universalization of norms," based on shared ethical values and not on political expediency, with Muslims being taken seriously in forging a consensus on common grounds about how to live together.[78] Aware that he is departing from the exegesis of others, particularly the dominant teachings of the mosque movement in the United States, Kasim insists that the Qur'an promotes the idea of pluralism. He affirms that salvation also is available to believers among the People of the Book.[79]

For a short time there was the expectation that perhaps the proponents of the so-called Progressive Islam would provide new leadership, particularly after the government undermined the existing leadership of the Muslim community by raiding their homes, offices, and business establishments. In the aftermath of 9/11, a new generation of Muslim scholars has gained some prominence for their advocacy of this Progressive Islam.[80] Omid Safi edited a book by that title at the University of North Carolina. The book received some attention as the authors also sought to dissociate Islam from Wahhabi interpretation and rejected any understanding of Islam that cast it as violent, misogynist, or exclusivist. The book attempts to redefine Islam as governed by justice, including gender and racial justice. Some of the authors set up websites devoted to discussions of an Islam based on concepts of justice, gender equality, and pluralism. They were catapulted into prominence by the media. While at first it was welcomed as a refreshing new interpretation, Progressive Islam soon receded in popularity among young Muslims as its authors went beyond what is acceptable as Islamic morality, particularly concerning openness to a gay life style.

A few members of the group chose to confront tradition by holding a co-ed Friday service in New York City, led by Professor Amina Wadud of Virginia Commonwealth University. Some observers interpreted the service as a publicity stunt to promote journalist Asra Nomani's book, *Standing Alone at Mecca*. The event once again focused the negative attention of the press on the Muslim community. Despite the fact that their efforts were not welcomed by the majority of the Muslim community, they did make some impact by highlighting the restricted role of women in American mosques. The traditional mosque organizations issued guidelines instructing mosques to open leadership positions for women members. Several women were propelled into positions of leadership: ISNA elected Ingrid Mattson of Hartford Seminary as its first woman president, and MSA elected Hadia Mubarak as its first woman national president.

Amina Wadud is noted for her work championing gender pluralism. In her book *Qur'an and Woman* she calls for a new hermeneutic and advocates women's engagement with the exegesis of the Qur'an. She notes that there is an absence of women's voices in interpreting the text of the Qur'an, which she identifies as the effort of traditional society to silence women. She calls for an alternative exegesis that takes into consideration women's insights in order to foster a holistic Islamic message.[81] Her ideas about "gender jihad" have resonated among Muslim feminists, several of whom began to echo her demand for gender pluralism and a women's interpretation of the Qur'an. These include, among others, Asma Barlas, Aziza al-Hibri, Kecia Ali, and Nimat Hafiz Barazangi. Also calling for gender pluralism is African-American Gwendolyn Zohara. She writes, "Frankly, I am tired of the contortions, the bending over backwards, and the justifications for the oppressive, repressive, and exclusionary treatment of women in majority Islamic societies as well as in minority Muslim communities in the U.S.A."[82]

Zohara also questions racial discrimination by immigrant Muslims against African-Americans. The fissure between immigrant Muslims and African-American converts was exacerbated when Warith Deen Muhammad, the late leader of the African-American Muslim community, appeared on PBS's *Tony's Journal* and said that his followers have the true Islam and they should not look to Muslims overseas for understanding what true Islam is about. African-American scholar Sherman Jackson, now King Faisal Chair of Islamic Thought and Culture at the University of Southern California, is one of the most articulate voices calling attention to the fact that immigrant Muslims exclude African-Americans from their deliberations on the meaning of Islam. He warns against commitment to ideologies imported from the Middle East that are exclusionary and do not accommodate different interpretations, contrary to Islamic tradition that has made room for competing interpretations that at times are even contradictory. For Jackson, the future of Islam in the United States, particularly after 9/11, is contingent on a pluralistic, nonviolent, tolerant, and egalitarian interpretation of the faith that is inclusive of America and makes room for differences in interpretation. For a true pluralistic Islam, it has to promote the "collective enterprises of good."[83]

More recently, as a new generation of American-born Muslims has come of age, and as the American government has tried to undermine the leadership of the Muslim community, the GWoT generation has been left to fend for itself. A recent survey of college students identified a different set of Muslim scholars whom they look up to as the "rock stars" of Islam. What is interesting in the survey is the lack of any reference to immigrant scholars. Every Muslim on the list is a convert to Islam, and the majority tend to promote Islam as a lifestyle rather than an ideology, an Islam that is more spiritual, more Sufi in orientation than Wahhabi. Among white converts, the following were noted: Yahya Rhodus, Nooridin Durkee, Abdul Hayy Moore, Suhaib Webb, Yusuf Estes, Hamza Yusuf, and Umar Faruq Abdullah. Two transnational Muslim scholars were also singled out as important in formulating the thinking of young Muslims: Timothy James Winter of the United Kingdom, and the American Nuh Ha Mim Keller, who has a center in Amman, Jordan, frequented by American Muslim youth. Several African-American leaders were listed, including Murad Kalam, Imam Siraj Wahhaj, Sherman Jackson, and Zaid Shakir. These leaders call on Muslim youth who are alienated from their parents' imported rigid culture to engage in dialogue with the West while maintaining their commitment to the traditional teachings of Islam. Their authority stems from the fact that they have studied overseas under the tutelage of recognized Muslim scholars.

One of the most popular of the "rock stars" is Hamza Yusuf, founder of the Zeituna Institute in California. Hamza Yusuf originally became popular because of his sharp criticism of the United States, its decadence, lack of spirituality, and injustice in its foreign policy. After 9/11, however, he was invited to the White

House, where he seems to have undergone a "conversion" in thinking. Rather than focusing on what makes Muslims angry about American policy, he began to focus on the relation between Islam and the West and urged his Muslim listeners to look at the good things in Western society. This transformation in his message has earned him the criticism of some in the Muslim community who consider him a collaborator, even calling him former President George W. Bush's "pet Muslim."[84] He has expressed regrets over his former outspoken criticism of American foreign policy in the Middle East as inappropriate, and has since criticized political Islam. "September 11 was a wake-up call for me. I don't want to contribute to the hate in any shape or form. I now regret in the past being silent about what I have heard in the Islamic discourse and being part of that with my own anger."[85] He urges the youth to return to their spiritual heritage in order to set their relationship with God on the right path.

Like Sherman Jackson,[86] Hamza Yusuf sees a role for Muslims in the West in fashioning a new interpretation of Islam based on the classical foundation of the faith. He is seen as an important link between American culture and Muslim youth who face the travails of integration and assimilation. He and the other convert "rock stars" embody the struggle for the meaning of being an American Muslim. He is a white convert who is idealized by nonwhites because he has rejected the allures of American culture and found fulfillment and meaning in Islam. He now criticizes "Muslim fascists" who peddle a theology of hate. As for Muslims who are critical of the West, he is quoted as saying, "if they are going to rant and rave about the West, they should emigrate to a Muslim country."[87] Yusuf is a popular television personality. He appears on "Journeys with Hamza Yusuf," which is broadcast on Middle East Broadcasting Corporation (MBC) via satellite to the Arab world. He presents Islam as part of the Abrahamic tradition, sharing its values with Christianity and Judaism, and does not necessarily oppose freedom and democracy. He notes that "it is Islam that has prevented the Islamic world from blowing up in rage—not the opposite."[88]

The new generation of Muslim youth in the West, both in North America and Europe, children of the Global War on Terror, is looking for new leadership. Part of this search is a consequence of the American government's efforts to undermine the leadership that existed prior to 9/11. The other reason is that parents are now more laid back; they realize that the institutions they established may have saved their children from the pornographic, drug-infested subculture of America, but it has also placed them under the suspicion of the security agents of the government. Unlike their older siblings, the new youth have more freedom to explore different avenues of being Muslims in America. They have no allegiance to their parents' identity and are eager to shed some of its restrictive culture. The question is how to go about setting up new institutions where they can be truly American, truly Muslim.

One of the most interesting and challenging new interpretations to come from this cohort of young Muslims is that of Umar Faruq Abdullah, which calls specifically for the creation of an American Islam. The parent's generation was raised on the idea that Islam as a way of life is a prototype that needs to be replicated wherever the religion takes hold. It promoted a specific culture that was to be implemented so all Muslims will walk and talk and hold their posture in a particular manner. Abdullah draws attention to the fact that the Prophet and the companions were not at war with the cultures of the world, nor did they try to eradicate ethnicities and to fit everyone into a preconceived mold. More importantly, they did not have a bipolar view of cultures that divided them into good and evil, a division that is a characteristic of Islamist literature.[89]

What Abdullah is calling for is not tinkering with or trying to repair Islam as it has been conveyed through tradition, but a new project that embraces American culture as a vehicle for engaging Islamic values. "In China, Islam looked Chinese; in Mali, it looked African."[90] Why, he asks by implication, should Islam in the United States not look American? He criticizes Islamist rhetoric as falling "short of Islam's ancient cultural wisdom assuming at times an unmitigated culturally predatory attitude."[91] For him, it is incumbent on the new generation of Muslims to construct an American culture where they can be at home being Muslim and American.

Conclusion

Most of the writing of Muslim authors on issues of pluralism has focused not only on the need for a *modus vivendi* with American society, but also on the necessity of developing pluralism in the Muslim community itself. It emphasizes the awareness of the great diversity among Muslims, not only of nationalities they come from but also issues of race, color, language, and theological and ideological commitments. The literature advocates tolerance of differences in practice and beliefs among Muslims who adhere to distinct schools of law and a moratorium on efforts to force people to conform to one school. It looks forward to a future when Muslims will learn to celebrate their internal differences.

Muslims living in the United States are in an unprecedented situation, in that they are living as a religious minority with equal rights granted to all the citizens in the nation. While some Muslims continue to focus obsessively on anti-Muslim sentiments and Islamophobia, others have chosen to call attention to the guarantees of the Bill of Rights, with the potential for Muslims to have input into all aspects of the public square. As was true for other religious minorities of the past, like Catholics and Jews, Muslims can become full constituents of American society.[92] They hold on to the promise of America as a pluralistic society and hope that the day that America will make room for them as Muslims is not far off.

The need to emphasize the diversity of Muslims, the pluralism within American Islam, becomes imperative as Western governments appear to hold their Muslim citizens potentially guilty by association with a faith that has been deemed by some to be violent in nature. There appears to be an incipient hope, if not expectation, that once Western societies are enlightened about the true nature of Islamic pluralism, they will incorporate Islam and Muslim culture, not as a novelty consigned to ghettoes of difference, but as an integral part of Western society.

As a British Muslim academic summed up the Muslim situation vis-à-vis pluralism, "The fundamental obligation on us all, then, is to ensure that our societies accept all the challenges of pluralism, religious and secular. For Muslims and Islamic states, this is about remembering that the pluralism on which Islam flourished as a civilization is no longer sufficient for the multiple religious and secular discourses of our contemporary world. The Qur'anic verse, 'Had God willed he would have made you all one,' must translate into a re-visioning of society where Muslim communities can truly accept that religious diversity may possibly be God's will, challenge and blessing on earth. The imperative on us is how we free ourselves from dogmatism and prejudice and be allowed to interpret the Qur'an in such a way that translates meaningfully with human diversity at a local, national and global level."[93]

Notes

1 Michael Wolfe et al., *Taking Back Islam: American Muslims Reclaim their Faith* (Emmaus, PA: Rodale, 2004).

2 Hatem Bazian, "Virtual Internment: Arabs, Muslims, Asians and the War on Terrorism," *Journal of Islamic Law & Culture* 9 (2004): 1.

3 George Bush, "Remarks by the President at Islamic Center of Washington, D.C.," available at http://www.whitehouse.gov/news/releases/2001/09/20010917-11.html, accessed September 22, 2005.

4 Muzammal Siddiqui, "Unity and Diversity: Islamic Perspective," available at http://www.crescentlife.com/spirituality/unity_and_diversity_islamic_perspective.htm, accessed June 3, 2007.

5 Ismail Raji al-Faruqi, "Common Bases between the Two Religions in Regard to Convictions and Points of Agreement in the Spheres of Life," reprinted in *Islam and Other Faiths*, Ataullah Siddiqui, ed. (Leicester: Islamic Foundation and International Institute for Islamic Thought, 1998), 220.

6 Muhammad Abduh, *al-A`mal al-Kamila* (Beirut, 1980), III, 289.

7 Abduh, Ibid., III, 291–292.

8 Abduh, Ibid., III, 290.

9 `A'isha `Abd al-Rahman, *al-Isra'iliyyat fi al-Ghazu al-Fikri* (Cairo 1975); Anwar al-Jindi, *Afaq Jadida li-al-Da`wa al-Islamiya fi `Alam al-Ghar* (Beirut: 1984), 20–22; Salim `Ali al-Bahnasawi, *al-Ghazu al-Fikri li-al-Tarikh wa al-Sira bayn al-Yamin wa al-Yasar* (Kuwait, 1985), 111–147; `Ali `Abd al-Halim Mahmud, *al-Ghazu al-Fikri wa al-Tayyarat al-Mu`adiya li-al-Islam* (Riyadh, 1984); Hassan Muhammad Hassan, *Wasa'il Muqawamat al-Ghazu al-Fikri li-al-`Alam al-Islami* (Mecca, 1981); `Abd al-Halim Mahmud, *al-Ghazu al-Fikri wa-Atharuhu fi al-Mujtama` al-Islami al-Mu`asir* (Kuwait, 1979); `Ali Muhammad Jarisha and Muhammad Sharif al-Zaybaq, *Asalib al-Ghazu al-Fikri li-al-`Alam al-Islami* (Cairo, 1977); Muhammad Faraj, *al-Islam fi Mu`tarak al-Sira` al-Fikri al-Hadith* (Cairo, 1962); Muhammad Jalal Kishk, *al-Ghazu al-Fikri* (Cairo, 1975).

10 ʿAbd al-Rahman, *al-Isra'iliyyat*, 58–59.

11 Sayyid Qutb, *Fi Zilal al-Qur'an* (Beirut, 1980), II, 816.

12 Ibid., II, 828.

13 Ibid., II, 829.

14 Ibid., II, 874.

15 Ibid., III, 1564. For further reflection on the issue, see Fahmi Huwaydi, *Li'l-Islam Dimuqratiyya* (Cairo: 1993), 32–34.

16 Qutb, *Fi Zilal*, II, 908.

17 Ibid., II, 910.

18 Ibid., II, 915.

19 Ibid., III, 1620.

20 Ibid., III, 1633.

21 Rajab Madkur, *al-Takfir wa al-Hijra Wajhan li-Wajh* (Cairo: 1985); Nuʿman ʿAbd al-Raziq al-Samirra'i, *al-Takfir: Judhuruh- Asbabuh- Mubarriratuh* (Jiddah: 1984); Salim al-Bahnasawi, *al-Hukm wa Qadiyyat Takfir al-Muslim* (Kuwait: 1985); Hassan al-Hudaybi, *Duʿat la Qudat* (Beirut: 1978); Yusuf al-Qaradawi, *al-Sahwa al-Islamiyya bayn al-Juhud wa al-Tatarruf*, Kitab al-Umma #4 (Doha, Qatar:1985); Yusuf al-Qaradawi, *Zahirat al-Ghuluww fi al-Takfir* (Kuwait: 1985); Muhammad ʿAbd al-Hakim Hamid, *Zahirat al-Ghuluww fi al-Din fi al-ʿAsr al-Hadith* (Cairo: 1991).

22 Muhammad Arkun, *al-Hawamil wa-al-Shawamil: Hawl al-Islam al-Muʿasir* (Beirut: 2010), 16.

23 Mustafa Farghali Shuqayri, *Fi Wajh al-Mu'amara ʿala Tatbiq al-Shariʿa al-Islamiya* (al-Mansura: 1986), 20.

24 The Symposium took place in Amman, Jordan, October 25–7, 1986, and the proceedings were published in *Majallat al-Ufuq al-ʿArabi*, #9, 1987.

25 The Symposium on Political Pluralism in the Arab World was sponsored by the Center for Arab Unity in Amman, Jordan, March 26–8, 1989. The proceedings were published in *Muntada al-Fikr al-ʿArabi*.

26 Mustafa Mashhur, "al-Taʿaddudiyya al-Hizbiyya," *al-Shaʿb*, October 4, 1993; Salah al-Sawi, *al-Taʿaddudiyya al-Siyasiyya fi al-Islam* (Cairo: 1992).

27 The proceedings are published in *Majallat Minbar al-Sharq*, vol. 1, 1992.

28 Muhyi al-Din ʿAtiyya, "al-Taʿaddudiyya: Qa'ima Biblioghrafiyya Intaqat," *Nadwat al-Taʿaddudiyya al-Hizbiyya wa al-Ta'ifiyya wa al-ʿUrqiyya fi al-ʿAlam al-ʿArabi* (Herndon, VA: IIIT, 1993). The bibliography included the papers delivered at a Symposium on Pluralism in Political Parties, Sects, and Race in the Arab World sponsored by the International Institute of Islamic Thought in Herndon, Virginia, November 26–December 1, 1993.

29 ʿAbd al-Rahman al-Rashid, "Bayʿal-Iʿlam al-ʿArabi," *al-Majalla*, #707, August 14–20, 1994, 13.

30 Jabir Saʿid ʿAwad, "Mafhum al-Taʿaddudiyya fi al-Adabiyyat al-Muʿasira: Murajaʿa Naqdiyya," *Nadwat al-Taʿaddudiyya al-Hizbiyya wa al-Ta'ifiyya wa al-ʿIrqiyya fi al-ʿAlam al-ʿArabi* (Herndon, VA: IIIT, 1993), 2.

31 For a study of recent reflections on the role of Christians in an Islamic state, see Yvonne Yazbeck Haddad, "Christians in a Muslim State: The Current Egyptian Debate," in *Christian-Muslim Encounters*, Yvonne Yazbeck Haddad and Wadi Zaidan Haddad, eds. (Gainesville: University Press of Florida, 1995). Cf. ʿAbd al-malik Salman, "al-Tasamuh Tijah al-Aqalliyyat Kadarura li al-Nahda," *Nadwat al-Taʿaddudiyya*

al-Hizbiyya wa al-Ta'ifiyya wa al-`Irqiyya fi al-`Alam al-`Arabi (Herndon, VA: IIIT, 1993).

32 Zaki Ahmad, "al-Ta`addudiyya al-Hizbiyya fi al-Fikr al-Islami al-Mu`asir," *Nadwat al-Ta`addudiya al-Hizbiyya wa al-Ta'ifiyya wa `Irqiyya fi al-`Alam al-`Arabi* (Herndon, VA: IIIT, 1993), 1.

33 Available at http://www.islamonline.net/english/index.shtml.

34 Yusuf al-Qaradawi, *Ghayr al-Muslimin fi al-Mujtama`al-Islami* (Beirut, 1983).

35 Ibid., 7–12.

36 Ibid., 49.

37 Ibid., 20–23, 41.

38 Ibid., 80–81.

39 See for example: (S. 6:98–99; 35:27–28; 30:22; 49:13). Ahmad, "al-Ta`addudiyya," 6. Cf. Sa`d al-Din Ibrahim, *al-Ta`addudiyya al-Siyasiyya wa al-Dimuqratiyya fi al-Watan al-`Arabi* (Amman: 1989). Proceedings of a conference held March 26–28, 1989.

40 Huwaydi, *Li'l-Islam*, 22.

41 Ismail Raji al-Faruqi, "The Role of Islam in Global Inter-Religious Dependence," reprinted in Siddiqui, ed., *Islam and Other Faiths*, 72.

42 Ismail Raji al-Faruqi, "Islam and other Faiths," reprinted in Siddiqui, ed., *Islam and Other Faiths*, 149.

43 al-Faruqi, "Role of Islam," 74–75.

44 Ibid., 91–92.

45 al-Faruqi, "Islam and Other Faiths," 140.

46 Ibid., 138.

47 Ismail Raji al-Faruqi, "Islam and Christianity: Diatribe or Dialogue," in Siddiqui, ed., *Islam and Other Faiths*, 269.

48 al-Faruqi, "Islam and Other Faiths."

49 al-Faruqi, "Role of Islam," 72–73.

50 Muhammad `Amara, "al-Ta`addudiyya: al-Ru'ya al-Islamiyya wa al-Tahadiyat al-Gharbiyya," *Nadwat al-Ta`addudiyya al-Hizbiyya wa al-Ta'ifiyya wa al-`Irqiyya fi al-`Alam al-`Arabi* (Herndon, VA: IIIT, 1993), 3–14.

51 al-Faruqi, "Role of Islam," 103.

52 Fazlur Rahman, *Major Themes of the Qur'an* (Minneapolis, MN: Bibliographica Islamica, Inc., 1980), 165–166.

53 Mohamed Fathi Osman, *The Children of Adam: An Islamic Perspective on Pluralism*, Occasional Papers (Washington, DC: Center for Muslim-Christian Understanding, 1996), 13.

54 Ibid., 31.

55 Mahmoud Ayoub, "Islam and Pluralism," *Encounters* 332 (1997): 103–118. See also his "Islam and Christianity Between Tolerance and Acceptance," *Islam and Christian-Muslim Relations* 2, no. 2 (December 1991).

56 Ayoub, "Islam and Pluralism," 103–118.

57 Khalid Abou El Fadl, *The Authoritative and the Authoritarian in Islamic Discourse: A Contemporary Case Study* (Dar Taiba, 1997), 16.

58 Sulayman S. Nyang, "Seeking the Religious Roots of Pluralism in the United States of America: An American Muslim Perspective," *Journal of Ecumenical Studies* 34, no. 3 (Summer 97): 402.

59 Ibid., 402.

60 Ibid., 402.

61 Farid Esack, *Qur'an, Liberation and Pluralism* (Oxford: One World Publications, 1997), 78.

62 Ibid., 179.

63 Abdullahi A. An-Na`im, *The Second Message of Islam* (Syracuse: Syracuse University Press, 1987).

64 Ibid., 11.

65 Abdullahi A. An-Na`im, "Religious Minorities under Islamic Law and the Limits of Cultural Relativism," *Human Rights Quarterly* 9 (1987): 10–11.

66 An-Na`im, *Second Message*, 17.

67 An-Na`im, "Religious Minorities," 10.

68 Abdulaziz Sachedina, *The Islamic Roots of Democratic Pluralism* (New York: Oxford University Press, 2001), 139.

69 Abddulaziz Sachedina, *The Qur'an on Religious Pluralism*, Occasional Paper Series (Washington, DC: Center for Muslim-Christian Understanding, 1999) 11.

70 Ibid., 13.

71 Ibid., 16.

72 Ibid., 19.

73 Sachedina, *Islamic Roots of Democratic Pluralism*, 11–14.

74 Mona Siddiqui, "Islam: Issues of Political Authority and Pluralism," *Political Theology* 7, no. 3 (2006): 338.

75 http://archives.cnn.com/2001/US/11/06/gen.attack.on.terror/.

76 M.A. Muqtedar Khan, "Living on Borderlines: Beyond the Clash of Dialogue," in *Muslims' Place in the American Public Square*, Zahid H. Bukhari, et al., eds. (Altmira Press, 2004), 90–93.

77 Khalid Abou El Fadl, *The Place of Tolerance in Islam*, Joshua Cohen and Ian Lague, eds. (Boston: Beacon Press, 2002), 17.

78 Husein Kasim, *Legitimating Modernity in Islam, Muslim Modus Vivendi and Western Modernity* (Lewiston, ME: Edwin Mellon Press, 2005), 138–146.

79 See Yvonne Yazbeck Haddad, "Islamist Depictions of Christianity in the Twentieth Century," *Islam and Christian Muslim Relations* 11, no. 3 (October 2000): 75–94.

80 Omid Safi, *Progressive Muslims: On Justice, Gender and Pluralism* (Oxford: One World Publications, 2003).

81 Amina Wadud, "Alternative Qur'anic Interpretation and the Status of Women," in *Windows of Faith: Muslim Women Scholar-Activists in North America*, Gisela Webb, ed. (Syracuse: Syracuse University Press, 2000), 3–21. See also Amina Wadud, *Inside the Gender Jihad: Women's Reform in Islam* (London: One World, 2006).

82 Gwendolyn Zohara Simmons, "Are We Up to the Challenge? The Need for a Radical Reordering of the Discourse on Women," in Safi, ed., *Progressive Muslims*, 235.

83 Sherman A. Jackson, *"Islam(s) East and West: Pluralism between No-Frills and Designer Fundamentalism,"* in *September 11 in History: A Watershed Moment?* Mary L. Dudziak, ed. (Durham, NC: Duke University Press, 2003), 112–135.

84 Jack O. Sullivan, "Profile: If You Hate the West, Emigrate to a Muslim Country," *Guardian*, October 8, 2001, Features Pages, 4.

85 Ibid.

86 Sherman Jackson, *Islam and the Black American: Looking Toward the Third Resurrection* (New York: Oxford University Press, 2005).

87 Sullivan, "Profile: If You Hate the West," 4.

88 Don Lattin, "North American Muslims Ponder Effect of 9/11 on Them," *San Francisco Chronicle*, September 2, 2002, A3.

89 Umar Faruq Abd-Allah, "Islam and the Cultural Imperative" (Chicago: A Nawawi Foundation Paper, 2004), 4.

90 Ibid., 1.

91 Ibid., 2.

92 Nyang, "Seeking the Religious Roots of Pluralism," 402.

93 Siddiqui, "Islam: Issues of Political Authority and Pluralism," 348.

CHAPTER 8 | Buddhism, Art, and Transcultural
Collage: Toward a Cultural History
of Buddhism in the United States,
1945–2000

THOMAS A. TWEED

IN THE EAST ROOM of the White House on a fall afternoon in 1965, President
Lyndon B. Johnson signed the Highway Beautification Act. It was a bill that his
wife, Lady Bird, had advocated, and he had leaned on members of Congress
to pass it. Earlier that year, the First Lady had campaigned to "beautify" the
nation's capitol (see Figure 8.1). Her frequent automobile trips between Texas
and D.C. had convinced her that the nation's highways, with their crass billboards, had become eyesores. "Ugliness is so grim," she complained. "A little
beauty, something that is lovely, I think, can help create harmony which will
lessen tensions."[1] It is difficult to say if the national campaign to add "masses
of flowers where masses pass" eased the considerable tensions of 1965, a time
when many Americans were watching images of a war in Southeast Asia and
witnessing a violent domestic battle over, among other things, civil rights.
Nonetheless, she managed to extend the reach of her beautification efforts.
The result—Public Law 89–285—prescribed new guidelines for maintaining
the federal highways. The beautification of America had begun.[2]

During the ceremonial signing of the Highway Beautification Act that
October afternoon, President Johnson interpreted the federal program in
nationalist and religious terms. "We frequently point with pride and with
confidence to the products of our great free enterprise system—management
and labor." Industry, he proposed, is "actually a part of America's soul." There
"is more to America than raw industrial might," however. The beautiful natural landscape—"the forests and flowers"—is "another part of America's soul
as well."

In this chapter, I identify yet another component of postwar America's
"soul"—Buddhism—and analyze another less systematic aesthetic process—
the transcultural collage that led to the Buddhification of the American cultural landscape.[3] A hyperbolic term that playfully evokes Lady Bird's emphasis

Figure 8.1 Lady Bird Johnson and two children inspect the results of her "beautification" project on a tour of Washington D.C. on April 26, 1966.
LBJ Library photo by Robert Knudsen.

on "beautification," *Buddhification* refers to the complex transcultural process
whereby a confluence of forces that originated in the late nineteenth century
and intensified between the 1940s and the 1960s allowed some decontextualized Buddhist beliefs, practices, and artifacts to circulate widely, especially
among Americans who did not identify with that tradition. As representations
circulated in English-language communication systems after the "Zen boom"
of the Fifties, I argue, Buddhism became associated with conflict and violence
in the public imagination during the Vietnam Era, not only among Johnson
administration officials overseeing the war but also in print media and television news. Yet Buddhism's Asian and American popularizers managed
to break that representational link—as Islam's advocates could not—and the
Asian tradition emerged in the second half of the twentieth century as a tolerant spiritual alternative and an adaptable cultural implement, as I illustrate by
analyzing prescriptive literature and visual art. Some middle- and upper-class
Americans selectively and creatively appropriated the "Buddhism" that circulated so widely in books, magazines, television, and museums to meet their
own needs. That religion—especially what I call *Suzuki Zen*—could meet varied needs because it had been removed from its institutional context (the discipline of the monastery and the authority of the priest) and from its ritual
forms (the rigors of seated meditation and the aims of *kōan* practice). Liberated
from the constraints of precedent and released from tradition's inertial force,
Buddhism could become almost anything in the transnational flow of representations. It was an almost blank slate onto which Americans could inscribe

their own desires. Or, to change the metaphor to fit my focus, Americans who were not born into Buddhist households appropriated the received representations in a process that resembled collage, much as twentieth-century artists like Marcel Duchamp and Robert Rauschenberg pasted together varied materials, including found objects, to assemble new cultural forms. After tracing the complex history and diverse expressions of that cultural influence, I discuss how-to literature and focus on the fine arts, especially Buddhist-inspired painting and video art.

This case study gestures toward a fuller cultural history of Buddhism in the United States since 1945, but it does more than that. It considers both what happened (Buddhism exerted influence) and how it happened (religious decontextualization and transcultural collage). Yet it also contributes to conversations about the meaning and function of "pluralism" in America. However we talk about pluralism—and the term has referred to both the social fact of diversity and attitudes toward that demographic reality—this case study reminds us that any adequate analysis will do more than count adherents. It also requires assessing cultural impact. Sometimes sheer numbers of new Americans have prompted change, as with the transformations produced by the migration of Roman Catholics in the nineteenth century. In other cases, as with Buddhism, cultural influence can be disproportionate to numbers. Because new immigrants transformed the local landscape and, as I show here, some Americans appropriated decontextualized beliefs and practices flowing in transnational circuits, Buddhism's cultural impact since 1945 has been so great that it is only a slight exaggeration to talk about the Buddhification of America.

Conflict and Disaster: Representations of Buddhism in LBJ's America

Religious diversity had long been present in the United States, but before and after Lyndon Johnson's presidency, Protestantism continued to be the dominant cultural force in most regions and most media. Nonetheless, at least since the late-nineteenth century—and for Protestants concerned with foreign missions, as early as the 1810s—many middle-class Americans had some sense that the religious world reached beyond Protestantism and Catholicism, though the idiom for representing that diversity varied during the twentieth century.[4]

Johnson, who left the Baptists for the Disciples of Christ at the age of 11, was a firsthand witness to some of America's postwar religious diversity, which was mostly framed in terms of a "triple melting pot" and the "Judeo-Christian" tradition.[5] His mother, like most of his relatives, was a Baptist, and he befriended the evangelist Billy Graham.[6] His wife was an Episcopalian, and one of his daughters, Luci Baines Johnson, converted to Roman Catholicism. In Washington, D.C., he attended not only his own church, National City Christian Church, but also St. Mark's Episcopal with Lady Bird. With Luci, who was married in Washington's National Shrine of the Immaculate Conception in 1966, he knelt in the pews of local Catholic churches filled with images of saints that had not been part of the Protestant material culture of his childhood home or local congregation.[7] As Lynda Johnson Robb recalled, "God was in a very big tent for him."[8] There is little evidence, however, that his personal piety or ecumenical impulses included America's "third faith," Judaism, or any Asian tradition.

From intelligence briefings as well as news media, however, President Johnson knew that Buddhism was the majority faith of the Vietnamese he spent so much of his time worrying about, and the source of his representations of that religion illustrate a larger interpretive pattern: during and after the Sixties, Buddhism sometimes entered Americans' field of vision when it was associated with conflict or disaster.[9] During the John F. Kennedy and Johnson Administrations, Buddhism became linked with violence and the Vietnam War. A clash developed between South Vietnam's Catholic leader, President Ngo Dinh Diem, and the Buddhists he had antagonized with his restrictive policies. As historian Michael Hunt notes, that collision erupted in South Vietnam's major cities, supposedly Diem's strongholds, and it culminated in a clash on May 8, 1963, in Hue between government troops and those celebrating the Buddha's Birthday. "The encounter proved deadly," Hunt suggests, "and it set off protests that spread in June to Saigon and other cities." Most important for the course of the war and the representations of Buddhism, "soon headlines in American dailies and pictures on the television registered sensational self-immolations by monks, dramatic government raids, and harsh language by Diem's sister-in-law about the barbecuing of religious opponents."[10]

Surviving records show that LBJ, and other members of the Kennedy and Johnson Administrations, talked regularly about Vietnamese Buddhists as they planned and assessed military interventions.[11] For example, in 1965 President Johnson displayed his understanding of Buddhism's annual ritual cycle—perhaps he recalled the violence two years earlier—when he suggested to the U.S. Ambassador to South Vietnam, Maxwell D. Taylor, that they might temporarily stop the bombings on Buddha's Birthday: "...the days of Buddha's birthday seem[s] to me to provide an excellent opportunity for a pause in air attacks which might go into next week and which I could use to good effect with world opinion."[12] World opinion and U.S. attitudes were increasingly negative, and Johnson and other officials attributed that, in part, to the Buddhist peace and reform movement in Vietnam. In a National Security Council meeting on June 22, 1966, for instance, LBJ said, "I think that public approval is deteriorating, and that it will continue to go down. Some in Congress are disgusted about the Buddhist uprising and are talking about pulling out."[13]

Other officials agreed that it was "the Buddhist uprising"—and especially the published and televised images of the self-immolations by the protesting monks—that triggered the negative American perceptions.[14] An oral history interview with CIA official William E. Colby recounts the perceived impact of media images on the administration and the people.[15] Referring to the famous 1963 photograph of the Buddhist monk Thich Quang Duc immolating himself on a busy street in Saigon (see Figure 8.2), Colby suggested that "the Buddhist

Figure 8.2 The self-immolation of Thich Quang Duc on June 11, 1963, on a street in downtown Saigon.
(AP Photo/Malcolm Browne)(630611023).

revolt, which blew up in June of 1963, had its major impact not in Vietnam but in the United States." "When that picture of the burning bonze [monk] appeared in *Life* magazine," Colby recalled, "the party was almost over in terms of the imagery that was affecting the American opinion... 'How can you possibly support a government that has people doing this against it?'"[16] Other officials, including Ambassador Henry Cabot Lodge, noted the same representational pattern. Lodge blamed it on the media and implied that the awestruck journalists were naïve and the protesting Buddhists were insane. "The success which the Buddhists have in winning the American press over to them is marvelous to behold... practically all of the U.S. press takes the Buddhists at face value," Lodge wrote to President Johnson on June 1, 1966. "Every burning seems to be treated by our journalists with awe and wonder. Yet I imagine one could get some pretty lurid TV footage in some of our mental institutions at home—not an unfair equivalent of most of these self-immolations."[17]

One stream of Buddhist interpretation during and after the Vietnam War linked that Asian religion with conflict and disaster—as with American representations of Islam, which long had highlighted violence and had reaffirmed that thematic link after the 1979 Iranian Hostage Crisis, during the Bosnian "ethnic cleansing" of the 1990s, and after the World Trade Center attack of 9/11.[18] Consider, for example, television news. Buddhists managed to get some limited coverage on the major network evening news programs, averaging about four per year between 1968 and 2005. That average is misleading, however, since the number of stories varied widely—from zero in 1980 to 17 in 2000. According to the holdings of the most extensive archive of evening news broadcasts, there were 142 stories about "Buddhists" during this period.[19] Judy Muller reported on Buddhism's "growing appeal" among converts in the United States in a 1994 story on the ABC Evening News, but a bit more than half of those other stories (79) dealt with conflict, violence, or disaster. As with many other topics, Buddhists seemed newsworthy to journalists when something was going wrong. For example, nine stories followed the effects of the tsunami in Buddhist Asia in 2004 and 2005. Six chronicled the Taliban's destruction of Buddhist images in Afghanistan in 2001, just as a half dozen stories had focused on the People's Republic of China's destruction of Tibetan monasteries in 1987. Seven stories reported on the 1991 murder of Thai Buddhists outside a temple in Arizona, and one recounted the destruction of a Buddhist shrine in Hawley, Massachusetts, by several Vietnam veterans. Earlier, between 1968 and 1978, Vietnam had figured prominently in the coverage of Buddhism: almost all of the 33 stories about Buddhists in those years focused on Southeast Asia and the war.

Despite those widely circulated representations of Buddhists in conflict or crisis, including the memorable image of Quang Duc's self-immolation, many Americans continued to support the war: *The Ballad of the Green Berets* was the top single in 1966, and 43% of Americans polled by Gallup that April thought that the war was "a necessary evil" while only 15% thought "we should get out." Some Americans also had negative impressions of Buddhism, as did Colby, who years later still remembered those Vietnamese Buddhist reformers as "very, very strange." As for President Johnson, there is no evidence that Buddhism positively influenced his own religious beliefs or practices in any significant way. Yet by the time of Johnson's death in 1973, the process of Buddhification was already underway in the United States. Initiated in part by LBJ's signing of the Immigration and Naturalization Act beneath the Statue of Liberty on October 3, 1965—that law would allow more Buddhist priests and laity to enter in the decades ahead—and propelled by other more sympathetic interpretive streams in other media—including the print media's fascination with Zen and Tibet—Buddhism would only grow in cultural influence for the remainder of the twentieth century.[20]

The Cultural History of Buddhism in America, 1945–2000: An Overview

Buddhism's influence originated in the late nineteenth century, when thousands of middle-class, urban Americans sympathized with the tradition or defended Christianity against the widespread championing of Buddhism as a tolerant and scientific tradition well-suited for modern America.[21] Yet the first late-Victorian vogue of Buddhism had begun to fade by about 1912. The preoccupation with the First World War, and the concomitant shift in mood, combined with other social and economic forces—including the racist restrictions of the 1924 immigration act and the devastating impact of the Great

Depression—to cut off the flow of new Buddhist immigrants and diminish the interest among European-Americans, even if Buddhism remained the primary religious alternative, and main religious foe, for many U.S. intellectuals between the world wars.[22]

After World War II, however, Buddhism again began to exert some cultural clout in popular piety and popular culture. As Wendy Cadge and Robert Wuthnow persuasively argued in an important sociological study, Buddhism's influence in the United States "increased considerably" during the last decades of the twentieth century.[23] Some of that influence can be measured by the number of adherents—those who identify themselves as Buddhists or have connections to Buddhist institutions. No one knows exactly how many Buddhists there were in the United States by 2000, however. Reasonable estimates range from 1.4 to 4 million, and it seems safe to suggest that there were *at least* two million Buddhist adherents by 2007.[24] The majority of those adherents were Americans of Asian descent, both lifelong Buddhists and those who affirmed (or reaffirmed) Buddhist identity after emigration, but there also seemed to be hundreds of thousands, and maybe more than a million, European-American, Latino/a, and African-American converts.[25]

Counting adherents, however, does not reveal the scope of Buddhist presence since 1945. There seem to have been many nightstand Buddhists, sympathizers who did not identify fully or exclusively with the tradition but whose meditation manual on the nightstand signaled their interest in Buddhist beliefs and practices.[26] And as Cadge and Wuthnow show, a "significant minority of Americans have had contact with Buddhists and Buddhism and/or been influenced by it..."[27] In their analysis of a nationally representative survey of 2910 adults in the United States in 2002 and 2003, they found that one American in seven claimed to have a fair amount of contact with Buddhists and that one person in eight reported that Buddhist teachings or practices "have had an important influence on his or her religion or spirituality."[28] That means that "a sizeable number of Americans—as many as 25–30 million"—reported contact with Buddhism, and one-quarter of the American public claimed "to be very or somewhat familiar with the teachings of Buddhism."[29] Further, unlike perceptions of Islam, the media's conjoining of Buddhism and conflict after Quang Duc's "fiery protest," did not have an enduring negative impact. Survey data suggests that by 2003 "relatively small proportions of the American public thought negative words, such as violent (12%) and fanatical (23%) applied to the Buddhist religion, and, continuing nineteenth-century patterns, "a majority thought this about positive words such as tolerant (56%) and peace loving (63%)."[30]

These relatively positive perceptions of Buddhism and the relatively widespread reports of contact seem to have been propelled along by the swirl of both supply-side and demand-side forces: after 1945, and especially after the Sixties, attractive representations of Buddhism were more available in the spiritual marketplace, and more Americans sought out what was available.[31] That Buddhist presence was mediated by communication and transportation technology and by movements and institutions, including immigrant and converts groups that brought new religious leaders, texts, artifacts, and practices to the United States.[32] The so-called New Age Movement—with its retreat centers, regular workshops, and mail-order catalogs—exposed some Americans to Buddhism.[33] So did university classrooms and martial arts centers as well as the alternative medicine and holistic health care movements. Thich Nhat Hanh, the exiled Vietnamese Buddhist, led a transnational movement that emphasized "mindfulness," the practice of attending fully to each moment. Nhat Hanh's *The Miracle of Mindfulness*, to mention just one of his many books, sold more than 125,000 copies between 1975 and 2000, and its principles were applied in hospitals, clinics, and therapists' offices to reduce stress and enhance mental and physical health.[34] In that sense, a therapeutic Buddhism emerged from the writings of Nhat Hanh (and others like Jon Kabat-Zinn), but the Vietnamese monk also was connected with Buddhist activism.[35] Martin Luther King, Jr., nominated Nhat Hanh for the 1967 Nobel Peace Prize, and Nhat Hanh's influence extended also to organizations connected with "engaged Buddhism," a loosely organized movement emphasizing social action to promote benevolence, nonviolence, and social justice. It found some of its first expressions among Vietnamese and Indian Buddhists during the 1960s and, resonating with long-standing American activist impulses, grew in influence in the United States in the 1990s.[36] Engaged Buddhists visited prisoners, and correctional institutions also were sites where some inmates had the opportunity to read sacred texts and learn meditation practices.[37] Some churches and synagogues sponsored meditation workshops, and the film, music, fashion, advertising, and television industries also circulated Buddhist images and represented Buddhist practices.

So did publishing companies, and the scope of Buddhism's popular impact was evident in the national print media.[38] A search of one index identified 330 pieces on Buddhism in popular U.S. magazines between 1945 and 1980. Although there is more complexity than this periodization indicates, three overlapping periods emerge. First, although some accounts appeared earlier, in most ways Zen Buddhism entered the American scene between 1957 and 1963. In 1957, *Time* introduced "Zen," and *The New Yorker* profiled D. T. Suzuki, a major interpreter of the tradition to the West. Two other influential interpreters joined the conversation the next year: Nancy Wilson Ross answered the question, "What Is Zen?" for *Mademoiselle*, and in 1961 *Life* offered a portrait of Alan Watts, "Eager Exponent of Zen." The press even tried to distinguish authentic and inauthentic forms of the tradition in several pieces, including "Zen, Beat, and Square" in 1958 and "Real Spirit of Zen?" in 1959. In a second phase of interest, Zen continued to be a topic for the magazines between 1964 and 1979, for example, the American Zen teacher Philip Kapleau wrote a piece for *The New York Times Magazine* in 1966, and two years later, just after the Summer of Love, *Time* published an account of Tassajara, the first Zen monastery in the United States.[39]

TABLE 8.1 Buddhism in National Print Media: Periodicals, 1935–75.

DECADE	NUMBER OF PIECES ON BUDDHISM
1935–1945	44
1945–1955	48
1955–1965	168
1965–1975	90
Total	321

SOURCE: *Reader's Guide Retrospective* (Bronx, New York: H.W. Wilson, 2004).

Buddhism in Vietnam and Southeast Asia took center stage in periodicals between 1963, when the monks' protests began, and 1972, when the war waned. The decade between 1955 and 1965, then, saw the largest number of articles, in part, because reporting on the Zen boom and the Buddhist protests coincided (See Table 8.1). Some of the articles on Buddhism in Vietnam included coverage of Quang Duc's self-immolation—such as the *U.S. News and World Report* piece, "When a Monk Became a Human Torch"—and coverage of later immolations as well, including *Time*'s story on the "Second Buddhist Priest to Burn Himself to Death." Broader coverage of the Buddhist peace and reform movements appeared in the pages of national magazines too, including a piece on "Buddhist Revolt" in the *New Republic*. The leading Protestant and Catholic periodicals also pondered events in Vietnam: *Catholic World* considered "Religious Liberty: Buddhist Protests and Catholic Principles," and so did the Protestant periodical *Christian Century* ("Rome and Saigon"). Even *Business Week* observed in 1966 that "Vietnam's Buddhists Emerge as Key Power."[40]

As the conflict in Southeast Asia ended—or at least changed form—a third period in the print media representations of Buddhism shifted focus to Tibetan traditions and the Dalai Lama. That period began in 1973, just as some of the first Tibetan practice centers were emerging, increased when the Dalai Lama won the 1989 Nobel Peace Prize, and continued into the late 1990s. In 1967, Tarthang Tulku, a Tibetan Buddhist of the *Rnying Ma* (*Nyingma*) lineage, arrived in Berkeley, and in the next decade periodicals began to include accounts of his meditation center as well as others, like Chogyam Trungpa Rinpoche's Naropa Institute in Boulder. Continuing the hoary Western tradition of exoticizing Tibet, travel accounts provided glimpses of the "hidden splendors" of that "adventureland." American general interest and religious periodicals also covered the visits of the Dalai Lama, and, as with television news coverage, that leader of the exiled Tibetan community got a good deal of press after his 1989 Nobel Peace Prize. With celebrities like Richard Gere and Steven Seagal affiliating with Tibetan Buddhist lineages, the vogue of things Tibetan seemed to peak during the 1990s. National magazines reviewed several films showing in American theaters—*Little Buddha*, *Kundun*, and *Seven Years in Tibet*—and at the height of public interest in 1997, the cover of *Time* proclaimed "America's Fascination with Buddhism." That periodical printed an interview with Brad Pitt, who starred in *Seven Years in Tibet*, and ran a cover story on "Buddhism in America."[41]

Zen and the Art of Everything: Buddhist Themes in Prescriptive Literature

Some interpreters pondered the implications of Tibetan Buddhism for daily life, and prescriptive literature illustrates the tradition's cultural impact after 1945. An article in *Psychology Today*, for example, applied the insights of the *Tibetan Book of the Dead* to "the art of dying."[42] The same strategy of applying Buddhist principles—especially what had come to be understood as "Zen"—found expression in an astonishingly wide range of prescriptive literature after 1957. Some of that literature appeared in national magazines. The science fiction author Ray Bradbury's piece on "Zen and the Art of Writing" was published in 1958. The next year Calvin Tomkins offered an article on "Zen in the Art of Tennis," and *The New Yorker* linked Zen and food in a 1962 story, "Macrobiotics: Zen Diet at Musubi Restaurant."[43]

These articles, and the hundreds of prescriptive books that followed, were indebted to the influence of mid-century Zen popularizers such as Nancy Wilson Ross, Arthur Waley, and Alan Watts, and especially to the Japanese Rinzai Zen Buddhist SUZUKI Daisetz Teitarō (1870–1966) and the German philosopher Eugen Herrigel (1884–1955).[44] As scholars of Japanese Buddhism have shown, the popular conception of Zen emerged as advocates of the "New Buddhism" [*Shin Bukkyō*] responded to governmental persecution during Japan's Meiji period (1868–1912).[45] Those Buddhist leaders, including Suzuki's teacher SŌEN Shaku, presented Buddhism as a modern scientific tradition well suited to the progress of the Japanese nation. In later decades, an image of Zen circulated in the transnational flow of representations, which portrayed the tradition, as Robert H. Sharf has argued, "as an iconoclastic and antinomian tradition which rejects scholastic learning and ritualism in favor of naturalness, spontaneity, and freedom."[46] As William James's emphasis on "religious experience" influenced Japanese thought in the first decade of the twentieth century, Zen came to be understood as "pure experience itself," and that transhistorical personal experience, the popular interpretation goes, has shaped all aspects of Japanese culture, which is spiritually and aesthetically superior.[47] Although others in Japan and the United States played a role—including HISAMATSU Hōseki Shin'ichi (1889–1980)—Suzuki's writings and lectures were exceptionally influential in the United States, especially between 1936 and 1957, as he turned his attention to the relation between religion and culture in books such as *Zen and Its Influence on Japanese Culture*; and between 1957, when he published *Mysticism: Christian and Buddhist*, and his death in 1966, Suzuki returned to the earlier emphasis on experience and compared forms of Eastern and Western mysticism.[48]

Herrigel also exerted some influence. The English translation of Herrigel's international bestseller *Zen in the Art of Archery* appeared in 1953, and it leaned on a presupposition derived from D.T. Suzuki's writings: "In his *Essays in Zen Buddhism*, Herrigel proposed, "D.T. Suzuki has succeeded in showing that Japanese culture and Zen are intimately connected and that Japanese art...cannot be understood by anybody not acquainted with it."[49] Some scholars have suggested that Herrigel was a credulous Westerner who traveled to Japan to find the timeless mysticism and religious culture he had come to expect from Suzuki's accounts and, in his popular book, the German traveler offered a distorted account that exaggerated the link between archery and Zen as well as between Zen and other Japanese cultural practices.[50]

The prescriptive literature influenced by Suzuki and Herrigel provides an angle of vision on Buddhism's impact on personal piety and popular culture, and, for a cultural history of Buddhism in the postwar United States, it does not matter that the received representations did not faithfully or fully portray the complexities of Zen as it had been practiced by monks and laity in Japanese temples for centuries. Americans received a notion of Zen as a tradition that centered experience, eschewed constraints, encouraged spontaneity, shaped culture, and inspired art. And, most important for the prescriptive literature published in America, this decontextualized Zen emerged as a tradition that seemed to be applicable to all aspects of everyday life.

An analysis of the books on Zen published in the United States since the 1950s indicates that they included not only the many translations and guidebooks designed to enhance religious practice—such as Philip Kapleau's *Three Pillars of Zen* and Shunryu Suzuki's *Zen Mind, Beginner's Mind*—but also texts that claimed to apply Zen principles to a wide array of activities. In 2006, *Books in Print* listed 319 books with "Zen" in the title, and 133 of them were prescriptive texts of one sort or another. Some were written by those with long-standing experience in Zen practice, while other writers, like the author of *The Zen of Organizing: Creating Order and Peace in Your Home, Career, and Life*, claimed no expertise. "Although I am not a serious student of Zen," wrote the professional organizer, "I deeply admire its precepts and am drawn to its simplicity." Further, despite her lack of expertise, she recommended three "aspects of Zen"—beginner's mind, concentration on the breath, and mindfulness—and felt able to detect the application of those Zen principles: "I recognize a Zen-organized environment the minute I enter one. It's the *feel* of the room, not just its *appearance*."[51]

Zen, in her view, is not a religion but a "practice," but some interpreters classified Zen as religious and explored the relation between Zen and other faiths, as in *Zen for Christians* and *Zen Judaism*. Some books dealt with science and technology—*Zen Computer* and *Zen and the Art of Systems Analysis*—while others addressed mental health (*Zen Therapy*) and physical well-being (*Zen and the Art of Diabetes Maintenance* and *Zen of Bowel Movements: A Spiritual Approach to Constipation*).[52]

More than two dozen volumes applied Zen principles to daily activities and domestic tasks. Those books included some that claimed to help with the design and organization of the home: not only *Zen of Organizing* but also *Zen Style: Balance and Simplicity in Your Home*. There were books on eating (*Zen of Cooking*) and, for those who ate too much, books on losing weight (*Zen of Permanent Weight Loss*). Volumes not only offered advice about the kitchen but also the bedroom, as in *Zen Sleep: Enlightenment for a Good Night's Rest* and *Zen Sex: The Way of Making Love*. Before sex comes romance, and there were prescriptive books for that too: *Zen and the Art of Falling in Love*. In turn, how-to volumes for dealing with children, including, *Zen Parenting* and *Zen and the Art of Changing Diapers*, also were published. Others offered suggestions about work spaces and professional activities, including *Career Development: Zen and the Art of Making a Living, The Zen of Selling*, and *Zen and the Art of Public School Teaching*.[53]

Extending the interpretive trajectories initiated by Suzuki and Herrigel, prescriptive books also considered the significance of Zen for recreation and leisure—*Zen Golf, Zen and the Art of Quilting*, and *Zen and the Art of Poker*—and a number of practices that involve some sort of artistry—including flower-arranging, gardening, archery, sword-fighting, and karate. In a similar way, other how-to books promised to stimulate creativity (*Zen of Creativity: Cultivating Your Artistic Life*) and, as with *Zen of Creative Painting*, helped readers to master the visual and performing arts: music, calligraphy, drawing, and painting.[54]

Buddhism and American Art

Zen of Creative Painting points to another important area of Buddhist influence—the fine arts—and another institutional mediator of influence—the museum.[55] Beginning in the 1940s and escalating after 1957, Buddhism shaped other cultural arenas, as psychotherapists, philosophers, and fiction writers engaged the tradition, especially what might be called *Suzuki Zen*, a distinctive interpretation that emerged from D. T. Suzuki's writing and lectures.[56] Buddhism also shaped visual culture. In the 1990s that impact was evident in film, advertising, television, and the Internet.[57] Yet, as I suggest in the remainder of this chapter, Suzuki Zen also combined with Japanese aesthetics and Dada iconoclasm to shape some movements in American painting after the 1940s and some movements in video art after the 1970s.

Buddhism's influence on American artists, collectors, critics, and museums began in the nineteenth century, when the Paris Exhibition of 1867 introduced some American travelers to Japanese art.[58] Around that time the American painter John LaFarge began collecting Japanese art, and other American artists, including Frederick Edwin Church, James Abbot McNeill Whistler, Winslow Homer, and Mary Cassat, were struck by Japanese woodblock prints' bright colors, stylized patterns, simplified detail, and flattened perspective. During the 1870s and 1880s some elite Americans, not only Lodge but also Ernest Fenollosa, Edward S. Morse, and William Sturgis Bigelow, traveled to Japan. Some of them—Fenollosa and Bigelow—formally embraced Buddhism, while others sympathized with the tradition or, as with Church and Whistler, simply admired Japanese aesthetic principles.

Before and after the "golden age of collecting" (1893–1919), other elites, who admired Japanese aesthetics but did not embrace Buddhism fully or formally, displayed East Asian Buddhist images in their homes.[59] Detached from their original ritual context, devotional "living images" became domesticated exotic artifacts.[60] Consider a few examples. An 1884 photograph shows that Church, the Hudson River School painter, had a silk temple scroll, which portrayed the Buddha's entrance into nirvana, hanging above the stairway in his hilltop New York home.[61] Friends in Japan gave Joseph M. Wade, a Theosophist who presided over an esoteric magazine, *Occultism*, a large portable shrine with a wooden statue of Amida Buddha, who stands on a lotus and bends slightly at the waist as he glances toward the right. As a 1902 photograph indicates, Wade displayed that image on a table in the "occult room" of his home in Dorchester, Massachusetts.[62] Not far away, in that same year the Bostonian Isabella Stewart Gardner had a "Chinese Room" in her home—and later her museum—that included a variety of Asian artifacts, including a Japanese temple hanging, a large Chinese embroidery, and a Tibetan prayer wheel.[63] To mention a final example, encouraged by Whistler and Fenollosa, the self-made millionaire Charles Lang Freer, who had some personal interest in Buddhism, began collecting East Asian art in the 1890s, and some of those Japanese pieces—as well as Whistler's Japanese-inspired *Princess from the Land of Porcelain*—were originally displayed in his Detroit home.[64]

More important for a cultural history of Buddhism in America, Japanese Buddhist art—distanced again from its ritual setting—also found its way into museums, and Western reconstructions of Japanese aesthetic principles influenced art education.[65] In 1906, Freer donated his collection of religious and secular artifacts to the Smithsonian Institution in Washington, D.C., and the gallery that bears his name opened to the public in 1923. Freer, in turn, helped other museums establish collections of East Asian art—in Cleveland, Chicago, Minneapolis, and Philadelphia.[66] The earlier collecting efforts of Bigelow and Fenollosa also found an institutional home in Boston's Museum of Fine Arts. Fenollosa sold his collection to Charles Weld in 1886, and in 1889 the pieces collected by the three Japanophiles came to form the most impressive holding of Japanese artifacts outside Asia.[67]

So Fenollosa, who also served as curator of the Boston collection from 1891 to 1896, helped to establish a popular institutional center that would display Buddhist artifacts—from Buddhist sculpture to temple scrolls. Through his own writing and the work of his assistant at the Museum, Arthur Dow, he also directly and indirectly shaped art criticism and art education. Fenollosa had penned a piece on "Contemporary Japanese Art" for a magazine in 1893, but it was his two-volume *Epochs of Chinese and Japanese Art* that secured his cultural clout. Interpreting what he learned from his extensive contacts in Japan, Fenollosa explored the "aesthetic motive" of each epoch of East Asian art and emphasized the importance of "line, spacing, and colour." In what came to be called the Dow-Fenollosa approach, Dow promoted the same formalist principles in his important volume, *Composition*, which appeared in 1899. Dow's students at Brooklyn's Pratt Institute and Columbia's Teachers College included major American artists, such as Max Weber and Georgia O'Keefe, whose work reveals Dow's emphasis on line, color, and *notan*, light and dark relationships.[68]

Transcultural Collage: Buddhist Themes in American Art, 1940–1960

It was after the 1920s, when O'Keefe reached her mature style, that the converging influence of Japanese aesthetics, Dada, and Suzuki Zen began to be felt in art museums and art movements.[69] That impact was evident during the 1940s and 1950s. For example, in 1953 more than 420,000 American visitors, including President Eisenhower, saw an exhibit of 91 Japanese paintings and sculptures that traveled to five cities—Washington, New York, Seattle, Chicago, and Boston. That traveling exhibition, which was sponsored by the Japanese government and aimed at intercultural understanding in the postwar period, was widely covered in the press, so even readers of national magazines such as *Life* and *Time* who never made it to the show had some exposure to the aesthetic principles embedded in the "treasures from Japan."[70]

Before and after that exhibition some American artists also were turning east. For example, two American Abstract Artists of the 1930s and 1940s, Mark Tobey (1890–1967) and Morris Graves (1910–2001), gained prominence around 1940, and both claimed Buddhist and Japanese inspiration.[71] Tobey's work between 1910 and 1930, when he lived in New York, showed some resemblance to O'Keefe's. In that sense, Tobey's art seems indirectly linked with the Fenollosa-Dow tradition.[72] He had independent influences too, however, since he knew Arthur Waley, author of the influential *Zen Buddhism and Its Relation to Art*, and in 1935 Tobey spent a month in a Zen monastery outside Kyoto, where he studied painting and calligraphy. He came to emphasize abstraction and what he called "moving lines," as in the 1944 painting *New York*, a tempera on paperboard piece that consists of a dense crossing of black and white lines.[73]

Abstract Expressionism, nonrepresentational art that expressed the artist's emotion, predominated during the 1940s and 1950s, and the non-gestural abstract expressionism of Ad Reinhardt, and his emphasis on color harmonies and formal relationships, showed the influence of Japanese aesthetics and Suzuki Zen. Like Tobey, Reinhardt attended Suzuki's Columbia University lectures in the early Fifties. He read Suzuki's books, as well as Waley's account of Zen and art.[74] Earlier, between 1947 and 1949, Reinhardt made vertical paintings that resembled the Buddhist temple scroll that Church had hung in his home, and Reinhardt's work, for example *Calligraphic Painting*, showed the influence of Japanese aesthetics. After 1950, and especially after his trip to Japan in 1958, he started to make monochromatic oil paintings, like *Abstract Painting* (1960), flattened meditative spaces that experimented with slight variations of black or grey.

Those canvases reflected his understanding of Zen and the aesthetic principles it implied or declared. In a diary entry written during this trip to Japan, Reinhardt listed Zen's 11 "elements." Seven of those—asymmetry, simplicity, naturalness, unconventionality, inner quietness, humor, and freedom—were especially important for Reinhardt and other American artists in the 1950s and 1960s.[75] As with Reinhardt, some other mid-century art movements revealed the direct and indirect influence of Suzuki: Jasper Johns's and Robert Rauschenberg's Neo-Dadaism, which kept alive the earlier movement's revolt against artistic practice and expansion of "art"; Rauschenberg's "assemblage" art, which emphasized three-dimensional objects assembled by collage techniques; and the Happenings, partly planned and partly spontaneous events that combined elements of theater and visual arts that were initiated in 1952 by the composer, poet, and artist John Cage (1912–1992), who also attended Suzuki's Columbia lectures and visited him in Japan.[76]

It was, above all, Cage who became a "conduit" of Suzuki Zen, by assigning it in his classes at Black Mountain College, the experimental school in North Carolina, and by talking about it with his friends, including Johns and Rauschenberg. Even though a major retrospective minimized this Buddhist influence, it was important for Johns's work. In fact, some of that work makes little sense without excavating the influence of Suzuki Zen. For example, in 1955, shortly after he traveled to Japan and read Herrigel's *Zen and the Art of Archery*, he began his famous series of *Target* paintings. Suzuki Zen informed Rauschenberg's approach to art too. Consider his 1951 account of his all black and all white paintings, which dealt with "the suspense, excitement and body of an organic silence, the restriction and freedom of absence, the plastic fullness of nothing..."[77]

Cage, who was influenced by Rauschenberg's all-white paintings, which "caught whatever fell on them," once staged a late-night public reading—it started at 11 PM—of the teachings of the Chan master Huangbo Xiyuan (d. 850), who emphasized non-dualism and one mind.[78] Cage also reflected on the artistic significance of themes that he took from Suzuki, including emptiness, freedom, and silence. For example, in 1949 at the Artist's Club on Eighth Street in New York City, Cage gave his famous "Lecture on Nothing." It was written in the same rhythmic structure he had used in his innovative musical compositions of the time, including *Sonatas and Interludes*. It began "I am here." Then, after the first of many patterned pauses, it continued "and there is nothing to say." Part of the lecture's structure came from the repetition—he said it 14 times—of the refrain "If anyone is sleepy let him go to sleep." Both that lecture, and his staged responses afterward, were not universally embraced at the time, as Cage recalled.

> Jeanne Reynal stood up part way through, screamed, and then said, while I continued speaking, "John, I dearly love you, but I can't bear another minute." She then walked out. Later, during the question period, I gave one of six previously prepared answers regardless of the question asked. This was a reflection of my engagement in Zen.[79]

In this and other ways, Cage's mediation of Suzuki Zen did have widespread influence on American art, but there were other influences converging in the work of Johns, Rauschenberg, and Cage. As Watts noted in 1954, "it is not quite correct to say that a 'Zen influence' is simply being imported and imitated." "It is rather," Watts continued, "a case of deep answering to deep, of tendencies already implicit in Western life which leap into actuality through an outside stimulus." When he made that observation, Watts apparently did not have Dada in mind. But that movement was one of the crossing cultural currents that converged in the middle of the twentieth century to shape American painting. Or, to use a different metaphor, it is one of the found objects that artists used to assemble new forms of art. In that regard, it is significant that Cage's introduction to Zen in 1936 came in a lecture by Nancy Wilson Ross on "Dada and Zen Buddhism." He was very impressed, Cage recalled, because both seemed to champion "experience and the irrational rather than...logic and understanding."[80]

As Cage knew, Dada was an artistic movement in music, art, poetry, and performance that had begun in 1915 in Zurich and found autonomous but parallel expression in New York between 1915 and 1922. Although its proponents—including the German painter and sculptor Jean Arp, the German filmmaker Hans Richter, and the Romanian poet Tristan Tzara—were fond of claiming that it was not a movement, they also were fond of offering manifestos. In the first Dada Manifesto, Hugo Ball suggested that Dada (and the label was a nonsensical word, *hobbyhorse*, in French) was international in scope, antagonistic to society, and sought to change conventional attitudes and practices in aesthetics. That iconoclastic transnational movement arrived in Japan in 1920, and combined with Buddhism in the work of some Japanese literary and visual artists, but it is not clear how much European Dada was shaped by Buddhism. Tzara's 1922 "Lecture on Dada," for example, anticipates some of the themes of Cage's "Lecture on Nothing." Tzara spoke of "the Nothing." He even equated it with Dada: "Everyone knows," Tzara suggested, "that Dada is nothing." Further, he also defined the movement as a pre-modern (or anti-modern) Buddhist state of mind: It is a "calm level state of mind that makes everything equal and without importance." "Dada," he continued in that 1922 lecture, "is not at all modern. It is more in the nature of a return to an almost Buddhist religion of indifference." One scholar who explored the possible Buddhist sources of Tzara's Dada concluded that the evidence suggests only thematic parallels and not causal links. In their shared emphasis on cultivating a certain state of mind, as well as in celebrating spontaneity and "nothingness," European Dada and Japanese Zen seemed to have "striking parallels."[81]

In America, the French-born artist Marcel Duchamp, whom Cage befriended in the early 1940s, was associated with Dadaism, at least after he contacted the Dada group in Paris in 1916. Even before then, however, Duchamp expressed the iconoclastic inclinations that came to be associated with the transnational movement. The dynamism that artists like Tobey would find later in Japanese calligraphic aesthetics, Duchamp found in other sources, and that sense of movement was captured in his controversial 1912 painting, *Nude Descending a Staircase*. More important for art at mid-century, Duchamp, disillusioned by the medium of painting, turned his attention to ordinary objects, which he called "readymades," in several pieces he produced in the 1910s, including *Bicycle Wheel*, *Bottle Rack*, and *Fountain*, a porcelain urinal he presented as an art object.[82]

The Vernacular Glance and the Meditative Gaze: Buddhist Themes in American Art After 1960

In a process of transcultural collage, then, some American artists between the 1940s and the 1960s assembled found objects—Dadaism, Japanese aesthetics, and Zen—to create new art forms that valued spontaneity and irreverence, experimented with line, color, and space, and emphasized the *vernacular glance* and the *meditative gaze*. An art historian, who did not recognize the Buddhist sources of the impulse he identified, introduced the phrase "the vernacular glance" to analyze Rauschenberg's focus on the ordinary.[83] A similar impulse can be seen in Johns's use of ordinary objects such as beer cans and light bulbs, as in his 1968 image, *Lightbulb*, which focuses the viewer's attention not only on a common object but also on the dangling cord that seems to lead to the anticlimax of the darkened bulb at the bottom of flattened masonite surface. With some limited and indirect Buddhist inspiration, this vernacular glance also found expression in other figurative movements that echo the themes of Neo-Dada, like the pop art of Andy Warhol's soup can.[84]

A second way of seeing is produced, I propose, by this transcultural assemblage—the meditative gaze, a concern to cultivate in the artist an attentive focus on the abstract canvas and to prompt a similar encounter by the viewer. For example, Rauschenberg's white paintings and Reinhardt's black paintings invite the viewer to attend carefully to the play of hue and space, and they demand that onlookers inscribe meaning onto the relatively blank meditative surface. If Rauschenberg saw those nonrepresentational paintings as instantiations of "the plastic fullness of nothing," Reinhardt saw his black paintings, for example *Abstract Painting*, as Zen-inspired expressions of "pure painting," which is "spaceless" and "timeless." Like Johns's *Target*, which not only recalls Herrigel's *Zen and the Art of Archery* but also functions as a sort of mandala (a square or circular diagram that represents the cosmos and is used for the practice of visualization), these paintings focus the reader's gaze in a way that tries to parallel the focused attention of meditation.[85]

The vernacular glance and meditative gaze also inform some video and computer art since the 1970s. Those impulses were at work in the installations of one of the genre's founders, Nam June Paik (1932–2006), who was inspired by Cage and Suzuki. Consider Paik's *TV Buddha* (1974) in which a cross-legged Buddha gazes back at a projected image of himself on a television, one of the most ubiquitous objects in American homes. Kimsooja's *A Laundry Woman— Yamuna River, India* (2000), in which a woman with her back to the viewer watches the debris—including flowers, trash, and ashes—from nearby crema-tions float down a river, also explores the transformative power of mindfully attending to everyday surroundings. And the vernacular glance and meditative gaze are present in different ways in the work of video artists who have prac-ticed Buddhism, including Mariko Mori, the Japanese-born artist who divides her time between Tokyo and New York, and Bill Viola, the American-born artist who has lived in Japan, where he also studied Buddhism.[86]

To illustrate larger patterns, I want to focus on the early video art of Viola, who first encountered Buddhism during college: "I went to university in the late 1960s, when change and social transformation were in the air. A com-plete reordering of spiritual practice was part of this revolution, and ancient Eastern religions like Hinduism and Buddhism were freely circulating across American youth culture.... I took several workshops in meditation on campus and started reading books like *The Tibetan Book of the Dead*."[87] That introduction to Buddhist practice and teaching shaped his early work, including *Migration* (1976).[88] As Viola proposed in his notebook, that video is "a slow, continuous journey through changes in scale, punctuated by the sounding of a gong."[89] It opens with the viewer's vision obstructed by a screen with vertical lines. Slowly the obstruction is removed, and we can see through the screen into a room. A man with a green striped shirt and white trousers enters and sits on a wooden chair in a meditative position, with hands in his lap. Back erect, as in *zazen*, he gazes ahead at rather ordinary objects on a square wooden table: a red bowl, two pieces of fruit, and a box of cornflakes. The scale narrows more and more until the viewer's attention focuses on a single drop of water that drips in slow motion from a small metal tube in front of the seated man. The seven-minute video ends as the viewer sees the man's reflection in that single drop. As Viola suggested, "the piece evolves into an exploration of the optical properties of a drop of water, revealing in it an image of the individual and a suggestion of the transient nature of the world he or she possesses within."[90] Recreating the perceptual experience he found during his first attempts at meditation, in *Migration* Viola celebrates the transformative power of mindful attention to the most ordinary of objects—a box of corn flakes and a drop of water. In that sense, this video draws on the vernacular glance and the medita-tive gaze.

Viola does the same in many other works too, including *Ancient of Days* (1980), which he produced during a year of residence in Japan in 1979–80, when he also began to study Buddhism more formally and practice it more regularly.[91] It was then, Viola claimed, that he had his first "real encounter with Buddhism."[92] He has recounted his deepening interest in Buddhism: "After moving away from my Christian upbringing, I got interested in Eastern culture, and I went to Japan, and I was practicing Zen meditation and so on. Then when I came back from Japan, I studied more intensively people such as the great Japanese lay Zen scholar Daisetz Suzuki...."[93] His experience at temples in Japan converged with what he had been reading and thinking about—westernized Zen and Japanese aesthetics—and that transcultural collage self-consciously informed *Ancient of Days*, a video that opens with an enflamed table on a beach, continues with urban and natural landscapes from the United States and Japan, and ends with a clock ticking on a table as the image hung on the wall slowly changes before the viewer's gaze. This "video haiku," as Viola called it, is imagined as "pure seeing."[94] "This sense of seeing...is what I have been after.... The object doesn't change, you do. This is what is behind the Buddhism brought from India to China to Japan."[95] Viola explained his aim for "my Japan piece": "I want to look so close at things their intensity burns through your retina and onto the surface of your mind. The video camera is well suited to looking closely at things, elevating the commonplace to higher levels of awareness."[96]

In *Ancient of Days*, Viola's "elevation of the commonplace," his intense transformative gaze at ordinary objects—like the clock ticking on the table—also included the wider landscape, from slow-motion images of pedestrians on a Tokyo street to the micro-changes observed during a day's filming at the Washington Monument. The landscape in Washington D.C. and across the nation had been transformed by 1980, when Viola finished that video, yet the process of Buddhification continued during the next two decades.

Conclusion

The Buddhification of the landscape has included a dramatic increase in the number of Buddhist temples and centers in the United States since 1945, and especially since 1965, when President Johnson signed not only the Highway Beautification Act but also the new immigration act. The confluence of immigrant piety and convert interest propelled efforts to build new structures or transform homes and churches to worship spaces, from the Washington Buddhist Vihara in D.C., a modest Sinhalese Theravada Buddhist temple founded in 1965, to Hsi Lai Temple in California, a large Chinese Mahayana Buddhist complex built in 1988.[97] One guidebook to Buddhist institutions counted more than one thousand centers in 1998, with only about 2% of those founded before 1964; another source, the Pluralism Project's Directory, listed 2147 Buddhist centers in the United States in 2006.[98]

There is no evidence that President Johnson or Lady Bird ever met, or even heard about, the Asian-born monk who founded Washington Buddhist Vihara

Figure 8.3 Altered billboard. The Billboard Liberation Front Creative Group. April 28, 1998. U.S. Highway 101, San Carlos, California.
Photo by Jack Napier.

in 1965. In an interesting development in later years, however, Buddhist impact on the American landscape extended beyond local Buddhist worship spaces—and beyond bookstores, health care centers, and museums—and out to the highways that Lady Bird had tried so hard to "beautify." For example, Apple's controversial 1998 "Think Different" advertising campaign put the enormous image of another monk, the Dalai Lama, the spiritual leader of Buddhist Tibet, on billboards across America. Even if the former First Lady did not express public dissatisfaction about this addition to America's visual culture, some others did. In April 1998, one of the Dalai Lama billboards along U.S. Highway 101 in San Carlos, California, was altered by "culture jamming," the practice of parodying ads and highjacking billboards as a form of protest. The protestors from the Billboard Liberation Front, a group dedicated to "redressing the imposition on public space," did not disturb the image of the Tibetan Buddhist monk but changed the Apple symbol to a skull and revised the slogan to read "Think Disillusioned" (see Figure 8.3). In this way, and many other ways, Buddhification was a contested process. Although not in the ways that Lyndon or Lady Bird might have imagined—though the president did address his remarks at the 1965 signing ceremony to "all other lovers of beauty"—Buddhism had begun to transform—and, for some, even "beautify"—the American cultural landscape, from billboards on the highways to video installations in museums.

To describe this contested process is to do more than contribute to the conversation about the cultural history of Buddhism in the United States, though I hope it does that too. I have offered some hints about *how* it happened. I have argued that representations of a tradition that was detached from its institutional setting circulated in transnational communication systems. In a process of transcultural collage, some American readers and viewers then selectively appropriated those circulating representations—affixing some of this to some of that—to assemble an almost infinitely malleable Buddhism that exerted wide cultural influence and met multiple needs. Like the other chapters in this volume, this essay also refines our understanding of how "pluralism" has operated in America since World War II. Analyzing religious pluralism is not only a matter of using telephone surveys or demographic records to estimate the number of adherents; nor does it mean only using city directories or congregational studies to count the number of buildings that dot the landscape. As the case of Buddhism vividly illustrates, assessing cultural influence can be important, and that impact can be disproportionate to the number of devotees that scholars can count.

Notes

1 I am grateful to Erika Doss, Katie Lofton, Linda Dalrymple Henderson, Richard Jaffe, and David Morgan for comments on an earlier draft. The quotation from Lady Bird, and the one below about "masses of flowers," are included in the supporting materials, "Topics in Focus," for the 1981 PBS documentary film *Lady Bird Johnson: Portrait of a First Lady*, MacNeil/Lehrer Productions and KLRU (Austin). Available at http://www.pbs.org/ladybird/shattereddreams/shattereddreams_report.html, accessed February 27, 2006. See also Lady Bird Johnson, *A White House Diary* (New York: Holt, Reinhart, and Winston, 1970).

2 See "Some Enchanted Evening!: House Approved Highway-Beautification Bill," *Time*, October 15, 1965, 30–31. See also "Beauty and the Billboards: OAAA Support Beautification Act," *New Republic*, April 23, 1966, 8–9.

3 "Transcultural collage" is a phrase that draws on two images. First, it proposes an analogy between cultural exchange and collage, the practice of assembling multiple artifacts, sometimes found objects, to creatively construct something new. That metaphor has the advantage of emphasizing agency, and it works well with the focus of this essay, the Buddhist influence on American art. Second, by using the term "transcultural," I allude to a term that the Cuban anthropologist Fernando Ortiz coined in 1940—*transculturation*—to move beyond the limits of the idea of acculturation, and its presupposition of a simple unidirectional process. As Ortiz and I use it, transculturation suggests a complex and multidirectional process of contact and exchange that transforms all participants and practices. In this chapter, however, I emphasize the ways that the exchanges with Asia, especially Japan, shaped American culture. Of course, it went in the other direction too—and often in many directions at once. Fernando Ortiz, *Cuban Counterpoint: Tobacco and Sugar* (Durham, NC: Duke University Press, 1995), 97–103.

4 Sometimes observers simply called it *diversity*, as in a 1954 account of "Religious Diversity and American Education." P. A. Bertocci, "Religious Diversity and American Education," *School and Society*, August 21, 1954, 55–56. More often, interpreters turned to other terms or phrases. The phrase most widely used between the 1910s and the 1940s was *melting pot*, a metaphor that expressed a desire about

what would happen with the diverse peoples coming to America's shores. They would acculturate. As early as 1915, the sociologist Horace Kallen challenged that metaphor as incompatible with democratic principles and sanctioned an alternate term, *pluralism*, which by the 1920s came to mean an attitude or policy of welcoming religious and ethnic diversity. Horace M. Kallen, "Democracy Versus the Melting Pot: A Study of American Nationality," *The Nation* 100, Febraury 18, 1915, 190–194. Diana Eck suggested that Kallen was probably the first to use the term pluralism to describe "an alternative vision": *A New Religious America: How a "Christian Country" Has Become the World's Most Religiously Diverse Nation* (San Francisco: HarperSanFrancisco, 2001), 57. William R. Hutchison argued that even though its fundamental meaning—the welcoming of diversity—has been around much longer, the term pluralism "was not coined for this particular usage until the 1920s": *Religious Pluralism in America: The Contentious History of a Founding Ideal* (New Haven, CT: Yale University Press, 2003), 4. The term *pluralism* appears in American popular usage early in the twentieth century, and it has shown some lasting power. According to the *Reader's Guide Retrospective*, it appeared in 112 articles between 1911 and 1982, including several that appeared in a Catholic periodical the same year that John F. Kennedy was elected president: L. C. McHugh, et al., "Our Post-Protestant Pluralism," *America*, March 5, 1960. That term continued in use and made a comeback in the last decades of the twentieth century. Using slightly different language, some scholars had begun to talk about the *world religions* as early as the 1920s. On that see Tomoko Masuzawa, *The Invention of World Religions: Or, How European Universalism Was Preserved in the Language of Pluralism* (Chicago: University of Chicago Press, 2005). On the use of *world religions* in popular media, see, for example, "World's Great Religions," *Life*, March 7, 1955, 78–98. The predominant model for understanding religious diversity in the United States during the middle decades of the century was the notion of a *Judeo-Christian tradition*. That notion emerged in the 1930s, as neo-orthodox Protestant theologians focused on the Jewish roots of early Christianity, and the phrase gained widespread usage during the 1940s as a progressive alternative to the notion that America was a "Christian nation" and as a tool for fighting fascism, anti-Semitism, and "godless" communism. On that see Mia Sara Bruch, "Religious Pluralism in One Nation Under God: American Islam and the Legacy of the 'Judeo-Christian Tradition,'" Paper delivered at the American Historical Association Annual Meeting, Philadelphia, Pennsylvania, January 2006. For a use of the term *Judeo-Christian* as a category, see Milton Himmelfarb, "On Reading Matthew," *Commentary* 40 (October 1965): 56–65. In 1942, for example, the National Conference of Christians and Jews released a list of beliefs shared by Protestants, Catholics, and Jews, and, even though the melting pot metaphor persisted, some sociologists and historians challenged it. Others advocated the notion of a "triple melting pot," expanding the metaphor's reach to include Protestants, Catholics, and Jews. On the 1942 declaration by the National Conference of Christians and Jews, as well as the term Judeo-Christian, see Hutchison, *Religious Pluralism in America*, 197–198. For challenges to and expansion of the notion of the "melting pot," see R. J. R. Kennedy, "Single or Triple Melting Pot?" *American Journal of Sociology* 58 (July 1952): 56–59; Nathan Glazer, "America's Ethnic Pattern: Melting Pot or Nation of Nations?" *Commentary* 15 (April 1953): 401–408; and Will Herberg, "Triple Melting Pot," *Commentary* 20 (August 1955): 101–108. That same year, Herberg popularized the notion of the "triple melting pot" in *Protestant,*

Catholic, Jew: An Essay in American Religious Sociology (New York: Doubleday, 1955). After Johnson's death in 1973, other rhetoric predominated—including talk about *multiculturalism*. For an assessment of the usefulness of *multiculturalism*, which was prominent in the 1970s, see A. J. Arnold, "Sometimes Words Fail, and the Word That's Failed Us Most is Multiculturalism," *Maclean's*, July 24, 1978. Sean McCloud traces the changes in print journalists' representation of "fringe" religious groups during the second half of the century in *Making the American Religious Fringe: Exotics, Subversives, and Journalists, 1955–1993* (Chapel Hill: University of North Carolina Press, 2004). More recently, in a rhetorical practice that constricts the range of diversity while it attempts to construct bridges between Islam, Judaism, and Christianity, after 9/11 some interpreters have emphasized the interconnectedness of the three *Abrahamic faiths*. Some scholars referred to the *Abrahamic faiths* before 2001: for example, F. E. Peters's *Children of Abraham: Judaism, Christianity, Islam* (Princeton, NJ: Princeton University Press, 1982). It became a somewhat more popular term after 2001. See for example, David R. Smock, *Building Interreligious Trust in a Climate of Fear: An Abrahamic Trialogue* (Washington, DC: U.S. Institute of Peace, 2003); and James L. Heft, ed., *Beyond Violence: Religious Sources of Social Transformation in Judaism, Christianity, and Islam*, Abrahamic Dialog Series No. 1 (New York: Fordham University Press, 2004).

5 For biographical information and analysis of LBJ's presidency see, for example, Paul Keith Conkin, *Big Daddy from the Pedernales* (Boston: Twayne, 1986); Robert Dallek, *Lyndon B. Johnson: Portrait of a President* (New York: Oxford University Press, 2004); and Mark K. Updegrove, *Indomitable Will: LBJ in the Presidency* (New York: Crown, 2012). Robert A. Caro has published a multi-volume series of studies called *The Years of Lyndon Johnson*, including the fourth volume on 1958 to 1964: *The Passage of Power* (New York: Knopf, 2012).

6 For archival evidence of Johnson's relationship with Billy Graham, see the 31 Daily Diary Cards for the Reverend and Mrs. Billy Graham between December 1963 and January 1969 in the archives at the LBJ Library.

7 Besides his visits with his daughter, Johnson also visited Catholic churches at other times. For example, on June 28, 1966, a time when a new bombing campaign had begun in Vietnam, he visited St. Dominic's Catholic Church in Washington, D.C., from 10:24 to 10:36 PM. See Daily Dairy Cards, June 28, 1966, LBJ Library. On this visit see also Lady Bird Johnson, *A White House Diary*, 391.

8 Quoted in Updegrove, *Indomitable Will*, 182.

9 There is a great deal of literature on Johnson and Vietnam. For example, see Michael H. Hunt, *Lyndon Johnson's War: America's Cold War Crusade in Vietnam, 1945–1968* (New York: Hill and Wang, 1996) and Lyndon B. Johnson, *Lyndon B. Johnson's Vietnam Papers: A Documentary Collection* (College Station: Texas A&M University Press, 1997). This pattern also seems to be true for the Korean War, though more research is needed to trace the history of those representations. See "No Truce at Home: Monks in Seoul," *Newsweek*, August 15, 1955, 32.

10 Hunt, *Lyndon Johnson's War*, 63.

11 Besides the other archival sources cited below, see also the following: President Johnson referred to Buddhists in response to a question about Thich Tri Quang, leader of the Buddhist opposition, in a news conference on May 21, 1966; he also referred to Buddhists in his remarks to the American Alumni Council on U.S. Asian policy

on July 12, 1966, in a statement about "the peace we seek in Asia." Both documents are available at the American Presidency Project, Public Papers of the Presidents, University of California, Santa Barbara. Available at http://www.presidency.ucsb. edu/ws/, accessed July 9, 2006. Some items related to Buddhists can be found in the Drew Pearson Papers, Lyndon B. Johnson Library, Austin, Texas: Box G 302, 1 of 3 folders, "Vietnam"; Box G 288, 1 of 3 folders, "Laos;" Box G 301, 3 of 3 folders, "Vietnam 1967." A good source for documents relating to Buddhists and Vietnam is volume one, and the other six published volumes on Vietnam for 1964–1968, of the Foreign Relations of the United States: John P. Glennon, ed., Office of the Historian, Department of State, Department of State Publication 9934, *Foreign Relations of the United States: Vietnam, 1964*, vol. 1 (Washington, DC: U.S. Government Printing Office, 1992). For the online versions of all seven volumes see U.S. Department of State, Office of the Historian, Foreign Relations of the United States, Johnson Administration, available at: http://www.state.gov/r/pa/ho/frus/johnsonlb/, accessed July 9, 2006. "Buddhists" also came up in seven recorded telephone conversations between Johnson and government officials. Those are archived in the LBJ Archives and Museum's Reading Room and include discussions with McGeorge Bundy, Dean Rusk, and Robert McNamara: 5245, Bundy, 8/28/64, 10:17A, WH6408.40, PNO 18; 7016, Rusk, 3/4/65, 10:41A, WH6503.01, PNO 16; 9918, Rusk, 3/28/66, 4:44P, WH 6603.09, PNO 11; 10013, WH Situation Room, 4/5/66, 7:45A, WH6604.01, PNO 13; 10021, McNamara, 4/7/66, 7:45A, WH6604.02, PNO 6; 10029, Rusk, 4/9/66, 9:48A, WH6604.02, PNO 14; 10032, Rusk, 4/11/66, 10:50A, WH 6604.03, PNO 2. There are other archival records, too, that indicate some awareness of or contact with Buddhists, for example, a meeting between Johnson and representatives of five South Vietnamese universities, including Thich Minh Chau of Van Hanh (Buddhist) University: Daily Diary Cards, November 9, 1967, LBJ Archives and Museum. I am grateful to Barbara Constable, archivist at the LBJ Library, for her generous assistance in helping me find information on Buddhists in Johnson's papers and in government documents.

12 LBJ to Ambassador Taylor, May 10, 1965, reprinted in David M. Barrett, ed., *Lyndon B. Johnson's Vietnam Papers: A Documentary Collection* (College Station: Texas A&M University Press, 1997), 155.

13 Barrett, ed., *Johnson's Vietnam Papers*, 353.

14 Print media representations of the Buddhist protests, and maltreatment of Buddhists by Diem, included the following: "Diem's Other Crusade: Against Vietnamese Buddhists," *New Republic*, June 22, 1963, 5–6; "Same Old Diem," *The Nation*, June 29, 1963, 538; "Buddhist Crisis," *Time*, July 26, 1963, 24–26.

15 For information about Buddhism found in intelligence accounts during Johnson's administration, see National Security File (NSF), Country File, Vietnam, "S.E. Asia—The Asia Foundation Buddhist Study," LBJ Archives and Museum. In the same archives, see also NSF, Komer-Leonhart File, "Buddhists and Catholics," LBJ Archives and Museum.

16 Transcript, William E. Colby Oral History Interview I, 6/2/81, by Ted Gittinger, Internet Copy, LBJ Library, 20. On the Buddhist reform and peace movement in Vietnam during this period, see Robert J. Topmiller, *The Lotus Unleashed: The Buddhist Peace Movement in South Vietnam, 1964–1966* (Lexington: University Press of Kentucky, 2002). That work focused on the developments after 1963, but Topmiller

does mention Thich Quang Duc in several passages (for example, pp. 3 and 134). The story that Colby mentions is "Angry Buddhist Burns Himself Alive," *Life*, June 21, 1963, 24–25. For other print media coverage of Quang Duc's self-immolation, see also "Trial by Fire," *Time*, June 21, 1963, 32; "Fiery Protest," *Newsweek*, June 24, 1963, 63; and "When a Monk Became a Human Torch: What U.S. Has at Stake," *U.S. News and World Report*, June 24, 1963, 3. The religious press commented too: for example, see "Diem Rebuked," *America*, June 29, 1963, 895; and "Brutality in Vietnam," *Christian Century*, July 31, 1963, 950. For analysis by religious studies scholars, see Russell T. McCutcheon, *Manufacturing Religion: The Discourse on Sui Generis Religion and the Politics of Nostalgia* (New York: Oxford University Press, 1997), 167–77; and Sallie B. King, "They Who Burned Themselves for Peace: Quaker and Buddhist Self-Immolators during the Vietnam War," *Buddhist-Christian Studies* 20 (2000): 127–50. For an insider analysis see Thich Nhat Han's *Vietnam: Lotus in a Sea of Fire* (New York: Hill and Wang, 1967).

17 Barrett, ed., *Johnson's Vietnam Papers*, 344.

18 At least since the nineteenth century, Western interpreters have represented Buddhism as nonviolent and "tolerant," as I argued in Thomas A. Tweed, *The American Encounter with Buddhism, 1844–1912: Victorian Culture and the Limits of Dissent* (Chapel Hill: University of North Carolina Press, 2000), 32–33, 66–67, 96–103. Yet, as some scholars have noted, "there have been numerous individual and structural cases of prolonged Buddhist violence." Michael K. Jerryson, "Introduction," in *Buddhist Warfare*, Michael K. Jerryson and Mark Juergensmeyer, eds. (New York: Oxford University Press, 2010), 3. In the United States, Buddhism managed to retain its association with peacefulness, even during and after the Vietnam War, while Islam continued to be interpreted as a violent tradition. On that see Thomas A. Tweed, "Why Are Buddhists So Nice?: Media Representations of Buddhism and Islam in the United States since 1945," *Material Religion* 4, no. 1 (March 2008): 91–93. Television News Archive, Vanderbilt University. Available at http://tvnews.vanderbilt.edu, accessed March 5, 2006. There were 52 stories on the evening news broadcasts between 1978 and 1980, most focusing on Iran. Again, between 1994 and 1996, during and just after the war in Bosnia, there were 209 stories on Muslims. Between 2001 and 2005, the major networks broadcast 568 stories on their evening newscasts. Most of those linked Islam with terrorism or war. As Mark Silk notes, "conflict stories play a large part in religion stories" (41), but he goes on to suggest that it can be useful to note also the underlying presuppositions and values of journalists—Silk calls them *topoi*—and the ways those find their way into media coverage of religion (55): Mark Silk, *Unsecular Media: Making News of Religion in America* (Urbana: Illinois University Press, 1995), 41, 55.

19 Television News Archive, Vanderbilt University. Available at http://tvnews.vanderbilt.edu, accessed March 5, 2006. All the statistics I cite here were derived from this archive. The number of stories is probably larger, since I searched only the term "Buddhists." A search of related key words might turn up more stories that deal with Buddhism directly or indirectly.

20 Eck, *New Religious America*, 6. As enacted, the new immigration act (H.R. 2580) is Public Law 89–236 (79 Stat. 911). In his remarks at the signing ceremony, Johnson called it "one of the most important acts of this Congress and of this administration": "President Lyndon B. Johnson's Remarks at the Signing of the Immigration

Bill, Liberty Island, New York," October 3, 1965, *Public Papers of the Presidents of the United States: Lyndon B. Johnson, 1965,* vol. II, entry 546 (Washington, DC: Government Printing Office, 1966), pp. 1037–1040. The next day that speech was printed in the *New York Times* (October 4, 1965, SU 1, pp. 1–2), and the Congressional signing of the bill had made the front page a few days earlier: Cabell Phillips, "Congress Sends Immigration Bill to White House," *New York Times,* October 1, 1965, pp. 1–2.

21 Tweed, *The American Encounter with Buddhism, 1844–1912.* For overviews of Buddhism in America, see Richard Seager, *Buddhism in America* (New York: Columbia University Press, 1999); and Thomas A. Tweed, "United States [Buddhism in the]," *Encyclopedia of Buddhism,* Robert E. Buswell, Jr., ed (New York: Macmillan, 2003), vol. 2: 864–870.

22 Reinhold Niebuhr, for example, suggested in 1937 that Buddhism was Christianity's only competitor in a piece entitled "The Christian Church in a Secular Age." See Tweed, *American Encounter with Buddhism,* 161.

23 Robert Wuthnow and Wendy Cadge, "Buddhists and Buddhism in the United States: The Scope of Influence," *Journal for the Scientific Study of Religion* 43, no.3 (September 2004): 378.

24 On the number of Buddhists in the United States, see Tweed, "United States [Buddhism in]"; and Wuthnow and Cadge, "Buddhists and Buddhism in the United States," 364.

25 Studies of Chinese immigrants, for example, show that many affirmed or reaffirmed Buddhism in the United States. See Noel Lin, "Finding Buddha in the West: An Ethnographic Study of a Chinese Buddhist Community in North Carolina," M.A. Thesis, University of North Carolina at Chapel Hill, 2001; and Carolyn Chen, *Getting Saved in America: Taiwanese Immigration and Religious Experience* (Princeton, NJ: Princeton University Press, 2008).

26 On nightstand Buddhists, and other sorts of adherents and sympathizers, see Thomas A. Tweed, "Who is a Buddhist?," in *Westward Dharma: Buddhism beyond Asia,* Charles Prebish and Martin Baumann, eds. (Berkeley: University of California Press, 2002), 17–33.

27 Wuthnow and Cadge, "Buddhists and Buddhism in the United States," 365.

28 Ibid., 363.

29 Ibid., 364–365.

30 Ibid., 365.

31 Roger Finke has suggested that the eastward turn during the late 1960s and 1970s was a product of both supply-side and demand-side factors: Roger Finke, "The Illusion of Shifting Demand: Supply-Side Interpretations of American Religious History," in Thomas A. Tweed, *Retelling U.S. Religious History* (Berkeley: University of California Press, 1997), 111.

32 The Buddhist presence has been mediated by other sorts of institutions, including philanthropic institutions and wealthy patrons. A cultural history of Buddhism would acknowledge the role of those foundations and patrons, including Cornelius Crane, Stephen Rockefeller, Peter Lynch, and Mitchell Kapor. I am indebted to Richard Jaffe for reminding me of this philanthropic connection. On the ways that religion is mediated by technology, see Thomas A. Tweed, *Crossing and Dwelling: A Theory of Religion* (Cambridge, MA: Harvard University Press, 2006), 124–127.

33 Wuthnow and Cadge, "Buddhists and Buddhism in the United States," 367. On the New Age Movement see P. Heelas, *The New Age Movement: The Celebration of the Self and the Sacralization of Modernity* (Cambridge, UK: Blackwell, 1996) and N. Drury, *Exploring the Labyrinth: Making Sense of the New Spirituality* (New York: Continuum, 1999).

34 Originally published in 1975, Thich Nhat Hanh's *The Miracle of Mindfulness* appeared in a revised edition with Beacon Press (Boston: Beacon, 1987). The sales figures I cite are from officials at Beacon Press. I originally cited them elsewhere, where I also offered a brief biographical account of Nhat Hanh: Thomas A. Tweed and Stephen Prothero, eds., *Asian Religions in America: A Documentary History* (New York: Oxford University Press, 1999), 268. On the uses of mindfulness practice for stress reduction, see Tweed, *American Encounter with Buddhism*, xiii. Mindfulness has been applied in other ways too. For example, in *Turning the Wheel: Essays on Buddhism and Writing* (New York: Scribner, 2003) the novelist Charles Johnson ponders "the elusive art of mindfulness" as an approach to writing.

35 For an example of this sort of therapeutic Buddhism, see Jon Kabat-Zinn, *Coming to Our Senses: Healing Ourselves and the World through Mindfulness* (New York: Hyperion, 2005). For a critique, see Wakoh Shannon Hickey, "Meditation as Medicine: A Critique," *Crosscurrents* (June 2010): 168–184.

36 On the movement see Christopher S. Queen, *Engaged Buddhism in the West* (Boston: Wisdom, 2000). In India, the movement is linked with the civil rights leader B. R. Ambedkar, who converted to Buddhism in 1956 and reached out to India's Untouchables between 1956 and 1966. As Queen notes, parallels also can be found among Buddhist activists in Thailand, Japan, Cambodia, and Myanmar (5). The movement also has found expression in the United States, for example in the outreach activities of the Zen Center of New York. On that, see Tweed and Prothero, eds., *Asian Religions in America*, 285–288. The religious and secular press in America took notice of both Nhat Hanh and Ambedkar at the time: see P. O. Philip, "Ambedkar now Buddhist," *Christian Century*, December 19, 1956, 1493–1494; and "Thich Nhat Hanh," *The New Yorker*, June 25, 1966, 21–23.

37 For example, see Jenny Philips, ed., *Letters from the Dhamma Brothers: Meditation Behind Bars* (Onalaska, WA: Pariyatti Press, 2008). There are guides for inmates about Buddhist practice in prisons: for example, Kobai Scott Whitney, *Sitting Inside: Buddhist Practice in American Prisons* (Boulder, CO: Prison Dharma Press, 2002). That volume was published by one of the groups that aim to bring Buddhism to prisoners; the Prison Dharma Network was founded in Colorado in 1989. Other groups include the National Buddhist Prison Sangha, the Prison Meditation Network, and the Buddhist Peace Fellowship's Prison Program.

38 Local print media is important too, of course, though coverage varies from place to place. That variance depends, in part, on local demographics, i.e., the number of Buddhists and Buddhist temples in the area. A study of dailies would offer another helpful angle of vision on Buddhism's presence. Here I focus on national magazines.

39 "Zen," *Time*, February 4, 1957, 65–66; W. Sargaent, "Profiles [D.T. Suzuki]," *The New Yorker*, August 31, 1957, 34–36; Nancy Ross Wilson, "What Is Zen?" *Mademoiselle* 46 (January 1958): 64–65; Allen Watts, "Eager Exponent of Zen," *Life*, April 21, 1961, 88A-B; "Zen, Beat, and Square," *Time*, July 21, 1958, 49; "Real Spirit

of Zen?" *Newsweek*, September 21, 1959, 121–122; Philip Kapleau, "All Is One, One is None, None is All," *New York Times Magazine*, March 6, 1966, 26–27; "Zen with a Difference: Tassajara Monastery in California," *Time*, October 18, 1968.

40 "When a Monk Became a Human Torch," 3; "Death v. the Family: Second Buddhist Priest to Burn Himself to Death," *Time*, August 16, 1963, 23; E. Wulff, "Buddhist Revolt," *The New Republic*, August 31, 1963, 11–14; J. B. Sheerin, "Religious Liberty: Buddhist Protests and Catholic Principles," *Catholic World* 197 (September 1963): 339–342; "Rome and Saigon," *Christian Century*, September 4, 1963, 1067; "Vietnam's Buddhists Emerge as Key Power," *Business Week*, April 23, 1966, 38–40.

41 "Teaching Tulku: The Tibetan Nyingmapa Meditation Center," *Saturday Review of Education* 1 (March 1973): 66; "Pious Master of the Mountains: Naropa Institute," *Time* 109, Febraury 14, 1977, 86; G. Baeyens, "Adventureland: The Himalayas," *Vogue* 167 (May 1977): 180; A. R. Topping, "Journey to Tibet: Hidden Splendors of an Exiled Deity," *The New York Times Magazine*, December 9, 1979, 68–72.

42 D. Goleman, "Art of Dying: Tibetan Book of the Dead," *Psychology Today*, April 1977, 58–59; David Van Biema, "Buddhism in America," *Time*, October 13, 1997, 72–81; The *Tibetan Book of the Dead* is the title given by Walter Yeeling Evans-Wentz (1878–1965), its first Western-language editor, to a collection of Tibetan ritual and literary texts concerned with death. On that, see "Tibetan Book of the Dead," in *Encyclopedia of Buddhism*, 2: 859. On Western interpretations of Tibet, see Donald S. Lopez, Jr., *Prisoners of Shangri-La: Tibetan Buddhism and the West* (Chicago: University of Chicago, 1998).

43 Ray Bradbury, "Zen and the Art of Writing," *The Writer* 71 (October 1958): 5–10; "Macrobiotics: Zen Diet at Musubi Restaurant," *The New Yorker*, August 25, 1962, 22–23; C. Tomkins, "Zen in the Art of Tennis," *The New Yorker*, August 8, 1959, 24–26.

44 Arthur Waley, *Zen Buddhism and Its Relation to Art* (London: Luzac, 1922). On Waley, see John De Gruchy, *Orienting Arthur Waley: Japonism, Orientalism, and the Creation of Japanese Literature in English* (Honolulu: University of Hawaii Press, 2003). See also Nancy Wilson Ross, *The World of Zen: An East-West Anthology* (New York: Random House, 1960), and Alan Watts, *The Spirit of Zen: A Way of Life, Work, and Art in the Far East*, 3rd ed. (New York: Grove Press, 1960).

45 James Edward Ketelaar, *Of Heretics and Martyrs in Meiji Japan: Buddhism and Its Persecution* (Princeton, NJ: Princeton University Press, 1990); Robert H. Sharf, "The Zen of Japanese Nationalism," in *Curators of the Buddha: The Study of Buddhism under Colonialism*, Donald E. Lopez, Jr., ed. (Chicago: University of Chicago Press, 1995), 107–39; Judith Snodgrass, *Presenting Japanese Buddhism to the West: Orientalism, Occidentalism, and the Columbian Exposition* (Chapel Hill: University of North Carolina Press, 2003); YOSHINGA Shin'ichi, guest editor, Special Issue: The *New Buddhism* of the Meiji Period: Modernization through Internationalization, *Japanese Religions* 34, no. 2 (July 2009).

46 Sharf, "Zen of Japanese Nationalism," 107.

47 Ibid. That emphasis on experience in Suzuki's work, I have argued, also came from the influence of Emmanuel Swedenborg. See Thomas A. Tweed, "American

Occultism and Japanese Buddhism: Albert J. Edmunds, D.T. Suzuki, and Translocative History," *Japanese Journal of Religious Studies* 32, no. 2 (2005): 249–281.

48 I have argued that it is useful to identify distinguishable but overlapping stages in Suzuki's intellectual development, and different Suzukis: a Rinzai Suzuki, Rationalist Suzuki, Experiential Suzuki, Occult Suzuki, Philological Suzuki, Aesthetic Suzuki, Existentialist Suzuki, Psychological Suzuki, and Mystical Suzuki; Tweed, "American Occultism and Japanese Buddhism," 262–264.

49 Eugen Herrigel, *Zen in the Art of Archery* (New York: Pantheon, 1953), 22–23.

50 YAMADA Shōji, "The Myth of Zen in the Art of Archery," *Japanese Journal of Religious Studies* 28, no. 1–2 (2001): 1–30. YAMADA Shōji, *Shots in the Dark: Japan, Zen, and the West*, trans. Earl Hartman (Chicago: University of Chicago Press, 2009). In that book, Yamada analyzes the Japanese and Western reception of Herrigel's best-selling book on archery, as well as Ryōanji's famous dry-landscape rock garden, and documents Suzuki's ambivalence about *Zen and the Art of Archery* (207–210). I am indebted also to Yamada for the insights he shared during a visit with him and several other scholars to Ryōanji in October 2011, when he pointed out that the staff at that Kyoto temple had removed a sign describing the history of the garden after his alternative historical account appeared.

51 Philip Kapleau, *The Three Pillars of Zen*, 25th anniversary edition (1965; New York: Doubleday, 1989); Shunryu Suzuki, *Zen Mind, Beginner's Mind: Informal Talks on Zen Meditation and Practice* (1970; New York and Tokyo: Weatherhill, 1986); Regina Leeds, *The Zen of Organizing: Creating Order and Peace in Your Home, Career, and Life* (Indianapolis, IN: Alpha Books, 2002), xix–xx.

52 Kim Boykin, *Zen for Christians: A Beginner's Guide* (San Francisco: Jossey-Bass, 2003); David M. Bader, *Zen Judaism: For You, a Little Enlightenment* (New York: Harmony, 2002); Philip Toshio Sudo, *Zen Computer* (New York: Simon and Schuster, 2001); Patrick McDermott, *Zen and the Art of Systems Analysis: Meditations on Computer Systems Development* (Lincoln, NE: Writers Club Press, 2002); David Brazier, *Zen Therapy* (New York: John Wiley & Sons, 1996); Charles Creekmore, *Zen and the Art of Diabetes Maintenance: A Complete Field Guide for Spiritual and Emotional Well Being* (Alexandria, VA: American Diabetes Association, 2002); Kathy A. Price, *Zen of Bowel Movements: A Spiritual Approach to Constipation* (Santa Barbara, CA: Rock House, 1995).

53 Jane Tidbury, *Zen Style: Balance and Simplicity in Your Home* (New York: Universe, 1999); Lucille Naimer, *The Zen of Cooking: Creative Cooking with and without Recipes* (New York: Overlook, 2002); Mark D. Fussner, *The Zen of Permanent Weight Loss* (Frederick, MD: PublishAmerica, 2004); Eric Chiles, *Zen Sleep: Enlightenment for a Good Night's Rest* (Austin, TX: Pilatus, 2003); Philip T. Sudo, *Zen Sex: The Way of Making Love* (San Francisco: HarperSanFrancisco, 2005); Brenda Shoshanna, *Zen and the Art of Falling in Love* (New York: Simon and Schuster, 2003); Judith Costello and Jurgen Haver, *Zen Parenting: The Art of Learning What You Already Know* (Beltsville, MD: Robins Lane Press, 2004); Sarah Arsone, *Zen and the Art of Changing Diapers* (Pacific Palisades, CA: Arsone, 1993); Laurence G. Boldt, *Zen and the Art of Making a Living* (New York: Penguin, 1999); Stan Adler, *The Zen of Selling* (New York: American Management Association, 1998); John Perricone, *Zen and the Art of Public School Teaching* (Frederick, MD: PublishAmerica, 2005).

54 Joseph Parent, *Zen Golf: Mastering the Mental Game* (New York: Doubleday, 2002); Sarah Detrixhe, *Zen and the Art of Quilting: Exploring Memory and Meaning in Patchwork* (Cincinnati, OH: Adams Media, 2004); Larry Philips, *Zen and the Art of Poker: Timeless Secrets to Transform Your Game* (New York: Plume, 1999); John Daido Loori, *The Zen of Creativity: Cultivating Your Artistic Life* (New York: Ballantine, 2005); Jeanne Carbonetti, *The Zen of Creative Painting: An Elegant Design for Revealing Your Muse* (New York: Watson-Guptill, 1998).

55 In this second case study of Buddhist influence I do not attempt a full history of the tradition's impact on all forms of American art during all periods. I offer only a few episodes and works that illustrate the larger patterns of appropriation and reception. Art historians have long acknowledged the Japanese influence on nineteenth-century American painting but came to recognize Buddhism's impact on twentieth-century art only during the 1990s. The major survey of religious influence on art was the exhibition catalog *The Spiritual in Art: Abstract Painting, 1890–1985* (New York: Abbeville for the Los Angeles County Museum of Art, 1985), but it overlooked Asian influence. Five years later, however, a brief exhibition catalog provided helpful clues about Buddhism's impact on some artists: Gail Gelburd and Geri De Paoli, *The Transparent Thread: Asian Philosophy in Recent American Art* (Hempstead, NY: Hofstra University; Annandale-on-Hudson, NY: Bard College, 1990). A few studies of selected periods followed, including Helen Westgeest, *Zen in the Fifties: Interaction in Art between East and West* (Zwolle: Waanders; Amstelveen: Cobra museum voor moderne kunst, 1996). Two other volumes offered more profiles of artistic impact: Jacquelynn Bass and Mary Jane Jacobs, eds., *Buddha Mind in Contemporary Art* (Berkeley: University of California Press, 2005); and Jacquelynn Bass, *Smile of the Buddha: Eastern Philosophy and Western Art from Monet to Today* (Berkeley: University of California Press, 2005). After I submitted the revised version of this chapter, another important exhibition volume appeared: Alexandra Munroe, ed., *The Third Mind: American Artists Contemplate Asia, 1860–1989* (New York: Guggenheim Museum Publications, 2009). That book, edited by the Guggenheim's senior curator of Asian art, is the best historical survey available. It offers further support for my argument about the impact of Buddhism on the arts in America.

56 By using the phrase "Suzuki Zen" I employ a category that acknowledges the important, though not exclusive, role of D. T. Suzuki in creating and circulating a certain notion of Zen. Others, including Ross, Waley, Herrigel, Watts, and Cage also played a role in the making of Suzuki Zen. But those popularizers acknowledged the decisive influence of Suzuki's interpretations, as Watts did in the preface to the first edition of his *The Spirit of Zen*: "I should never have been able to write this book if it had not been for the work of Daisetz Teitaro Suzuki of the Otani Buddhist College at Kyoto. . . ." Alan W. Watts, *The Spirit of Zen: A Way of Life, Work, and Art in the Far East*, 3rd ed. (New York: Grove Press, 1960), 12. Following Suzuki's lead, some pondered the relation between Zen and existentialism, and Zen and psychotherapy. The psychotherapists included Eric Fromm and Karen Horney. On Existentialism, see George Cotkin, *Existential America* (Baltimore, MD: Johns Hopkins University Press, 2003).

57 UC Berkeley's Center for Buddhist Studies and Institute of East Asian Studies sponsored a conference on "Speaking for the Buddha?: Buddhism and the Media," Febraury 8–9, 2005. Nancy Lin's helpful summary of the proceedings, which included

discussion of film, advertising, and print media, can be found at http://ieas.berkeley.edu/events/2005.02.08–09.html. Institute of East Asian Studies, 2005, accessed March 1, 2006.

58 Warren I. Cohen, *East Asian Art and American Culture: A Study in International Relations* (New York: Columbia University Press, 1992), 19–20. As Cohen notes (20, 29), two other exhibitions in the United States also were important for the reception of East Asian art: Philadelphia's Centennial Exposition in 1876 and Chicago's World's Columbian Exposition in 1893. Earlier exhibitions in Europe also played a less direct role, including the world's fairs in 1851 (London) and 1855 (Paris). On those exhibitions and other events, see the helpful "chronology" compiled by Ikuyo Nakagawa in Munroe, ed., *The Third Mind*, 378–397.

59 On this "golden age" of collecting East Asian art, see Cohen, *East Asian Art and American Culture*, 37–73. On religious art displayed in American homes between 1840 and 1940, see Colleen McDannell's *The Christian Home in Victorian America, 1840–1900* (Bloomington: Indiana University Press, 1986) and *Picturing Faith: Photography and the Great Depression* (New Haven, CT: Yale University Press, 2004). For a qualitative study of art in domestic spaces in late twentieth-century New York: David Halle, *Inside Culture: Art and Class in the American Home* (Chicago: University of Chicago Press, 1993). Halle found, for example, class differences in the landscapes displayed: In the upper-class homes on Manhattan's East Side, Japan was portrayed more often than any other foreign space, while the working-class homes in Greenpoint tended to display landscapes representing the residents' country of origin, especially Poland or Italy (81).

60 On Buddhist images as "living images" see Robert H. Sharf and Elizabeth Horton Sharf, eds., *Living Images: Japanese Buddhist Icons in Context* (Stanford, CA: Stanford University Press, 2001).

61 Photograph, the Court Hall at Olana, 1884, OL.1980.1259, Archives, Olana State Historic Site, Staatsburg, New York. For a report on this scroll in the archives, see Christine M. E. Guth, "Report on a Painting of the Buddha's Nirvana in the Collection of Frederick Church (acquired before 1884)," June 20, 1997, Archives, Olana State Historic Site. I am grateful to Karen Zukowski, Curator, Olana State Historic Site, for assistance.

62 Photograph, "Amhikiki Buddha" [sic], Joseph M. Wade Collection, Dorchester, Massachusetts, May 22, 1902. I have a copy of the photograph in my own files. The information listed above is written on the bottom of the photograph. On this image see "A Sacred Buddha in Wood," *Light of Dharma* 2 (August 1903): 109–110. On Wade, see Tweed, *American Encounter with Buddhism*, 55, 75, 82.

63 Alan Chong, "Introduction: Journeys East," in *Journeys East: Isabella Stewart Gardner and Asia*, Alan Chong and Noriko Murai, eds. (Boston: Isabella Stewart Gardner Museum, 2009), 30, 38–44. As Chong points out, there were two "Chinese Rooms," the first from 1902 to 1914 and the second from 1914 to 1971. I analyze Gardner's interest in Buddhism—and compare it with the approach of her neighbor, William Sturgis Bigelow—in Thomas A. Tweed, "Smells and Bells: Buddhism, Catholicism, and the Therapeutic Aestheticism of William Sturgis Bigelow and Isabella Stewart Gardner," in *Inventing Asia*, Alan Chong and Noriko Murai eds. (Boston: Isabella Stewart Gardner Museum, 2013), 36–46.

64 On Freer, see Cohen, *East Asian Art and American Culture*, 49–64. I have considered Freer's interest in Buddhism and Japanese art in Thomas A. Tweed, "The Spiritual Origins of the Freer Gallery of Art: Religious and Aesthetic Inclusivism and the First American Buddhist Vogue, 1879–1907," *Japanese Journal of American and Canadian Studies* [Japan], no. 24 (2006): 41–59. For an archival source that documents Freer's interest in Buddhism see Charles Lang Freer to Dwight Tryon, June 17, 1895, from "Ano-no-Hashidate" (Japan), Dwight Tryon Papers, Freer Gallery of Art, Archives. See also Kathleen Pyne, "Portrait of a Collector as an Agnostic: Charles Lang Freer and Connoisseurship," *Art Bulletin* 78, no. 1 (March 1996): 75–97.

65 On this period, see Vivien Greene, "Aestheticism and Japan: The Cult of the Orient," in Munroe, ed., *The Third Mind*, 59–71.

66 Cohen, *East Asian Art and American Culture*, 55.

67 On the Japanese collection at the Museum of Fine Arts, Boston, see *Selected Masterpieces of Asian Art* (Boston: Museum of Fine Arts; Tokyo: Japan Broadcasting Publishing, Co., 1992), 6–121; Anne Ninshimura Morse and Nobuo Tsuji, eds., *Japanese Art in the Museum of Fine Arts, Boston*, 2 vols. (Boston: Museum of Fine Arts; Tokyo: Kodansha, 1998).

68 Ernest Fenollosa, *Epochs of Chinese and Japanese Art*, vol. 1 (New York: Dover, 1963), xxiii. On Dow and Fenollosa and their influence, see Matthew Baigell, *A Concise History of American Painting and Sculpture*, rev. ed. (New York: HarperCollins, 1996), 214.

69 I again use the phrase *Suzuki Zen* here to gesture toward that ritually decontextualized and historically conditioned cluster of beliefs, values, and practices that had a complicated relation to what happened in monastic institutions associated with Chinese Chan, Korean Seon, and Japanese Zen. Gregory Levine, a specialist in Japanese art, italicizes the phrase *Zen Art* for similar reasons—to signal that Zen-inspired art in the West and the paintings and calligraphies produced by East Asian monks and nuns are best "imagined as a field of converging and colliding objects, notions, and interpretations in which the visual is open to debate" (59). Gregory Levine, "Two (or More) Truths: Reconsidering *Zen Art* in the West," in *Awakenings: Zen Figure Paintings from Medieval Japan*, Gregory Levine and Yukio Lippit, eds. (New York: Japan Society; New Haven, CT: Yale University Press, 2007), 52–63.

70 "Treasures from Japan," *Life*, April 20, 1953; "Ambassadors of Good Will," *Time*, July 13, 1953, 52ff. The estimate of visitors to the exhibit, and the historical background, are found in Cohen, *East Asian Art and American Culture*, 139–143. As Cohen notes (139), John D. Rockefeller III, who served as president of the Japan Society, "played a key role" in this use of art as cultural diplomacy and transnational exchange. That is another example of how such institutions and elites—Rockefeller also had an important collection of Japanese art, which he donated to the Japan Society—shaped the American reception of East Asian Art.

71 On Tobey, Graves, and others see Kathleen Pyne and D. Scott Atkinson, "Landscapes of the Mind: New Conceptions of Nature," in Munroe, ed., *The Third Mind*, 89–99; and Bert Winther-Tamaki, "The Asian Dimension of Postwar Abstract Art," in Munroe, ed., *The Third Mind*, 145–157.

72 Westgeest, *Zen in the Fifties*, 46.

73 Ibid., 49.

74 Ibid., 67.

75 The entry from Reinhardt's diary is reprinted in Westgeest, *Zen in the Fifties*, 81–82. As Sally Promey notes, during World War II and the Cold War period, "freedom" was opposed to fascist and Soviet realisms, and it meant the "subjective" liberation from the task of reproducing the appearance of the visible world. It meant, in short, abstraction and formalism. Sally Promey, "Taste Cultures: The Visual Practice of Liberal Protestantism, 1945–1965," in *Practicing Protestants: Histories of Christian Life in America, 1630–1965*, Laurie F. Maffly-Kipp, Leigh Schmidt, and Mark Valeri, eds. (Baltimore, MD: Johns Hopkins University Press, 2006), 250–294. As Promey also points out, Alfred Hamilton Barr, Jr.'s influential book *What is Modern Painting?* (New York: Museum of Modern Art, 1943) associated expressivist styles with freedom.

76 On these developments see Munroe, "Buddhism and the Neo-Avant-Garde: Cage Zen, Beat Zen, and Zen," in Munroe, ed., *The Third Mind*, 199–215. The term "Happening" seems to have been coined by Allan Kaprow, a student of John Cage, in 1959, seven years after the event that is generally recognized as beginning this movement, which also had roots in Dadaistic theater and performance earlier in the century. On the term "Happening," see Ian Chilvers, *Oxford Concise Dictionary of Art and Artists* (New York: Oxford University Press, 2003), 272.

77 On Cage as a "conduit" of Zen, see Alberta Arthurs and Glenn Wallach, eds., *Crossroads: Art and Religion in American Life* (New York: The New Press, 2001), 237. Munroe also notes Cage's mediating role in her use of the phrase *Cage Zen*, which she helpfully defines as one of "three interconnected collectives of artists and artists" with links to Zen and other forms of Mahayana Buddhism. The other collectives she calls *Beat Zen* and *Bay Area Conceptual Art*: Munroe, "Buddhism and the Neo-Avant-Garde: Cage Zen, Beat Zen, and Zen," in Munroe, ed., *The Third Mind*, 200. As I see it, Munroe's *Cage Zen* is a subset of what I have called *Suzuki Zen*; Cage was one important node in the personal and institutional networks that circulated interpretations of Buddhism that can be traced to Suzuki's writings or lectures. On Black Mountain College, see Mary Emma Harris, *The Arts at Black Mountain College* (Cambridge, MA: MIT Press, 1987), and Vincent Katz, ed., *Black Mountain College: Experiment in Art* (Cambridge, MA: MIT Press, 2002). On the exhibition of Johns's work in 1996–1997 at the Museum of Modern Art, see Kirk Varnedoe, *Jasper Johns: A Retrospective* (New York: Museum of Modern Art; distributed by Harry N. Abrams, 1996). The information about Johns and the quotation from Rauschenberg are included in Gelburd and De Paoli, *The Transparent Thread*, 82, 95.

78 Cage's statement about Rauschenberg's white paintings is found in John Cage, *Silence* (Middletown, CT: Wesleyan University Press, 1973), 108. Cage's account of the reading of the Buddhist text is found in "John Cage, Interviewed by Martin Duberman," Phone Interview with John Cage, April 26, 1969, Martin Duberman Collection, Series 4 (Interviews), Box 6, North Carolina Department of Cultural Resources, Archives and Records, Raleigh, North Carolina. Cage revealed in "An Autobiographical Statement," originally published in the *Southwest Review* in 1991, that the text they read aloud was the 1947 translation by the British Buddhist John Blofeld, who published under the name Chu Ch'an: *The Huang Po Doctrine of Universal Mind* (London: The Buddhist Society, 1947).

79 Cage, *Silence*, ix.

80 Watts, *Spirit of Zen*, 15. The *Suzuki Zen* that Americans received already had been created in a transnational exchange, and included influences from William

James's philosophy and American occult traditions; that is another reason that the "tendencies" Watts noticed seemed "implicit" in "Western life." John Cage, "An Autobiographical Statement," *Southwest Review* (1991). For an online version of Cage's "Statement" see http://www.newalbion.com/artists/cagej/autobiog.html. Westgeest, *Zen in the Fifties*, 55.

81 Ko Won, *Buddhist Elements in Dada: A Comparison of Tristan Tzara, Takahashi Shinkichi, and Their Fellow Poets* (New York: New York University Press, 1977), 12, 90. For an online copy of Ball's manifesto see "Dada Manifesto (1916, Hugo Ball)," Wikisource. Available at: http://en.wikisource.org/wiki/Dada_Manifesto_(1916,_ Hugo_Ball), accessed December 7, 2006. The quoted passages from Tzara's 1922 "Lecture on Dada" is reprinted in Robert Motherwell, ed., *The Dada Painters and Poets: An Anthology*, 2nd ed. (Boston: G. K. Hall, 1981), 246–251.

82 On Dada in New York, see Francis M. Naumann and Beth Venn, *Making Mischief: Dada Invades New York* (New York: Whitney Museum of Art, distributed by Harry N. Abrams, 1996). On Cage and Duchamp see Erika Doss, *Twentieth-Century American Art* (Oxford: Oxford University Press, 2002), 140. Janis Mink, *Marcel Duchamp, 1887–1968: Art as Anti-Art* (Köln, Germany: Taschen, 2004), 43–67. Jacquelynn Baas has considered the possible Buddhist influences and parallels in the work of Duchamp: for example, *Draft on the Japanese Apple* (1911) portrays a Japanese woman sitting in a cross-legged position; one contemporary suggested that, by inverting the urinal in *Fountain*, Duchamp had turned the readymade into a Buddha; and Baas suggests that *The Coffee Grinder* is a *mandala* that "hints at Tantric influence": Jacquelynn Baas, *Smile of the Buddha: Eastern Philosophy and Western Art from Monet to Today* (Berkeley: University of California Press, 2005), 79–93.

83 Brian O'Doherty, *American Masters: The Voice and the Myth in Modern Art* (New York: Dutton, 1982), 201. Doss, *Twentieth-Century American Art*, 142–146.

84 On Neo-Dada see Susan Hapgood, *Neo-Dada: Redefining Art, 1958–1962* (New York: American Federation of Arts in association with Universe Publishing, 1994). One biographical profile notes that Warhol traveled to Asia in 1956, and his first film, *Sleep* (1963), reflected Cage's Buddhist-derived interest in silence and repetition. Yet it would be difficult to defend the claim that Warhol was a Buddhist-inspired artist in any direct or substantial way. Munroe, ed., *Third Mind*, 423.

85 David Morgan highlighted the notion of "the gaze" in *The Sacred Gaze: Religious Visual Culture in Theory and Practice* (Berkeley: University of California Press, 2005). The quotations from Reinhardt are included in Westgeest, *Zen in the Fifties*, 68. Monroe used slightly different language to represent Reinhardt's understanding of art as "a perceptual experience with the specific power…to purify consciousness through the act of concentrated contemplation": Munroe, "Art of Perceptual Experience: Pure Abstraction and Ecstatic Minimalism," in Munroe, ed., *The Third Mind*, 287. On Johns's "Target" as *mandala*, see Gelburd and De Paoli, eds., *Transparent Thread*, 82. Providing more evidence that the meditative gaze was at play in his work, Johns told an interviewer in 1964 that "I was just interested in enriching things as much as possible. One way to do this was to stare at a certain situation without allowing my attention to waver and focus my attention on it." Quoted in Baas, *Smile of the Buddha*, 149.

86 Brief analysis of the Buddhist influences on the work of Kimsooja, Mariko Mori, and Bill Viola, as well as some biographical information, is included in

Jacquelynn Baas and Mary Jane Jacob, eds., *Buddha Mind in Contemporary Art* (Berkeley: University of California Press, 2004), 212–19, 248–57, 258–63. On Paik's *TV Buddha* see Baas, *Smile of the Buddha*, 185–186.

87 Baas and Jacob, eds., *Buddha Mind in Contemporary Art*, 249. For an analysis of the Asian influences in Viola's work that emphasizes his "creative misunderstanding" of those sources and his recurrent use of the number five, which is important in Buddhism, see Elizabeth Ten Grotenhuis, "Something Rich and Strange: Bill Viola's Uses of Asian Spirituality," in *The Art of Bill Viola*, Chris Townsend, ed. (New York: Thames and Hudson, 2004), 161–179.

88 Bill Viola, "Migration" (1976), videocassette, color, mono, 7:00, in Bill Viola, *Selected Works* (Van Nuys, CA: AGF Media Services, 2001).

89 Bill Viola, *Reasons for Knocking at an Empty House: Writings 1973–1994* (Cambridge, MA: MIT Press, in association with the Anthony d'Offay Gallery, London, 1995), 44.

90 Viola, *Reasons for Knocking at an Empty House*, 44.

91 Bill Viola, "Ancient of Days," (1979–81), videocassette, color, stereo, 12:21, in Bill Viola, *Selected Works* (Van Nuys, CA: AGF Media Services, 2001).

92 Baas and Jacobs, ed., *Buddha Mind in Contemporary Art*, 249.

93 Viola, *Reasons for Knocking at an Empty House*, 282–283. Bill Viola confirmed my interpretation of these early videos of the 1970s and 1980s as Buddhist-inspired during an exchange we had at a conference session about his work at the American Academy of Religion's annual meeting in San Diego on November 17, 2007.

94 Viola, *Reasons for Knocking at an Empty House*, 79.

95 Ibid.

96 Ibid., 78.

97 For information on these centers, see not only the Pluralism Project directory but also the centers' web pages: Washington Buddhist Vihara, 2006, available at http://www.buddhistvihara.com/, accessed July 6, 2006; Hsi Lai Temple, 2006, available at http://www.hsilai.org/, accessed July 6, 2006.

98 Don Morreale, *The Complete Guide to Buddhist America* (Boston and London: Shambhala, 1998), xvi. The Pluralism Project, "Directory of Religious Centers," 2006, available at http://www.pluralism.org/directory/index.php, accessed July 6, 2006.

CHAPTER 9

Beyond Pluralism: Global Gurus
and the Third Stream of American
Religiosity

JOANNE PUNZO WAGHORNE

IN NOVEMBER OF 2007, the Hindu American Foundation (usually known as
HAF) celebrated the unanimous passage of a U.S. Senate resolution recogniz-
ing the "religious and historical significance of the festival of Diwali."[1] The
Senate resolution begins, "Whereas Diwali, a festival of great significance to
Indian Americans and the people of India, is celebrated annually by Hindus,
Sikhs, Buddhists, and Jains throughout the United States and the world;
Whereas there are more than 2,000,000 Hindus, Sikhs, Buddhists, and Jains
in the United States.... Whereas Diwali is a festival of lights, during which
celebrants light small oil lamps, place them around the home, and pray for
health, knowledge, and peace...." The Senate resolution, and indeed the work
of the Hindu American Foundation, appears to present a classic example of
"religious pluralism" as increasingly understood and even lauded in America:
a clearly identifiable community represented by a recognized organization
speaking for American values of peace and tolerance, and the recognition
of difference within common categories—in this case the celebration of one
common *Hindu* festival to enter into the national consciousness along with
Thanksgiving, Christmas, and Hanukkah that mark the year's end.

The Hindu American Foundation, a new organization based just outside
the Washington Beltway, "a non-profit 501(c)(3), non-partisan organization,
promoting the Hindu and American ideals of understanding, tolerance and
pluralism,"[2] managed to raise funds for the campaign and successfully lobby
Congress for its passage within a short time. The speed and unanimity of the
Senate on this resolution speaks not only to the savvy of the Hindu American
Foundation but also to the growing recognition of the presence and power
of this fast-growing minority—represented here not as Asian-Indians, as the
official census terms them, but as a *religious* community, as Hindus within
America's growing religious pluralism. However, for this vigorous organiza-
tion, which sees itself as the voice of the "2 million strong Hindu American

community," the line between ethnicity and religion blurs, as does the number of those Asian Indians who might not be comfortable, if asked, with having a Hindu organization speak for them.[3]

Prior to these more recent forays into political life in the United States, émigré Hindus made their public mark by practicing more visual acts of pluralism: building grand temples in New York City, Pittsburgh, Washington D.C., and in numerous smaller cities that parallel the many churches, mosques, and Buddhist temples sharing a new American religious landscape.[4] In *Diaspora of the Gods: Modern Hindu Temples in a Middle-Class Urban World*, I charted the growth of new Hindu temples among urban Anglophone Indians in Washington D.C., London, and Chennai (Madras), India (2004). In the American context these temples rarely became a religious home to those outside the Indian ethnic fold. They often include "community centers" in the basement or as a separate building to meet the needs of both second-generation and newly migrating Indians and people of Indian origin. Leaders of these temples participate as representatives of the Hindu perspective in interfaith councils that emerged in many American cities, especially after 9/11. Many Hindu American temples increasingly mirror the role of churches for their members, who are sometimes even referred to as the "congregation." Temples usually undertake the religious education of their youth in settings resembling Sunday schools. They foster volunteer social service work for the larger community and provide counseling for their own members.[5] Most are practitioners of liberal pluralism.

As Hinduism in the American context elides into a religio-ethnic identity for some Asian Indians (though not all), cultural and religious pride begins to demand tighter boundaries around the definitions of who is a Hindu. Debates have raged within the academy over "who speaks for Hinduism?" The energetic Dharma Association of North America now meets in conjunction with the annual meeting of the American Academy of Religion. Here, members of the HAF critique presentations of "Hinduism" within the educational system that fail to reflect the Hindu practices and principles which are taught within Asian-Indian homes. Debate always ensues. This is the harder edge to organizations like the HAF, whose members often identify with the increasing wealth and power of India as well as the growing economic and political clout of its diaspora in America. Older organizations like the VHP (Vishwa Hindu Parishad) and the even harder-edged RSS (Rashtriya Swayamsevak Sangh, "national service organization") push for a much closer identification of Hindus with India as quite literally "Mother India" (Bharata Mata). Such organizations may speak of pluralism in the American context but contest the Government of India's commitment to secularism in the mother country and support the increasing pressure on religious minorities in India, especially Muslims and Christians. The VHP and RSS reflect a growing, very modern conservatism, usually called Hindu Nationalism but often understood as a variant on worldwide fundamentalism.[6]

The current use of the term "pluralism"—like the title of this volume—reflects these realities on the ground as the situation of Hinduism in America *seems* to parallel—albeit in complex ways—the clash of "pluralism" with "fundamentalism." Pluralism continues to reflect much of the ethos of organizations like the Hindu American Foundation and the governing board of most Hindu temples in the United States. However, *pluralism* excludes the continuing presence of a *third stream* of mixing, matching, adopting, and adapting that also complicates—as I will argue—the lines between pluralism and fundamentalism. This *third stream* characterized the earliest period of American encounter with "Hinduism" and appears to be reemerging within the American religious context. Today this *third stream* comprises what many call "Hindu spirituality," widely practiced as mediation, alternate healing, and yoga taught by globally active *gurus* (*guru* meaning "teacher" but used for a religious master). Today, numerous Hindu-oriented gurus espousing "spirituality" and eschewing "religion" attract followers from the Indian émigrés, second-generation Indian-Americans, as well as many Euro-, Asian-, and African-Americans who can be seen sitting together chanting mantras, meditating, or listening in rapt attention to their global guru, who is visible in person or on screen via a projected DVD or sophisticated televideo link.

Thus I am identifying three modes of the globalization of Hinduism within the American context (there may indeed be more and many individuals mix these models): (1) the "liberal" mode of Hindu-heritage citizens identifying with the generalized system of *pluralism* as "Hindus" in a multireligious American domain, (2) the "conservative" mode of heritage of Hindus identifying their Hinduness (Hindutva) with an ethnic identity derived from India as the Motherland, and (3) the "spiritual" mode of Hindu consciousness and yogic practices as open to worldwide participation, usually via a *guru* and a guru-centered organization. This third stream marks the once dominant mode and—what I increasingly consider—the most enduring mark of Hinduness on the broader public consciousness of the United States. Practitioners of this third stream, involving the now familiar yoga and meditation, argue against boundaries or dualities of all kinds, including boundaries between bodies, the duality between mind and body, and between the body and the world. This mode is not primarily about peoples but about persons—and as we will see—this third stream also complicates any easy duality between pluralism and fundamentalism. The often reviled, and just as often revered, *gurus*, we cannot forget, came long before over a million (now almost two million) "Asian-Indians" built the temples and religious organizations that made "Hinduism" obvious even to the most oblivious eye. The confluence in the late nineteenth century of the beginnings of the language of pluralism *and* the first popular wave of Hinduness that led some Americans—at that time mostly middle- or upper-middle class white Protestants—to dabble with or outright join Hindu-based, guru-centered organizations requires some serious reflection.[7]

Swami Vivekananda Introduces Hindu Universalism, 1893

This earliest popular encounter with Hinduism came at one defining moment: an unknown handsome young saffron-robbed Indian *swami* ("master," usually referring to a renunciant who has mastered a yogic discipline) rose to speak for "Hinduism" on the floor of the World Parliament of Religion in Chicago in 1893. The organizers of the Parliament had hoped to add a human perspective to the grand World's Columbian Exposition of 1893[8] with its glorification of science and industry—the scientific progress made four hundred years after the "discovery" of America. The Parliament was to stress the equal progress achieved in human tolerance and understanding. The young swami had recently renounced the world after the death of his spiritual master, the famous Sri Ramakrishna. He had come to America to raise funds for social service projects in India. Swami Vivekananda learned of the Parliament, applied, and was asked to speak for "Hinduism." At the moment when scholars were at work constructing the differences between world religions and classifying Hinduism as locally confined to India, and when the conveners of the Parliament were also beginning to define the contours of liberal pluralism in an increasingly diverse nation, Swami Vivekananda's electrifying speech in the Parliament of Religions presented "Hinduism" as universal. Moreover, he left his audience with the suggestion that the catholicity of his Hinduism, its inherent inclusion of all, could serve as the very model for a rising new kind of universal religion:

> The Hindu might have failed to carry out all of his plans, but if there ever is to be a universal religion, it must be one which would hold no location in place and time, which would be infinite like the God it would preach, whose sun shines upon the followers of Krishna or Christ; saints or sinners alike; which would not be the Brahman or Buddhist, or Christian or Mohammedan, but the sum total of all of these, and still have infinite space for development; which in its catholicity would embrace in its infinite arms and formulate a place for every human being....[9]

With this giant leap over the widely accepted universality of Christianity, with some scholars including Islam and/or Buddhism as "universal" (see Masuzawa 2005), Vivekananda redefined the terms of the debate, but in subtle ways that moved between persons, bodies, nations, and races.

Swami Vivekananda spoke to certain members of the American public in a delightfully ambiguous and yet mutually intelligible language, which Srinivas Aravamudan has recently termed "Guru English."[10] Thus the "dawn of pluralism" and the beginnings of Hindu spirituality in America coincided and commingled when the young swami rose in the Parliament.[11] And even more intriguing, his triumphal reception and his equally powerful speeches on his return to India, mark—as some now argue—the beginnings of Hindu Nationalism. Swami Vivekananda, the first really popular voice for Hinduism in the United States, continues to stand at the intersection of the three modes of globalization of Hinduism in America—he appears simultaneously as the first to popularize Hindu spirituality, as official voice of Hinduism in the first pluralistic interfaith conference, and as an early voice in India for what would become Hindu Nationalism.

Swami Vivekananda's Curious Double Role

"Don Yellow Robes—Chicagoans to Imitate the 'Holy Men' of India," the *Chicago Daily Tribune* reported on July 11, 1897.[12] The article featured a group of Chicago "believers in occultism, meditation, concentration, and the general 'practice of yoga'" who would gather in Michigan with their swami "Abayananda" [Abhayananda], a French émigré, "the only woman monk in the world, and the latest follower of the yellow-robed order of East Indian religious mendicants." This "yellow-robed order" referred to those—including this Mme Marie Louise—initiated by Swami Vivekananda at Thousand Islands near the Canadian border of New York State.[13] At this moment in 1897 Swami Vivekananda had just returned to India after fruitful years of lecturing and writing in the United States and the United Kingdom. His newly founded Ramakrishna Mission was less than two months old and sadly he was within five years of his early death. Out of these brief years, the complex and often controversial life story of Swami Vivekananda came to signify seemingly opposite trends that continue to characterize the globalization of Hinduism: the coterminous relinking of Hindu religion to "a way of life" embedded within Indian cultural, ethnic, and *national* identity and the equally intriguing unlinking of Hindu religiosity from the very same ethnic-cultural and national ground. However, whether acting as spokesman for "Hinduism" at the Parliament in Chicago, teaching yoga to a few Western disciples in a Victorian cottage in upstate New York,[14] or speaking at triumphal gatherings in Madras,[15] Vivekananda came to be envisioned by the Indian and American public as he appeared in a popular poster widely distributed during the World's Parliament of Religions[16] and as he chose to present himself at the Parliament, a turbaned and saffron-robed *swami*.

Today such peripatetic world teachers, now more commonly called *gurus*, and the organizations that surround them remain deeply venerated by some yet suspected by others as they apparently were even in the 1890s. The *Chicago Daily Tribune* reported on Vivekananda at the World's Parliament in almost breathless terms describing him as he took the podium, "Dr. Nobel then presented Swami Vivekananda, the Hindoo monk, who was applauded loudly as he stepped to the center of the platform. He wore an orange robe, bound with a scarlet sash, and a pale yellow turban. The customary smile was on his handsome face and his eyes shown with animation."[17] Six years later the same newspaper would report on "Chicago Followers of Strange Religions," which included those Western followers associated with Vivekananda's teachings. Writing with undisguised cynicism in the same style as the earlier report on the woman swami, the reporter concluded, "all of the followers after strange gods and even stranger religions labor, talk, and practice their rites.... the 'sacred word' of the Hindoos, the Buddhists, the Confucians, the Brahmans,... the Persians, and the Mohammedans, alike is recited over and through Chicago daily."[18] At this point, many in the press seemed to make no distinction between the occult and what most textbooks now classify as the major religions of Asia.

This shift from awed veneration to sarcastic quips seems to parallel the two very public faces of global gurus: their function as spokespersons, apologists, and unifiers of the Hindu religion for Hindus in India and heritage Hindus in the United States as well as the broad-minded international public (for which they are respected) and their other role as synthesizers and creators of newer and more universalized religious forms that break the bounds of territory, race, and ethnicity (for which they and their followers are often treated with suspicion). Again the great Swami Vivekananda took on both functions—indeed he is credited with pioneering the current popular fusion of generalized Hindu spirituality and yogic techniques with pre-existing Euro-American esotericism.[19] The monks of the worldwide Ramakrishna-Vedanta missions that he initiated continue to serve, like their founder, both constituencies and to perform both functions, although not without tension.[20] Today this conflicting picture of Swami Vivekananda reappears as seemingly divergent organizations claim him as an icon of modern Hindu nationalism, or as an early apostle of a new world theology, religious pluralism, and even New Age movements.

Swami Vivekananda's Presence at the Second World's Parliament of Religions, 1993

After years of obscurity, reenactments of the World's Parliament of Religions once again made headlines and once again Swami Vivekananda's spirited defense and articulation of "Hindu religion," as he phrased it, reemerged along with the memory of his universal message. In 1993 the Vishwa Hindu Parishad of America (VHP) organized "Global Vision 2000" in Washington D.C. to mark the centenary of the Parliament in Chicago. At the same time the newly formed Council for a World's Parliament of Religions, in which the monks of the Ramakrishna-Vedanta Society of Chicago "played a leading role,"[21] held the second Parliament in Chicago exactly one hundred years later in 1993 with 8000 people attending. The second Parliament produced, as its organizers put it, "a groundbreaking document, *Towards a Global Ethic: An Initial Declaration* is a powerful statement of the ethical common ground shared by the world's religious and spiritual traditions."[22] This second Parliament intended to carry on—albeit in a distinctly modified form[23]—what Joseph Kitagawa described as the focus of the first Parliament, "not the critical, scholarly inquiry concerning religions, but rather the religious or philosophical basics for the unity of all religions."[24] Speeches at Global Vision 2000 also invoked Swami Vivekananda's "Universal Religion"[25] and spoke of "lifting the thoughts of people to higher ideals of peace, harmony and unity,"[26] but the emphasis as recorded in the speeches and the descriptions of the conference centered on "our culture" and the "great son of our motherland."[27] Although the event in Washington D.C. was very well attended, many other Indian-American organizations protested strongly before and during the conference, in part over the seeming co-optation of Swami Vivekananda. The *Washington Post* quoted one protester, "Swami Vivekananda's...message is very universal, but the World Hindu Organization takes a very narrow view, to exclude everybody else except those who accept their political agenda."[28]

Organizers of Global Vision 2000 retorted "that the Washington conference was purely a cultural and religious gathering intended to help reconnect Indian expatriates to their Hindu roots,"[29] and indeed many first- and second-generation Indian Hindus settled in the United States viewed the event as a celebration of their Hindu heritage. Speeches at Global Vision invoked Swami Vivekananda's message "to unify the religious vision of humanity" but one created, however, through particular Hindu religious sensibilities.[30] A speech by Sri Tarlabalu Jagadguru of Sringere on "Hindu Visions of Global Peace" affirmed, "To those who are enlightened and noble, the whole world is one family. Here is the Hindu vision of the whole world as one Global Family based on pure human love."[31] Others later reflected that the conference had succeeded in "deepening the understanding of our culture and what it stands for, and broadening our vision of the world we live in."[32] For others, Swami Vivekananda's universalizing message to a divided world elided into his brilliant articulation of a generalized Hindu religion to unify a divided nation. In a speech arguing that the "RSS fulfills the mission of Swami Vivekananda," a leader of the social service projects of this nationalist Hindu organization built the case through a careful selection of quotes from Swami Vivekananda that "His life mission was to rejuvenate and reestablish this Hindu nation." He quotes the foremost apostle of Sri Ramakrishna[33] as saying, "It is specially for the preservation of the Hindu race and religion that Bhagawana Sri Ramakrishna, the embodiment of mercy, has incarnated himself." He provided no reference for the quote.

While many who protested Global Vision 2000 and others who extolled the new World's Parliament of Religions saw clear contrasts between the universalism of *their* Swami Vivekananda and the icon of Hindu Nationalism constructed by the VHP, their differences are actually not so easy to theorize. The second World's Parliament of Religion and Global Vision 2000 shared a common sense that there are bounded religions in this world and that these boundaries should be accepted, even celebrated, but that an overall *commonality* exists on some generalized level under certain conditions. They also share common sensibilities that modernization acts on older systems and demands new configurations, reformation, and re-formation. Importantly, they *both* contrast with another realm of the modern religious world—now even more apparent as contemporary globalization exceeds the worldwide penetration of modernism at the time of the first Parliament of Religions—a *third stream* of highly syncretic, newly wrought or "discovered" religious systems. My major concern will be this "third component," which the Dutch scholar of New Age religions Wouter J. Hanegraaff also identifies in American-European culture[34] and which I also see as an important component of global Hinduism, especially in connection to the contemporary rise of guru-centered movements worldwide. A return to the first World's Parliament of Religions will reveal the complex tangled roots of pluralism, nationalism, and what is now often called "spirituality."

1893 Again: Shared Sensibilities Beyond Liberal Pluralism

On the opening day of the first World's Parliament of Religions, the Rev. John Henry Barrows, the prime organizer of this unprecedented congress, addressed the assembled invited representatives of the world's "major" religions:

> We are met as religious men, believing here in the capital of material wonders, in the presence of an Exposition which displays the unparalleled marvels of steam and electricity, that there is a spiritual root to all human progress. . . . We are met, I believe, in the temper of love, determined to bury, at least for the time, our sharp hostilities, anxious to find out wherein we agree, eager to learn what constitutes the strength of other faiths and the weakness of our own. And we are met as conscientious and truth-seeking men, in council where no one is asked to surrender or abate his individual convictions, and where, I will add, no one would be worthy of a place if he did.[35]

Barrows's brief address simply assumes distinct and even codified religious traditions with clear "representatives"—all in common consort with the engineering miracles of the century and the lauded *progress* of modernity tempered by religious values. The very notion of "representatives" and even the term "parliament" assumes a democratic polity. Interestingly, the organizing committee invited only the "leading representatives from the great Historic Religions of the world"[36] and apparently assumed that the common language would be English. Representatives delivered their addresses in this de facto lingua franca. "Delegates" included African-American Christians and several prominent women. Notably absent[37] were any of the popularly known Native American chiefs and holy men, like Sitting Bull, who had recently died violently in the hysteria to end a Native American messianic movement in 1890.[38] The religions of Africa, still the "Dark Continent," were apparently too shadowy to notice, and delegates from Latin America was similarly excluded: "a particularly conspicuous absence given that the celebration of Christopher Columbus's achievements was the occasion for the event."[39]

Here were the earmarks of classic American religious liberalism: the acceptance of diversity—within carefully defined limits—the assumption of a representative democracy, English as the obvious cosmopolitan language, and the affirmation of material progress defined within a capitalist world tempered by religious values. However, Richard Seager observes a paradox in the Parliament in Chicago heralded as a sign of the growing "religious pluralism in our nation": while the conveners of the Parliament assumed a growing liberal Protestant agenda, "the assembly embraced an extraordinary variety of positions simultaneously."[40] These included a delegation of Theosophists from the new world headquarters in Madras (now Chennai), India, as well as scientists with a religious bent:

> One suspects that such eclectic religious sensibilities, although rarely studied sympathetically, are quite prevalent in many quarters today. But they were also there on the Parliament floor, a harbinger of a later day when religious humanism would not be synonymous with liberal Christianity.[41]

These understudied and underestimated *shared eclectic religious sensibilities* were indeed alive in 1893.

Diana Eck, the most articulate and passionate spokesperson for *pluralism*, provides clear distinctions between several modes of religious encounter in *Encountering God: A Spiritual Journey from Bozeman to Banaras*, also published in 1993 during the centenary of the World's Parliament:

> First there is the exclusivist response: Our community, our tradition, our understanding of reality, our encounter with God, is the one and only truth, excluding all others. Second there is the inclusivist response: There are, indeed, many communities, traditions, and truths, but our way of seeing things is the culmination of the others, superior to the others, or at least wide enough to include the others under our universal canopy and in our terms. A third response is that of the pluralist: Truth is not the exclusive or inclusive possession of any one tradition or community. Therefore the diversity of communities, traditions, understandings of truth, and visions of God is not an obstacle, but an opportunity for our energetic engagement and dialogue with one another.[42]

After further delineating the important distinction between the pluralist and inclusivist perspective, she explains the inclusivist sense that "the other is not so much dangerous as immature and in need of further enlightenment"; this was "the kind of thinking that lay behind Swami Vivekananda's mission to bring spiritual growth to the immature materialist West."[43] A few pages later, Eck discusses relativism, "Relativism for me and for many others becomes a problem when it means the lack of commitment to any particular community or faith.... There is no beloved community, no home in which the context of values are tested, no dream of the ongoing transformation of that community. Thus the relativist can remain uncommitted, a perpetual shopper, set apart from a community of faith, suffering from spiritual ennui."[44]

While deeply committed to his nation and its common community of fellow Hindus—a wide community sense that he helped to articulate and construct—Vivekananda remains an inclusivist. Yet in many ways he is "set apart" from his community and continued to live in the world of religious shoppers as the founder of the first Hindu mission to the West. Something is simply missing from this charting of exclusivism, inclusivism, and pluralism. And as an inveterate "uncommitted" shopper, like many others, with an ambiguous sense of *my* community, I think these elusive yet powerful *shared eclectic religious sensibilities* remain unacknowledged and misunderstood within the pluralist framework. Hence I choose not to discuss "Hinduism" here as community property, but the *other* Hinduism of that first global guru as the carrier of that kind of *eclectic universalism*.

These shared eclectic religious sensibilities, evidence suggests, were more global in range than American liberal Protestantism but equally a part of the growing worldwide middle class. Many in the United States and the United Kingdom, as well as throughout the British Empire and beyond, shared a modern outlook derived from the Enlightenment which was not *liberal* and certainly not *pluralistic*. They challenged borders between nature and culture, between nature and science, and between human and divine. It was these *unspoken religious values* that the many speeches would now make public in this first global arena. Swami Vivekananda's presentation of Hinduism as the model for a new universalism is perhaps the most famous, the most contentious, and the most problematic for the liberal world of pluralism—then and now. Rather than framing this as inclusivist, I say rather call it *eclectic*—the difference is important if global gurus can be understood as doing more than "selling spirituality."[45]

Changing Bodies, Changing Minds

To return to the paradox of Vivekananda's message, Swami Vivekananda as he emerges in contemporary scholarship also assumes a Janus face: one side looks toward the West, and the other to India. "Ecumenical and almost Unitarian during his sojourn in the United States, Vivekananda demonstrated his chauvinistic colors on his return to South Asia,"[46] or "In India, the swami hotly defended Hinduism against attacks while simultaneously urging renewal and programs of humanitarian reforms that frightened orthodox Hindu leaders. In the West, meanwhile, he undertook a separate work, launching the first Vedanta societies in the United States and Europe to disseminate Hinduism to Western people."[47] Just how separate were these two faces of the swami?

In Elizabeth De Michelis's *A History of Modern Yoga: Pañjali and Western Esotericism*, Vivekananda emerges not only as a disseminator of Hinduism but more importantly as a conduit for a rising interest in esotericism not only in American cities but also in the capital of British India, Vivekananda's hometown of Calcutta. She provides an important clue in her description of Vivekananda's ease in settling into the many parlors of his American admirers during his two sojourns in the United States:

> It was…the social group corresponding to the Bengali [language and people around Calcutta] cultic milieu from which he himself came. Except that these American circles were far more widespread, affluent, secularized, individualistic and far more intent on engaging in "occult" endeavours.…It was therefore not surprising that, with relatively minor adaptation on both sides, he was readily accepted and accepting. This pattern of social interaction continued throughout his stay in the West: embraced by the more fluid, unchurched, affluent strands of the cultic milieu, he in turn adapted to them. Flattered by their admiration and support, he also admired them, and the reciprocation of positive feelings led to mutual admiration.[48]

In short, many upper middle-class young Hindus in Calcutta and the other colonial port cities of the Empire already shared *religious sensibilities* with their American, and indeed British, counterparts.

De Michelis points to common international organizations like the Free Masons. Another group, the Theosophists, had also recently moved their headquarters to Adyar in Madras city and would begin a century of close interactions between Europeans, Americans, and a rising Indian middle class. A small but powerful segment of urban Indians and urban Americans shared a common milieu at the turn of the nineteenth century—that milieu was far more radical than our clichés of the Victorian period usually allow. Vivekananda adapted a growing movement called Neo-Vedanta. *Vedanta* usually refers to a system deriving from ancient Hindu texts—the Veda but most especially the Upanishads—the primary texts for Hindu meditative and yogic practices. Neo-Vedanta, much like the Protestant reformation, saw itself as moving back directly to the earliest sources of Hinduism with an increased emphasis on the *person* as the location of religious renewal. As De Michelis explains, "Vivekananda gave shape to Modern Yoga by blending Neo-Vedantic esotericism and avant-garde American occultism. Thus Neo-Vedantic ideology became an integral part of Western occultism and, conversely, Western occultist ideas were integrated into Neo-Vedanta."[49] The important point here: much of this happened *within* an American context amid the highly receptive, increasingly wealthy American middle classes of the late nineteenth century.

In the American context, Vivekananda's teachings began with the *person* as the site of religious experience and not with the community as a whole. Without a doubt these persons *joined* Vedanta Centers in the United States— with a few joining the Ramakrishna Missions and Cultural Centers in India— but these remained voluntary organizations, not the kinship groups associated with belonging "naturally" to a Hindu family and to a jati/varna ("caste"). Their goal, after all, was some form of "personal salvation"—to borrow an evangelical term. These early years of the turn of the century saw the rise of a worldwide middle class unmoored from older community configurations and increasingly operating as individuals. At the same time, scholarship also focused on the *person*—the middle-class person. Dr. Freud analyzed the ills of society through the neurotic gestures and dreams of his affluent patients. Max Weber built a theory of the rise of capitalist modernity out of the "this-worldly" but *personal* asceticism of Protestant merchants—interestingly in the midst of a visit to the United States. Weber also created his long-standing theory of charisma—a personal quality of the leader—as the key to new community formation. So too in Calcutta, the group of mostly university-educated, middle-class young men and older householders gathered around Ramakrishna, each looking to him as *their* teacher while he fashioned them into an inner and outer *circle* of disciples—the *antaranga* and the *bahiranga*.[50] Interestingly, the Sanskrit term *ranga* can be translated "circle" in the sense of an "assembly" but has its root connotations in arena, theater, and stage.[51] The term perfectly captures the ambiguity in this kind of teaching via the revered guru: Were minds or bodies transformed? I ask this in full cognizance of Sigmund Freud's movement of the ailing body into the mind and his apparent incorporation of insights on Ramakrishna's "oceanic feeling" into his later *Civilization and Its Discontents*,[52] or Weber's strange circle from asceticism—which was corporal—to his arguments over the processes of "rationalization" through which discourse appears to devalue bodily practice—issues Foucault would surely raise. Recall that the issue of bodily change/mental change has implications for the globalization of Hinduism and the possibility for that *third stream* of "de-ethnicized" universalism. In other words, is there some middle ground between a Hindu identity based on "birth"—that is, having the right kind of body and belonging *naturally* to a community, and the other model based on the "universal" religion of Christianity (or Islam or Buddhism) that requires—supposedly—only a confession of "belief"?

From Thousand Islands, New York, to Calcutta, India—A Place in the World

In his preface to *Ràmakrishna: His Life and Sayings,* one of his rare books on contemporary India, Professor Friedrich Max Müller, the famous Oxford scholar of ancient Hindu scriptures, declares, "We need not fear that the Samnyâsins [monks, renouncers] of India will ever find followers or imitators in Europe, nor would it be at all desirable that they should...".[53] But just a few years before Müller wrote these lines, a small band of Americans were meeting in Thousand Islands Park, New York, in the summer of 1895 to do exactly that. A published record of this event is now widely available through the devoted eyes of Vedantist Mary Louise Burke, "the movement's most indefatigable scholar"[54] as part of her six-volume series on Swami Vivekananda's two visits to America, in 1893–1896 in connection with the Parliament of Religions, and again in 1899–1900. The Thousand Islands meeting attracted a very small company but Vivekananda wrote, "I have arranged to go to Thousand Islands, wherever that might be. There is a cottage belonging to Miss Dutcher, one of my students, and a few of us will be there in rest and peace and seclusion. I want to manufacture a few 'Yogis' of the material of these classes."[55] And according to Burke, he indeed initiated several of them. She reverently describes the fruit of his work:

> His desire, as he often intimated, was to see many hundreds of men and women of the West formally renounce the world. "The yellow robe of the sannyasin is the sign of the free," he said in one of his last classes at Thousand Islands Park. "Give up your beggar's dress of the world; wear the flag of freedom, the ochre robe."[56]

And, she comments:

> Was not his stay at Miss Dutcher's cottage only the occasion, then, for releasing a flood of spiritual energy into the very heart of the nation? Was he not teaching generations of Americans in those few weeks? One cannot but think that the immense power generated by Swamiji's teaching day and night at the height of spiritual consciousness must have far transcended and out distanced its effects in the lives of the twelve students who gathered around him and asked, "What have we done to ever deserve this?"[57]

Mary Louise Burke thoroughly enmeshed the swami into the American landscape—not only in this passage but also throughout her text—and he in turn liberally borrowed potent American tropes. Swami Vivekananda will give real freedom to those in the land of the free. He will revitalize America from its own heartland.

However, the most curious feature of these potent weeks in upstate New York remains Swami Vivekananda's reconstruction of what Elizabeth De Michelis terms "Modern Yoga." De Michelis positions Vivekananda's stay at this "camp" as the key moment of his refashioning of yoga. She sees him emerging from this retreat with his "basic tenets" for a practical and universalized type of yoga and ready to dictate his soon-to-be very popular *Karma-Yoga* followed by his most famous work, *Raja Yoga*.[58] Her intriguing study carefully unravels the ingredients of multiple Western occult ideas that Vivekananda blended with classical yoga to produce a new "secularized" practical and pragmatic formula for worldwide consumption. But whereas her interest is in this East-West process of mutual interpenetration, mine is to return to the issue of the possibilities of a de-ethnicized Hinduism. We are both concerned with bodies because Vivekananda chose to present his "teachings" as yoga, always a bodily practice even in its most meditative forms. Ethnicity also is identity perceived, assumedly, in bodily practice and bodily form—such identity requires birth into the fold—or to put it another way, the right kind of "body." She shows us how Vivekananda constructed yoga within an American milieu and on American soil. Here like De Michelis I have "to piece together...the hidden or untold parts,"[59] but at this point in an even more speculative manner than her exhaustive work. I ask, why did Vivekananda turn to yoga at all and why did he develop his Raja Yoga here in the United States but on returning to India, redefine a unifying Neo-Hinduism for an emerging Indian nationalism?[60] In other words, what is this Janus face about and how does it relate to a "universalized" Hinduism?

As De Michelis presents Vivekananda's *Raja Yoga*, "Its message was what many in cultic milieus worldwide had been waiting for: a flexible set of teachings that would meet their craving for exotic yet accessible and ideologically familiar forms of practical spirituality."[61] The key here is *practical, accessible*, and accommodating a worldwide following. To this end, Vivekananda, De Michelis argues, presents two models of yoga, the *Prana* Model and the *Samadhi* Model. The Prana Model begins with processes of gaining control, via control of the vital breath, over "'gross' and 'subtle', 'internal' and 'external' aspects of the cosmos."[62] In the Samadhi Model, "the more prominent," Vivekananda

> ...construes yoga in terms of the mind undertaking a proprioceptive journey back to the "source of intelligence" through various levels of meditative practice. Each individual mind is part of "universal mind," he postulates, and by accessing higher or "superconscious" states (*samadhi*) each of us can tap into the omniscience of the universal mind and obtain gnosis. *This profound transformative effect on the adept*, eventually brings to the fore his or her forgotten almighty, omniscient, and divine nature.[63]

At the risk of summarizing too much of this careful history of borrowings and reinterpretations, I understand De Michelis as making several major suggestions. Swami Vivekananda "tries to salvage the 'natural laws' of the Enlightenment with their materialist and empiricist principles" by reworking this model of humans as part of nature and under its laws into another model of humans *homologized* to nature. Hence by "occultist" sensibilities, comes the formula that what persons do with their bodies, they do with the world:

> An equation between "knowledge," "power" and "control" underlies Vivekananda's recommendations for practice: if one becomes aware, feels, perceives gross and subtle energy movements within oneself... then one will come to know and control fully.... Further still, if one controls one instant (usually one's own *prana*, one's own body), then one will control all (all *pranas*, all bodies).[64]

Vivekananda harnessed a whole series of conceptions at that time which saw no distinction between the material and spiritual in the multiple theories of universal energies or fluids that moved between divine and material principles. These are "magic correspondences of microcosm and macrocosm" that Vivekananda "activates."[65] In this sense the "religious" becomes "secular" via occultist sensibilities that understand the material world as infused with what others would call "otherworldly" or "transcendent" powers, now available to the human transformed through yogic practices.

I continue to question why Vivekananda would release such potent power initially to his American followers. Certainly persons in India may have had some knowledge of these practices, but his fellow Bengali middle-class, university-educated cohort would have been as unlikely as Americans to take up practices which until then would have remained within an ascetic milieu, within the world of renouncers, not householders. Jeffrey Kripal argues that Ramakrishna, a temple priest and, although unconsummated, nonetheless married, had already broken this "householder/renouncer division" and begun to teach his more "secret" practices to selected members of both.[66] De Michelis describes a series of teachers from the Calcutta intelligentsia who became renouncers of sorts, but all of this was a break from tradition and affected a very few in Calcutta. Vivekananda on the other hand looks first to producing a "few yogis" *in America* and then hopes for "many hundreds of men and women from the West" to undergo this profound transformation. The key here is the transformative power of yoga, the power to heal, to purify, to rebuild a subtle body from the gross body. I would suggest—in what I recognize is a controversial leap of interpretation—that Vivekananda never let go of his sense of the spiritual superiority of the Indian person and of Indian religious sensibilities to grasp these powers. But Indians remained too bounded by tradition and by the multifold communities at that moment, and would require another kind of transforming release. The American person, on the other hand, required a personal (bodily) transformation to move onto and into this new universal religion that Vivekananda had introduced on the floor of the World's Parliament of Religion just three years before.

On returning to Calcutta and prior to his departure, Shamita Basu argues in an equally fine grained and sensitive study, *Religious Revivalism as National Discourse: Swami Vivekananda and New Hinduism in Nineteenth-Century Bengal*, that Vivekananda constructed a "universal Hinduism" for a new nationalist India. Her argument moves through some of the same Hindu philosophical concepts and the same nineteenth-century Indian reformers that De Michelis mentions, but she sets these within their Bengali and finally all-Indian context. She summarizes his project:

> This is the national context in which the Advaita principles of Universalism was [sic] to be employed: to organize the sociologically decentralized people by invoking a single absolute core of Hindu philosophy of non-dualism that is supposed to represent and incorporate all sectarian beliefs, practices, and institutions of various communities. The universalization of Hinduism was the task that Vivekananda had set himself to achieve in his nationalist endeavor.[67]

Both she and De Michelis focus on Vivekananda's creative use of Advaita (non-dualist) philosophy, but, rather than frame her reading in the context of common occult sensibilities, Basu uses theories of language, politics, and the public intellectuals to frame her analysis. In her introduction she presents her selected material and methods for *Religious Revivalism as National Discourse:* "[Vivekananda's] commentaries on Hinduism, which I have sought to study as part of a history of thought, are treated as a document, and his appearance in America as a form of performative utterance: an event in the history of the genesis of nationalism in nineteenth-century Bengal."[68] Basu presents Vivekananda's "discursive practices" as generating powerful, performative words but nonetheless concludes that Vivekananda maintained what is frequently termed the Enlightenment compromise, "The Swami wanted to advocate a form of Hinduism that was a far cry from the parochial version of religion which the orthodox Hindu leaders wanted to popularize. Vivekananda followed the Reformation model in *depoliticizing* Hinduism, confining in a Lutheran manner the *spiritual to the private sphere of life.*"[69] At one point she describes his words as "a classical example of the language of ideology."[70]

However, her own choice of language throughout her text makes me suspicious that something more than performative language was at work in Vivekananda's teachings, even in Bengal. For example (the emphases are mine):

> To Vivekananda, the personality of Ramakrishna was the embodiment of the idea of national unity: a practical illustration of how Hinduism could be conceived in the context of heterogeneity and could be successfully used as the organizing factor in creating *a collective self.*[71]

And:

> Within the neo-Hindu philosophy, the nation which is now generally represented as Nationalism, to Vivekananda, was an act of self-revelation, *a going back to the origin of this Hindu self, and a Hinduism rising to self-consciousness.* In the subsequent period of nationalistic struggle those who adopted the religious idiom and rose in defense of Hinduism often borrowed from Vivekananda this gigantic conception of Hinduism as the *custodian of universal enlightenment.*[72]

Later, Basu argues that "Vivekananda made religious discourse open to rational analysis, and spiritual realization *as exclusively a subjective affair.*"[73] But then she adds:

> Neo-Vedantism was created as...the spiritual source of the combative spirit, the inner strength, and the sublime knowledge of the *eternal freedom of the soul* which could never be held in subordination, be it political bondage, social discrimination or material deprivation. It was *the pure unconquered self* which was the seat of God.[74]

What is this national "self"? Within these passages in Shamita Basu and within Vivekananda's own speeches and teachings, the problem of the political and the religious reemerges with full force but in some very tricky ways. At stake here is Basu's unspoken but clear intension to bracket Vivekananda and his religious nationalism from the current Hindu Nationalism of the RSS and the then ruling BJP party. And, indeed, recall that the Ramakrishna Mission in the United States helped to initiate the second World Parliament of Religions, staying clear of the VHP-sponsored *Global Visions* 2000. She reads Vivekananda as initiating a transformation of a multitude of individual subjects into a realization of their commonality. But how corporate and how intense was this "collective self" to be? Is this incorporation a matter of brilliant performative discourse that would transform minds, or was this a subtler in-corporation, a "magical" means of creating a national body? Reading De Michelis's discussion of the occultism in Vivekananda into the India context, I would argue that not only are the microcosm and macrocosm of some inner and outer universe homologized—as in his eclectic American-made Yoga—but also that here Vivekananda may be homologizing the public sphere and the private sphere as well. The Indian people may well be invited into a massive yogic exercise, to *realize* their unity to willingly become a part of this glorious Whole.

The Third Stream in a Confluent World

This is the tricky part of the Swami's two faces—one does point almost uncomfortably close to the trope of the Nation as Person used by the Hindu Nationalists—images of Mother India, the divine holy land, Our Nation, "Our Culture," "Our Heritage." But here Swami Vivekananda's "occultism" and his "yoga" cannot be ignored. As both Basu and De Michelis make clear: Vivekananda in his role as guru/swami begins and ends his discourse within the person, within the self, not the community. Yoga does more; there is physicality here with talk of *forces* that are understood as instrumental in a "scientific sense" or, as De Michelis suggests, in the sense of a new "magic." His scientizing, his occult naturalism, forces his language into a notion of the human body and the earth as composed of universal substances, energies, and forces working under a common, albeit occult, "laws." I do not claim that Vivekananda abjured all of the many racial theories of his day that were rife among his fellow occultists, especially Theosophists,[75] but that his ontology was so thoroughly universalistic—and yes, literally *inclusive*—that his nationalism never merged into an exclusive ethnicity but assumed the very Hindu sense that mind and matter entangle within the human self. So while his yogic spell meant to re-form Indians into a single body—a powerful religio-political entity fit to be free, his American yogis needed to re-form their bodies, to build a self, fit to learn and to teach. In classical terms they needed to gain *adhikara*—the right to learn and the right to teach. Vivekananda then, as global gurus now, released what had been an exclusive birthright of certain caste communities into anyone willing to undergo that transformation of the self-body-senses that the guru's touch and teaching can effect.

Although one need not accept all of the implications of Jeffrey Kripal's controversial book, *Kali's Child*, his insight into the physicality of the guru-disciple relationship cannot be easily put aside. Whether the disciple touches or even washes the guru's feet, or receives a chaste touch on the forehead, or a massive hug, or, as in the case of Vivekananda, beholds a shining countenance, more than a verbal message is shared. A transformation of the *self* involves a transformation of the body—in the context of acquiring a new discourse. Here I think Srinivas Aravamudan is right and yet wrong that the modern gurus constructed a new cosmopolitan language, "Guru English," and that this new language fits perhaps dangerously well into our postmodern consumer world. Aravamudan views the ambiguity of Guru English and its almost empty message as part of the world of style participating "in an era when value has resolutely shifted from mechanical to mental labor, and where consumer culture is meeting the challenge by rising to target levels of immaterial lifestyle, experience, and ethos that can bypass the cruder measures of material product."[76] However, I would counter that this new worldwide guru-engendered "theo-linguistics"—to use Aravamudan's term—rides on a body of more than words. These are not simple dialogues or even encounters—but a baptism of fire. They are felt within the person. The question as to whether they spell the end of metaphysics or onto-theology, or whether they herald a strange return of magic, a "re-enchantment" must remain in debate—but I no longer think that either the liberal language of pluralism, nor of ethnic "identity politics" can contain them.

Notes

1 The HAF website carried the full text of the final Senate Resolution 299, dated August 3, 2007. Full versions of the earlier House version are also posted in the press release at http://hafsite.org/media_press_release_sen_res_299.htm, accessed January 11, 2008.

2 As described on its website at http://www.hinduamericanfoundation.org, accessed January 7, 2008.

3 The Hindu American Foundation appears to count Sikhs, Jains, and Indian Buddhists among the Hindus. Not all of these groups would agree. The figure of two million parallels the estimated number of Asian-Indians in the United States, many of whom may not identify as Hindu. Here the HAF follows the logic of nationalist groups like the VPH and RSS, who consider any religious movement generated within India as part of the Hindu fold. Hence Christians and Muslims are firmly outside this category, while, for example, Buddhists are not.

4 All of these are well documented by the ongoing Pluralism Project founded by Diana Eck at Harvard in 1991. Eck, one of the first scholars to see this changing landscape, fully comments on the process in *A New Religious America: How a "Christian Country" Has Become the World's Most Religiously Diverse Nation* (San Francisco: HarperSanFrancisco, 2001). See the website of the Pluralism Project at http://www.pluralism.org/.

5 Joanne Punzo Waghorne, "The Hindu Gods in a Split-level World: The Sri Siva-Vishnu Temple in Suburban Washington, DC," in *Gods of the City*, ed. Robert Orsi (Bloomington: Indiana University Press, 1999), 103–130; idem, "Spaces for a New Public Presence: The Sri Siva-Vishnu and Murugan Temples in Metropolitan

Washington DC," in *American Sanctuary: Understanding Sacred Spaces*, ed. Louis P. Nelson (Bloomington: Indiana University Press, 2006), 103–127.

6 Thomas Blom Hansen, *The Saffron Wave: Democracy and Hindu Nationalism* (Princeton, NJ: Princeton University Press, 1999).

7 Carl T. Jackson, *Vedanta for the West: The Ramakrishna Movement in the United States* (Bloomington: Indiana University Press, 1994), 97–99.

8 See the excellent website dedicated to the history of this major event at http://columbus.gl.iit.edu/.

9 John Henry Barrows, ed., *The World's Parliament of Religions* (Chicago: The Parliament Publishing Company, 1893), 977.

10 Srinivas Aravamudan, *Guru English: South Asian Religion in a Cosmopolitan Language* (Princeton, NJ: Princeton University Press, 2006).

11 Richard Hughes Seager, "Pluralism and the American Mainstream: The View from the World's Parliament of Religions," *Harvard Theological Review* 82, no. 3 (1989): 301–324.

12 *Chicago Daily Tribune*, July 11, 1897, p. 25.

13 Marie Louise Burke, *Swami Vivekananda in the West: New Discoveries*, vol. 3 (Calcutta: Advaita Ashrama Publications, 1985), 125, 127.

14 His talks to those disciples at Thousand Islands, New York, were published as *Inspired Talks: My Master and Other Writings* (New York: Ramakrishna-Vivekananda Center of New York, 1987). The Ramakrishna center celebrated the centenary of this event in 1995: see http://ramakrishna.org/activities/events/MEvents2.htm, accessed December 28, 2006.

15 Vivekananda left for Chicago via Madras and returned the same way, stopping there in 1897 as he made his way back to Calcutta. For Vivekananda's connection to Madras, see the website of the Sri Ramakrishna Math, Chennai, e.g., the page at http://www.chennaimath.org/about-us/history-of-chennai-math, accessed May 11, 2013.

16 The poster and the photographs that served as models can be seen at http://www.rkashrambailurmath.org/blog/?p=321, accessed May 11, 2013.

17 *Chicago Daily Tribune*, September 20, 1893, p. 10.

18 Ibid., April 16, 1899, 46.

19 Elizabeth De Michelis, *A History of Modern Yoga: Pañjali and Western Esotericism* (London: Continuum, 2004), 110, 112.

20 Gwilym Beckerlegge, *The Ramakrishna Mission: The Making of a Modern Hindu Movement* (New Delhi: Oxford University Press, 2000), 61, 81.

21 Jackson, *Vedanta for the West*, xii.

22 http://www.kusala.org/udharma/globalethic.html, accessed May 3, 2013. The statement was initially drafted by Dr. Hans Kung, the controversial Catholic theologian currently president of the Global Ethic Foundation for Intercultural and Interreligious Research, Education, and Encounter, for which see http://www.weltethos.org/index-en.php.

23 See Eck, *New Religious America*, 366, 370.

24 Joseph M. Kitagawa, "Humanistic and Theological History of Religions with Special Reference to the North American Scene," *Numen* 27, no. 2 (1980): 199.

25 "Swami Vivekananda's Message–Modern Perspective," by Dr. Mahesh Mehta. Posted on the website "Global Hindu Electronic Network: Swami Vivekananda Study

Center sponsored by the Hindu Student Council." Report on the Global Vision 2000, http://www.hindunet.org/vivekananda/mm_gv.txt, accessed December 29, 2006.

26 "World Vision 2000 Success /Failure?" by Nagulapalli Srinivas, http://www.hindunet.org/vivekananda/ns_success_failure, accessed December 29, 2006.

27 "Vision 2000–Vivekananda Celebrations Report," http://www.hindunet.org/vivekananda/jm_report, accessed December 29, 2006.

28 Laurie Goodstein, "Protesters Call Hindu Fest Politically Motivated," *Washington Post*, August 9, 1993, p. D1.

29 Ibid.

30 Mehta, "Swami Vivekananda's Message."

31 In "Global Vision 2000 Theme II: The Cosmos is One Family."

32 Srinivas, "World Vision 2000 Success/Failure."

33 As termed in the official website of the Ramakrishna Mission Institute of Culture, http://www.sriramakrishna.org/, accessed January 2, 2006.

34 See Roelof van der Broek and Wouter J. Hanegraaff, eds., *Gnosticism and Hermeticism from Antiquity to Modern Times* (Albany: State University of New York Press, 1998), x; Wouter J. Hanegraaff, *New Age Religion and Western Culture: Esotericism in the Mirror of Secular Thought* (Albany: State University of New York Press, 1998); Joscelyn Godwin, *The Theosophical Enlightenment* (Albany: State University of New York Press, 1994). The source of the term "third stream" is unclear, but Hanegraaff has popularized the concept of an important strain of early and continuing "Western esotericism" that has been used subsequently by De Michelis in her excellent study of yoga and Swami Vivekananda. The term is also used in music for a new confluence of jazz and contemporary new music.

35 Barrows, ed., *World's Parliament of Religions*, 75

36 Ibid., 18.

37 One very short paper on "The Religion of the North American Indians" was presented by Alice C. Fletcher, whom Seager identifies as "an anthropologist and student of Franz Boas," in "Pluralism and the American Mainstream," 316.

38 The slaughter of almost 400 Sioux participants in the Ghost Dance movement at Wounded Knee, South Dakota, by the U.S. military was headline news in late 1890. The conveners of the conference could not have failed to know the names of many of these Native American religious leaders.

39 Richard Hughes Seager, *The Dawn of Religious Pluralism: Voices from the World's Parliament of Religions, 1893* (La Salle, IL: Open Court, 1993), 7.

40 Seager, "Pluralism and the American Mainstream," 312.

41 Ibid., 315.

42 Diana L. Eck, *Encountering God: A Spiritual Journey from Bozeman to Banaras* (Boston: Beacon Press, 1993), 168.

43 Ibid., 185.

44 Ibid., 195.

45 Jeremy Carrette and Richard King, *Selling Spirituality: The Silent Takeover of Religion* (London; New York: Routledge, 2005).

46 Aravamudan, *Guru English*, 56.

47 Jackson, *Vedanta for the West*, 5.

48 De Michelis, *History of Modern Yoga*, 114.

49 Ibid., 110.

50 Jeffrey J. Kripal, *Kali's Child: The Mystical and the Erotic in the Life and Teachings of Ramakrishna*, 2nd. ed. (Chicago: University of Chicago Press, 1998), 11.

51 See Monier-Williams's classic Sanskrit dictionary, *A Dictionary, English and Sanskrit* (Lucknow: Akhila Bharatiya Sanskrit Parishad, 1957 reprint of 1851 original), 862 columns b and c.

52 Aravamudan, *Guru English*, 57; Sudhir Kakar, *The Analyst and the Mystic: Psychoanalytic Reflections on Religion and Mysticism* (Chicago: University of Chicago Press, 1991).

53 Friedrich Max Müller, *Ramakrishna: His Life and Sayings* (New York: Charles Scribner's Sons, 1899), vi.

54 Jackson, *Vedanta for the West*, 32.

55 Quoted in Burke, *Swami Vivekananda in the West*, 109.

56 Ibid., 129.

57 Ibid., 119.

58 De Michelis, *History of Modern Yoga*, 124–125.

59 Ibid., 5.

60 Shamita Basu, *Religious Revivalism as National Discourse: Swami Vivekananda and New Hinduism in Nineteenth-Century Bengal* (New Delhi: Oxford University Press, 2002).

61 De Michelis, *History of Modern Yoga*, 150.

62 Ibid., 151.

63 Ibid., 153.

64 Ibid., 167.

65 Ibid.

66 Kripal, *Kali's Child*, 11, 14.

67 Basu, *Religious Revivalism*, 71.

68 Ibid., 10.

69 Ibid., 127, my emphasis.

70 Ibid., 128.

71 Ibid., 82.

72 Ibid., 39.

73 Ibid., 190.

74 Ibid., 191.

75 Gauri Viswanathan, *Outside the Fold: Conversion, Modernity, and Belief* (New Delhi: Oxford University Press, 1998), 177–207.

76 Aravamudan, *Guru English*, 268..

PART IV | Impact of Religious
Pluralism: I

| # The Impact of Religious Pluralism on American Women

R. Marie Griffith

TO CONTEMPLATE (AS I have been asked to do) the topic of "women" in a book devoted to religious pluralism in modern America is, first, to ask whether there has been something noteworthy, special, or unique about women's engagement with pluralism. Indeed, if Ann Braude is correct in arguing that "women's history *is* American religious history"—meaning that women's preponderant numbers in American congregational and extra-ecclesial life have essentially made religious institutions possible throughout U.S. history, and that women ought therefore to be at the center rather than the margins of the stories we tell about that history—then one can hardly cast doubt on the claim that religious pluralism entails deeply gendered dimensions and consequences.[1] Two premises require our initial agreement in this regard. The first is that the chief sociological feature shared by those who are called "women" (who are, otherwise, an impossibly diverse group of people) is a basic, even if variable, differential in power compared to men, once other social variables such as race, class, and educational status have been taken into account. The second premise is that, on account of this power differential, one issue of pressing interest to modern American women (though by no means the only one) has involved questions of institutional leadership, authority, and influence in relation to men. Together, these points help focus our attention on a precise, empirically driven question: how has religious pluralism affected women's view of their gendered status within religious as well as other social institutions?

Giving a precise empirical answer is, not surprisingly, more difficult than posing the proper question. Thanks to the wealth of scholarship over the past quarter century devoted to debates over women's formal religious leadership in various sectors of the Abrahamic religions, we do know a great deal about women and gender roles in particular communities and traditions. Various scholars have opened our eyes to the gendered disparities that recur even in those sectors that appear to have fully accepted the notion of a female rabbi, priest, or minister.[2] This work, some of which I will cite in this paper, provides important context for thinking about how ordinary women have responded to the realities of religious multiplicity, encounter, conflict, and cooperation in modern America. But however important this body of literature, it does not yet offer a satisfyingly thorough answer to our question; and hence the points that I will make in this paper are of necessity partial and incomplete.

The simplest and most concise response to our initial query about the impact of religious pluralism on American women would begin by pointing to two discernible historical trajectories: the first is the path toward acceptance of female leadership, and we would note in this regard that most institutions now allowing women to serve as leaders at the highest levels formalized this egalitarian stance around the same time, in the wake of the second wave of the feminist movement. The second trajectory flows in the opposite direction, and we would have to remark upon the fact that those groups that do not allow women's authoritative leadership have in recent times grown more robust in their defenses of female submission to male clerical leadership. (I'm thinking particularly of the Southern Baptists and some other evangelical and Pentecostal groups, but of course one could broaden this out quite expansively beyond the conservative Protestant tradition). If we consider that one of the effects of pluralism is simply new knowledge—albeit of varying degrees of accuracy—about how other groups treat important issues such as gender, then we can ponder the interesting ways in which American religious groups have reacted to reported stories about women in other religions by making shifts in their own gendered arrangements or at least their ideals.

Let me illustrate this point with an event that occurred during the course of my first fieldwork project, which resulted in the book *God's Daughters: Evangelical Women and the Power of Submission*. At one of the large national Women's Aglow Fellowship conferences that I attended, nearly a decade before 9/11 brought Muslims to the center of attention in religious media, the culminating worship service peaked in a massive outpouring of prayer for Muslim women, who were portrayed as dark-skinned and frail, mysterious and foreign-looking to the masses of white middle-class women who were in attendance at the Nashville Convention Center. Above all, Muslim women were depicted as the abused victims of swarthy, arrogant, self-centered Muslim men. After a good 30 to 45 minutes of lively spiritual warfare prayer against the evil forces perceived to be so oppressive to Muslim women and so threatening to their evangelization, a large standing tomb-like structure onstage broke open to reveal a live woman outfitted in a full black *burqa* (doubtless an Aglow woman in costume). No part of her body showed through the heavy cloth, but the slumped posture and head hanging low suggested deep shame and sorrow for her fate. With this downcast persona projected on larger-than-life film screens surrounding the conference center auditorium, thousands of evangelical women reacted vociferously to the hopelessness and the victimization that this Muslim female image was meant to convey—wailing loudly for Jesus to save this poor woman and all women like her across the world.[3]

This was not a moment of cheerful pluralism. It was, rather, a vivid encounter between conservative American Christian women (evangelical, Pentecostal, and Catholic) and an imagined Muslim "other," a perceived female victim whom the Christians desperately wished to help and to rescue. The episode recalls women's mission endeavors a century earlier, in which images of "heathen" women in Asia, Africa, and South America appeared regularly in church periodicals and fund-raising materials. Indeed, Aglow leaders in the mid-1990s were making personal visits to Egypt in an explicit attempt to witness to Jesus' saving grace to female followers of Allah, whatever the risks. The message that these Christian women repeatedly reinforced and conveyed to others in their religious circles was, in effect, a form of quasi-feminist evangelical consciousness-raising: they insisted upon a direct contrast between the enslaved women of the Muslim Middle East and their own enlightened freedom through Christ, a freedom that could be shared and that Islamic women should be glad to receive once they understood it properly and realized that such freedom could easily be theirs too.

At the same time, it grew clear that not all of the Aglow women wholly believed their own rhetoric about the contrast between Christian freedom and Muslim enslavement regarding gender. Something about this head-on confrontation with other women's perceived oppression, in fact, made these evangelical women rethink their own positioning vis-à-vis men in their institutions. It was precisely during this time that Aglow leaders reversed course and began to speak forcefully against the doctrine of female submission to male authority in the church: a doctrine they had once vehemently defended. The morals of this story may be multiple, but my particular point in retelling it is to accentuate the significance of interpretation (including misinterpretation) of "other" women's religiously gendered lives in these conservative Christian women's rethinking or restructuring of their own.

Having laid out a few introductory ideas, I want to turn more directly to the subject at hand, beginning with "pluralism" itself. Scholars such as Diana Eck and William R. Hutchison have developed complex and subtle models for thinking about religious pluralism in America, both historically and in the present context. Both have argued eloquently that pluralism is a more robust conceptual commitment than its critics have allowed, that it (to cite Hutchison) "emphatically does not imply 'lack of all conviction,' either for historically dominant American faiths and their adherents or for the society at large." And each has pointed out, in different ways, that the question facing us is not *whether* we will choose to deal with diversity and pluralism but *how* we will do so; in the powerful closing words of Eck's book, "The ongoing argument over who 'we' are—as religious people, as a nation, and as a global community—is one in which all of us, ready or not, will participate." Likewise, the sociologist Robert Wuthnow has argued that genuine religious pluralism in the American context can and should "move beyond wishy-washy acceptance." Historically, Wuthnow continues, "our sense of the destiny we share and the fundamental values we stand for have always been expressed in relation to those we deemed to be different from ourselves. It is not less true today." These cautions against knee-jerk conservative critiques of religious pluralism, on the one side, and empty (or sloppy) liberal celebrations of diversity, on the other, remind us of the confusion that still bedevils the very notion of "pluralism" and the need for richer discussion and debate such as this book intends to foster.[4]

It remains tempting, nonetheless, when the subject is women and religious pluralism, to forget the qualifications and simply celebrate the gains of diversity. Indeed, the few existing efforts that do try to tackle this topic align themselves, more or less, with this narrative: *Look at all of these amazing women whose religious faith has motivated them to be progressive activists, and see the wonderfully harmonious communities these women have helped to create.* There seems to be an implicit presumption in some of this work, such as reflections on the U.N.-sponsored international women's conferences [Mexico City (1975), Copenhagen (1980), Nairobi (1985), and Beijing (1995)], that women rise above theological and ethnic differences more readily than do men and that herein lies the potential for a global feminist movement.

Plainly such cooperation exists in a number of settings and organizations, and there are historically grounded reasons why various modes of female religious collaboration continue to flourish. But the need to find happy stories of pluralistic partnerships across religious differences could mean that we miss other modes of engagement between women of diverse religious traditions. My hope here is to present a multifaceted picture of this complicated dynamic as seen in scholarly work on American religion, that is, to portray a range of possibilities that come to the fore when religious multiplicity pinpoints women.

In this chapter, I consider the impact of religious pluralism on American women in several distinctive settings, with reference to a wide array of helpful work by scholars of American religion. The first section looks back to the developments that took place in the wake of the World's Parliament of Religions, held in Chicago in 1893; there I focus particularly on how a number of scholars have begun to debate white Protestant women's encounters with Asian religions. The second draws upon the work of Catholic historians to describe the encounters of immigrant Catholic women with American culture; both the data and the interpretive models of these scholars have a great deal to tell us about American women's engagement with religious diversity as well as the difficulties that work to prevent a thoroughgoing pluralism. The third section enlists the help of scholars who analyze religions of the African diaspora as they have been transplanted to the United States, in order to analyze women's particular roles there. Finally, I will offer further reflections and some preliminary hypotheses concerning women in recent U.S. history and their encounters with religious "others."

White Protestant Women and Asian Religions in America in the Early Twentieth Century

The United States in the decades after the Civil War, we well know, witnessed major changes in the social, political, economic, and religious realms. Immigration patterns contributed to these changes, with new immigrants numbering approximately 10 million between 1860 and 1890 and increasing to 15 million between 1890 and 1914. Southern and Eastern Europeans composed the majority of new immigrants, while Mexicans, Chinese, and Japanese were also part of the pattern. Waves of Protestant anti-Catholicism, along with some anti-Semitism, signaled the strain felt by many white Protestants toward these newcomers who appeared so foreign. Religious multiplicity could be celebrated, as in the 1893 World's Parliament of Religions, but it also remained, for many, a persistent source of tension and unease.

Gender was a key feature of the period's debates over religious multiplicity. Consider, by way of example, the case of Mabel Potter Daggett (1871–1927), a journalist, temperance activist, and progressive reformer (like many others, she supported the eugenics movement for the creation of a "better race"). Her 1912 article entitled "The Heathen Invasion of America" lambasted the "mystics," yogis, and "turbaned teachers from the East" who began arriving with the World's Parliament of Religions. This problem had deeply gendered aspects, in Daggett's view, for "a Swami's following recruits its largest numbers among women." American females were all too often falling into the seductive traps of these swarthy and exotic proselytizers, who knew well how to lure the ladies with the "promise of eternal youth" at the center of these "pagan religions." Women's gullibility in the face of these false promises, she warned, inevitably led to their de-Christianization (and to the falling away of Jewish women as well). "Placing the Hindu scriptures, the Bhagavadgita [sic], or the Persian scriptures, the Zend Avesta, above their Bible are women who were formerly Baptists and Presbyterians, Methodists, Episcopalians, Catholics, and daughters of Abraham." Led astray by their own vanity, women were subject to the tragic results of "domestic infelicity and insanity and death."[5]

Daggett detailed several accounts of prominent women who, to her mind, had suffered the "devastation that follows in the wake of the trailing robes of the 'masters' from the East." Her examples included the alleged insanity of Sarah Farmer ("the study of many religions unbalanced her mind"), the ill health of May Sewell (who was "said to be a physical wreck through the practice of yoga and the study of occultism"), and the wife of Purdue University President Winthrop Stone (she "abandoned home and husband and children to join the sun worshipers in the study of yoga"). These and other women were drawn to Asian religions in the belief that they were pursuing "beautiful philosophies," not realizing that they had embarked instead on the "descent to heathenism." Daggett approvingly cited the famous Indian convert to Christianity Pandita Ramabai for bringing to Westerners' attention the sorry plight of Indian women, bound to primitive gods and degrading rituals; in Daggett's lamentation, American women had "forgotten Pundita [sic] Ramabai" and were paying a horrific price for their short memories. But all too soon, Daggett warned, these women would come to recognize the sheer contempt in which they were held by the Oriental impostors who were mucking up American ideals.[6]

A number of other condemnations of Indian religiosity shortly appeared in the American press. As the historian Stephen Prothero has documented, this "theme of Hindu swamis as seducers of naïve women" recurred in Mrs. Gross Alexander's 1912 article, "American Women Going after Heathen Gods" (published in the *Methodist Quarterly Review*) as well as Elizabeth A. Reed's 1914 book *Hinduism in Europe and America*.[7] Most notable of all was the best-selling if highly controversial 1927 book, *Mother India*, published by the journalist Katherine Mayo (1867–1940). *Mother India* set out to prove, in no uncertain terms, the legitimacy of British rule in India and the horrors of Indian culture due, at least in part, to Hinduism. (A review of the book on the front page of the *New York Times Book Review* described Mayo's book as unequivocally promoting the "gospel of empire.") Once again, the journalist's most venomous criticism pinpointed the exploitation of women by ruthless Indian men, here focusing on the disturbing condition of child brides and teen motherhood that resulted in the physical debilitation of the entire Indian population. Although she documented the ways in which Indian women appeared to consent to their own subjugation and then instilled these gender norms in their own children, Mayo's account did not blame them alone, for she acknowledged how deeply the worship of their husbands was bred into young girls from infancy. Still, Mayo—an Anglophilic Episcopalian and Republican—left little room for doubting the superiority of Christianity over Hinduism in the cause of women's advancement.[8]

Two years later, Mersene Sloan's *The Indian Menace* (1929) returned the focus to the encroachment of Indian customs upon American women, expanding upon Daggett's argument about brainwashed women being the chief victims of Indian gurus. Sloan's incendiary account, more even than Daggett's, depicted women as quite stupid:

> When American women by such delusion come under continued influence of a swami, they are easy victims to whatever suggestions may be proposed. It is said that a certain Hindu fakir of this breed successfully fooled a class of several hundred "high-brow" New York women into the belief that he was Christ reincarnated and had occupied the new body for towards a thousand years. When he died of TB, they refused to credit it. Another swami influenced a prominent and wealthy woman in New York to marry him. Several rich women of that city have bought fine homes for such Hindu teachers who had claimed to be Christs, and even God. I know a woman of superior natural ability who came under such influence until she now claims to be the first person to attain super-human life and power. She claims power to confer eternal life upon whom she will, and makes other insane claims. Such are the effects of oriental so-called philosophy that India has for us and is selling us!...
>
> Women pupils practicing yoga often reach a point of perplexity, even a condition of felt danger, when they seek advice from the swamis....The deluded women will do whatever the swamis suggest. At this stage the women have been alienated from their husbands and families...and become victims of abnormal erotic urge.[9]

The full weight of this body of work, Prothero concludes, led to the dire conclusion that "Hinduism's obsession with sex...was crossing the oceans to the United States," carried over by swamis hungry for power and sexual exploitation. This menace, concluded such authors, was leading to the corruption of American Christian women.[10]

Of course, not all female writers were as hostile to Indian religions as these authors. Well before the anti-Hinduism writings of Daggett, Mayo, and Sloan reached their audiences, American women suffragists were writing about Hindu leaders such as Swami Vivekananda in ways that show the attraction of Eastern religions to female reformers. The historian Kathi Kern has been working to piece together this forgotten story of suffragist encounters with Hinduism. Although her work remains preliminary, already the sources she has gathered make plain, in her words, "the complexity of women reformers' reactions as they encountered new religions and the people who professed them." Kern's work promises to open up to new interpretations "the shifting contours of Anglo-American Orientalism and the centrality of gender to it."[11]

At first glance, these contrasting narratives seem merely to confirm what we may think we already know about America's religious multiplicity and pluralism: liberals are religious pluralists, conservatives are not. But when it comes to women and issues of women's rights, this dichotomy clearly does not hold. For women in the United States, debates over the gendered dimensions of religious diversity have centered on the treatment of women in faiths that appear foreign; put differently, liberal no less than conservative women have voiced exceedingly negative statements about religions other than their own when they perceive these to oppress female adherents. Bringing this point back to the fore, it becomes clearer how liberal *women* might well value religious pluralism far less than their male colleagues who have been better documented in the historiography as liberal pluralists. A few further examples from the history of Catholicism in America will help to illustrate this point.

Catholic Women Encounter American Culture

The Catholic church long bedeviled Protestant liberals and conservatives alike, women no less than men. American anti-Catholic sentiments against the despotism of priests and popes served the interest of women's rights activists to denounce what one female writer in 1849 termed Catholicism's entwined problems of "POPERY, DOMESTIC SLAVERY, POLITICAL DESPOTISM, AND THIS ARISTOCRACY OF SEX." The furor over pulp accounts such as *The Awful Disclosures of Maria Monk* (1851), we well know, often centered on the supposed sexual exploitation of Catholic women and nuns at the hands of unsavory priests.[12] Well into the twentieth century, many Protestant women's reform and rescue societies built successful fund-raising campaigns by describing in vivid detail Catholic ill-treatment of women and children.

The historian John McGreevy has noted these "tensions between Catholicism and women's rights advocates" during the nineteenth century, and he cites the increasing frequency of feminist anti-Catholicism after the Civil War, as suffragists such as Elizabeth Cady Stanton worked to attain the vote for women (other scholars, of course, have noted the racist overtones of Stanton and other reformers, as they grew to resent African-American men's earlier success in this arena). Stanton, like many other liberals of her time, seemed convinced that Catholicism was inherently opposed to American notions of democracy, writing in 1869 that "it is not possible for a foreigner and a Catholic to take in the grandeur of the American idea of individual rights, as more sacred than any civil or ecclesiastical organization." Still more, she noted, "The human mind is ever oscillating between the extremes of authority and individualism; and if the former—the Catholic idea—finds lodgment in the minds of this people, we ring the death-knell of American liberties." McGreevy gives clear documentation of other suffragist writers arguing sharply against the "idolatrous perversions of the Romish faith," seeing the Catholic church as having been ever "the deadly opponent of progress and freedom."[13]

But by the end of the nineteenth century, the impact of the women's movement on American Catholics was palpable. The historian Leslie Woodcock Tentler documents these changes in her book *Seasons of Grace: A History of the Catholic Archdiocese of Detroit*:

> An important minority among Catholic women now envisioned their lives in less limited terms than their mothers and grandmothers had done. Catholic women began in the 1890s to join benefit societies in large numbers, and in that same decade they were instrumental in organizing and sustaining a surprisingly large number of parish groups devoted to adult education. In different ways, these developments in women's church-related organizations reflect the growing sense of their members that women not only possessed a clear individuality apart from the family but that they might in good conscience enlarge the boundaries of "woman's sphere."[14]

Jay Dolan has documented the ways in which Catholic women and men of the period, no less than their Protestant counterparts, debated the notion of the "new woman" and sought to come to terms with the challenges this emergent ideal presented to traditional gender hierarchies. Catholic writers such as Mary Dowd echoed evangelical feminists such as Frances Willard who combined traditional notions of female virtue and domesticity with arguments for women's suffrage, arguing that women ought to receive the vote, if for no other purpose than to reform society along moral lines.[15]

Of course, not all Catholics agreed with Dowd, and debates about women's proper roles in both church and society have continued to divide Catholics to this day. Indeed, there is no greater fault line between Catholic traditionalists and progressives than that relating to gender; as the ethicist Aline Kalbian has reminded us in her smart and succinct book *Sexing the Church*, debates relating to abortion and sexuality in the Catholic tradition have everything to do with the gendered order that church leaders deeply believe characterizes God's world. Having thoroughly analyzed a century's worth of official Catholic documents on sex, marriage, and reproduction, Kalbian concludes:

> [S]tructures of authority pervade the official Catholic teachings on marriage and reproduction. The primary goal of the teachings is to maintain order in its different dimensions. The order that is most at stake in these documents is the right relationship of male and female. Attitudes about gender are, in some sense, both the starting point and the endpoint of Catholic discourse about sex.[16]

Catholic feminists from the academic theologian Rosemary Radford Ruether to the pro-choice activist Frances Kissling (not to mention former Catholics such as Mary Daly and gay Catholic scholar-activists such as Mark Jordan) have battled Rome's authority on these gendered grounds. The subservient role played by women in the Church has also generated important critiques on the part of those women who have left the Church (what the Catholic scholar Debra Campbell has termed "graceful exits").[17]

Gendered arguments about Catholicism have been important, then, both for Catholic insiders (including those who deem themselves "recovering" Catholics) and for those who wish to denounce the Church's alleged authoritarianism and debauchery from outside its bounds. Just as gender has been one critical source of Protestant anti-Catholicism for much of American history, moreover, it remains a live source of political debate today. Witness, for instance, the conflicts between religious liberals who want to retain women's right to safe abortions in the 50 states, to secure rights for gay men and women equivalent to their heterosexual counterparts, and to establish universal access to comprehensive sexuality education in the public schools; and those religious conservatives (Catholic and Protestant) who vehemently oppose such efforts. Those religious debates have many components, of course, but they have a great deal to do with gender and with religious groups' disparate views of the proper ordering of male and female in home and society. As with Protestant women's treatment of Hinduism in turn-of-the-century America, moreover, contemporary arguments against the so-called Religious Right often rest their case solidly on gendered grounds, for instance when feminist liberals complain that criminalizing abortion and instituting abstinence-only sex education will cause inordinate harm to women. Once again, then, we see a case of religious conflict being enacted on gendered grounds.

Women and Religions of the African Diaspora

When it comes to African-American women, the history of race, racism, and slavery in America deeply complicates any picture we otherwise may wish to draw of successful pluralism. How can there be genuine celebration of religious diversity in the United States when problems of racism, compounded by sexism and related forms of discrimination, remain alive and well? A growing body of work on African-American women and religion, and on women and religion in the African diaspora, addresses this paradox (although it is worth noting here that this literature seldom invokes the conceptual framework of "pluralism"). In this section I attempt to trace out some salient lines of investigation and interpretation that help shed light on the ways in which attention to race in the African-American context complicates the broader picture of pluralism's impact on American women.

At least since the Civil Rights movement, a number of scholarly works have attempted to forge a path toward thinking about the interracial aspects, including cooperative engagement but also conflict, of African-American women's religious work in American history. Notable recent examples include Evelyn Brooks Higginbotham's important 1993 book, *Righteous Discontent*, and Judith Weisenfeld's underappreciated but equally valuable 1998 work, *African American Women and Christian Activism*. As these two examples suggest, however, most of these inquiries have focused their attention on women working within the single (albeit highly varied) tradition of Protestant Christianity. The shadow of America's "peculiar institution" of slavery has loomed large over this literature, as has the interpretive model of white paternalism, even among otherwise progressive Christian feminists. As more and more scholars have turned their attention to other traditions, as well as to transnational forms of Afro-Christian religions, Christianity itself has undergone vigorous critique as an inevitable source of racism that precludes authentic encounter across the black-white divide.[18]

According to the anthropologist Carolyn Moxley Rouse, for instance, black Muslim women in the United States strongly believe that, while Christianity has promoted racism and sexism, Islam "balances the rights and responsibility of men and women with the need for community cohesion and social justice." Rouse fleshes out these views in her 2004 book, *Engaged Surrender: African American Women and Islam*:

> Muslims have often reiterated to me that Islam showed them that they were "made in excellence." Through continued immersion in Islamic scholarship, my informants say they have been able to reverse a self-loathing made worse by the church. This emotional trajectory has roots in the Nation of Islam and in the teachings of Elijah Muhammad, who encouraged his followers to rid themselves of their internalized self-hatred.... In many ways I believe the Muslim community's most profound corrective has been its grassroots initiative to undo self-hatred.

Having given up on the possibility of reforming the Christian tradition from within, these African-American converts have instead forged their own path to Islam, many drawn first to the Nation of Islam before moving on to the Sunni tradition.[19]

But why would African-American *women* choose to convert to a religious tradition that so many Americans continue strongly to believe is not merely sexist but outright misogynistic? Rouse cites a manual for Muslim girls written by Gail Madyun, an African-American convert who turns the tables to address how the Bible and Christianity have legitimized Western patriarchy:

> Another misconception which has hampered our development has been the image woman has received under Christianity as practiced in our society. Even though you were not raised as a Christian, the prevailing concept of what a woman is in our society comes from the Christian doctrine. The Creation myth propagated in the Bible…places the blame for the downfall of man on Eve's weakness. It is she who tasted the forbidden fruit which in Christianity condemned man to toil and struggle on Earth. As further punishment for woman, the Bible says she is also condemned to suffer pain in childbirth because of her "sin."…So it is no wonder that we as women have entered the race for human progress at a disadvantage. The earliest images we receive are not nurturing of a positive self-concept both as non-Europeans and as females. But again, with a clear image of who we really are, Allah promises us much more.[20]

Through a close reading of texts such as this one and her intensive fieldwork with African-American female converts to Islam, Rouse develops a persuasive argument about the subtle forms of agency that are to be found in these women's submission to Islamic teaching.

Since most of the women in Rouse's account come from traditional black Christian backgrounds, the book works on one level as a sort of case study of religious encounter between these disparate traditions. Her evidence plainly demonstrates that female converts to Sunni Islam, no less than their counterparts in the Nation of Islam, continue to view Christianity as a slave religion that even in the twenty-first century imparts a "slavery mentality" to its African-American members. As a convert identified as Maimouna tells Rouse, however, "If you're only submitting to Allah you really can't be a slave to anybody else. So that wipes out a whole range of oppressions that would afflict people: Gender issues, age issues, race issues." Only the weak and unenlightened would continue to adhere to particular forms of surrender demanded by Christianity, this woman and others tell Rouse; indeed, Muslim women here are seen as the only liberated women in the United States. As Rouse remarks in her conclusion, "African American women have surrendered to Islam because of the way Islam has been used in the community as a legitimate framework for challenging racism, sexism, and economic exploitation. Islam is their epiphany. It is the nexus of their social history, personal reality, and liberation theology.…Islam gave them a language and methodology for challenging [multiple] systems of oppression."[21]

When we turn from Rouse's innovative study of African-American women and Islam to other studies of women and religion in the African diaspora (Vodou, Candomblé, Santería, and so forth), divergent interpretive models emerge. Whatever their differences, however, one similarity insistently recurs in the scholarly emphasis upon the empowerment that is supposedly achieved by African-American women in appropriating such traditions for themselves. I have already noted the focus upon agency that appears in Rouse (as well as in

Higginbotham, Weisenfeld, and countless other studies of African-American religions, including Marla Frederick's marvelous recent ethnography, *Between Sundays: Black Women and Everyday Struggles of Faith*), and I must confess here my ambivalence toward what has come to seem the inevitability of this interpretive focus. To linger so assiduously on agency, however, suggests that authors may protest *too* much: in other words, what is increasingly missing from this literature is a clear and sustained analysis of gendered power within black religious traditions and institutions.[22]

More to the current point, very little if any of this work speaks directly to modes of encounter and engagement that occur across religious lines—that is, attention to pluralism seems minuscule at best.

Conclusion: American Women Encounter Religious Others

The abbreviated case studies that I have gathered in this chapter suggest some hypotheses about the impact of religious pluralism on American women, propositions that demand further thinking and refinement before I would claim them as empirical arguments. Before outlining these points, let me reiterate my earlier qualification that the literature investigating this subject remains scanty and that any conclusive statements made here are inevitably partial and preliminary. More research surely needs to be done on women and religious pluralism in American history before grand interpretive schemes can begin to emerge.

Plainly, encounters between women across religious boundaries have often resulted in profound disagreements that are explicitly grounded in gender norms and values. White Protestant women who condemned Hinduism at the turn of the twentieth century regularly couched their denunciations not so much on competing theological truth claims as on the perceived sexism and misogyny of that tradition. Likewise, disputes between Catholic and Protestant women as well as between Muslim and Christian women, as the examples here begin to show, have frequently hinged on accusations of women's mistreatment at the hands of unscrupulous male leaders from competing traditions. American women, in short, have consistently used gender as a critical gauge for assessing religious traditions other than their own, as well as for articulating both the virtues and the vices of the religious communities to which they themselves belong.

It is important to note the obvious fact that such gendered judgments made by women about other religions' treatment of women have very often relied for their persuasiveness on caricature, speculation, and outright fear rather than concrete encounters with a religious other whom they seek to know. Such a lack of genuine openness to others removes this mode of encounter from the pluralist paradigm, which is based instead on a disciplined, enthusiastic, and empathic-yet-critical engagement with those who see the world differently from oneself. The stock falsehoods that repeatedly circulate in order to fuel these negative evaluations suggest that something deep is at stake for both the women and the men who promote them in the face of little evidence (not to mention evidence to the contrary). The stakes differ according to context, of course, but probing more deeply into these divisions may begin to clue us in to the meaning of gendered contestations in the realm of religion.

But if women's critiques of "other" religions have often rested on gendered grounds, so too have the models of cross-religious cooperation that appear in contemporary feminist accounts of women and pluralism. Examples here might include the recent film by Rachel Antell, "Acting on Faith: Women's New Religious Activism in America," or the stories of religious pluralism and women that recur in large multi-religious organizations such as Church Women United. In these settings and many others, American women have joined together across religious boundaries, and they have done so precisely on the basis of a common discontent with a perceived patriarchal religiosity and the faith that things can and should be otherwise. Evidence for this point emerges clearly from this chapter's use of secondary literature, particularly the recurrent focus on terms such as "empowerment" and "agency" in much of the literature on women and religion in the African diaspora; and one could multiply examples to strengthen this point. Whether opposing the religions of one another or joining together in pluralistic celebration of their multiplicity, women have often made their case on gendered grounds.

Notes

1 Ann Braude, "Women's History *Is* American Religious History," in *Retelling U.S. Religious History*, Thomas A. Tweed, ed. (Berkeley: University of California Press, 1997), 87–107.

2 I do not know of Muslim communities that accept the notion of female imams.

3 R. Marie Griffith, *God's Daughters: Evangelical Women and the Power of Submission* (Berkeley: University of California Press, 1997).

4 William R. Hutchison, *Religious Pluralism in America: The Contentious History of a Founding Ideal* (New Haven, CT: Yale University Press, 2003), 235; Diana L. Eck, *A New Religious America: How a "Christian Country" Has Become the World's Most Religiously Diverse Nation* (San Francisco: HarperSanFrancisco, 2001), 385; Robert Wuthnow, *America and the Challenges of Religious Diversity* (Princeton, NJ: Princeton University Press, 2005), 105.

5 Mabel Potter Daggett, "The Heathen Invasion of America," *Missionary Review of the World* 35 (March 1912): 210–214: reprinted in R. Marie Griffith, *American Religions: A Documentary History* (New York: Oxford University Press, 2007), 384–389. See also Daggett, "The Heathen Invasion," *Hampton-Columbian Magazine* 27 (October 1911): 399–411.

6 Daggett, "Heathen Invasion," 385 and 386.

7 Stephen Prothero, "Mother India's Scandalous Swamis," in *Religions of the United States in Practice*, Colleen McDannell, ed., 2 vols. (Princeton, NJ: Princeton University Press, 2001), 418–432.

8 Katherine Mayo, *Mother India* (New York: Harcourt, Brace & Co., 1927); P.W. Wilson, "India is Her Own Worst Enemy," Review of *Mother India*, *New York Times Book Review* (June 5, 1927), BR1.

9 Mersene Sloan, *The Indian Menace: An Essay of Exposure and Warning Showing the Strange Work of Hindu Propaganda in America and Its Special Danger to Our Women* (Washington: The Way Press, 1929); reprinted in Thomas A. Tweed and Stephen Prothero, *Asian Religions in America: A Documentary History* (New York: Oxford University Press, 1999), 212–215.

10 Prothero, "Mother India's Scandalous Swamis," 420.

11 Kathi Kern, "Woman Suffrage, Hinduism, and American Orientalism," unpublished paper presented to the Department of Religion, Princeton University, February 21, 2007; 3–4, 5. Kern's earlier work on radical feminists' religious experimentation is also instructive here; see Kern, *Mrs. Stanton's Bible* (Ithaca, NY: Cornell University Press, 2001).

12 See Jenny Franchot, *Roads to Rome: The Antebellum Protestant Encounter with Catholicism* (Berkeley: University of California Press, 1994).

13 This paragraph relies on John T. McGreevy's argument in his important book *Catholicism and American Freedom: A History* (New York: W. W. Norton, 2003), 95. McGreevy's citations (see p. 333, notes 20–22) are to Elizabeth Wilson, *A Scriptural View of Woman's Rights and Duties, in All the Important Relations of Life* (Philadelphia, 1849), 252; Elizabeth Cady Stanton, "The 'Catholic World' on Woman's Suffrage," *Revolution*, April 29, 1869: 264; "Christianity and Woman's Suffrage," *Woman's Journal*, August 24, 1878: 268; and T.W.E., "A Suffragist's Reply to a Roman Catholic Bishop," *Woman's Journal*, March 24, 1877: 93.

14 Leslie Woodcock Tentler, *Seasons of Grace: A History of the Catholic Archdiocese of Detroit* (Detroit, MI: Wayne State University Press, 1990), 213, cited in Jay P. Dolan, *In Search of an American Catholicism: A History of Religion and Culture in Tension* (New York: Oxford University Press, 2002), 119–120.

15 Dolan, *In Search of an American Catholicism*, 121.

16 Aline H. Kalbian, *Sexing the Church: Gender, Power, and Ethics in Contemporary Catholicism* (Bloomington: Indiana University Press, 2005), 135.

17 Debra Campbell, *Graceful Exits: Catholic Women and the Art of Departure* (Bloomington: Indiana University Press, 2003). For representative works, see, for instance, Rosemary Radford Ruether, *Sexism and God-talk: Toward a Feminist Theology* (Boston: Beacon Press, 1983); Frances Kissling, *A Feminist's Reflection of the Women's Movement in the Philippines: A Dialogue with Frances Kissling on Reproductive Freedom* (Quezon City, Philippines: Center for Women's Resources, 1989); Mary Daly, *Beyond God the Father: Toward a Philosophy of Women's Liberation* (Boston: Beacon Press, 1985, orig. 1973); Mark D. Jordan, *The Silence of Sodom: Homosexuality in Modern Catholicism* (Chicago: University of Chicago Press, 2000). For Campbell's discussion of Daly, see *Graceful Exits*, passim, esp. 79–106.

18 Evelyn Brooks Higginbotham, *Righteous Discontent: The Women's Movement in the Black Baptist Church, 1880–1920* (Cambridge, MA: Harvard University Press, 1993); Judith Weisenfeld, *African American Women and Christian Activism: New York's Black YWCA, 1905–1945* (Cambridge, MA: Harvard University Press, 1998).

19 Carolyn Moxley Rouse, *Engaged Surrender: African American Women and Islam* (Berkeley: University of California Press, 2004), 40, 42–43.

20 Gail Madyun, *Being Muslim: A Rites of Passage Manual for Girls* (Los Angeles: Gail Madyun, 1993), 2–3, cited in Rouse, *Engaged Surrender*, 44.

21 Rouse, *Engaged Surrender*, 93, 216–217.

22 As the coeditor of a collection of essays on women and religion in the African diaspora, I consider this a self-critique as much as a critique of other works in the field. See R. Marie Griffith and Barbara Dianne Savage, *Women and Religion in the African Diaspora: Knowledge, Power, and Performance* (Baltimore, MD: Johns Hopkins University Press, 2006).

| Popular Religion and Pluralism, or, Will Harry Potter Be Left Behind?

PETER W. WILLIAMS

"POPULAR RELIGION" IS A term that shares something important in common with pornography: it's hard to define, but we usually know it when we see it. It also is a term that seems intuitively useful in talking about the American religious scene, since the protean character of religion in this country even before it became an independent nation has long been a source of bemusement to observers both domestic and foreign. Since the First Amendment has from our national beginnings prohibited any "establishment of religion"— that is, an official or state religion—the way has been clear for Americans to adapt, borrow, or invent religion in any form they choose and practice it within the very broad boundaries set by the courts. As opposed to the "folk religion" of Europe and its colonies, which was dependent on the existence of a state-enforced cultus on which local communities could weave creolized variations, Americans enjoyed an abundant variety. They were free to express their religious imagination in ways that had not been possible in premodern societies, which were officially religiously homogeneous. Moreover, the confluence of democracy, industrialization, and communications technology in the United States made this nation the cradle of popular culture, a phenomenon that, while by no means identical with popular religion, nevertheless has exerted important "elective affinities" with the latter and dramatically influenced its course of development.

In terms of definition, the phrase "popular religion" is always destined to be elusive because of the ambiguity of the terms here coupled together to form an even more elusive amalgam. The problems with defining "religion" are too manifold and manifest to even mention. The term "popular" is also highly ambiguous: it may refer to something that enjoys widespread popularity; it may indicate an origin among "the people," whoever they may be; it may be synonymous with "populist," more about which later; it may mean the same as "mass culture," the distinctive form of cultural expression in a capitalist economy employing sophisticated technologies for the production and communication of cultural products; and it may connote a value-judgment, especially if one is inclined to privilege the cultural production of an elite over that of the "people" (or vice versa). All of these shades of meaning are relevant and useful in this discussion.

In my early work, I attempted to define "popular religion" as symbolic expression and action with at least two of the following three characteristics:

1. Popular religion is *extra-ecclesiastical* religion, that is, religious activity taking place outside organized social frameworks such as denominational bureaucracies and hierarchies;
2. Popular religion, similarly, is transmitted outside the normal channels of official religious communication;
3. In terms of content, popular religion tends to manifest itself in the form of supernaturalism, such as spiritually-induced healings, providential interference in the course of historical events, or other phenomena in which the order of natural causation is seemingly interrupted or reversed.[1]

A fourth category might be added in hindsight: an elective affinity with popular culture. There is no shortage of definitions of the latter, but popular culture is usually associated with a capitalistic system of cultural production and a technologically sophisticated system of mass distribution of these products. Moveable-type printing provided the technical basis for the earliest Euro-American popular culture, as the circulation of words and images now was no longer confined to oral transmission. By the twentieth century, a host of rapidly developing new communications technologies—tabloid newspapers, radio, film, television, paperback books, the Internet—all converged to make the past dozen or so decades a time in which a new mass culture transcended local, regional, and national boundaries and transformed the consciousnesses of Americans—and everyone resident in what media analyst Marshall McLuhan christened the "global village"—not only with undreamt of masses of information but with new vistas of the imagination, both free and for sale.

It is not surprising that religion—one of the most primal and protean of human impulses—began to adapt itself to the possibilities of these new media. The affinity of different religious communities for these media, however, was by no means uniform. The mainstream radio and television industries, leery of controversy, generally tended toward the bland and predictable, as did the mainline denominations that occasionally provided programming for them. (Occasional exceptions, such as Roman Catholic Bishop Fulton Sheen's enormously popular series, "Life Is Worth Living," which vied with Milton Berle's comedy hour for a massive TV audience during the 1950s, generally proved the rule.) The shapers of the emergent film industry recognized their opportunity but generally steered clear of confessional controversy. Directors such as Cecil B. DeMille found religious themes to be highly profitable from the inception of film in the 1920s.[1] By the 1950s, lavish biblical epics such as "The Ten Commandments" and "Ben Hur" appealed to a mainstream interdenominational audience in their combination of secular action and dramatic supernaturalism.

In contrast with mainline religious groups—Will Herberg's trinity of "Protestant, Catholic, Jew" that had emerged by the 1950s as respectable manifestations of middle-class American religiosity—evangelical and fundamentalist Protestants, whose commitment to an aggressive spreading of the faith was part of their self-understanding, seemed to sense intuitively that emergent mass media could readily be separated from the secular contexts in which they had originated and domesticated and harnessed for religious purposes. This community, though scattered throughout a multitude of denominations, institutions, and networks, nevertheless possessed a unified message, and believed that its effective distribution was essential to a nation that otherwise possessed no common faith. At the other end of the religious spectrum, an even more diffuse network of "seekers" of truth(s) variously identified as "harmonial" or "metaphysical" was similarly comfortable with mass media, even though its messages more often took the form of broad themes expressed in what might appear to be secular guises.[2] The goal here paralleled that of the evangelical focus on individual religious conversion and social moral transformation, but in a far more individualized and eclectic fashion, with no central scriptural text as the basis for canonical norms.

Although other religious phenomena and movements might be considered to be "popular religion"—for example, the ethnic and popular variants on Roman Catholic themes studied by Robert Orsi, or a variety of movements once known as cults but now usually designated as "New Religious Movements" (NRMs)—it makes sense here to focus on what we shall hereafter refer to as the evangelical and metaphysical strains in our attempt to understand what relationship popular belief and practice have to the issues of religious pluralism in American life.[3] While movements arising at the periphery of established religions, such as the Roman Catholic Church or Hinduism, or entirely new religions, such as Scientology, certainly illustrate religious pluralism, they seldom become sufficiently widespread to have more than a local and passing influence upon American pluralism, although they may test the boundaries of the First Amendment. (Mormonism, of course, is a major exception.) On the other hand, both evangelical and metaphysical religion are pervasive in American life, both past and present, although the forms they have taken and their relationship to the broader culture have been in continual flux. It is their stories that we shall now narrate, with an eye to how understanding each, individually and in their interactions, can illuminate some of the dynamics of religion in a pluralistic American society. We will consider each in terms of the first three definers of popular religion advanced earlier, and conclude with two telling examples of their manifestations in contemporary American popular culture.

The roots of American evangelicalism extend to the earliest British colonial foundations in what is now the United States, especially to New England Puritanism. Although the foundational scholars of this movement, particularly Harvard's Perry Miller, stressed the elite dimensions of Puritan culture, more recent work, particularly David Hall's *Worlds of Wonder, Days of Judgment*, rejects a sharp elite/popular or clergy/lay dichotomy in favor of a more nuanced, cultural interpretation of the colonial New England scene.⁴ Hall argues persuasively that a distinctively Protestant culture had been borne across the Atlantic by the Puritan emigrants, in which literacy was nearly universal and the process of the desupernaturalization of nature was well under way. Nevertheless, belief in the occult, for example, was pervasive not simply among the putatively ignorant "folk" but among the clerical leadership as well.

Jon Butler's *Awash in a Sea of Faith*, published a year after Hall's *Worlds of Wonder*, examines a broader spectrum of early American religious practice from a vantage point very similar to Hall's. Butler, like Hall, explicitly interests himself in "popular religion," which he defines as "the religious behavior of laypeople." He maintains that, during the colonial and antebellum periods, popular religion was sometimes anticlerical and anti-institutional, and sometimes not; similarly, it might or might not be rooted in folk traditions of the occult.⁵ Butler throughout emphasizes what he calls America's "spiritual pluralism," and regularly attempts to deconstruct or de-center attempts to overemphasize the continuity, homogeneity, or inevitability of evangelical hegemony.

In the early Republic, tension arose rapidly between popular and elite denominations. Although the First Amendment forbade any establishment of religion at the federal level, states were still free to support churches, and Massachusetts did so until 1833. Those denominations—Congregational, Episcopal, Presbyterian—that required a learned clergy were identified with local and national elites, and provoked both religious and social opposition from popular movements such as Baptists, Methodists, and Campbellites. The de facto hegemony that Episcopal clergy enjoyed prior to the Civil War in the chaplaincy of Congress was a sign that, in a land in which all religious groups enjoyed a de jure equality under law, some denominations were de facto more equal than others. As popular movements succeeded in gaining adherents who later became more settled and prosperous, these movements tended to become routinized into denominations, losing or modifying the apparent spontaneity that had characterized their early, effervescent phases.

Metaphysical movements were similarly extra-ecclesiastical, though for the most part only implicitly anti-ecclesiastical. If we are to take the entire range of phenomena that Catherine Albanese identifies as "metaphysical" in the colonial and antebellum eras as normative, we are confronted with a vast array of religious and cultural phenomena that includes European, Native, and African constituents. These bore only a highly generic resemblance to one another, but they converged at various points and in various ways as these three broad social/racial categories began to interact with and influence one another as a distinctively American people and culture began slowly to take shape. Here, more obviously than among evangelicals, does not only cultural pluralism but creolization—appropriation and new synthesis, as manifest in New Religious Movements—begin to make itself manifest. In any case, metaphysical belief and practice, broadly and loosely defined, emerge both at the edges of the dominant society—among native peoples, enslaved Africans, and socially marginalized Euro-Americans—and within the dominant society itself, that is, in the folk beliefs and lore shared by elites and white "plain folk."

Only after the Revolution—in the midst of what Alice Felt Tyler long ago labeled "freedom's ferment"—did organized groups begin to arise that incorporated metaphysical themes into their teaching and practice. For the most part, however, these did not parallel the denominations busily springing up around explicitly Christian confessional cores. Instead, they took a variety of other forms, ranging from the under-the-radar practice of "hoodoo" and "conjure" by African-Americans to the highly respectable—and often resented—elitist form of Freemasonry, as well as the very loosely organized intellectual coterie known, to the dismay of some who fiercely resisted structure and essentialist labeling, as Transcendentalists. Albanese identifies Latter-day Saints, Shakers, and Universalists as New Religious Movements, or at least new popular denominations, that were ostensibly Christian but nevertheless incorporated some important aspects of metaphysical teaching into their practice. Other appropriations of metaphysical religion were spread by traveling lecturers and practitioners self-identifying as Mesmerists, phrenologists, Fourierists, and spiritualists, who were essentially independent, itinerant entrepreneurs— much like their evangelical revivalist counterparts from George Whitefield onward. The era before formal professional education and licensing began to dominate medical practice provided an ethos in which what would now be called alternative therapies could flourish, since mainstream medicine could not demonstrate a very impressive record of success before it had acquired a firm scientific foundation. Similarly, as Nathan Hatch has noted, the impossibility of governmental mandating of professional requirements for the clergy benefited popular practitioners of all stripes, then as now.[6] One would, in short, look in vain to find a metaphysical church or even a coherent community. Rather, as Albanese notes, metaphysical religion usually spread through networks of the like-minded who did not assemble for common worship but rather participated in a very loosely organized shadow society that lacked formal organizational structures or mandatory belief systems.

With regard to our second definitional point—the transmission of information through other than denominational channels—evangelicals and metaphysicians manifested some important similarities. In both cases, oral communication was highly important, although it took significantly different forms. For evangelicals, the sermon—the preached Word—was normative, as it was in the elite traditions they challenged, although it was now aimed at the heart rather than the mind. For the metaphysical set, preaching directed at the emotions was inappropriate, since *harmonialism*—the alternative term

Sydney Ahlstrom coined to describe this community of discourse—was essentially a rational rather than an affective construct. The lecture, therefore, was a more typical mode of communication, exemplified in Ralph Waldo Emerson's fame as an itinerant speaker of edifying thoughts, as well as in the somewhat later Christian Science movement's employment of *readers*. At a lower social plane, communication took place by word of mouth in a one-on-one or small group context. In addition, for both evangelicals and metaphysicals, the proliferation of print culture—as Albanese, Hall, and Hatch all note in various contexts—was transformative of the communications infrastructure that underlay the spread of these movements in early America. The ability to put one's thoughts into written form and distribute them widely at little cost across growing distances overcame the obstacle of geographical isolation. It also made it possible for the seeds of new religious ideas to be planted in individuals and small groups without the necessity of personal mediation or ecclesiastical structures.

A third characteristic of popular religion is the focus of attention on this-worldly supernaturalism—that is, the ability to induce and experience concrete manifestations of divine power in an earthly setting. For evangelicalism, the primary manifestation of this-worldly supernaturalism has been the experience of conversion. In the holiness-pentecostal strain of evangelicalism that originated in the nineteenth century as a reaction to the denominationalization of Methodism, the direct experience of the Holy Spirit became enhanced by the possibility of physical and emotional healing through faith, which might take place through a variety of means and in a variety of social contexts, including, eventually, electronic transmission.

In the metaphysical strain of popular religious practice, a considerable variety of possibilities presented themselves throughout the nineteenth and into the twentieth centuries. These included divination and other "occult" practices engaged in by a variety of folk, including the young Joseph Smith; the foretelling of future events through astrology; communications with the spirits of the departed in séances with mediums or through Ouija boards or "channelers"; and physical and psychic healing through any number of means ranging from formal Christian Science practice through alternative holistic medicines through the wearing of crystals. Religious practice in both strains is this-worldly and pragmatic; the supernatural is relevant not only, or even primarily, as a means of ensuring ultimate spiritual transformation and salvation, but also as a practical agenda for dealing with the pains and losses of everyday existence.[7]

The development of each of these strains of popular religion in the twentieth and twenty-first centuries was profoundly affected by the broader transformations in American society and culture. *Mobility*, in both its geographical and sociological senses, accompanied the urbanization of the United States both through in-*migration* of native-born Americans from the nation's small towns and rural areas, as well as the *immigration* of millions, mainly Europeans, into the rapidly industrializing urban centers of the Eastern seaboard and, especially, the Great Lakes. Beginning in the wake of World War II, and abetted by the GI Bill, another exodus—this time out of these same cities—took place in the form of *suburbanization*, with a resultant homogenization of the children and grandchildren of the earlier urban immigrants characterized by both geographical and social mobility. Still later, accompanied by a new kind of immigration from Asia and the Middle East promoted by the Hart-Celler Act of 1965 and an economic transformation from a manufacturing to a service economy, millions of new- and old-stock Americans alike began to reassemble in new patterns, focused in the Sun Belt and clustered in *exurban* aggregates of various sorts in the geographical and social space lying beyond the postwar suburbs. Accompanying these new patterns of settlement and employment was an ongoing revolution in technology, transportation, and communications that further altered the ways in which Americans could acquire information and relate to one another—and to the realm of the supernatural. Mass-circulation periodicals, radio, television, computers, and cellular telephones paralleled the development of interstate highways and affordable jet travel. All of these affected both strains of American popular religion profoundly.

First, the metaphysical strain took some dramatic new turns in the context of the American city. At one end of the spectrum, Christian Science arose in the midst of what Sydney Ahlstrom dubbed a now-irrecoverable subethos of boarding houses, among marginalized in-migrants, many of them women, who now lacked a natural community within which the tasks, trials, and passages of life could be undergone and interpreted.[8] Where the mainline churches offered new communities on the old parish model, and evangelicals responded in ways we will address later, urban metaphysical religion was largely individualistic. Although the Christian Science movement acquired many of the appearances of denominational religion and liturgical worship, it never attempted to generate much in the way of communal life, relying instead on individual appropriation of an intensely verbal message through oral testifying at weekly assemblies or through the distinctive innovation of the "reading room." Various forms of New Thought, the early twentieth-century movement that derived many of its themes from Christian Science, manifested themselves in institutionally more diffuse and less authoritarian ways, and relied primarily on the written word in the form of magazines and pamphlets for the dissemination of their messages among individuals. Similarly, organizations for the promotion of various "occult" movements loosely derived from Asian or other exotic traditions, such as Vedanta or Rosicrucianism, were highly intellectualist and individualistic.

After the vogue for New Thought had subsided, metaphysical religious activity became somewhat dormant for several decades, until the countercultural movement of the later 1960s and early 1970s provided a fertile ground for its revival. The Beat movement of the 1950s, with its quest for new knowledge through such unorthodox channels as drugs and Asian religiosity, had foreshadowed this resurgence on a much smaller scale. The growing unpopularity of the war in Southeast Asia catalyzed a larger pattern of youthful disillusionment with the "conventional wisdom" of the dominant society, and the panoply of cultural experimentation that had already begun, particularly in California, provided a variety of themes and avenues that could now be selectively appropriated for the quest of eclectic wisdom, frequently in the metaphysical tradition broadly understood. Once again, the quest here was for *usable knowledge*—alternative ways of acquiring not only information seldom available through conventional means, but also paths to wisdom that would lead to a complete transformation in the character and quality of one's way of living.

The individual components available to the "seekers" who now proliferated on college campuses, hippie communes, and other places where the young, especially, congregated were manifold. In some cases actual institutions provided access to the means to experiential wisdom, for example, therapeutic centers such as Esalen at Big Sur and academic or worship communities based on Asian traditions, such as the San Francisco Zen Center or the Naropa Institute in Colorado. Independent entrepreneurs, often oblivious to or exempt from the certification required of many professionals, offered alternate forms of health care and spiritual access, such as channeling the spirits of the dead. Shops devoted to New Age literature and paraphernalia such as crystals flourished. Even further from conventional social sources were consciousness-altering or mind-expanding drugs, especially marijuana and LSD, which became abundantly available, though never legal. Travel to sacred sites was another means of potential access to wisdom: to Asia, especially India, in quest of residence at ashrams led by gurus in the Hindu tradition; to domestic sites sacred to native peoples, who often were less than enthusiastic about their appropriation by those not imbued in their traditional cultures; to Latin America and the Caribbean, in search of more powerful hallucinogens.

Metaphysical religion persists as an important strain in American culture, albeit one that tends to exist close to the ground and under the radar of much of the media. Protean in character, it can take any form from daily newspaper horoscopes to acupuncture. It has no centralized organization, and its members tend to view claims to absolute or exclusive religious authority with suspicion. Eclecticism is the rule, and those in search of wholeness, both bodily and spiritual, usually have little compunction about entertaining beliefs and practices from radically different sources simultaneously. Many of these "seekers" belong to the mainline Christian denominations, which themselves have become accommodating to such practices as meditation—a practice with a long history in Christianity as well as in Asian religions—and the walking of the labyrinth as an aid to meditation. In *Habits of the Heart*, sociologist Robert Bellah and his research associate coined the eponym "Sheilaism" from a young woman they interviewed who described her own spiritual eclecticism and suggested that one might call her a "Sheilaist," that is, one whose religious position is a unique blend chosen from an array of elements to harmonize with one's own distinctive outlook and needs.[9]

Unlike the Religious Right, the metaphysical community is too individualistic and resistant to authority and regimentation to constitute a predictable political bloc. In general, however, its sympathies tend toward the liberal, although directed more toward movements and issues than toward personalities or parties. Environmentalism is an obvious major concern for those who find religious significance in nature, and the Green Party is one of the few organized political entities that have attracted support from this quarter. Enfranchisement for women and minority groups also follows naturally from what is an essentially universalistic theology, in which distinctions among humans are subordinated to the idea that transformational knowledge and experience are potentially open to all.

The other, and much more visible, strain of popular religiosity we have identified is evangelicalism—what Randall Balmer has called "America's folk religion."[10] During most of the nineteenth century, evangelicalism could be more accurately characterized as the nation's informally established religion: Protestant communities ranging from the elite denominations (Presbyterians and "low church" Episcopalians) to popular movements that had now acquired middle-class denominational status (Baptists and Methodists) to "ethnic" communities ("English" Lutherans, German Methodists) to most African-American forms of Christianity—all would most likely have self-identified as practitioners of evangelical Christianity.

A major shift began toward the end of the nineteenth century when internecine quarrels over the related issues of Darwinian evolution and biblical criticism drove a wedge within and between denominations. "Fundamentalism" emerged early in the twentieth century as a self-identified movement, and the Scopes Trial of 1925 brought these issues into a national media spotlight, to the detriment of the fundamentalists. An important corollary of this event was the linkage that it wrought between antimodernist Protestantism and populist politics, with both embodied in the person of William Jennings Bryan. As Edward J. Larson has argued, Bryan saw himself as defending not only the authority of a literally interpreted Bible, but also the right of local communities to make their own choices about the proper education of their children.[11] This suspicion of and even hostility toward elites goes back to the earliest years of the Republic and even beyond, as has already been mentioned with regard to early Methodism's emergence. Since religious groups were among the few professional communities in the nation that had escaped the drive for licensing and other forms of governmental and peer-group regulation that had characterized the Progressive era, it was through their agency that an antimodernist, countercultural campaign could focus in a nation in which these "culture wars" were taking shape following the breakup of the evangelical hegemony of the previous century.

This counterculture stayed low to the ground during the ensuing several decades, although in the South and parts of the Midwest it was in fact the dominant culture. It was propagated not by any centralized authority, such as that which directed the Catholic Church's similarly alternative social and cultural constructions of the same era, but rather through the systems of networking that also characterized metaphysical practice. Somewhat more elaborate and extensive than those of the latter, these networks were maintained through Bible schools, summer camps, periodicals, radio (and later television) stations, itinerant revivalist preachers, and other means that fell short of fully articulated denominations. This is the milieu out of which the young Billy Graham arose in the late 1940s, a man who became a national instrumentality and symbol in six subsequent decades for the transition of evangelicalism from a regional subculture to a national phenomenon.

With the visibility thrust upon evangelicalism by the candidacy of "born-again" Southern Baptist Jimmy Carter in the 1976 presidential election, conservative Protestantism began not only to grow rapidly but also to advance in a number of directions. Many who identified as evangelicals began to move in the direction of "mainline" status, adhering to the movement's traditional theological definers but demonstrating a willingness to accommodate to and even appreciate many aspects of contemporary intellectual culture. The emergence of a number of institutions, publications and publishers, and scholars and scholarly associations that embraced the term *evangelical* but eschewed antagonism toward their mainline and secular counterparts clearly removed this entire wing from designations such as "popular" or "populist." An emergent distancing from the populist Religious Right also manifested itself by the mid-2000s in the National Association of Evangelicals' refusal to privilege symbolic issues of morality over others, such as environmentalism and hunger, which had a broader ethical appeal.

The emergence of the Religious Right as a distinctive and potent force in American political life in the 1970s highlighted the populist character of this branch of evangelicalism. This politicized form was most characteristic of the fundamental wing, although it gained appeal not only among other evangelical strains, such as pentecostalism, but went even further in its outreach to socially conservative Roman Catholics, to whom its constituents would have been openly adversarial in an earlier era. This adversarial quality of the movement harkened back to the days of the Second Great Awakening when evangelical leaders such as Timothy Dwight and Lyman Beecher vilified Catholics, deists, and the French as agents of evil. This scapegoating took on metaphysical as well as political dimensions in both the postmillennial and premillennial forms that evangelicalism assumed as it developed and bifurcated over the next two centuries. By the time of the heyday of the Religious Right at the end of the twentieth century, the two forms tended to blur in such fictionalized expressions as the "Left Behind" series of popular fiction and in Pat Robertson's attempt to find a loophole through which premillennial events might be delayed as he saw growing hope for moral improvement through political means in the here-and-now.[12]

In addition to the hard-edged political organizing and symbol-making by the Religious Right, latter-day evangelicalism began to generate a culture far removed from that of its pre–World War II predecessors, described in contemporary vestigial form in some of Balmer's chapters. Where earlier evangelicalism had sought to distance itself from the dominant culture, its successors eagerly imitated the means through which latter-day capitalism had succeeded in transforming the nation itself into a consumption-obsessed society. This impulse manifested itself in a fascination with and mastery of cutting-edge communications technology; the generation of a vast amount of evangelically themed print matter and material culture; marketing techniques such as a "Christian Yellow Pages"; biblically oriented theme parks; television programming modeled on secular talk-show formats; and so on almost indefinitely.[13]

Perhaps the most distinctive innovation of this sort is the *megachurch*. The megachurch is a place for worship for congregations numbering from 2000 to as many as 15,000 or more, with an adjoining physical plant for a whole panoply of activities appealing to the religious, educational, social, and recreational needs of the various cohorts that make up the larger community of believers. Although sometimes affiliated with organized denominations such as the Southern Baptist Convention or the Assemblies of God, many of these churches are either independent or, increasingly, affiliated with California-based religious "franchises" such as Saddleback or Vineyard.[14] The establishment and "growing" of these churches echoes the early Methodist circuit-riders and Baptist farmer-preachers since many such ecclesiastical entrepreneurs today possess little in the way of theological credentials, but instead may have valuable experience in the areas of business and communications. These churches are, moreover, a tactical response to the broad-based phenomenon noted earlier of exurban in-migration, the latest form of the distinctively and pervasively American phenomenon of mobility. Megachurches offer instant community for people on the move.

The theologies that underlie these enterprises are also in transit. While many of the earlier megachurches, such as Chicago's Willow Creek, formally espouse a traditional, even fundamentalist, set of beliefs—although these are often not flaunted, especially among newer members—more recent "franchises" seem to be moving toward a theological vocabulary that has the soft-edged quality of New Age rhetoric.[15] In addition, many of these churches are openly oriented toward the achievement of worldly success, both in terms of size of membership and income of members. Robert Schuller, whose "Crystal Cathedral" in Anaheim is an architecturally spectacular early version of a megachurch, pioneered this strain through his doctrine of "Possibility Thinking," a direct continuation of the "Positive Thinking" promoted by his mentor, Norman Vincent Peale. The "name it and claim it" rhetoric of TBN (Trinity Broadcasting Network), a hugely successful television enterprise with large minority appeal, is another version of this sort of this-worldly supernaturalism we earlier identified as a distinguishing trait of popular religion.[16]

With regard to pluralism, it is reasonable to conclude that the metaphysical community as it exists in the United States today is highly compatible with religious and cultural pluralism in the context of contemporary American society. Although metaphysical philosophy is avowedly monistic—affirming the ultimate oneness of all that is, and denying the ultimate separation of such seemingly disparate categories of being as matter and spirit—the praxis of metaphysical religion is in fact remarkably pluralistic. We have already seen that eclecticism is the hallmark of contemporary metaphysical practice, and that members of this very loosely defined and bounded community of believers, practitioners, and sympathizers are loath to restrict their pursuit of wisdom to any particular path. Given the value placed on the religious lore of such disparate traditions as Buddhism and those of Native American peoples, it would be a major contradiction if such seekers after truth among varied paths were to take a hostile or suspicious attitude toward any culture on the grounds of its difference from their own—which is always in process and never sharply delineated or defined. In fact, hostility toward the metaphysically minded has come not only from such predictable sources as Protestant fundamentalism, which insists on its exclusive possession of religious truth, but also, and more ironically, from native peoples who resent what they see as attempts to appropriate and exploit particularistic spiritual resources that are the cultural property of, and possess efficacy for, only those who are bonded by a common ancestry, both genetic and cultural.

Evangelicalism—the other broad-based strain of contemporary American popular religion—is more ambiguous with regard to the issue of pluralism. "Neo-Evangelicals," as they are sometimes designated—the sort who read *Christianity Today*, belong to the NEA or Sojourners, and have been educated at Calvin or Wheaton College—probably do not differ greatly from most Americans in their attitude toward such issues. Although they by definition privilege Christianity among religions, they are not necessarily hostile to the practitioners of other religions, whom they may well regard as people of good will who are mistaken on some important particulars. The enormous popularity of evangelicalism, especially in its pentecostal form, among Latinos is another marker of diversity within the highly pluralistic evangelical community.

On the other hand, latter-day fundamentalists, who are often sympathetic with or active in the congeries of movements known as the Religious Right, have little tolerance for those who disagree with them, although they differ from their predecessors in their willingness to enter into pragmatic alliances with Catholics, Jews, and others who share their moral and political aims. Intolerance for difference extends beyond the censuring of false belief to a desire to regulate the moral practice of others through the exercise of the powers of a government believed to be founded on evangelical principles. Although race and ethnicity are no longer primary categories of difference, religion—both liberal and "alien"—most definitely is, as exemplified in Franklin Graham's denunciation of Islam as "a very wicked and evil religion."[17] Fear of and hostility toward the "other" is manifested not only in a neo-nativist political agenda but also, more obliquely, in a focus on "moral" issues such as abortion and homosexuality. In both cases, fear of penetration of the human body by alien instrumentalities can be read as a projection of anxiety about penetration of the pure social body—the United States—by the impure "other," once Communism, now primarily Islam. Accurate information, whether about the ideological origins of the United States or about the character of contemporary Islam, is subordinated to a mythology informed by fear and desire.

In conclusion, we can see that what we have been calling "popular religion" is a distinctively, if not uniquely, American phenomenon. It has historically been generated and nurtured by the de jure prohibition of established religion; the de facto flourishing of religious institutions and behavior under the protection of the same First Amendment; the exemption of religious personnel from the licensing requirements imposed on most other professions; the individualistic and entrepreneurial character of American society; ongoing immigration from the rest of the entire world; and the phenomenal mobility of the American people, both geographically and socially.

Although popular religion has been protean in its expression, it has nevertheless tended to cluster into the two strains we have labeled as "metaphysical" and "evangelical." The first represents an optimistic view that misfortune and limitation can be overcome through proper knowledge and individual effort without extensive reliance on institutions and professionals. The second is based on a more pessimistic view of human possibility, combined with a fundamental insecurity about the prospects of a nation lacking deep roots and a settled social order. As a result, the need to regulate human behavior and to protect both the individual and the social body from all enemies foreign and domestic has often been a leitmotiv, especially in the fundamentalist camp.

The two enormously popular cultural products of the late 1990s and early 2000s alluded to in this chapter's title are illustrative of these two strains. The first six of the British author J. K. Rowling's series of novels, aimed at a young audience but enjoyed by readers of all ages in both book and film form, had already sold over 325,000,000 volumes by the time of the release of the seventh and ultimate volume, *Harry Potter and the Deathly Hallows*, in 2007.[18] These stories are set at the Hogwarts School of Witchcraft and Wizardry, which appears to exist in a dimension parallel to that of the mundane life world of the "muggles," or nonmagical folk (i.e., the bourgeoisie). The series is essentially a *Bildungsroman*—a coming-of-age novel—which, though situated in the realm of the imagination rather than the bourgeois reality of earlier practitioners of the genre, nevertheless focuses on the theme of self-realization through successful encounters with adversity. It is in many ways a retelling of George Lucas's *Star Wars* epic series of films (six films, 1977–2005), which itself was deeply influenced by that *auteur*'s engagement with Joseph Campbell's popular work on comparative world mythologies.[19] Both can be read as archetypal story-telling, dealing with universal themes in human life and the human psyche, which find expression in all religions in varying forms but which are retold by both Rowling and Lucas without reference to any explicit religious framework.

Despite its vast popularity, the Rowling oeuvre has encountered criticism—perhaps not surprisingly, primarily in fundamentalist circles—for its utilization of magical themes and its omission of any Christian references. (C. S. Lewis, an earlier English fantasist, has been lionized by evangelicals because such references are fairly transparent in works such as *The Lion, the Witch and the Wardrobe*.) In the United States, occasional calls for removing the *Harry Potter* saga from public schools have been made on the grounds not only that it promotes sorcery and witchcraft but also that it advocates a specific religion, Wicca, and its inclusion in curricula violates First Amendment guarantees of religious neutrality. Such calls have met with little success, and more moderate evangelical voices, such as *Christianity Today* magazine, have praised the series as harmonious with Christian values. (Rowling herself is a member of the Church of Scotland, and she turned to more explicit Christian references in her final volume.)

The relevance of this British series to religious pluralism in the United States resides in its universalistic appeal. While for many—probably most—American Christians the series is compatible with or actually supportive of Christian values, its message is not couched within an explicitly Christian vocabulary. With the gradual erosion of a common literary canon within the American educational system, the nearly universal popularity of this series—even among young people not infatuated with the printed word—can be read as an affirmation of a system of values congruent with that of many contemporary religious communities but not limited to any, as well as lore that has appeal to many outside the boundaries of institutionalized religion. This stress on values over specific creeds and symbols has roots in the liberal Protestant movement of the early twentieth century, and is appealing to those who see a shared moral vision as more valuable to the social fabric than a divisive appeal to more particularistic belief systems. The *Harry Potter* saga, in short, has a distinctively "metaphysical" character and has highly positive implications for a pluralistic worldview.

Inhabiting a virtually parallel universe in the realm of contemporary American popular culture is the *Left Behind* series, which consists of 16 novels created by Tim LaHaye and Jerry B. Jenkins between 1995 and 2007, almost exactly the same time span as that of *Harry Potter*. The series, which has sold approximately 65 million copies to date, has not done as well as the more internationally popular *Potter*, but its statistics are nonetheless impressive.[20] *Left Behind*, like *Potter*, is also based on a mythic framework, but a very different one. The underlying paradigm for the series comes from the doctrine of dispensational premillennialism, formulated in the 1830s by the British clergyman John Nelson Darby and popularized in the United States through the annotations to the *Scofield Reference Bible* (1909). Distinctive to this theology is the notion of a sequence of apocalyptic events, based on a reading of the Book of Revelation, commencing with the Rapture, in which the faithful will be bodily removed from earth immediately prior to the reign of a figure of cosmic evil known as the Antichrist. Under the latter's reign, those not worthy of rapture nevertheless have a chance to demonstrate their faith in the face of horrendous persecution. The raptured have little dramatic interest, while the story of those "left behind" has much—enough, in fact, to fill 16 volumes.

If *Harry Potter* is a *Bildungsroman*, *Left Behind* might be compared with the medieval morality play genre in that it presents protagonists caught between good and evil with a binary choice rather than a process of nuanced development. It is more American than medieval, however, in that it partakes of the ethos of many distinctively American film genres, such as the private eye and the Western, which in their heydays (the Cold War era) reflected a sense that a once-and-for-all choice—similar, perhaps, to the evangelical conversion experience—was necessary in both the private and the social realm. John Wayne, whether cast as cowboy or Marine, was the Hollywood archetype of genre protagonist here. The theological dimensions tend toward the dualistic, in which good and evil as cosmic forces are matched against each other, with humans having to choose unequivocally between them.

The implications of the *Left Behind* series are practically a mirror image of those of *Harry Potter*. Where the latter series is based on what is implicitly a universal paradigm of moral growth and transformation, the former is explicitly sectarian in its message that only strict conformity to a highly particularistic belief system can bring about personal redemption and forestall the moral collapse of the social order. If America, in short, is to survive, it must eschew the temptations both of secularism as well as the demonic international order of which the United Nations and other transnational organizations are symbolic in this universe of discourse. The success of the series, however, appears to be due to its appeal to an audience beyond that of the fundamentalist community. The fast-moving narratives, with far more violence than the world of Hogwarts, have elicited critical praise from such unlikely sources as the *New York Times*, and the books have been widely distributed in supermarkets and "big box" stores as well as "Christian" (i.e., evangelical) bookstores.

In conclusion, one might observe that the proliferation and persistence of popular religion in the United States has itself been a manifestation of religious pluralism from our beginnings as a nation, and that the founding document of that nation has continued to guarantee the possibility of that pluralism. One can also argue that some strains of popular religion, especially the metaphysical, have themselves been essentially pluralistic, as manifest in their eclecticism, their fascination with the exotic, and their resistance to institutionalization. On the other hand, evangelicalism has generally proven less receptive to coexistence with religions that do not share its own interpretation of Christianity. For some, this lack of openness to other religious expressions has been restricted to the realm of personal decision and focused on the conversion of individuals, who might organize into small groups and distance themselves from the broader culture. Contemporary fundamentalism, however, with ideological roots stretching back to New England Puritanism and to the Second Great Awakening, is clearly committed to a species of tribalism manifesting itself in a nationalistic commitment to an idealized—and never actually realized—America that has little room for religious dissent or pluralistic expression. For such believers, figures like Harry Potter, who do not overtly conform to the norms of social and religious orthodoxy, will and must indeed be left behind.

Notes

1 Peter W. Williams, *Popular Religion in America: Symbolic Change and the Modernization Process in Historical Perspective* (Englewood Cliffs, NJ: Prentice-Hall, 1980); reissued by the University of Illinois Press (Urbana and Chicago, 1989).

2 "Harmonialism" is used by Sydney E. Ahlstrom in his *A Religious History of the American People* (New Haven, CT: Yale University Press, 1972, 2004); "metaphysical religion" is favored by Catherine L. Albanese in her *A Republic of Mind and Spirit: A Cultural History of American Metaphysical Religion* (New Haven, CT: Yale University Press, 2007). Much of the discussion of metaphysical religion in this essay is derived from Albanese's narrative and arguments.

3 Robert Orsi, *The Madonna of 115th Street: Faith and Community in Italian Harlem, 1880–1950* (New Haven, CT: Yale University Press, 1985), 4; and Orsi, *Thank You, St. Jude: Women's Devotion to the Patron Saint of Hopeless Causes* (New Haven, CT: Yale University Press, 1996).

4 David D. Hall, *Worlds of Wonder, Days of Judgment: Popular Belief in Early New England* (New York: Knopf, 1989).

5 Jon Butler, *Awash in a Sea of Faith: Christianizing the American People* (Cambridge, MA: Harvard University Press, 1990), 4.

6 Nathan O. Hatch, *The Democratization of American Christianity* (New Haven, CT: Yale University Press, 1989), 16.

7 Albanese, passim.

8 Ahlstrom, *Religious History of the American People*, 1022. The language quoted here is remembered from an orally delivered discourse on this topic.

9 Robert N. Bellah, et al., *Habits of the Heart: Individualism and Commitment in American Life* (Berkeley and Los Angeles: University of California Press, 1985), 221, 235.

10 Randall Balmer, *Mine Eyes Have Seen the Glory: A Journey into the Evangelical Subculture in America*, 4th ed. (New York: Oxford University Press, 2006), 7.

11 Edward J. Larson, *Summer for the Gods: The Scopes Trial and America's Continuing Debate over Science and Religion* (Cambridge, MA: Harvard University Press, 1997), 39–40, and passim.

12 Paul S. Boyer, *When Time Shall be No More: Prophecy Belief in Modern American Culture* (Cambridge, MA: Harvard University Press, 1992), ch. 10.

13 Balmer, *Mine Eyes Have Seen the Glory*, ch. 10, and passim.

14 Donald E. Miller was among the first to identify and analyze this phenomenon in *Reinventing American Protestantism: Christianity in the New Millennium* (Berkeley and Los Angeles: University of California Press, 1997).

15 I am indebted to my student Myev Rees for this observation.

16 See Kathleen M. Hladky, "'Modern Day Heroes of Faith': The Rhetoric of Trinity Broadcasting Network and The Emergent Word of Faith Movement," M.A. thesis, Miami University, 1997.

17 NBC Nightly News, November 16, 2001. See also http://www.covenantnews.com/graham.

18 http://en.wikipedia.org/wiki/Harry_Potter#Origins_and_publishing_history.

19 E.g., Joseph Campbell, *The Hero with a Thousand Faces* (Princeton, NJ: Princeton University Press, 1968).

20 http://en.wikipedia.org/wiki/Left_Behind; see also Bruce David Forbes and Jeanne Halgren Kilde, *Rapture, Revelation and the End Times: Exploring the Left Behind Series* (New York: Palgrave Macmillan, 2004).

CHAPTER 12 | "Finding Light through Muddy
Waters": African-American
Religious Pluralism

STEPHANIE Y. MITCHEM

IN MY FAMILY, SOME folks are members of the African Methodist Episcopal
(A. M. E.) Church, a historically black Christian church. Some are Muslim
and not Christian at all. Some belong to Unity and some are Seventh-day
Adventists, both groups understanding Christianity in much different frames
from those in the A. M. E. Church. Other family members are Unitarian, a
creedless religion. A couple of folks are Episcopalians, and some are Catholics.
At least a couple of us practice Yoruba religious traditions on top of what we
normally follow. And we're all in one family. My family's experiences are not
unique; rather they are rendered invisible because discussions of pluralism in
African-American religious life flatline in mainstream scholarship.

Religious diversity and religious pluralism are given short shrift as statistically insignificant in black communities and thereby rendered invisible.
The invisibility does not reflect the realities of black religious experiences;
rather, it reflects a preponderance of misleading data that is ultimately based
on the reduction of black people to a pigeon-holed category: aren't all black
folks evangelical and/or Baptist? There are reasons that these erasures happened; there are reasons that new light is beginning to shine on black religious pluralism.

Throughout this chapter, I will use the terms pluralism and diversity interchangeably because black American religious pluralism is bound up with a
primary lack of recognition of religious diversity. I cannot discuss all aspects of
black religious pluralism/diversity but will focus on several areas to encourage
more extensive exploration: the status quo and invisible black American differences; some historic reasons for erasure of black religious diversity; and new
foci on black religious pluralism.

The Status Quo: Invisibility

That black Americans are viewed as a nearly monolithic group is also true for understanding their religious lives. A 2009 report by the Pew Research Center exemplifies this view, presenting what it terms a "religious portrait of African Americans" that underscores an indivisible black-world.[1] Based on data from a Pew Center 2007 survey of American religious life,[2] the authors of the report write that "The vast majority of African-Americans are Protestant (78%), compared with only 51% of the U.S. adult population as a whole. By a wide margin, African-Americans stand out as the most Protestant racial and ethnic group in the U.S."[3] Attempting to expand this vision, the report continues that black folks belong to three Protestant groups: evangelical, historically black, and mainline Protestant churches. Yet, years ago, Martin Luther King, Jr., called Sunday morning the most segregated time in America. That black people attend black churches is not news. One problem with this Pew report is that it sheds no light on the meanings: the numbers are crunched, and humans are absent. The Pew report is a discussion of religion without the contexts of those who are "studied." It continues a scholarly tradition reflected in a comment of novelist and anthropologist Zora Neale Hurston: "I have been amazed by the Anglo-Saxon's lack of curiosity about the internal lives and emotions of the Negroes."[4]

The Pew study's conclusions assume the motivations of those black people who are members of Protestant churches. The questions are never asked: are the Protestant church selections made from among a clear set of worshipping community choices in those black neighborhoods? Have Hindu temples or Buddhist meditation centers, as examples, eschewed opening sites in black communities? Might the absence of other religious networking and affiliation opportunities in black neighborhoods provide one reason why black people are more likely to participate in Protestant or historically black churches? A related conclusion in this report, that black women are more likely to be members of congregations than men, underlines the same point: Are social opportunities—to meet partners or spouses; socially interact; discuss politics; go to dances and dinners; secure social opportunities or Sunday school for offspring in neighborhoods with little public transportation—are these the greatest motivations for black involvement in Protestant religious congregations?

The same unreflective identity compression happens as the Pew report discusses black religious beliefs. "African-Americans also express higher levels of religious belief than do Americans overall. Compared with the population, for instance, African-Americans are more likely to believe in God with absolute certainty...interpret Scripture as the literal word of God...and express a belief in angels and demons."[5] This statement continues the emphasis on the alleged Protestant beliefs held by the majority of black folk. Statements such as these imply an exclusively Christian understanding of terms like "God," "Scripture," "angels," or "demons." But more than this understanding, the terms are used in an undifferentiated way that implies all Christians—black or white, poor or rich, from one denomination to another, and across regions of the country—believe the same things when using these terms. Based on such equivalencies, it is consistent that the Pew report on black people would also contend that black people are more politically conservative, the researchers again equating their ideas of "conservative" with that of all black folk.

When efforts to interview and gauge subjects' meanings do not take place, the meaning that is assigned may merely reflect the researchers' beliefs. A strictly quantitative approach is dangerous in the best of conditions when there is a solid knowledge of the people being studied. When the researchers do not know the definitions and interpretations of the research subjects, the results must be questioned. (In the case of the Pew report, no black religious scholars were included among the authors.) The context for this discussion of religious pluralism in black Americans' lives is still, and sadly, race. The rationale for such a context is found in the ways that African-Americans—black people—are continually constructed to fit white imaginations. Such constructions happen across the social spectrum. Some years ago, an essay written in the *Village Voice* pointed out some interesting distinctions when white and black people perform racialized material: "Whites doing 'black' material...are expected to acknowledge their debt, even by calling themselves blue-eyed soul singers if their derivation is too overt. But blacks doing 'white' material...rarely acknowledge the fact. It would call into question the assumption that whiteness is the core around which everything else revolves."[6] Unstated assumptions and polite avoidance of issues arising from the constructions of race help to maintain the status quo. Ultimately, such research as the Pew "Portrait of African American Religious Life" is skewed and the flaws make it unacceptable to actually define black religious life, much less the existence of pluralism.

It would be generally unacceptable for white researchers to "speak" for black people today—unless it is in the field of religion. Religion can be thought of as performance, as the *Village Voice* essay points out, with whiteness again becoming the core around which everything is supposed to revolve. White standards were used to set so-called American culture, and this includes how Americans should worship; this overarching structure included expectations of African-Americans' behavior. Some reasons that religion continues to be portrayed so narrowly can be found among the popular television and movie renditions of black religious life.

Seldom shown in complex ways, religion is a comedic gold mine for black comedians. Flip Wilson, Richard Pryor, Cedric the Entertainer, and Eddie Murphy have used a stereotypical figure of a black pastor: greedy, licentious, and dishonest. Despite the public ministries of the Reverend Martin Luther King, Jr., or Bishop Desmond Tutu, the stereotyped, silly minister is embedded in the public imagination as representative of black religious life. A stereotyped black religious woman may be portrayed by some male comedians, such as Tyler Perry's Madea, a woman who is masculinized, loud, and demanding. Despite the gospel singing of Mahalia Jackson or the serious witness of praying women in the Civil Rights movement, the image of the ridiculous black religious woman continues.

The inability to "see" the pluralism in African-American religious life is, on one level, consistent with the statement of Zora Neale Hurston about a lack of interest in the internal lives of black people. Taking this idea one step further, the lack of interest creates a vacuum in understanding black life that is filled in with the white imagination's view of black people; thus, the enduring power of stereotypes.

Yet, there is another side to understanding the contemporary views of black American religious life. The social history that helped build current views, especially that construction now called "the black church," requires some attention. This history and a sampling of thinkers who contributed to the black church concept indicate the idea's development. The history and the thinkers built an almost exclusively Christian "black" church. Both history and thinkers indicate other differences from white American Christian theological streams. And both helped to build the blinders to black American religious pluralism.

The Construction of a Monolith

The development of an idea of a normative Christianity in black communities denies the complexities of history. Another way to consider how Christianity became prominent in black communities is through the sociopolitical stories of cash-strapped, socially confined people. Racial segregation was a powerful force for the creation of an image of black people stripped of diversity, imagination, and creativity. Conversely, that image was also motivation for blacks to resist the dehumanization of enslavement. Plantation owners, politicians, and white religious leaders began questioning the suitability of baptizing enslaved Africans; to do so could (and did) lead to rebellious slaves being able to hold regular meetings on Sunday, further spreading rebellion. Instead, white leaders attempted to develop catechisms for the black communities, enforcing the divinely sanctioned status of "obedient" slaves. But, as black religious historian Gayraud Wilmore pointed out, enslaved Africans took another path:

> Despite the deliberate distortion of Christian doctrine and stringent restrictions upon religious activity, a distinctive African-American form of Christianity—actually the new religion of an oppressed people—slowly took root in the black community. This black folk religion contained a definite moral judgment against slavery and a clear legitimation of resistance to injustice....It was the slaves' African past that did the most to influence their style of religious life, their rejection of the spiritual and political despotism of the whites.[7]

It could be said, therefore, that the beginnings of religious pluralism in black American communities happened in the experiences of enslaved Africans in their encounters with Christianity. The resulting "Christianity" was not that of the plantation owners, and these differences are still not understood widely.

Throughout American history, black Christian churches were sources of support for black communities from enslavement through Jim Crow, providing

community organization, news, and political information. Black denominations were the forces behind most historically black colleges, networks of
elementary schools and hospitals, all important for the Jim Crow era of legal
segregation. Black preaching and musical styles developed consistently with
black cultures; again, legal segregation ensured maintenance of black cultures.
Even as many white Americans viewed black religious styles with disdain,
black Americans found in religious life a home, a haven, a refuge from what
happens in the rest of the world.

To build well-grounded discussions of black pluralism and religious diversity, the construction and use of the term "the black church" must be considered. The term has a significant history and speaks in particular ways to black
Americans. In some ways the "black church" could be considered a construction of the late twentieth century; earlier references did not use that term. But
the analysis of religious life was central for African-American scholars.

In 1921, Carter G. Woodson wrote one of the first histories of the Negro
Church. Standing in the Jim Crow era among survivors of enslavement,
Woodson considered the conservative and the progressive sides of Christian
churches as the main analytical streams for his time. The difference between
conservative and progressive, he believed, was found in the degree of social
activism promoted by the church. The conservative church, under Woodson's
definition, wanted only to promote a life of prayer and thankfulness to God.
"The conservatives believed that the individual should sacrifice all for the
church. On Sunday, they would come from afar to swell the chorus of the
faithful, and there they would remain during the day, leaving their net earn-
ings in the hands of management, given at the cost of a sacrifice placed on a
common altar."[8]

Woodson's concepts of conservative or progressive church members were
based upon how, coming from different traditions, they approached living in
the United States under oppressive conditions. Progressive religious ideas
in particular extended into the political sphere. So Denmark Vesey planned
and implemented the beginnings of a rebellion of the enslaved population in
1822 through the A. M. E. church in Charleston, South Carolina. Throughout
American history, black activists often used religion as the basis from which
they called for an end to enslavement and later Jim Crow, all forms of oppression including violence and racism.

The conservative strand of religious life that Woodson identified had an
important purpose, despite how often it was decried by black people (on the
progressive side) as inhibiting black American resistance to oppression. The
so-called conservative black folk may not have been as mindless and fearful as
they are portrayed. Their insistence on quiet, on letting God alone take care
of any problems, or seeming compliance offered a form of black resistance
against oppression and even hope for some members in a climate where any
sign of active resistance to enslavement, segregation, social marginalization,
and extremely limited life options could mean a violent death. In other words,
powerlessness definitely shaped black Americans' religious lives, in one way

or another. Religion became a way to reflect on powerlessness and oppression and, hopefully, to chart a course into fuller citizenship and realized freedom.

Relations with white Americans and power structures were not alone enough to create what is referred to as the black church. The cultures that helped to shape a people played a significant role in the constructions of religious life. Like the conservative/progressive approaches, the links with culture began before the end of enslavement. A seminal study of slave culture by Sterling Stuckey more than 60 years after Woodson's included a focus on an African religious dance ceremony as being pivotal for defining black culture:

> Wherever in Africa the counterclockwise dance ceremony was performed—it is called the ring shout in North America—the dancing and singing were directed to the ancestors and gods, the tempo and revolution of the circle quickening during the course of movement. The ring in which Africans danced and sang is the key to understanding the means by which they achieved oneness in America.[9]

With these words, Stuckey isolated key elements of the cultural basis of black religious life, which are important for understanding the layers behind the conservative/progressive concepts. The ring shout in particular identified something that had been a source of argument among scholars of black life: whether or not there was a real link to be found between black people in the United States and those on the continent of Africa. One line of argument had been that black Americans had a distance of centuries away from the shores of Africa, had endured enslavement, and had lost other facets of culture, such as language. But Stuckey's demonstration strengthened the other line of argument, that there was a link with Africa, and so scholars could interpret aspects of black culture in new ways. His work was critical for African-American scholars of religion, providing a basis with which to explore the "invisible institution," as black Christian churches were called, since before Emancipation.

Stuckey was not the first or only scholar to explore African-American culture and roots in relation to religion. Arthur Huff Fauset, for instance, wrote *Black Gods of the Metropolis: Negro Cults of the Metropolis*—now considered a classic—in 1944. The title indicates the book's tendency to view different black religions, such as Father Divine's 1920s New York ministry, and to identify how black people used religions to further their own ideas.[10] The author, an anthropologist, has left a record of black religious movements that we would otherwise have lost. Fauset's approach was based on interviews and extensive time spent with members of different religious bodies. In the foreword to the 2001 edition of the work, Barbara Dianne Savage points explicitly to its exposition of African-American religious variety: "The historical significance of Arthur Fauset's work endures. This book still teaches much about the appeal of black religious sects and the spiritual creativity that drove them. The work stands as a reminder of the religious diversity that existed among African-Americans then and now." Savage also cautions that terms like "black church" and "black religion" often "obscure more than they illuminate."[11]

Some extant records of black religious creativity and diversity are found in the Library of Congress Works Progress Administration collections. Other records that can be found at some historically black colleges, such as Hampton, add a bit more information. Other than the Fauset book, though, additional records may be difficult to locate.

There is one exception readily available today. Anthropologist Zora Neale Hurston researched black religious life in the South. Many of her papers were never published, although she sharply defined cultural distinctions of African-Americans' religious thought. A slim volume published in 1981 paints a portrait of black religious life that is grounded in a cultural view, some of which can be traced to African conceptualizations.[12]

The 1950s and 1960s created new opportunities for African-Americans to attend white universities and colleges, some continuing on to get doctorates and becoming part of the wider mainstream scholarship in new ways. Among the scholars who deconstructed racist religious views and reconstructed theological statements pertinent to black communities was James H. Cone, whose *Black Power and Black Theology* was written in 1969.[13] As the title indicates, Cone brought a theological reflection to the concept of black power, one that he deemed critically important to understand even as he observed at the book's beginning that "some religionists would consider Black Power as the work of the Antichrist."[14] This distance between what black communities identify as important and what remains invisible to scholars or "some religionists" is continued with the Pew report. Cone's book served as a watershed in theological scholarship because he brought the people's conversations into the academy.

The 1970s and 1980s saw the beginning of the exploration of African-American religious thought in multiple ways from the perspectives of black Americans. George Eaton Simpson's *Black Religions in the New World*,[15] for instance, discussed religious lineages, drawing from history and linking enslaved Africans with the regions on the African continent from which they were taken. Simpson identified a diversity of black religions beyond Christianity, including African traditions and their hybridized presences in various forms of Christianity.

It was during this 1970s–1980s time frame that the term "the black church" moved into common usage. C. Eric Lincoln, a preeminent scholar of black religion, declared the death of the Negro Church as he identified sweeping social and political changes, including civil rights and black power movements, along with the growth of black theology and the Nation of Islam. "The Negro Church accepted death in order to be reborn. Out of the ashes of its funeral pyre there sprang the bold, strident, self-conscious phoenix that is the contemporary black Church."[16]

The concept of the black church was empowering to black communities that were struggling with the post–Civil Rights world of the 1970s and 1980s. The images of an institution that belonged to black communities, stretching back through history, establishing norms for dealing with the present and the future, were powerful for black communities. The structure and identification of this black church powerhouse may have created stereotypes in many white minds, but black imaginations were also captured by these visions. The concept of the black church gathered a sense of "we" into African-Americans' consciousness. This location of religion under a black church rubric became an enduring center of black identity construction.

Differences in religious beliefs in black communities were ignored as a mythical unity was proclaimed among black American community members. Yet, such proclamations were not true. Even differences among Christians were ignored. Black Catholics, whose historical lineage in the United States is actually older than that of black Protestants, often felt excluded by the "black-church-equals-Protestant" equation. Black Americans ignored differences of beliefs in favor of honoring the potent and poetic black church concept construction. Among white Americans and the general public, black religious differences were further suppressed by the general climate of stereotypes, aided and abetted by their distribution throughout the media.

In the twenty-first century, a groundbreaking introduction to "Black Church Studies" attempted to broaden the lens and to encompass a wide range of black religious thought. The authors provide this framework: "For the sake of simplicity and efficacy, the term *Black Church* became a euphemistic generalization for the collective identity of African American Christians in both academic and societal contexts."[17] The authors present the black church in global terms, not just a United States' construction: "The term...moves beyond historic, denominational affiliations and toward a more expansive understanding of the Black Church as an African Diasporan reality."[18]

Black communities, even when confessing Christianity, have never been monolithic. Certainly, communities are shaped by social systems, but black communities have parallel yet distinctive histories of oppression that produce additional components. Regional differences contribute to differing cultural frameworks regardless of race, but race still ties black Americans into a group. How can black religious life be studied in a way that will account for the rich differences and not collapse black people into a single unit? Black scholars have continued to explore questions that began with James Cone's reflections on the life of the folks who are religious. When will insights from years of black theological analysis become part of mainstream scholarship?

In the meantime, scholars of black religion have been making the internal pluralism of African-American communities much clearer. Building on the work of such thinkers as historian Carter G. Woodson or sociologist C. Eric Lincoln, drawing from other disciplines such as anthropology, ethnography, and literature, some scholars of black religion are uncovering the dynamism of black religious life. The authors of *Black Church Studies: An Introduction* make this statement: "For our purposes, we consider the Black Church tradition not as a fixed historical product but rather a *fluid historic process* in which Black Christians engage one another, invent, embrace, and inherit this tradition that they argue over and care deeply about."[19] Pointing out the fluidity and historicity of "the Black Church tradition" recognizes the differences and dynamism within black religious life. There is need, however, for more explicit and intense analysis of the differences, including religious pluralism.

A Call to Reconsider Black American Religious Pluralism

But might a different definition of pluralism be needed in order to encompass black religious life? An example that points to the need is found in American black gospel music. Gospel is a form often identified with black Christianity. In fact, black gospel music may be more cultural than theological or dogmatic. The language of black gospel music indicates the different theology, called by Gayraud Wilmore "a distinctive African-American form of Christianity—actually the new religion of an oppressed people." Gospel music, while considered Christian, might be about the human condition, as one popular song focuses on getting up after we fall. This kind of nonspecific but reflective gospel lyric stretches back to the spirituals. For instance, a song about feeling like a motherless child is not a specifically Christian theological concept. I have seen non-theologically specific gospel music used during one black American Yoruba-derived worship service. Prosperity churches in black communities change the lyrics but keep the rhythm to draw in members and emphasize their own theologies. Perhaps pluralism needs to incorporate analyses of culture as integral to the shape of religious lives.

In his day Carter Woodson analyzed the Negro Church from the aspect of conservative or progressive. That lineage has continued, sometimes even leaning toward alternatives that move beyond the progressive. An example is the Shrine of Black Madonna, a church that split off from a United Church of Christ community in the 1970s in Detroit, Michigan. The Shrine is black nationalist and understands itself as the inheritor of Harlem Renaissance era Marcus Garvey's African Orthodox Christianity. The Shrine now has communities in Houston and Atlanta as well as some landholdings in South Carolina. That leadership of the church drew from black culture and the social/personal yearnings of the black communities. Global political contexts are taken into account deliberately as part of the church's theological reflection. The church uses social developments to craft its theological meanings, remaining true to its black nationalist roots. The analysis of race remains central to their theology and ritual, a continuing concern across the arc of history and the oppressions of enslavement. While race is often excluded from consideration of pluralism, is it not always invisible in most analyses and constructions? Perhaps, as with black analyses, it is time to address racial content through any religious pluralist analyses. Theologian James Cone challenges this invisibility: "From the time I was conscious of being black and Christian, I recognized that I was a problem for America's white politicians and invisible to most of its practitioners of religion."[20] To what degree do constructions of pluralism treat race as if it has no meaning in constructions of pluralism?

The economic power of black churches also creates some important differences among them. As Shondrah Nash and Cedric Herring have stated, "The black church has been a primary source of economic and community development as well as empowerment in cities and towns across the United States."[21] Yet, despite its importance to black American religions, a solid analysis of the pluralism and diversity through the lens of economics has yet to be developed.

One other aspect must be raised for future explorations of black religious pluralism: the exploration of religious dynamics that are not Christian. One author, Anthony Pinn, has drawn attention to African-American religious practices beyond Christian borders. He turned the call for analyzing black religious pluralism on other black religious scholars when he stated, "The narrow agenda and resource base of contemporary African American theological reflection troubles me because it limits itself to Christianity in ways that establish Christian doctrine and concerns as normative."[22] In *Varieties of African American Religious Experience*, Pinn discusses Vodou, Santería, Islam, and Humanism in detail, presenting views of black religious life that have nothing to do with Christianity. All of these traditions warrant extensive examination in themselves, but they also raise a question: is it time to avoid using typologies as the primary way to analyze religions? Is there an approach to discussing pluralism that does not lionize or diminish one particular religion and yet provides greater intelligibility about the human capacity for belief and spiritual growth?

Reconsidering black American religious pluralism, then, I am suggesting that four notes should be included in future analyses. Culture should be taken into account, especially as it creates differences in religious understandings. Race should be a component in future analyses. The constructions of religious pluralism or diversity through economics have played an important role in black religions and need to be incorporated in future analyses. Finally, the veil of invisibility should be removed from black religious pluralism by recognizing that black people are more than only Christian and that other aspects of our religious lives need analysis.

Notes

1 Pew Research Center Forum on Religion and Public Life, "A Religious Portrait of African-Americans," released January 30, 2009, http://pewforum.org/A-Religious-Portrait-of-African-Americans, accessed August 2010.

2 Pew Research Center Forum on Religion and Public Life, *U.S. Religious Landscape Survey: Religious Affiliation: Diverse and Dynamic* (Pew Research Center: Washington, DC, 2008). The poll was conducted in 2007 and is available at http://religions.pewforum.org/pdf/report-religious-landscape-study-full.pdf.

3 Pew Research Center Forum, "A Religious Portrait of African-Americans," released January 30, 2009, http://www.pewforum.org/a-religious-portrait-of-africa n-americans.aspx.

4 Zora Neale Hurston, "What White Publishers Won't Print," in *I Love Myself When I am Laughing...And Then Again When I Am Looking Mean and Impressive: A Zora Neale Hurston Reader*, Alice Walker, ed. (New York: The Feminist Press, 1979), 169.

5 Pew Research Forum, "Religious Portrait of African-Americans."

6 Richard Goldstein, "White Shtick," *Village Voice*, December 17, 1996, 49.

7 Gayraud S. Wilmore, *Black Religion and Black Radicalism: An Interpretation of the Religious History of Afro-American People*, 2nd ed. (Maryknoll, NY: Orbis Books, 1993), 25–26.

8 Carter G. Woodson, *The History of the Negro Church* (Washington, DC: The Associated Publishers, 1921), 251.

9 Sterling Stuckey, *Slave Culture: Nationalist Theory and the Foundations of Black America* (New York: Oxford University Press, 1987), 12.

10 Arthur Huff Fauset, *Black Gods of the Metropolis: Negro Cults in the Urban North* (Philadelphia: University of Pennsylvania Press, 1944).

11 Barbara Dianne Savage, "Foreword" to the 2001 edition, *Black Gods of the Metropolis*, xvi.

12 Zora Neale Hurston, *The Sanctified Church* (Berkeley, CA: Turtle Island Foundation, 1981).

13 James H. Cone, *Black Power and Black Theology* (New York: Seabury Press, 1969).

14 Cone, *Black Power and Black Theology*, 1.

15 George Eaton Simpson, *Black Religions in the New World* (New York: Columbia University Press, 1978).

16 C. Eric Lincoln, *The Negro Church in America/The Black Church Since Frazier* (New York: Schocken Books, 1974), 105.

17 Stacey Floyd-Thomas, Juan Floyd-Thomas, Carol B. Duncan, Stephen G. Ray, and Nancy Westfield, *Black Church Studies: An Introduction* (Nashville, TN: Abingdon Press, 2007), xxiv.

18 Floyd-Thomas, et al., *Black Church Studies*, xxiv.

19 Ibid., emphasis mine.

20 James H. Cone, *Risks of Faith: The Emergence of a Black Theology of Liberation, 1968–1998* (Boston: Beacon Press, 1999), xii.

21 Shondrah Nash and Cedric Herring, "The Black Church and Community Economic Development," in *African Americans in the U. S. Economy*, Cecilia A. Conrad, John Whitehead, Patrick Mason, and James Stewart, eds. (Lanham, MD: Rowman and Littlefield, 2005), 363.

22 Anthony B. Pinn, *Varieties of African American Religious Experience* (Minneapolis, MN: Fortress Press, 1998), 1.

PART V | Impact of Religious Pluralism: II

CHAPTER 13

From Consensus to Struggle:
Pluralism and the Body Politic
in Contemporary America

CHARLES H. LIPPY

"FROM THE PLANTING OF the Virginia and Plymouth colonies forward, professions of faith in God—usually what George Washington called 'that Almighty Being who rules over the universe'—have been at the center of the country's public life."[1] So wrote Jon Meacham in the opening chapter of his best-selling *American Gospel: God, the Founding Fathers, and the Making of a Nation*. Meacham went on to note that this intricate and intimate link between faith and public life, between religion and politics, should be no surprise, despite the proverbial etiquette mavens who urge sophisticated folk to avoid discussion of either in polite company. Indeed, the heritage stemming from those English colonies that first formed the United States has disproportionately drawn on religious images most common among the New England Puritans to create a sense of what the American people are all about. In popular perception, the American enterprise was an exodus from the Old World akin to Israel's leaving Egypt for a promised land and its people also chosen by God to be an example to the entire world. Even if at first the physical location of the nation lay along the Atlantic coast, it was its manifest destiny, guided by divine providence, to span the continent.[2]

Jon Meacham explained this connection between religion and national identity by pointing out that the American is, after all, what Mircea Eliade called *homo religiosus*, a being who naturally looks beyond the self for a canopy of meaning for both personal and collective existence. Meacham might also have pointed out, as did Eliade, that *homo religiosus* necessarily seeks to plant an *axis mundi*, literally a pole on which the earth rotates. For the preindustrial societies that Eliade studied, that center of meaning was often an object or place, but one that would be fixed anew should people move to a different location. Eliade's conceptuality retains import even for urban, industrial societies such as that of the United States, but for those cultures the *axis mundi* is more a focal point for meaning and identity, a symbolic center of ideas and images around which to orient and organize common life. Like an *axis mundi* of old, this symbolic cluster serves as a link to the realm of the gods or, in the American context, God.[3]

These observations serve as a useful backdrop for examining the curious and evolving relationship between religion and the body politic in the United States over roughly the last half century. I shall look at how leaders, both religious and political, crafted images of the religious character of the United States to promote particular notions of national identity and, to use Eliade's term, to construct an *axis mundi* around which Americans could find a world of meaning for their shared experience as Americans. Not all of these efforts have endured, and sometimes the proposed images clashed with empirical reality.

One continuing source of potential conflict comes from the increasing religious diversity or pluralism that has marked American life since the close of World War II. Of course, scholars are not of a single mind themselves in understanding precisely what words such as diversity and pluralism connote. Some use them interchangeably, since both suggest simply "more than one" of a kind exists. Others see diversity as a term that implies a sometimes reluctant toleration of variations of a single theme (in the American context, perhaps religious groups emerging from the orbit of Judaism and Christianity). For them, pluralism includes a positive affirmation of the goodness not just of diversity, but of a multiplicity of religious truths. This chapter presumes first that both point to the empirical reality that multiple religious options exist in the United States. It also presumes that as those options expand, particularly as they move beyond the strands of Christianity and Judaism foundational to the American experience, a more thoroughgoing pluralism prevails, for then there may be vastly different religious worlds in conversation, if not competition. Another source of potential conflict is the expanding number of visions for the nation within the body politic itself, many of which draw on religious images and ideals. What American national identity means for a Back Bay Boston brahmin long accustomed to wealth and power may be radically different from what it suggests to the undocumented Latino/a immigrant working for minimum wage or less as an unskilled laborer. So, too, how one views one's place in the body politic differs according to circumstances.

As I probe this delicate connection, my argument is that, first, in the decade and a half or so following the close of the Second World War, the tone of that relationship was to emphasize unity—sometimes perhaps a veneer of unity—while affirming a selective religious diversity. The *axis mundi* offered by key political and religious figures fixed the United States as a righteous nation with a unique relationship with God. But midway through the 1950s and surely through the turbulent 1960s, the theme became one of reluctantly acknowledging disunity when it came to our common life, but a disunity that prevailed amid an expanding religious diversity. The *axis mundi* crafted after the war no longer functioned to provide meaning, and a new constellation of shared images had not yet emerged. Out of that lack of a center of meaning emerged the third motif that, with some earlier roots, came to the fore by the middle of the seventies, with mass circulation magazines dubbing 1976, the year marking the bicentennial of the United States as an independent republic, as also "the year of the evangelical."[4] That motif reveals a contrived unity masking diversity. A "moral majority," as some called it, but one propelled by religious forces, staked a claim to dominance in political life as it attempted to recast the *axis mundi* that had served so well in the 1950s. However, this effort to refurbish an old sense of national identity ultimately failed, for it was predicated on the continuing cultural dominance of those explicit religious traditions that in the 1950s had clustered under the rubric of the Judeo-Christian tradition. By the dawn of this century, the religious diversity was rapidly continuing its metamorphosis into a pluralism that went beyond strands of Christianity and Judaism. That metamorphosis was giving a painful and often awkward birth to a fourth pattern in the relationship between religion and the body politic. This pattern represents the struggle to find and affirm a common ground, a sense of political unity, an *axis mundi* for the American *homo religiosus*, when an ever-expanding pluralism has stripped the collective life and experience of the American people of a shared religious base. In other words, the question today is whether it is even possible to find a symbolic cluster of images that gives an overarching meaning to the common life of all the peoples called American.

Informing this argument are several underlying notions. Most important is the assumption that although those who seek to lead, shape, or interpret American common life may attempt to construct a constellation of symbolic images (an *axis mundi*) that they believe will give meaning to the shared experience of the body politic, no single set of images will function this way for every single person. Dissenting views are part of the overall picture, although they cannot be dissected carefully in what follows. Likewise there has never been a single perception of national identity.

A cognate assumption is that this *axis mundi* and national identity exist in a symbiotic relationship. They are not identical, but they are intertwined. In one sense, both are artificial constructs offered by those in positions of power as ways to legitimate their own understanding of the meaning of the American nation. Some are more compelling than others because they resonate more with the lived experience of greater numbers of people. Likewise, some will falter because they lack such a correlation with lived experience. Nonetheless, the effort to make sense out of what it means to be an American and how that identity gains plausibility in part through its appeal to religious images, through a symbolic *axis mundi*, remain central to the American experience of fusing many peoples into one body politic. At the same time, the ever-growing diversity and expanding pluralism challenge all attempts to do so simply because the more diverse the worldviews of different clusters of Americans become, the more difficult it is to reach consensus or to formulate a notion of shared identity that actually grips the nation as a whole.

Unity amid Selective Diversity

On that cold January morning in 1953 when Dwight Eisenhower took the oath of office as the first Republican president elected in nearly a quarter of a century, the nation hushed as the war hero turned university president and now politician called the American people to prayer before beginning his formal address. Although by the last inauguration in 2013 it had become commonplace to include multiple formal prayers by a host of religious figures presumably representing the array of faiths practiced by Americans, when Eisenhower offered his brief prayer in 1953, he injected into the inaugural ceremony a rite that had never been there before. The content of the prayer pales in comparison to its symbolic import, for it signified to the whole world that religion and the body politic in the United States were far from strange bedfellows, but belonged together. They were two sides of the same coin, as it were. More importantly, this alliance between a simple expression of religious faith and political life marked what set apart the United States and its mission in the world from its archenemy in the Cold War era, the communism—often the "godless" communism—of the expanding Soviet empire.[5]

Eisenhower's action at his first inaugural ceremony points to the initial theme, the stress on political unity amid a selective religious diversity. At the time, few Americans knew much if anything about Eisenhower's personal faith; he had yet to become a church member, although he soon affiliated with the National Presbyterian Church in Washington. Eisenhower regularly had prayer at cabinet meetings, and at one point, he is reputed to have claimed that American government "makes no sense unless it is founded on a deeply felt religious faith—and I don't care what it is."[6] Although historians of religion have often made light of this latter statement, it highlights the need to push for some kind of unity in common life, an *axis mundi* for the body politic, while affirming that there may well be some differences that prevail when it comes to personal appropriation of religious faith. If godless communism were even more dangerous than the recently defeated Hitler and his cohorts, it was essential to have at least a semblance of common identity, of shared values, in the political realm in the United States.

Thus, in 1954, in a move still debated today, the Congress enacted legislation that added the two words "under God" to the Pledge of Allegiance to the flag. It was as important not to define the word God doctrinally as it was to have the word inserted into the pledge. Any effort at definition would have revealed the diversity that prevailed among religious traditions, among denominations, among congregations, and surely among the 150 million individuals called American. But when all said those two words, there was a sense of shared values, of common identity, of national unity. The nation had a symbolic *axis mundi*. That same year, other legislation extended to all U.S. coins and currency the words that had appeared on some for many years: "in God we trust."

The push in the public arena to stress unity over difference, regardless of any overt political intention, is also evident in what pundits of the day called mainline Protestantism. Over the centuries, mainline bodies had sometimes engaged in fierce debates over issues of doctrine and practice, such as whether to baptize infants or whether one's eternal destiny was a matter of free will or predestination, but in the decade and a half after the end of World War II, such matters were seldom part of public discourse. In the age of expanding suburbia, mainline Protestant bodies muted their differences; ecumenism or cooperation became the ideal. Consequently, such bodies began to lose their distinctive identities, at least in the popular mind, and in many respects were regarded pretty much as equivalent to one another.

Three examples illuminate this mainline surge toward emphasizing unity. One was the reorganization in 1950 into the National Council of Churches of what had formerly been the Federal Council of Churches. This body, with ties to the World Council of Churches formed in 1948, allowed mainline Protestant bodies to speak with a common voice, share concerns, and work together—sometimes in areas of social justice and welfare that drew adherents directly into the political arena. The symbol of this ecumenical spirit was the construction of the Interchurch Center in New York City, with President Dwight Eisenhower participating in the ceremonies marking its cornerstone laying and dedication. The political and the religious sectors were thus brought together in a show of common identity. Across the nation, state and local councils of churches, as well as interfaith agencies, augmented this ecumenical mood, directly and indirectly supporting the perception that the United States was a bastion of faith and righteousness, in contrast to godless communism.[7] Perhaps the most vibrant signal of this ecumenical ethos came in 1960 when the Presbyterian Eugene Carson Blake, a noted leader in interdenominational cooperation, issued a call in tandem with Episcopal bishop James Pike in a sermon at San Francisco's Grace Cathedral for American Protestant bodies to move toward organic union, not just working together to promote common interests; that call in turn gave birth to the Consultation on Church Union and then, in a later incarnation, to the Churches of Christ Uniting.[8]

The second illustration comes into focus with the publication in 1955 of Will Herberg's classic *Protestant, Catholic, Jew: An Essay in American Religious Sociology*.[9] Herberg himself in many ways represents the move toward consensus when it came to the public and therefore political expression of religion. A onetime labor union organizer and a Jew by religious identity, Herberg was a professor at a Methodist theological school when this seminal work appeared. One strand of his argument asserted that by mid-century, it no longer made any practical difference in the public arena whether one was identified with any of the many strains of Protestantism, with Roman Catholicism, or with one of the branches of Judaism; in the public square, all were seen (along with the Eastern Orthodox Christian tradition) as nurturing adherents in the sort of ethical and moral values that made one a good citizen. Religious identity thus became a badge of trustworthiness—regardless of what that label was. The other major strand of Herberg's thesis is perhaps more unsettling. As one groomed in the biblical heritage, Herberg bemoaned this sort of amalgamation that he found most obviously manifested in what he dubbed the "religion of the American way of life" with its roots in a capitalist economic system that sacralized conspicuous consumption.

The final illustration is more symbolic. In 1954, evangelist Billy Graham launched a crusade in a Britain that was still in the throes of recovering from the ravages of World War II. Already becoming a household name in the United States, Graham gained international stature as a result of this revival campaign. In 1957, he took his crusade to New York City, holding daily rallies for several months at Madison Square Garden and capping the event with an outdoor service at Yankee Stadium. A Southern Baptist by birth and inclination, Graham intentionally sought out endorsement for his evangelistic endeavors from a wide array of religious leaders across the Christian spectrum; the New York City campaign, for example, relied heavily on the support of what was then called the Protestant Council of the City of New York, an ecumenical agency. By inviting leaders from a host of particular denominations to join him on the platform at preaching services, Graham advanced the perception that unity superseded diversity. When his preaching repeatedly and vigorously assailed enemies to national well-being, from juvenile delinquency to the communist menace, it became clear why: Righteousness marked American common life in a stunning way. Graham also fused the religious and the political, becoming personally acquainted with every U.S. president from Harry Truman on and, while his health permitted, often blessing the political sector by appearing at inaugurations to offer prayer, regardless of the particular political party of the president (once prayers became standard components of the celebration).[10]

Different religious bodies still existed, to be sure, and diversity lurked beneath the surface. But the veneer of unity prevailed to a large degree because of its political utility in promoting a sense of a common American identity. The difference beneath the surface percolated in 1960 when the Democratic Party nominated John F. Kennedy, a lifelong Roman Catholic, for the presidency of the United States. In 1928, a scant generation earlier, when the first Roman Catholic received the nomination of a major political party, the campaign unleashed some vitriolic anti-Catholic sentiment that no doubt contributed to the victory in that election of the Republican Herbert Hoover. But things were different in 1960. There was still a murmuring of anti-Catholic fear and concern, a sign that some uncertainty over how to deal with diversity remained, but Kennedy was able to quell much of that when he openly proclaimed that his personal religious faith was entirely a matter of the private sphere that would in no way have bearing on his political agenda or in any way influence decisions he would make as president. In a stunning speech delivered to members of the Greater Houston Ministerial Association in Texas, folk presumed likely to harbor anti-Catholic sentiments, Kennedy drew a sharp contrast between religion and politics, between personal faith that was a private matter and public leadership that was part of the common life of the whole people. "I believe in an America that is officially neither Catholic, Protestant, or Jewish," Kennedy insisted, "where no public official either requests or accepts instructions on public policy from the pope, the National Council of Churches, or any other ecclesiastical source—where no religious body seeks to impose its will directly or indirectly upon the general public or the public acts of its officials—and where religious liberty is so indivisible that an act against one church is treated as an act against all."[11] In retrospect, the insistence on a divide between religion and the body politic, that affirmation of a political *axis mundi* and shared identity that acknowledged a selective but muted religious diversity linked to personal identity, may have allowed Kennedy to achieve a narrow victory over Richard Nixon when voters went to the polls. When Kennedy took the oath of office on the Capitol steps in 1961, the unity that allowed Americans to stand as one in the face of godless communism was paramount, as was the nod to diversity that came as Boston's Richard Cardinal Cushing implored divine blessing on the nation and the fledgling administration in a lengthy inaugural prayer.

By the time of that historic inauguration, there were ample signs in American life that the united front provided by interfaith ecumenical cooperation and the political necessity of bolstering national consensus to withstand godless communism in the Cold War was crumbling. The *axis mundi* fixed in the years after World War II that celebrated the unity of Protestants, Catholics, and Jews who were part of "one nation under God" was about to collapse and cease to provide a symbolic center for the American body politic. Indeed, the roots of a political disunity amid expanding religious diversity were about to end the illusion of a single framework of meaning for the nation and all its peoples. Perhaps there could no longer be one understanding of national identity that had widespread support or one framework of meaning for the American body politic. Religious images and religious language might still permeate the public sphere, but without the consensus that marked an age when a righteous America was pitted against a godless communism.

Disunity amid Expanding Diversity

In December 1955, the same year that sociologist Will Herberg argued that there was a functional unity among the major religious traditions in the United States in their promotion of the common good, Rosa Parks refused to give up her seat on a Montgomery, Alabama, bus. Her action marks the symbolic beginning of the modern civil rights movement that challenged political authority and the legal status quo throughout the nation, building on the landmark Supreme Court decision of 1954 (*Brown v. Board of Education*) that declared "separate but equal" unconstitutional in its reversal of the decision issued in *Plessy v. Ferguson* in 1896. But the civil rights movement was much more than simply an effort to dismantle legalized segregation and recall the body politic to its foundation in liberty and equality. It was also intertwined with religion in a variety of ways.

The leadership of the civil rights movement came largely from the ranks of the clergy and from members of religious bodies, both African-American and white. The Rev. Martin Luther King, Jr., pastor of Dexter Avenue Baptist Church in Montgomery when Parks's defiance of local law launched a long boycott of public transit there, and his Southern Christian Leadership Conference are only the most obvious examples. Countless religious leaders joined in demonstrations and sit-ins; northern white seminarians lost their lives when they attempted to organize efforts to register black voters in the South. Those who steadfastly refused to abandon racist ways also often turned to religious worldviews to justify their opposition to ending legalized segregation.[12] Godless communism remained a national threat, but the racial divide in the nation became the more immediate sign that American democracy, the political being of the nation, was in peril.

Martin Luther King took the movement to the symbolic center of national political life with the March on Washington in the summer of 1963. His oration at the Lincoln Memorial, like virtually all of his civil rights speeches, was packed with religious and biblical imagery. Coming scant months before the assassination of President John F. Kennedy, the March on Washington transformed the civil rights movement into a religious revival even as it spawned alternative modes of action that were more radical and drew on rather different religious visions of the nation. Malcolm X, the fiery Black Muslim leader prior to his personal participation in the annual pilgrimage to Mecca, was one of those more strident voices.

Churches and other religious institutions were as divided as the nation. The public watched with anguish, for example, as two Methodist bishops (one Euro-American and one African-American) were arrested as they attempted to enter the Galloway Memorial Methodist Church in Jackson, Mississippi, to worship on Easter Sunday 1964.[13] In 1964, the General Conference of the Methodist Church took steps to begin dismantling an administrative structure based on racial separation. Yet, as scores of later commentators recalled, King pointed out, likely quoting his Morehouse College mentor Benjamin E. Mays, that the worship hour on Sunday mornings remained the most segregated time of the week.[14] Members of the revived Ku Klux Klan drew as well on their religious heritage in the calls to sustain a racially separated republic. Was there an *axis mundi* orienting the life of the body politic?

Complicating the matter was the mounting apprehension over American military engagement in Southeast Asia, popularly dubbed the Vietnam War. Protest against political policies that repeatedly called for an expanded war effort tapped into the same religious reservoir as the civil rights movement. The nation watched in horror as Roman Catholic priests such as the brothers Daniel and Philip Berrigan, nuns, and others broke into offices housing Selective Service System records and destroyed files. In an address delivered on April 4, 1967, at New York City's Riverside Church, across the street from the Interchurch Center, Martin Luther King linked the war protest movement to the civil rights enterprise, proclaiming that both racism and the war effort signaled that a moral decay had polluted the nation's political life, tainting all programs and endeavors.[15] If the ecumenical movement in the 1950s stood as a beacon for a united front pitting American political integrity against a morally bankrupt, godless communism, the formation of the interfaith Clergy and Laity Concerned about Vietnam crossed barriers of denomination and faith to become the ecumenical emblem of increasingly strident opposition to political ploys to promote the war effort. Disunity, rooted in both religious and political difference and dissent, seemed to have replaced the unity of "one nation under God" of the previous decade.

Alongside these currents came a series of Supreme Court decisions in the 1960s and early 1970s that affirmed the increasing religious diversity within the nation and sought creatively, but often in painfully convoluted ways, to apply the principles captured in the First Amendment to the Constitution to a social and political context that was becoming ever more diverse. The controversial decisions in 1962 (*Engel v. Vitale*) and 1963 (*Abington v. Schempp*) that banned required devotional prayer and mandatory reading of the Bible in the nation's public schools in one sense simply acknowledged that the rich diversity of religions and religious belief systems precluded privileging any one, even if it were the artificial and amorphous Judeo-Christian tradition that had long provided a sacred canopy of meaning for the body politic. For those who feared the courts were legislating morality (or immorality), the most shocking Supreme Court decision came in 1973 when the majority ruled in *Roe v. Wade* that many of the laws restricting a woman's access to abortion were unconstitutional. In time a host of religious voices would come together as "pro-life" opponents of this decision, claiming that abortion was little short of legalized murder. Some of the "pro-choice" voices also had religious roots, drawing on the second-wave feminism unleashed by the civil rights movement as it moved into religious communities in calls for the ordination of women to professional ministry as well as claims that there was a religious right for women to choose whether to bear a child.

In the midst of all the disarray, disorder, and disunity came a growing intrigue with religious traditions and practices associated with Asia that reshaped the diversity and pluralism at the heart of American religious life. As with cognate shifts, this one also had ramifications for American political culture. Fascination with Asian philosophy and religion in itself was not entirely new. The Transcendentalist writers and thinkers of the nineteenth century, for example, delved into Asian religious texts, but their interest was largely intellectual. Immigrants from China and Japan had brought their indigenous religions with them to the West Coast, yet their influence remained small thanks to early restriction on that immigration, a willingness to adapt the familiar to American models, and then—especially during the years of World War II—overt hostility and internment. The presence of representatives of non-Western religions at the World's Parliament of Religions held in Chicago in 1893 in conjunction with the Columbian Exposition introduced more Americans to Asian ways of thinking and being religious, especially when some, such as Vivekananda, went on a lecture circuit of American cities and founded groups like the Vedanta Society. Yet like the Transcendentalists, most of those who pursued things Asian were propelled by intellectual curiosity and had no desire to become practitioners of these exotic religions.[16]

Even in the 1950s, when public life celebrated a veneer of religious unity, interest in Asian thought began to percolate. Some was the result of American military folk being introduced to Asian culture during World War II; Asian "war brides" in many cases brought with them their own approaches to religion, at least for a time. The writers of the "Beat Generation" sparked a concern for Zen Buddhism; Alan Watts, although critical of the way such writers portrayed Buddhism, became a respected conduit for bringing Zen thought to American literary and academic culture.[17] Also kindling popular fascination with Asian religious expression were the sustained exposure of military personnel during the Vietnam era to aspects of Asian life, the association of mass culture figures like the Beatles with Asian gurus such as the Maharishi Mahesh Yogi, and the efforts of some Asian religious figures to become aggressive in seeking converts among Americans. One thinks here especially of the arrival in the United States in 1965 of His Grace A. C. Bhaktivedanta Swami Prabhupada, the founder of the International Society for Krishna Consciousness, and of others such as the Guru Maharaji and his Divine Light Mission and in time of Sun Myung Moon and the Holy Spirit Association for the Unification of World Christianity. By the late 1960s and early 1970s, men and women wearing saffron robes chanted on urban street corners throughout the nation, urged travelers passing through the nation's airports to purchase copies of the Bhagavad Gita, proclaimed their message of truth to motorists stopped at rest areas on the developing interstate highway system, and sometimes went door-to-door through residence halls on college and university campuses. What was different was the effort to secure American converts whose commitment went beyond intellectual curiosity to actual practice. Controversy followed, much of it with political overtones. The proselytizing techniques raised questions of free speech and free exercise of religion, while anxious families believed their youth had been kidnapped and brainwashed, and with increasing frequency sought to kidnap them back and deprogram them. Such actions, of course, had numerous political and legal consequences. If the most obvious appeal of these strains of Asian religiosity faded with the passing of the counterculture after overt American military engagement in Southeast Asia ended, they left behind a new stratum within American religious pluralism that would continue to challenge the hegemony of an artificial Judeo-Christian tradition and the functional equivalency in the public arena of Herberg's Protestant-Catholic-Jew triad.

In the midst of this religious turbulence came an event that in retrospect had even greater implications for the interplay of religion and politics in American life. In 1965, the year Krishna Consciousness came to the United States, in a ceremony that received much less public attention than anything associated with the civil rights movement, or controversial Supreme Court decisions, or street-corner gurus chanting mantras, President Lyndon B. Johnson signed legislation that radically revamped national immigration policy. Such policy, like civil rights, carried heavy religious and political baggage. In the 1920s, when federal legislation placed tight controls on both the total number of immigrants who could enter the nation in any one year and the number who could come from any one country, matters of religion and ethnicity were of critical importance. In the major wave of immigration between the end of the Civil War and the outbreak of World War I, immigration shifted largely away from Northern and Western Europe, its major sources (besides Africa) for more than two centuries. In this epoch the bulk of immigrants came from Central, Southern, and Eastern Europe. As well, the overwhelming majority were Roman Catholic, Eastern Orthodox, or Jewish. The diversity and pluralism, both religious and ethnic, of that wave of immigration spurred Evangelical Alliance executive secretary Josiah Strong by the 1880s to pen his now widely quoted *Our Country*, in which he saw the mushrooming numbers of Catholics and Jews especially as endangering the "least common denominator" evangelical Protestantism that he believed central to American political well-being.[18]

The diversity and pluralism that followed the change in immigration laws in 1965 would prove in time to have even greater significance, for pluralism was taking on a new face. No longer would it be possible to see the Protestant-Catholic-Jewish triad as the only model, and the political ramifications were profound. Added to the political and cultural shifts accompanying the civil rights movement, second-wave feminism, angst over the Vietnam war, intrigue with new religions, and the way Supreme Court decisions prodded the nation to accommodate religious diversity, the new immigration was one more factor that prompted some religious leaders and political figures to seek to reassert some expression of common identity, to fix an *axis mundi* for the body politic, or perhaps to construct one where none actually existed. What was clear, however, was that the cluster of symbols and values provided by an *axis mundi* predicated on unity within one nation under God had ceased to function.

Contrived Unity Masking Diversity

The emergence of a more strident, explicitly evangelical Protestant voice in the public sector during the 1970s comes as no surprise. For half a century, those who saw themselves as a "righteous remnant" that had been shoved to the margins of American common life after the fundamentalist-modernist upheavals of the 1920s willingly separated themselves from active political engagement. Pundits at the time mistakenly believed that the Scopes Trial (1925) had made the premillennial dispensationalist interpretation of scripture and history that informed fundamentalism seem not only anachronistic but also intellectually absurd. Part of the reason why fundamentalists who were more inclined to separatism were in the 1920s willing to disengage themselves from active participation in the body politic was their widespread sense that American society still had an undercoating of biblical religion, even if those who spurned fundamentalist premillennial dispensationalism were misguided in their personal beliefs and practices. The larger issues brought by the Great Depression, World War II, and then the specter of godless communism fostered the conviction among the most theologically conservative Protestant rank and file that the nation, although misdirected in its rejection of fundamentalist principles, was not totally bankrupt spiritually. During the 1950s, as attendance at religious services plummeted throughout Western Europe, for example, participation and membership in the United States moved toward record highs. The decades on the margins allowed fundamentalists to build a stunning network that connected those of like mind together, ranging from independent Bible schools and colleges to religious publishing houses, radio programs, and even the widespread use of the Scofield reference edition of the King James Version of the Bible.[19] So long as the nation retained its veneer of shared religious ideals and political values, fundamentalists were content to remain aloof from the public square. But the disunity of the 1960s and 1970s, alongside the new religious diversity and pluralism, created a perception that the very heart of the nation was at risk. The collapse of the "least common denominator" Judeo-Christian *axis mundi* that had buttressed political life and informed public discourse required action, lest the soul of the nation perish.

Two events that marked the year of the national bicentennial set the stage for the emergence of a concerted effort to claim a single religious vision for the American body politic, albeit one that was artificial and contrived. The first is the successful presidential campaign of Democrat Jimmy Carter. A Southern Baptist from south Georgia, Carter in his campaign talked more freely than had any previous presidential candidate about his personal religious faith and how that faith undergirded decisions he had made and policies and programs he had advocated during his tenure as governor of Georgia. He spoke often about being "born again" and thus tapped into the linguistic reservoir that fed into much of American Protestantism. A Sunday school teacher himself, Carter also suggested that his religious values would continue to inform his political perspective once in the Oval Office and on many occasions noted that the writings of the Protestant theological ethicist Reinhold Niebuhr, who had been an advisor to the Department of State during the Truman administration, had long influenced his thinking. Americans of a conservative religious bent, especially those inclined to fundamentalist ways, resonated with Carter's testimony and looked to his administration to halt the decline in American common life stoked by the expanding pluralism and abandonment of the 1950s veneer of unity. Carter owed his electoral success to being forthright about his religious convictions and how they played into his political perspective. His approach was in effect the reverse of that taken by the Catholic John Kennedy in the 1960 campaign.

The other event was the proclamation by *Newsweek* that 1976 was also the "year of the evangelical" in the United States. The *Newsweek* piece noted that the nation's evangelical congregations were growing at a much faster pace than others, many of which were actually losing members in record numbers. Among the nation's youth, the Jesus Movement had caught popular attention. Within the largest Protestant body in the country, the Southern Baptist Convention, those inclined toward a fundamentalist position had moved aggressively to secure their hold on the organizational and bureaucratic apparatus of the denomination. More and more Americans identified themselves as "born again" evangelicals, although their social and demographic profile was not necessarily the same as that of fundamentalists of the 1920s. For example, rates of divorce and also of substance abuse were roughly the same among those "born again" as among the population at large. Among second-wave feminists, there were countless signs of a style of feminism that blended the new identities of women as women with an evangelical posture. Some, however, resisted the inroads of second-wave feminism and continued to call for the "servant leadership" of men within families and to consign women to a paradoxical role that was presumably equal but yet subordinate to that of the male servant leader.

Not long after Carter entered the White House, evangelicals lost their enthusiasm for the president who was unabashedly "born again." When the Carter administration proved reluctant to advocate the political and social policies promoted by many evangelicals, particularly with regard to overturning *Roe v. Wade* and the Supreme Court decisions regarding devotional prayer and Bible reading in the public schools, some vocal evangelical leaders on the far religious right called for direct political action. In 1978, for example, independent Baptist preacher and television personality Jerry Falwell organized the Moral Majority, a political action group that called for the election only of candidates whose views were in keeping with their own politically conservative position. Falwell toured the country touting the evils of abortion, pornography, homosexual rights, and second-wave feminism, drawing large crowds to rallies that melded the religious and the political. In the 1980 presidential election, Republican candidate Ronald Reagan aggressively sought the support of groups like the Moral Majority, creating the impression that if he were victorious, his administration would advance causes supported by the religious right.[20] It mattered little that Reagan himself rarely attended religious services; his campaign rhetoric resonated with the religious right more than did that of the born-again Carter, who had continued to teach Sunday school even while in the White House.

Although Reagan won, with groups like Moral Majority boasting that their efforts were integral to his success, for pragmatic reasons he too did little to promote the political and cultural causes espoused by the religious right. What remained significant, however, was the fact that, by 1980, many religious conservatives who had once voluntarily withdrawn from overt political activity, who had been content to be on the margins for two generations, now enthusiastically engaged in working on campaigns for favored candidates and in many locales began to seek office themselves. What propelled them was the perception that the continuing disunity unleashed in the sixties and the ever-expanding pluralism and diversity in the nation had somehow shattered the nation. They longed for an *axis mundi* like that which had given a semblance of unity to American common life in the years immediately after the end of World War II. Earlier, as noted above, such folk were content to remain on the sidelines because they thought the larger culture retained a common moral base, even if a misguided, misdirected one. That common moral base now seemed demolished, and a radical response was in order. Throughout the decade of the 1980s, religious conservatives stepped up the pace of their political engagement. Hence in 1987, the onetime Southern Baptist law school student Pat Robertson, by then head of a vast evangelical media enterprise, launched the Christian Coalition, another political action group similar in aim and focus to Falwell's Moral Majority, which actually disbanded as a formal organization the following year. All these groups jettisoned the working distinction between religion, a matter of the private sphere, and politics, a matter of the civic order, that had dominated American thinking since the eighteenth century.

By the time that these political action groups were trying to recreate a center of meaning for the American experience that presumed a Protestant Christian underpinning, the consequences of the change in immigration law in 1965 were becoming apparent and in their own way undermined efforts to have a single religious base for national identity. Because it ended most earlier restrictions, the revamped immigration law opened America's doors for thousands—now millions—from Asia, Latin America, and the Near East. Like immigrants of an earlier day, they brought with them their own religious styles and worldviews. Unlike earlier immigrants, however, these were more inclined to regard themselves as full participants in American common life without having to adapt their religious mores to prevailing ways, to accommodate the supposed Judeo-Christian majority culture, or to jettison what simply did not fit in.[21]

Even if the majority of those who came from Asia and Latin America identified in some way with the Christian tradition, their way of expressing that religious identification was often different. Many from Asia and the Near East brought with them their Buddhist, Hindu, and Muslim allegiances and had no intention of abandoning those commitments in order to fit in to American society and political culture.[22] Slowly but steadily Hindu temples began to appear throughout the nation, various Muslim groups established mosques to serve the faithful, and Buddhist centers that were as vital to sustaining ethnic integrity as to promoting religious practice formed wherever immigrant communities were to be found. Even though many strands of the Buddhist tradition had historically sought converts through proselytizing, and the Muslim tradition was noted for its efforts to impress its truth on potential converts through aggressive witness, in the United States much of this activity was muted; developing mechanisms to survive as minority religious and ethnic communities took precedence.

Numbers tell a stunning story of steady growth. In 1964, the year before the immigration law changed, estimates suggest that in all of North America, including Central America and the Caribbean, there were just 38,000 Muslims, 29,000 Hindus, and 171,000 Buddhists. More than one-third of the Buddhists were part of the Buddhist Churches of America, a group with roots in nineteenth-century immigration that had changed its name as part of the process of cultural accommodation. By 1970, in the United States alone, the Muslim population had reached at least 800,000, the number of Hindus had climbed to around 100,000, and the Buddhist population totaled 200,000. Three decades later, the United States was home to around four million Muslims, one million Hindus, and two million Buddhists.[23]

As the nation was becoming home to millions who had no ties to the Jewish and Christian traditions, American Catholics, or at least the hierarchy of the church in the United States, also became more politically assertive. The Second Vatican Council (1962–1965), along with John Kennedy's election to the presidency in 1960, emboldened the Catholic leadership to speak out on a range of social and political issues without the fear of an anti-Catholic backlash that might have ensued in an earlier era.[24] Although some of the pronouncements that came from the hands of the nation's Catholic bishops seemed less likely to create alliances with politically engaged conservative Protestants—especially those that had to do with economic justice, war, and the like—there was common ground on some matters. For example, the Roman Catholic Church had for centuries opposed abortion, except in cases where the mother's life was at risk; so did many on the Protestant religious-political right. A tradition that formally rejected the idea of having women in the priesthood, Catholicism—or at least the bishops speaking collectively—could ally with conservative Protestants who thought second-wave feminism would lead to the destruction of the nuclear family as a viable social unit. Although champions of equal rights for homosexuals, like second-wave feminists and a host of others, drew inspiration from the larger civil rights movement, official Catholic aversion to seeing homosexuality as anything but a sinful aberration also drew Catholic leaders into political associations with like-minded conservative evangelical Protestants.

Thus, from rather disparate religious clusters came ever more shrill calls not only to inject a moral and ethical dimension into the common life of the American people, but also to give explicit religious sanction only to certain political policies, programs, and candidates. This yearning for a return to the ideals of a supposedly Christian America was in actuality a desire to recapture the fabricated unity of the 1950s, the *axis mundi* that revolved around the artificial construct of a shared Judeo-Christian tradition that allowed "one nation under God" to stand as a bulwark of righteousness opposing godless communism. The difference now was that the enemy had become those who affirmed diversity and multiculturalism. Even in some academic circles there was a longing to create a mythic past. When Robert Bellah in 1967 published his widely publicized essay on "Civil Religion in America,"[25] he was in effect bemoaning the diversity and seeming disunity that had come to prevail and hoping to bolster a set of common values grounded in a fusion of nationalism and religion that was in retrospect an artificial construction itself.[26]

An unintended consequence of the ever-expanding political engagement of ultra-conservative religious folk was the widening of the racial divide that the civil rights movement had sought to overcome. This unwitting result came because some white leaders conflated religious conservatism, political conservatism, and cultural conservatism.[27] Theologically, many African-American religious leaders shared views that were compatible with those of white religious conservatives. But the history of slavery, segregation, and racism had infused African-American religion with a social ethic and sense of social justice that was often not in keeping with the political and cultural conservatism that so readily accompanied religious conservatism among whites. Although Sunday mornings remained the most racially segregated hours of the week as whites and blacks worshipped separately, African-American concern for issues such as increasing the minimum wage, having access to health care, reducing the large proportion of black single-parent families, and kindred matters meant that it was often difficult for African-Americans to lend their political support to the candidates touted by white religious conservatives.[28] In many cases, those candidates were precisely the ones whose positions were antagonistic to those thought by African-American leaders to advance the well-being of black Americans.

At the same time, the changes in the immigration laws in effect since 1965 continued to compound the intricate ways religious identity and the public order were intertwined. Not all the change related to the new pluralism signaled by the dramatic growth in the nation's Muslim, Hindu, and Buddhist population. Outstripping immigration from Asia and the Near East was the influx from Latin America. By the time of the 2000 census, it was clear that Latino/a Americans had become the largest ethnic minority in the United States, outnumbering African-Americans. Of course, these immigrants represent a host of nationalities and ethnic subgroups. But the overwhelming majority are Christian. Their style of Christianity, whether informed by Roman Catholicism or various expressions of Protestantism, is decidedly charismatic or Pentecostal. Of more import for the body politic, these immigrants tend to hold conservative positions on a range of social issues that have obvious moral dimensions. Most, for example, oppose abortion rights, and most oppose extending rights associated with marriage to homosexual couples, however those legal rights are construed. This social conservatism carries over into how the growing millions of Latino/a Americans scrutinize candidates for public office. As they attain citizenship in ever larger numbers, they will bring to American common life a rather different understanding of how religious faith shapes political decisions.

The Struggle for Common Ground

The increasing pluralism in American religion, as well as the reaction to it, represents only some of the strains in the delicate relationship between religion and the body politic in the United States in the opening years of the twenty-first century. As evangelicals associated with groups such as the Moral Majority and the Christian Coalition raised their voices to recapture a presumably fading Christian nation, other evangelicals injected a different perspective into the national conversation. One example comes from those evangelicals who look to figures such as Jim Wallis and the Sojourners community. Wallis and his associates gained renown when his *God's Politics: Why the Right Gets It Wrong and the Left Doesn't Get It* zoomed to the top of the best-seller lists after it appeared in 2005.[29] Suggesting that he offered "a new vision for faith and politics in America,"[30] Wallis sought to craft a call for social justice, particularly in areas relating to economics, based on a solidly evangelical reading of the Gospel. Evangelicals themselves had begun to speak with multiple voices when it came to applying their faith to their politics. Another example comes from the results of a more recent multi-year, soul-searching study regarding matters of race and ethnicity in American life on the part of faculty at Trinity Evangelical Divinity School and Wheaton College, two of the nation's premier evangelical institutions. They, too, issued a call for continued transformation toward an ethnically inclusive society, with public policies to match, that was firmly grounded in an evangelical reading of scripture.[31]

At the same time, injecting religious language into the political arena has become a matter of course, although there remains considerable concern as to what that language denotes. After Jimmy Carter in 1976 described himself as "born again," the evangelical vocabulary became almost the norm among candidates, particularly at the national level. Unlike John Kennedy, who was forced to downplay his own religious allegiance, later candidates faced an electorate that expected them to indicate how their personal faith—whatever it might be—would influence policy, programs, and leadership. By the 1990s, "born again" imagery had become so commonplace that to careful analysts it was becoming devoid of meaning. So in 1992, both the Baptist Bill Clinton, for whom an evangelical Christian vocabulary was second nature, and the Episcopalian George H. W. Bush, for whom such imagery was not second nature, described themselves as born again. In 2000, it was the Democratic candidate for vice-president, Senator Joseph Lieberman, who was able to make the most compelling use of religious language; echoing Herberg's Protestant-Catholic-Jew triad, Lieberman could speak in explicitly religious terms in part because common perception granted legitimacy and an expectation of overt religious practice and belief to Orthodox Jews. George W. Bush deftly drew on religious language and imagery to promote not only his own candidacy, but his own vision for the nation in part by claiming in political debate that Jesus was the philosopher who had most deeply influenced his life and thinking.

By the dawn of the twenty-first century, polls indicated that many Americans expected political figures to be forthright about their personal faith and to indicate how that faith would relate to the controversial issues of the day, from stem cell research to gay marriage. The shift over the past couple of decades is worth noting. A poll commissioned by the *New York Times* in 1984 demonstrated that just 22% of Americans thought it appropriate for presidential candidates to discuss their personal religious faith while campaigning and three-quarters indicated that such discussion should not be part of the quest for office at all. Twenty years later, 42% wanted candidates to talk about their faith, while the number finding this fusion of religion and politics inappropriate dropped to 53%. Mark Silk, head of Trinity College's Greenberg Center for the Study of Religion in Public Life, observed that the shift represented not only the enduring impact of the evangelical influence on common life, but also a recovery of a form of public discourse where religious language is routine.[32] There may not be a coherent set of symbols to serve as an *axis mundi*, but use of religious rhetoric abounds.

When George W. Bush entered the White House, he launched an effort to engage religious institutions more directly in the body politic, calling for government funding of selected charitable and social welfare programs sponsored and administered by religious groups. These faith-based initiatives, as they were popularly dubbed, provoked immediate controversy. Some feared that they would breach the traditional barrier between religion and government, the venerable wall of separation between church and state. Others feared that such agencies could easily use religious tests or coerce religious allegiance when determining who qualified to receive the assistance that they administered. But the idea resonated across the country, with many local communities following suit in forging alliances between government agencies and religious groups presumably engaged in promoting the commonweal. The thornier issue of whether some religious groups forfeited access to such initiatives because of the nature of their beliefs and practices remained unresolved, despite a host of policies indicating that only activities that were secular in nature could receive government funding. As religious pluralism continued to mushroom, however, drawing the line between what was religious and what was secular became an ever greater challenge.[33]

Another issue complicating the process of determining what was religious and what was secular emerged from a growing awareness that the increasing pluralism was questioning older ways in which diversity had operated. To some it seemed as if all groups were forced into a mold that reflected an understanding of religion germane only to the Protestant-Catholic-Jew model, or perhaps only to those religions that some scholars call the Abrahamic traditions in order to include Islam. If so, an authentic pluralism was undermined. Jacob De Roover, a Belgian analyst of comparative culture, has suggested, for example, that much of the glorification of American pluralism presumes a single understanding of religion, however secularized, that emphasizes belief and regards all religions as holding certain sets of beliefs, even if the content of those beliefs varies considerably.[34] He argues, for example, that the idea of belief in God, however constructed among the Abrahamic religions, cannot be found in quite the same way in the newer religions to take root on American soil, such as Hinduism. If the ways of being religious and of understanding the very nature of the religious enterprise lack common ground, linking religion to the body politic in a way that would enhance the common good of all becomes almost impossible, and the casual association of religion and politics becomes ruptured.

The struggle for common ground, for a religious sensibility that sustained an increasingly pluralistic social order, also came to the fore following the 2006 national elections, when voters sent to the U.S. Congress two Buddhists and one African-American Muslim, more Jews (43) than Episcopalians (37), and a total of 15 members of the Church of Jesus Christ of Latter-day Saints. With 154 adherents in the House and the Senate, the Roman Catholic Church had more than any other single group.[35] This diversity challenged the notion of a common religious base for public life when Keith Ellison, the African-American Muslim, announced his intention to place his hand on the Qur'an when taking the symbolic oath of office, rather than on a Bible. The trend accelerated in subsequent elections. The 2012 Congressional races, for example, resulted in the election not only of the first Hindu but also of the first representative to list "none" for religious affiliation.[36] The latter echoed the steadily increasing proportion of Americans to declare themselves to pollsters as having no particular religious affiliation.

Reactions to the candidacy of Mitt Romney, the former Republican governor of Massachusetts who is a member of the Church of Jesus Christ of Latter-day Saints (LDS), for the Republican presidential nomination in 2008 provide another illustration of the ongoing struggle to find common ground, as well as a sign that the body politic harbors lingering religious prejudices. A survey reported by Damon Linker in the *New Republic*, for example, indicated that 43% of Americans would not vote for a Mormon candidate for the nation's highest political office.[37] Another indicated that a majority of Americans (55%) believed that the nation was not ready for a president aligned religiously with the LDS; that particular survey showed 60% of respondents thinking that the United States was ready for a woman to be elected president and fully 63% convinced that the nation was ready for an African-American commander-in-chief.[38]

Democrat Barack Obama, an African-American, was victorious in both 2008 and 2012. In the latter election, he indeed faced Mitt Romney in what many at first anticipated would be a close race. Interestingly, Romney's religious affiliation became a matter of concern only in some primary contests. Once he secured the Republican nomination, the religious issue virtually disappeared. Romney himself, although never trumpeting his Mormon identity, worked diligently in the campaign to show that his political positions were close to those of many Protestant evangelicals. Even though Obama became the first incumbent since Dwight Eisenhower in 1956 to win re-election with more than 51% of the popular vote, Romney succeeded in carrying heavily evangelical states. Whether enthusiastically or reluctantly, many evangelical Protestants who identified as Republicans jettisoned their long-standing apprehension of Mormonism to vote for Romney. The gradual erosion of their angst over candidates from other religious groups, such as Roman Catholics and Mormons, reveals how deeply appreciation of the nation's religious diversity has penetrated.

Hence the model that may best capture the present relationship between religion and the body politic is the lack of a common religious base for public life, coupled with the hope of finding one. In other words, there is still no *axis mundi* around which to fix common meaning, but a yearning that one might emerge. At the same time, the religious mix of the American peoples is becoming ever more diverse and pluralistic, making the quest for shared religious values that might undergird the commonweal ever more elusive. Elsewhere I observed that the "burden of the 21st century [is] whether Americans can craft a symbolic configuration of symbols and associated practices that will support a common identity for all the peoples called American and grant them social cohesion."[39] In other words, can the American *homo religiosus* erect an *axis mundi* that functions to provide an overarching framework of meaning for the body politic? That question also describes well the dilemma in the relation between religion and the political order in the United States over the last half century. In that period, Americans have moved from an artificial religious consensus to sustain national identity through an era when there seemed to be little political or religious unity to a time when a contrived religious unity in the form of a public evangelical Protestantism masked growing religious diversity. Now we have arrived at a time when diversity and pluralism mean that a struggle to find common ground pervades every facet of the links between religious culture and political life. That the way religious images and national identity are linked changes over time is not surprising or unexpected; such transformation is a natural consequence of diversity and increasing pluralism. But the shifts in the United States over the last 60 years suggest that it may no longer be possible to construct one world of meaning, one sense of what it means to be an American, or one *axis mundi* around which the common life of the American peoples revolves. Without a fixed center, the nation faces having to juggle multiple worlds of meaning engaged in an ongoing contest for primacy in interpreting the common life of all. But such juggling, with no one worldview achieving consensus or remaining stable for an extended period, raises another question, namely how to sustain and support a shared political order when fragmentation and discord become the norm. In a radically pluralistic and diverse society, how does one find common ground for civil order or for erecting an *axis mundi* for the American *homo religiosus*?

Notes

1 Jon Meacham, *American Gospel: God, the Founding Fathers, and the Making of a Nation* (New York: Random House, 2006), 14.

2 Many of the primary sources articulating this perspective are excerpted in Conrad Cherry, ed., *God's New Israel: Religious Interpretations of American Destiny*, rev. ed. (Chapel Hill: University of North Carolina Press, 1998).

3 These ideas receive classic elucidation in Mircea Eliade, *The Sacred and the Profane: The Nature of Religion*, trans. Willard R. Trask (New York: Harcourt, Brace & World, 1959), esp. ch. 1.

4 Kenneth L. Woodward, et al., "Born Again!" *Newsweek* 90 (October 25, 1976): 68–76.

5 Some of the ethos that pitted a godly, righteous America against ungodly or godless communism is captured in Richard Crossman, ed., *The God That Failed* (New York: Bantam Books, 1950), and in Thomas O. Kay, *The Christian Answer to Communism* (Grand Rapids, MI: Zondervan, 1961), a study guide prepared under the auspices of the National Association of Evangelicals.

6 Quoted in Will Herberg, *Protestant, Catholic, Jew: An Essay in American Religious Sociology*, rev. ed. (Garden City, NY: Doubleday, 1960), 95, from the *New York Times* (December 23, 1952). On the mood inspired by Eisenhower more generally, see Martin E. Marty, *Modern American Religion*, vol. 3: *Under God, Indivisible: 1941–1960* (Chicago: University of Chicago Press, 1996), 294–312.

7 A useful resource on a host of topics relating to the ecumenical movement, the National Council of Churches, and American involvement in the World Council of Churches is Nicholas Lossky, et al., *Dictionary of the Ecumenical Movement* (Grand Rapids, MI: Eerdmans, 1991).

8 For an overview, see H. George Anderson, "Ecumenical Movements," in *Altered Landscapes: Christianity in America, 1935–1985*, David W. Lotz, Donald W. Shriver, and John F. Wilson, eds. (Grand Rapids, MI: Eerdmans, 1989), 92–105.

9 Herberg's classic study first appeared in 1955, although I worked from the revised edition mentioned in n. 6 above.

10 The standard scholarly, but appreciative, biography is William Martin, *A Prophet with Honor: The Billy Graham Story* (New York: Morrow, 1991). On the crusade in Britain, see Martin, 173–185; on the New York crusade, 221–238.

11 The full text of the speech is included in John F. Kennedy, *"Let the Word Go Forth": The Speeches, Statements, and Writings of John F. Kennedy, 1947 to 1963*, selected by Theodore C. Sorensen (New York: Delacourt, 1988), 130–136, quotation from p. 131.

12 Charles Marsh, *God's Long Summer: Stories of Faith and Civil Rights* (Princeton, NJ: Princeton University Press, 1997), ably demonstrates how religious worldviews moved some to engage in civil rights activism and others to work against the movement. Still helpful for the larger story are David J. Garrow, *Bearing the Cross: Martin Luther King, Jr., and the Southern Christian Leadership Conference* (New York: Morrow, 1986), and the two volumes by Taylor Branch: *Parting the Waters: America in the King Years, 1954–63* (New York: Simon and Schuster, 1988), and *Pillar of Fire: America in the King Years, 1963–65* (New York: Simon and Schuster, 1996).

13 For the full story, see W. J. Cunningham, *Agony at Galloway: One Church's Struggle with Social Change* (Oxford: University Press of Mississippi, 1980).

14 Marsh, *God's Long Summer*, 127. For the Mays attribution, see "The Conservative Illusion that Racial Pressures Are Not a Factor in College Dropout Rates," *Journal of Blacks in Higher Education* 16 (Summer 1997): 26–28.

15 Martin Luther King, Jr., "Beyond Vietnam," mimeographed copy sent to Fellows of the Society for Religion in Higher Education with permission of Clergy and Laity Concerned About Vietnam.

16 Insightful on how Emerson and those inclined toward Transcendentalism drew on Asian philosophy is Leigh Eric Schmidt, *Restless Souls: The Making of an American Spirituality* (San Francisco: HarperSanFrancisco, 2005), 25–62. On the impact of the World's Parliament of Religions, see Richard Hughes Seager, *The Dawn of Religious Pluralism: Voices from the World's Parliament of Religions* (LaSalle, IL: Open Court, 1993).

17 See Patrick Allitt, *Religion in America since 1945: A History* (New York: Columbia University Press, 2003), 140–144. D. T. Suzuki's portrayal of Zen had an especially strong influence on Beat writers Jack Kerouac and Allen Ginsberg. For Suzuki, see William Barrett, ed., *Zen Buddhism: Selected Writings of D.T. Suzuki* (Garden City, NY: Doubleday Anchor, 1956); see also D. T. Suzuki, *An Introduction to Zen Buddhism* (New York: Grove Weidenfeld, 1991). Kerouac's classic work, first published in 1958, is *The Dharma Bums* (New York: Penguin, 1976). A good introduction to Watts is Monica Furlong, *Zen Effects: The Life of Alan Watts* (Boston: Houghton Mifflin, 1986). Among Watts's voluminous works are *The Way of Zen* (New York: Vintage, 1989) and *The Spirit of Zen* (Rutland, VT: Tuttle, 1992). His critique of the Beat writers comes to the fore in his *Beat Zen, Square Zen, and Zen* (San Francisco: City Light Books, 1959).

18 Josiah Strong, *Our Country*, ed. Jurgen Herbst (1886; Cambridge, MA: Belknap Press of Harvard University Press, 1963).

19 Joel Carpenter, *Revive Us Again: The Reawakening of American Fundamentalism* (New York: Oxford University Press, 1996).

20 Helpful on the "new religious right" are William C. Martin, *With God on Our Side: The Rise of the Religious Right in America* (New York: Bantam Books, 1996), and Matthew C. Moen, *The Transformation of the Christian Right* (Tuscaloosa: University of Alabama Press, 1992).

21 See William R. Hutchison, *Religious Pluralism in America: The Contentious History of a Founding Ideal* (New Haven, CT: Yale University Press, 2003).

22 The best known study that concentrates on Hindu, Buddhist, and Muslim inroads in U.S. religious life is Diana Eck, *A New Religious America: How a "Christian Country" Has Become the World's Most Religiously Diverse Nation* (San Francisco: HarperSanFrancisco, 2001).

23 For the numbers, see Charles H. Lippy, "Christian Nation or Pluralistic Culture: Religion in American Life," in *Multicultural Education: Issues and Perspectives*, James A. Banks and Cherry A. McGee Banks, eds., 6th ed. (Hoboken, NJ: Wiley, 2007), 127, and *Information Please Almanac, Atlas, and Yearbook: 1965*, Dan Golenpaul, ed., 19th ed. (New York: Simon and Schuster, 1964), 420.

24 Some Catholic thinkers were privately chagrined at the hard line Kennedy drew between his faith and his politics. A comprehensive study is found in Thomas J. Carty, "Cultural and Regional Responses to John F. Kennedy's Catholicism in the 1960 Presidential Campaign" (Ph.D. diss., University of Connecticut, 1999). More specifically, see also Fletcher Knebel, "Democratic Forecast: A Catholic in 1960," *Look* (March 3, 1959): 13–17, and Timothy J. Sarbaugh, "Champion or Betrayer of His Own Kind: Presidential Politics and John F. Kennedy's *Look* Interview," *Records of the American Catholic Historical Association of Philadelphia* 105 (Spring/Summer 1995): 54–70.

25 Robert N. Bellah, "Civil Religion in America," *Daedalus* 96 (Winter 1967): 1–21, and Robert N. Bellah, *The Broken Covenant: Civil Religion in Time of Trial* (New York: Seabury, 1975).

26 I explore this point in more detail in my "American Civil Religion: Myth, Reality, and Challenges," in *Faith in America: Changes, Challenges, New Directions*, vol. 2: *Religious Issues Today*, Charles H. Lippy, ed. (Westport, CT: Praeger, 2006), 19–36.

27 Helpful here is Marla Frederick McGlathery and Traci Griffin, "'Becoming Conservative, Becoming White?': Black Evangelicals and the Para-Church Movement," in *This Side of Heaven: Race, Ethnicity, and Christian Faith*, Robert J. Priest and Alvara L. Nieves, eds. (New York: Oxford University Press, 2007), 146–161.

28 For a challenging perspective written by one who was at the time the sole African-American Republican serving in the U.S. House of Representatives, see J. C. Watts, Jr., with Chris Winston, *What Color Is a Conservative? My Life and My Politics* (New York: HarperCollins, 2002).

29 See Jim Wallis, *God's Politics: Why the Right Gets It Wrong and the Left Doesn't Get It* (San Francisco: HarperSanFrancisco, 2005).

30 These words appear on the dust jacket of the cloth-bound edition.

31 See Priest and Nieves, eds., *This Side of Heaven*.

32 Laurie Goodstein, "Page Two: Politicians Talk More about Religion, and People Expect Them To," *New York Times*, July 4, 2004.

33 A brief overview of the debate regarding Bush's "faith-based initiatives" is found in Anthony E. Cook, "From Southern Strategy to National Strategy: How the Christian Right Is Transforming Church-State Relations," in Lippy, ed., *Faith in America*, 2: 83–85.

34 De Roover's research was reported in a January 22, 2007, posting on www.india-forum.com, as noted in Jean-Francois Mayer, "American Pluralism and Hinduism at Odds?" *Religion Watch* 22 (February 2007): 4.

35 See "Current Research," *Religion Watch* 22 (February 2007): 4.

36 "Faith on the Hill: The Religious Composition of the 113th Congress," *The Pew Forum on Religion and Public Life*, http://www.pewforum.org/government/faith-on-the-hill--the-religious-composition-of-the-113th-congress.aspx, updated January 2, 2013, accessed February 18, 2013.

37 See "Mormon Candidacy Stirs New Religion-Politics Debate," *Religion Watch* 22, no. 4 (February 2007): 1–2.

38 These results came from a poll commissioned by the American Association of Retired Persons reported in the *AARP Bulletin* 48 (February 2007): 4.

39 See Charles H. Lippy, "Religious Pluralism and the Transformation of American Culture," in *Our Diverse Society: Race and Ethnicity—Implications for 21st Century American Society*, David W. Engstrom and Lissette M. Piedra, eds. (Washington: NASW Press, 2006), 103.

CHAPTER 14 | Piety, International Politics,
and Religious Pluralism
in the American Experience

PAUL BOYER

IS AMERICA A CHRISTIAN nation? Some writers, caught up in the cultural wars
of our own day, insist that it is—and they invest the term with levels of meaning far beyond the obvious fact that most Americans profess one form or
another of Christianity. These polemicists see Christ hovering over America
with special concern, choosing its leaders in times of crisis, guiding its actions
to advance God's purposes for humanity. Proponents of this theocentric view
typically rely on pious myths and selectively cherry-pick their evidence. Many
factors—economic, strategic, political, and religious—have shaped U.S. history. To single out only one is to distort historical reality beyond recognition.
American foreign policy, like that of every nation, involves calculations of
power, prestige, and national interest. The Constitutional prohibition against
an establishment of religion, erecting what Jefferson famously called a "wall
of separation" between church and state, while never unchallenged, has been
and remains a robust force in American thought about religion and politics.
The Founders were products of the Enlightenment, espousing a Deist creed far
removed from the evangelicalism of their day or our own.[1]

When all this has been acknowledged, however, it is true that American history, including American foreign relations, cannot be fully understood without
attention to the way religious belief has influenced, or added a sacred aura to,
governmental policies and Americans' foreign involvements. The importance
of religion, among the many forces shaping America's world role, can be seen
in leaders' actions and pronouncements; in missionary activity and philanthropic ventures; and in the climate of opinion within which policymakers
function. All of these offer useful perspectives on our topic, and this chapter
addresses all three.

The essay focuses primarily on the years since World War II. We begin,
however, with a look at the decades from the Colonial era through World War I.
These early episodes will, I hope, contextualize the later material, underscoring

how deeply embedded in American history are the religious perspectives on America's world role that survive so strongly in our own era. The concluding section reflects on the implications for religious pluralism in contemporary America.

Religious Influences on American Foreign Relations and Global Interactions from the Colonial Era to World War I

From the beginning, Americans have viewed foreign conflicts through a religious lens. In the imperial struggle between France and Great Britain known in America as the French and Indian War (1754–1763), colonial preachers justified the war on biblical grounds, casting the French Catholics of Canada as agents of the Antichrist, the demonic end-time foe foretold in the Book of Revelation. Siding with Britain, writes historian Nathan Hatch, colonial ministers saw little distinction "between the Kingdom of God and the goals of their own political community."[2]

As the tables turned and Britain began to tighten control of its American colonies, religion became both a bone of contention and an ideological weapon. New England Congregationalists and others denounced the Church of England's attempts to establish an American episcopate as a threat to religious freedom. Boston's Jonathan Mayhew, warning of this alleged plot in a celebrated sermon of 1750, described resistance to tyranny as a Christian duty. The colonists also condemned on religious grounds Parliament's 1774 Quebec Act granting religious freedom to Quebec's Roman Catholics and extending Quebec's administrative authority southward to the Ohio River and westward to the Mississippi. This act, they charged, threatened Protestantism's hegemony in North America. (The colonists' anti-Catholicism did not, however, prevent them from seeking support from Catholic France once the Revolution began.)[3]

During the Revolutionary War itself, some Patriot ministers echoed Jonathan Mayhew in interpreting the conflict as a divinely sanctioned struggle against a tyranny. Some even cast the conflict in apocalyptic terms, linking George III to the Antichrist and finding intimations of America's destiny in biblical prophecies of a coming Millennium of justice and peace. Even preachers who did not employ millennialist imagery argued that victory in the war would advance the Protestant cause and end threats to religious liberty by the British oppressor.[4]

In the Early National era, American settlers migrated into southwestern territories claimed by Mexico, independent since the 1820s but strongly Roman Catholic thanks to three centuries of Spanish rule. Anti-Catholic prejudice, still endemic in Protestant America, helped fuel assertions of America's "manifest destiny" to absorb these territories and carry Protestantism to the Pacific. Such religious claims ran high during the U.S.-Mexican war (1846–48).[5]

Meanwhile, Protestant missionary activity, a manifestation of the evangelistic fervor that gripped many American denominations in the nineteenth century, had significant foreign-policy implications. From 1820 on, Protestant missionaries sent to Hawaii by the interdenominational American Board of Commissioners for Foreign Missions not only sought converts but also promoted U.S. interests, culminating in U.S. annexation in 1898. In the 1840s, American missionaries in Oregon vigorously backed U.S. claims in a boundary dispute with England that at times threatened war. As the ranks of Protestant missionaries burgeoned in the mid- and later-nineteenth century, they inevitably played a role in U.S. relations with European colonial powers and in America's own developing political and economic involvements abroad. In *Our Country* (1885), the Rev. Josiah Strong viewed missionaries as crucial to the spread of Christianity and "Anglo-Saxon" civilization. Under the banner of world evangelization, missionaries recruited by the Student Volunteer Movement (1888) further extended America's religious, political, and cultural influence. After the Spanish-American war and U.S. suppression of the Filipino independence movement (1898–1903), Protestant missionary activity expanded to Cuba, Puerto Rico, and the Philippines. By 1900, nearly six thousand U.S. Protestant missionaries labored around the globe. American Roman Catholics established foreign missions as well, sometimes in direct competition with Protestants, as did the Church of Jesus Christ of Latter-Day Saints (Mormons), thus projecting abroad key divisions within American religion.[6]

The missionary movement's relationship to Western imperialism and to America's quest for informal empire was complex. To be sure, U.S. missionaries often arrived in the wake of European colonizers. In today's Zimbabwe, for example, the empire-builder Cecil Rhodes in 1898 granted U.S. missionaries of the small Brethren in Christ denomination 3000 acres in Matabeleland, the scene of recent anticolonial unrest. "Missionaries are better than policemen," observed Rhodes, "and cheaper." U.S. diplomats in Asia saw missionaries as advance agents for American entrepreneurs. "Missionaries are the pioneers of trade and commerce," the head of the U.S. diplomatic mission in China, Charles Denby, candidly wrote in 1895. "The missionary, inspired by holy zeal, goes everywhere, and by degrees foreign trade and commerce follow."[7]

For the missionaries themselves, of course, religious motivations were paramount. Indeed, some criticized Western colonizers, encouraged indigenous leadership, and even supported anticolonial movements. They also battled social conditions that offended their values. Female missionaries, for example, criticized patriarchal oppression of native women. But an aura of cultural condescension proved hard to avoid, breeding resentments. A central theme of *Re-thinking Missions* (1932), a critique of the missionary movement funded by the Baptist layman John D. Rockefeller, Jr., was (in the words of a reviewer) that the enterprise "must be modified so as to avoid unpleasant implications of superiority on the part of missionaries."[8]

By the mid-twentieth century, liberal Protestants had largely abandoned proselytizing missionary work in favor of education, medical programs, and social services. Evangelical and Pentecostal denominations took up the slack, however, sending thousands of missionaries abroad, seeking converts to their fundamentalist faith. Overall, American missionaries over the years have spread not only Christianity but American cultural values, interpreted foreign cultures to U.S. churchgoers, and advanced (or sometimes criticized) U.S. interests abroad. William R. Hutchison's judgment that the entire missionary enterprise constituted a "moral equivalent for imperialism" is perhaps overly harsh, but without question missionary activity, a quintessential institutional expression of American religious zeal, has played a role in the nation's global emergence, and thus constitutes a central and continuing part of our story.[9]

Shifting from the cumulative influence of thousands of missionaries to the influence of a single leader in a moment of crisis, one finds a dramatic instance of the potency of religious belief in molding national attitudes on a vital foreign-policy issue as President Woodrow Wilson, the son and grandson of Presbyterian clergymen, led the nation into war. The reasons for U.S. intervention in the war that erupted in Europe in 1914 are complex, but in Wilson's own formulation, religious considerations loomed large. By joining on the side of England and France, Wilson insisted in his April 1917 war message, America would help realize the Christian vision of a redeemed world order. Indeed, he proclaimed, the decision for war had "come about by no plan of our conceiving, but by the hand of God.... We can only go forward, with lifted eyes and freshened spirit, to follow the vision. It was of this that we dreamed at our birth. America shall in truth show the way."[10]

Inspired by such rhetoric, so redolent of the pulpit, the nation's religious leaders, especially from the liberal, reform-minded churches, rallied behind the war and embraced Wilson's understanding of its spiritual meaning. In a typical effusion, the Rev. William Barton, an Illinois Congregationalist, proclaimed: "God is on the side, not of America against Germany, but... of humanity against inhumanity,... of justice against injustice. We shall win... because we have allied ourselves with... God's own cause." Disillusion would soon set in, but for a bright shining moment, God's purposes and American policy seemed at one.[11]

A generation later, under different circumstances and facing a different foe, many Americans, including key policymakers, would again define the nation's world role in sweeping religious terms. Indeed, the continuity of this theme across time and under very different conditions bears witness to its importance in American foreign policy and the larger history of America as a global actor.

Religion and Foreign Policy in the Cold War

As new power alignments arose from the wreckage of World War II, many Americans and some of their leaders again invoked religious assumptions as they envisioned the nation's postwar role. Since Colonial days Americans had tended to view their disputes with other nations, whether France, Britain, Mexico, or Germany, as confrontations of righteousness and evil with cosmic significance, and this habit of mind persisted into the later twentieth century, with first the Soviet Union and then Islamic terrorists, if not Islam itself, cast in the demonic role.

As the Soviet Union, officially atheistic in ideology, emerged as the new adversary, the sense of America's divinely ordained destiny, always near the surface, surged back to prominence. Through nearly 50 years of confrontation, the religious dimensions of the struggle with "godless communism" loomed large. Heavily underscoring the Cold War's spiritual aspect, Congress in 1956 added the phrase "under God" to the Pledge of Allegiance, adopted "In God We Trust" as the nation's motto, and added the latter phrase to U.S. currency. (It had appeared on coins since the Civil War.)[12]

The impulse to cast the U.S.-Soviet geopolitical rivalry in theological terms became especially pronounced during John Foster Dulles's tenure as secretary of state (1953–59). Like Woodrow Wilson, the son of a Presbyterian clergyman and himself a prominent Presbyterian layman, Dulles sometimes seemed more Protestant pope than diplomat. Sir Oliver Franks, the British ambassador to the United States in the 1950s, observed: "Three or four centuries ago,... in an age of wars of religion, it was not so rare to encounter men of the type of Dulles. Like them he came to unshakable convictions of a religious and theological order. Like them he saw the world as an arena in which forces of good and evil were continuously at war."[13]

Also a sophisticated corporate lawyer, the grandson and nephew of secretaries of state, Dulles in actual negotiating situations displayed hard-headed realism. Nevertheless, his belief in a divinely ordained moral and historical order in which America had a God-given role to play undergirded his understanding of the Cold War's deeper meaning. In a 1949 lay sermon at the First Presbyterian Church of Watertown, New York (where his father had been pastor), Dulles criticized the Truman Administration's failure to recognize the Cold War's spiritual dimension. "[M]oral power does not derive from any act of Congress," he declared; "It depends on relations of a people to their God. It is the churches to which we must look to develop the resources for the great moral offensive that is required to make human rights secure and to win a just and lasting peace." He reiterated this theme in an influential *Life* magazine essay in 1952, applying it specifically to the Cold War: "There is a moral or natural law not made by man which determines right and wrong," he wrote, "and in the long run only those who conform to that law will escape disaster. This law has been trampled by the Soviet rulers, and for that violation they can and should be made to pay. This will happen when we ourselves keep faith with the law in our practical decisions of policy." These religious convictions, argues historian Andrew Johnston, underlay Dulles's dissatisfaction with George Kennan's containment strategy, and his enunciation, in the same *Life* essay, of "a policy of boldness" committed to rolling back Soviet power and threatening "massive retaliation" (widely assumed to be nuclear) against Soviet expansion anywhere. As secretary of state, Dulles proved more cautious than his fire-breathing pronouncements suggested, particularly as the Soviets gained nuclear parity and after the U.S. failure to support the 1956 Hungarian uprising. Nevertheless, his rigidly moralistic worldview remained firmly in place until his death in 1959, shaping his understanding of America's global role. As Johnston concludes: "Religion, per se, may not have been always present in his thought (although it was more than in any other Secretary of State), but he organized his conception of history and morality on a religious basis."[14]

Religious considerations shaped Cold War diplomacy in specific ways. The selection of Ngo Dien Diem, a devout Roman Catholic, to head the U.S.-backed South Vietnamese government in 1954 won support from Dulles and from such prominent U.S. Catholics as Senator John Kennedy and Francis Cardinal Spellman. Diem's relentless promotion of Catholic interests in a heavily Buddhist society contributed to his unpopularity and eventual assassination in 1963. In the Middle East, argues Rachel Bronson, Washington's Cold War alliance with Saudi Arabia rested not only on the economics of oil, but also on a shared aversion to atheistic communism.[15]

A preponderance of U.S. religious leaders shared Dulles's view of the Cold War as a spiritual as well as strategic confrontation. "[O]nly as millions of Americans turn to Jesus Christ," declared the evangelist Billy Graham, "...can this nation possibly be spared the onslaught of a demon-possessed communism."[16] Further out on the politico-religious spectrum, the John Birch Society, founded in 1958 by candy-maker Robert Welch, saw America's "Judeo-Christian" heritage as crucial to its anticommunist mission. Indeed, the eponymous John Birch was a Southern Baptist missionary (and U.S. army intelligence officer) shot by Chinese communists in 1945. Billy James Hargis's Christian Crusade (1950) and Fred C. Schwartz's Christian Anti-Communist Crusade (1953) placed anticommunism at the heart of their ministries.[17]

The religious intensity of the Cold War faded somewhat in the turbulent, conflict-ridden 1960s, but it revived in the 1970s as evangelical Protestantism enjoyed a resurgence, and in the early 1980s President Ronald Reagan gave it forceful expression. Although not a churchgoer, Reagan sprang from a conservative evangelical upbringing, and both his private musings and public utterances are rich in religious imagery. He often quoted John Winthrop's biblical trope of the "city on a hill" (subtly enhancing it to "a *shining* city on a hill") to suggest America's redemptive mission in the world. In 1983, addressing the National Association of Evangelicals, an alliance of conservative Protestant denominations, Reagan, like Wilson and Dulles before him, aligned the United States firmly with God's plan for humanity. America's sense of purpose, he declared, was grounded in the "realization that freedom prospers only where the blessings of God are avidly sought and humbly accepted." "[Y]ou...are keeping America great by keeping her good," he assured the assembled preachers; "Only through your work and prayers and those of millions of others can we hope to survive this perilous century." As for Russia, he said: "[L]et us pray for the salvation of all of those who live in...totalitarian darkness—pray that they will discover the joy of knowing God. But until they do, let us be aware that while they preach the supremacy of the state...and predict the eventual domination of all peoples on the Earth, they are the focus of evil in the modern world."[18]

Reagan's apocalyptic language particularly resonated with millions of Americans who embraced a system of Bible-prophecy interpretation known as *premillennial dispensationalism*, formulated by the nineteenth-century British churchman John Darby. Assembling an array of biblical proof texts in jigsaw-puzzle fashion, Darby predicted dramatic and unsettling developments as the present "dispensation" approaches its end: wars; natural disasters; increasing wickedness; and, crucially, the Jews' return to Palestine, promised by God to Abraham (Genesis 15:18). These converging events, Darby taught, will culminate in the Rapture, when true believers will join Christ in the air. After a seven-year Tribulation, a horrific interlude when the Antichrist rules the world, Christ will return to defeat Antichrist's armies at Armageddon, an ancient battle site in Israel. From a rebuilt Temple in Jerusalem, Christ will reign over the earth for a thousand years—the Millennium foretold in Revelation.[19]

Darby's interpretative scheme won many American adherents, especially after 1970, when conservative evangelical, fundamentalist, and Pentecostal churches burgeoned while the liberal denominations hemorrhaged members. Dispensationalist belief was promulgated by local pastors; radio and TV evangelists; and Hal Lindsey's *The Late Great Planet Earth* (1970), a slangy paperback popularization that sold millions of copies. In a 1983 Gallup poll, 62% of Americans expressed "no doubts" that Jesus will return to earth.[20]

Lindsey and other prophecy popularizers ingeniously wove current events into their end-time scenario, thereby influencing believers' understanding of global trends and U.S. foreign policy. The atomic bomb and a nuclear World War III, they argued, are foretold in such Bible passages as II Peter 3:10 ("[T]he elements shall melt with fervent heat, the earth also and the works that are therein shall be burned up"). The United Nations, the European Union, and other international bodies; multinational corporations and financial institutions such as the International Monetary Fund and the World Bank; and the globalized mass culture symbolized by the Beatles and communications satellites, they contended, foreshadow Antichrist's world rule. Prophecies in the Book of Ezekiel foretelling the destruction of "Gog," a mysterious northern kingdom, they insisted, prophesy the doom of Russia, America's Cold War enemy. For dispensationalists, the policy implications of all this seemed obvious. The U.N. and other international bodies must be shunned at all costs. Efforts for disarmament or reduced Cold War hostilities are pointless, since thermonuclear war and Russia's destruction are foreordained.[21]

Prophecy believers hailed Israel's creation in 1948 and Israel's recapture of the Old City of Jerusalem and occupation of the West Bank and Gaza after the 1967 Six-Day War as steps in God's unfolding plan for the Jews. By the same token, dispensationalists rejected Palestinian claims as contrary to God's division of land in the Middle East. Some even identified the Palestinians and the larger Islamic world with the Antichrist. From this perspective, peace proposals aimed at addressing Palestinian grievances or resolving the larger Arab-Israeli conflict, like attempts to promote better relations between America and the Soviet Union, were not only pointless, but opposed to God's end-time scenario, which by the 1970s seemed to be unfolding with breathtaking speed. While the liberal Protestant denominations represented by the National Council of Churches tempered their backing of Israel with support for the Palestinian cause, evangelical support for Israel, buttressed by dispensationalist belief, became increasingly vocal and uncritical.[22]

To argue for the foreign-policy importance of these beliefs is not to claim (despite Ronald Reagan's well-documented interest in prophecy) that administration officials themselves embraced dispensationalism and shaped U.S. policy accordingly. Indeed, as *The Economist* magazine has noted, "America's foreign-policy elite is...one of the most secular groups in the country."[23] But the prevalence of these beliefs, and their tireless promotion by televangelists, paperback writers, and local pastors unquestionably affected the political climate within which policymakers operated, making it easier for them to espouse positions that coincided with believers' worldview, and harder to pursue policies that ran counter to that worldview. This was particularly true during the Republican ascendancy that began with Reagan's election in 1980, since evangelicals, politically mobilized by Jerry Falwell's Moral Majority (1979) and other organizations, constituted a key Republican voting bloc.

But religion's influence in shaping America's global role and foreign policy in these years was not monolithic. If some prominent religious figures and millions of Christian believers saw Russia's annihilation and a coming nuclear holocaust as divine imperatives, others found these interpretations dismaying. From August 1945 onward, some churchmen criticized the atomic bombing of Japan and the ensuing nuclear arms race. Within days of Hiroshima, writing in the liberal *Christian Century* magazine, Professor Fred Eastman of Chicago Theological Seminary, a Congregationalist school, offered an anguished *cri de coeur*: "King Herod's slaughter of the innocents—an atrocity committed in the name of defense—destroyed no more than a few hundred children. Today, a single atomic bomb slaughters tens of thousands of children and their mothers and fathers. Newspapers and radio acclaim it a great victory. Victory for what?" Thirty-four prominent Protestant clergymen issued an open letter to President Truman condemning the atomic bomb. Harry Emerson Fosdick of New York's Riverside Church, a liberal Protestant leader and longtime pacifist, declared in a nationally broadcast radio sermon: "When our self-justifications are all in, every one of us is nonetheless horrified at the implications of what we did. Saying that Japan was guilty and deserved it, gets us nowhere. The mothers and babies of Hiroshima and Nagasaki did not deserve it." To argue that the "mass murder of whole metropolitan populations is right if it is effective," Fosdick went on, was to abandon "every moral standard the best conscience of the race has ever set up."[24]

The criticism of U.S. foreign policy by an articulate minority of religious leaders, continuing as the Cold War and the nuclear arms race accelerated, peaked during the Vietnam War. While Cardinal Spellman supported the war as vital to the anticommunist struggle, Catholic antiwar activists, notably the Jesuit priests Daniel and Philip Berrigan, vehemently opposed it. The Berrigans were jailed for their antiwar protests, including burning draft-board records and symbolically attacking nuclear missiles on U.S. bases. While Billy Graham and the National Association of Evangelicals endorsed the U.S. role in Vietnam, other Protestant leaders, including Martin Luther King, Jr.; Yale chaplain William Sloan Coffin, Jr.; and the veteran pacifist A. J. Muste, protested. An antiwar umbrella organization, Clergy and Laymen Concerned about Vietnam (1966), attracted 40,000 members, mostly liberal Protestant ministers and laypersons, but also Catholic priests and Jewish leaders (notably Rabbi Abraham Heschel, a leading theologian). Their rallies and lobbying activities mobilized antiwar sentiment in churches and synagogues. Christian activists on college campuses, influenced by the theologians Dietrich Bonhoeffer and Paul Tillich, protested the war as part of their quest for authenticity in putting their faith in practice.[25]

The early 1980s' Nuclear Weapons Freeze campaign again energized sectors of America's religious communities. By 1983 at least 15 national church bodies, Protestant, Catholic, and Jewish, had adopted resolutions or otherwise spoken out against the nuclear arms race. *The Challenge of Peace*, a 1983 pastoral letter by the National Conference of Catholic Bishops, criticized America's nuclear-weapons build-up and the use of the bomb in World War II. "[W]e must shape the climate of opinion which will make it possible for our country to express profound sorrow over the atomic bombing of 1945," the bishops wrote; "Without that sorrow, there is no possibility of finding a way to repudiate future use of nuclear weapons." Attacking the freeze campaign in several speeches, President Reagan blunted its political momentum with a March 1983 speech calling for a national missile-defense system.[26] From the 1940s through the 1980s, in short, successive Cold War foreign-policy issues were often formulated and debated within a framework of religious meaning.

Religion and America's World Role in the Contemporary Era

The Cold War's sudden end around 1990 radically reconfigured global realities, but, once again, religious belief continued to influence many Americans' perceptions of the nation's foreign relations and international role, and to inform many citizens' view of, and engagement with, the larger world beyond America's borders. Circumstances changed, but for many, the basic interpretive template remained in place. The view of America as a "redeemer nation" (in Ernest Lee Tuveson's phrase) remained alive and well as the United States moved deeper into its third century.

As conservative Protestant churches continued to grow and mobilize politically, the most impassioned activism came from this part of the religious spectrum.[27] Thousands of U.S. missionaries from evangelical, fundamentalist, and Pentecostal churches carried their religious message and cultural values to

Latin America, sub-Saharan Africa, Asia, Russia, and Eastern Europe. By the early twenty-first century, the Southern Baptist Convention, America's largest Protestant denomination, sponsored more than 5000 missionaries in 153 countries. The Calvary Chapel Fellowship, tracing its origins to 1965 when "Pastor Chuck" Smith came to a small church in Costa Mesa, California, today numbers around 1000 congregations in some 50 nations—more than 30 each in Mexico and the Philippines, 26 in Russia, and on down the list. Thanks to communications satellites and global TV operations like Pat Robertson's Christian Broadcasting Network (CBN) and Paul Crouch's Trinity Broadcasting Network (TBN), American televangelists reach a worldwide audience. The best-selling *Left Behind* series of prophecy novels by Tim LaHaye and Jerry B. Jenkins, published between 1995 and 2007, has been translated into nearly 30 languages, from Afrikaans to Thai. While many historians have explored the global penetration of American popular culture and consumer goods, from Mickey Mouse and jazz to Coca Cola and MacDonalds, the worldwide diffusion of U.S.-based evangelicalism and the implications of the spread of the dogmas and cultural values of this subset of American Protestantism remain fertile fields for further investigation.[28]

Post–Cold War evangelicals also made their voices heard on political issues, domestic and global. "After many decades of isolation," wrote Michael Cromartie of Washington's Ethics and Public Policy Center in 1989, "American evangelicals have plunged into the political arena with enthusiasm," in the process voicing "strong views on foreign policy."[29] Revering the Bible as inerrant, most evangelicals viewed all Scripture, including the prophetic and apocalyptic passages, as authoritative. The belief that all history is foreordained, including end-time events about to unfold, promulgated by televangelists, Internet websites, megachurch pastors, glossy magazines such as *Midnight Call,* and a torrent of mass-market paperbacks, thus continued to shape the worldview of millions. The phenomenally successful *Left Behind* series offered a fictional popularization of dispensationalism, beginning with the Rapture and concluding with a final apocalyptic battle between the forces of good and evil. In a 1996 poll, 42% of the U.S. respondents agreed with the statement: "The world will end in a battle in Armageddon between Jesus and the Antichrist."[30] As during the Cold War, these beliefs had foreign-policy implications.

With the Soviet Union's collapse, prophecy popularizers downplayed (without wholly abandoning) the theme of Russia's coming destruction while highlighting other features of the dispensationalist scenario. They monitored international developments for signs of the Antichrist's coming rule. *The New World Order* (1991), by Pat Robertson, head of CBN and founder of the conservative Christian Coalition, successor to Falwell's Moral Majority, offered a relentlessly conspiratorial view of history, with the Masons, the Rothschilds, the World Bank, the U.N., the Beatles, and the European Union all preparing the world for the Antichrist. "A giant plan is unfolding," Robertson wrote; "Everything is perfectly on cue."[31]

Robertson was not alone in demonizing international organizations. In both the *Left Behind* novels and Hal Lindsey's 1996 prophecy novel *Blood Moon*, the U.N. secretary general is unmasked as the Antichrist. In *Blood Moon*, U.N. troops herd evangelical Christians into concentration camps. And since the Antichrist, according to Revelation, will first pose as a man of peace, the U.N.'s peacekeeping efforts only underscored its sinister nature. For Tim LaHaye, a veteran right-wing activist, the *Left Behind* novels simply provided another outlet for his anti-U.N. message.[32] In the 1999 film *Omega Code*, the Antichrist is a media mogul like Rupert Murdoch, who gains control of the European Union as a steppingstone to world dictatorship. American suspicion of internationalism has many sources, including Jefferson's 1801 warning against "entangling alliances," but in the contemporary era, prophecy believers' conviction that the U.N. and other international organizations are literally demonic has added a compelling religious imperative to this strand in the nation's political culture.

Environmental issues also caught the prophecy popularizers' attention. Biblical prophecies of a darkened sun, blood-filled rivers, monsters arising from earth and sea, and hideous sores on people's bodies are, they contended, foreshadowed by contemporary reports of air and water pollution, the threat of genetic mutations and skin cancers as the ozone layer thins and solar radiation increases, and predictions of flooding, drought, and ecological catastrophes caused by global warming. From this eschatological perspective, countermeasures are pointless; all is foreordained. As Hal Lindsey commented after Hurricane Katrina hit the Gulf Coast in September 2005: "It seems clear that the prophetic times I have been expecting for decades have finally arrived."[33] For many prophecy believers, the George W. Bush administration's repudiation of the Kyoto Accords, a multinational initiative against global warming, and its broader skepticism toward environmental protection made perfect sense.

Above all, post–Cold War prophecy expositors focused on Islam and the Middle East—an ancient motif in Christian eschatology that now took on fresh urgency. The medieval Crusaders had battled to free Jerusalem from Muslim control to prepare the city for Christ's millennial rule, and later interpreters had demonized the Islamic Ottoman Empire as Antichrist's domain. This theme had faded after 1918 as the Ottoman Empire fragmented and the Soviet Union emerged, but with Saddam Hussein's 1990 invasion of Kuwait and the subsequent Persian Gulf War, it surged back to prominence. "Islam is fighting a *holy war* for control of the world!" declared one prophecy writer in 1995; "To *the Muslim...*, violence and bloodshed are the highest expression of religion and the surest way to eternal reward."[34]

To post-1990 prophecy writers, the Genesis account of God's curse on Ishmael, Abraham's son by the servant girl Hagar, and God's blessing of Isaac, Abraham's son by his wife Sarah, portended eternal conflict between their descendants, Arabs and Jews. In Lindsey's prophecy novel *Blood Moon*, a Muslim fanatic, *Ishmael* Mohammed, plots to launch nuclear missiles on Israel. But Israel's military leader, *Isaac* Barak, foils the attack with a preemptive nuclear assault that vaporizes "every Arab and Muslim capital...along with the infrastructures of their nation." When a band of Muslims mobilize to avenge this attack, a supernatural "wave of heat" incinerates them.[35] Genocide, in short, finally fulfills God's plan for the Middle East.

Saddam Hussein drew special attention. In 1991, the Jews for Jesus organization ran full-page newspaper ads declaring: "[Saddam] represent[s] the spirit of Antichrist about which the Bible warns us." The prophecy popularizers particularly noted Saddam's plan to rebuild Babylon, the fabled capital of King Nebuchadnezzar, who in 586 B.C. destroyed Jerusalem and took the Jews captive. Revelation describes Babylon (near modern Baghdad) as evil incarnate—"a great whore...with whom the kings of the earth have committed fornication"—and prophesies its destruction by fire. Most Bible scholars view the "Babylon" of Revelation as a coded allusion to Rome, but in the political climate of the 1990s, many popularizers interpreted this passage literally, and found great prophetic significance in Saddam's rebuilding project. *The Rise of Babylon: Sign of the End Times* (1991), by Charles Dyer of Dallas Theological Seminary (a center of dispensationalist teaching), juxtaposed images of Saddam and Nebuchadnezzar on its cover. Saddam's project, wrote Dyer, offered "thrilling proof that Bible prophecies are infallible." "When Babylon is ultimately destroyed," he continued, "Israel will finally...dwell in safety."[36] In the *Left Behind* novels, the Antichrist moves the U.N. to a rebuilt Babylon, laying the groundwork for the simultaneous destruction of *two* sinister symbols of satanic power.

The September 11, 2001, terrorist attacks by Muslim jihadists intensified prophecy believers' concentration on the Middle East and lent new urgency to the ancient Islam=Antichrist equation. The televangelist and prophecy writer John Hagee, pastor of a San Antonio megachurch, argued that 9/11 heralded the final apocalyptic struggle between Islam and Israel. Franklin Graham, Billy Graham's son, denounced Islam as "a very evil and wicked religion." Michael Evans's best-selling prophecy paperback *Beyond Iraq* (2003) labeled Islam "a religion conceived in the pit of hell." Rush Limbaugh and other radio talk-show hosts praised Evans's book; CNN and Fox News interviewed him.[37] Meanwhile, General William G. (Jerry) Boykin, Deputy Undersecretary of Defense for Intelligence, delivered apocalyptic sermons in full-dress uniform in evangelical churches that reinforced such views: "Why do [radical Muslims] hate us so much?" he asked; "[B]ecause we're a Christian nation..., and the enemy is a guy named Satan." Satan's earthly agents will be defeated, Boykin added, only "if we come against them in the name of Jesus.... The battle won't be won with guns. It will be won on our knees."[38]

Having focused for a decade on Saddam's prophetic significance, prophecy writers welcomed George W. Bush's post-9/11 call for his overthrow. Hal Lindsey's website featured a cartoon of a fighter plane adorned with a U.S. flag and a Star of David, carrying a missile targeting "Saddam." The caption quoted the prophet Zechariah: "[I]n that day...I will seek to destroy all the nations that come against Jerusalem." In November 2002, John Hagee in a sermon broadcast via TBN on 127 TV stations and 82 radio stations, called the looming Iraq invasion "the beginning of the end" and a sign of Christ's imminent Second Coming. Beyond these "birth pains," he noted reassuringly, lay "a thousand years of peace in the millennial reign." Endorsing Hagee's message, House majority leader Tom DeLay proclaimed: "[W]hat has been spoken here tonight is the truth from God." When the Iraq invasion began in April 2003, 87% of white evangelicals supported it. *Left Behind* coauthor Tim LaHaye pronounced the war "a focal point of end-time events." Addressing a prophecy conference in Houston in October 2003, LaHaye declared: "Christians are suspicious of globalism,... as maybe a precursor of Antichrist.... I wouldn't be surprised... [if] the United Nations and the European Common Market... gradually grow together and join other countries... against the United States, and... move the center of government to Iraq." By early 2006, with overall U.S. support for the Iraq War at an anemic 37%, 68% of white evangelicals still approved of the conflict. Political writer Howard Phillips overstated the case when he saw America's "tens of millions of true believers viewing events through a *Left Behind* perspective" as *the* force driving U.S. Iraq policy, but this potent electoral bloc unquestionably made it easier for neoconservatives in the Bush administration to pursue the war.[39]

Prophecy popularizers continued to delineate the Jews' prophetic destiny, including a rebuilt Jerusalem Temple and Israel's expansion to the boundaries God promised to Abraham, from the Euphrates to "the river of Egypt." A contributor to *Midnight Call* magazine, writing about international efforts to take land from Israel and turn it into "so-called 'autonomous' territories," declared that "God's judgment [would]... come upon the nations with all severity because they have laid their hand upon Israel.... God's promises for Israel are so closely connected with Himself that every blow against Israel touches Him." In *Final Dawn over Jerusalem* (1998), John Hagee agreed: "The man or nation that lifts a voice or hand against Israel invites the wrath of God.... There can be no compromise regarding... Jerusalem, not now, not ever.... Israel is the only nation created by a sovereign act of God, and He has sworn... to defend... His Holy City." Jerry Falwell joined the denunciations, earning the gratitude of Israeli hardliners. When Prime Minister Benyamin Netanyahu came to America in 1998, he first visited Falwell in Lynchburg, Virginia, and only then called on President Bill Clinton. Addressing an audience of 3000 prophecy-believing evangelicals, Netanyahu declared: "We have no greater friends and allies than the people sitting in this room."[40]

When the George W. Bush administration floated its so-called road map for peace in 2003, envisioning Israel's partial withdrawal from the West Bank and Gaza, shared governance of Jerusalem, and a Palestinian state, dispensationalists recoiled in horror. "The only Road Map for peace is the Bible," declared Michael Evans; "God gave [the Jews] that land and forbade them to sell it." Gary Bauer, a prominent evangelical and 2000 Republican presidential candidate, told AIPAC, the American-Israel Public Affairs Committee: "God owned the land; he has deeded it to the Jewish people, a deed that... cannot be amended—even by a president." Tom DeLay, defying the State Department, rushed to Israel to denounce the road map, earning him the 2003 "Defender of Israel" award from the Zionist Organization of America.[41] Hal Lindsey joined the protest chorus: "[T]he United States is leaping at the same old bait offered by the Palestinians. Secretary of State Condoleezza Rice, following the orders of our dear but naïve president, is shoving Israel toward a disastrous agreement to grant a Palestinian state." Wrote a *Midnight Call* columnist: "Old Testament promises made to national Israel will literally be fulfilled.... [C]ast your allegiance with the literal Word of God, lest we be found fighting against God and His Sovereign plan." For many evangelicals, this writer continued, Israel was "the central issue" determining their vote in upcoming national elections.[42]

Early in 2006, the tireless John Hagee formed a new lobby, Christians United for Israel (CUFI). The inaugural event at Washington's Hilton Hotel, attended by 3500 evangelical Christians and other supporters, was broadcast live by Daystar, a Christian TV network. Featured speakers included Tom DeLay, conservative Republican senators Rick Santorum and Sam Brownback, and GOP national chairman Ken Mehlman. President Bush sent greetings. Hagee himself proclaimed the Israeli-Arab conflict a "war of good versus evil." In *Jerusalem Countdown* (2006), Hagee added: "This is a religious war that Islam cannot—and must not—win.... The end of the world is rapidly approaching.... Rejoice and be exceedingly glad—the best is yet to be." At CUFI's 2007 rally in Washington, Senator Joseph Lieberman compared Hagee to Moses as "a man of God" and "leader of a mighty multitude." Tom DeLay, asked by a reporter about the Rapture, and how it related to his support for Israel, responded: "Obviously, it's what I live for.... And obviously we have to be connected to Israel in order to enjoy the Second Coming of Christ." Commenting on Hagee's movement and its links to powerful Washington figures, Dennis Ross, a U.S. envoy to the Middle East under presidents George H. W. Bush and Bill Clinton, observed that while prophecy-believing evangelicals had long backed Israeli hardliners, they "didn't really appear on the radar screen. Now they are an important part of the landscape."[43]

This is not to argue that evangelicals think in lockstep, or that televangelists and popularizers like Lindsey, LaHaye, Hagee, Evans, and the late Jerry Falwell speak for all evangelicals. As early as 1989, sociologist James Davison Hunter found great ideological diversity among the "evangelical elite" (theologians and seminary students) on a broad range of issues, including foreign-policy matters. When asked whether the United States "should do everything it can to support Israel," for example, Hunter found that only 38% of evangelical seminarians agreed, while 30% disagreed and 31% adopted a neutral stance.[44] But if Lindsey, LaHaye, Hagee, and their brethren lacked standing among the "evangelical elite," they wielded potent media megaphones and exerted great grassroots influence.

This influence peaked after 2000 as the George W. Bush administration cultivated evangelical voters and especially leaders of the religious Right who embraced its agenda. Evangelicals overwhelmingly supported Bush in 2000. Commented the always quotable General Boykin: "[Bush] is in the White House because God put him there for a time such as this."[45] In 2004, self-identified evangelicals, together with Mormons, traditional Catholics, and other religious conservatives, composed nearly 60% of the Bush vote. A born-again Christian himself, Bush avidly courted his evangelical base. After his 1986 religious conversion, Bush often mentioned God's role in directing his career and indeed all of American history. While still in Texas politics he said: "I could not be governor if I did not believe in a divine plan that supersedes all human plans." In the 2000 campaign he declared: "[O]ur nation is chosen by God and commissioned by history to be a model to the world." Once in the White House, Bush and his advisors conferred regularly with evangelical leaders, including Richard Land, Washington lobbyist for the Southern Baptist Convention; James Dobson, head of the Family Research Council, a Washington lobby, and of Focus on the Family, a radio, paperback, and magazine empire; and Ted Haggard, pastor of a Colorado Springs megachurch and head of the National Association of Evangelicals until his resignation in 2006 amid a sex scandal.

As Bush's pronouncements became increasingly apocalyptic after 9/11, religion's role in the public sphere and its use as a foreign-policy rationale had rarely seemed more prominent and overt. "[O]ur responsibility to history is already clear," the president declared at Washington's National Cathedral on September 14, 2001; "To answer these attacks and rid the world of evil." "We are in a conflict between good and evil, and America will call evil by its name...[and] lead the world in opposing it," he proclaimed in June 2002. At a 2003 White House prayer breakfast he spoke of "the hand of a just and faithful God... [b]ehind...all of history." As the Iraq War dragged on, Bush subtly modified his eschatological imagery. "The road of Providence is uneven and unpredictable," he acknowledged in his February 2005 State of the Union Address, "yet we know where it leads: It leads to freedom." At a military event a few weeks earlier, he had made the same point even more sweepingly: "We Americans have a calling from beyond the stars to stand for freedom."[46] Abraham Lincoln in his Second Inaugural Address had been more circumspect about whether anyone, even a president of the United States, can fully know God's purposes. Nevertheless, Bush's language echoed a worldview deeply rooted in the American past, and embraced by millions of his fellow citizens.

While describing global realities in apocalyptic terms, Bush also exuded an optimism reminiscent of Progressive-Era Social Gospel advocates and "postmillennial" theologians who foresaw an inexorable advance of righteousness before Christ returns to reign over an already redeemed world. In a classic formulation of what Robert Bellah has called America's civil religion, Bush, like Wilson, Dulles, and Reagan before him, saw the United States as a chosen instrument of God's purposes.[47] As Bush's evangelical speechwriter Michael Gerson commented in denying that such speeches sent coded messages to the religious Right: "They're not code words. They're our culture."[48]

Bush's words certainly summed up the culture of *many* Americans—and this group generally applauded his post-9/11 foreign policy. For this constituency, the administration's apocalyptic "war on terror"; invasion of Saddam Hussein's Iraq; downgrading of the Israeli-Palestinian peace process; hostility to the U.N.; repudiation of international treaties, including the Kyoto Accords; and dismissive attitude toward environmental hazards all accorded with God's end-time plan.

As during the Cold War, however, religion's influence on post–Cold War foreign policy was far from monolithic. The (liberal Protestant) National Council of Churches and the mainstream liberal Protestant denominations, despite their loss of members, remained politically engaged, endorsing the Kyoto Accords, supporting the U.N., criticizing the Iraq War, condemning the holding of prisoners without trial at Guantánamo Bay, and in general reaffirming their historic commitment to peace, social justice, and humanitarian causes. Influential voices within the Catholic and Jewish communities similarly criticized the religious Right and advocated positions historically associated with the more humanitarian and peace-oriented strands of American religious life and thought.[49]

Even some evangelical leaders urged more attention to peacemaking; social justice; environmental hazards; poverty, disease, and malnutrition in the developing world; and specific humanitarian issues such as the genocide in Somalia's Darfur region. Ronald Sider, founder of Evangelicals for Social Action (1973), won wide attention for his 1977 book *Rich Christians in an Age of Hunger* and many subsequent works. Jim Wallis, founder of the Washington-based Sojourners movement, similarly called on his fellow evangelicals to address a broader social agenda, from global warming to income inequity.[50]

James Davison Hunter in 1989 found a "political drift among evangelical elites...from the Right to the Left," and this trend continued in the succeeding years. (The evidence for the evangelical laity, bombarded by televangelists and paperback writers with their hard-line apocalyptic message, is less clear.) In 2004 the National Association of Evangelicals issued a manifesto, "For the Health of the Nation: An Evangelical Call to Civic Responsibility." A compromise document designed to achieve consensus, it espoused predictable positions on abortion, pornography, gay marriage, the international sex traffic, and so forth. On other issues, however, particularly relating to foreign policy, it diverged sharply from the Bush administration and the religious Right. Governments must "pursue thoroughly nonviolent paths to peace before resorting to military force," it asserted, and wage war only "in the service of peace and not merely in their national interest....God did not call [Christians] to bring in God's kingdom by force." On the environment, the manifesto upheld "the principle of sustainability..., to conserve and renew the Earth rather than to deplete and destroy it." "Because clean air, pure water, and adequate resources are crucial to public health and civic order," it went on, "government has an obligation to protect its citizens from the effects of environmental degradation." Citing the U.N.'s Universal Declaration of Human Rights, the NAE called on governments to "change patterns of trade that harm the poor" and "make the reduction of global poverty a central concern of American foreign policy." In dealing with the developing world, it went on, governments should aggressively address "unfair socio-economic structures..., extreme poverty, lack of health care, the spread of HIV/AIDS, adequate nutrition, unjust and unstable economies, ... and government cronyism and graft." Declared Ronald Sider, the document's coauthor: "No longer dare one accuse evangelicals of being... focused exclusively on one or two issues."[51]

In an open letter to President Bush in 2007, prominent evangelicals called for renewed efforts to resolve the Israeli-Palestinian conflict, including support for a Palestinian state and recognition of Palestinian territorial claims. Along with the ever-present Ronald Sider of Evangelicals for Social Action, the signers included officials of World Vision International, an evangelical relief agency; the president of Fuller Theological Seminary, a leading evangelical institution; and the editor of *Christianity Today*, a widely read evangelical periodical. "Bible-believing Christians will scoff at that message," jeered John Hagee,[52] but mounting evidence pointed to a widening rift within the evangelical camp, and challenged any suggestion that evangelicals march in lockstep on all issues. Ideological differences aside, many evangelicals grew disaffected with the Bush administration for pragmatic reasons, concluding that it courted them at election time with little concern for their interests otherwise. Black evangelicals, of whom an estimated 75% retained Democratic loyalties dating to the New Deal era, were especially skeptical of evangelicalism's de facto alliance with the Republican party.[53]

As we saw in considering the nineteenth-century missionary movement, American religion's contemporary world role involves more than its influence on foreign policy. Along with global missionary activity (now mostly under evangelical auspices), this role now includes a host of church-sponsored relief and welfare organizations. Even a cursory overview suggests the scope of this activity. The Seventh-day Adventist Church supports over 160 hospitals and sanitariums, and some 450 clinics and dispensaries worldwide. American Jewish World Service (founded in 1985) sponsors programs and college-age volunteers in projects ranging from water purification in Honduras to flood relief in Mozambique. Catholic Relief Services, founded by the U.S. Catholic bishops in 1943 to aid war refugees, operates in nearly 100 countries, assisting victims of war, natural disasters, and political conflict. World Vision International, a global relief agency focused on child welfare, was founded in 1950 by Robert Pierce, an evangelical missionary in Korea. In the 1970s its director was W. Stanley Mooneyham, formerly with the National Association of Evangelicals and the Billy Graham organization. In 2006, World Vision, with its deep evangelical roots, had a $2 billion budget and 23,500 employees in 97 countries. The Quaker-sponsored American Friends Service Committee (1917) and the Mennonite Central Committee (1920) sponsor programs to promote peace, social uplift, disaster aid, and international understanding worldwide.[54] The global activities of these and countless other church-sponsored organizations, in all their doctrinal diversity, underscore the range and complexity of religion's role in shaping American interactions with the outside world.

With liberal religious leaders reasserting their influence and evangelicals growing increasingly restive, not to mention the U.S. missionaries and church-sponsored welfare organizations operating worldwide, confident generalizations about American religion's effect on international politics seem ill-advised. One conclusion, however, proposed at the outset, merits reiteration here: one cannot begin to understand America's contemporary world role, or the forces shaping U.S. foreign policy, without close attention to the religious beliefs of millions of citizens and the way those beliefs have influenced the political culture and Americans' engagement with the world.

American Religion and World Realities: Implications for Religious Pluralism

How does this essay relate to this book's larger theme: religious pluralism in America? When applied to American religion, *pluralism* is both an objective description and a sought-after goal. As a descriptive term, the word simply characterizes the kaleidoscopic U.S. religious scene in the early twenty-first century: a Roman Catholic Church coping with ethnic, cultural, and ideological differences; a sprawling Protestant world of baffling diversity; a Jewish community vigorously debating religious, cultural, and political issues; five million Mormons; a growing Muslim population; several million native-born and immigrant Buddhists (itself an umbrella term covering a variety of beliefs, practices, and national traditions); increasing numbers of Indian-American Hindus; home-grown Wiccans and New Age adherents; a small but vocal minority of atheists, agnostics, and skeptics. "Pluralism" indeed!

Beyond this obvious statement of fact, however, "pluralism" also describes a hopeful goal: that all these groups will develop greater mutual respect and understanding. It is in this second sense of the term that the developments discussed in this essay may be relevant. As one reflects on how religion's influence on U.S. foreign policy and America's world role relates to the goal of increasing understanding among the nation's religious groups, the impact seems, at best, mixed.

In some respects, the foreign-policy issues and global activities explored in this essay, particularly since World War II, have strengthened links across creedal and denominational lines. Relief organizations sponsored by different religious bodies have cooperated in responding to natural catastrophes and conflicts throughout the world. A shared anticommunist ideology, particularly during the early Cold War, helped Protestants and Catholics overcome centuries-old prejudices. In the 1950s this rapprochement found expression in a generic "civil religion" that some critics found thin and unsatisfying. For many, President Eisenhower's much-quoted (and misquoted) 1952 comment epitomized this superficiality: "'[O]ur Government has no sense unless it is founded in a deeply felt religious faith and I don't care what it is.'"[55] Few, however, favored returning to the blatant prejudices of earlier times. The enthusiastic support for Israel by many evangelical Christians seemed to create bonds of common interest across what had once been barriers of misunderstanding and prejudice.

In other respects, however, the international developments and engagements examined in this chapter have intensified both inter-group and intra-group religious divisions in America, and made the pluralist ideal more elusive. Aggressive proselytizing by evangelical and Pentecostal missionaries in Mexico and Latin America, along with Protestant televangelism and Spanish-language print materials, has stirred resentment among Roman Catholic leaders, from local parishes to the Vatican. Tensions have flared, too, between American Jewish groups devoted to Israel and Christian leaders and organizations critical of Israel's treatment of Palestinians. Even the apparent alliance between some Christian evangelicals and some U.S. Jewish groups in support of Israel's most hard-line and expansionist parties arose from fundamentally different theological and eschatological positions, and was inherently unstable.

Differing perceptions of global realities have also deepened division *within* America's major religious bodies. In conflicts over the Vietnam War, nuclear disarmament, and other issues, Roman Catholics have experienced severe tensions between those who embraced the traditional patriotism of the immigrant church, including strong support for the military, and those who have insisted on the Church's duty to promote peace and question state power. American Jews have divided sharply over how to balance support for Israel with Judaism's historic concern for the suffering and oppressed—including the Palestinian people.

Within American Protestantism, a chasm yawns between the liberal, so-called mainstream, churches, with their commitment to tolerance, social justice, peace, and international understanding, and a highly politicized evangelical subculture that stresses personal salvation; strict standards of personal—especially sexual—morality; and an aggressive, intensely nationalistic, and black-and-white worldview, shaped by apocalyptic readings of Bible prophecy, that sees the forces of righteousness and the forces of evil in a cosmic conflict that is rushing toward a cataclysmic denouement. The evangelical camp itself is torn by divisions, with some voices calling for a more nuanced, less doctrinaire application of evangelical values to contemporary world problems. Not only Revelation, but also the Sermon on the Mount and the Beatitudes, these dissidents insist, are part of the Bible that evangelicals profess to revere.

Finally, the Persian Gulf War, 9/11, the conflicts in Iraq and Afghanistan, and continued terrorist alarms—the grim realities of a post–Cold War era that began so hopefully—have vastly complicated efforts to promote religious understanding in America, most especially between U.S. Muslims and non-Muslims, and toward the Islamic world as a whole. Despite the insistence by public figures that the enemy is not Islam or the world's 1.3 billion Muslims but specific jihadist groups engaging in criminal activities, this distinction has often been obscured in the public discourse, including the pronouncements of religious figures who claim the mantle of biblical authority. As a delegate to John Hagee's 2007 CUFI conference told a reporter: "We're fighting what's behind the Muslim people, which is Satan."[56]

As elsewhere in this essay, then, we conclude with a mixed assessment. In some respects, the global developments, foreign-policy issues, and international engagements by U.S. church groups since World War II have advanced the pluralist goal of overcoming barriers and promoting dialogue and mutual respect across religious lines in America. In other important ways, sadly, these same developments have exacerbated divisions, both among the major religious groups, and within these groups. In a shifting and volatile era, long-range trends are frustratingly difficult to discern. As a statement of an ideal, however, pluralism remains an elusive goal, not yet the reality, of American religious life.

Notes

1 Frank Lambert, *The Founding Fathers and the Place of Religion in America* (Princeton, NJ: Princeton University Press, 2003); Isaac Kramnick and R. Laurence Moore, *The Godless Constitution: The Case Against Religious Correctness* (New York: W.W. Norton, 1997). For the "Christian nation" interpretation of American history, see Mark A. Beliles and Stephen K. McDowell, *America's Providential History* (Charlottesville, VA: Providence Foundation, 1989) and three volumes by Peter Marshall and Daniel Manuel: *The Light and the Glory* (Grand Rapids, MI: Baker Publishing Group, 1980); *From Sea to Shining Sea* (1989); and *Sound Forth the Trumpet* (1998).

2 Nathan O. Hatch, *The Sacred Cause of Liberty: Republican Thought and the Millennium in Revolutionary New England* (New Haven, CT: Yale University Press, 1977), 43; Paul Boyer, *When Time Shall Be No More: Prophecy Belief in Modern American Culture* (Cambridge, MA: Harvard University Press, 1992), 72.

3 Jonathan Mayhew, *Discourse Concerning Unlimited Submission and Non-Resistance to the Higher Powers* (Boston: D. Fowle and D. Gookin, 1750). On the Episcopate Controversy, see Patricia U. Bonomi, *Under the Cope of Heaven: Religion, Society, and Politics in Colonial America*, updated ed. (New York: Oxford University Press, 2003), passim. On the Quebec Act, see Charles P. Hanson, *Necessary Virtue: The Pragmatic Origins of Religious Liberty in New England* (Charlottesville: University Press of Virginia, 1998), passim.

4 Hatch, *Sacred Cause of Liberty*; Ernest Lee Tuveson, *Redeemer Nation: The Idea of American's Millennial Role* (Chicago: University of Chicago Press, 1968); Ruth H. Bloch, *Visionary Republic: Millennial Themes in American Thought, 1756–1800* (New York: Cambridge University Press, 1985); Boyer, *When Time Shall Be No More*, 72–75; Melvin B. Endy, Jr., "Just War, Holy War, and Millennialism in Revolutionary America," *William and Mary Quarterly*, 3rd Series, 42 (1985): 3–25.

5 Ted C. Hinckley, "American Anti-Catholicism during the Mexican War," *Pacific Historical Review* 31 (1962): 121–137; John C. Pinheiro, "'On Their Knees to Jesuits': Nativist Conspiracy Theories and the Mexican War," in *Nineteenth-Century America: Essays in Honor of Paul H. Bergeron*, Todd Groce and Stephen V. Ash, eds. (Knoxville:

University of Tennessee Press, 2005); Pinheiro, "'Religion Without Restriction': Anti-Catholicism, All Mexico, and the Treaty of Guadalupe Hidalgo," *Journal of the Early Republic*, 23 (2003): 69–96; and "'Extending the Light and Blessings of Our Purer Faith': Anti-Catholic Sentiment among Soldiers in the U.S.-Mexican War," *Journal of Popular Culture* 35 (2001): 129–152.

6 William R. Hutchison, *Errand to the World: American Protestant Thought and Foreign Missions* (Chicago: University of Chicago Press, 1987); Joel A. Carpenter and Wilbert R. Shenk, eds., *Earthen Vessels: American Evangelicals and Foreign Missions, 1880–1890* (Grand Rapids, MI: Wm. B. Eerdmans, 1990); Dana L. Robert, "Foreign Missions," in *Encyclopedia of the United States in the Nineteenth Century*, Paul Finkelman, ed. 3 vols. (New York: Charles Scribner's Sons, 2001), II, 347–348; Jane Hunter, "Missionary Movement," in *Oxford Companion to United States History*, Paul Boyer, ed. (New York: Oxford University Press, 2001), 507–508; Angelyn Dries, O.S.F., *The Missionary Movement in American Catholic History* (Maryknoll, NY: Orbis Books, 1998), esp. pp. 63ff, "Catholic Reactions to Protestant Missionary Efforts."

7 Thomas J. McCormick, *China Market: America's Quest for Informal Empire, 1893–1901* (Chicago: Quadrangle Books, 1967), 66; H. Frances Davidson, *South and South Central Africa: A Record of Fifteen Years' Missionary Labor Among Primitive Peoples* (Elgin, IL: Brethren Publishing House, 1915); E. Morris Sider, *Nine Portraits: Brethren in Christ Biographical Sketches* (Nappanee, IN: Evangel Press, 1978), "Hannah Frances Davidson," 159–212, Rhodes quotation on p. 168. See also Lloyd C. Gardner, Walter F. LaFeber, and Thomas J. McCormick, *Creation of the American Empire*, 2nd ed., 2 vols. (Chicago: Rand McNally College Pub. Co., 1976).

8 William E. Hocking, *Rethinking Missions: A Layman's Inquiry after One Hundred Years* (New York: Harper & Bros., 1932); Guy W. Sarvis review, *American Journal of Sociology* (November 1934): 381–383, quotation on p. 382.

9 Hutchison, *Errand to the World*, quoted in Robert, "Foreign Missions," p. 348; Dana L. Robert, *American Women in Mission: A Social History of Their Thought and Practice* (Macon, GA: Mercer University Press, 1996); Carpenter and Shenk, eds., *Earthen Vessels;* Hunter, "Missionary Movement."

10 James H. Moorhead, *World Without End: Mainstream American Protestant Visions of the Last Things, 1880–1925* (Bloomington: Indiana University Press, 1999), 152.

11 Moorhead, *World Without End*, 149–158, quotation on p. 151. See also Ray Hamilton Abrams, *Preachers Present Arms: The Role of the American Churches and Clergy in World Wars I and II, with Some Observations on the War in Vietnam* (Scottdale, PA: Herald Press, 1969).

12 U.S. Department of the Treasury, "Fact Sheets: Currency & Coins: History of 'In God We Trust,'" http://www.ustreas.gov/education/fact-sheets/currency/in-god-we-trust.shtml.

13 Quoted in Townsend Hoopes, "God and John Foster Dulles," *Foreign Policy* 13 (Winter 1973–74): 154.

14 John Foster Dulles, "A Policy of Boldness," *Life*, May 19, 1952: 151–152; Henry P. Van Dusen, ed., *The Spiritual Legacy of John Foster Dulles: Selections from His Articles and Addresses* (Philadelphia: Westminster Press, 1960); Andrew Johnston, "Massive Retaliation and the Specter of Salvation: Religious Imagery, Nationalism, and Dulles's

Nuclear Strategy, 1952–1954," *Journal of Millennial Studies* 2 (Winter 2000): 1–18, quotation on p. 9, and quoted passages from Dulles's 1949 sermon and 1952 *Life* essay, pp. 12, 13.

15 Seth Jacobs, "'Our System Demands the Supreme Being': The U.S. Religious Revival and the 'Diem Experiment,' 1954–1955," *Diplomatic History* 24 (2001): 589–624; Seth Jacobs, *America's Miracle Man in Vietnam: Ngo Dinh Diem, Religion, Race, and U.S. Intervention in Southeast Asia, 1950–1957* (Durham, NC: Duke University Press, 2004); Rachel Bronson, *Thicker than Oil: America's Uneasy Partnership with Saudi Arabia* (New York: Oxford University Press, 2006).

16 Quoted in Johnston, "Massive Retaliation and the Specter of Salvation," p. 6.

17 Fred C. Schwartz, *You Can Trust the Communists (to be Communists)* (Englewood Cliffs, NJ: Prentice Hall, 1960); "Evangelist Billy James Hargis Dies: Spread Anti-Communist Message," *Washington Post*, November 30, 2004, p. B6.

18 Ronald Reagan, "Address to the National Association of Evangelicals," March 8, 1983, in *Reagan as President: Contemporary Views of the Man, His Politics, and His Policies*, Paul Boyer, ed. (Chicago: Ivan R. Dee, 1990), quotations on pp. 166, 168, 169.

19 Boyer, *When Time Shall Be No More*, 86–88.

20 Paul Boyer, "The Evangelical Resurgence in 1970s American Protestantism," in *Rightward Bound: Making America Conservative in the 1970s*, Bruce Schulman and Julian E. Zelitzer, eds. (Cambridge, MA: Harvard University Press, 2008), 33–43; Boyer, *When Time Shall Be No More*, 1–15 (Gallup poll: p. 2).

21 Boyer, *When Time Shall Be No More*, chaps. 4, 5, 8 (115–180, 254–290).

22 Ibid., 187–208; Timothy P. Weber, *On the Road to Armageddon: How Evangelicals Became Israel's Best Friend* (Grand Rapids, MI: Baker Academic, 2004), chaps. 8–9 (213–268).

23 "In the World of Good and Evil," *The Economist*, September 16, 2006: 37–38, quotation on p. 38. See also "God and American Diplomacy," *The Economist*, February 8, 2003: 33.

24 Fred Eastman, Letter to the Editor, *Christian Century*, August 29, 1945; Harry Emerson Fosdick, *On Being Fit to Live With: Sermons on Postwar Christianity* (New York: Harper & Brothers, 1946), 20, 76, 77. Eastman and Fosdick quoted in Paul Boyer, *By the Bomb's Early Light: American Thought and Culture at the Dawn of the Atomic Age* (New York: Pantheon Books, 1985), 196, 200. On the ministers' letter to Truman, see "Godless Götterdämmerung," *Time*, October 15, 1945, p. 62.

25 Boyer, *By the Bomb's Early Light*, chaps. 17–18 (196–229); Warren Goldstein, *William Sloane Coffin, Jr.: A Holy Impatience* (New Haven, CT: Yale University Press, new ed, 2006); Jo Ann O. Robinson, *Abraham Went Out: A Biography of A. J. Muste* (Philadelphia: Temple University Press, 1988); Murray Polner and Jim O'Grady, *Disarmed and Dangerous: The Radical Lives and Times of Daniel and Philip Berrigan* (New York: Basic Books, 1997); Mitchell K. Hall, *Because of Their Faith: CALCAV and Religious Opposition to the Vietnam War* (New York: Columbia University Press, 1990); Leo P. Ribuffo, Review of *Because of Their Faith* by Mitchell K. Hall, *American Historical Review* 96 (1991): 1326–1327; Doug Rossinow, *The Politics of Authenticity: Liberalism, Christianity, and the New Left in America* (New York: Columbia University Press, 1998). On evangelical support for the Vietnam War, see Anne C. Loveland,

American Evangelicals and the U.S. Military, 1942–1993 (Baton Rouge: Louisiana State University Press, 1997), chaps. 9–11 (118–164).

26 "American Religious Organizations and the Nuclear Weapons Debate," *Science, Technology, and Human Values* 8 (Summer 1983): 39–40; National Conference of Catholic Bishops, *The Challenge of Peace: God's Promise and Our Response* (Washington, DC: United States Catholic Conference, 1983), quotation on p. 92; David S. Meyer, *A Winter of Discontent: The Nuclear Freeze and American Politics* (New York: Praeger Paperbacks, 1990); Paul S. Boyer, "Selling War: Ronald Reagan's Strategic Defense Initiative," in *Selling War in a Media Age: The Presidency and Public Opinion in the American Century*, Kenneth Osgood and Andrew K. Frank, eds. (Gainesville: University Press of Florida, 2010), 196–223.

27 On the growth and political mobilization of evangelical Protestants, see William Martin, *With God on Our Side: The Rise of the Religious Right in America* (New York: Broadway Books, 2005); Howard Phillips, *American Theocracy: The Peril and Politics of Radical Religion, Oil, and Borrowed Money in the 21st Century* (New York: Viking Adult, 2006), Part II, "Too Many Preachers," 99–264; Michelle Goldberg, *Kingdom Come: The Rise of Christian Nationalism* (New York: W.W. Norton, 2006); Clyde Wilcox and Carin Larson, *Onward Christian Soldiers? The Religious Right in American Politics*, 3rd ed. (Boulder, CO: Westview Press, 2006); Michael Northcott, *An Angel Directs the Storm: Apocalyptic Religion and American Empire* (London: Tauris, 2004); and Esther Kaplan, *With God on Their Side: How Christian Fundamentalists Trampled Science, Policy, and Democracy in George W. Bush's White House* (New York: New Press, 2004).

28 On the worldwide reach of American televangelists and its implications, see Michael Serazio, "Geopolitical Proselytizing in the Marketplace for Loyalties: Rethinking the Global Gospel of American Christian Broadcasting," *Journal of Media and Religion* 8, no. 1 (2009): 40–54; Jeffrey K. Hadden, "The Globalization of American Televangelism," *International Journal of Frontier Missions* 7, no. 1 (January 1990): 1–10; and Robert S. Fortner, "Saving the World? American Evangelicals and Transnational Broadcasting," in *American Evangelicals and the Mass Media*, Quentin J. Schultze, ed. (Grand Rapids, MI: Zondervan Academic Books, 1990).

29 Michael Cromartie, ed., *Evangelicals and Foreign Policy: Four Perspectives* (Lanham, MD: University Press of America, 1989), vii.

30 Angus Reid Group, Cross-Border Survey, "Canada/U.S. Religion and Politics," October 11, 1996, 80, provided to the author by Professor Mark Noll. Of the U.S. respondents, 28% "strongly" agreed with this statement, and 14% "moderately" agreed, for a total of 42%. In a 1998 Gallup/*USA Today* poll, 39% of the respondents considered it either "very likely" (23%) or "somewhat likely" (16%) that "the World will come to an end because of Judgment Day or another religious event in the next century." Poll findings provided to the author by George H. Gallup, Jr., October 15, 2000.

31 Pat Robertson, *The New World Order* (Dallas, TX: Word Books, 1991), quotation on p. 176.

32 For an overview of LaHaye's career see Rob Boston, "Left Behind," *Church & State* 55 (February 2002): 8–13.

33 Boyer, *By the Bomb's Early Light*, 331–336; Hal Lindsey, "International Intelligence Briefing," Trinity Broadcasting Network, September 9, 2005, online at http://mediamatters.org/items/200509130004.

34 Dave Hunt, *A Cup of Trembling: Jerusalem and Bible Prophecy* (Eugene, OR: Harvest House, 1995), 196, 202. Italics added in second sentence.

35 Lindsey, *Blood Moon*, 312, 313.

36 *New York Times*, March 18, 1991, A9; *Boston Globe*, March 28, 1991, 22 (Jews for Jesus ads); Charles H. Dyer, *The Rise of Babylon: Sign of the End Times* (Wheaton, IL: Tyndale House Publishers, 1991), 14, 20. See also Joseph Chambers, *A Palace for the Antichrist: Saddam Hussein's Drive to Rebuild Babylon and Its Place in Bible Prophecy* (Green Forest, AR: New Leaf Press, 1996).

37 John Hagee, *Attack on America: New York, Jerusalem, and the Role of Terrorism in the Last Days* (Nashville, TN: Thomas Nelson Publishers, 2001); "Should Christian Missionaries Heed the Call in Iraq?" "Week in Review," *New York Times*, April 6, 2003, 14 (Graham quote); Michael D. Evans, *Beyond Iraq: The Next Move* (Lakeland, FL: White Stone Books, 2003), 79; Christopher Dreher, "Religion Publisher's First List Delivers Crossover Hit," *Publishers Weekly*, August 18, 2003 (on Evans's book); "Apocalyptic Theology Revitalized by Attacks," *New York Times*, November 23, 2001.

38 "The Boykin Affair: A Long Career of Marching with the Cross," *Time*, November 3, 2003; "Church Event Set for Base Stirs Concern," *New York Times*, April 6, 2003, A15; William M. Arkin, "The Pentagon Unleashes a Holy Warrior," *Los Angeles Times*, October 16, 2003.

39 For the cartoon by John Rule, which originally appeared on a now-defunct website, "Hal Lindsey Oracle," see http://www.oneimage.org/Images/pages/29cartoon54Zachariah12-9.htm, "The End is Nigh," *The Texas Observer*, December 12, 2002, http://www.texasobserver.org/article.php?aid=1192; Steven Kull, Principal Investigator, *Americans on Iraq: Three Years On*, TheWorldPublicOpinion. org/Knowledge Networks Poll, March 15, 2006 (on overall U.S. support for Iraq War); Charles Marsh, "Wayward Christian Soldiers," *New York Times*, January 20, 2006 (statistics on evangelical support for the war); "Left Behind," ABC Radio, "The Religion Report," October 22, 2003, on the web at http://www.abc.net.au/rn/talks/8.30/relrpt/stories/s972452.htm (LaHaye "Christians are suspicious" quote); Phillips, *American Theocracy*, quoted in Christine Rosen, "In God's Country," *Washington Post Book World*, April 9, 2006, 5. See also Sarah Posner, "Lobbying for Armageddon," AlterNet, August 3, 2006, http://www.alternet.org/story/39748/.

40 Norbert Lieth, "How the Conflict in the Present World Situation Can Be Explained," *Midnight Call*, June, 2002, 11; John Hagee, *Final Dawn Over Jerusalem* (Nashville, TN: Thomas Nelson Publishers, 1998), 34, 131, 150; David Cohen, "Liberty University to Send 3000 Students on a Study Tour of Israel," *Chronicle of Higher Education*, September 25, 1998, A51; Deanne Stillman, "Onward, Christian Soldiers," *The Nation*, June 3, 2002, 26–29, Netanyahu quotation on p. 27. See also Weber, *On the Road to Armageddon*; Irvine H. Anderson, *Biblical Interpretation and Middle East Policy: The Promised Land, America, and Israel, 1917–2002* (Gainesville: University Press of Florida, 2005); and Gershom Gorenberg, *The End of Days: Fundamentalism and the Struggle for the Temple Mount* (New York: Oxford University Press, 2002).

41 Evans, *Beyond Iraq*, 94, 104; Gary Bauer, address to AIPAC 2003 policy conference, http://www.tampabayprimer.org/index.cfm?action=articles&drill=viewArt&art=751#Bauer; "DeLay's Foreign Meddling," *Los Angeles Times*, August 1, 2003; Lou Dubose, "The Righteous Brothers," *The Texas Observer*, December 5, 2003: http://www.texasobserver.org/article.php?aid=1513 (DeLay at Hagee rally).

42 Hal Lindsey, WorldNetDaily Exclusive Commentary, "Beware of 'hudnas,'" posted Febraury 10, 2005, online at http://worldnetdaily.com; Thomas Ice, "Is Modern Israel Fulfilling Prophecy?" *Midnight Call* (February 2003): 15; Ice, "What Do You Do with a Future National Israel in the Bible," Pre-Trib Research Center Website, Febraury 21, 2005: http://www.according2prophecy.org/1israel.html.

43 Posner, "Lobbying for Armageddon"; "Christian Zionist Mobilizes for Israel," *Capital Times* [Madison, WI], July 29–30, 2006, A6 (reprinted from *The Wall Street Journal*); "For Evangelicals, Supporting Israel is God's Foreign Policy," *New York Times*, November 14, 2006; Max Blumenthal, "Rapture Ready," *The Nation*, July 27, 2007, at http://www.thenation.com/blog/rapture-ready. See also http://www.youtube.com/watch?feature=player_Embedded&v=mjMRgT50-Ig (Lieberman and DeLay quotations); "We People of Faith Stand Firmly with Israel," statement by Ralph Reed, chairman of the Georgia Republican Party and former director of the Christian Coalition, *New York Times*, May 2, 2002. This statement appeared as a public-service ad sponsored by the Anti-Defamation League.

44 Hunter, "The Shaping of American Foreign Policy," in Cromartie, ed., *Evangelicals and Foreign Policy*, 74.

45 "In the World of Good and Evil," 37; Steven Waldman, "Heaven Sent: Does God Endorse George Bush?" *Slate*, posted September 13, 2004, http://www.slate.com/id/2106590/ (Boykin quote). See also "The Faith Factor," *Time*, June 21, 2004, 28; Garry Wills, "With God on His Side," *New York Times Magazine*, March 30, 2003, 26–29.

46 Fred Nielsen, "With God on Our Side," History News Service, http://www.h-net.org/~hns/articles/2003/032003a.html ("[O]ur nation is chosen by God..."); Matthew Rothschild, "Bush's Messiah Complex," *The Progressive*, February 2003, 8–10 ("I could not be governor..."); "President Bush Addresses the 51st Annual Prayer Breakfast," White House website, February 2003: http://www.whitehouse.gov/news/releases/2003/02/20030206-1.html; "Bush and God," *Newsweek*, March 10, 2003, 24 ("We are in a conflict between good and evil"); Mark Danner, "Taking Stock of the Forever War," *New York Times Magazine*, September 11, 2005 ("rid the world of evil"); George W. Bush, "State of the Union Address," Febraury 2, 2005, White House website: http://www.whitehouse.gov/news/releases/2005/02/20050202-11.html; "President Thanks Military, Guests, at 'Celebration of Freedom' Concert," January 19, 2005, White House website: http://www.whitehouse.gov/news/releases/2005/01/20050119-15.html.

47 Robert N. Bellah, "Civil Religion in America," *Daedalus: Journal of the American Academy of Arts and Sciences* 96 (Winter 1967): 1–21.

48 Peggy Noonan, "It's Policy, Not Poetry," WSJ.com, posted December 16, 2004, online at http://www.opinionjournal.com/columnists/pnoonan/?id=110006032.

49 The National Council of Churches criticized the George W. Bush Administration's foreign policy in a number of areas; the NCC's website for

December 14, 2006 (http://www.councilofchurches.org/), for example, contained links to "NCC Welcomes Iraq Study Group Report"; "Churches Speak out on Iraq, Cloning, Global Warming"; "'Honor the Legacy': Campaign Asks Rededication to Geneva Conventions, International Law"; "Peaceful Ends Through Peaceful Means: A Witness for Peace in Israel and Palestine"; and similar entries. The Mennonite Central Committee, the American Friends Service Committee, and the Washington-based Friends Committee on National Legislation strongly opposed the Iraq War and other Bush Administration policies.

50 Jim Wallis, *Agenda for a Biblical People* (New York: Harper & Row, 1976) and *God's Politics: Why the Right Gets It Wrong and the Left Doesn't Get It* (San Francisco: HarperSanFrancisco, 2005); Ronald J. Sider, *Rich Christians in an Age of Hunger: A Biblical Study* (Downers' Grove, IL: InterVarsity Press, 1977). Sider went on to publish many other books, most recently *The Scandal of the Evangelical Conscience: Why Are Christians Living Just Like the Rest of the World?* (Grand Rapids, MI: Baker Books, 2005). Sider teaches at Philadelphia's Palmer (formerly Eastern Baptist) Theological Seminary.

51 Hunter, "Shaping American Foreign Policy," 76; National Association of Evangelicals, "For the Health of the Nation: An Evangelical Call to Civic Responsibility" (2004), on the NAE website: http://www.nae.net. For an expanded version, see Ronald J. Sider and Diane Knippers, *Toward an Evangelical Public Policy: Political Strategies for the Health of the Nation* (Grand Rapids, MI: Baker Books, 2005). See also "Evangelical Leaders Adopt Landmark Document Urging Greater Civic Engagement," NAE news release, October 8, 2004.

52 "Coalition of American Evangelicals Issues a Letter in Support of a Palestinian State," *New York Times*, July 29, 2007, A15.

53 "In the World of Good and Evil," 37–38 (on the role of religion in shaping U.S. foreign policy). See also David O. Moberg, *The Great Reversal: Evangelicalism versus Social Concern* (Philadelphia: Lippincott, 1977); "Pastor Chosen to Lead Christian Coalition Steps Down in Dispute over Agenda," *New York Times*, November 28, 2006; Robert Lanham, *The Sinner's Guide to the Evangelical Right* (New York: NAL Trade, 2005), 15 (on black evangelicals' Democratic allegiance); Thomas Frank, *What's the Matter with Kansas: How Conservatives Won the Heart of America* (New York: Metropolitan Books, 2004), on the Republican use of moral issues to court conservative religious voters; Andrew Greeley and Michael Hout, *The Truth About Conservative Christians: What They Think and What They Believe* (Chicago: University of Chicago Press, 2006), on the diversity of political and social views among religious conservatives; David Kuo, *Tempting Faith: An Inside Story of Political Seduction* (New York: Free Press, 2006), on the dismissive view of evangelicals Kuo found in the George W. Bush White House.

54 "Seventh-day Adventist World Church Statistics," www.adventist.org/world_church/facts_and_figures/index.html; American Jewish World Service: http://www.ajws.org/; "A Brief History of CRS": www.crs.org/about_us/who_we_are/history.cfm; "World Vision's History": www.worldvision.org/worldvision/comms,nsf/stable/history; J. William Frost, "American Friends Service Committee" in Boyer, ed., *Oxford Companion to United States History*, 32; Robert S. Kreider and Rachel Waltner Goosen, *Hungry, Thirsty, a Stranger: The MCC Experience* (Scottdale, PA: Herald Press, 1988).

55 *New York Times,* December 22, 1952, 16, quoted in Patrick Henry, "'And I Don't Care What It Is': The Tradition-History of a Civil Religion Proof-Text," *Journal of the American Academy of Religion* 49 (March 1981): 37. Henry's entertaining article traces the vicissitudes of this quotation, in various mangled versions, in the work of Sydney E. Ahlstrom, Will Herberg, Robert Bellah, and others.

56 CUFI delegate interviewed in Blumethal, "Rapture Ready."

| "Courting Anarchy"?: Religious
Pluralism and the Law

SHAWN FRANCIS PETERS

LATE IN THE SUMMER of 2007, a group of Amitabha Buddhists bought dozens of live animals from fish markets in the Chinatown section of New York. Advocates of Pure Land Buddhism, they had no intention of eating the frogs, eels, and reptiles they purchased, nor did they want to keep the animals as pets. Buddhists believe that humans can be reincarnated in the form of reptiles, and members of the Amitabha sect hoped that their purchases could in their subsequent lives "go back to the world as good people and go to heaven," as one of them put it. To help further that process, members of the sect traveled to the nearest body of fresh water, the Passaic River in New Jersey, and performed a religious ritual: they released the reptiles into the water.[1]

The Buddhists' rite alarmed public officials in New Jersey—not because they were bothered by its religious trappings, but because they feared its potential environmental impact. In recent years, a number of ecosystems throughout the country have been disturbed by the introduction of non-native invasive species, the most pernicious being the snakehead fish. To help control the spread of such potentially disruptive animals, New Jersey requires anyone intending to stock wildlife to first obtain a permit from the fish and wildlife division of the state's environmental protection agency, which can determine if the particular species are appropriate for release. Because the Amitabha Buddhists had failed to take this step before performing their ceremony at the Passaic River, state authorities asserted that they might face possible fines of up to $1000.[2]

Such church-state disputes—or, in this case, temple-state disputes—are hardly a new feature of the American social and political landscape. Throughout the nineteenth and twentieth centuries, devout individuals from a variety of faiths wrangled with state authorities who, in the name of maintaining public order, sought to regulate their religious conduct. Mormon polygamists, Jehovah's Witness proselytizers, Christian Science healers, Amish parents—all found themselves in court when secular authorities challenged particular religious practices. What makes the brewing dispute over the Amitabha

Buddhists' religious practices revealing is that the potential defendants, unlike those earlier litigants, are not Christians.

Before the 1970s, nearly all significant legal disputes over the First Amendment's provision safeguarding the free exercise of religion, and analogous measures in state constitutions, involved members of Christian churches. These tended to be faiths on the perceived margins of mainstream Protestantism, with beliefs and practices that seemed aberrant to most Americans. As many contributors to this volume have noted, a "new religious America" (to borrow Diana Eck's apt description) flowered after the enactment of the Immigration and Nationality Act of 1965, significantly altering the face of religion in America. That change was mirrored by a similar shift in the kinds of religion cases heard by the courts. Litigation over purportedly "fringe" religious behavior increasingly involved Muslims, Buddhists, Hindus, and members of "new religious movements" (NRMs) or "cults,"[3] many of which had roots or connections outside the United States.[4] Now, Jehovah's Witness proselytizers were joined in the courts by Hare Krishnas, whose practice of *Sankirtan*—an aggressive form of religious proselytizing—led to a succession of prosecutions in states across the country starting in the 1970s.

Legal protections for faith-based practices are part of the bedrock of religious pluralism in America. It is difficult to imagine such a diverse array of faiths flourishing for so long—and with, relatively speaking, so little repression, official or otherwise—without the elegant combination of safeguards and limitations for religion codified in the First Amendment (and subsequently redefined by courts at all levels). Since immigration laws were liberalized in the mid-1960s, how the courts have delimited the scope of those boundaries for religion vis-à-vis non-Christians and purported "cultists" has shaped the contours and character of religious pluralism in the United States, helping to continually define and redefine the limits of both the religious conduct of individuals as well as the operation of religious bodies. Similarly important over the last four decades have been the sometimes rancorous secular political processes by which states have attempted to regulate religious customs and organizations that previously had been relatively uncommon on these shores (if not entirely unknown). This interplay between law and religion demonstrates not only that the state can and indeed *will* impose limits on religious pluralism, but also that those parameters can wax and wane—often in unexpected and perhaps troubling ways—in response to the broader social, political, and cultural forces that shape American life as a whole.

With its attention long focused on such matters as economic regulation, the U.S. Supreme Court got off to a relatively late start in interpreting the religion clauses of the First Amendment. Indeed, it was not until 1947, in *Everson v. Board of Education*, that the Court rendered a truly significant ruling in an Establishment Clause case.[5] The belated development of these lines of constitutional jurisprudence was due in large part to the long-prevailing notion that the provisions of the Bill of Rights were applicable strictly to actions by the federal government and not individual states. Only in the twentieth century, when the court began its piecemeal incorporation of the First Amendment's safeguards of civil liberties into the due process clause of the Fourteenth Amendment, did the court begin to seriously examine the conditions under which states regulated such matters as speech and religion.

Because the underlying legal dispute occurred in what was then a federal territory (Utah), the high court's first major case dealing with the free exercise of religion preceded the process of incorporation. In *Reynolds v. United States* (1879), the Supreme Court considered a challenge made by a Mormon named George Reynolds to a federal statute banning polygamy. The longest and most significant part of Chief Justice Morrison Waite's opinion addressed Reynolds's claim that the federal law compromised his religious liberty. Waite began his discussion of this issue by stressing that Congress lacked the authority to pass any law that would abrogate the religious liberty of individuals living in territories such as Utah. Waite simply did not believe, however, that polygamy was a bona fide religious practice and thus beyond the regulatory authority of Congress. (He decried it as little more than an "odious" custom.) Moreover, marriage, for all its religious trappings, was at bottom "a civil contract," and as such it was "usually regulated by law."[6]

The chief justice went on to make a crucial distinction that would influence free exercise jurisprudence for decades to come. "Laws are made for the government of actions," Waite wrote, "and while they cannot interfere with mere religious belief and opinions, they may with practices." George Reynolds, in short, was free to believe anything he wished, but his conduct remained very much subject to regulation by the state. That this conduct might have been inspired by a religious belief did not mean that the First Amendment protected it. "Can a man excuse his practice to the contrary [of an established law] because of his religious belief?" Waite asked. "To permit this would be to make the professed doctrines of religious belief superior to the law of the land, and in effect to permit every citizen to become a law unto himself. Government could exist only in name under such circumstances."[7]

The Jehovah's Witnesses, who trooped before the high court more than two dozen times between 1938 and 1946, gave the *Reynolds* precedent its first sustained challenge. Persecuted throughout the United States during the World War II era because of their obstreperous proselytizing activities and refusal to salute the American flag (they considered the ceremony idolatrous), the Witnesses repeatedly sought judicial safeguards for their imperiled civil rights. Among the most significant Witness cases of this era was *Cantwell v. Connecticut* (1940), in which a church member challenged a state law requiring religious proselytizers to obtain a municipal permit before they canvassed in public. *Cantwell* proved to be a watershed for religious liberty. The Supreme Court used the Witness case to incorporate the First Amendment's Free Exercise clause into the protections afforded by the Fourteenth Amendment, meaning that religious practices could be shielded from state (and not simply federal) regulation. And in striking down the Connecticut measure as unconstitutional, the Supreme Court applied a heightened level of judicial scrutiny to the permit requirement.[8]

The Supreme Court built on *Cantwell* and other Witness-related opinions in several subsequent cases involving members of other faiths and further fortified judicial protections for religious liberty. For instance, in *Sherbert v. Verner* (1963), a case involving a Seventh-day Adventist, the justices introduced a three-pronged test for evaluating religious liberty claims. In addition to gauging whether state action burdened a claimant's religious liberty, the court would assess whether there was a "compelling state interest" in applying a particular regulation and whether or not granting an exemption to such a rule would undermine that interest. (Using this heightened level of scrutiny, the court issued a ruling in favor of Adell Sherbert, a Seventh-day Adventist who had claimed that she had been denied unemployment benefits because of her refusal to work Saturdays, the Adventist Sabbath.)[9] For many observers, *Wisconsin v. Yoder* (1971) marked the apogee of this trend toward more expansive protections for religious liberty, with the high court holding in favor of Old Order Amish parents who opposed a compulsory school attendance law in Wisconsin on the grounds that it forced them to violate the tenets of their faith. (The Amish believed that sending their children to school past the age of 14, as state law required, would make the youngsters too "worldly" and thereby fray their connections with the church.)[10]

With judicial precedents like *Sherbert* and *Yoder* in place, it seemed as though the courts were poised to inaugurate an era in which all but the most outlandish religious practices were beyond the reach of state regulation. And, indeed, there were indications that religious claimants, even those hailing from what researchers categorized as "marginal" religions, fared better in the courts in the 1970s than they had several decades previously—surely a positive sign for the members of faiths that began to proliferate after the nation's immigration laws changed in the mid-1960s. According to one careful study, the litigants making free-exercise claims over the next decade benefited from those safeguards: in judicial opinions reported between 1970 and 1980, they prevailed on the merits in nearly 37% of cases. (That figure represented more than three times their success rate between 1946 and 1956, when judicial protections for religious practice were less stout.) In leafleting, soliciting, and proselytizing litigation reported in that decade, members' "marginal" faiths prevailed in 35 out of 43 cases. This rate of success led two scholars to conclude in 1983 that "at long last marginal or dissident religions have found a measure of constitutional protection."[11]

Or had they? Even as scholars were looking back on the apparent gains for religious liberty made in the 1970s, courts in a variety of jurisdictions, including the U.S. Supreme Court, had begun a process of whittling away at them. By 1990, *Yoder* would be but a distant memory, replaced as the law of the land by *Employment Division v. Smith*, an opinion in which Justice Antonin Scalia all but mocked the standards that had been established in earlier free-exercise litigation, suggesting at one point that rigorous application of the compelling interest standard would amount to nothing less than "courting anarchy."[12] In response to *Smith*, Congress enacted the Religious Freedom Restoration Act (RFRA), which had as its explicit goal to restore many of the constitutional protections articulated in decisions like *Sherbert* and *Yoder*, most significantly the "compelling government interest" standard, which required proof that laws infringing on individuals' free-exercise rights satisfied some significant state interest. But this, too, the Supreme Court found unconstitutional, in *Boerne v. Flores* (1997).[13]

One revealing method of surveying the road leading from *Yoder* to *Boerne* and beyond is to examine contentious litigation involving the religious faiths that have flowered in the United States since the mid-1960s, such as the Hare Krishnas. Their practice of *Sankirtan*—an assertive form of religious proselytizing with roots dating back to at least the ninth century—repeatedly put them at odds with public authorities throughout the United States in the 1970s and early 1980s. From reading the somewhat hyperbolic judicial opinions that were published in this period, one might get the impression that the nation's fairgrounds, airports, and bus depots were in danger of being overrun by overly aggressive members of a sect who sought to disseminate information regarding their religious faith and coerce unwilling individuals into providing financial donations. Hare Krishnas repeatedly fought restrictive permit and licensing requirements that were reminiscent of the strictures that states and municipalities attempted to impose on a comparably persistent and unpopular religious minority—the Jehovah's Witnesses—during the World War II era. It was apparent to at least one judge that sect members encountered so many legal obstacles in part because of sheer intolerance. Reviewing the rejection of the Hare Krishnas' 1977 application to stage a demonstration in Manhattan's Washington Square Park, Justice Hortense W. Gabel of the Supreme Court of New York wrote, "It is clear to this court that the major, if not exclusive, reason for rejection was the unpopularity of the [sect] and the community's dislike and fear of its religious beliefs and practices." (Gabler then drew the obvious conclusion that "fear and dislike cannot provide a constitutional basis for denial of this permit.")[14]

The animus directed toward Hare Krishnas was evident in their ongoing battle to freely practice *Sankirtan* on the grounds of the New York State Fair. After receiving numerous complaints about sect members' proselytizing activities at previous fairs, authorities resolved in 1977 to restrict Hare Krishnas to a stationary booth—where, presumably, they would be less intrusive. When the Krishnas filed suit, claiming that the requirement violated both their right to free exercise of religion and right to free speech, the case wound up before Judge Howard Munson of the U.S. District Court for the Northern District of New York. Munson's opinion in *International Society for Krishna Consciousness v. Barber* provided an encyclopedic account of sect members' alleged misdeeds at previous sessions of the fair, which included what he termed "fraudulent accosting and misrepresentation." (Devotees would force ostensibly free record albums onto fairgoers, for instance, and then demand "donations" in return.)

Given that history of misbehavior, Munson had little difficulty finding that fair authorities merely sought to impose a constitutionally permissible restriction on the time, place, and manner of the Hare Krishnas' soliciting. This would, Munson wrote, help mitigate sect members' "illicit acts."[15]

The Hare Krishna solicitation cases reached a climax in 1981, when the U.S. Supreme Court heard *Heffron v. International Society for Krishna Consciousness*. This was another fairgrounds solicitation case: authorities in Minnesota wished to limit all distributors of literature at the state fair, including Hare Krishnas', to fixed locations. It was resolved as *Barber* had been a year earlier, with the court holding that sect members' activities were subject to reasonable time, place, and manner restrictions, even if they were engaged in religious activities. Writing for the Court's majority, Justice Byron White asserted that the regulations served "a significant governmental interest" by safeguarding the "safety and convenience" of individuals in the public space of the fairgrounds.[16]

In and of itself, *Heffron* by no means represented a death blow to judicial protections for religious liberty vis-à-vis the kinds of faiths that began to emerge in the United States after the mid-1960s. But it was certainly emblematic of how those faiths—almost all of them lacking in secular political clout—struggled with a variety of forms of governmental regulation throughout the 1970s and 1980s. Perhaps no two religious bodies were more profoundly affected by state regulation than the Worldwide Church of God (WCG) and the Unification Church. After a tangled and somewhat irregular legal proceeding, the WCG—founded by Herbert Armstrong, whose ministry began in the 1930s—was actually taken over by the state of California for a brief period in the late 1970s. The dispute centered on the alleged misappropriation of church funds for personal use "on a massive scale" by Armstrong and six codefendants. Prodded by a dissident faction of church members headed by Armstrong's son, California's attorney general filed a complaint in state court seeking to put the WCG into receivership. The attorney argued that the WCG was, like every charitable organization, subject to some measure of state control, in part because the church itself and its affiliated institutions (these included a college) "enjoyed substantial public subsidies," primarily in the form of tax exemptions. This argument proved successful, if only temporarily: a state superior court judge appointed a receiver "to take possession and control of the church and all its assets" and "supervise and monitor" its financial dealings and records. He further permitted the attorney general's office to conduct "a full and complete financial examination and audit" of the WCG's holdings, which had an estimated worth of $80 million.[17]

Although the WCG itself might not have enjoyed broad public support, a number of secular and religious organizations rallied to its defense after it came under attack by California's attorney general. When the church sought a hearing before the state supreme court in order to dissolve the receivership, religious bodies as diverse as the Unification Church and the Archdiocese of Los Angeles sought to file friend-of-the-court briefs branding the state's efforts to regulate the church as patently unconstitutional. This "outpouring of support," as the WCG termed it, included a particularly strong claim from the archdiocese, which argued that "a more complete departure from the long-established constitutional principles and tradition of religious freedom can scarcely be imagined."[18] Such protests failed to sway the court—it refused to rein in the attorney general—but they resonated in the state legislature. Concerned by what one lawmaker decried as the abuses of "overzealous prosecutors," legislators responded to the WCG imbroglio by curbing the attorney general's power to take legal action against religious bodies.[19] After Governor Jerry Brown signed the bill in the fall of 1980, the attorney general dropped his inquiry into the WCG, and the receivership was terminated.

After the WCG prevailed, its attorney exulted that his faith "in the legislative process and this country's commitment to preserve religious freedoms" had been restored.[20] But he might have adopted a less sanguine view had he undertaken a broader examination of how "the legislative process" was affecting NRMs (New Religious Movements) in other states. According to one sobering account, a "legislative assault on new religions" took place at both the state and national levels in the late 1970s and early 1980s. Often prodded into action by anticult activists, lawmakers in Pennsylvania, Maryland, and Massachusetts, among other states, conducted broad-ranging inquiries into the practices of groups that purportedly relied on (in the words of one piece of legislation) "improper mind control techniques in their recruitment and subsequent retention of members." (Typically, this meant the Hare Krishnas, the Church of Scientology, and the Unification Church.) These efforts were duplicated in Washington, where the likes of Kansas Senator Bob Dole and New York Congressmen Richard Ottinger called for more sweeping and intensive examinations of the practices of NRMs. Dole held several widely publicized hearings on cult practices, and Ottinger inserted into the *Congressional Record* a damning report entitled "Cults and Their Slaves." He also introduced in the House of Representatives an implicitly anticult resolution that advocated changing federal law to "provide penalties for certain deceptive and coercive practices used by certain organizations in recruiting members, and for other purposes."[21]

Although Ottinger's resolution went nowhere, it typified efforts being made by lawmakers throughout the country in the late 1970s and early 1980s to regulate "cult" practices. So many anticult measures were introduced in this period that one observer concluded, "The welter of legislation has been staggering." In Nebraska, legislators felt compelled to investigate what one resolution termed "the problem of cult activity." Their counterparts in Illinois considered no fewer than seven measures aimed at regulating cults and their members. One 1981 bill was aimed at preventing cult members from engaging in "deceitful practices" in recruiting new members and using "menticide techniques" to control them once they joined. The caustic tenor of these proposals reflected an increasingly widespread public perception that many cults and NRMs were potentially dangerous organizations that merely masqueraded as religions in order to escape state scrutiny.[22]

The Unification Church and its leader, the Rev. Sun Myung Moon, came under particularly intense regulatory scrutiny in this period. In 1978, lawmakers in Minnesota amended that state's registration and disclosure requirements for charitable organizations in a manner that appeared to be specifically directed at the controversial church. Religious organizations long had been considered exempt from those regulations, but state legislators altered them so that the exemption would cover only those religious bodies that received more than half of their total contributions from members or affiliated organizations. There seemed to be little question that the revision was aimed at groups like the Unification Church and the Hare Krishnas, whose members aggressively solicited donations in public. One lawmaker admitted as much, stating that the change was aimed at giving closer scrutiny to "the people that are running around airports and running around streets and soliciting people." Another legislator, who clearly was less enamored of the revision, wondered, "I'm not sure why we're so hot to regulate the Moonies anyway."[23]

The Unification Church challenged the revised law as a violation of the First Amendment's establishment clause, arguing that it amounted to the state granting preference to certain religions over others. Minnesota responded that Moon's church was not a bona fide religious organization at all and thereby failed to qualify for *any* kind of exemption under the charitable contributions measure. In *Larson v. Valente* (1982), the U.S. Supreme Court held in favor of the Unification Church. Writing for the Court's majority, Justice William Brennan asserted that the state's action in creating the 50% threshold for oversight—a threshold that would affect only a few unpopular churches—established "precisely the sort of official denominational preference that the Framers of the First Amendment forbade."[24]

The Rev. Moon himself was somewhat less fortunate in his dealings with the federal government, which zealously pursued him on tax-evasion charges in the early 1980s. During a six-week trial, prosecutors alleged that Moon had committed fraud by filing inaccurate federal tax returns and engaged in a criminal conspiracy to cover up his crime. They deliberately downplayed the religious dimensions of the case, referring to Moon as "an ordinary high-ranking businessman" rather than the founder and leader of a religious organization. Perhaps not surprisingly, Moon's formidable defense team—including Harvard Law School's Laurence Tribe—took the opposite tack: it asserted that he was being prosecuted precisely because he was a religious leader, and an unpopular one at that. (One defense attorney complained that the government pursued Moon to satisfy a "public bloodlust.") A jury convicted Moon, and he was sentenced to an 18-month term in prison and fined $25,000.[25] Even this punishment failed fully to satisfy federal authorities: following his conviction, they raised the possibility of having the Immigration and Naturalization Service initiate deportation proceedings against Moon, who was a resident alien. However, a federal judge, determining that Moon already faced sufficient punishment for his misdeeds, ruled that he could remain in the country. (He would spend over a year incarcerated at the Federal Correctional Institution in Danbury, Connecticut.)[26]

As was amply demonstrated by the experiences of the Hare Krishnas, the Worldwide Church of God, and the Unification Church, religious organizations stigmatized with the "cult" label were prime targets for state regulation in the 1970s and 1980s—this despite the U.S. Supreme Court's apparent bolstering of judicial safeguards for religion in such opinions as *Sherbert* and *Yoder*. In retrospect, it seems apparent that a variety of factors contributed to governmental efforts to restrict, if not simply suppress, the activities of these religious organizations. To be sure, "cult" members were not always model citizens. Many resorted to overly aggressive or downright deceptive proselytizing tactics, and their apparent subordination of new members left them open to the accusation that they engaged in "mind control" tactics. The most extreme example of cult misbehavior occurred in Guyana in 1979, when Jim Jones, leader of the Peoples Temple, coerced nearly one thousand followers into ingesting poisoned Kool Aid. (Congressman Leo Ryan, who had traveled to Guyana to investigate the group, also was assassinated by Jones's followers just before the mass suicide.)[27]

But, their actual misdeeds aside, many religious movements appear to have been deemed suspect—and therefore ripe for regulation—because of their foreign origins and their ideological distance from mainstream Christianity. What might have made Sun Myung Moon appear so menacing, for instance, was that he had been born in Korea and bore a distinctively Asian name. So too with the Hare Krishnas, whose dress and practices (which included ritual chanting) heralded the group's South Asian origins. And, of course, neither the "Moonies" nor the Hare Krishnas espoused doctrines that were even remotely aligned with the nation's prevalent Catholic or Protestant denominations. Indeed, in many cases (such as *Larson v. Valente*), several public officials who sought stricter oversight of the operations of the Unification Church asserted that such organizations were not even bona fide religions at all.

Such cultural factors might also have inspired and complicated efforts to regulate even more established non-Christian faiths that burgeoned in the United States after immigration restrictions were relaxed in the mid-1960s. Sikhs, for instance, were rarely (if ever) involved in noteworthy litigation in any American jurisdiction prior to the 1960s. By the end of 1990s, however, an advocacy group known as the Sikh Coalition could issue a summary of landmark decisions relating to Sikh religious identity. Several of these cases involved two of the essential symbols of Sikh identity: long hair and the *kirpan*, a short ceremonial knife that is to be worn at all times. (For adherents to the faith, it signifies an obligation to safeguard the weak.) A prolonged legal dispute in California involved a group of Sikh children challenging the application to them of that state's statutory ban on weapons in public schools. After failing to reach a compromise with the Livingston Union School District, the youngsters' families went to federal district court to obtain an injunction allowing them to continue carrying the knives. Restrictions on the wearing of the ceremonial knives, they asserted, violated their First Amendment right to the free exercise of religion. Under the Religious Freedom Restoration Act (which the Supreme Court subsequently ruled unconstitutional), the district court issued a preliminary injunction ordering the school district to permit *kirpans*, provided that the knives met certain restrictions regarding length, sharpness, and accessibility.[28] The American Civil Liberties Union helped to broker an eventual settlement permanently exempting Sikhs from the weapons ban. Lawyers representing one of the families called it "an important achievement for religious liberty."[29]

A *kirpan* case in New York forced one judge to acknowledge how difficult it is for the courts to, as he put it, "effectuate a fair and rational balance between religious freedoms and the enforcement of criminal statutes designed to protect, among others, the very citizens and residents who...assert their religious right to observe certain customs and traditions inherent in their faith." The case began early in 1986 when a Sikh named Partap Singh was arrested for carrying his *kirpan* while waiting on a subway platform. Police charged Singh with violating a New York City law prohibiting individuals from wearing or displaying knives in public view. The judge who heard Singh's case, John A. Milano, recognized that the Sikh did not have a "lawful purpose" for carrying the knife, as the statute mandated. Thus, there was "no basis for dismissal [of the charges] as a matter of law." But, after exhaustively reviewing the development of Free Exercise jurisprudence and carefully delineating Sikh beliefs and practices, Milano exercised his discretion and set the charges aside. He asserted that, even though the defendant might have violated the narrow stipulations of the knife law, allowing Singh to be prosecuted for wearing a religious emblem "would not be in the furtherance of justice."[30]

The terrorist attacks of September 11, 2001—carried out by Muslims purporting to act from religious motivations—helped to create an entirely new constellation of challenges to the religious liberty of non-Christians in the United States. Extra-legal confrontations, such as attacks on individuals and places of worship, occurred in communities throughout the country. Moreover, a wide range of new state and federal regulations that were aimed at improving security (and thereby preventing future terrorist attacks) wound up threatening to circumscribe non-Christian religious traditions. Many Sikhs, for instance, encountered obstacles when they attempted to pass through the beefed-up airport security checkpoints that came under the purview of the new Transportation Security Administration (TSA). In 2007, that agency promulgated guidelines allowing the nation's 43,000 airport screeners to pull aside travelers for more intrusive "secondary screenings" simply because they wore turbans. A group of U.S. senators, led by Democrat Richard Durbin of Illinois, drafted a letter of protest to the TSA that cited the unpleasant experiences of several Sikh travelers who had been screened under the policy. The senators asserted that "it seems that travelers are being singled out for secondary screening solely on the basis of physical manifestations of their religious beliefs." The TSA eventually relented, adopting a new policy that seemed to better accommodate religious head coverings.[31]

Perhaps not surprisingly, Muslims and their religious traditions were particularly imperiled after 9/11. When the Council of American-Islamic Relations (CAIR) issued in early 2002 a dismal summary of the status of Muslim civil liberties in the United States, it found pervasive discrimination against members of the faith. In addition to suffering from an egregious array of hate crimes, some had been terminated from employment, or denied it altogether; others had been denied accommodation of their religious practices in schools, prisons, and places of employment. "All of these experiences," the CAIR concluded, "have common elements of setting religious and ethnic features of Muslim life or Muslim religious and political and religious views apart from what is considered normal and acceptable."[32] Noting the ongoing erosion of legal protections for members of the faith, subsequent reports on the status of Muslim civil liberties in the United States were scarcely more upbeat. CAIR's report for 2005 lamented the "growing disparity in how American Muslims are being treated under the law on many different levels."[33]

This was perhaps most evident in the U.S. Department of Justice's apparent stretching of federal law to detain Muslims with suspected links to terrorist activity. As the American Civil Liberties Union (ACLU) and Human Rights Watch noted in a 2005 report, after 9/11 the Justice Department detained 69 Muslims under a federal "material witness" statute. Although the measure was designed to allow for the brief detention of individuals possessing critical information about specific crimes, the Justice Department invoked it to hold Muslim witnesses with only the barest connections to terrorist activity for periods lasting as much as a full year, and nearly half of them never wound up testifying before a grand jury or in court. The ACLU asserted that the federal government abused the material witness statute "to buy time to conduct fishing expeditions for evidence to justify arrests on criminal or immigration charges." The Justice Department itself eventually acknowledged some merit to this accusation: it apologized to more than a dozen of the men for having wrongfully detained them.[34]

Muslims in many communities also ran into opposition when they endeavored to build or modify mosques. In 2000, Congress passed the Religious Land Use and Institutionalized Persons Act (RLUIPA), a measure designed in part to prevent governments at all levels from "impos[ing] or implement[ing] a land use regulation in a manner that imposes a substantial burden on the religious exercise of a person, including a religious assembly or institution," unless they could demonstrate a "compelling interest" for doing so.[35] The federal measure made it more difficult—at least in theory—for municipalities to create or enforce burdensome zoning restrictions to block the erection of places of worship. But even with the provisions of RLUIPA on their side, Muslims hoping to build or expand mosques after 9/11 often found themselves "encountering vehement opposition" from citizens and their elected representatives, according to one account.[36]

When opponents invoked the strictures of zoning ordinances to block mosque construction, they often cited practical concerns, such as the disruptions to community life that might be caused by increased traffic flow or decreased property values. However, an undercurrent of religious intolerance sometimes flowed just beneath this legalistic surface. In 2002, for instance, Muslims in Marietta, Georgia, sought a zoning variance for the construction of a new mosque that featured a 70-foot-tall minaret. When the local zoning board denied the request, there were accusations that its members had caved in to bigotry and rebuffed those hoping to build the mosque "purely because they were Muslims."[37] A similar dispute erupted in 2007 in Walkersville, Maryland, when the Ahmadiyya Muslim Community sought permission to build a worship facility and retreat on a large farm parcel. Local officials were not warm to the proposal, one allegedly even going so far as to furnish financial support and advice to a citizens' group opposing the construction. An attorney representing the Muslims called on the federal Justice Department to investigate whether the town had violated RLUIPA. "This is one of the most blatant examples of hostility to a particular religious group that I have ever seen," the lawyer asserted.[38]

Hindus utilized RLUIPA for protection as well. Throughout the early 2000s, members of the Sri Venkateswara temple in Bridgewater, New Jersey, engaged in a prolonged battle to expand its facilities. Local zoning authorities, citing concerns over traffic and noise pollution, initially denied all of the temple's requests for expansion, but they relented partially after being named in a lawsuit, allowing for the expansion of the temple itself and the construction of detached housing for ten priests and their families. The sticking point remained a variance that would allow for the replacement of the temple's cultural center with a much larger structure. This expansion was critical, the Bridgewater Hindus argued, because the building hosted essential religious events, including performances and celebrations. Apparently eager to address community concerns, representatives of the temple repeatedly modified their plans for the cultural center and even offered to mitigate traffic congestion by funding improvements for a nearby highway. The board still refused to give in, and another lawsuit followed, with the temple this time losing. The legal dispute was still grinding on in mid-2007 as the temple contemplated, as a kind of final legal recourse, invoking the provisions of RLUIPA in order to gain the necessary zoning variances for the cultural center's expansion. One land-use expert observed that the Bridgewater Hindus had "a lot going for them" in their challenge under the federal statute.[39]

Prisoners from a variety of religious traditions also turned to RLUIPA, which prohibited correctional institutions from imposing a "substantial burden" on their religious exercise unless they could demonstrate a "compelling governmental interest" in doing so. One comprehensive survey found 46 reported cases involving prisoners who had filed claims under RLUIPA during its first four years. These ranged from challenges to diet and grooming restrictions to protests against limits on group worship and access to religious literature.

Muslim prisoners turned to RLUIPA for a variety of reasons: to gain religious exemptions from prison regulations that prohibited the wearing of beards; to force prison authorities to establish separate worship services for Sunnis and Shiites; and to enable them to possess Islamic prayer beads. Another Muslim case, *Tayr Kilaab al Ghashiyah v. Wisconsin Dept. of Correction*, involved a prisoner who had been deprived of access to ceremonial oil, incense, and candles (described by prison authorities as potentially lethal "incendiary materials" that could be used to set fire to the facility) and prohibited from using his Muslim name (which had been legally changed from John Casteel).[40]

In his seminal book *Religious Outsiders and the Making of Americans*, published in 1986, R. Laurence Moore assessed the experiences of a range of non-mainstream religious groups in the United States, among them Mormons, Christian Scientists, and Christian Fundamentalists. Moore provocatively argued that in dissenting from doctrinal orthodoxy (sometimes at an enormous price), members of such groups were equipped with "strategies for success...badges of respectability and at least sometimes, a path to upward social mobility and greatly enhanced power." Nonconformity, in short, broadly translated into opportunity for these purported outsiders. Moore even went a step further, arguing that "a characteristic way of inventing one's Americanness" has involved identifying as an outsider.[41]

As Moore and others have noted, the courts often have provided a powerful forum for religious outsiders to assert their rights and gain status, even when they do not prevail on particular legal issues. The Jehovah's Witnesses provided the classic example of this phenomenon. Their ongoing legal campaign, which began in the World War II era and has stretched into the present day, has helped to transform them in public perception from suspicious "cultists" into harmless (if still slightly annoying) members of a generally respectable church. The fact that they have so willingly engaged in a secular political process, and have so often invoked the nation's core values in doing so, has made them seem less threatening.

It remains to be seen if a similar process—legitimization through litigation, if you will—has been taking place for the "religious outsiders" whose ranks in the United States have swelled over the past four decades. Cult members, Hare Krishnas, Sikhs, Hindus, Muslims, and Buddhists all have run afoul of public authorities intent on tightening government regulation of religious practices or the operation of religious organizations. This inherently adversarial process has not always helped these devout individuals achieve, in the words of Moore's paradigm, "greatly enhanced power." To cite the most glaring example: in the name of protecting national security, some laws have been stretched in unprecedented ways to target Muslims specifically. Their desultory experiences since 9/11 have demonstrated in especially dramatic fashion how secular political processes—lawmaking, the application of those laws by public authorities, and their interpretation in the courts—can profoundly affect religious individuals and the communities they form. So too with the Worldwide Church of God, which faced the prospect of essentially a state takeover in California.

One struggles to see how such manifestations of state control might foster religious pluralism, especially as they seem to reflect an implicit animus toward non-normative religions in general and non-Christian faiths in particular. But neither laws nor the people who implement them are static; both change over time in response to developing social, political, cultural, and economic conditions. Even in these fluid circumstances, the likes of Amitabha Buddhists might not accrue much political clout; indeed, like the Amish, they might very well spurn the entire notion of participating in secular governance as a form of "worldly" corruption. Yet their increased and ongoing presence in the public square—sparking debate over how laws relating to religious conduct and the governance of religious organizations are to be implemented and interpreted—might in itself help to shape the parameters of religious pluralism for decades to come.

Notes

1 Samantha Henry, "Buddhist Animal Ritual Gets Vegans in Trouble," *The Record* (Bergen, New Jersey), August 14, 2007, L1.

2 Sachi Fujimori, "State May Work with Buddhists on Wildlife Release," *Herald News* (Passaic, New Jersey), August 30, 2007, C1.

3 Opponents of particular religious groups often employ "cult" as an epithet meant to denote a group with purportedly aberrant beliefs and practices. I use it here as a neutral term of religious sociology.

4 Diana Eck, *A New Religious America: How a "Christian Country" Has Now Become the World's Most Religiously Diverse Nation* (San Francisco: HarperSanFrancisco, 2001).

5 *Everson v. Board of Education*, 330 U.S. 1 (1947).

6 *Reynolds v. United States*, 98 U.S. 145 (1879).

7 *Reynolds v. United States*, 153–168.

8 *Cantwell v. Connecticut*, 310 U.S. 296 (1940).

9 *Sherbert v. Verner*, 374 U.S. 398 (1963).

10 *Wisconsin v. Yoder*, 406 U.S. 205 (1972). For a more comprehensive account of this case, see: Shawn Francis Peters, *The Yoder Case: Religious Freedom, Education, and Parental Rights* (Lawrence: University Press of Kansas, 2003).

11 Frank Way and Barbara Burt, "Religious Marginality and the Free Exercise Clause," *American Political Science Review* 77 (1983): 652–665.

12 *Employment Division v. Smith*, 494 U.S. 872 (1990), 888.

13 *City of Boerne v. Flores*, 521 U.S. 507 (1997).

14 *International Society for Krishna Consciousness v. Lang*, 398 N.Y.S. 2d 20 (1977), 21.

15 *International Society for Krishna Consciousness v. Barber*, 506 F. Supp. 147 (1980), 148–173.

16 *Heffron v. International Society for Krishna Consciousness*, 452 U.S. 640 (1981), 642–656.

17 Sharon Worthing, "The State Takes Over a Church," *Annals of the American Academy of Political and Social Science* 446 (1979): 136–148; Russell Chandler,

"Church Receivership Dissolved by Court," *Los Angeles Times*, March 2, 1979, B29; Russell Chandler, "Second Receiver Named in Church Dispute," *Los Angeles Times*, March 13, 1979, A8.

18 Russell Chandler, "Rights Groups Back Church's Court Plea," *Los Angeles Times*, November 13, 1979, A6.

19 Russell Chandler and Lois Timnick, "Bill to Cut State's Power to Probe Religious Groups' Abuses Gains," *Los Angeles Times*, June 17, 1980, B3.

20 Russell Chandler, "Deukmejian Dropping 12 Inquiries Into Church Groups," *Los Angeles Times*, October 14, 1980, A3.

21 Jeremiah Gutman, "The Legislative Assault on New Religions," in *Cults, Culture, and the Law: Perspectives on New Religious Movements*, Thomas Robbins, William Shepherd, and James McBride, eds. (Chico, CA: Scholars Press, 1985), 101–110.

22 Frank K. Flinn, "Criminalizing Conversion: The Legislative Assault on New Religions et al.," in *Crime, Values, and Religion*, James Day and William Laufer, eds. (Norwood, NJ: Ablex Publishing, 1987), 153–191.

23 *Larson v. Valente*, 456 U.S. 228 (1982), 231–273.

24 *Larson v. Valente*.

25 Arnold Lubasch, "Moon is Sentenced to 18-Month Term," *New York Times*, July 17, 1982, 1.

26 E.R. Shipp, "Judge Bars Deporting Rev. Moon on Tax Conviction," *New York Times*, August 11, 1982, A20.

27 David Chidester, *Salvation and Suicide: Jim Jones, the Peoples Temple, and Jonestown*, rev. ed. (Bloomington: Indiana University Press, 2003).

28 *Cheema v. Thompson*, 67 F.3d 883 (1995), 884–894.

29 Charles McCarthy, "Livingston Schools say Sikh Knives are Allowed," *Fresno Bee*, June 12, 1997, B1.

30 *People v. Singh*, 516 N.Y.S. 2d 412 (1987), 413–416.

31 The Sikh Coalition, "U.S. Senators Weigh in on TSA Turban Screening Policy," http://www.sikhcoalition.org/advisories/TSASenatorLetter.htm, accessed November 15, 2007.

32 Council on American-Islamic Relations, "The Status of Muslim Civil Rights in the United States 2002: Stereotypes and Civil Liberties," http://www.cair.com/CivilRights/CivilRightsReports/2002Report.aspx, accessed November 15, 2007.

33 Council on American-Islamic Relations, "The Status of Muslim Civil Rights in the United States 2005: Unequal Protection," http://www.cair.com/CivilRights/CivilRightsReports/2005Report.aspx, accessed November 15, 2007.

34 American Civil Liberties Union, "U.S.: Scores of Muslim Men Jailed Without Charge," http://www.aclu.org/safefree/detention/17616prs20050627.html, accessed November 15, 2007.

35 42 U.S.C. § 2000cc-1.

36 Donna Leinwand, "Muslims See New Opposition to Building Mosques since 9/11," *USA Today*, March 9, 2004, A1.

37 Leinwand, "Muslims See New Opposition," A1.

38 Philip Rucker, "Board Draws Back From Mosque Fray," *Washington Post*, October 26, 2007, B1. For discussion of the controversy over building a mosque

and Islamic community center near Ground Zero in lower Manhattan, see Bret E. Carroll's essay in this volume.

39 Nyier Abdou, "Hindu Temple Trying New Legal Remedy," *Star-Ledger* (Newark, NJ), May 17, 2007, County News, 22.

40 Derek L. Gaubatz, "RLUIPA at Four: Evaluating the Success and Constitutionality of RLUIPA's Prisoner Provisions," *Harvard Journal of Law and Public Policy* 28 (1995): 501–606.

41 R. Laurence Moore, *Religious Outsiders and the Making of Americans* (New York: Oxford University Press, 1986), 46.

American Atheists, 58

American Board of Commissioners for
Foreign Missions, 322

American Civil Liberties Union (ACLU),
356–357

American Council of Learned Societies,
38–39

American Ecclesiastical Review (AER),
129–130

American Friends Service
Committee, 336

American Indian Movement
(AIM), 81–82

American-Israel Public Affairs
Committee, 332–333

American Jewish World Service, 336

American Native People
Organization, 84

American Religious Identification
Survey (ARIS), 105

American Revolution, 3, 142–143, 321

American Revolutionary Settlement of
Religion, 1, 3–5

American Society for Muslim
Advancement, 56

Amerindians (*see* Native Americans)

Amin, Idi, 179

Amish, 347, 350–351, 360

Amitabha Buddhism, 347–348, 360

Anglicanism: in the colonial Mid-
Atlantic, 2, 66–68; decline of,
4–5; and denominationalism,
26–27; as an established church
in the colonies, 44–45, 321; and
global Christianity, 109 (*see also*
Episcopalianism)

Antell, Rachel, 263

Antichrist, 110, 279–281, 321, 326,
329–332

anticlericalism, 45, 269

Anti-Defamation League, 57, 344n43

Anti-Semitism, 4, 13–14n14, 142, 154,
157, 214n13, 255

Arab-Israeli conflict, 167, 172, 176,
326–327

Aravamudan, Srinivas, 231, 245

Arctic National Wildlife Refuge, 71

Arizona, 69, 84, 198

Arkansas, 72

Armageddon, 326, 329

Armstrong, Herbert, 352

Arp, Jean, 208

Ashkenazi Judaism, 141, 143–144, 155

Asian Americans, 50, 72–73,
228–229, 305

Assemblies of God, 109, 276

Association for the Sociology of
Religion (Catholic Sociological
Association), 135

astrology, 271

atheism: American intolerance of, 4, 29,
50–52; and anti-Soviet propaganda,
324; and evangelicalism, 113; and
pluralism, 337; prevalence in the
Pacific region of the United States,
79; rise in unbelief in the United
States, 10–11 (*see also* agnosticism;
"nones")

atomic bomb, 326–327

Augustine of Hippo, 131

Azhar, al- (University), 172

Babalú Ayé, 77, 80

Bahá'í, 11–12, 46, 58, 79

Baker Book House, 107

Ball, Hugo, 208

Balmer, Randall, 274–276

Baptism, 116, 134, 286, 301

Baptists: and African-Americans, 283;
and colonial America, 2, 5, and
female submission, 252; and Lyndon
Johnson, 195–196; megachurches
and, 276; in the Midwest and South
regions of the United States, 68,
71–72; persecution and populism in
colonial and early republic America,
43–46, 269

Barazangi, Nimat Hafiz, 184

Barlas, Asma, 184

Barlow, Philip L., 11

Barrows, John Henry, 235

Barton, David, 9

Barton, William, 323

Basu, Shamita, 242–244

Baum, Gregory, 128, 137
Beat Movement, 272, 306
Beatles (music group), 306, 326, 329
behaviorism, 25
Beecher, Lyman, 275
Belgium, 132
Bellah, Robert, 79, 273, 312, 334
"Ben Hur" (film), 268
Benedict XVI, 137
Benesch, Klaus, 60
Berger, David, 158–159
Berger, Peter, 51
Berle, Milton, 267
Berrigan, Daniel, 304, 328
Berrigan, Philip, 304, 328
Bhagavad Gita, 255, 306
Bible: and American nationalism, 37,
     305, 308–309, 315; centrality of,
     2, 5; and Eastern religion, 255; and
     evangelicalism, 27, 106–108, 114,
     118; and legitimation of Western
     patriarchy, 261; literalism, 274, 332;
     prophecies, 326, 329; revelation of,
     39, 331, 338
Bigelow, William Sturgis, 205
Bill of Rights, 3, 76, 142–143, 187,
     348–349
Black Hills, 70, 81, 83, 89
Black Mountain College, 207, 225n77
Black Power, 289
Blake, Eugene Carson, 301
Boerne v. Flores, 351
Bonhoeffer, Dietrich, 328
Borglum, Gutzon, 81–83
"born again" Christianity, 2, 26,
     105–106, 114, 118, 275, 308–309, 313
Bosnia, 197, 217n18
Boston, 205–206, 321
Boston Museum of Fine Arts, 205
Boykin, William G. (Jerry), 331,
     333–334
Boy Scouts of America, 10
Bradbury, Ray, 202
Braude, Ann, 251
Brazil, 109
Brennan, William, 354
Brethren in Christ, 322

British Empire: American apologists
     for, 256; Protestant ideology of,
     1, 4; and Swami Vivekananda,
     237–238
Bronson, Rachel, 325
Brown, Jerry, 353
Brown v. Board of Education, 303
Brownback, Sam, 333
Bryan, William Jennings, 274
Buddha, 196, 205, 210
Buddha statues in Bamyan, 183, 198
Buddhism: alternative medicine
     and, 200; decontextualization
     of Buddhist beliefs in the United
     States, 193–194, 203, 224n69;
     and the environmental
     movement, 83–84; and
     ethnoreligious enclaves, 74, 228;
     and evangelicalism, 107, 112–113;
     and the fine arts in the United
     States, 204–211; and its growth in
     the United States after World War
     II, 8–12, 29, 195, 199–202, 310–312;
     litigation over religious freedoms,
     348–360; in the Mid-Atlantic
     region of the United States, 68;
     and pluralism, 33–34, 44, 46, 58;
     and popular religion in the United
     States, 277; its prevalence in the
     Pacific and New England regions,
     69, 72–73; and Renewal Judaism,
     159; and sacred space, 64, 86; self-
     immolation of monks, 196–198; as
     therapy in the United States, 200;
     viewed as a peaceful and tolerant
     religion among Americans, 194,
     217n18; widespread recognition
     of, 48–51
Burke, Mary Louise, 239–240,
     245–246n6
burned-over district, 45
burqa, 252–253
Bush, George H. W., 313, 333
Bush, George W., 46, 48, 113, 183, 186,
     313–314, 330–336
Butler, Jon, 3, 269
Byrne, Peter, 40

Cadge, Wendy, 199
Cage, John, 207–210, 222n56, 225n77
Cairo, 176
Calcutta, 237–238, 242
California, 69, 78, 134, 273, 352, 355, 359
Calvin College, 277
Calvinism, 37
Campbell, David E., 10
Campbell, Debra, 259
Campbell, Joseph, 278
Campbellites, 269
Campus Crusade, 115
Canada, 148–149, 321
Cantwell v. Connecticut, 349–350
capital punishment, 110
capitalism: and evangelism, 276;
    likened to religious diversity, 1; and
    the Muslim world 170–171; and
    popular religion, 266–267;
    and sacralization of conspicuous
    consumption, 302; and Weber's
    theory, 239
Caribbean (*see specific countries,
    ethnicities, and religions*)
Carroll, Daniel, 126
Carroll, John, 125–126
Carter, Jimmy, 275, 308–309, 313
Cascade-Siskiyou National Movement, 71
Cassat, Mary, 204
caste system, 238, 244
Catholic Relief Services, 336
Catholic University of America,
    129–130
Catholic World, 201
Catholicism: and its acquiescence to
    authoritative regimes, 128; and
    African-Americans, 137, 283,
    290; among American elites,
    47; American Protestant hostil-
    ity toward, 4, 255–259, 275 (*see
    also* tests, religious); Boomer
    Catholics, 135; in colonial America,
    1–2, 62; and communism, 130,
    132; and the demographics of the
    United States, 47, 77; détente
    with evangelicals in America,
    110–111; and education, 24; and

environmental movement, 83–84;
    and ethnoreligious enclaves,
    74–75, 78; exclusivism, 125;
    French Catholicism in Canada,
    321; and gender, 252–253, 259;
    Hispanic, 69; immigration and,
    5, 195, 338–339; influence on early
    American Judaism, 143–144;
    integration within the United
    States after World War II, 49,
    128–133, 302–303, 311; Luci
    Johnson's conversion to, 195–195;
    in the Mid-Atlantic and Midwest
    regions of the United States,
    66–68; prevalence in New
    England region, 72–73; in Utah,
    76–77; after Vatican II, 134–138
Cedric the Entertainer, 285
Central Intelligence Agency (CIA),
    196–197
Chabad-Lubavitch, 151, 155, 158–159
Charleston, 143–144, 287
Chennai (Madras), 229, 236
Chicago, 107, 205–206, 231–232,
    254, 276
Chicago Daily Tribune, 232
China: and evangelicalism, 109, 116,
    211; and immigration to the United
    States, 8, 255, 305; and Islam, 187;
    and Tibetan Buddhism, 198
Christian Broadcasting Network
    (CBN), 329
Christian Century, 6, 327
Christian Coalition, 310, 313, 329
Christian Science, 5, 271–272, 347, 359
Christianity and Christians: civil
    religion in the United States,
    298–303, 320; in colonial America,
    3, 26; demographics in the
    United States, 51, 105–106; and
    the environmental movement,
    83–84; and ethnoreligious enclaves,
    74; and Global South, 108–110;
    and Islam, 167–171, 177; religious
    pluralism and, 44, 114, 118; slave
    religion, 261–262; and threat of
    modern liberalism, 38 (*see also*

Catholicism; Orthodox Christianity; Protestantism)

Eastern Europe: and immigration to the United States, 5–6, 127, 141, 144, 255, 307, 329 (*see also specific countries and religious groups*)

Eastern Orthodoxy (*see* Orthodox Christianity)

Eastern religions (*see specific religion*)

Eastman, Fred, 327

Eccles, Robert S., 25

ecclesiology, 126 (*see also* churches)

Eck, Diana, 8, 30–31, 33–35, 39, 44, 49, 51, 60, 74, 87, 89, 236, 253, 348

ecumenism: and American Catholicism during Vatican II era, 130, 132, 134–138; and Diana Eck, 33; and Judaism, 146–148; liberal Protestantism and, 23; and Lyndon Johnson's faith, 195–196; and postwar national unity, 301, 305; and sacred space, 89; and Swami Vivekananda's message, 237–239

Edgell, Penny, 53

education: and American Protestantism, 22–30; and gender, 25; literary canon within, 279; and non-Western religion, 49, 229; and religion in the classroom, 21–23; and sexuality education, 259; Western forms opposed in the Muslim world, 170 (*see also* colleges and universities; schools)

Edwards, Jonathan, 37

Egypt, 112, 172–174, 176, 179

Eisenhower, Dwight D., 7, 154, 206, 300–301, 315, 337

Eisenstein, Ira, 149

Eliade, Mircea, 28, 33, 61, 297–298

Ellis Island, 8

Ellison, Keith, 9, 315

Emancipation Proclamation, 288

Emory University, 181

Employment Division v. Smith, 350–351

Engel v. Vitale, 305

England (*see* United Kingdom)

Enlightenment, 40, 50, 133, 236–237, 241, 243, 320

entrepreneurs, religious, 45

environmentalism: and Native American spirituality, 82–84, 89; and the Pacific Northwest, 70–71; and popular religion, 274; prophecy of the Bible, 330; and the Shundahai Network, 76

Episcopalianism, 26, 47, 109, 195–196, 255, 269, 274, 283 (*see also* Anglicanism)

Esack, Farid, 179, 181

Estes, Yusuf, 185

esotericism, 5, 232–233, 237–238

Ethical Culture Society, 145

eugenics movement, 255

Europe (*see also specific European nations, ethnicities, organizations, and regions*)

European Union, 326, 329–330

Evangelical Alliance, 27–28, 307

evangelicalism: and African-Americans, 283, 336; among American elites, 47; civil religion after World War II, 299–303; during the colonial and early republic periods in America, 269–271, 320; "counterculture" in the Pacific Northwest, 70–71; demographics in the United States, 4–5, 47, 105–106; denominationalism, 26–27, 40n9; dominance in the South region of the United States, 71–72, 80–81, 89; evangelical theology, 107–108; and gender, 252–253; holiness-pentacostal strain of, 271; its inherent pluralism, 116–118; as opposed to mainline Protestantism, 46; politicization of, 48, 275, 325; and popular religion in the United States, 277; and transnationalism and missions, 85–90, 338–339

Evangelicals for Social Action, 335–336

Evans, Michael, 331–333

Everson v. Board of Education, 348

evolution, 113, 274

Gere, Richard, 201
Germany, 6, 27, 45, 132, 323
Gerson, Michael, 334
Ghannushi, Rashid al-, 176
Ghazali, Muhammad al-, 176
Gibbons, James, 127
Giuliani, Rudolph, 56
Glass, Matthew, 82
globalization: and electronic
    communities of faith, 85–90;
    and evangelical Christianity, 109,
    120–121n24; and Hinduism, 232;
    and Islam, 180
Global South, 109–110
Global Vision 2000, 233–234, 244
Global War on Terrorism (GWoT),
    167–168, 185–186 (see also
    terrorism)
God: in American civil religion, 4, 79,
    297–303; covenant with Israel, 332;
    defined as the "ultimate concern"
    according to Tillich, 28–29; lack
    of belief in, 10–11, 38–39, 145, 151;
    and religious pluralism, 51–52; and
    Shamblin's weight loss program,
    116; transcendence of, 37, 63;
    unity of in Islam, 182; unity of in
    Judaism, 141
Gospel: as central in Lumen Gentium,
    135; and evangelism, 106–108 (see
    also evangelicalism; scripture;
    social gospel)
Gospel music, 291–292
Graham, Billy, 108–109, 115, 195, 275,
    302, 325, 328, 336
Graham, Franklin, 277, 331
Graves, Morris, 206
Great Depression, 69, 198–199, 308
Greater Houston Ministerial Association
    (Texas), 302
Green Party, 274
Gregory XVI, 126
Griffith, R. Marie, 118
Ground Zero, 56–58, 62
Guantánamo Bay, 335
Gulf War, 179, 330, 338

Guru Maharaji, 306
gurus, 230, 232, 256, 273, 306
Guthrie, Stan, 111
Guyana, 355

Hagee, John, 331–333, 336, 339
Haggard, Ted, 334
Haiti, 75, 77, 134
Hall, David D., 269, 271
Hanegraaff, Wouter J., 235, 247n34
Hanh, Thich Nhat, 200, 219n34
Hannerz, Ulf, 85–86
Hanukkah, 151, 154–155, 228
Hare Krishna (see International Society
    for Krishna Consciousness)
Haredi Orthodox Judaism, 148–150,
    152–153
Hargis, James, 325
Harlem, 75–76
Harlem Renaissance, 291
Harris, Sam, 10
Harry Potter, 278–281
Hart, D. G., 30, 38–39
Hart-Cellar Act (1965), 58, 80, 89, 272
    (see also immigration)
Harvard Divinity School, 28, 35
Harvard Pluralism Project, 43, 58,
    211–212, 245n4
Harvard University, 33, 58
Hasidism, xi, 141–142, 150–151, 152, 158
Hatch, Nathan, 270–271, 321
hate crime, 58, 91n8
Hawaii, 69, 322
health care, 27, 114, 200, 212, 273,
    312, 336
"heathenism": as a capacious category, 6;
    used to describe Native American
    religions, 3; used in women's
    missions endeavors, 253–257
Hecht, Richard D., 64
Heffron v. International Society for
    Krishna Consciousness, 352
Heinze, Andrew, 159
Henry, Carl F. H., 110
Herberg, Will, xi, 7, 15n30, 44, 66,
    214n4, 301–303, 306, 313

immigration acts: of 1924, 7, 134, 176, 198–199; of 1965, 7, 11, 46, 134, 198, 217–218n20, 307, 311, 348

imperialism, 172 (see also colonialism)

India: and American exoticization of its religious traditions, 237, 273; and Catholic immigration to the United States, 134; and global Christianity, 109, 112; government's commitment to secularism, 229; and Hindus in America, 228; and the Rushdie controversy, 178

Indiana, 68, 200

Indiana School of Religion, 24

Indonesia, 112

Ingersoll, Robert "Bob," 10

Interchurch Center, 301, 305

interfaith cooperation, 25, 70–71, 83–84, 89, 107

Interfaith Network, 83–84, 89

International Churches of Christ (ICOC), 116

International Monetary Fund, 326

International Peace Day, 58

International Society for Krishna Consciousness, 306, 348, 351–354, 359

International Society for Krishna Consciousness v. Barber, 351–352

Iran, 112, 172–173, 178

Iranian Hostage Crisis, 197

Iranian Revolution, 167, 172–173

Iraq, 332

Iraq War, 332, 334–335, 338

Ireland, 45

Irish, 127

Isaacs, Harold, 63

Islam and Muslims: and African-American women, 260–262; and Christian conversion efforts in the United States, 111–112; and ethnoreligious enclaves, 74, 78–79; and evangelicalism, 107, 113, 277–278; and globalization, 85; and immigration of practitioners to the United States, 8–9, 46, 310–312; and interfaith dialogue, 175–176; Islamist fundamentalism, 22; Islamic militancy, 30; Islamic presence in American colonies, 3, 6; litigation over religious freedoms, 348–360; in the Midwest and New England regions of the United States, 68, 72–73; perfectionism, 43; pluralistic theology, 56–58, 107–108, 176–177; its prevalence in the Pacific region, 69; reaction to American materialism, 180; and sacred space, 64; and September 11, 87–89, 167–168, 183–187; Sufism, 30, 33, 187; and Western liberalism, 169–170; widespread recognition in the United States, 9–12, 33–34, 48–51 (see also Shi'ism; Sufism; Sunnism)

Islamic Circle of North America (ICNA), 176

Islamic Society of North America (ISNA), 175, 184

Islamism, 170–172; and pluralism, 178

Islamo-fascism, 168, 186

Islamophobia, xi, 4; after September 11, 167–168

Israel: and American Jews, 148–149, 155, 159; Ancient Israel, 4; evangelical support, 337–338; Israeli-Palestinian Conflict, 334–336; and the Muslim world, 172, 176, 187; tension between American Jewish and Christian groups over, 338; Zionist movement seen as fulfillment of prophecy by evangelical and fundamentalist Christians, 326–327, 331

Istanbul, 176

Italians, 127

Italy, 45, 132

Jackson, Mahalia, 285

Jackson, Sherman, 185–186

Jacoby, Susan, 50

Jagadguru, Sri Tarlabalu, 234

national anxieties about Islam, 87–89; from Northern Europe, 5, 45, 274; Vivekananda's religious structure in light of, 243; after World War II, 46

Madinah, 176
Madras (see Chennai)
Madyun, Gail, 260–261
Maharishi, Mahesh Yogi, 306
Maine, 72
Malaysia, 112
Malcolm X, 304
Mali, 187
Manifest Destiny, 321
March on Washington, 304
Maritain, Jacques, 132–133
"market share" of religion, 4–5
marriage: interfaith marriage among Catholics, 49, 128, 135–136, 139n9, 258–259; interfaith marriage among Protestants, 46, 49; intermarriage and Judaism, 49, 156–158; same-sex marriage, 124n70, 312, 314, 315; and the state, 349
Marsden, George, 37–38
Marty, Martin, 60, 63, 114
Marxism, 170–171
Maryland, 2, 66, 129, 353, 358
Massachusetts, 72, 87, 205, 353
Massachusetts Bay Colony, 45
Mattson, Ingrid, 184
Mawdudi, Abu-al Aʻla al-, 176
Mayhew, Jonathan, 321
Mayo, Katherine, 256–257
Mays, Benjamin E., 304
McCutcheon, Russell, 30, 39
McGreevy, John, 257
McKean, Kip, 115–116
McLuhan, Marshall, 267
Meacham, Jon, 297
Mead, Sidney, 60
Mecca, 86, 178, 181, 184, 304
meditation, 61, 194, 199, 232, 240
Meiji Restoration, 202
Mennonite Central Committee, 336

Mennonites, 3; in the colonial Mid-Atlantic, 66–68
Mesmerism, 270
Metcalf, Barbara, 86
Methodism: holiness strain in, 271; interdenominational cooperation, 26; in the Midwest and South regions of the United States, 68, 71–72; and the "Plantation Mission," 5; pluralism, 34–35, 45–46; and populism in antebellum America, 4–5, 269, 274 (see also African Methodist Church; African Methodist Episcopal Church; United Methodist Church)
Mexico, 69, 134, 137, 255, 321, 323, 329, 338
Meyer, Michael, 145
Miami, 74, 77
Michigan, 68, 232, 291
Micronesia, 109
Mid-Atlantic, as a religious region, 66–67, 78
Middle East, 58, 68, 73, 87, 176, 185–186, 253, 272, 325–326, 330–333 (See also specific countries, ethnicities, and sects)
Middle East Broadcasting Corporation (MBC), 186
Mid-West: and national anxieties about Islam, 87–89; as a religious region, 67–69, 274
Milano, John A., 356
Miller, Perry, 269
Miller, William, 45
Millerites, 45 (see also Seventh-day Adventism)
"mindfulness," 200, 203
Minneapolis, 205
Minnesota, 9, 68, 352, 354
missions: Catholic, 127; Christian efforts to convert Jews, 111–112; Christian evangelicals and cultural imperialism, 321–323; Christians in the Muslim world, 169–170;

national unity, 21, 299–303

Nationalism: in the Arab world, 170–172, 176; civil religion and identity in the United States, 299–303; and Hinduism in India, 231–232, 243–244

Native American religion: influence on religion during colonial and antebellum era, 1, 3, 269–270; messianic movement, 235, 247n38 and popular religion in the United States, 277; prevalence in the Pacific, Northwest, and West regions of the United States, 69–71, 81–84, 89; and sacred space, 64

Native Americans: 43, 70; during colonial and antebellum period, 1, 3; and controversy over Mount Rushmore, 81–83, 89; Pueblos, 1

natural law, 114, 133, 241, 324

Nazism, 130, 148–150, 156

Nebraska, 68, 353

Nebuchadnezzar, 331

neoconservatism, 332

neoorthodoxy, 37–40

neo-paganism, 10, 130

Netanyahu, Benjamin, 157, 332

Netherlands, the, 132

Neuhaus, Richard John, 9, 110

Nevada, 69

New Age Movement, 71, 84, 200, 233, 235, 273, 337

New Amsterdam, 3

"New Buddhism," 202 (see also Zen Buddhism)

New Deal, 129, 336

New England: Catholic and Protestant dominance in, 66, 72; church establishment in, 4, 269; and Hindu presence, 87; and national anxieties about Islam, 87–89; and Puritanism, 2–4, 269, 297–298, 321; and religious diversity, 77; as a religious region, 67, 72–73

New Hampshire, 72

New Jersey, 2, 26, 66, 78, 347

Newman, William M., 74

New Mexico, 69

New Netherland, 2

New Religious Movements (NRMs), 268, 270, 348–360

New Republic, 201, 315

New Spain, 69

Newsweek, 309

New York (city), 184, 229, 301–302, 347; and ethnoreligious enclaves, 74–75, 86–87, 145, 206–207, 210

New York (state), 66, "burned over district," 45; and the Ramakrishna Mission, 232

New York Times, 7, 9, 27, 111, 148, 200, 280, 314

New Yorker, 200, 202

Niebuhr, H. Richard, 37

Niebuhr, Reinhold, 14n24, 37, 218n22, 308

Nigeria, 109, 112, 120n22, 137

nirvana, 205

Nixon, Richard M., 110, 303

Nobel Peace Prize, 200–201

Noll, Mark, 5, 37–38, 109, 112

Nomani, Asra, 184

non-Christian faiths: and early American history, 1, 3, 8–10; and evangelical Christian conversion efforts, 111; religious diversity, 107–108 (see also specific faiths)

"nones" (non-religion), xii, 10–11, 46–47; prevalence in Pacific Northwest, 70–71 (see also agnosticism; atheism)

non-Western religion: acceptance into American society, 49–52, 62–63; and population demographics of the United States, 43, 46, 48–49

Noonan, John T., Jr., 132

North Carolina, 71, 207

North Dakota, 68

Nuclear Weapons Freeze, 328

Nyang, Sulayman, 179–181

gender, 253–263; global religious pluralism, x, 85–90; its growth out of liberal Protestantism, 25–30; in historiography of American religion, 11, 12, 30–37, 44; integration of Hindu spirituality into American Protestantism, 231–233, 235–237; and loss of religious certitude, 50–51; "melting pot" metaphor and, 6, 34, 44, 213–214n4; and non-Western religion, 46–51; origin of term "Judeo-Christian," 6; and People of the Book, 175; and Protestant idealism, 22–25, 30–37; and September 11 attacks, 9, 50, 56–58, 87–89; and spatial dynamics, 60–65; in urban environments, 72–79

Plymouth, 297

Polish, 127

political action committees, 179

"popular" religion, 266–281

Portier, William L., 111

postmodernism, 86, 108, 159, 245

Prabhupada, A. C. Bhaktivedanta Swami, 306

Pratt Institute, 206

prayer, 61, 252; and Catholicism, 125; campaign of 2007, 115; and civil religion in the United States, 113, 154, 300, 302–303, 305, 309; and gender politics, 252; Islamic prayer beans, 359; and Jewish tradition, 143, 145–146, 148–149, 151, 153, 155, 159; and sacred space, 56, 61, 84, 90n2, 155, 359; Tibetan prayer wheel, 205

premillennial dispensationalism, 307–308, 326–327, 332

Presbyterianism: among American elites, 47, 269, 274; and denominationalism, 2, 26, 46; and the environmental movement, 83–84; and the Scotch-Irish in the colonial Mid-Atlantic, 66–68; and the split with the Disciples of Christ, 5

Progressive Islam, 184

prophecy, biblical, 326, 329–332, 338

prophets, 3, 178

Protestant Council of the City of New York, 302

Protestantism: and African-Americans, 284, 290; and American education, 22–25, 38–40; the American idealism of, 30–37; Asian Americans and, 69; Catholic views of, 125; civil religion and mainline Protestantism, 299–303; in the colonial period, 1, 2, 62, 321; current demographics, 47, 49, 77, 105–106; and diversity of, 33–34; dominant cultural force in the 1960s, 195–196; and gender, 252–253; integration of Hindu spirituality into American Protestantism, 231–233, 235–237; liberal vs. conservative Protestantism in the United States, 25–30, 45–46; the "Protestant Establishment," 31–32; Protestant nationalism, 1, 3–4, 44; transnationalism and missions, 338–339; in Utah, 76–77

Prothero, Stephen, 256–257

Pryor, Richard, 285

psychology, 25

public sphere (see public square)

public square, 48, 89, 113, 179, 187, 301, 308

Puerto Rico, 75, 322

Pure Land Buddhism, 347

Puritanism: established church in New England, 2, 4, 44–45, 269, 297–298; forebears of contemporary fundamentalism, 280–281; and the social gospel, 31–32

Putnam, Robert D., 10

Pyle, Ralph E., 54n26

Qaeda, al-, 171–172

Qaradawi, Yusuf al-, 175, 182

United Kingdom, 26, 178, 185, 232, 237, 302, 321–323
United Methodist Church, 46, 78
United Nations, 132, 172, 176, 280, 326, 329, 331–332, 334–335
United States, 1, 11, 22–23, 29; and civil religion, 79–84; and evangelicalism, 110; immigration and, 5–6; influence of Hindu yogi practices, 230–233; influence of Japanese aesthetics on, 202–213; in the Muslim world, 170, 179; Protestantism and, 4–5, 11–12, 297–298; public opinion of the Vietnam War, 196–198; religious diversity, 43, 79; and religious pluralism, 30–37; religious regions, 65–73; sacred spaces within, 60–65; and transnationalism, 85–90
Unity, 283
Universal Declaration of Human Rights, 335
universalism, 24, 232–234, 237, 242–244, 270
University of Central Florida, 183
University of Chicago, 29, 178
University of Delaware, 183
University of Iowa, 25
University of Judaism (Los Angeles), 150
University of North Carolina, 184
University of Southern California, 24, 185
University of Virginia, 182
Upanishads, 238
Urey, Harold C., 7
Urry, John, 60
US News and World Report, 201
Utah, 69–70, 75–76, 349

Vatican II, 133–138; criticized within Islamic pluralist discourse, 177; and politicization of Catholicism in the United States, 311
Veda, 238, 255
Vedanta Society, 11, 233, 237–239, 272, 306
Vermont, 72

Vesey, Denmark, 287
Vietnam, 134, 201; Buddhist peace and reform movement in, 196–198
Vietnam War, 32, 194, 196–198, 304, 306–307, 327–328, 338
Vineyard Church, 276
Viola, Bill, 210–211
violence, religious, 43–44, 58–60, 64; ascribed to Islam, 112, 168, 184, 187–188; justified by Qutub's Islamic imperative, 171 (see also hate crime)
Virginia, 2, 71, 297
Vishwa Hindu Parishad (VHP), 229, 233–234
Vivekananda, Swami, 27, 231–234, 236–245, 257, 306
Vodou, 261, 292

Wade, Joseph M., 205
Wadud, Amina, 184
Wahhabism, 180, 183–185
Wahhaj, Imam Siraj, 185
Waite, Morrison, 349
Waley, Arthur, 202, 206, 222n56
Wallis, Jim, 313, 335
Warhol, Andy, 209
Warner, R. Stephen, 8
Washington, D. C., 66, 79, 193, 195, 205–206, 211, 229, 233–234
Washington, George, 297
Washington (state), 70, 83–84
Washington Buddhist Vihara, 211
Washington Post, 234
Washington's Ethics and Public Policy Center, 329
Watts, Alan, 200, 202, 208, 306
Webb, Suhaib, 185
Weber, Max (artist), 206
Weber, Max (social theorist), 239
Welch, Robert, 325
Weld, Charles, 205
Wentz, Richard E., 65
Wertheimer, Jack, 150
West Bank, 332
West Virginia, 71
Westminster Assembly, 26